NEW YORK REVIEW BOOK
CLASSICS

T0274886

THE LETTERS OF WILLIAM GADDIS

WILLIAM GADDIS (1922–1998) was born in Manhattan and reared on Long Island. He attended Harvard during World War II, but left without a degree in 1945. He was a fact-checker at *The New Yorker* for a little over a year, during which time he began writing short stories. In 1947 he embarked on a course of travel, living in Mexico, Panama, Spain, and France, while writing his first novel. *The Recognitions* was published in 1955 to largely negative reviews, though it developed an underground following. Over the next twenty years, Gaddis was employed by various companies as an industrial writer and taught part-time while working on his second novel, *J R*, which was finally published in 1975, winning the National Book Award. Ten years later he published his third, *Carpenter's Gothic*, which was also well-received, followed nine years later by *A Frolic of His Own*, winning his second National Book Award in 1994. Just before his death in 1998 he finished a novella, *Agapē Agape*, which was published in 2002 along with a collection of nonfiction, *The Rush for Second Place*. He was the recipient of grants and awards from the Rockefeller Foundation, the Guggenheim Foundation, the MacArthur Foundation, and the Lannan Foundation, and was a member of the American Academy and Institute of Arts and Letters.

STEVEN MOORE is the author/editor of several books and essays on William Gaddis, and has written about many of Gaddis's literary acquaintances in *My Back Pages: Reviews and Essays*. He is also the author of *The Novel: An Alternative History* and of books on Ronald Firbank and Alexander Theroux.

SARAH GADDIS was born in New York City and educated at Swarthmore. She is the author of the novel *Swallow Hard*, and has published short fiction in *The New Yorker*, *Faultline*, *Paris Passion*, and *AGNI*.

THE LETTERS OF WILLIAM GADDIS

Revised Edition

Edited by
STEVEN MOORE

Afterword by
SARAH GADDIS

NEW YORK REVIEW BOOKS

New York

THIS IS A NEW YORK REVIEW BOOK
PUBLISHED BY THE NEW YORK REVIEW OF BOOKS
435 Hudson Street, New York, NY 10014
www.nyrb.com

The bulk of these letters are held by Washington University Libraries and are published with their permission.

Library of Congress Cataloging-in-Publication Data
Names: Gaddis, William, 1922–1998, author. | Moore, Steven, 1951– editor of compilation.
Title: Letters / by William Gaddis ; edited by Steven Moore.
Other titles: Letters of William Gaddis
Description: New York : New York Review Books, 2023. | Series: New York Review
    Books classics | Includes index.
Identifiers: LCCN 2021037264 (print) | LCCN 2021037265 (ebook) | ISBN
    9781681375830 (paperback) | ISBN 9781681375847 (ebook)
Subjects: LCSH: Gaddis, William, 1922–1998—Correspondence. | Authors, American—
    20th century—Correspondence. | LCGFT: Personal correspondence.
Classification: LCC PS3557.A28 Z48 2022 (print) | LCC PS3557.A28 (ebook) | DDC
    813/.54 [B]—dc23/eng/20211220
LC record available at https://lccn.loc.gov/2021037264
LC ebook record available at https://lccn.loc.gov/2021037265

ISBN 978-1-68137-583-0
Available as an electronic book; ISBN 978-1-68137-584-7

Printed in the United States of America on acid-free paper.
10 9 8 7 6 5 4 3 2 1

CONTENTS

ILLUSTRATIONS

*Reproduced courtesy of Special Collections, Washington University.

INTRODUCTION

IT'S HARD to say whether William Gaddis would have approved of this book, hard to judge whether he was serious or joking when he wrote to his mother in 1949 to state, "Our correspondence should never be published." Publically, he insisted that only a writer's published work matters and "the rest is not our business" (as his revered T. S. Eliot wrote). He submitted to interviews reluctantly—and not until the second half of his career—gave no readings, and regarded biographical details as irrelevant. He planted his views early in his first novel, *The Recognitions* (1955), and thereafter directed inquiring critics and interviewers to this passage: "—What is it they want from a man that they didn't get from his work?" the reclusive painter Wyatt Gwyon asks his wife Esther. "—What do they expect? What is there left of him when he's done his work? What's any artist, but the dregs of his work? the human shambles that follows it around. What's left of the man when the work's done but a shambles of apology" (95–96). He reiterated the point twenty years later in his second novel, *J R* (1975): when Rhoda, the teenage squatter at the 96th Street apartment, tells the composer Edward Bast that he's not very "interesting," he sputters, "—Well why should I be interesting! I mean, I mean I want my work to be interesting but why do I have to be interesting! I mean everybody's trying to be interesting let them I'm just, I'm just doing something I have to do..." (561). Gaddis admired Justice Oliver Wendell Holmes for "ordering all his papers burnt & letting his Opinions stand for themselves nobody's business how he got there," as he writes in one of the letters in this volume, and in another marveled at Faulkner's "ambition to be, as a private individual, abolished and voided from history, leaving it markless, no refuse save for the printed books." I can imagine what he would think of strangers reading his mail.

And yet, he did not burn his papers. As essays, doctoral dissertations, and then books on his work began to appear, Gaddis resigned himself to becoming the subject of a biography someday and to seeing his letters published after his death. He addressed the latter "threat" (as he called it) in the letters themselves; when I wrote to him in 1984 requesting permission to view some letters held by the Bruce Peel Special Collections Library (University of Alberta), he reluctantly granted permission,

> although as you're surely aware it's an entire area I've never condoned. Some of my reasons have been noted in relation to my reticence re interviews though here they go further: like many fledglings, my early letters were many times written with the vain notion of eventual publication & thus obviously much embarrassing nonsense; & of the later ones, those of substance will probably never be seen for equally fortunate if exactly different reasons. (I don't know if you happened upon a review of Hemingway's letters by Hugh Kenner, might have been in that same *Harpers* with my piece 2 or 3 years ago, but he does use them to flay the writer & point up frailties in his work as glimpses of the 'real' Hemingway, I think really these things go quite the opposite, the letters are the detritus &c).

Later that year, when I was stepping up my efforts to collect Gaddis's letters—both for my own work and to secure those to former friends and contacts while they were still accessible—he snapped "no one's [letters] are written for publication (unless they *are* in which case they're probably full of lies)."

Privately, however, he kept carbon copies of some of his letters and maintained his archives over the years, and near the end of his life carefully prepared them for eventual sale to a university library, telling his children that he relished the idea of scholars poring over his papers and making all sorts of discoveries. At any rate, his letters are neither full of lies nor the mere detritus of his life; they do indeed offer glimpses of the "real" Gaddis, and rather than providing the means "to flay the writer & point up frailties in his work," they foster a deeper appreciation of the writer and his work.

It's ironic that Gaddis complained—in a 1948 letter to his mother after reading about dramatist Eugene's O'Neill's early vagabond days—that he was "furious that one can no longer live as he did—just wandering about, one job, one ship to another," for Gaddis led what sounds today like an almost mythic young writer's life. Born near the beginning of the Roaring Twenties (29 December 1922), he went off to boarding school at age five, learning to negotiate the trains between Manhattan and Berlin, Connecticut, and writing numerous poems while still a child. In high school he contracted a rare tropical disease that baffled his doctors and kept him home from school for a year and a half (detailed in his letter of 13 December 1986). During the summer before his senior year, he sailed to the Caribbean and visited Haiti and

Venezuela, and in 1941 was accepted by Harvard, the only college he applied to, but had to leave after a few months because of complications from his earlier treatment. He sailed through the Panama Canal (the week the Japanese bombed Pearl Harbor) to California and stayed at a ranch in Arizona for a few months, breaking horses and hitchhiking through the southwest before driving an old woman and her mentally unstable son to St. Louis, where he spent a month and a half living on a government ship on the Mississippi River "building a pipeline for a dredge in big hip boots," then went back west to celebrate Cheyenne's Frontier Days with enough gusto to get thrown in jail, then headed down to Colorado to work at a mine near Leadville before returning to Harvard in the fall of '42, a few months before his twentieth birthday.

There he became editor of the *Harvard Lampoon*, but after a minor public disturbance (drunk and disorderly) that wouldn't raise an eyebrow today, he was asked to leave Harvard in January 1945. Unwilling to return under Harvard's conditions, he quickly snagged a job as a copy-editor at the *New Yorker* and lived in Greenwich Village (at the same address where Wyatt Gwyon forges his paintings), writing stories and raising hell until the spring of 1947, when he and a friend drove down to Mexico in a Cord convertible, an adventure recounted in a long letter (9 March 1947) that reads like a comic outtake from Jack Kerouac's *On the Road*. A few months later he returned to New York for "grand and often wild times" amid "the drug ambience" of Greenwich Village (as he recalled in one of the last letters he wrote), falling in love with an enigmatic junkie/artist/*Vogue* model named Sheri Martinelli, until he hopped a plane for Panama City, hoping to begin a career as an international journalist but settling for working on the canal locks for a few months, and then left for next-door Costa Rica and participated in its brief 1948 revolution before returning to New York on a Honduran banana boat. He wasn't there five months before he shipped out to Spain, where he lived on and off for the next two and a half years: staying a week in a monastery, trying out Paris for a year (avoiding the other expats on the Left Bank, whom he found pretentious), engaging himself to a fellow American named Margaret Williams, vacationing in Italy, spending a Christmas in England, visiting Robert Graves on the island of Majorca, and working on a film in North Africa before returning to the States in 1951 at the age of twenty-eight.

All that time, from Mexico in 1947 onwards, Gaddis worked on what would become *The Recognitions*, finishing it in 1954. Its publication the following year marks a low point in American book reviewing, for it was almost universally panned, sending Gaddis to look for freelance work and a five-year stint as a writer for Pfizer Pharmaceuticals to support himself and his new family. (He had married Pat Black in 1955, and they had two children: Sarah in September 1955, Matthew in January 1958.) He returned to freelance work in 1962—and would continue to take on projects through the late '70s—and continued to travel widely: to Germany in 1964 to work with the U.S. Army on a film about the Battle of the Bulge, through the Far East (Thailand, the Philippines, Japan) in 1976 on a speaking tour for the U.S. Information Agency, vacations in Haiti (1979) and Greece (1980), Italy in 1984, Russia in 1985 with a delegation of American writers (including his friend William H. Gass, who published accounts of the trip), Australia, New Zealand, England and Bulgaria for book promotions and conferences in 1986, and back a few times in the late 1980s and 1990s to Germany, where he was greeted with movie-star adulation unthinkable in his homeland. He even appeared in a blaxploitation vampire film with his second wife, Judith Thompson (*Ganja and Hess*, 1973).

The chief value of these letters is not their documentation of a colorful life but their revelation of how chaotic the composition of Gaddis's novels were. The published works have such an aura of Olympian confidence and authority that it is startling to learn how hard Gaddis *struggled* to produce these novels. His vision for each of them was often clouded by self-doubts and periods of exasperated indecision, not to mention the distractions of financial hardship and the more enjoyable commitments to his family and friends. During the writing of *The Recognitions*, as these letters reveal, Gaddis moodswings between such excitement for his novel that he can barely get the words down (see the spring 1948 letter to Charles Socarides) and such disgust that he sounds like his worst reviewer. The composition of *J R* stretched over twenty years, interrupted by countless claims on his attention until he reached the point when he told his son Matthew that the most satisfying thing about finishing it was that he would "NEVER HAVE TO READ THE INFERNAL BOOK AGAIN!" After it came out in 1975, Gaddis never wanted to write another novel; when he realized he had to for financial reasons, it took him four years to come up with the idea for *Carpenter's Gothic*, and even then he had to struggle to find some aspect of it to challenge him. In several letters to legal advisors in the late 1980s while writing *A Frolic of His Own*, Gaddis confesses he's over his head in legal complications and doesn't know how to get out of the mess he's created. After its triumphant appearance in 1994, winning Gaddis a second National Book Award (after *J R*), he cast about for something new to write about, and in 1996 decided to resurrect a book he had begun fifty years earlier, *Agapē Agape: The Secret History of the Player Piano*, and struggled with that for a year or so—just as Jack Gibbs struggled with the same work decades earlier in *J R*—before deciding to convert it to a novel, finishing it just before he died on 16 December 1998, two weeks before what would have been his seventy-sixth birthday.

It's interesting to see that most of Gaddis's characteristic elements of style were in place at an early age: a rather formal tone—it's difficult to believe a nineteen-year-old wrote the letter of 26 January 1942—a preference for British spellings, a fondness for literary allusions (especially to Eliot: he seems to have memorized *Four Quartets*), and the use of the European dash to indicate dialogue—not an avant-garde affectation, as some reviewers charged, but simply what Gaddis grew used to seeing in Spanish and French books while in Central America and Europe. In later letters there are long, tortuous, punctuation-free sentences that rival those in his novels, punched up with active verbs, colorful imagery, sardonic wit, and (toward the end) some touching whimsy and nostalgia. Though not written for publication, these letters offer many of the same linguistic delights as his published works.

His literary tastes and aesthetics were also in place from an early age: his lifelong love for the great Russian novelists of the nineteenth century, for T. S. Eliot and Evelyn Waugh, for parody and burlesque (nurtured by the *Lampoon*), and his conviction that, once written, a work must stand on its own. In a 1949 letter to his mother Edith—who is the heroine of the first half of this book: his confidante, research assistant, financial benefactor, his everything—Gaddis says of one of his stories: "Yes, it is supposed to end as you quote it—heaven knows if it should or not—but I can't tell now, it is none of my concern now the thing is written I am through with it." He would reiterate that point to every critic who approached him in later years.

Gaddis had mixed feelings about writing letters, often considering them an annoying distraction and putting off responding to incoming mail for months—or years, in the almost comical case of David Markson. (In later years, a good percentage of his letters begin with an apology for not writing sooner.) "Correspondence a good thing," he conceded to his mother in January 1948, "though even it often seems a waste to me," going on to rail against "the vanity of letter-writing" a few months later in a remarkable letter to Katherine Anne Porter (7 April 1948). In a 1967 letter to his future second wife, he counters Judith's claim that she "can't bear this letter writing business because mine are so marvelous" by insisting "they're not, no, and I almost think it would be terrible if we became adept, exchanged sparkling & accomplished correspondence, things mustn't get to that point! No, our letters have to stay awkward & just blundering around [...]." On the other hand, as he indicates in one to his friend Saul Steinberg, he sometimes welcomed the opportunity to write a letter in order to clarify his thoughts by setting them down on paper. And he certainly enjoyed writing to his children, as the selection included here should indicate. He took care over his letters: he would often write and correct a draft before sending one—no shoddy goods left his workshop—and favored friends received beautifully handwritten letters that are superb examples of calligraphy (see p. 320–21). In many cases, his letters contain "Material, one might say, for a novel," as he quipped to his mother (28 November 1950): some of his early letters contain passages that went straight into *The Recognitions*, and in later letters there are many situations and sentiments that would be reworked in his novels. Watching how he transformed experience into art, recognizing the base materials that he alchemized into gold, may be the most rewarding aspect of this collection. Gaddis used a different metaphor: "They would fill out the endless ups & downs of this writer's life & provide such a terrific record of the battlefield," as he wrote his agent late in life (10 August 1995).

William Gaddis would not have approved of this book, but I can't imagine anyone interested in modern American literature agreeing with him.

Since the principal justification for publishing Gaddis's letters is to enable greater insight into his work, I've favored those in which he discusses his writing, his reading, his views on literature (and related fields like criticism, publishing, and book reviewing), along with a few concerned letters to politicians and enough personal matter to give the volume continuity, allowing it to function as a kind of autobiography in letters. This selection represents maybe a quarter of his extant correspondence.

Gaddis's letters are transcribed virtually verbatim, including idiosyncratic punctuation, spelling, careless errors, and so on; only obvious misstrokes and insignificant misspellings have been corrected, such as "canot" to "cannot." I have occasionally supplied a bracketed correction, or a *sic,* but otherwise it can be assumed any irregularities are in the originals. Again, these letters were not written for publication—except for a few to the editors of periodicals—and a close transcription will keep that front of mind throughout. I've retained Gaddis's preference for British orthography, his habitual misspellings (e.g., tho, envelop[e], compleat, thot, magasine, Shakespear), his habit of closing up phrases (as in "eachother") and number quantities ("3000miles," "4months"), outdated contractions like "'phone," abbreviations ("$ly" = "financially"), occasional malapropisms ("attentions" for "intentions"), inconsistent punctuation, and other personal choices. (However, I have not replicated his occasional use of German-style quotation marks: „like so.") In a few cases I've retained a deleted word to indicate Gaddis's first thought, where interesting. Underlined words have been set in italics, except for a few places where the underline has been retained for emphasis, especially when Gaddis used a double underline. Gaddis wasn't consistent in the treatment of book titles—sometimes he underlined them (especially when writing by hand), more often he used all caps, or nothing at all—but for clarity and consistency the titles of all books, periodicals, movies, artworks, and ships have been italicized. On the other hand, I haven't italicized foreign words unless Gaddis did so. He used a variety of paragraphing forms—including subparagraphs within paragraphs, many of which I've run together—and likewise placed dates and addresses in a variety of positions over the years. Most often, his address and the date appear at the bottom of the letter, to the left of his signature. But for ease of reading and reference a consistent physical layout has been imposed on all the letters. (The dates are transcribed verbatim.) For those from the same address, the first gives the complete street and city address, but subsequent ones only the city. Closing signatures are verbatim; in some cases, one isn't present, either because it's a carbon copy or a draft. Some abridgments of mundane matters have been made—and they are merely mundane matters, no shocking secrets or libelous insults—indicated by bracketed, unspaced ellipses ([...]); Gaddis's own ellipses are spaced (. . .), and have been regularized thus. (Sometimes he used two periods . . , sometimes more . . . . . .) Some postscripts and marginalia have also been omitted. Material deleted at the request of the Estate is indicated thus: {* * *}.

Acknowledgments

FIRST, I want to thank Sarah and Matthew Gaddis for the opportunity to edit this collection, a dream I've had for the last thirty years. Gaddis's second wife, Judith, gave her blessings and was enormously helpful with both letters and information. Thanks also to the Andrew Wylie Agency's Adam Eaglin, Scott Moyers, and especially Carrie Smith for facilitating the project, and to Jeremy M. Davies at Dalkey Archive.

Second, my thanks to all the individuals who generously shared their letters with me over the years, especially those—like James Cippio and David Madden—who took the trouble to supply contextual material. And to Anne Posega and especially Sarah Schnuriger of Olin Library's Special Collections department at Washington University (St. Louis, Missouri), where Gaddis's archives are held. I am especially grateful for a travel grant from the library that allowed me to spend an eye-opening week there in May 2011.

I also wish to thank the staffs of the following libraries for supplying letters: The Beinecke Rare Book and Manuscript Library, Yale University Library; Bentley Historical Museum, University of Michigan; the Bruce Peel Special Collections Library, University of Alberta, Edmonton, Alberta; Harry Ransom Center (University of Texas at Austin); Stanford University Library, Stanford, California; Special Collections, University of Maryland Libraries; Rush Rhees Library, University of Rochester; Vassar College Library, and the University of Chicago Library. I would also like to thank the rare-book dealers Lame Duck Books, Ralph Sipper Books, Chandler Gordon of the Captain's Bookshelf, and Ken Lopez for sharing their merchandise, and Julia Murphy for sharing some late faxes.

Particular thanks go to photographers Miriam Berkley and Mellon Tytell.

And for help with various details, I am indebted to Crystal Alberts (who performed valuable preservation work on the Gaddis letters when they arrived at Washington University), Stephen Burn, Nicholas Fargnoli, Gerry Fenge, Mike Gladstone, Mark Hale, Victoria Harding, Brian Lamere, Mark Lewis, Bernard Looks, James M. Morris, Allen Peacock, Julián Ríos, Richard Scaramelli, Michael Silverblatt, Emmett Stinson, Joseph Tabbi, A. Robert Towbin, Edward Tudor Pole, Alexander Waugh, and Greg Werge.

Ann Arbor
Autumn 2012

Revised Edition

IN ADDITION to adding several new letters and photographs, I have revised and updated many editorial notes, and corrected various typos, errors, and mistranscriptions in the hardback edition—though most of Gaddis's own misspellings have been retained per the earlier editorial principles. I also slightly abridged some previously published letters, and restored passages to a few others I had originally cut that now strike me as useful. I am deeply indebted to Edwin Frank of New York Review Books for allowing me to prepare this new, expanded edition rather than offsetting the earlier book (and for paying for rights to one of the new photographs), and to managing editor Sara Kramer for seeing the book through the press with the same eagle eye for detail that she brought to NYRB's reissues of Gaddis's first two novels in 2020.

To the earlier names above, I want thank first and foremost Joel Minor for help above and beyond his duties as curator of the William Gaddis Papers at Olin Library; and then David Abel (Passages Bookshop), Jamie Diamond, Catherine Gass and Mary H. Gass, Kate Goldkamp (Olin Library), Jill Krementz, Kaitlyn Krieg (Morgan Library and Museum), Ken Lopez, Dave Moore, John Soutter, Ken Taylor, and Michele Wilbanks (George A. Smathers Libraries, University of Florida). Finally, I want to thank Adam Hess for typesetting this behemoth, and Joe Meyerson for proofreading it.

Abbreviations

AA   *Agapē Agape* (Viking, 2002)

CG   *Carpenter's Gothic* (Penguin, 1999)

FHO *A Frolic of His Own*, the first American and British editions (1994), not the repaginated paperback.

JR   *JR* (Penguin, 1993). Because WG sometimes cites page numbers from his first two novels, they have not been changed to those of the recent NYRB editions.

ODQ *The Oxford Dictionary of Quotations* (London: Oxford University Press, 1949, 6th impression). This often-used reference book was given to WG in 1950 by Ormonde de Kay in Paris.

R   *The Recognitions* (Penguin, 1993), sometimes cited by part/chapter (e.g., III.5)

RSP *The Rush for Second Place* (Penguin, 2002)

WG William Gaddis

1. GROWING UP

1930–1946

Children enjoy eating outdoors at Merricourt

WG at Merricourt, c. 1928, "that blond pageboy off to
boarding school age 5" (see letter of 9 November 1994).

To Edith Gaddis

[*WG's mother, née Edith Charles (1900–70); see WG's capsule biography of her in his letter of 14 March 1994. In 1922 she married William T. Gaddis (1899–1965), but they separated three years later. WG's earliest letters date from 1929, when he was attending the Merricourt School in Berlin, CT. Most are addressed to Mrs. Gaddis's work address: 130 E. 15th St., New York, NY, the office of the New York Steam Corporation, which later merged with ConEdison. (Her work there was the subject of a feature in the* New York Times: *6 April 1941, Society News, p. D4.) The first two are included because they refer to WG's first "book," his earliest reading, and document his first creative effort.*]

> Merricourt
> Dec. 9, 1930

Dear Mother.
    Our vacation is from Sat. Dec. 20. to January 4.
    We are making scrapbooks and lots of things. We are learning about the Greek Gods.
    I am making an airplane book.

> With love
> Billy

To Edith Gaddis

> Merricourt
> Jan. 23rd, 1932

Dear Mother.
    [...] We just came back from the library but I didn't get any books.
    I finished *Bomba the Jungle Boy* and I have started *Bomba the Jungle Boy at the Moving Mountain*. I wrote a poem and it went like this

EASTER
Easter is on Sunday
But today is Monday
And Easter is 11 weeks away
At Easter the bunny hides eggs all over,
Some in the grass, some in the clover.

Did you like it

With love
Billy

Bomba the Jungle Boy [...] *Moving Mountain*: the first two (both published 1926) in a
series of boys' adventure novels by the pseudonymous Roy Rockwood.

To Edith Gaddis

[*Most of WG's early letters home are brief, cheerful bulletins about school activities, but
the following one about the three-hour train-ride between New York City and Berlin
conveys some of the anxiety that Jack Gibbs recalls of his boarding-school days in* J R:
"—End of the day alone on that train, lights coming on in those little Connecticut towns
stop and stare out at an empty street corner dry cheese sandwich charge you a dollar
wouldn't even put butter on it, finally pull into that desolate station scared to get off scared
to stay on [...] s*chool car waiting there like a, black Reo touring car waiting there like a
God damned open hearse think anybody expect to grow up..." (119).]*

Merricourt
Oct. 24, 1933

Dear Mother.

I got here safely, but got mixed up because it was dark and didn't think it
was Berlin. Carl, Warren, and David were there to meet me and we enjoyed
the rest of the Oh-Henry. The darn train stopped up over the bridge to
let another one pass it and I was wondering where the station was when we
started up and rode by the station (nearly) and the boys had to race with the
train. [...]

With love Billy

To Edith Gaddis

[*After Merricourt, WG attended public school on Long Island from seventh through twelfth grades. In the summer of 1940, he sailed to the Caribbean on the SS* Bacchus, *the first of many voyages he would make throughout the Western hemisphere over the next dozen years.*]

Port-au-Prince, Haiti

[24 August 1940]

Dear Mother

Well everything is coming along fine. I was pretty under the weather the first 2 days out but after that fine. The other passengers are fine especially 4 of the men who are swell. And the crew are too. I have become the bos'n's "apprentice." He has taught me to splice rope etc. and is a corker. A good part of the crew are colored but they're OK too.

As I write this it is 5 AM and we are lying in at Port-au-Price. I slept on the bridge last nite and this morning got up early and am watching the sunrise over the mountains to the east of the town. Last nite 3 of the men (passengers) and I went ashore and saw a little of Haitian nite-life, of which we saw *very* little. All the stores were closed as they didn't expect the ship 'til this morning so the town was almost dead. Mr Romondi's prophesy, however, has come true. There are a good many palm trees on the island and I was under one last nite.

The town is quite beautiful with the mountain behind it and all the white buildings and a flaming cloud to the right and the sun rising to the left.

We go ashore this morning to the souvenir shops etc. Oh boy!

We lift anchor at 10 AM for Aruba or La Guiara—I forget which.

I read *Black Majesty*—a fellow on the boat has it.

Hope I don't get stuck in a record store in Port-au-Prince and miss the boat—

Love

Bill

Mr Romondi: unidentified.

La Guiara: on the coast of Venezuela, WG's next port-of-call.

Black Majesty: a biography of Henri Christophe, king of Haiti (1767–1820), by John W. Vandercook (1928).

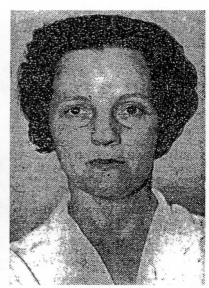

Left: WG piloting the SS *Bacchus*, 1940. Right: Edith Gaddis, 1941 (Times Wide World).

To Edith Gaddis

[*WG entered Harvard in September 1941, but almost immediately began experiencing medical problems. (Thirty years later he recalled it as mononucleosis.) As a result, he left after the first term and headed west for his health.*]

> Harvard University
> Cambridge, Massachusetts
> [10 September 1941]

Dear Mother

First the business before I forget and then the news. As you can see a typewriter ribbon will be welcome at the first opportunity, and then there is the problem of the desk lamp. They have nice ones like my room mate's at the Coop for $5.98, but if you can get one and send it all right; any how I think it must be settled soon as classes start today and they are starting assignments off with a bang. Also I understand that note books seem to be required to some extent in many of the courses, so if you happen on one it will be welcome up here. I have been spending to a fair extent, having gotten all of my books and other little things such as writing paper, joining the Coop, etc., and so the latest contribution was very welcome. And speaking of contributions, have you heard anything from the Christy affair?

I've had two classes: in English and French, and you should see the assignments. Boy, they aren't waiting for anything. The food is good so far, and with classes starting we are beginning to get settled down to a more regular life. Boy it is really some life, and promises to become more so to the nth degree. We are beginning to realize just about what the courses are going to be, how much work connected with them, etc. Although my course is not a stiff one, and the courses aren't as hard as they are dry, uninteresting, and only requirements, I am looking forward very apprehensively to the Latin course, in which my classes start tomorrow. V (my room mate just did this—for Victory—in the November hour exams I guess).

I guess you got my card asking for the jacket; I was figuring I might take it down to this Max Keezer and get a trade in on that corduroy jacket which I think is going to be the thing to wear to classes.

Well, that's about all, I guess; I'll write and let you know how things are when we get really settled.

Love,
Bill

the Christy affair: a high school prank pulled on a local businessman named J. I. Christie; for details, see Marilyn Parke Weir's "William Gaddis: A Previously Unpublished Memoir," *Los Angeles Review of Books*, 16 October 2013, https://v2. lareviewofbooks.org/article/william-gaddis-a-previously-unpublished-memoir.

Max Keezer: a menswear shop founded in 1895, located in Harvard Square at the time.

To Edith Gaddis

Matthews Hall – 31
Cambridge, Massachusetts
[19 October 1941]

Dear Mother—

Could it be that Dolly and her ilk are slipping? They seem to be failing us. I don't know, here it is Saturday afternoon and I'm still flat listening to the Dartmouth game. My temp stays right around 100 tho it's been down to 99 and up to 101 but I feel like hanging up. Harvard just made a touchdown and the stands are going crazy—me too only for a different reason—because I'm not there. I'll bet there'll be a hot time tonite.

Well I've decided one thing—they told me that they can't keep you here if you insist on going so come Tuesday or Wednesday and I'm still the same I'm leaving and see if I'll get well outside on my own. I'm not getting anywhere here—only disgusted.

The food here is supposed to be good but I think it's pretty sad and not half as good as Union food.

They're still making their crazy blood tests which never show a thing—what a bunch of jerks!

Hoping to have better reports soon—

Love
Bill

To Edith Gaddis

Cambridge, Massachusetts
[23 October 1941]

Dear Mom—

I'm feeling a lot better and I think the temp has been dropping a little—not normal yet but someday I suppose. The only effects are my ankles are very weak and I have a pot belly! But I guess exercise will cure both. I'm not up long enough to feel dizzy—not on my treks to the bathroom anyway. [...]

The only studying I've done is that 100 pages of French outside reading—the exam in it is today so I guess I'll have to make it up too. Somehow this place isn't condusive to study and I haven't felt like it until the last couple of days.

I'm only taking 4 subjects—which is minimum—but 2 (Physics and Eng[lish literature] I) are pretty tough. However there's no backing down or changing now—I'll just hang on and hope for the best.

Love
Bill

To Edith Gaddis

Cambridge, Massachusetts
[4 November 1941]

Dear Mother—

Gosh Dr. Contratto must have written you an encouraging letter—we were so certain I'd be out for the next Army game and now you don't mention it, but say you're coming up—I tell you gee—I feel *good* and have no temperature at *all*—always normal now; only a small stomach which seems to be going down slowly—I still think I'll be out for Saturday's game—I can't see why not, and yet this whole thing is so screwy and is getting me so mad—that is, if I don't get out by Saturday.

I'd like to know what those two thot about the ultimate outcome—I don't see why I can't make up 4 weeks' work—I'm not worrying about that—my English A is almost made up already; my Eng I reading is getting done; Physics

Gaddis and fellow members of the Class of 1945. First row: John Callahan, Ormonde de Kay Jr., Charles Gardner; second row: John Snow, Charles Socarides, Francis Ware. From the *Harvard Freshman Red Book* (1941).

and French I'm letting go, but I think I might be able to catch up on them even without tutors, tho tutors might prove to be adviseable. I don't see why I should worry about being a freshman next year—unless Dean Leighton suggested it—because I can do this work and I'm getting out soon, or know why.

As for talk of my graduating class—I doubt if many of us will graduate. That is far ahead any way, and even so I'll be draft-meat in a couple of years, and I'm going to beat them to it. [...]

Love
Bill

Dr. Contratto: Dr. Andrew W. Contratto, who practiced in Cambridge at this time, and taught medicine at Harvard.

Dean Leighton: Delmar Leighton (1897–1966), Dean of Freshmen from 1931 to 1952.

To Edith Gaddis

Cambridge, Massachusetts
[13 November 1941]

Dear Mother—

The freighter to L.A. sounds great—just perfect and I'd like it best if possible. 10,000 tons is a fair sized ship—it sounds good and ought to ride well. I think the Japs are the least of our worries—time seems to be the thing now. I might stay in L.A. for a couple of days and send ahead to find out about right reservations to my destination. I think as for cost it may be even if not slightly less, considering 21 days aboard ship with meals is equivalent to 3 weeks of boarding *somewhere*.

That's swell about the 15% on American Airlines and it would be fairly and comparatively inexpensive to fly to Baltimore with time at home such a premium.

If it is at all possible please pull every string to make the freighter trip possible—it would be just what I wanted and would work out more perfectly and best for me if it can be done—

Love
Bill

P.S. She's a midget
P.P.S.—What is time of sailing from Baltimore?

the Japs are the least of our worries: three weeks later the Japanese would bomb Pearl Harbor.

To Edith Gaddis

[*WG left Harvard on November 21, and a week later shipped out from Baltimore on the SS* West Portal.]

> Barker Hotel
> 2000 Miramar Street
> Los Angeles, California
> [2 January 1942]

Dear Mom.

It is such a long time since I wrote and I don't know what customs in Panama let thru that I'll have a hard time remembering everything.

We were half way thru the Canal when Japan declared war, having arrived at Colon early that morning (Atlantic side). At 7 o'clock the canal was blacked out except for guide lights on the banks and the ship ran with only running and mast head and stern lights. We reached Balboa late that nite (pacific side) and despite war went ashore while ship took on oil. Panama City wasn't blacked-out and it was really an intriguing city. Then we returned to the boat and sailed late the next afternoon. About 9 that nite however things in the Pacific were getting pretty lively as we swung around and were anchored in Panama Bay next morning. We stayed there for nine days, with quite a few other ships—twenty five at once sometimes—blacked out always and continuously shifting position. Altho we didn't get ashore often, and when we did we couldn't go further than Panama City (I mean across the isthmus to Cristobal) for comparitively short times as the ship was likely to leave any minute—awaiting naval orders and even the captain wasn't sure. I did get a room mate in Panama—his name was "Davey" Abad, a native Panamanian who was light weight (I think) boxing champion of the world! He was really quite a character—sort of genial, sloppy, tough, and paunchy, about 34, and his only faults that I think of now were really ripping nightmares he would get and bounce around in the top bunk and yell out in Spanish until I thot it might be unsafe to room with him; one night he was really going and kicked the light right off of the ceiling!—I used to have to light a match when I came in at night and say "It's me, your room mate, Davey—" and be ready to duck. They subsided however and we got along quite well. Then he used to come into the dining salon patting a large tan stomach, usually exposed by a shirt with one button, and one night Ross had a miserable time trying to eat cherries while Davey sat slapping his bare stomach after supper. And aside from these and the horrible manner in which he mangled and distorted the English language he was all right and really *took* me around Panama City one nite where every one seemed to know him.

Then there was a one year old baby whom I knick-named "Wetsy" (and it stuck) very appropriately because she seemed quite unable to control herself; indeed, some times she seemed almost proud of the little pools she left behind, and at *least* she was nonchalant about it. This little animated mass of sodden diapers took a liking to me—probably a strange fascination, and it was quite a mystery to everyone, including myself, because of the way I treated her. Despite the way I sort of kicked her as she walked unsteadily down the deck, or squirted her milk in her face to see her squint, or pulled her hat down over her eyes, or tempted her toward unsafe perches on the edge of the hatch or near the rail and told her mother about the dire plans I had for her future in the way of "hot-foots" or seeing if she would float, or the way I sort of carried her slung under one arm and bounced and shook her (which she actually seemed to enjoy), she would spread her arms out and get a downright jolly look on her face and make weird gurgling noises (resembling the Bronx cheer) and weave an unsteady path toward me, usually ending up on her face, when ever she saw me. Needless to say her mother was slightly worried and probably expected me to come back from one of our jaunts with a bloody mass under my arm, but Wetsy weathered them all—she really could take it. Her mother couldn't see her resemblance to a cocker spaniel puppy which I pointed out, and looked sort of horrified when I mentioned King Herod or Jonathan Swift's "Modest Proposal" after Wetsy had put in a particularly hard nite at our expense, but all in all was a remarkably good sport through it all.

Mr. Byrne has been fine, and we have gotten along very well except for a streak when he sort of tried to "hold me down"—not that I wanted to do any thing—it's just that any one doesn't like to be "with strings on"—that was in Panama and now in L.A. we get along like regular chums and he is really quite jolly and as a matter of fact was sort of the life of the whole trip.

There was another nice fellow on the way up from Panama—a twenty-seven year old sailor serving in the navy in Panama. He and I got along wonderfully and were usually partners in conspiring where Wetsy's future was concerned. However I really took a kidding where Massapequa was concerned—it seemed as if it was brought up in every conversation—but when I got here I saw in the *L.A. Daily News* a *large* picture of a bonfire of Japanese made goods in "Massapequa, Long Island!" I tried to get one but it was an early edition.

At any rate we finally did leave Panama and tho the run up was completely uneventful it was at the same time very exciting. As we got nearer L.A. precautions were much greater—no smoking on deck and absolutely no lights. Lifeboats were slung out and ready, provisioned with food and water, lifebelts always handy, and I had my watch and money and papers in an oilskin pouch always with me. We really expected trouble—in fact Mr. Byrne and I had a two dollar bet on when it would come!—but things quieted as we neared L.A.

Christmas on the boat was a beautiful day but that's about all, tho we did have a more sumptuous spread than usual. I had gotten a good burn the day before in the sun, but Christmas it was easier. And to top things off I was presented with a present!—my *dirtiest* pair of pants wrapped up in wooden cheese boxes!!! My most unique present yet!

Well now we're getting settled in Los Angles—it's quite a large town—spread all over etc. Happy New Year!

Love
Bill

Japan declared war: by bombing Pearl Harbor on 7 December 1941.

"Davey" Abad: born 1907, professionally active from 1921 to 1937.

Ross: J. Ross Byrne, WG's traveling companion.

King Herod or Jonathan Swift's "Modest Proposal": Herod, bent on killing Jesus, ordered all children of Bethlehem under two to be murdered (Matt. 2:16); Swift's satirical essay (1729) advises the Irish to sell their children to the rich as food.

Massapequa: WG's hometown on Long Island; his mother owned a house at 40 Jerusalem Avenue.

To Edith Gaddis

[*WG spent three months at a ranch about 14 miles northwest of Tucson.*]

Cortaro, Arizona
[12 January 1942]

Dear Mom—

Well settled at last; "Sahuaro Vista Desert Ranch—Cortaro, Ariz." is the new address. I left Ross in Yuma Saturday, after calling here to be sure of reservation, and got to Tucson that nite. The rates here, all over Arizona are much higher than before, because of war in Calif., and because Calif. weather is a bit cold. Mrs Adams, the proprietress here, told me her rates were higher and that I might stay at $90 a month because she had already quoted this rate. I think it is good because Ross is paying $40 per on a just regular "farm" in Yuma for room and board, and here they have horses etc. and the land is much nicer, Yuma being poor, and just dirty desert, while here they have plenty of giant cactus and mesquite etc. It looks like it's going to be wonderful. [...]

And lest I forget—please get me another birth certificate whenever it is convenient (no hurry) and send it out, as I had trouble in Panama and L.A. landing without it. I suppose I should always carry it when I travel.

And I haven't time now to tell you about it, but Brad Brown showed me a wonderful time in Hollywood—had many plans for this (past) weekend, but I thot I should get started for Arizona.

I haven't seen much here—it is compairtively quiet as there are only two guests now, but soon there will be 18!, and I'll probably get some mail from you in Tucson today, so I'll stop now as we're going very soon (it's about 14 miles).

And *say*, if you haven't seen *H. M. Pullham Esq.* don't miss it. I saw it in Tucson Saturday nite. It is *wonderful*, Rob't Young is superb and Hedy Lamarr is extremely good too. I have not *really* been *extremely* lonely since I left, but after that I just felt *lost*. I can see where the book must have been very good—

Lots of love
Bill

$90 a month: $1440 in buying power today. ($1 in 1942 = $16.00 in 2022.)

Yuma: on the Arizona–California border.

Brad Brown: unidentified.

H. M. Pulham Esq.: 1940 film directed by King Vidor (based on a novel by John P. Marquand) about a stuffy Bostonian businessman who livens up his dull life with a fling.

To Edith Gaddis

Cortaro, Arizona
[17 January 1942]

Dear Mom—

[…] Well everything is coming along fine out here. I've been riding every day for two or three or four hours and it is wonderful.

However I can see where I made a sad mistake. I did as I have been waiting to do since I left, and for my Christmas present bought a handsome pair of boots for $19. They are good looking, but no inlay except around the top. At any rate I was well pleased until I started riding in them, and altho I do really like them—they fascinate me—this land is so rough, and what with riding through greasewood and cactus etc they now by the end of the week are getting pretty scratched up. Every time I pass a bush or cactus that scratches them I feel like it was tearing my own flesh! […]

As for wanting anything else—well there are things down here that make me froth just to look at them!—belts such as I never dreamed of—rings— *beautiful* silver and leather work—but I figure I don't need any of it now and will let it go until I've been around a bit more and seen more of these things that I've always known *must* exist *somewhere*!

My pictures turned out quite well on the trip 'round. I'm sending them under separate cover with the negatives in case you want to see them and you may keep them so I won't lose them. They most all turned out—some taken in Panama Bay of sunsets which is <u>restricted</u> and I almost lost every thing—and say I don't know whether or not I told you about what happened at Norfolk— I was caught taking pictures on the pier—trailed all over town by two Naval Intelligence men and finally "relieved" of any film. They said they would develop it and send me any pictures they approved—so if any thing comes to you there from them that resembles photographs please take a look and send them on—there may be some good shots. [...]

I can't think of any thing I'd want from Saks—perhaps a tux but that will be a long time—I really don't know what they handle—so why don't you get yourself something and then later things will straighten out. There just isn't much in the east that I can think of wanting—except clothes when I return— these wallets and belts and rings and other silver and leather creations out here are just things I have always dreamt of.

Well everything's fine—just riding—rocking back and forth (what I mean *rocking*) in these saddles. It's quite warm tho the natives comment on the "chilliness!" Tell Gram I'll write and tell her all about Brad and thank her for her letter.

Love
Bill

Gram: aka Granga, WG's great-aunt, Ida Williams Way (see headnote to 16 November 1943), whom he regarded as his grandmother.

To Edith Gaddis

Cortaro, Arizona
[26 January 1942]

Dear Mother—

I received both your letters Saturday and the box that evening; thanks so much for the check (I paid it down on my "rent"), and the box—I still get a kick out of opening packages and presents!

And then as you say this slightly ironic setup—about my father. But I suppose we shall do just what might be expected, and wait . . . things always do take care of them selves, and, as "most of our troubles never happen," by the same token plans and worries often make an unexpected outcome that much harder to meet. As you said it has not been a great emotional problem for me, tho it does seem queer; you see I still feel a little like I must have when I said "I have no father; I never had a father!," and since things have been as they have, I have *never* really missed one—honestly—and only now does it seem queer to me. All I know of fathers I have seen in other families, and in reading, and somehow thru the deep realization I have gained of their importance; of father-and-son relations; and families: not just petty little groups, but *generations*—a *name* and honour and all that goes with it—this *feeling* that I have gained from other channels without ever having missed its actual presence: somehow these are the only ties I feel I have with him. You understand, not so much personal feelings, but the sort of feeling that I feel must exist between the father and son of a family as fine and as noble as I feel the name of Gaddis to represent; something far above such stuff as the *Good Will Hour* thrives on.

The package contained a very handsome pigskin wallet—a very fine gift, and I shall write him and thank him.

I suppose all we can do is wait, and not *hope* but *know* that it will all turn out perfectly. And while I realize that perhaps it is an affair between father and son, and I shall try to carry my end thru as a gentleman would, for apparently now I have reached the place where I am old enough to think for myself and act accordingly, and be expected to carry things thru like a man, at any rate Mother, if there is any part of this that you want me to do "your way," or any advice you wish to give me on any part of it, please do so, and rest assured that I will do as you wish, for far from making a mess of things or being unfair to me at any point, you have done a wonderful job of the whole thing, and people who have never seen you or have just met you to whom I speak of you telling me that you must be a very wonderful woman only substantiate my feelings and make me realize all the more how much I owe not only a wonderful mother but a wonderful person as well for everything good I have and am today, or ever will be—

Love
Bill

Good Will Hour: a radio advice program (1937–45) hosted by John J. Anthony.

To Edith Gaddis

Cortaro, Arizona
[19 February 1942]

Dear Mother—

Everything out here is fine as per usual and after receiving your letter and request for a picture I got my roll developed and here's one of me on "Johnny"—

WG in Arizona, 1942.

the wildest jumpiest horse here; I ride him daily and he's slowly getting broken in—but today he ran off with me and I came through still on top this time but a slight rip on my head from a passing tree limb. However he's a good horse and we're getting along better all the time. It is a poor picture but at least shows I'm still alive and able to get around.

And say—about those pictures I sent of my *West Portal* trip—was the negative roll with them? I don't know what happened—the manila envelop they were in must have broken.

I don't know about registering—but some time if you see George (Castor) or Arvid you might ask them.

We made a trip to Nogales (Mexico) Saturday and had a fine time. They had buckskin jackets there for $10—one of the fellows got one—but I'm in too deep all ready—and what with the rodeo coming up. I do want to get started and work and pretty soon am going to give this edima an ultimatum. I've got an offer of a job down near Elgin near the border where a fellow's running cattle and sort of needs a helper. Would only be for board and I'd have to bring bed-roll and perhaps saddle—but experience is the thing and I guess I'd get it there.

Well we'll see I suppose—but I do want to get going—

Love
Bill

West Portal: the name of the ship WG took through the Panama Canal.

George (Castor) or Arvid: Castor, like Arvid Friberg, was a Farmingdale High School friend.

edima: i.e., edema, an abnormal accumulation of fluid beneath the skin or in a body cavity. Several of WG's unpublished letters from Arizona deal with this problem.

To Edith Gaddis

Cortaro, Arizona
[23 March 1942]

Dear Mom—

Things are still in a sort of state of waiting; I was going to Yuma about the middle of last week but Mrs. Adams talked me out of it—but a couple of days ago I got a letter from Ross in Yuma asking me to drop down and see him.

And so here's how it stands: you see the old gal who runs this place—Mrs Adams—is a little—well—eccentric—putting it mildly. At any rate there haven't been any guests here for a while, and no wrangler, so I've been doing part time work—taking care of horses—for $1 a day off my board. Now she's starting things rolling again (she says) and there's a possibility of my getting a job—I don't know. If it's not working the horses I won't take it. She's made me propositions now and again but she seems to be given to—well—fabricating etc etc. and I can't keep up with her. And so if I should get a job here I'll stay for a while—until I clear up the albumin in the urine. Otherwise down to Yuma to see Ross, and then I'd like to go out to L.A. just to see how things are looking. You see the edima is about gone—the doctor thinks it is negligible; I haven't had swelling in the ankles for the last month or two as the boots are tight and keep it out—just the upper legs—but the doc thinks that's cleared up. He says I can work but doesn't advise the sea until I clear up this albumin condition.

And then just to complicate things an old seaman is working here—gardening—and we get together and he really can tell me the stories. He says he doesn't think that there is so much danger—he thinks one has a good chance. Then for further complication a pretty brunette is staying over at the "Picture Rocks" Ranch a little ways away. Her name is Petrillo—you know the Petrillos in the song writing and A.S.C.A.P. etc—that's her—I ride over and see her every so often—gee not like that Ford—this saddle only seats one! [...]

Well that's about the size of it now—have been reading H.M. Stanley's auto biography—it's wonderful (at present he is going to sea!)

Love
Bill

---

the Petrillos: James Petrillo (1892–1984) was president of the American Federation of Musicians (1940–58) and would have dealt with the American Society of Composers, Authors, and Publishers.

H. M. Stanley's auto biography: Sir Henry Morton Stanley (1841–1904), explorer in Africa; his *Autobiography* was posthumously published in 1909.

To Edith Gaddis

Rancho de los Caballos
Yuma Valley, Arizona
Tuesday [31 March 1942]

Dear Mom—

Well I got started at last—hitch hiked over here yesterday in six hours and am seeing Ross who sends his best.

It is certainly hot here out on the desert, and I think I'll get started for L.A. soon—perhaps this afternoon—for I think I can get a ride as far as El Centro. I just want to go out to the coast to see how things are.

For the last two or three or four weeks I'd been working at S— V— Ranch for Mrs Adams with horses and dudes—$1 off per day—and so when paid up

$28 to leave on. That will be plenty to get me to the coast and back—and I'll be back in Tucson soon I'm sure—unless something good should turn up in L.A.

Love
Bill

To Edith Gaddis

The Rosslyn Hotels
111 West Fifth Street
Los Angeles, California
[early April 1942]

Dear Mom—

Well it took me over 500 miles of hitch hiking—but now you may set your mind completely at rest; I went down to San Pedro today—and the U.S. Maritime Commission—and the sea seems at least post poned for a while—next summer perhaps. But I had to come out and settle it for myself. I got out to San Diego and on the ride up from there saw miles of the Pacific, so I guess I'm cured for a while.

I have been here since last evening, when I arrived, and after this second good look at L.A. plan to start back in the morning.

I had a haircut this morning (first in 3 months!!) and the barber whom I got to know here in January said that I looked better. You should have seen the hair tho—it was really long—what I mean—and curly too!

Well should be back at the Ranch by the weekend unless some thing intriguing intervenes!

Love
Bill

To Edith Gaddis

Cortaro, Arizona
[6 April 1942]

Dear Mom—

Well—back at last, and what a trip. I got here yesterday afternoon about two P.M., having got a ride thru from near Yuma.

That hitch-hiking works out well. I "cheated" once—took a bus from L.A. to Indio; I never could have gotten a ride out of L.A.

And so now I'm going to start looking around here for a job. I could have got one out on the coast but I don't like it a bit out there, and it seems any thing but healthful.

What I'd like to do is work around here until the beginning of May and then start out and see the north west and west and work east in June.

There's an ad in the paper today by a 'large electrical firm' for 'young men 18 to 22' so I'm going to see what's cooking.

Came back from L.A. with three dollars so my one week's thousand mile trip wasn't so expensive after all—and I got a hair cut!—First since January fifth!

Love
Bill

P.S. How do you like my new 'G' in Gaddis on the envelop? I think it's better.

To Edith Gaddis

Cortaro, Arizona
[8 April 1942]

Dear Mom—

Well this is just to tell you about the latest intriguing offer and plans.

There is a couple here—an elderly deaf woman and her feeble minded son (!) from Saint Louis Mo.—and they plan to return the fifteenth. However they want someone to drive them—that is share driving with the son—only about 200 miles a day apiece! They have a '38 Buick—and have offered me the job!—They pay all car expenses—and my quarters at nite—leaving me only meals to pay for—so I think I'll do it.

As it looks now we leave the fifteenth—Wednesday—and so around the twentieth I can receive mail at Gen'l Delivery–St. Louis.

Love
Bill

To Edith Gaddis

St. Louis, Missouri
[20 April 1942]

Dear Mom—

Well here in St. Louis at last—we got here Sunday afternoon—and what a trip. You see this woman is hard of hearing—and her son Otto, who's about 23—is sort of—simple. He went thru college—then started in at Harvard (!) and then cracked up it seems.

Anyhow we got here—after going thru Carlsbad Caverns etc.—and I figured on staying here with these people until I could get myself a job—or a river boat down to New Orleans—then back to Tucson; but chances for jobs on boats were very slim, and I finally ended up down on the river where the government is building a levee—so tomorrow morning I am to go down and see about a job there—it looks good, and I saw the boss yesterday and he said that if I came back in the morning he thot chances looked good. It is 55¢ an hour—you board and room on the boat there—and it amounts to about $22 a week cleared. I figure that if I work there for about two or four weeks I can make a good enough stake to get back to Arizona.

I know just how things are at home—I mean no car—and George, Henry Cliff and probably Arvid gone—and I'd thot about it that way—so here's what I figure. You see Ross may buy an *old* car and start east around the thirtieth of May, so I may go with him. That would get me home around the middle of June—just right to see some of my old friends graduate etc.—and then, Mom—if you'll do me a favour, and please see Gerald Haggerty and see how much chance I'd have to ship out in coastal or South American waters around June twenty-fifth—or do you think it would be better if I wrote him myself? At any rate that's what I want to do. That would just round things out right.

Well that's how things stand now—of course I may not get a job—then I'll do as you said and go to a nice hotel and send for money. But other wise things should work out well; I have $4. which will keep me over until I get this job—then things will be fine.

I saw De Mills' secretary and told her to send you the bill (and also told her what I thot of his $5 a call services and what they'd done for me!); also to the laboratory, for similar purposes!

I have shipped a box by express from Tucson (my old overcoat and a pair of steer's horns)(collect) and intend to ship my big suit case today—I don't need the shirts and pants in it (by express)(collect).

Will write tomorrow and let you know about the job—in the mean time don't worry—I'm not.

Love
Bill

[*on back of envelope:*] P.S. When does Harvard June session start?

Otto: the name of a major character in *R*, who likewise went to Harvard and eventually "cracked up." But see also notes to 29 October 1950.

Carlsbad Caverns: a popular tourist attraction in New Mexico.

Henry: Henry Parke, older brother of Marilyn Parke (see 23 November 1945) and one of his best friends during high school.

Gerald Haggerty: unidentified.

De Mills: apparently another doctor WG consulted.

To Edith Gaddis

Water Tower Station
2102 East Grand
St. Louis—Mo.
U.S. Quarterboat #1
Tuesday afternoon
[21 April 1942]

Dear Mom—

Started work last nite at 4 P.M.; am on the 4–12 shift working eight hours a day. It is some job. I live with about seventy other fellows on the quarter boat—a big boat tied up here on the Mississippi east bank across from St. Louis.

I am getting 55 cents an hour, and after paying board here on the boat it comes out to about $21 a week. I think that after a couple of weeks I'll have enough to go back to Tucson. Or perhaps I'll work longer if I like it, tho I doubt this. You see Ross plans to get an *old* car and we might drive east together about the end of May, taking a week and a half or two I suppose. Then I might go to sea from New York, if it could be worked out, or get work in the east somewhere—perhaps on a dude ranch—or even come back west.

But then of course if you think it would be good to enter Harvard in June, that would change everything. I might come east from here, or get Ross to drive east early.

And so please send me the date for entry in June; it was probably in that *Accelerated Programmer* book, but I think I sent it back with that bag I shipped. So please tell me which you think would be best—Harvard in June, or a little more working around, until fall.

I seem to be in good physical condition; I had a physical exam and the doctor wrote 'good'; the work is pretty hard (building a pipeline for a dredge in big hip boots etc!) and I'll watch myself and if anything looks like it's going wrong will go to the doc—however I think this work will build me up—if *anything* will, and it is an experience. The boys here are a ripping bunch, and the food good and plenty (4 meals a day). And they all think I'm an Arizona cowboy! We do have fun!

Love
Bill

To Edith Gaddis

St Louis, Missouri
[26 May 1942]

Dear Mom—

I know you had a hard time getting the birth certificate—and as for shipping out of New Orleans—I wouldn't do that even if I did get down there—and I don't expect to do that now—unless I'm fired and it should work out that way conveniently.

However I am planning on coming home in June—very definately unless something radical should happen—then we'll plan from there—and at least have time to talk over the sea before I go, if I should.

We paint and scrape daily and pretty hard too, down below deck, but Frank (the captain) doesn't seem to think we're fast enough—so I may leave (by request!) any day! And say tell Granga I expect to be leaving this town about the eighth—she said she might come out here and I'd like seeing her. I expect to work thru the weekend of the 7th—then leave and come home slowly—stop in Chicago—Indiana—Ohio—but of course the job may move or end before then, so I can't be sure.

We go out once in a while but not often—I haven't had a day off since I started so can't do much and work next day. The time passes fast enough on the job it is rather monotonous and so this evening I went down to some 2nd hand book stores—saw a *beautiful* copy of Omar Khayam's *Rubaiyat*—leatherbound—I've read it and like it a great deal—but it was $6 so I left with a copy of Ibsen's plays to help pass the time—

Love
Bill

Omar Khayam's *Rubaiyat*: 12th-century collection of Persian poems, especially popular in Edward FitzGerald's 19th-century translation.
Ibsen's plays: his *Peer Gynt* (1867) plays an important role in *R*.

To Edith Gaddis

Saint Louis, Missouri
[1 June 1942]

Dear Mom—

Well everything still under control—and June 9th drawing closer every day! Boy it's going to be good.

Still painting down in the hold, tho today I worked out on the shore line.

I think I'll have enough money when I leave here to start home—I get paid Friday the 5th and have some debts to collect so think it will turn out all right

Am quite sure I won't be home by next week-end—right now I expect to work through Saturday—then off 8 hours, go back out at midnite 'til 8 Sunday morning—then plan to drive down to Cape Gerardo about 135 miles south, with some of the boys with whom I work here on the boat. They're a swell bunch and have been wanting me to go down for some time—so we'll go Sunday morning—and back Monday afternoon; then perhaps see Granga Monday or Tuesday nite—(preferably Monday evening) and leave next day for Chicago. So if you'll see what her hotel will be so I can look her up Monday nite (or Tuesday nite if this isn't possible) it will work out fine.

Well it won't be too long now—I expect to stay in Chicago—and around in Indiana and perhaps Sandusky Ohio—however that trip is uncertain—and say is Henry driving a school bus?? George said so.

Love
Bill

Cape Gerardo: i.e., Cape Girardeau.
Sandusky Ohio: WG's journal indicates he met (or intended to meet) a Carole Potter there on 16 June.

To Edith Gaddis

The Mark Twain Hotel
Eighth and Pine Streets
Saint Louis
[7 June 1942]

Dear Mom—

Well can you believe it?! Free at last! And in a hotel room with bed! and tub! and easy chair! And tonite I go out and sink my teeth into a *thick juicy red* steak—haven't had any red meat since I started!

And say but these dress pants feel good after a month and a half of those heavy work pants!

I heard from Gram and planned to meet her the 13th in Indianapolis—but now is changed to Keokuk, Iowa the 9th—so I'll see her there and then wander on east thru Chicago and Indianapolis etc. and home—I don't know when but probably around the end of the week of the fourteenth. But will let you know when I'm definately headed for New York.

And say, I forgot to mention—but you might write Dr. Gumere or some such—Mr Garrett's friend; he's the dean of admissions at Harvard and probably the boy who'd know.

Well I'll write and keep you posted—and you'll probably get a letter from Gram soon telling you I look ragged or something—but I haven't changed a bit—my watch still fits just like it did and pants etc— I've hit a 'bottle neck' and my regular life ab'd the boat apparently hasn't helped—or done bad—I guess I'm lucky—

Love
Bill

Dr. Gumere: Richard M. Gummere (1883–1969), Dean of Admissions at Harvard from 1934 to 1952. Mr. Garrett is unidentified.

To Edith Gaddis

[*After meeting his great-aunt in Keokuk, WG arrived in New York on 18 June, but changed his mind about returning to Harvard and headed back west on 18 July.*]

Cheyenne, Wyoming
[25 July 1942]

Dear Mom—

Thanks so much for the letter and check. And I do hope that you haven't wondered too much about me—I haven't had a chance to write, and that last letter I didn't have a 6¢ stamp.

At any rate here it is Saturday evening and having seen a wonderful rodeo and 'Frontier Days' we're going north tomorrow—to his ranch just for a little—a few days—then back south I guess.

And now a tale of which I don't know what you'll think. You see we got up here late Friday evg., met a couple of cowboys in town, and proceeded to celebrate 'Frontier Days,' until, Mother, we were taken to the local 'calabozo' to spend the rest of the night. Don't worry—we're out and every thing's all right—no fingerprints etc.—and *quite* an experience. You know a newspaper-man must see things first hand—and the Cheyenne jail is some thing to see! I am getting rid of the bed-bug itches I acquired and will soon be back to normal.

Don't know when I'll write again as mail is infrequent from the ranch—but everything's fine—

Love
Bill

Frontier Days: a celebration held in Cheyenne on the last ten days of July ever since 1897.

calabozo: Spanish for jail.

To Edith Gaddis

Cheyenne, Wyoming
[4 August 1942]

Dear Mom—

Well back at last to civilization—electric lites and running water etc. But I mean that ranch was the real stuff!! We were finished branding (yes *we*—you should have seen me holding down the back ends of those calves!) about Friday but H— convinced me I ought to stay thru the week end so I left this morning and came down to Cheyenne—a little over two hundred miles. The ranch was swell tho—and so were the 'boys'—his father and two uncles—and I saw and did it all—branding, herding, driving cattle & horses, fixing fence, killing rattle snakes (!), washing dishes, and myself less frequently, and riding most of the time, and it was wonderful.

I plan on going down to Denver tomorrow—we'll see if Mr. Keating is there or Pueblo or where—then down to Colorado Springs to see this Harvard 'class mate' of mine for a day or two—then if Mr Keating's around I'll contact him. That's as far as real plans go, but expect to continue on down to Tucson after this.

Am trying to keep expenses at a minimum—because I do want to get some new clothes when I come home in the fall, as these two shirts and levis are all I've gotten in recent times. Harold did run me in a little, as he was broke when we hit Denver and I staked him to various stuff—and then the rodeo and room etc in Cheyenne, but it was worth it with that time at the ranch to pay off! And speaking of clothes I was looking at cur[rent] *Esquire* today, and gee—I love this west etc. etc. but do you think there is *any* chance of Harvard in the fall? The trip is swell but it is really sort of escapism—I do want to go back there this fall more than anything, and after I talk to Franny in Colo. Spgs. I hate to think how I'll feel. Gosh I'd kiss the ground Dr. (?) Williams walks on or blow his brains (??) out if I thot either would do any good. The more I think of a southern college the less I think of it—ye gods I could wear coats—even sweaters—even a sterno stove under my bed—— I really think they were utter fools to let such a point drive them to such drastic lengths. In short I am still quite disgusted but hopeful—'bloody but unbowed'—and Mom if there is *anything* you can do—tell 'Byard' I spent a nite in jail and have been branding calves—it may help.

Love
Bill

Mr. Keating: unidentified.
Franny: Francis C. Ware Jr., his roommate at Harvard.

Harold: the H— mentioned in the first paragraph, but otherwise unknown.
Dr. Williams: unidentified.
'bloody but unbowed': from the once-popular poem "Invictus" by British writer William Ernest Henley (1849–1903) expressing determination: "Under the bludgeonings of chance / My head is bloody, but unbowed."
'Byard': unidentified.

To Edith Gaddis

Colorado Springs, Colorado
[8 August 1942]

Dear Mom—

Well everything is still under control, and I'm presently enjoying a fine time in Colo. Springs as Francis' guest. I rolled in about Wednesday evening and have been entertained royally since.

You have probably received a card asking you to send the field boots (and the barracks bag if you haven't sent them yet) to Leadville—it is up in the mountains and there's a big job of some sort going on there; it is really at 'Pando' which is just outside of Leadville but I doubt if they have a post office. At any rate I expect to go up there and work for a while.

Harold was a fine fellow—real 'Wyoming'—and believe me the ranch was wonderful.

Having been here since Wednesday I do feel rather guilty but Francis is having a party on Sunday and they want me to stay for that, so I'll probably be off for Pando around Monday or Tuesday.

It did feel good getting back into shoes and a coat and tie and bath after the ranch, and in Denver I hit another book store and got a nice leather bound copy of O'Neill's sea-plays, *Vanity Fair* and *Crime and Punishment* to catch up a little.

Well Pando is supposed to be pretty tough—one of the toughest towns out here, as it's just a camp, and I've met men who wouldn't stay because of their familys, so I mayn't last long but it does sound interesting and worth a try—

Love
Bill

O'Neill's sea-plays: probably Eugene O'Neill's *Moon of the Caribees and Six Other Plays of the Sea* (1919).
Vanity Fair [...] *Crime and Punishment*: classic novels by William Thackeray (1848) and Fyodor Dostoevsky (1866).

To Edith Gaddis

Pando, Colorado
[15 August 1942]

Dear Mom—

Well am settled for a few days—not more—because this is *some* job; cold in the morning and now we are working 12 hrs. per day—½ hr. off for lunch—go on at 5:30 A.M. and off at 5:30. We are 2 miles high but the alt. seems all right tho it is cold especially mornings. Don't know how long it will last.

Well I can't write any college because I don't know where I'm going to be—I do expect to be home early in September and then will start out for school again. And so since there isn't any chance for Harvard just pick out any southern college with a nice name—I think Tulane sounds better than Tucson—and let H— send what ever they have to. I don't know and it doesn't particularly matter.

I got the check at the Springs and thanks tho I shan't need it for a while unless I'm fired which is very probable.

I think it's foolish to try an urinalysis—besides have no place to so just tell Williams and all his buddies to find some other where to peddle their bottles and pills—I'm all thru with them.

The address is just Pando Colo. and the boots will probably come in a few days—

Well must get to bed to get up at 4:30 tomorrow morning—

Love
Bill

To Edith Gaddis

[*WG returned to Harvard in September* 1942.]

Harvard University
Cambridge, Massachusetts
[25 September 1942]

Dear Mom—

Well it began today—classes, I mean—and oh boy! Now the devil to pay for eight months hence I guess.

I had a talk with Dean Leighton—am only supposed to take 2 subjects but have signed up for 4—think I can talk Dr. Bach into it. Am taking Eng. A (required), French C (required—*lousy* course—just *lousy* right thru to the last day, but required), Eng I—good course—history of Eng. literature—open to freshmen and sophs—and psychology I—a 2nd year course—had to get permission from the instructor to take it—reputed to be tough but a good course. Also books have been changed for all courses but Eng A—so today spent practically $10 on books—still lack three.

The extra $100 for tuition is OK—all the boys had trouble—many with own checking acc'ts—were stymied—but they don't catch up for a day or two and by that time it will be straightened out.

Got a letter from Underwood—they say the typewriter is on the way—I already owe a 600 wd. theme! Boy they don't waste time.

I got my lamp back from Neil and the clock—and am going to get the rug as soon as I have time!

Francis is OK for roommate—very conservative—quiet—extremist really—may be he'll be a good influence.

John is still the same—and the old crowd—same bunch—you know I feel like an upper classman—all upper classmen around me etc.—it's wonderful.

Love
Bill

Say when you get a chance could you start the following things on their way up here to make our room more habitable[:] the leopard skin on the lodge closet door—the spurs on the floor nearby—both of Smokey's pictures—the small rug—both machetes and the little Mexican knife & sheath & chain to the right of the east hayloft windows (one machete is over hayloft door—the other on edge of balcony)—also any thing else you think might look intriguing on our wall—oh yes the *steers' horns*—

Thanks
Bill

P.P.S. [*He continues with another page of requests.*]

———————

John: John Snow; see headnote to 13 March 1994.
Smokey: WG's Labrador; spelled Smoky below.

———————

To Edith Gaddis

Eliot House D-31
Cambridge, Mass.
[4 October 1942]

Dear Mom—

Back again into this wonderful old life—but for how long? Gee, it's got me—not worried, but thinking, and wondering sometimes it seems so futile, but this is so good I wish it might last.

Thanks for the letters—and it's so swell that the raise worked out, probably to buy me a sea chest a sailor sent or something! The package came too.

Am trying to keep work up, and to the best of my knowledge am up in it all—am recovering now from a film we had today in psychology of a dog with half a brain!! boy they have everything here.

Also have made a new discovery—the music room here, with fine record player and all kinds of classics—*Afternoon of a Faun* and the *Bolero*, *Porgy & Bess*, *Scheherazade*—everything.

I saw Cliff Mon. evening—lent him $25 to buy a little cocker spaniel which is very cute—don't be alarmed tho—I have his check and am going to cash it tomorrow—I left him and went down to 42nd St.—up to 500 to a place Eddie South was supposed to be playing but he wasn't there—then Café Society uptown—saw Hazel Scott—wonderful—and got a late train up—slept all the way—

Must get back to my English—

Love
Bill

Cliff: mentioned earlier (20 April 1942), but unidentified.

Eddie South: African-American jazz violinist (1904–62).

Hazel Scott: African-American pianist (1920–81). The Café Society was a nightclub on 58th Street between Lexington and Park Avenue (an offshoot of the better-known one down in Greenwich Village).

To Edith Gaddis

Cambridge, Massachusetts
[5 October 1942]

Dear Mom—

Thanks so much for the letter and bond—gee it will save things—I need three books for French (must read *Tovaritch*—in French—isn't that awful?!!). We are also waiting to get some slip covers for our couch ($4!).

And thanks for sending the stuff—it will look swell up here. It's all right about Smoky's pictures—will get 'em later— And then thanks for the pen—it will be swell I know—

Don't know about the rug but there's time for that— *And* thanks for *Bacchus*—it will look handsome too. I know.

And now I have a bit of bad news—you remember the raincoat I was *so* proud of—and saw me thru from Panama to L.A.—and Arizona and everything—any how I lost it—registered at Memorial Hall for school—went out and walked half a block—remembered I'd left it in the chair—ran back—practically immediately—and it was *gone*—checked with janitor and lost–found—no sign—some body picked it up so apparently it's gone—we were thinking of a new top coat—they have water repellant top coats—sort of combinations— might get one of them—what's your word?—keep present coat for winter cold.

Saw the Penn game here Saturday—we lost but good game—have been seeing John and company recently too—everything swell so far except French C—but can't have everything—excuse hurry but must read some Middle English Drama and psychology for tomorrow—will write again soon—

Love
Bill

Tovaritch: stage comedy by Jacques Deval, adapted as a film (1935).

Middle English Drama: undoubtedly *Chief Pre-Shakespearean Dramas*, ed. Joseph Quincy Adams (Cambridge: Houghton Mifflin, 1924), which WG used for *R* and retained all his life.

To Edith Gaddis

[*A rare typewritten letter, which is what WG means by the opening phrase.*]

Cambridge, Massachusetts
[12 November 1942]

Dear Mom

This may seem like a queer way to write but am in the midst of another one of those D— themes for English which is unimportant anyhow, and am taking a breather.

Say I have only got one hour mark back: an 83 in English which is about a B which suits me *fine*! It is the only course I really care about—I mean really like and want to get the most out of. The psyc is good but getting tough—we're getting into physics which I hadn't expected but it is still interesting. The French is of course still all right, and am trying to get a good basic knowledge of it; the exam is tomorrow. Sometimes I get disgusted with it but something always comes—this time it was the French film of *Crime and Punishment* that we saw down in Boston—to make me realize what a beautiful language it is and what fun it would be to know it well and all of the gates that would be open to one who did understand it.

English A is still as inane as ever—I write the themes, work on them, but that's all—I didn't take the inconsequential hour exam in it; you see that was one good reason I went up to Stillman. It wasn't a stomach ache, but 'uncontrollable nausea,' which finally came up to get me after celebrating that game we won last Saturday (Princeton) and then studying hard for the hour exams during the week. I was just upset that day but got right over it and now am back at it again.

I'm beginning to wish I had been able to squeeze Philosophy A in somewhere this year. I was over in John's room late last nite and we 'got into it,' and it was really fun. Have been reading Nietzsche and Schopenhauer and got a book of Kant's out of the library today. Incidentally, we have the most wonderful house library in Eliot: all kinds of books, but an accent on classics and such, and big leather covered chairs etc. Gee it's all really wonderful.

Glad to hear about that $5 for that coat; everything here seems to come in 5's; for the radio which I just got out of 'hock' 5 for the student council, 5 for our venetian blinds, which is about all our rooms has, aside from the $4 couch!

Yale next week! Boy it's going to be something; John is taking some woman from locally here, a swell girl a bit on the 'debby' side, you know, that way of talking etc., but nice; we went over and had tea at their home about a week and a half ago. And my amazing Puritan room mate with a girl coming from Cleveland; he never fails to amaze me with something new like this!

And how the time passes; it seems like November just started, and here it is almost half done, and I owe a theme for December in one course already! It is snowing just a little today, and I saw the handsomest Christmas cards down at the Coop with pictures of the Eliot House gate in colour; gee it's all as good as it ever could be, except for one detail, spelled A-r-t-h-u-r-M-u-r-r-a-y. Ware and I were hashing it over this afternoon, and I guess I'll have to do something one of these days.

Love,
Bill

French film of *Crime and Punishment*: Pierre Chenel's *Crime et châtiment* (1935).
'debby': a high-society debutante.
A-r-t-h-u-r-M-u-r-r-a-y: name of the founder of a chain of dance studios.

To Edith Gaddis

Cambridge, Massachusetts
[27 November 1942]

Dear Mom—

Well—here we are—another envelop of bills—see how they come.
Neil and I stayed in town Sunday night—saw *Native Son*—liked it a great

deal; finally got a bus up after the show—but it was worth it. Gee, he is some guy, isn't he?! It was some mess but worked out fine I guess.

Last evening Camilla Sewell (the girl whom John had down to the Yale game) had a lovely and very formal tea dance—you know, butlers in tails etc.—but *nice*!

Tonight same bunch—I say bunch—of opera players are doing *Carmen* down in Boston—we may go down, I don't know. I can't figure whether it would be better to see it done poorly than not at all—we'll see—

Have some psyc. to catch up on—

Love
Bill

Native Son : Richard Wright's 1940 novel was adapted for the stage the following year.

To Edith Gaddis

Cambridge, Massachusetts
[3 December 1942]

Dear Mom—

Just a note—have to study for exam tomorrow—in English A.— And so angry now am about to fly—my section man recommended a book to me he said was an exposition of the theory of history's repeating itself etc.— I got it and turns out to be history of Communism and Socialism—Marxism—enough to make me actively ill—so don't care about mark in this test but am going to tell him what I think of his *lousy* piggish socialism &c— some times I think he's turned that way—he recommends many such books—so I'm going to tell him how stinking I think it is and not worry about an E.

Have got Christmas cards—50—do you know where that plate I had for engraving is? It must be perhaps in my desk or somewhere—I'd like to have them done and mailed from here if possible—would appreciate it if you should run across it to send it up.—

Can hardly wait for Christmas—it will probably be the last "home from college" Christmas and I hope it will turn out well. We're having a house formal here Saturday night but think I will abstain—the Christmas recess is more important. Quite a few of the fellows are going to be in town and will probably see them then and be in New York a good part of the time—

Well it isn't long now—

Must get back to work—

Love
Bill

P.S.—Have gotten a couple of W. Saroyan's books—wonderful—but G Stein is still a little beyond!

E: Harvard's failing grade.

W. Saroyan: William Saroyan (1908–81), American short-story writer, novelist, and playwright, at the peak of his fame in 1942.

G Stein: Gertrude Stein (1874–1946), American writer and art patron.

To Edith Gaddis

Eliot House
11 January [1943]

Dear Mom—

Everything is fine and thanks for the check.

The work has been rather lax recently but only because the finals are coming up—@!!☆ brother—then we get it! My first exam is next Monday—English I—my last one Monday the 25th in psychology. I think I shall be home Monday (25th) evening—OK? And say, how do you think the $ situation will be about then—I'd like to try to erase that mess I made of Christmas week if it's possible and try to see some shows—plan ahead I mean and *work it out* like you have always said— [...]

Charles Gardiner is going to be in town over the weekend too, and wants me to see a show or two with him—more complications. He is just 18 but mature—*well* read etc.—*good* mind etc.—remembers *Dead End—Winterset* etc. Quite a guy.

Got a card from Francis this AM—he's gone for good I guess—I am to send his last box out to him—'end of an era!—'

Say, I hear you're having gasoline trouble!! How are you coming out with the coupons? I suppose we did unnecessary driving, but I think it came out the same as if I hadn't come home at all—and hadn't got the 4 'A' stickers from Granga.

We have been living quite a life this past week but now everyone is going into seclusion for midyear preparation—me too—it now being 1 AM and am starting *She Stoops to Conquer* for Eng I—wonderful course.

Love
Bill

P.S.—Tue AM—just got inductment papers—to report here the 14th—Thursday—so my next letter I'll either be 4F or in His Majesty's Army!

Charles Gardiner: Charles Wesley Gardner Jr. (1924–2013) of Bridgeport, CT, who later became a psychiatrist and professor of psychiatry at Yale. WG consistently misspelled his surname (which has been silently corrected hereafter), until his letter of 28 December 1947.

gasoline troubles: in 1942, gas rationing went into effect. An "A" sticker on a car was the lowest priority of gasoline rationing.

Dead End—Winterset: movies that came out in 1937 and 1936, respectively.

She Stoops to Conquer: classic comedy by Oliver Goldsmith (1773).

To Edith Gaddis

Cambridge, Massachusetts
[16 January 1943]

Dear Mom—

Tried to get into Merchant Marine—couldn't because of albumin; had draft board changed to Cambridge—will probably be inducted in early February but think I shan't be drafted.

Thanks for Sak's letter—since it looks like I'll be here and do need a suit—well what do you think? I need it and they have my measurements—couldn't they send it up?

Well everything under control, and except for owing Weidner library a small fortune and wanting to get a newspaper job *immediately*, having just seen Cary Grant in *Once Upon a Honeymoon*, I guess things will stay under control—

Love
Bill

Once Upon a Honeymoon: 1942 film in which Grant plays a radio correspondent in Europe.

To Edith Gaddis

Cambridge, Massachusetts
[11 February 1943]

Dear Mom—

Just about able to sit up and write after my first fencing—first physical ed. I've had in years—and it was wild! Exercises I never knew existed. My right leg is *sore* from them and practicing lunges etc. I do hope I can stay with it. It is some sport.

Thanks for the watch—it's good to have it again—and the gloves are *beautiful* thanks so much for both—and the checks. I paid 22.75 on the Coop's bill and got $8 change—now I can charge until March 10th. That bill is right I guess and will check up some more. Now I can pay Callahan—and get a ticket to the ballet—the Ballet Russe de Monte Carlo is going to be up here next week—*Scherherezade* Thursday night—the *Afternoon of a Faun* Saturday night—I don't know which—those are the ones I want to see—

Last evening my room mate and I and some others (one fellow from India, one from Puerto Rico,—Afghanistan etc.) were invited to dinner at Mr. Finley's—the house master's—quarters—quite an affair—beautiful furniture, silver service etc.—an Australian flier was here and did a great deal of talking but otherwise it was quite an event—

Right now it's time to stop—Stanley Gould just came over—from 'Watch Hill' in Connecticut—who practiced drums for 6 years—and my room mate—and a record named Chasin' with Chase are all going at once—so—I'd better get to work

Love
Bill

Callahan: there are two Callahans in the *Harvard Freshman Red Book*: I suspect this is John Anthony Callahan of Plainfield, NJ, who lived on campus (the other lived at home).

Stanley Gould: (1926–85), later became a well-known Greenwich Village hipster/junkie. He was the model for Anatole Broyard's "Portrait of a Hipster" (*Partisan Review*, June 1948) and for Ross Wallenstein in Kerouac's novel *The Subterraneans* (1958), in which WG also appears (as Harold Sand).

Chasin' with Chase: a jazz tune recorded by vibraphonist Lionel Hampton.

To Edith Gaddis

Cambridge, Massachusetts
[19 February 1943]

Dear Mom—

We did see the ballet last night and it was beautiful—we had wonderful seats—middle of back, orchestra circle, 1st row, *Scheherazade* was—well just — — — don't have the right words. We're going again tomorrow night—*Afternoon of a Faun* (Callahan cashed a check!).

I have been quite busy all week, and waiting around for George, who I thot might show up. He set out the 17th and I wanted him to stop here on his way down—then looked at the map and saw how far out of his way it is, so I'm really not surprised not seeing him. I hope I do before he goes, tho.

Red and I have furnished the room some what—an easy chair, lamp, and pillows for the couch, and now it is quite liveable—strange how much these little things do. It runs into $ but certainly is worth it.

We haven't been asked for any ration books up here—they just feed us tripe and that is that. However I see no reason for not getting my number 2 book, as we can't tell how long I'll be here.

I'm quite busy—an hour exam in psyc. next week, 5000 words (which is quite a lot when you stop to count them up) on the short story form in the *New Yorker, Atlantic Monthly* etc.—I had a talk with Mr. Elman—he is quite all right—in fact I gave him a story I wrote for him to look at and criticize—which he probably *will*!

John is taking a secretarial course in Washington—and not exceedingly happy with it—but it will clear up I guess.

And by now (when you get this letter) you will probably know all about it—tho it may not happen—but Charley Socarides is coming soon to try to get into some medical school in NY—plans to stay at the Biltmore and may look up Mrs. Garrett! So—it's out of my hands—I'd like to have come down with him, but $ and work and I guess it's best I'm not—a good long weekend.

The news about J— Osborne quite astounding—but keep me posted—I don't know if I'll be down in April—no Easter vacation—

Love

B—

---

ration books: issued in World War II to control consumption of high-demand products. Book 2 was issued in January 1943.

Mr. Elman: unidentified.

Charley Socarides: Charles W. Socarides (1922–2005), American psychiatrist and author, known for his belief that homosexuality was a curable illness. He graduated from Harvard in 1945, and stayed in touch with WG for years.

J— Osborne: Jim Osborne, apparently a high-school friend.

To Edith Gaddis

Cambridge, Massachusetts

[25/27 February 1943]

Dear Mom—

Thanks so much for the check—and now if I can collect from my roommate I can see Sylvia Sidney in *Pygmalion* this weekend too! I suppose that it was extravagant to go to the Ballet Russe—twice—and good seats, but can never regret it; the first night was better than the second, but the latter was worth seeing just for the *Afternoon of a Faun* which they did beautifully. Of course it was quite short but delightful all the same.

And now the best news: I have gotten out of that time wasting french class—I was really getting nothing out of it that it hadn't had already, and the only reason for taking it was language requirement for a degree. So, after much trouble, I got admitted to English 3b, the 'form of the drama, from Lope de Vega to Odets,' and am effervescent with delight! It is quite late to be starting a course (they all started when I came back—1st of feb), it is essentially an upperclass course, and there is a rule that no freshman may take more than two courses on the same subject, but I made it; now to try to get through it! I have had to get new books for it, and charged them at the Coop, and so dont know what this next bill will be, but it isn't necessary to pay it; I have got all I need there and it can go until convenient. And so here I am, three English courses and one in psychology! Perfect. And what with the room furnished I enjoy staying at home and studying such stuff instead of going off as last half. However we do have fun; a new game called 'International Spy,' (sound like 4 year-olds?); we have two rival spy rings, Charlie S— and myself, and the other is Gardner and Callahan; we try to outwit each other at any opportunity. A few nights ago they locked us in their bathroom, and we had to climb out the window and in someone else's bathroom window (only 2nd floor) to escape. So now we call them 'junior spys' (Callahan is 190 lbs, Gardner 180) and they do not like it. And so we go!

Say before I forget, please send me a sheet or two; I only had three and two of them have worn through and torn. Mrs. Trask (our biddie) told me to be sure to see about it! [...]

Well, back to reading 'dramas,' and an hour exam in psyc friday, and a three thousand word paper for english A, and a conclusion to compose (about 700 words) for Coleridges (assinine) poem 'Christabel.'

Love
Bill

I forgot to tell you about the best bargain. there is a book i have been wanting —poetic drama is the name of it, a $5 book—beautiful thing, poetic drama from the greeks to edna st v— millay. i went to a book store where it had been marked down, gave them my french texts, and got the book for $1! isnt that grand?!

written Thursday—now am mailing it Saturday—have been busy—Jim Osborne showed up—will write again—

Sylvia Sidney in *Pygmalion*: American film and stage actress (1910–99); *Pygmalion* (1913) is one of George Bernard Shaw's most popular plays.

'Christabel': a Gothic ballad composed 1797–1800, but not published until 1816.

poetic drama: *Poetic Drama: An Anthology of Plays in Verse from Ancient Greek to Modern American*, ed. Alfred Kreymborg (Modern Age Books, 1941).

edna st v— millay: American poet and dramatist (1892–1950).

To Edith Gaddis

Cambridge, Massachusetts
[17 March 1943]

Dear Mother

Just a letter between plays—what a race this is. Hour exams this past week, and just out of Stillman. What work—enough to have to make up the regular work for the exams—but this English course—just reading play after play day and night. I am in the Restoration drama and the class doing Chekov! The exam is Thursday. I can't get any of the notes from the lectures; I have missed just half the course!—between getting in late and then the measles just did it. The man who gives the course is Theodore Spenser! Really a *plum*—and a grand one too. I don't know how I'll come out in the exam and the course, but I'm enjoying it immensely and he is really a *top* man as you know. His lectures are wonderful and I regret having missed the ones I have. But we're getting into modern work now which is really going to be interesting.

I am going to have to write 4000 words and chose O'Neill when we study him in a week or two. Would it be too much to ask for you to send my copies up? I would appreciate it.

There is one book I need—*Masters of the Drama*—Gassner—for this course and would have helped in the exam but couldn't get it at that @!?// Coop—they could 'order' it for me—a week later—but Gardner hasn't had a check recently!—and I owe him $5 anyhow—oh I got the shoes—$3 but *handsome*—practically new.

Also thanks for the ration books—and Mrs. Trask and I both send thanks for the sheets!

Love
Bill

Chekov: Anton Chekhov (1860–1904), Russian playwright and short-story writer.

Theodore Spenser: Spencer (1902–49) taught at Harvard from 1927 until his death. He also published fiction, poetry, and edited James Joyce's *Stephen Hero* (New Directions, 1944).

O'Neill [...] my copies: WG mentions buying O'Neill's sea plays in his letter of 8 August 1942.

Masters of the Drama: a historical overview by John Gassner (Random House, 1940).

To Edith Gaddis

[*First mention of the* Harvard Lampoon, *the well-known undergraduate humor maga-zine founded in 1876. WG's first contribution appeared in the 1 October 1943 issue; he became its president in spring 1944, and published over 60 items (poems, stories, reviews, essays, cartoons, jokes) there by the time he left Harvard in January 1945.*]

> Cambridge, Massachusetts
> [18 April 1943]

Dear Mother

[...] George just left today—came up and stayed on Friday and Thursday night and we had a fine time—went to see *Cry Havoc* in Boston, which was all right but nothing special.

And speaking of 'drama'—guess who is property man for Harvard Dramatic Club—?! They are putting a play on in about 3 weeks, and I got the job—no great position but contacts and experience!

And Kibby Home—a fellow I know on the *Lampoon*—has told me to come on down and try it—that I stand a good chance!—things really developing! [...]

Well must get back to work—a 4000 word paper in attempt at psycho-analysis of some of Eugene O'Neill's more serious plays—! and not much time with play rehearsals every night (I have been reading the part of a spinster for the last week—I hope one shows up!)—

> Love
> Bill

Cry Havoc: a 1943 film with an all-woman cast about nurses during warfare.

To Edith Gaddis

> Cambridge, Massachusetts
> [22 July 1943]

Dear Mom—

Sorry I haven't written. John Snow has been up here for a week and just left about an hour ago. I haven't got too much work done (have kept up, read-ing plays for Spencer and learning lines from Shakespeare) etc.—but I have plenty of psychology to do for tomorrow.

Thru John I got to know Mac Osburne—president of *Lampoon* (and of A— D— Club)—he's a fine fellow as I had heard—urges me to come down and try out so I must think up something witty to write. Looks like I do have a chance! [...]

> Love
> Bill

A— D— Club: an all-male club founded in 1836 (an offshoot of Alpha Delta Phi fraternity).

To Edith Gaddis

> Cambridge, Massachusetts
> [12 August 1943]

Dear Mother—

Thanks for the last check—debts etc cleared up and my clothes cleaned—so now am prepared to appear in public! Say I just realized about Labour Day weekend—I'll have 4 or 5 days off! What do you think?

We were up last night writing Charley's radio script—his 'Man About Boston' programme—he and Gardner write the script, panning everything in town, having seen about ⅛ of it—but it's a lot of fun.—

I am beginning to get scared—hour exam in psyc. next week—what a horrible course! But the others are coming along well. I don't suppose you know W. H. Auden—a modern poet—Hazel probably knows him. I met him a few days ago—Mr. Spencer introduced me. Boy I was quite thrilled. And then we saw Rex Ingram do the *Emperor Jones* up here too.—and see him in the street occasionally.

If you haven't sent Johnson Smith don't bother because Mac was in a hurry for this thing I was writing—wanted it for the forthcoming issue—so I wrote it on what I could remember—it came out all right tho I don't know yet whether he's going to print it or not.

There is little else doing—somehow we don't feel the heat up here—and all your subtle cajolling can't get me to Revere Beach! Just a jump in the pool downstairs when things get warm, or to wake up in the mornings is enough—and if things get too hot I just settle down with *Vanity Fair* which I am about halfway through. But I may start to row once in a while soon. Don't know yet.—am going down today for a physical exam—and if they make me take conditioning—@!?☆/!

> Love
> Bill

W. H. Auden: the British poet (1907–73) was teaching at Swarthmore at the time.
Hazel: Hazel Bond of Yellow Springs, Ohio, a maternal relation.

Rex Ingram do the *Emperor Jones*: the protagonist of Eugene O'Neill's 1920 play is a plum role for African-American actors like Ingram (1895–1969).

Johnson Smith: a mail-order company specializing in novelty items. The thing WG was writing apparently wasn't published.

To Ida Williams Way

[*WG's great-aunt (d. 1951), daughter of music educator Samuel E. Williams (1855–1937) and a pianist and bass violinist in his family orchestra. She was a supervisor of music in public schools until 1920, after which she became a businesswoman.*]

> Adams House B 34
> Cambridge, Massachusetts
> [16 November 1943]

Dear Gram

Thanks so much for the idea and the invitation—and financial backing!—but this is the one weekend we expect to turn out up here.

First off the first big dinner at the *Poon* this year, and after dinner we have our pictures (*Poon* staff) made for the '45 yearbook—I won't get in any other way—as a member of the class that is—so I'd at least like to get in as a member of the *Lampoon*!

Then Saturday is our one big football game—I don't expect to go, but anyhow it will probably turn out to be a pretty big weekend. I would love to come down of course, but now see how it is—and then too, I have reason to believe that I can work the Thanksgiving weekend so I can get down—not sure of course, and something's liable to crop up—probably will—but there's a chance.

Everything up here is coming along wonderfully—including my work (!). A new issue ought to be out within a week and a half—I'll send a couple of copies down when it does. And I'm glad (and somewhat surprised) that Aunt Emma liked it!

Thanks again—and I hope I'll see you around Thanksgiving

> Love
> Bill

---

new issue: dated 19 November, it contains four items by WG.

Aunt Emma: Emma Bond, Mrs. Way's cousin.

To Edith Gaddis

[*At this point, WG began eschewing capitals in his typed letters.*]

WG (center) with some *Lampoon* staff, 1944 (photo by Chester T. Holbrook).

Cambridge, Massachusetts
[10 December 1943]

dear Mother

terribly sorry i haven't written, and this time i can really say that i have been pretty busy well right through until tonight—haven't had time to get a haircut and so you can imagine what i look like by this time!

we had *'Poon* deadlines through that first week, and what with the dearth of prose writers i was called on and kept busy, as i am afraid the next issue will attest to. in fact, i even wrote the editorial! then of course there was that quantity of Spinoza which i had to get through my head (though i did get a B– on the quiz, so i feel all right about it) and a story to write (which i just got back with an A! he liked it and thought parts admirable—really gives me a lift.)

and no sooner had that got by than an hour exam in Eng 5, and *Bleak House* seemed to go on interminably. the exam was today, and also more Spinoza quiz, and one in the criminology course, all of which give me a sort of warm feeling, because i think i did fairly well.

ever and above these banal and mundane topics, however, my social life seems to have taken a turn for the better. i am not sure, but Middendorf informed me that i had been elected to the Hasty Pudding, though that was some days ago and i haven't heard anything about it. but also the Speakers Club has invited me to two punches, and i seem to know quite a number of the fellows (many of whom are *'Poon* men), so i may make a club yet.

thanks so much for the check and money—and please don't think that this letter is merely to enclose the Coop bill (which is rather high this month, but as always with the beginning of a term, mostly books), and the impending 7.80 for *Poon* dues, though there is not any rush—i'll be there whenever they want me!

i don't think i told you that Mr Dick (Amer Field Ser)'s son is on the *'Poon*! it may not help, but then again . . . i haven't had time to get to the Boston office, but plan to do it soon, perhaps the weekend.

heard from Mark, having a simply terrible time in texas with a bunch of illiterates, and *prays* for a letter. really, it sounds pretty bad.

must write a 4500 word story this weekend too, so will probably be occupied far into the night. but i don't mind, if i can get into the subject.

that's about all—will let you know how things work out

Love   Bill

next issue: published 10 December, it contains five contributions by WG, including two short stories ("I Want You for Christmas" and "The Kid in Upper Five").
Bleak House: Charles Dickens' esteemed legal novel (1852).
Hasty Pudding [...] Speakers Club: the first was founded in 1770, the oldest college social club in America; the second was founded in 1908 as an intellectual, not social, club.
Mr Dick (Amer Field Ser)'s son: C. Mathews Dick (class of '46); the American Field Service was founded in 1915 as a corps of ambulance drivers before becoming a student-exchange program.

To Edith Gaddis

Cambridge, Massachusetts
[12 February 1944]

dear Mother

how are things going?—and are we still hanging on? i haven't realized that we were so involved, or at least that i had got you so involved. i thought that everything was just about breaking even. and now i do want to stay on here, unless i get thrown out by the language requirement which is sort of a mess. but aside from these problems seemingly everything at hartford college are going quite well.

discounting my last letter, i shall start this angle out again freshly; you remember telling me to fall in love (i am afraid that i am going to be throwing that up continually!). there is an awfully nice and attractive girl whom i have been coming across twice a week in my short story writing class. i thought that i was the only one that knew about her, but was suddenly surprised when i met her with Bob Ward over at the *Lampoon* a few evenings ago—and Saturday evening he was with her at the *Lampoon* dance. and so as the evening wore on and we all wore on i danced with her(!) though you could hardly call it dancing i'm afraid because i spent most of the time standing and looking at her and just being pretty happy about the whole thing. her name—Jean Campbell. she is really awfully nice, but early in the morning (at the moment) i can't get onto just what i want to say. but she's going to be up here until october, and i am hoping to be able to get to know her better. i think that spring is on its way!

i still find it difficult to conceive that another term is ending. probably when exams are done i'll realize it, and they are quite imminent. except for this girl, things should be easier next term, because so many are leaving, and i suppose a lot of the little temptations will be gone. my class graduates in february, you know. and a number of the little outlets for flings will be carried off. but i do want to see more of Miss Campbell.

my sophomoric troubles will be done with the twenty fourth, and we come back the sixth of march. do you think that it would help things out if i were to stay up here and get a job for a few days. at this point (and you may say that it is Miss C— if you wish, tho she is only a contributing factor) i want to hold on at hartford college if it can be worked out.

Love
Bill

Jean Campbell: born in Vermont, Campbell (1922-2001) graduated from Radcliffe in 1944 and went on to become a writer and Beauty Editor of *Seventeen*.

To Edith Gaddis

Adams House B 34
Cambridge, Massachusetts
[17 February 1944]

Dear Mom—

[...] The *Lampoon* is printing a story of mine in the next issue and of course I am on top of the world. And incidentally your letter of encouragement helped a lot—I really feel 'ready' now! Osbourne seems to like my stuff—in fact I was talking to Mahoney (a very effete artist on our staff), about getting in. He said he'd heard them discussing my stories—and in quite a favorable light too! The point is one must have 4 pages of material accepted—they have taken my stuff, but it's not really accepted until they really decide to put it in. I may get some credit working on the business board—just to get me on—but you know the literary board is really the right and top side of the 'Poon to be on—so I don't know how long it will be.

And say at your first opportunity could you send me that dirty bedraggled copy of the Johnson Smith catalog which is probably on the hayloft bookcase. I want to try a story from those old fashioned amusement books they advertise—a Rediscover the American Home affair. I did write one and Mac told me to take that part and build it up. [...]

Things are coming along well—so far. I have been giving a good deal of time to the *Lampoon*, and am beginning to realize what this psychology course is! No kidding—the reading is *incredible*! Trying to explain and form theories for personality—which I have decided is quite futile. I don't know why the devil I ever got involved with it.

But otherwise things are quite grand, tho the heat does discourage sitting down to study for very long at a time. On the whole tho I am afraid I am quite exuberant—the room is fine (tho I can hear it every time someone dives down in the pool, and some fool is learning to play 'As Time Goes By' across the court on a trumpet.)

If it weren't for the $ end, I was thinking it would be nice if you could come up some weekend—after all I was a green freshman last time you saw the place. The Coop bill may be sizeable this month—books, a pair of pants and shirt etc.—and I don't know when the $65 from the '*Poon* will be due—

Well I have 30 lines of *Romeo and Juliet* to learn for tomorrow.

Love
Bill

---

story of mine: perhaps "Suffer the Little Children," which didn't appear in the next
   issue (1 April) but the one after that (15 May). Or WG could be referring to one of the
   short fables he was publishing at the time.
'As Time Goes By': song by Herman Hupfeld (1931) popularized in the movie *Casablanca* (1942).

To Edith Gaddis

The Harvard Lampoon, Inc.
Cambridge 28, Massachusetts
[27 February 1944]

Dear Mother—

Sunday—and the first chance I have had to write—really it has been quite a week!

Exams all last week of course—only two—but they lasted all week—and after being up for four nights it was quite a feeling Thursday with the 'press' lifted and really nothing to worry about.

The *Poon* had its final tremendous affair for the season—and really for all time, since so many are leaving. A very pleasant dinner at the Pudding and then the dance—of course I got mixed up and went to a punch and forgot to get my black shoes from the shoemaker whom I'd taken them to be shined—so I ended with tuxedo and those dirty white buckskins.

Peter Jenks—don't know whether I've mentioned him—he did the drawings for my poem—has left, and everything looks sort of blue—and then that woman being in Florida—if only she might have been up for the *Poon* dance—because it was the last of the neat ones. [...]

Everyone it seems is going to New York—all I hear is 'See you in Larue (a 58th St. spot!) and I'll probably get pretty fed up with this. I would like to get home before it goes(!)—and if it will be easier for you I certainly think it's the only thing to do. Perhaps next weekend? I don't know. I do want to get a pair of shoes—and the ballet is so important—as she is. Don't know about scholarship—but I might as well get the beneficiary business—and perhaps borrow something from them. Will write again when I get a little further with $ matters. [...]

Love
Bill

Peter Jenks [...] my poem: Jenks illustrated WG's poem beginning "Once came upon a quiet college town" in the 11 February issue of the *Lampoon*.

this job: WG had just picked up a part-time job "taking attendance."

Larue: one of the most fashionable restaurants of the time.

To Ida Williams Way

Harvard Lampoon
Cambridge 38, Massachusetts
2 April 1944

dear Gram

sorry to have missed you in Grand Rapids, and am writing this in plenty of time to make Winchester. having spent the better part of the night thus far preparing for an exam in abnormal psychology, mostly involved with experiments on rats, which is getting pretty sordid and seems a far cry from human mental disorders, i am ready for a release for a few minutes.

thanks a great deal for the check; it did arrive at a most opportune moment. however, instead of paying my Pudding bill i think i'll pay my first bill from the Speakers Club (35$). it is a dinner club which is pleasant and fun to belong to since i have known most of the members for some time. Pudding bill has run for so long that it might as well run on a while longer. i didn't make Delphic, but i think that it is just as well for a number of reasons, first the financial angle, not just initiation fee but the subsequent monthly dues which tend to pile up.

and then the group is hardly exciting or for that matter very interesting—just a bunch of 'good guys' with whom i really have little in common—nothing like the *Lampoon*! on the whole i think things have turned out quite well.

perhaps Mom mentioned that i had got a 100$ scholarship—subject of course to withdrawal if something drastic happens or if my marks tend to reach toward the lower depths. however, i am hoping that such will not be the case and that it will turn out all right.

perhaps Mom also mentioned my new interest in life up here. Her name is Jean Campbell, and really a singular person, interested in writing and all that sort of thing. She is twenty two and expects to graduate this fall, and what with her and work and the *Lampoon* i have little time to just sit and think!

as for the forthcoming issue of the *'Poon*, i shall send a copy—it will probably be ready in a little over a week. however, you will probably not enjoy it, unless you go for that '*Lampoon* wit,' since it is a reprint issue of old stuff from other years, and neither i nor any of the present members have written for it. however (and i admit this only to myself and members of the family! though i am sure others realize it) i am proud of my name at the top of the mast head.

with exams current and imminent my life is in rather a whirl—i can hardly realize that the term is almost half done, and another deadline for the *Lampoon* hanging dangerously close!

must get back to my rats and their neurotic personalities. regards to the Cheneys and congratulations to Bill.

> Love
> Bill

Winchester: in Indiana, where Way lived.
forthcoming issue: dated April 1, it lists WG as president on the masthead; he contributed a farcical introduction to this issue.

To Edith Gaddis

> Cambridge, Massachusetts
> [5 April 1944]

dear Mother

well it never seems to end. it is just like being seasick. after one bit of running excitement you don't see how it can keep on, but it does. [...] this elementary spanish is insidious; the abnormal psyc is good but a great amount of reading which as yet remains only touched, and an exam imminent; the social psyc is terrible—can you imagine, it seems to be a never ending discussion on politics, for which i see no reason and am beginning to dislike cordially. the short story course is the only thing that seems to be going evenly, but the fool wants the long (5000 word) story in about two weeks, right when hour exams come and the *Lampoon* deadline, which is really going to be bad and take time, since i seem to be the only one that holds it together and gets it moving. and must go down and read proofs for this issue very soon. [...]

well such are things now, if any of it has been clear. the only thing i am sure about at the moment is the way i am getting along with Her, which is singularly well.

Love
Bill

Her: Jean Campbell. In a letter to his mother two weeks earlier, WG wrote: "as for Her, we had a little trouble last evening. heavens i wish i could fall in love like a rational person and not rush it and get involved before things have started and then miss the boat and stand and watch it sail away. you can see that I am in rather a state."

To Edith Gaddis

Cambridge, Massachusetts
[20 April 1944]

dear Mother

am slowly getting there—though i am not sure of the destination. i spent most of last week and up for two nights studying for a spanish and then a psychology hour exam, and up until after 5 this a m writing my long story for english a 4.

and over it hangs this *Lampoon*—supposedly a deadline this week but hardly any one is coming around or doing anything, and so tonight i plan to spend trying to put it partially together and filling in prose, though i hardly feel like writing anything clever and witty. [...]

affairs with the Campbell girl are coming along very well. that is all i am certain of.

Love

---

this *Lampoon*: the 15 May issue has nine contributions by WG: an editorial, two stories, two poems, two drawings, an essay, and a facetious crossword puzzle.

To Edith Gaddis

Cambridge, Massachusetts
[23 July 1944]

dear Mother

[...] only one mark so far—a B on an english paper—pretty poor and drab course. Hillyers english course is more pleasant, and have seen him once—he is my tutor. that will be one bright spot in the academic end of it all. finally resorted to a modern art course, which is fun i suppose if one likes modern art. and the french is as bad as—no, not as bad as the spanish—but not much good, and i await the hour exam with qualms. do you think i shall ever write and not be muttering about the courses I am taking? really, it seems like i should be about ready for a phd by this time.

you have a copy of the *Itching Parrot*, don't you? could you possibly send it up as soon as possible? Jean needs it for her thesis and cant get a copy up here. [...]

aside from Jean there is little of interest—except our next issue of the *Lampoon*—devoted to politics. hmmm. at the moment Jean is busy on her thesis but we get together often enough. i don't know. also a very undignified corn like business on the underside of my left big toe

Love

Bill

Hillyers: poet Robert Hillyer (1895–1961), who taught at Harvard from 1926 until 1944. In an April 1943 letter, WG wrote to his mother: "Have been auditing Robert Hillyer's course on poetry for a while now—what a person he is—and grand lecturer—I mean, when he talks about 'having poets like Edward [*sic*] Arlington Robinson to a tea he gave' etc—adds *so* much." For an example of the kind of feedback Hillyer gave WG, see Marshall Klimasewiski's "William Gaddis and the Thoughts of Others," *Conjunctions* 70 (2018), 333–34.

Itching Parrot: a novel by José Joaquín Fernández de Lizardi (1816), translated by Katherine Anne Porter (1942).

To Edith Gaddis

Cambridge, Massachusetts
[28 November 1944]

dear Mother

you must not bandy that term 'free and gay' about so unadvisedly. i am on probation, and have lost my room permission among other things BUT (well this deserves a new paragraph):

Olsen and Jonson have a show in Boston, and they and their company of chorines etc. came out to the 'Poon Sunday afternoon at the invitation of one of our old (class of '01) members. we entertained them to the best of our respective abilities—and i came out quite well. Olsen (Jonson didn't show up) talked with me or rather to me for some time. and finally ended by asking me to come to the show as his guest, take notes on it, and write him a report of my reactions! critic! haha. and (This deserves a new one too):

one of the young ladies showed a rather abnormal rate of intelligence and we talked at length; she intends to leave and go onto *Life* magazine—one of her 'dearest friends' is foreign editor of *Life* etc. at any rate she is very nice and wants to come out and look Harvard over seriously and so forth. so i am left little choice. she has been a torch singer too. do i sound 18 yrs old? i guess. but do not be concerned. as you have no doubt guessed she is a bit taller than your son, and i feel pretty self conscious with her. i went back stage last night and was very impressed, or intrigued at least.

it is the biggest thing that has happened to the *'Poon* in some time.

thanx for the $. what with probation and three papers to write (and Jean expects to come down in December) i am not going to make Vermont [for Thanksgiving]. anyhow do not be concerned—this is all harmless and quite exciting. of course old 'Poonsters are saying 'while the cat's away...' but that is very silly.

Much Love
B

Olsen and Jonson: Ole Olsen and Chic Johnson, a vaudeville act best known for their *Hellzapoppin'* satiric revue. (In 1976, William H. Gass praised *J R* for its *Hellzapoppin'* energy when giving it the National Book Award.) The vaudeville revue WG refers to was called *Laffing Room Only!*, which tried out in Boston before moving to New York City for an extended run (December 1944–July 1945).
one of the young ladies: Frances Henderson: see next letter.

To Edith Gaddis

Cambridge, Massachusetts
[7 December 1944]

dear Mother—

not having heard from you for some time—specifically, not since i wrote you about having met this dancer, Miss Henderson. i am not worried, and ascribe it to your probably having a pretty difficult time getting settled in town etc. but i hope there is a letter tomorrow condoning, not mentioning, or even mild censure. Where are you living? and what arrangements? i hope it's all all right.

matter of fact, things have turned out much better than i ever could have expected. she is very nice and seems to know everything and everybody. and last evening i had dinner with her and Mr Olsen. this may sound like i am getting like Jan and preparing to run off with the Tom show; it is not a Tom show (though i did see it and was not at all as much intrigued as hellzapoppin or sons o fun) and the idea of going backstage is very exciting. i want to tell you all about it and also convince you it has not been like backstage at Minskys or Barnum and Baileys. something very funny and flattering—my being prex of the *Lampoon* seems to carry some weight! and the stage manager etc are especially nice to me. the whole thing is pretty new and eye opening.

i finally put the Christmas issue of *Lampoon* together at 9 this morning— that is certainly a load off. but in light of recent developments it looks like it's worth the work.

i have only got one mark this term so far, and it was B plus, and have two papers to do this week. then Christmas. Jean expects to come down here right after Christmas, but there are no plans, except that i get out the 22nd.

must make an eleven oclock class.

Love,
B

PS—Jean 'knows about' Miss Henderson and is quite approving about it, if that has been troubling you.

Miss Henderson: Frances Henderson, who appeared as a dancer in several numbers of *Laffing Room Only!* See headnote to 13 March 1946.

Jan: WG's uncle Jan Williams (1884–1981), a clarinetist who began playing with the John Philips Sousa Band when still a teenager, and eventually played for the New York Symphony and other orchestras. He became musical director of the Ernest Williams School of Music in 1947, founded by his brother (1881–1947), a cornet player.

Tom show: a blackface minstrel revue, based loosely on *Uncle Tom's Cabin*.

sons o fun: another Olsen/Johnson revue (1941–43).

Minskys: notorious burlesque show in New York City.

To Edith Gaddis

[*In January 1945, after an incident involving the Cambridge police (creating a public disturbance while drunk), WG was asked to leave Harvard. He moved to Manhattan and was hired by the* New Yorker *as a fact-checker, where he worked from late February 1945 to April 1946. In the summer of 1945 he went on vacation to Canada.*]

Mount Royal Hotel
Montreal, 2, P.Q.
[1 August 1945]

Dear Mother—

Frankly the more I move along the more I find that every city is quite like the last one. Perhaps there are sights in Montreal which I have missed (I have not visited the Wax Museum). But I feel little like gaping at anything.

At any rate tonight the boat leaves for Quebec and I expect to be on it.

Jacob did not arrive—and though I felt he might not when he did not show up I found myself vaguely disappointed. Really, in the little kicking about I have done I think I have had enough of wandering around cities alone. And shall probably be home before very long—

Love
Bill

Jacob: Jake Bean (1924–92), a Harvard friend who later became a connoisseur of Italian and French drawings; he was the curator of drawings at Manhattan's Metropolitan Museum of Art for thirty-one years.

To Edith Gaddis

Hotel Louis XIV
3 Place Royale
Quebec
[4 August 1945]

Dear Mother—

Coincident with yr letter came news from Beth that Je— plans to be married as soon as possible, to this fellow.

Oh—the thoughts that run through you as you read this—they are similar to mine, I know. Consequently I shall try to say little.

Yes, it is very difficult, but there is finality, and therefore something on which to build. I have nothing more to add—I shall leave here soon and see you the earlier part of the week, both of us a little stronger people, I think.

Again thanks, and love

B

To Marilyn Parke

[*Marilyn Anne Parke (1925–1993) was the younger sister of WG's friend Henry Parke, and later wrote a memoir of WG's younger days: see note to 10 September 1941.*]

The New Yorker
No. 25 West 43rd Street
[postmarked 23 November 1945]

Dear Marilyn—

Many thanks for yr. invitations, and since any wit of mine seems to be lost as a college memory, I can not be very clever about my answer. At any rate, for some time a costume party of sorts has been in the works here, and is supposed to consummate itself in a loft somewhere in New York that weekend. The last time I saw yr. brother, I was trying on a regalia in which I intend to pass myself off as a leper.

Except for a very occasional weekend in Cambridge, I spend all of my time here in town, doing largely nothing. Though most of the little money I squeeze out of this magasine seems to go into books of one sort or another.

At the moment my only plans for an out-of-town expedition involves the trip to New Haven to watch the Yales beat the Harvards in a game which otherwise holds less interest for me than politics. But it can be fun to see old friends for just long enough until they start to get boring—as it seems most of the end of Harvard that attends football games is inclined to do.

Thanks again for the invite—perhaps I shall see you up here later in the winter.

Yrs.
Bill

To Edith Gaddis

[*Final surviving page of undated letter on* New Yorker *stationery.*]

[late 1945 or 1946]
[...] received notice from draft board concerning occupational reclassification[.] needless to say at this point in my career I am rather terrified—how I *hate* to be manipulated.

meanwhile job goes awfully well—worked until 8 tonight
B

To Frances Henderson Diamond

[*The dancer WG mentions in his letters of 28 November and 7 December 1944. Henderson (1924–2019) was raised in Canada and at age 16 won a scholarship to study ballet in New York City; she joined Olsen and Johnson's vaudeville troupe a few years later. (See the headnotes to 6 April 1964 and 2 March 1976 for her remarkable later career.) WG apparently visited Henderson in Canada in the summer of 1945, but by 1946 she was living in Hollywood, and on 3 March 1946 she married Jack Diamond (1910–64), then in the publicity department for Warner Bros. and later Publicity Director for Universal Studios. (Humphrey Bogart was best man, Lauren Bacall matron of honor.) WG wrote to Henderson in early 1946 (not extant), and the letter that follows—handwritten on*]

New Yorker *stationery—responds to her letter to him dated 22 February 1946 (which opens "Willie, my pet"). WG was living on Horatio Street in the East Village at this time, the same street on which Wyatt Gwyon in* R *commits his art forgeries.*]

No. 25 West 43rd Street
[postmarked 13 March 1946]

My dear Frances—

Needless to say, yr. lovely letter caused a small flurry of excitement at quiet 79 Horatio Street—and further comment on how good it was to hear from you seems unnecessary. Of course you said just the things I wanted to read in a letter from you—but left me a little dark about just what you have been up to since you left Canada last summer. First I heard from friends still in Cambridge that just recently you had done a show in Boston—however, they had not seen it, nor you, and so I doubt the whole thing. Then this business of Hollywood. The name of the place connotes only one pursuit to the American mind (of which I have one—small) and so dear lady I gather that you are involved with the screen. You must tell me. I love you for the way you say things.

So much for you for the moment. I think that I probably told you all of what is happening to me. As for what has happened, the business of the ruptured courtship was long, ghastly, and pretty unhealthy. And really quite the best thing. Looking back on it now it is difficult to believe that it could have had the proportions it did in my mind. All that I can comment now is that it was a compleat experience and before it was done embraced any angle of such a piece of life that I can imagine. Briefly, if I had married her in May, as she so much wanted, things would have gone on—where I can not say, and am afraid to imagine. We had been living on in such a way that she was gradually getting tired and discouraged with the whole thing—and New York was hardly the right climate. She was in a great hurry, and I was lapsing, as I still am, certain that when the time comes to speak I shall know what to say, but am not ready now. Publishing a story in any of the local magasines would give no satisfaction, and I find the picture of making money (especially as an end to such a means) bores me. As for the girl, I wonder occasionally what is becoming of her—somehow it seems that she will always be disappointed. I am a little afraid for her because of that. One can not regret that she is incapable of suffering—I mean an emotional experience that takes one over compleatly for a little time, and leaves something of value. But that what she will always want will be a little bit beyond her. How terrible that she can never really, entirely, be happy. The goals she puts before her are *not* her goals.

Sorry I put in that business of my being "in a rut". I didn't mean it, really. The truth is that this job could become a rut, but for the time being it is reasonable and balanced. At the moment I have fond hopes of getting to Amsterdam with the Associated Press, which may well fizzle—but little matter if it does. The things I want are not in any country, nor in any job. As yet I am not quite sure where they are, but am coming nearer to the conclusions that they are latent in myself, and that through reading the thoughts, the *impressions*, and the creations of responsible minds I shall come nearer to discovering them. And then if I can articulate I shall be set. No hurry about that—my only thought now is to make progress as a human being.

How wonderful you have always been to listen to me—I should want so to talk with you now. But I think that I have said all that I shall have to say for some time. I am happy now, and hope earnestly that you are. Some of us deserve it, and some of us, it seems, can not escape it.

You must be happy now, I know—but you must tell me why.

my Love—
WG

---

ruptured courtship: years later Anatole Broyard met Jean Campbell at a party and they discussed their mutual friend: "When she broke off with him, she said, he climbed into the window of her apartment and burned her clothes in the fireplace" ("Remembering William Gaddis in the Nineteen-Fifties," *New England Review* 17.3 [Summer 1995]: 13).

Frances Henderson (courtesy Jamie Diamond).

2. THE RECOGNITIONS

1947–1955

To Edith Gaddis

[*In the spring of 1947, WG left New York for several years of traveling as he worked on* The Recognitions. *He first headed south for Mexico in a Cord convertible with a friend named Bill Davison.*]

New Orleans, Louisiana
[6 March 1947]

dear Mother—

after much fortune and misfortune we are off to Mexico I hope this afternoon. I trust that you got my wire, so that when we reach Laredo I shall have birth certificate and be able to get visa. It must be a student's visa, however, which disclaims any attentions on my part to get a job while there, since they have a sort of protective immigration. The point being that it will take a little while after I get to Mexico City to arrange through any contacts I may have to get a job, a little to one side of authority, as it were. I hope that you will be able to send me some money there—can you conveniently? We are leaving here with next to nothing, as you may imagine, and are taking on a passenger, the fellow who has been our host, and who I gather will be able to finance a good part of the trip from here on. You may gather from my letters the state that things have been in. But I just feel that once we get to Mexico city, and if you can send me some money there, that things will start to shape up well. The address is c/o Wells Fargo Express Company, Mexico D. F., Mexico, and to be marked Please Hold.

Also to add a touch of trouble, my leather suitcase stolen from the car last night, therewith all of my shirts, neckties, and all of the work I was taking with me. As for the work, it is too bad, but perhaps for the best since I plan to start rather freshly with writing when I get down there, and now will not have these things which I have written over the last year or two to distract me. The business of the shirts and ties, of course—infuriating. and the bag.

I want of course to write you a real letter, describing the pleasant parts of the trip, and what this city is like—certainly how much you would like it. But one minute we are to stay; the next, to leave; the next, to leave with a passenger. And now suddenly when it looks like we may get off in about an hour things are rather flurried. Health, and such things that may be worrying you, are all all right.

My love,
W

To Edith Gaddis

Rhodes Apartment Hotel
611 La Branch St.
Houston, Texas
9 March 1947

dear Mother—

Here we are, our plans made for us this time by a pretty ghastly breakdown of the car. and so I can take the opportunity to write you rather more of a letter than I have been able to manage in some time. And perhaps modify a few things which have perhaps troubled you; coming as they have in peacemeal sentences as bulletins on a consistent state of calamity.

Still I know what you are feeling under it all: even if there are occasional concerns (I imagine that the story of the suitcase gave you rather a turn) it is much better because things are happening, and moving, and alive, and not in one corner of Greenwich Vill. —and as long as I am eating and sleeping &c everything is all right. Good. I feel just that way.

Washington, as you could gather, was a pretty messy business, chiefly because of the cold. So windy and cold, and the blizzard, and sleeping on Mike's floor, chiefly difficult because we were both so discouraged at being stuck so near to NewYork, as if we might never get further. And so when we could leave we streaked out for South Carolina, and stopped at Chapel Hill. There a man of about 40 named Noel Houston teaches, and I have read a few of his pieces in the *New Yorker*, quite good. Well over a year ago a girl named Alice Adams who was at Radcliffe whom I knew quite well, mostly through Jean and later (and in New York) through Mike &c had told me that she wanted me to meet him. At any rate, we got there in the middle of the afternoon, drove out to his house and introduced ourselves, and spent until almost 7pm having a couple of drinks, and he talking at length about the *NYer* and its stories, the business of writing, &c&c, all in all very pleasant. We had, having heard of how affable he was, hoped that he might put us up somewhere for the night, but on arrival discovered that his wife and two children were ill, and so could hardly presume. Decided that the only thing to do was drive straight through to Atlanta and warm weather, Chapel Hill being similarly cold to everyplace we had left. Well, the drive that night was about the coldest thing I have ever managed. Oil being eaten up by the car, so that we must stop and try to pound holes in oil cans with nails and a rock, dark, and our hands and fingers like sticks. The only thing that saved it was good humour and a little profanity, for Davison is good in both. Finally, after one of those nights we always remember because they defy ever coming to an end, we got to Atlanta for breakfast, about eight. And never again mention Peachtree Street to me. It may have been magnificent after the War Between the States, but now the most tumblesome hurly-burly of trollycars, pedestrians, idiot drivers, and unattractive storefronts I have ever seen. We escaped about an hour later. The most infuriating thing, of course, was the weather—Georgia was quite as cold as Washington had been. And then at a town called Newnan, the radiator, which had to be flushed out, boiled, dipped, and all manner of endless treatments. The only thing was 2$ worth of room for the night. Which we needed. And so found it, and there a bath, shave, and suddenly nothing to do at 6pm. Odd dismal supper, and now 6.45—what but the movies? Two or three glasses of beer might have passed a pleasant hour, but no beer in Newnan. And so we sat through (and I am afraid almost enjoyed) a monstrosity called *The Strange Woman*, as Hedy Lamarr preached against such sins as Newnan probably never dreamt. Out on the street (in the courthouse square, needless to say), the clock struck—one could know the number of tolls before they were over—it was 9pm. Not a soul stirring, and a beautiful night. Stars, and not a sound. And so, after a brief walk, back to our home, where we collapsed.

The next day was another dedicated to the search for warmth, consisting of thundering out of Newnan and arriving in Mobile late in the evening. There we drank much coffee, ate many doughnuts, and finally drove down a long sideroad to sleep, for the first time on this 'camping trip', out-of-doors in our sleeping bags. Of course you know what happened. About 1am we were aroused by the gentle southern rain, teeming down upon our bland upturned faces. After what passed for sleep in the car, the road which he had driven down in the dark hours earlier proved one magnificent bank of mud, and I still marvel that we managed to reach the highway; obviously there was reason, for any fate which was attending us had more gruesome circumstances than a mere Alabama mudhole to address us to.

For just about cocktail time (I use it only as a figure of speech, to indicate the hour, for no one thought of such an amenity) we arrived in New Orleans. There the fun started. And it was so consistently folly that I cannot take it from day to day. Enough to say that we slept in the car for a few nights (I have not thought it necessary to mention that it was raining—rain such as Malay gets once in a generation), being low enough on funds to consider selling the car and sailing across the Gulf (until we were told that sailboats bring around 1500$), and other similarly unfelicitous notions. We spent one night in a great house belonging to friends of Bill's family, who apparently had not been posted on his standing (though one look at either of us should have told them that we were not exactly eligible bachelors). The living room was so big that a grand piano was passed quite unnoticed in one corner; there were, as a matter of fact, two kitchens, abreast of one another for no reason that my modest eating interests could resolve, and a dining room which should have been roped off and ogled at. By this time we had become rather legendary mendicants, with a good part of the city crossing the street when we approached. Fortunately New Orleans has a French Quarter. I was pulling at what was becoming a rather eager mustache and waiting for the time-honoured greeting: "Hello, friend. Where are you from?", this being the first step to any southern or western jail on a vagrancy charge, when we were introduced to a young man by a girl who had not the sense to see the desperation in our characters, and pictured us fondly as Bohem...This southern gentleman (for he is, or rather was before he became involved with us) found something in us which prompted him to offer an apartment which was kicking around in his hands. And therewith another resolve: sell the automobile, live for a little time in New Orleans, perhaps even work, and then go to Mexico in somewhat less sportive fashion than a Cord car. Oh, the gladsome effect of plans and resolution. We moved out of the car, into the apartment, had the lights and gas turned on, bargained with a passerby to sell the Cord for 300$, I wrote you a letter giving my address and settled state of mind, clothes were taken to be laundered and cleaned, and we drank a quiet glass of absinthe in what was once Jean Lafitte's blacksmithshop and went 'home'. As was well to be expected, dawn broke the following morning and so did everything else. The real-estate company appeared with legal forms which practically made us candidates for the penitentiary for our brief tenancy. The man who had made arrangements to buy the car had talked with some evil companion who convinced him that nothing could ruin him so quickly as a Cord (which is something I cannot quite deny flatly at the moment), and once more we were free to blow our brains out in the streets. But even New Orleans has laws against that, so what could we do but take miserable pennies to Lafitte's and invest them, this time in defeatingly tiny glasses of beer?

The proprietor of Lafitte's is a man whose name has passed me without ever leaving a mark. He is quiet, pleasant, 42, and believes that everyone should have a quiet little pub of his own, at least fifty yards from his. I approached

him modestly simply to ask if he had any sporting friends who thought life
had come to such a pass that they would enjoy sporting about the Quarter in
a long low and very moderately priced automobile. From there we went on to
the intellectual world, bogged through its vagaries for a little while, and after
I had proved my metal by reciting a few lines from T S Eliot, he encouraged
us with tasteful portions of absinthe and loaned me 10$.

Mr Hays, introduced earlier in the letter simply as a 'southern gentleman',
being about our age, took it upon himself at this point to be our host, until
some stroke of God, like an earthquake or tidal wave, could waft us out of his
city (have I mentioned that it was still raining?). His mother, a true southern
lady who proved herself so by retaining her sanity throughout the whole thing,
was at first reasonably horrified to see us appear with our natty sleeping bags
and recline in what were to us perfectly familiar contortions on her living
room floor. Two days later, when she was beginning to manage to breathe
again, I picked up a cold which dissolved the forepart of my face to such an
extent that even an ourangatang (spelling, you see, is again a distant world) 's
mother instinct would have leapt with succour. From then until we disappeared, carrying her son with us, she was splendid.

Her son, familiarly known as Sam, paints. In fact, he is doing that just at
the moment. He is facing one of the most terrible architectural monstrosities
that the Catholic Church ever erected, for some cabalistic reason, behind our
hotel. Houston, in what I trust was a surge of civic pity, displays the thing on
coloured picture postals, and I shall send you one so that you, too, may marvel.

As I have intimated, Sam, being at what we like to call 'loose ends', decided
to throw in his lot with us, and, he having a small but at this time of the world
provident allowance, we decided that it would be all for the best. And so the
next morning (I say loosely, having no idea just what it was next after) we went
down to the car. Since one of my suitcases had been stolen, there was more
room for his luggage, and at this point it matters very little whether I appear
shirtless and tieless in any of the capitols of the world. We fled. Have I said
that it was still raining? If so, it was stark understatement. Driving through
the bayous of Louisiana was like an experimental dive with William Beebe,
and, except for the shimmering streams that poured through the crevices
around the 'convertible' top, into our huddled laps, the Cord might have been
a Bathysphere. Lonely cows on the highway appeared as splendid Baracuda,
and the dismally soaked Spanish moss luxuriant submarine vetch. Across one
Huey Long bridge after another, until we stopped in a town called Houma,
having taken a wrong turn so that we were headed blithely for the Gulf of
Mexico. We ate, considered, reconsidered, and started again west, stopping
at a gas station for water (as, I have neglected to say, we have been doing every

score of miles since we left). There was a small dog, the black spots of his coat blending gently into the white with the aid of the automobile grease in which he slept, and eyebrows which curled distantly away from his unreasonable cheerful face. He joined the caravan, which set forth again into a downpour which would have made Sadie Thomson play the Wabash Blues until Pago Pago slid into the sea.

There is a town in Texas called Orange, for reasons which only a native could know. Here came the scene of the final depredation. The Cord began to make the most terrifying, and, to one so much attached, sickening noises, that the only thing to do was motor down a sideroad, pretend that there simply was no top on the car, and be lulled into a delicious and thoroughly sodden unconsciousness. When we awoke, the one watch in the company indicated that the morning was well along. The amount of water that was cascading down between us and any hope of heaven made the time a compleatly negligible factor. There was nothing to do but drive down the road and get stuck in someone's driveway. That is what we did. It was cold, and the rain so near to being one mass of moving water that we stood like three creatures in different worlds, shouting to each other as one might from inside an incandescent lamp.

We eventually recovered the car, now powered only in first and fourth gears, and limped into Houston. We had such a stroke of luck here as to convince me that we are being fitted out for the most violent end—something like driving unexpectedly into a live volcano-mouth in that country to the south, for here in Houston we have found one of the only Cord mechanics in the southwest. The Cord is now hanging in his establishment, where the most amazing array of toothless gears are exhibited on the floor. The whole thing is under the constant surveillence of Houma, the folly-ridden animal who remains, in spite of his new lot, our friend, looking up from his bed of transmission grease with the ingenuous faith which I have been mistakenly looking for in human beings.

Our apartment in Houston has a living room, bedroom, bath, kitchen, and breakfast nook. Last night we prepared a magnificent dinner (hamburger-with-onion, pan-fried-potatoes-with-onion, spinach-with-onions), and are now looking forward to this evening's culinary adventure. During the day we saunter through the streets and stare at the citizens, or stand in our parlour and stare at the atrocity which I mentioned earlier. We smoke a brand of aptly-named little cigars Between-The-Acts, and blow ponderous rings. We discuss only earth-shaking topics, such as whether or not there really is a sun, or were we brought up with a heat- and light-emanating mirage. We smile stupidly at one another, drink coffee, and nod our heads in answer to nothing at all.

While the world of fact drowns us, that of probability supplies an occasional bubble of life, and we plan (I use the world plan as an indication of my vocabulary weakness) to arrive gloriously in Laredo sometime toward the end of the week, Friday sounding as likely as any day I can call to mind at the moment. In these ensuing days I hope to work (there is another word) on something which has been on my mind (and another) for a couple of weeks, and since all of the deathless prose which I had expected to work on was purloined with the gay vestments of my formal existence, perhaps I shall be able to make a fresh start in the world of art.

Living in a world of my own, I have no notion of the US mails. This is undoubtedly Sunday, because the steepled monstrosity across the street has been breathing a regular stream of Texan Catholics in and out of its gabled nostrils all day—and you may get this message near the middle of the week. And so I cannot say whether you will find me at the Rhodes Apartment Hotel by mail, for the moment that the auto is able to stand by itself it is in for a fast drumming south. I trust that you got my frantic wire, asking for a means of proving my identity (the only other thing I had was a Harvard Bursar's card, in the stolen suitcase, which I suppose might not have got me a visa), and even that the birth certificate is now filed under general delivery at Laredo. The picture of $ still confounds me—it continues to leak in somewhere, and until it stops no appeals will be made. I do think, as I mentioned in another letter, that once in Mexico DF, with no job immediate, that I shall have to hold out an open and empty palm. Until then, here are probable addresses— c/o Wells Fargo, Monteray (you might check on what county of Mexico that's in, and also make certain that they have an agency there), and then, in perhaps a couple of weeks, c/o W— F—, Mexico D.F., Mexico.

I hope, trust that everything is well, you, and the things around you. I shall think of NewYork tonight as I wash my socks and underpants, articles which have seen considerable service.

My love,
Bill

Mike: Mike Gladstone (see headnote to 26 June 1952), who was staying at his sister's apartment then.

Noel Houston: an Oklahoma native (1909–58), author of the novel *The Great Promise* (1946).

Alice Adams: prominent fiction writer (1926–99), raised in Chapel Hill.

The Strange Woman: 1946 film about a scheming woman's affairs with three men.

Jean Lafitte: a pirate who worked out of New Orleans in the early nineteenth century.

Mr Hays: see endnote to 15 January 1948.

William Beebe: American naturalist and deep-sea explorer (1877–1962).

Sadie Thomson [...] Pago Pago: a prostitute in W. Somerset Maugham's early story "Miss Thompson" (later retitled "Rain") working the South Pacific island of Pago

Pago, best known in movie adaptations (*Sadie Thompson*, 1928; *Rain*, 1932). "Wabash Blues" is a popular song from the early 1920s that Sadie plays on her phonograph.

To Edith Gaddis

Houston, Texas
[16 March 1947]

Dear Mother—

You, I know, have spent much time in lesser cities of the United States—but never let fate hold anything for you like Houston, Texas. It is really pretty ridiculous, pretty dull, pretty bad. But we are leaving tomorrow—Monday—having had quite a "rest". I have written one story here, whose merits I find less each time I think of it, and at the moment have no idea of what to do with it. That, however, is hardly a major worry just now.

To explain the wire—and many thanks for sending the 35—they require much identification here to cash a money order, and, since my wallet was in the stolen suitcase, I have absolutely none—living in constant fear of being picked up for vagrancy before we reach Laredo, since I do not look like a leading citizen in my present attire.

Heaven knows, now, whether we shall make it or not—but we are again starting off. I only hope that the border will not present too many foolish difficulties, since one look will convince any official that we are not young American tourists with untold financial resources—but once across the border I shall feel much better about all sorts of things, including the hopeful sproutings of a mustache, which at the moment is as unedifying as it is rigorous in its growth.

Love—Bill

I have written one story: "Mr Astrakan Says Goodnight," set in Houston.
wire: on 15 March WG wired a Western Union cable that reads: "VAGUE INSANITY PREVAILS. 35 DOLLARS WOULD SUSTAIN THIS HOUSTON IDYLL. SEN[D] TO ROBERT DAVISON CARE OF WESTERN UNION HOUSTON EXPLANATION FOLLOWS MY BEST INTENTIONED LOVE= BILL"

To Edith Gaddis

Hotel Casa Blanca
Mexico City
[7 April 1947]

Dear Mother—

Well— Finally Wells-Fargo opened—Mexico, you see, has been enjoying a four-day holiday for Santo Semana—Thursday through Sunday, everything closed. And so we have been living on about 2 pesos a day—borrowed, and now repaid as is our hotel bill.

Will I continue to disappoint you, cause you wonder? Because no big long talks with an American magazine editor here who gives the same story as all—no money to Americans in Mexico, unless they are "in on something." The *Mexico City Herald* finally told me to come back in 2 or 3 weeks—and I finally understood that the best I could do there was about 10 pesos a day, for 8 hrs. proofreading.

But do not be disappointed immediately—for here is something heartening I hope. I have been working very hard. Many days. On a novel. It is something I have had in mind for about a year—had done some on it in fact, and the notes were stolen in New Orleans. But now I am on it, and like it, and believe it may have a chance. Right now the title is *Blague*, French for "kidding" as it were. But it is really no kidding. Silly for me to write about it here, though it is practically the only thing I think about. Now: Davison's father is attorney for Little Brown & Co., the Boston publishers. And so I can be assured that if I can do it to my satisfaction, it will be read and if anyone will publish it, it will stand best chance there, since he has some "influence." The really momentary problem is whether to do the first part, and an outline (which I have done) and try to get an advance—or to finish it now if I can.

What we hope to do—is sell the car, buy some minor equippage, including two horses, and set out and live in the less populous area of Mexico. And there I hope to finish this thing, while Davison lives outdoor life which he seems to desire, and I am not averse to as you know.

Could you then do this?: Send, as soon as it is conveniently possible, to me at Wells-Fargo:

My high-heeled black boots.
My spurs.
a pair of "levis"—those blue denim pants, if you can find a whole pair
the good machete, with bone handle and wide blade—and scabbard—if
    this doesn't distend package too much.
Bible, and paper-bound Great Pyramid book from H— Street.
those two rather worn gabardine shirts, maroon and green.
Incidentally I hope you got my watch pawn ticket, so that won't be lost.

PS My mustache is so white and successful I am starting a beard.

Santo Semana: i.e., Semana Santa (Holy Week), which culminated on Sunday, 6 April 1947.

Davison's father: at the top of the page, WG added: "He is R. H. Davison—15 State Street—Boston, if you want to communicate with him for any reason."

Blague: its full title was *Blague, called the 'lie with circumstance'* (cf. *As You Lie It* 5.4.96). In a later letter (7 April 1948) WG describes this as "an allegory, and Good and Evil were two apparently always drunk fellows who gave driving lessons in a dual-control car," but that was only the frame-tale. Within are stories of the lives of New Yorkers similar to the Greenwich Village sections of *R*.

Great Pyramid book: Worth Smith's *Miracle of the Ages: The Great Pyramid* (Holyoke, MA: Elizabeth Towne, 1934), a cranky book that translates apocalyptic messages from the Great Pyramid of Giza (predicting Armageddon in 1953), which WG took seriously and cites a few times in *R*. H— Street is his Horatio Street apartment.

To Barney Emmart

[*A lifelong Harvard friend (1923–89) who earned a doctorate at the University of London, worked in marketing in the 1950s, and later taught journalism at the University of Massachusetts. He was the son of A. D. Emmart: see letter of 29 October 1950.*]

Mexico City
April, 1947

dear Barney,

Just a note of greeting. And to say that I earnestly wish you were here, because I am working like every other half-baked Harvard boy who never learned a trade—on a novel. Dear heaven, I need your inventive store of knowledge. Because of course it is rather a moral book, and concerns itself with good and evil, or rather, as Mr. Forster taught us, good-and-evil. You see, I call out your name, because other bits of life proving too burdensome, I have taken to the philosophers—having been pleasantly involved with Epictetus for about a year, and now taking him more slowly and seriously. And of course I come upon Pyrrho, and see much that you hold dear, and why. Also David Hume, whose style I find quite delightful.

Shall I describe Mexico City to you? It is very pleasant, and warm, and colourful of course—and we are here, and cannot get jobs because we are tourists, and live on about 30¢ worth of native food a day. And I'm sure you would like it. Also, we grow hair on our faces. And plan, as soon as we can manage to sell the Cord—beautiful auto—to purchase two horses, and the requisite impedimenta, and go off and live in the woods, or desert, or whatever they have down here. There I shall finish *Blague*—that is the novel. And have George Grosz illustrate it—he has the same preoccupation with nates that I do—grounds enough to ask him.

Well old man, this is just to let you know dum spiro spero—I haven't learned Spanish yet—a noodle language if I ever heard one. Please give John Snow my very best greeting, tell him I shall write, would give anything for a drink and talk with you all. But must work. A dumb letter, but I am very tired.

Anyhow, my best—
Bill

Forster [...] good-and-evil: in *The Longest Journey* (1907), E. M. Forster writes, "For Ricky suffered from the Primal Curse, which is not—as the Authorized Version suggests—the knowledge of good and evil, but the knowledge of good-and-evil" (part 2, chap. 18).

Epictetus: Greek Stoic philosopher (c. 50–c. 135). WG owned George Long's translation of *The Discourses of Epictetus*.

Pyrrho: Greek skeptic philosopher (c. 360–c. 270 BCE). Otto relates an anecdote about him in *R* (130).

David Hume: Scottish skeptic philosopher (1711–76).

George Grosz: see postscript to the letter of 3–4 May 1947; "nates" are buttocks.

dum spiro spero: Latin, "While I breathe, I hope," attributed to Cicero, and the motto of many families and organizations.

To Edith Gaddis

Mexico City
[April 1947]

Dear Mother—

I do hope this will be the last time I shall have to put upon you so. And just now am in a sort of confident spirit because I believe *Blague* has something to say, if I can write it. If not, believe me, there is little else that interests me, but I shall do something which will take care of me, and I shall not have to keep you living in this perpetual state of waiting to hear that I need something. And so I add, could you within another week or so send 25$ more? And that will be all. Believe me, if *Blague* is done it will be worth it—you will like it. And if I can get an advance things will be rosy. As I say, I have the outline done, just what I want to take place from beginning to end. And each scene clear in my mind. I have only written about 5,000 words, and plan 50,000, comparatively short—ap. 200 pages.

We want to leave as soon as we can sell the car &c, out where living will be cheap.

Believe me, it will be worth it—I have never felt so single-purposed about a thing in my life. The novel will be the best I can write. And as I say, if it doesn't do, you won't have to put up with this foolishness any longer. Davison likes it much, and is very helpful. Am getting sun, and even on 20¢ a day enough food, eating in the marketplace. A grand city, but without a job or tourist money, no place to stay. So have faith for just a little longer—it will work out. Thanks, and love—

Bill

To Edith Gaddis

Mexico City
15 April '47

Dear Mother—

[...] You—and anyone—can usually be pretty certain, if you receive a letter of any length from me, that I am for the moment fed up with the novel. No offense—but, except for time we spend going marketwards for food—usually about 5 pm, the daily meal—or in the morning, for café-con-leche—I am here working on *Blague*. Of ap. 50000 words planned, I have 10000 fairly done—though now—tonight—must go carefully over all I have done, add wherever I can, clear up as much as possible—and even cut, wherever I use too many words—which is often. When I finish this part, am going to send it to Little Brown, where Davison's father will see that it gets read &c. And with any encouragement from them perhaps I can finish it in a couple of months.

The newspapers down here—very anti-communist &c, are practically fomenting war—at the moment much about Mr. Wallace. And so I have the idea—which as you know I have had for some time—that war comes soon. And *Blague must* be done before that, concerning itself with Armageddon &c. So we go. [...]

I have just discovered a new brand of cigarettes—Fragantes, which cost 4¢—and here we have been paying 5¢! Wasting our $. Great cigarettes, though they are inclined to come apart or go out—and are quite startling first thing in the morning. Someday—I look forward to Players again.

We have been to just one film since here—*Ninotchka*, with Spanish subtitles. A wonderful, delightful film. Admission is about the same as in the States, around 60–70¢, so we are debating about seeing *Comrade X* now playing.

I had a silly letter from Chandler Brossard, who wants particulars on living here. We may get him down here yet! Also letters from others, keeping me up on NYC, which sounds absolutely dull. But a safe distance off!

If the novel goes, I have thought of coming up in August. Possibly July. I cannot think of the Studio being so alone, and we might have a good piece of summer.

As for living here—anything you are curious about? I have given you most of it, I think. And it does not vary. My mustache seems to have stopped growing, now hanging down the corners of my mouth. To work.

Love, Bill

PS—We are leaving for Veracruz this evening (Wednesday). Everything fine. Will still get mail from W.F. And probably be back here soon enough.

Mr. Wallace: Alfred A. Wallace (1888–1965) denounced Truman's foreign policy in the *New Republic* (where he was editor in 1947), arguing it would lead to further warfare.

Ninotchka: 1939 film starring Greta Garbo.

Comrade X: a 1940 film derivative of *Ninotchka*.

Chandler Brossard: novelist and journalist (1922–93), WG's roommate in Greenwich Village for a period. Brossard based a character on WG in his first novel, *Who Walk in Darkness* (1952).

Studio: a converted barn next to Mrs. Gaddis's house in Massapequa, which WG (like Edward Bast in *J R*) used as a work space.

To Edith Gaddis

Mexico City
24 April '47

dear Mother—

A week in Veracruz. I could describe it to you now, here, in many pages—the incidents, &c., the changes in plans. But I must mention the trip. We were told before leaving that if we took one road we should go over the 'biggest god damn' mountain in the World'. I believe we did. At night. Do you remember driving from Hicksville home one night after the movies, fog so thick and we going 15mph, and did not speak for two days after? Imagine it like that, except a cloud instead of fog, heavy rain, roads of such incredible twists I shall have to draw them for you, and hills so steep that the heavy Cord, even in gear and with brakes, wouldn't stop. Honestly, it was wild. We went with what later turned out to be some sort of young confidence man, I believe, with a number of angles to work on us. The car finally sold, and at a pretty low price, but glad to get it done—after that ride, it really isn't worth much. The young man, Ricardo, was working so many deals that we finally escaped quietly. I wax to be captain of the boat his father owned, which sounded jolly, but never saw the boat. He had a place with one pleasant enough room bed &c., and behind it a shanty affair with mud floor where we slept. Down in the rather crowded residential section, near the market—residential for chickens, pigs, dogs, unnumbered barefoot children, radios, people. The noise at night!—cocks crowing, then burros and jackasses he-hawing, turkeys, dogs and dogs; and when eventually the sunrise put an end to the fracas, everyone leapt from bed and turned his radio to a different station. It never stopped. It is probably going on right now. I shall tell you, someday when I have more breath, of how I entertained hordes of tiny ninos (that is their charming word for children) by reading bible lessons in Spanish, putting lighted cigarettes in my mouth, swinging them about on my fingers. Or of how I entertained the (sic) adult population, after meeting the man who owned the entire market— a remarkably tremendous place—and he almost as much so, proportionately, we sat across the table from eachother, and after proving myself able to mouth bits of his language, a 5-gallon jug of pulque was brought out. We drank a glass (Salud!), then he poured me another, &c., until soon he was pouring me glasses and then drinking with me from the jug. When that was gone (a litre is about a quart) we had some tequila, to keep spirits up, and beer to make it a real comradeship. Entertained the populace, as I say, finally by falling off a rather vigourous streetcar. Huge joke. I think if I had actually split my head they would have died of laughter, but I can't go that far with them. They had enough fun as it was. Believe me, I am fine now.

And Mexico City looks good. I arrived to find quite a sheaf of mail from you, and shall try herewith to answer and straighten things out as they come. I gather from the tone of them that you have been having it rather rough, and I can imagine, and wish I were there to help you along instead of here, to keep you in a state of such running about.

First, immediate plans. We have just returned from the 'shopping district', carrying (picture this) two saddles, bits,—all the equipment for the equestrian. Bill has got himself a pair of boots, and we are ready to be off immediately for some sort of rustic nowhere. I cannot quite make out when you sent the boots and spurs. They are all that count really; the gabardine shirts would be fine, but don't really *need* them; hope you did not bother to send clean white shirt, no use for it; also the watch, which I didn't mean for you to try to send, but if you have don't worry about it; the machete doesn't matter, very cheap here; don't for heaven's sake worry about small-pox, no mention of it in our circles here; many thanks for NCB, but I don't see that you needed to bother, I never have enough money to carry on with banks, and as you shall see in the future don't plan to need a checking acc't; Look, many many thanks for sending the money (25$ WU April 10th, and just rec'd on return from Vera-cruz Thursday 25$ WU) But please don't send more money, it only leads us to confusion, and trouble for you. I don't need it now at all. We have plenty to get off from here for the sticks for a while. Honestly, I will let you know when I need it. I hate to sound excited about it, but when I need it I can let you know and you can always wire it just in care of the Western Union I wire from. OK? I am just tired of envisioning things like NCB machinations, that's what I came off to Mexico to get away from. So let's just leave it, I'll let you know if and when. OK?

The apartment: I really hope to not want it this fall. Here's what my hope is. To get out of here as soon as possible on horses to compleatly uninhabited country, for about two months, keeping in touch with Wells Fargo here or giving you an address so that we may correspond, but *away* from city machinations, all this business. Then, get back across Mexico to an eastern port town like Veracruz, Tampico, &c., end of May or early June or middle of June. From that port, start home, either working my way on a boat (talked to sailors on freighters in Veracruz, who say such things are still done), or (this is the only time I may need money) getting some sort of passage, and hoping to get back to NY late in June. Then coming to Long Island and working on the novel there this summer. How does that sound? At that point, of course, much depends on how the book comes along. But in the fall, especially if I have got any sort of money out of the book as a start, to leave NY again and go heaven knows somewhere. I cannot plan for that of course. And so don't want to say, dump the apartment. But feel sure enough about it to say, if there is anything brought up involving business about a new lease before I get back, to let the place go. I don't see great future for me in that old place, do you? Good if I could get back in late June and get books &c. together, so don't worry about such things until then. Many thanks for the addresses, we'll use them if there is any occasion.

Now. I hope that all of this, instead of unnerving you, has given a clear and rather bright picture. Honestly, I can see from your letters what a time you have been having, and feel like a fool having added such things as a machete for you to worry about. Needless to say how good I feel about the Halls, Mary, &c., all they have done. And pray, as they do I believe, for the day you can relax. Just relax. Anyhow you can about me now for a while. Or if you would rather get excited than relax, take a look at the enclosed pictures. In the large cabinet portrait, meet Mr Robert Ten Broeck (Bill) Davison. We are walking a main street in Mexico in the morning after coffee, not, as you might believe, discussing the missionary problem in Bengal or proofs of God. He is saying something rather violent about the cigarette he is holding, which has just gone out. I am reacting to his language. The beards, as you see, are not too exciting as yet. We do look ratty, but both are delighted with the picture. Also, a blurred indication of how we slept on the way down, unfortunately double-exposed, but if you look, I am in a sleeping bag, on my back looking up, with a cigarette-to-mouth, and above my head is the little dog we got in Louisiana (and lost eventually in Mexico). Me sitting down is me sitting down on the roof of the hotel Casablanca, where we call home, looking rather small-headed. The dog (named, fondly enough, 'Old Grunter') appears again in picture taken on the highway on the way down, cradled lackadaisacally (spelling!) in my arms. Great shot of the car. To top things off, a rather dull shot of a river from highway miles above. [...]

I hope all of this has settled the air. Off we go, into the hills. Davison for the first time on a horse. The whole thing should be fine, and whether the novel prospers (believe me I am going to try to help it do so) it will be healthful. I shall write, and get mail from W- F- until I let you know differently, though obviously for the next few weeks or two months letters farther apart. Believe me, we are fine, see no reason why things should not go off as planned, at least until I see you in the summer. My love to Granga, hoping to see her too.

Love—
Bill

PS Remind me sometime to tell you about the fox we had in Veracruz. Now there was a pet!

NCB: National City Bank.
Halls, Mary: Charles Hall, an antiques dealer, and Mary Woodburn, John Woodburn's wife and a close friend of Edith.
Old Grunter: a name WG used for family dogs.

To Edith Gaddis

Mexico City
[29 April 1947]

dear Mother—

I never do a thing, or if I do it immediately, it is wrong. So after that lengthy piece I mailed you this am concerning three suitcases being sent you, most of it is wrong, as I foolishly sent it before the bags. [...] If a sloppy package should arrive for you from Houston, Texas, it will be my handsome treasured Brooks Bros hat, being sent by the garage mechanic, since it was in a restaurant which was closed the night we left, and I couldn't retrieve it. I hope he gets around to sending it; if so, could you rescue it, and have it cleaned and blocked?

Then here are some books I shd appreciate your getting, sometime between now and June or July:

A Study of History by A J Toynbee Oxford Press 1 volume abridgement.

Aspects of the Novel by EM Forster Harcourt Brace $2.50

Steppenwolf by Hermann Hesse Henry Holt $2.75

The above are recent, in print. This below have no full information on, but may be available.

The Golden Bough by Frazer (well known book) or Frazier—a book on anthropology.

These are little paper-bound things, should be available, perhaps at Brentano's, or some college textbook place; published by The Open Court Publishing Company, La Salle, Ill.

The Vocation of Man by Johann Gottlieb Fichte 50¢

St Anselm: *Proslogium, Monologium, an Appendix on Behalf of the Fool by Gaunilon; and Cur Deus Homo.* (this is all one)— 60¢

The first two are most important to me, should be readily available (though the Forster is reprint, may be sold out quickly, and I would like to go over it carefully—for obvious reasons). So thank you, hopefully in advance.

We are now (29april) on the eve of leaving for life in the woods. Cannot imagine what will turn out, but don't fear: we have dysentary pills, all sorts of things, including horse equipage, blankets &c. So don't for a moment worry. It may last a week or two months, we hope to reach Tampico eventually.

Have had no word from you on how my spending the summer in Massapequa sounds. Because though I am working on my novel, and will these coming weeks, I know I can do best out there, quiet summer—regular tasty food (how I dream of it!). It has taken me all this trip and time to figure it out, now it needs writing, and not the sort I can manage sitting on the edge of a bed or a pile of rock. I hope the idea suits you—I picture it as being a good regular well spent couple of months, and we could have a good summer out of it.

Think of nothing else now, will instruct Wells Fargo to follow me about, and certainly don't worry if you don't hear for a week or two—simply mean we are not near a PO. Mexico is a pretty raggedy land.

Love, Bill

A Study of History: D. C. Somervell's 600-page abridgement of the first six volumes of Arnold J. Toynbee's classic study was published by Oxford University Press in 1947.

Aspects of the Novel: classic study first published in 1927.

Steppenwolf: Hesse's 1927 novel about the outsider nature of the artist was translated into English in 1929.

The Golden Bough: Sir James George Frazer's multivolume survey of magic and religion was published in abridged form in 1922, the edition WG used for several passages in *R*.

The Vocation of Man: a philosophical work first published in 1800; in *R* Otto quotes
   "Fichte saying that we have to act because that's the only way we can know we're real,
   and that it has to be moral action because that's the only way we can know other
   people are. Real I mean" (120).
St Anselm: Piedmont-born English theologian (1033–1109); WG named a major character in *R* after him, and quotes him a few times in the novel (382, 535). The edition
   WG asks for was published in 1939.
life in the woods: the subtitle of Thoreau's *Walden* (1854), a book WG knew well.

To Edith Gaddis

> Mexico City
> [3–4 May 1947]

dear Mother—

Just a few words to let you know the change of plans. The horse business
in Mexico didn't work out, simply because it seems impossible to buy horses.
One was offered, at 120$! Twice the price. So D—, still hell-bent on riding,
has the fancy of going somewhere in the Southwest US. I care little at this
point, having had a grand Mexico, which is to be topped off Sunday by a
bullfight. D. doesn't care about it, but I have persuaded him it is a spectacle
worth seeing. So we stay over and leave Monday for Laredo, thence I know
not where, care less, so long as there is a place for me to lie down in my
wretched bolster at night and sit up at this machine by day. All of which really
alters nothing, I still plan on returning in June, we can set the studio in
order, and I hope for a well-regulated summer in which *Blague* will either be
done or collapse. With all of our bumping around recently I have had no
chance to get at it, and feel guilty, limiting myself to scraps of notes on
paper. Anyhow I shall see you in June, and meanwhile write you when we get
some sort of flavourfully-western address, if we chance to settle near a stage
line. [...]

Little more of note. My beard looks at the point where it will not be very
edifying, even in another month, and need a haircut, the last having been
what seems months ago in New Orleans. Everything fine and in order, life is
great, will keep you posted. I have been on the roof, my usual quiet refuge for
working on the novel; but today, impossible. It is la Dia de las Cruces—Day
of the Crosses—and like a battlefield. The air absolutely full of explosions,
natives sending up fireworks. Became downright dangerous, as well as disconcerting—felt like a foreign correspondent reporting a Black and Tan
fracas so am back in the room.

My only Mexican expenditure, souvenir, and that through the munificence of D., a beautiful little pair of silver cufflinks with my old design which I am so fond of, and *so* neatly done. I am quite content, happy. Hope you are similarly so, and will write.

PS — In view of past mixups, I have have held this letter over until Sunday night, just before we leave simply to tell you that I have had two (2) wonderful *steaks—filets*—today, and the bullfight was grand.

Here is another book:— Being by Balzac, it may not be readily come on in modern book stores. But if so, if you should be able to come on it, how much appreciated. It is *Zeraphitus* by Honoré de Balzac. If not, don't trouble about it.

Love, Bill

PS

It is very late, I have been lying awake for some time, as I often do, thinking about—or rather being persecuted by this novel. With D— asleep I cannot make lights and notes, or work. At this point things usually get pretty wonderful, as you know about such possession. Anyhow, do you know of a German artist-illustrator named *George Grosz*? I know this is pretty excessive—he is well-known, brilliant &c (so this is rather *between us*, if it comes to naught, as it probably will)—but I have long liked his work, serious painting and cartooning—(he has done much satirical drawing on recent Germany)—but I want to try to get him to illustrate *Blague*. If only it could be done. His drawings would be exactly what I want for it—really *want* to *complete* it, as it were, besides obvious commercial advantages. He has written a book called *A Little Yes and a Big No*. It costs $7.50. If it could be managed, I should love to have it when I get back—and you would get a kick out of looking it over I know. If possible I want to show him my manuscript this summer (I think he lives in N.Y. now)—and *try*. Meanwhile, if it can be done not too strainingly, how I should appreciate his book.

Love, Bill

PS If you can and do get any of these books—*not to be sent*—I want to read them this summer in Massapequa. And thanks.

Black and Tan fracas: a British-supplied police force (named after the colors of their uniform) sent to Ireland in 1920 to help the Irish constabulary quell uprisings.

Zeraphitus: i.e.,, *Seraphita* (1835), a metaphysical story by the French novelist.

George Grosz: German artist (1893–1959) who emigrated to the U.S. in 1933. His autobiography, *A Little Yes and a Big No*, was published by the Dial Press in 1946.

Ormonde de Kay and WG at Donn Pennebaker's apartment in Greenwich Village, late 1940s (photo courtesy D. A. Pennebaker).

To Edith Gaddis

[WG returned to New York, but five months later he decided to leave again (the night of 28 November), this time for Panama "to launch my international news career" at El Pan-amá América, a bilingual newspaper, as he wrote thirty years later in his brief memoir "In the Zone" (New York Times, 13 March 1978, reprinted in RSP 33–37). It didn't work out. From this point on, WG begins sometimes signing his letters W (for Willie) rather than Bill. But he lapsed to neglecting to date his letters, so most are supplied from postmarks.]

Hotel Central
Plaza de la Catedral
Panama City, Panama
[late November 1947]

dear Mother— I had intended to write you a goodly letter about the fantastic business of being in 6 countries in one day, but by now the fantasy has got out of hand. I was met at the airport by four white-coated young gentlemen, escorted to a waiting Lincoln, and driven to my hotel, an establishment where

I have a room about the size of Madison Sq Garden and a private balcony overlooking the park. Then off for a few drinks and courtly conversation. Apparently I shall have a job, and no kidding, on this paper at 350$ a month; I am to have breakfast with the owner in the morning.

Fantastic.

That's all.

This is simply a note to let you know we are all alive, and I am breathing heavily, acting sophisticated and trying to carry on.

It is splendidly hot, and so am I, inside and out. When breathing begins to come more naturally again, I shall write.

Love,
W.

To Edith Gaddis

[*The new novel WG mentions below, initially called* Ducdame, *eventually became* The Recognitions.]

Panama City
[December 1947]

Dear Mother—

Here is one of those letters which makes it worth your while to have me 3000miles from home. Perhaps not. I don't know. I am quite confused.

I have just come back from coffee with a man named Scott, who is managing editor of the paper. He is very kind, and about to ship me off to a banana plantation. Roberto Arias—whose father and uncle are currently running against one another for the presidency—owns the paper. But the de la Guardia faction, my guardians, have rather put it upon his shoulders for my employment. He too is very kind, I had a pleasant lunch with him and his wife in their penthouse a day or so ago, and Roberto tells Juan Dias that I can have a job as a feature writer on the paper. Mr Scott, the kind NewZealander, finds the paper quite to his liking as it is. We go around and around in circles, there also being a matter of 225$ to be paid the P— government if I hang on and take such a job. Eh bien. With all of the Latin fooling around, bananaland sounds like the best bet. Everything here, in the city, is high; I have moved from the apartmento overlooking the park to a smaller, more airless cubicle, at 2$ the day. They give me no ashtray or (my favourite) cuspidor, so I must toss cigarette stubs on the floor. Not very pretty, but home.

At the moment I am waiting for a cable from somewhere to see if the Chiriqui Land Company wants an overseer. Imagine! Stalking through the jungle (of course *all* of my clothes for such a life are safely in Massapequa, as usual), and *Me*, who as moments go by takes a dimmer and dimmer view of bananas, telling hundreds of natives what ones to cut for shipment. The whole thing as fantastic as it seems always to turn out. But I am quite pleased.

The city is all one could ask, teeming with people and hot as it can be. There are occasional nice places where one could sit down and work, but I think that even with a comparatively substantial salary (Roberto mentions 350$ a month) the money and time would be gone as soon as it came, and I have honestly had enough of high life and sophistication for one season. From descriptions of bananaland, there is only the heat of the jungle, work to be done during the day, and the evenings and nights free. You can see, it sounds like a good place to work. The salary is pitifully small, but I gather one's needs are taken care of, and it is possible to save something each month.

I have started the plans for another novel. It all sounds so very possible, to spend a stretch on the old plantation, healthful outdoor life drenched with sun, and work on a book. And if the book does not work out, at least I should be able to escape with my life and leathery skin and enough money to get back to the states and figure out another immediate future. I hope that all this does not distress you. It shouldn't; at least for myself it looks good.

A good deal of my time is spent walking. I walk miles around the city alone, just looking and thinking. Then back to this palace to take off a wet shirt. I have still as little sympathy for the spanish language, and know just enough to be able to struggle through meals and get directions when I get lost, which is often.

You remember Davey Abad, the ex-prize fighter whose nightmares I shared on the ss *West Portal* some 6 years ago. I stopped in at a cantina a few evenings ago for a bottle of cervesa negra, fine dark beer, and there was Davey collapsed in a corner. He is taking cards at the gambling casino in the hotel Nacional, very ritzy, and I spent a pleasant hour or so recalling old times with him. Then I went into the casino and watched one man lose 100$ betting on the black on the roulette wheel—just like that, in two minutes, five spins, every number came up red, he with 20$ each time on the black—and a sad shattered American woman writing out 50$ travellers cheques like crazy to keep up with her losses. Fascinating, of course. The number 17 came up five times in twenty minutes, and I was fearfully tempted—but escaped quietly.

Everyone is kind. Strange to think that I have been here less than a week; I feel that the winter must be past in NY, and spring opening on LongIsland, that I have been away that long. But I gather that if the Chiriqui Land Company needs honest and competent (!) work done that it will seem years before I can manage to stroll into Brooks Brothers next fall and give them 47$ for one of their attache cases, and end this business of carrying papers and soap and a shaving brush in my pockets.

Again, thanks for so many things. I am getting on well, eating far more regularly than I ever managed in NY, &c &c. This address will reach me, I shall tell them to forward if the jungle calls.

Love
W

Roberto Arias: Panamanian lawyer (1918–99); his younger brother Tony was at Harvard with WG. Arnulfo Arias was first declared the loser in the 1948 presidential election, then declared the winner and held office from 1949 to 1951.

de la Guardia faction: in a later letter to his mother, WG mentions "Arturo de la Guardia & brother Gabriel, who was so kind to me in Panama" (11 October 1949). Arturo, another Harvard classmate of WG's, was the son of Ernesto de la Guardia (1904–83), president of Panama later in the 1950s.

Juan Dias: spelled Diaz in next letter, and later identified as a judge. Sometimes called "Juancho," his full name was Juan Octavio Díaz Lewis, and later worked at UNESCO in Paris when WG was there.

Chiriqui Land Company: a Panamanian fruit and vegetable vendor, a holding of Chiquita Brands, and still in business today.

To Edith Gaddis

Panama City
Thursday [December 1947]

Dear Mother—

Just a note to say I have your letter, and thank you. Honestly, it seems months since I left.

Also, best to call father and thank him for the Christmas present sentiment, but I think it somewhat dangerous to send anything here, with my plans as they are. This place will certainly forward mail, but you know the inter-American trouble that can happen with packages! Tell him I shall write.

Plans still uncertain—I hope the bananaland deal works out; it is the sort of exile I need. Am working hard at new novel—it is to concern *vanity*. I think I can write with some authority!

Well, you certainly sound like you are leading New York high life! Good— I do want you to have a good winter. No need to worry about sending me money—unless I have to pay my way out of bondage from the Chiriqui Land company!

Love to Granga, and you.

W.

To Edith Gaddis

Panama City
[28 December 1947]

dear Mother.

Another bulletin from the front. This one says that the Chirqui Land Co doesn't need the services of this old banana man. This old bananaman was pretty discouraged until today, now he is no longer discouraged but a bit alarmed. He has got a job with the canal, doing some kind of out-door work, something like helping overhaul a lock, whatever that is. I hope that you are not concerned that the fine education you gave me is producing nothing but a hemispherical bum, (let's say vagabond, sounds nicer), and one who even in his better moments can at best push a wheelbarrow. (I must interrupt here and say that I would rather push a w-b- and have my mind to myself and be able to laugh when I want to or spit or quit than be standing agued and wet-footed in a 40$ a week publishing-house in my favourite city, wasting the only treasure I have, the English language, constantly being angry with things which are wasteful to be angry at, &c &c, you know.) Anyhow the job doesn't open until january 5th, so I am sitting on the floor counting my fortune, and believe that I can hold out. I shall (I am given to believe) work from 7am to 3pm, and then have the rest of the day to count my blessings or anything else I have that can be counted, even monies, which I am told I will be given in return for my lock-overhauling efforts. Sounds fine, also healthful. I must buy some less-sporty pants than these I am wearing now, the white number originally Lusch's, which are becoming slightly soiled. And the tailor who built that white linen splendour for Mr. Winebaum 21years ago did not intend it to march on as it is trying hard to do, I believe. More often each day I am taken for something left here by a boat, which has cannily gone on without an undesirable member of its crew. Eventually I hope to send you my measurements and a portion of my earnings so that at your pleasure you can go to Brooks (I don't believe that they do have my measurements, they may) and have them send me one of those natural-colour linen suits they are hoarding on the 2nd or 5th floor. They are around 35$, and I find I would have to pay at least that here, without even getting the Brooks Brothers label, instead a suavely pinched-in waist which passes for fashion among these vain people but isn't quite what I have in mind as chic. And one might as well be chic if it is all the same price. Also it advances the chances of free meals, refreshments, and similar necessary vanities among the 'set' which I enter on occasion (occasion being the slightest hint of an invitation).

The two young gentlemen, Juan Diaz (a judge) and Guiellmo de Roux (an architect) continue to bear with me, and Sunday we motored again to the 50-mile-away beach and plundered the Pacific for all it was worth. I have a fine letter from Jake, whose plans for departure are practically realised, and I'm delighted; also one from Gardner, whose talents will never fail to arouse something akin to jealous envy in me. [...]

Love, W.

PS I have written to Father, a letter of news, greeting, and warning that perhaps it wouldnt be wise to try to send a gift right now.

Mr. Winebaum: poet, critic, and artist Bernard Winebaum (1922–89), a Harvard/ Village friend of WG, worked briefly in the advertising business (and wrote book reviews for *Time,* Alan Ansen told me), then spent most of his later life in Athens, where he owned a restaurant. He is the "Bernie" mentioned in the next letter.

Guiellmo de Roux: i.e., Guillermo de Roux (1916–2005), a prominent American-educated architect.

Gardner: see 11 January 1943.

To Edith Gaddis

Pedro Miguel, Canal Zone
[9 January 1948]

dear Mother.

Wouldn't it be nice if I could write a good novel? Well, that is what I have been trying to do all morning. Now it is near time for lunch, and then my presence and talents are required at the Miraflores lock until 11 pm, to take up with my crane. And coming in near midnight after that leaves me not wanting very much to jump out of bed in the morning for the great prose epic that is daily escaping from under my hand.

This is to thank you for the attaché case attempt—and to say that it's hardly a necessity. Because for the writing, I don't think I have anything really worthwhile carrying in one yet. I think the attaché case will just always be one of those distant beautiful images that lure us through this life and keep us believing that our intelligence is worthy. Meanwhile don't trouble about it. Perhaps, if in the summer I can get up there with something worth showing a publisher, one of the objects of (instant) beauty will be mine, and I shall have something worth carrying in it. As you may gather, I am not in very high nor triumphal spirits.

I enquired at the post office. There is no duty on anything sent for the recipient's personal use. If you get in touch with Bernie (PL81299) I'd like to know if he's in NY. or what. Also he has a small alarm clock, a little green one—and I need an alarm. Could you find where he got it? And if you could get and send me one like it?

Also badly need a haircut. I borrowed 10$ from Juan Diaz, my kind friend, so am seeing through quite well. Sorry about the trouble over the 'phone call. I don't understand about the 30th of Dec. call—I was at the 'phone station from 8^{50} until 9^{30}. They're all insane down here anyhow. But I'll call in a few weeks, after I get paid, just for the fun of it.

Love,
Bill

To Edith Gaddis

Pedro Miguel, Canal Zone
[12 January 1948]

dear Mother.

Well. I have been thinking about Mrs —, whatever the numberscope lady is—with something like horror. She has been rather remarkably right on the whole. But, she says January 6th to start new work which will carry through until September 19th. Does she mean spending 8 hours a day in the bottom of the Panama Canal?

The difficult part of such an existence is that having done a day's work of this nature, one is very tempted to do as the other men, who, with perfect right, feel that they have earned their place for the day, and relax. But I cannot. Infrequently the library here keeps me in good reading. Yesterday I had 2 plays and one novel, much for thought. And continue at work on my novel. I cannot work on it as I would—to sit down at the typewriter when I wish and write—because the machine makes so much noise as to disturb resting neighbors. So I try to write it in longhand, and to make continuous notes far in advance.

And then suddenly realise, in the midst of all this thought, here I am 25 and my education is just beginning. Honestly I wonder what I "studied" at Harvard.

I do hope to save enough here to be able to afford to go back—not necessarily to Harvard, preferably abroad—and study. And if I can do that and finish a credible novel by the fall it will be splendid. Oddly the things I want to study are not things I did at Harvard. Philosophy, comparative religions, history, and language. Well God knows often my hands are so tired from handling cables &c. that I do not do very well with this pen.

This is just an outburst—and regard it as such; suddenly like the whole bourgeois soul being terrified at time's passing, most especially furious to watch any of it wasted, as often the Canal seems to do. So much to learn and to think, no time for indulgences. I feel possessed. Soon will write a better letter.

Love,
W.

———

To Edith Gaddis

Pedro Miguel, Canal Zone
[15 January 1948]

dear Mother.

Many thanks for your letter. I can't do anything else now—purely nervous temper—so shall try to write you. I mean I can't work. It is 10³⁰ in the morning, I am to go out to work at 230—and somehow can't write. Largely this restriction on the typewriter and not being able to feel free and unrestrained—difficult anyway in the morning—and I can't work. I don't know what the right conditions are or even will be. Now I have the novel outlined, quite definitely (and continuously) in my mind. But for writing it that is the work. I am continuously upset, short tempered with most of the people I run into. I think what I shall do is work on here for about 3 more months, meanwhile reading, note-taking, trying to write. By then I should have saved around 300$. Then get a job on a boat going out of here for a couple of months. *Then* with a little money be able to do just as I wish. I don't know. I can't work unless it is in a place where I can come in at any hour of night put on lights and use the typewriter. We shall see. Meanwhile time is not being wasted I think because I am reading and thinking—sometimes with febrile excitement as a few days ago a play by Sartre called *Les Mouches* and also am making the money necessary to human dignity or at least solitary existence which is promised.

Of course letters from N.Y. excite me. I had a good one from Connie yesterday—and yours today with mention of Bernie &c. &c. You know he is rather simple, not a great mind—or at least not a good creative one (I am afraid, and he wants to be a good novelist, that is his tragedy, the more so since no one will see it as tragedy—can't take him seriously for long)—and I know it is simply indulgence to myself that makes me like to be with him, but I do miss him he is so kind, and there are few of those.

The only New Orleans person I can think of is Fischer Hayes. God knows what he is doing with a magazine—it couldn't be a very brilliant one. I heard he had married. Anyhow whatever the circumstances I *should* like to publish that story almost anywhere. So here is the next of the endless string of favours I ask of you. The name of the story—considerably rewritten since Hayes saw it—is "The Myth Remains." You may remember reading it. It is in Massapequa, and in a manila envelop with other stories, God knows where. But probably either on or in my desk or on the balcony. *Not* among the envelops on the landing, those are Chandler's (things I wouldn't be caught dead writing!). If you could pick it up next time you are out there, and meanwhile I shall hope to hear from whoever this New O— person is and write you.

Just before picking up your letter this morning I sent one off to father—brief cheery I think newsy bit. The prospect of publishing anything excites me as always. Bad business.

Now I remember the name of Bernie's clock is *Thrill*. And I should appreciate your sending me one very much. Yes the place is Tourneau—Madison at about 49th. (Lord how I miss New York! — You see what I am occupied with now is this whole business of the myth—tradition—where one belongs. And while disciplining myself to behave according as my intellect teaches me—that we *are* alone, and all of these vanities and seekings (the church, a wife, father &c.) are seekings for some myth by the use of which we can escape the truth of aloneness. Poor Bernie, he won't accept it, nor Jake that more successfully. But that is the whole idea (message) of my novel. I'd rather talk with you about it, the letter is so unsatisfactory but I have to write it down. I am afraid my letters are getting worse, also handwriting.

Again many thanks for the check. And *so* happy to know you are having the pleasant (pleasant hell it sounds hilarious) winter you deserve.

Love,
Bill

Les Mouches: *The Flies* (1943), an adaptation of the Greek story of Orestes and Electra avenging the death of their father; published in English translation by Stuart Gilbert in 1946.
Connie: probably Constance Smith: see note to 28 April 1948.
Fischer Hayes: called S. F. Hays in the next letter, apparently the painter "Sam Hays" mentioned earlier (9 March 1947).
Chandler's: unlike WG's stories, Brossard's were published in little magazines at this time.

To Edith Gaddis

Pedro Miguel, Canal Zone
[19 January 1948]

dear Mother—

Just a note to say I have heard from S. F. Hays, with a prospectus of the new magazine, which looks highly creditible. And to entreat you, on your first trip to Massapequa, to pick up that M.S.—"The Myth Remains". Now it must be in a large envelop with other stories, paper clipped. *Not* loose in a drawer—such might be an earlier version, and not to be shown. One of the other stories is "In Dreams I Kiss Your Hand, Madame." Don't bother with the other stories. I think the envelop has a large number 1 or I on the outside, and addressed to me from *Harper's Bazaar*—almost certain it is on top of the desk. Will you please send it to:

    Miss Cornelia P. Claiborne

    153 East 48th Street, N.Y.C. — and meanwhile I have written her a note asking her to return it to you if she doesn't want it.

Please pardon the outbursts I've been sending you. Now things are getting settled, I have a better system of time for myself. Coming in at midnight, I work on my novel until about 4 am—then sleep late. Tell G. S. B. to keep his shirt on. I am working hard, hope to have some money too when I show up there in the summer.

I am even drinking hot-water "lemon" juice when I get up! And have many good books from the library, and two new pairs of pants (not Chipp). The job isn't bad, except for the often hours of inactivity which madden me, any wasting of time now does. But the new novel, with incredible slowness, pieces itself together. And worthwhile thought is rampant. If I can stay with this life for a few months, perhaps I can show up with first novel draft, but not dependent on its success—so if it doesn't go I'll have money next fall to go abroad and study and continue to write.

Now it is past noon—I must make my little lunch (ham sandwich, peanut-butter sandw., and onion sandwich) (I keep the food in a drawer of my dresser) and be off for the breadwinning.

    Love to you,

        Will

PS. Another favour, if this incarceration is to last. If you could put aside the book review sections of the Sunday *Times*, and send them to me every 3 or 4 weeks, I should appreciate it greatly. Haven't seen it for so long, and get curious about current state of "literature".

"In Dreams I Kiss Your Hand, Madame": dated August 1947, this is an early version of Recktall Brown's Christmas party in *R* (II.8). It was posthumously published in *Ninth Letter* 4.2 (Fall/Winter 2007): 113–17, and reprinted in *Harper's*, August 2008, 29–32.

Cornelia P. Claiborne: an editor at the newly founded *Hudson Review*. In an undated March letter to his mother, WG mentions "A very good letter from *Hudson Review*— "I enjoyed [yr. MS.] very much and returned it with great regrets to yr mother . . . &c."

G. S. B.: unidentified.

Chipp: a men's clothing store in Harvard Square and later in Manhattan.

To Katherine Anne Porter

[American short-story writer and novelist (1890–1980). WG wrote to praise her superb but controversial essay "Gertrude Stein: A Self-Portrait" in the December 1947 issue of Harper's. (It was retitled "The Wooden Umbrella" in her Collected Essays.) *He would write two more letters to her in April and May of 1948.]*

Box 46

Pedro Miguel, Canal Zone

21 january, 48

My dear Miss Porter.

A friend at *Harper's* was kind enough to send me your address—I hope you don't mind—when I wrote him asking for it, in order that I might be able to tell you how much your piece on Gertrude Stein provoked and cleared up and articulated for me.

To get this out of the way, I am one of the thousands of Harvard boys who never learned a trade, and are writing novels furiously with both hands. In order to avoid the mental waste (conversation &c.) that staying in New York imposes, I am here working on a crane on the canal and writing the inevitable novel at night.

I have never written such a letter as this—never felt impelled to (but once, in college, an outburst which I fortunately did not mail to Markova, after seeing her 'Giselle') — But your piece on Gertrude Stein—and your letter that accompanied it—kept me occupied for three days. And since I have no one here to talk with about it—thank heavens—I presume to write you. Having read very little of your work—remember being greatly impressed by 'Pale Horse'—so none of that comes in.

How you have put the finger on Miss Stein. Because she has worried me—not for as long nor as intelligently as she has you certainly, but since I have come on so many acclamations of her work, read and been excited and consternated, and not realised that emptiness until you told me about it. I read your piece just nodding ignorantly throughout, agreeing, failing to understand the failure in her which you were accounting. Expecting it to be simply another laudatory article like so many that explain and analyse an artist away, into senseless admiration (the kind Mr. Maugham is managing now in *Atlantic*). Toward the end of your piece I was seriously troubled—how far can a writers' writer go? (v. "She and Alice B. Toklas enjoyed both the wars—") —until I found your letter in the front of the magasine. Then I began to understand, and started the investigation with you again. Thank God someone has found her defeat, and accused her of it. And it was a great thing because it should teach us afterward places where the answer is not.

Certainly she did it with a monumental thoroughness. Now "Everything being equal, unimportant in itself, important because it happened to her and she was writing about it"—was a great trick. And: "her judgements were neither moral nor intellectual, and least of all aesthetic, indeed they were not even judgements—" which in this time of people judging people is in a way admirable. But that her nihilism was, eventually, culpable—and that her rewards did finally reach her, "struggling to unfold" as she did, all wrong somehow and almost knowing it. Her absolute denial of responsibility—and this is what always troubled me most—made so much possible. And how your clearly-accounted accusation shows the result.

It must have been a fantastically big talent—and I feel that we are fortunate that she used it as she did, teaching by that example (when understood, as your piece helped me to do)—for in our time if we do not understand and recognise the responsibility of freedom we are lost.

I should look forward to a piece on Waugh; though mine is the accepted blithe opinion of "a very clever one who knew he was writing for a very sick time."

Thank you again, for writing what you did, and for allowing this letter.

Sincerely,

William Gaddis

Markova [...] 'Giselle': Alicia Markova (1910–2004), English ballerina, known for her starring role in Adolphe Adam's ballet standard *Giselle* (1841).

'Pale Horse': in Porter's short-story collection *Pale Horse, Pale Rider* (1939).

v.: an old scholarly abbreviation (*vide*: see) that WG occasionally uses.

Mr. Maugham: W. Somerset Maugham: English novelist and playwright (1874–1965). In 1947 Maugham began publishing a series of appreciative essays on classic authors like Flaubert, Fielding, Balzac, et al.

your letter: Porter explains that she has read virtually all of Stein's books and that Stein "has had, I realize, a horrid fascination for me, really horrid, for I have a horror of her kind of mind and being; she was one of the blights and symptoms of her very sick times."

Waugh: Evelyn Waugh (1903–66), English novelist (see letter of January 1949). Porter writes in the aforementioned letter in *Harper's* that long ago she read Waugh's *Black Mischief* and felt "that he was either a very sick man or a very clever one who knew he was writing for a very sick time."

To Edith Gaddis

Pedro Miguel, Canal Zone
[23 January 1948]

dear Mother—

Thanks, thanks again. And for having been so good as to take care of June Kingsbury. I must write them a letter. But can't think of them at the moment, somehow makes me nervous to do so.

If your letter sounded lecturish certainly it was warranted by the outbursts I've been sending you. For which I apologise. I think I am getting hold now: the job, though still at times maddening when I am unoccupied, goes on with a minimum of difficulty. And the novel (in the most excruciating handwriting you have ever seen) is now two unfinished chapters, but I think good, and am comparatively happy about it—when it goes well I am fine, when not; unbearable. A black girl in the place where I eat occasionally accuses me of looking "vexed"—which in this West-Indian dialect means angry. So I tell her I'm vexed at the small portion she has put on my plate, and she tries to make up for it.

Two good letters from John Snow, to which I sent a rather excited answer—he probably thinks me insane by now. Also Eric Larrabee at *Harper's* sent me the address of Katherine Anne Porter, a modern writer of some repute, and I have written her to say how much I enjoyed her piece on Gertrude Stein in the recent *Harpers*. Never done such a thing before, but that article certainly warranted it. Correspondence a good thing, though even it often seems a waste to me.

Please excuse my haste—my "lunch" (a munificent affair—one ham-cheese, one onion-cheese, one peanut-butter-marmalade sandw., all made by my busy hands) hangs from the light cord, so the ants won't get it—and I must pull it down and be off.

Love
Bill

June Kingsbury: unidentified, perhaps related to the Kingsburys of Merricourt.
Eric Larrabee: (1922–90), whom WG met at Harvard, was managing editor of *Harper's* from 1946 to 1958.

To Edith Gaddis

Pedro Miguel, Canal Zone
[29 January 1948]

dear Mother.

I have got the clock. What a charming little thing it is! to have the onerous duty of rousing me from good sleep or a good book—and I am finding so many—to send me out to the enclosed scene. And many thanks for sending off that story. Yes, it is supposed to end as you quote it—heaven knows if it should or not—but I can't tell now, it is none of my concern now the thing is written I am through with it. [...]

Each of my letters, you know by now, asks some favour of you. This one is less involved than many—a book which I can't get down here. In fact you may not be able to in N.Y.—it being only recently out in France. The author is named *Rousset*; the title *La Vie Concentrationaire* or *Le Monde Concentrationaire*. You might try a store called *Coin de France* on 48th St, or Brentano; and there's a good French book store on that Radio City promenade. Don't give too much effort to it, it may well not be available. [...]

A splendid letter from Jacob—after so many of the talks, the scenes I have been through with him, what I have seen him go through, you may imagine how happy I am that he can write: "When I'm alone I'm more content than I've been in years..." not that I don't watch him with some element of un-Christian jealousy!

Your mention of my "plans" sounding "glorious" is somewhat disconcerting. I must confess, they do not at all hold consistent, even from day to day. The illusion of studying again—at Oxford or Zurich or Neuchatel—something which I allow myself to indulge occasionally. If when the time comes I can manage it, all the better. But hardly 'plans'! At least I am (1) earning and saving (2) thinking reading and writing—which is not time wasted dreaming. The novel harrows me all the time, sometimes it looks all right, at others impossible. (The latter at the moment). It must take time and quiet writing: there is so much of desperation *in* it, that it cannot be written in desperation, if you follow me.

One thing though: to keep away from America. Except for New York and Long Island, but America I have such pity for, fury at, why are Americans so awful, their voices, every thing. You can't imagine Pedro Miguel, what the Americans have done in "civilising" this strip called Canal Zone, how they have *sterilized* it. And why do they feel it incumbent upon them to behave with rudeness every where away from home? Barren ignorance is most horrible when it is in power—the picture of the American soldier abroad will never cease to make me shudder. And the prospect of another war, wanting to fight the good fight and not finding it in my country's side, worst of all.

Sorry to end on a dismal note—end of paper.

Love,

W.

Rousset: *L'Univers concentrationnaire* (1946) by French political activist David Rousset (1912–97) is about the concentration camp at Buchenwald, where he was imprisoned. It was published in English translation as *A World Apart* in 1951.

To Ida Williams Way

Pedro Miguel, Canal Zone
18 Feb 48

dear Granga.

Many thanks for the Keystone View offer. I have been sitting over 3pm breakfast (I worked until 7 this morning) trying to think it out clearly. But first let me give you an idea of my present circumstances. I am, you know, spending all of my free time working on this novel; some times it looks good to me—as though it deserves all my time—and some times quite worthless. So clearly I am in no position to judge, and the only thing to do is to continue to work on it. Except for the fact that I lead a compleatly lonely life here, this life isn't too conducive to writing and clear thinking. Living in a large building where I can't use my typewriter because of other men resting &c. is one thing; then the Canal Zone, which is a sterile American monstrosity; and the job, which takes a good deal out of me. I am hoping now to hang on for about 8 more weeks, until early in April. And since I am living very close to the wall, spending as little as possible, by then I should have around 500$ put by, enough to travel down here, settle somewhere for a little while and write unhindered. Plan to be back in N.Y. around the middle of June.

Do you think it would be worthwhile? the photographing? And would it cost me, to get around here and take pictures? When I leave I'm going up into the interior—toward the Costa Rica border (and probably on to Costa Rica) to see what this jungle country really looks like. Certainly an opportunity for photography. But *you* will understand, I shan't have the money to spend traveling for that—for taking the pictures I mean. You see, I have a pretty vague picture of the set-up. It is awful to be this way, to have both time and money mean so much. But that's the corner I'm in. Also I must mention, no cameras allowed on the canal, if they should want some pictures here. Anyhow, if I had some better idea of how extensive a tour they wanted, and who would foot the bill, and what sort of remuneration, &c. And if, after all of this whining, it sounds feasible, you might let me know.

I wrote Uncle Oscar, and enclosed a picture card which may please him—and am half expecting, any day, to get an undecipherable answer.

And news from New York is good, although I am just as glad to be here for this winter.

Thanks for your letters—and the Valentine—and now I must get back down to business.

Love,
W.

Keystone View: a Pennsylvania company that produced stereoscopic images.
Uncle Oscar: Oscar Rhodes (1862–1949). The protagonist of *FHO* is named Oscar.

To Edith Gaddis

Pedro Miguel, Canal Zone
[late Feb/early March? 1948]

dear Mother—

An outburst. But I *have* to burst out somewhere. Having just spent 50$—
but on *what*. Two *magnificent* suitcases. All English made, beautiful leather,
locks, &c. Like Brooks sells for 45$ (the small one, I paid 18) and 87$ (big one
I paid 23.50$)—— Well. So now I *have* my little suitcase to carry about
manuscripts in and look like the Fuller Brush man. I should have been a fool
to miss it—and since it looks like I am going to spend a rather peripatetic
(that means doing things while moving about) youth, all the better.

I have your letter—and hope you do get to Virginia this weekend—I am
off to work now, go to Taboga at 6 am tomorrow. Hot spit. With typewriter.
This novel, dear God. If only I could stop *living* for a little and *do* it. But you
may imagine the sort of life I lead if packing 2 cans of beans, six of sardines,
a loaf of bread and a box of cinnamon buns, and going off to an island for 3
days alone excites me so that my handwriting gets like *this*. *Got* to write a
novel, *got* to work and save, *got* to go to Costa Rica, to Haiti, to Jamaica, *got*
to know people, write letters, *got* to read, study, think, learn—*got* (at the moment) to go to the dentist—— Isn't it fantastic? Wonderful?   I am going
off my trolley—*so* much. But most of all I *have* got to finish a good novel,
don't I. Because that's what I've set myself to do. And when one *forces* one's
self to rise above the idiotic futility of it *all*, the vanity of human wishes, the
acquisition of "things" (vis. luggage)—then it is splendid.

I had wondered about you and the Harvard Club—and am so glad it is as
good as you write it.

I don't think I could <u>stand</u> *Crime & Punishment* on the stage. Who was
this Dolly Hass—Sonia? What an opportunity *that* part would be for a young
actress. She could probably never play a part again.

Main reason for this, I have so many *ideas*, for writing. But they must be
written mustn't they? You see I suddenly find myself to engulfed with new
thoughts, interpretations, impressions, Revelations, that I can't sit still to
finish *one*. Well, you know. I'll get over *this*. (In psychology we call it Euphoria).

And many thanks. I await the civilised cigarettes and reading matter (if
that book doesn't sober me up, nothing will).

So *did* you go to Williamsburg? And be reckless enough (how you and I give ourselves gifts, with *such* guilty pleasure) to take a sleeper. I hope so.

Love,

W.

Fuller Brush man: archetypal door-to-door salesman of the early twentieth century.

the vanity of human wishes: title of a pessimistic poem (1749) by Samuel Johnson.

Crime & Punishment on the stage: opened in New York in January 1948, starring John Gielgud as Raskolnikov and German-born actress Dolly Haas as Sonia.

civilised cigarettes: in a letter mailed 2 February, WG wrote: "Some time when you are thinking of yr. loving son and how much you would like to do something to please his vagrant heart, but don't know just what—you might send him a box (10 pckgs.) of *PLAYERS* cigarettes, which he would enjoy and consider as a civilised respite in his present circumstance."

reading matter: apparently Rousset's *L'Univers concentrationnaire*.

To Charles Socarides

[*A Harvard friend; see note to letter of late February* 1943. *This is the earliest letter to explain the essential idea and plot of* R.]

Pedro Miguel, Canal Zone
[February or March 1948]

dear Charles.

First—please don't be alarmed by the weight of a correspondence which I may seem to be thrusting on you. But when you write a letter like this that I have just received, honestly I go quite off my head with excitement. Am fearfully nervous now.

All because I have been away for 3 days, on a neighboring island, working frantically on this novel. Which looks so *bad*. But here: you see, what you say in these letters—most specifically this last—upset me because the pictures you draw, the facts you offer, are just as this novel is growing. It is a good novel, terrific, the whole thread of the story, the happenings, the franticness. The man who (metaphorically) sells himself to the devil, the young man hunting so for father figure, chasing the older to his (younger's) death. And the "girl"— who finally compleatly loses her identity, she who has tried to make an original myth is lost because her last witness (a fellow who takes heroin) is sent to jail—the young man ('hero') the informer. Here the frantic point: that it all *happened*. Not really, maybe, but with the facts in recent life and my running, it *happened*. All the time, every minute the thing grows in me, I "think of" (or remember) new facts of the novel—the Truth About the Past (alternate title). (The title is *Ducdame, called 'some people who were naked'*). But this growing fiction fits so insanely well with facts of life that some times I can not stand it, must burst (as I am doing here). And *then* I *ruin* it by *bad writing*. Like trying to be clever—this perhaps because I am afraid to be sincere? But I watch myself ruin it. And then—because when I was writing in college I went so over board, now it must be reserved, understated, intimated. Or bad bits of writing just run on. Look: "There are few instances when we are not trying to control time; either frantically urging it on, or fearfully watching its winged chariot ragging by, spattering us with the mud that we call memory." Isn't that *awful*. You see, it just *happened*, was out of my control until the sentence reached the period. To be facile can kill what *must* be alive.

That's why I hated Wolfe—that he cried out so. Because my point is, no crying out, no pity. We are alone, naked—and nakedness must choose between vulgarity and reason. Every one of us, *responsible*. Still those lines you quote (Wolfe) excite me horribly. Not to have Forster's understatement. No room for Lawrence's lust. Perhaps Flaubert, or Gide. But I am not good enough as they. It is sickening this killing the best-loved—work.

How I should like to see you, if you could look at this thing, flatly condense (parts of) it—the writing, exposition. God I know all this fear, but have *no* sympathy with it. Fools. I can not afford to be one.

As though your letter anticipated what I am just putting down as fiction.

I can't come home before June. Because of *money*. Always that. After June I can live on Long Island, not before summer though, you see? Must work on this goddamned canal until April, hope to save around 600$, enough to live on until June and get home. I hate it, paid 12$ a day—or night—to *waste*. Now it is 10:15pm—and I must be at the canal at 11, "work" until 7am. But I have to because of money. Perhaps good I don't have money, crazy in love with the daughter of this local island's governor—not Mex, Panamanian, but Spanish. Splendid nose. Good Werther love, doesn't trouble her. It is hell not to have either the time nor the money to *live*.

Then there is a man here with a sail boat going to Sweden. And if the novel suddenly looks too *bad* I may go, he needs someone to work, a very small boat, sail boat.

God the running, running. You *understand* it, don't you? I almost do. But if I can't make a *good* novel then I must keep running, until I know all through me—not just as a philosophical fact, as *truth* which I "believe" and am trying to sell—but can sit down and know without having to try to sell it (writing) to *everybody*.

Thanks. I shall *write* you.

W.

Ducdame, called 'some people who were naked' : "Ducdame" is a nonsense word from Jaques's song in Shakespeare's *As You Like It*, which he facetiously defines as "a Greek invocation to call fools into a circle" (5.2.53). For more on the title, see the 7 April 1948 letter to Porter.

time [...] its winged chariot: an image from Andrew Marvell's poem "To His Coy Mistress" (c. 1650).

Wolfe [...] those lines you quote: perhaps Socarides quoted these lines near the end of *Look Homeward, Angel* (1929): "Inevitable catharsis by the threads of chaos. Unswerving punctuality of chance. [¶] Apexical summation, from the billion deaths of possibility, of things done." WG was so struck by the phrase "unswerving punctuality of chance" that he used it in all five of his novels (*R* 9, *J R* 486, *CG* 233, *FHO* 50, 258, *AA* 63).

Werther: the suicidal hero of Goethe's novel *The Sorrows of Young Werther* (1774).

To Edith Gaddis

Pedro Miguel, Canal Zone
[10 March 1948]

dear Mother.

You were so good to have sent this divination book right off. I have just got it; and of course it is in a way preposterous, and foolishness. But quite exactly what I wanted, and thank you.

Sometimes this life gets so horrid; but then, the time I have set myself runs out in 5 weeks! Dear God, to be 'free' again briefly. But then, the reading I have been doing recently (except for the New Testament, *such* a wonder)—has not been of a high character—Dostoevski's *House of the Dead*—an account of his Siberian imprisonment, and one cannot help but find analogies to the sterile barbarity of the Zone. Incidentally, we haven't had an extended talk about Americans. I am so glad you managed Virginia. When things are exceptionally woeful, I go in to Panama and simply walk. Such colours, and unarranged humanity, and rest. A lime-green building with brown trim, or another brown with blue, and pink, and so much wonderful white. Tomorrow night I am going in, and Juancho—this kind fellow who is a judge, and would 'write', so nice to me, humanly so—is going to play for me the *Messiah*, 35 sides to its recording! How I look forward to it, music is so badly missed.

A very distracting letter from John Snow. I shall show it you; he thinks he is well-off, but you may read it and may understand why I don't see going back to Harvard, where he is. Very sad.

And Granga and I seem to have got up a regular correspondence! Glad of course that you are passing such a jolly and busy winter. I trust you still attend your ceramic classes in the midst of all that gaiety! Eh?

Since I am on very bad terms with myself—writing going badly, so I have no sympathy *here*—I shall cut short, before I begin railing at something.

Love,
Bill

---

divination book: probably *The Book of Fate*, quoted a few times in *R* (137, 754). It is said to have been discovered by Napoleon's officers in Egypt, was first published in 1822, and has been reprinted often.

New Testament: in an undated letter around this time to his great-aunt, WG wrote: "And have reached Timothy in the New Testament! I go very slowly in it, underlining things I recognise, or do not recognise and want to in the future."

Dostoevski's *House of the Dead*: documentary novel first published in 1861–62.

35 sides: 78 rpm phonographs held only about 4 or 5 minutes of music per side.

To Edith Gaddis

Pedro Miguel, Canal Zone
[13 March 1948]

dear Mother.

One thing I do not understand. You know, I left N.Y. with comparatively little luggage. And now this room is *littered*. Junk all over the place, and all over the walls, &c. Apparently I am a real candidate for the studio; but I cannot understand how these things just *accumulate*.

This morning I rode into Balboa with the foreman on our job—he says he thinks it will last for 3 or 4 more weeks. And then I find that I cannot get the reduced rate back to the U.S.—that is 40$, the regular rate being 180$! So I guess I shall go up to Costa Rica as tenatively planned. Have recently been reading about Eugene O'Neill—and am furious that one can no longer live as he did—just wandering about, one job, one ship to another. No. To travel now—and this most especially for the woeful American—one must have money, and be ready to pay at every turn. [...]

Well—that little business can wait another couple of weeks—since I am just now getting no writing done at all, only making voluminous notes, and a few sketches for what should be splendid stage sets. (How one wanders, wanders, from one creative world to another—) (And this morning I got from the library a book on plays and two books of plays—perhaps the childhood influence of the ever-beautiful Frances Henderson—). [...]

Love, W.

Frances Henderson: see headnote to 13 March 1946. In an outline for *Blague*, the protagonist Charles Pivner recalls "a college romance with a dancer, which came to no
fruition, [...]" Marrying someone else, "He of course has failed to find in her the
beauteous innocence which he had endowed, and remembers in, Miss Horse (the
dancer's nickname)."

To Katherine Anne Porter

Panama, R.P.
7 April, 1948.

My dear Miss Porter.

Perhaps you can understand how well your letter was received, how many
times read; and how much I want to repay your kindness by trying very hard
to write you an honest letter. I find it difficult always (or rather of course make
it difficult for myself) to write an honest letter because I am not clear yet
about writing a letter, and especially as now when this writing I do is not
going well then to write a letter is more strange still because it becomes an
outlet which it should not be but the writing should be. Not that the writing
is an outlet, but as though the outlet is the purpose. Well when the writing
is consistently unsatisfactory then the purpose is all confused, and one may
run to letter-writing saying, —Here is what I have to say, you will see how
important it is, and what a worthy one I am ... no, I haven't quite finished the
story, the novel, the play, but meanwhile you must appreciate ... Well you
understand, that it can be like that morass of conversation. And so now often
in the middle of a letter I must stop and say, —What filthy little vanity is this,
Willie, that you are relishing so. And stop, furious with myself and also the
person who does not get the letter. Still it is all wrong, absolutely, to then turn
and revel in the idea of not being able to write a letter. You know, I have so
many letters from NY that start out, —I started to write you a letter last week,
but it turned out to be ..., and —I have written you twice, and the letters are
here unmailed. Well those people are writing to themselves, and would do
better to not bother using someone else's name at the head of the sheet as an
excuse. But the vanity of letter-writing, of shouting out for witnesses. I have
thought a great deal about this whole insistence on a witness that we all make,
that is certainly one reason why so many bad novels are so bad. Much of it
seems to be a very American thing too, I see the American with the camera
everywhere, that filthy silent witness; and to jump off of the aeroplane when
it lands in one country after another: no time to look at the volcano or feel
the air except to say to another how hot it is, but (because the 'plane will only
be in Guatamala, in Nicaragua, in Costa Rica, for fifteen minutes) that one
must get to the counter and send off postal cards with a picture of the volcano

he did not see, to witnesses. I have recently finished reading the New Testament, which makes much of witnesses. Now what did Jesus mean, (this is Matthew 9:30, 31, after he has healed a blind man) And their eyes were opened; and Jesus straitly charged them, saying, See that no man know it. But they, when they were departed, spread abroad his fame in all that country. Now certainly the largest reason he carried on these miracles was simply for witnesses, later he charges the apostles *as* witnesses. No; but getting back, everyone running about insisting on having them. (And that often splendid comedian Jimmy Durante's —Everybody wants to get into the act. Well.) Certainly a prophet needs witnesses, otherwise the whole thing is to little avail. But the instant a piece of writing takes on the note of, —See what I have done, where I have been, what I have read; but do not forget that these things cannot happen to you but through me…well then the whole thing is vile, will not do. And the other side of that dirty coin is all of the snivelling confessionals, they are the most infuriating and it seems to be the way the coin is falling now. Oh, these soft-handed little boys who suffer so with themselves and their boys and 'men', I am intolerant. Or of the loneliness of our lot, without a poet of stature that sensibility snivels. But Goethe's (I do not read German, I have learned some by rote—I am trying to be honest) Nur wer die Sehnsucht kennt weiss was Ich leide, Allein und abgetrennt von alle Freude—that that stands up in suffering; or Rilke's Who if I cried would hear me in the angelic orders. This distinction between loneliness and alone-ness. But to start this bad arguement at its beginning: Did you have trouble with people anticipating you? that an idea which you had discovered and formulated for yourself and then were working to deliver it, find it was not yours (in the mean sense) but (if you thought further, with courage and (if you were not mean) gratitude) eventually yours most because given to all, because perhaps one may have the brass to say it is a truth? Well, and so when you said in your letter of distinguishing loneliness and solitude, I was immediately troubled, even (witness this meanness) offended. Do you understand? As though, what business had you, to offer in some fifteen words, what I discovered finally some six or eight months ago, discovered with such triumph! And really what meaner more unchristian thing than one who would try to covet a truth. And these months past I have been running around pounding the board for recognition of aloneness and (this above all) the incumbent responsibility. Discovery indeed! And then to read Sartre's *Les Mouches*. This, if ever was, a time to find joy and triumph when truth is shared, and to tear out meanness where it grows, to be Christian. (The only poetry I have been reading here—after the tiresome disappointment of Auden's *The Age of Anxiety*—is Eliot; and I say this because a line suddenly comes up, —I am no prophet, but here's no great matter; I have seen my head (grown slightly bald) brought in upon a platter &c.)

The business of owning an idea, a line, an image. For instance, I remember finding the notion that some people are 'not big enough for tragedy', and believe me I have worked it out in a wonderful number of useless words: and then found it in Forster, in one sentence. (That was four or five years ago, I was in college.) But even now it has happened again, this time not a notion but a line, the title I had settled on for this work I am at now is *Some people who were naked*, that is what I want, it is the whole idea. And then I have just had recommended to read, and finally had the courage to read, a play by Pirandello, the title of course is *Vestire gl'ignudi*, Clothing the Naked. That was a start. Then, his heroine, Ersilia, says (with infinite sadness, but with a smile nevertheless) In that case, I shall not be the woman I was, nor the woman I am, but still another! (My Esme (even the name, you see) was one who was uncertain as to her identity, finally could not stand to be alone (knowing though that aloneness is essential) because without a witness she could not know if she had really done things, and finally loses all concept of being anyone at all) (Ersilia finishes the P— play with, —that I am dead...yes, and that I died naked!) My elder protagonist to be one who (exactly in the same manner of Faust, paraphrasus of the circumstances, dog and all) sells himself to the devil (a publisher, entrepreneur) to forge paintings. And to find P—'s protagonist sending the letter to Ersilia signed Faust. Well.

But you will see the whole thing clearly enough to understand that it cannot be simply this disconcerting discovery and relinquishing of ideas. Because there they are anyhow, and not new. And so one is forced to say 'style'? That word! And what ridiculous arguements, wasteful discussions it brings forth. I remember one, in which I had commented on what a fine style in David Hume; my antagonist started immediately with saying that Hume did not try to write in a style, but the style came about as he wrote writing to say what he had to say. You see where this arguement is going. Two people without style arguing on the same side against eachother; still I would try to say that, now that Hume is through, one reads him and sees an excellent style, after the fact. Glenway Wescott a fine stylist; and Rebecca West extraordinary: (so extraordinary, that once during the most recent war I was working on the *New Yorker*, and one of her pieces, a report on a trial for treason, described with such wondrous style a room in Lords, &c &c, that we could not eventually make out which room she meant: she did not once say, the fact simply wasn't there in all of that style.) And a preoccupation with style for itself is admittedly ruinous.

Penned in, in your letter (of writing): but it is fun, isn't it... well that was compleatly disconcerting, effacing, happy, infuriating. I don't know, when it begins to be fun then I know myself badly enough to immediately hold it suspect. You know, the temptations? Well, to be clever, for one. That is one of the worst, and how it kills. Then to preach and prophesy (Remember, it was I who told you this...); the tangent of going off and having fun for its own sake, no matter that it contributes nothing (though some do it infuriatingly well); and then the absolute necessity of making a character's experience *his* and not one's own, and that is certainly one of the most difficult requisites. To discriminate, perhaps that is the most important. Here is a line of Katherine Mansfield's, you may recognise it, from a book review of about 25 years back: —These are moments that set the soul yearning to be taken suddenly, snatched out of the very heart of some fearful joy, and set before its Maker, hatless, dishevelled and gay, with its spirit unbroken. (Now allow this presumption, simply for the sake of the hypothesis) That if I had written that I can imagine being very doubtful about it; but here I found it (the collection of reviews called *Novels and Novelists*) with fantastic pleasure, could not put it down, was troubled that it should be buried in an old book review. Or if I had been sure of it, should have wanted it published prominently, as mine, perhaps a little edition by itself. You see how 'lamentable' this is, will not do.

It is *enthusiasm* that I mistrust.

Presumption may not be the worst of sins (though it is when I think of it) but it is pretty bad. So there is the worry of pretentious and presumptious work. But I could no more sit down and write *When the mountain fell* (Ramuz) than ... well, the usual things people say, 'fly' for instance. Do you know the trouble I am in, right now, that any part of this letter may sound pretentious? I started a novel in Mexico last winter, it was an allegory, and Good and Evil were two apparently always drunk fellows who gave driving lessons in a dual-control car. Well, writing that was fun, so damn' much fun that it took me five months to realise how pretentious it was, and there is a kind fellow at an agency in NY (Harold Matson's) who wanted me to finish it, he wanted to sell it. Thank God a couple of publishers said no thanks &c and I came to Panama, to write an honest novel. Right now that is what he thinks I am doing. Oh dear.

In the Canal Zone I have done a great deal of 'thinking' (I want it to be) about our country, which depresses me but must not to the point of simply saying oh dear. (And then I came on this, in James, 1:23,24) For if any be a hearer of the word and not a doer, he is like a man beholding his natural face in a glass: For he beholdeth himself, and goeth his way, and straightway forgetteth what manner of man he was. And Paul to the Corinthians, 8:11 Now therefore perform the doing of it; that as there was a readiness to will, so there may be a performance also out of that which ye have.) At any rate, this Zone is all wrong, a transgression because of its *sterility*. Now (for a while) I am free of the concrete-buster and the air-hammers shaking me to pieces, and the crane, though all of that was good, to do work, it was the enforced idleness that was bad, being paid to be idle was horrible. It is terrifying that people can live here and for years, they bring up their children here and the children are empty boxes too, they usually stay, and so many of them are pale and I cannot love pale people in a sun country. Bloodless somehow, the Panamanians have blood, and the west indians who are niggers and are held off with disapproval and low wages but the Americans have radios, you can walk up a street past the house after house the same colour (that is the regulation, they are grey) and hear every radio playing the same programme, the mechanical-laugh programme from the States, the movies do well also new cars running around like crazy with the wives who are also some of them the young pretty ones pretty slick articles, but not when they stay and stay, then they are dumpy and sad and all the same colour but no one has told them they are sad so they do not know they are but talk to eachother instead. And no one goes into Panama except he is a man and then for the reasons that any sailor is glad to make a port, and as wearily ready to leave it.

To get to the war. Two years ago I wrote (badly) a story of a man who is devastated by a dream of Armageddon—with *no* idea that H. G. Wells had written a (bad) story called "A Dream of Armageddon"—and I have been worrying it since. Reading the prophesies in the Great Pyramid, of Nostradamus, and in Ezekial and Revelation. And have been obsessed with the idea of Armageddon coming in 1949. That we will live to see Good & Evil defined in battle? And then to have followed (with the lazy layman's eye, I confess) the developments in political geography since, and now. This thing (it is still just a thing) that I am trying to work on now ends with that; and so I have put myself under this insane press of time, that it must be done before, just before, this final violence comes. That we must *choose*, there is the trouble. And how are we equipped? All of the thesis of despair in "That is not what I meant at all" (and the Kaiser, after the other war—as Lawrence quotes him in *Women in Love*—This is not what I meant, this is not how I meant it to come out at all...) That intentions are most wasteful of the energies we spend, I believe. Except perhaps bitterness, somehow bitterness is the worst, the least pardonable, the most culpably wasteful.

When there was a civil war in Spain, the young Americans who wanted to fight the Good Fight went to fight Fascism, beside the Communists. And now see us. What is it? that in these countries without a middle class there is material only for the extremes, and that only the extremes war? Here is Costa

Rica. Where does one fight? Or is it two evils, which will not abide one another? These are not precious thoughts, and the precious will have to think
them and choose. And after there will not be one small voice saying, That is
not what I meant.

There is such an accumulation. Did you have the feeling, early when you
were writing, a novel, say, that you must get everything in? Everything. And
where will this fit? . . . and this? Idea, and incident, and image. It is as though
(I thought last night, thinking how should I say to you what it is like) one
were in deep water, and this accumulation bobbing all around, as far as can
be seen but all within reach; and that one may grab at any of them to present,
to say Look, does this not prove me worthy? and another to swim firmly past
them, through the water, while another still (and this somehow a woman)
not for a moment recognising the water, but at intelligent leisure take this,
and that, perfectly chosen, while further on one may float among it all on his
back and the eyes closed, while his considerate (civilised) neighbor drowns
with silent dignity. And as though I were in the middle of mine, beating the
water into a foam but not waves, shouting Whoopee, Look! Look! at all these
things of mine, they are mine, take any that you want. (They are mine.) And
then, with Mr Eliot, the moment of silence, I have heard the mermaids singing
each to each.   I do not think that they will sing for me.

I have tried to write you honestly. And have justified the lengthiness by
believing that you will read it all, if you were good enough to spend the time
for me that you did in the letter you sent to me. Of course, there are other
things, of vulgarity and reason, and Salvation wearing a political face (mostly
stolen from Mann). If it has seemed upset, I have quit the Canal Zone and if
I can get papers and this money together am going to fly to Costa Rica in the
morning. I have not put down an address (and even that has come to seem
presumptuous, to put a return on a letter, presuming an answer) because I
intend to have none for a while. Because I do not wish to say here why I am
going to San Jose, because anything I should say would be intentions, and
those I will not trust.

With it all, if things go as I 'intend', I hope to be back in New York June
or July, and if I could meet you, and talk, not chatter, perhaps you would talk.
Cordially, and sincerely,
William Gaddis

Jimmy Durante: (1893–1980), American comic actor and songwriter.
Goethe's [...] Freude: "Only one who yearns knows what I suffer, alone and separate
from all joy"—the opening lines from a once-famous song in Goethe's novel *Wil-
helm Meister's Apprenticeship* (1795–96).

Rilke's Who if I cried: the opening line of the first of his *Duino Elegies* (1923), quoted a few times in *R*.

Auden's *The Age of Anxiety*: book-length poem published in 1947.

I am no prophet [...] upon a platter: from "The Love Song of J. Alfred Prufrock" (1917), though lines reversed.

'not big enough for tragedy' [...] Forster: in his *Aspects of the Novel*, Forster writes: "For we must admit that flat people are not in themselves as big achievements as round ones, and also that they are best when they are comic. A serious or tragic flat character is apt to be a bore" (Harcourt, Brace, 1957, 111).

Pirandello [...] Clothing the Naked: a 1923 play by the Italian playwright and novelist Luigi Pirandello (1867–1936) about a young woman named Ersilia Drei and five men who try to "strip" her of the romantic fantasies she has created about herself as well as "clothe" her in their own fantasies about her. WG read Arthur Livingston's translation of *Naked* (as he titled it) in *Each in His Own Way and Two Other Plays* (Dutton, 1926).

Glenway Wescott: American novelist and journalist (1901–87).

Rebecca West: English novelist and journalist (1892–1983); she reported on the Nuremberg trials (1945–46) for the *New Yorker*.

Katherine Mansfield's [...] spirit unbroken: New Zealand short-story writer (1888–1923). As WG notes, the quotation is from her collection *Novels and Novelists* (1930); a favorite line of his, it is quoted thrice in *R* (125, 304, 716) and once in *J R* (486).

When the mountain fell (Ramuz): English title (Pantheon, 1947) of the 1937 novel *Derborence* by Swiss writer C. F. Ramuz (1878–1947).

kind fellow at an agency: Don Congdon (1918–2009), a well-known literary agent.

H. G. Wells [...] "A Dream of Armageddon": a 1901 story about a man who has premonitory dreams about the destruction new advances in technology will enable in the future.

prophesies in the Great Pyramid: in Worth Smith's *Miracle of the Ages: The Great Pyramid*, mentioned earlier (7 April 1947). Cf. WG to Sheri Martinelli, Summer 1953.

"That is not what I meant at all": another sentence from Eliot's "Prufrock."

Women in Love: in the final chapter of D. H. Lawrence's 1921 novel, Gerald cries, "'I didn't want it to be like this—I didn't want it to be like this,' he cried to himself. Ursula could but think of the Kaiser's: 'Ich habe as nicht gewollt'" (I didn't intend this [World War I] to happen).

I have heard the mermaids singing: the finest couplet in Eliot's "Prufrock."

Salvation wearing a political face [...] Mann: the German novelist and essayist Thomas Mann (1875–1955). In his address "An Appeal to Reason" (1930), he denounced the Nazis' appeal to mysticism: "This fantastic state of mind, of a humanity that has outrun its ideas, is matched by a political scene in the grotesque style, with Salvation Army methods, hallelujahs and bell-ringing and dervishlike repetition of monotonous catchwords, until everybody foams at the mouth. Fanaticism turns into a means of salvation, enthusiasm into epileptic ecstasy, politics becomes an opiate for the masses, a proletarian eschatology; and reason veils her face."

To Edith Gaddis

Pedro Miguel, Canal Zone
[7 April 1948]

dear Mother.

I am sorry that this will be just a note, to say that I am going up to San Jose tomorrow, and sorry that I haven't managed to reach you on the telephone. [...]

Now. Do you remember when we talked about Seabrook, the one who involved himself with the Arabs and travelled where there were no PostOffices? And your saying that you could picture me wanting to do just those things. No Arabs here, but my point is simply that I am going to Costa Rica, where they are having some disruption, and there may be postal problems, or I may get out of San Jose—because I do want to look at the country after being shut up in this sink—and may not have a mail-box at hand. That I shall try to write, and *please* don't be concerned (I know from my psychology books that this is idle pleading) if there are not many letters. Of course we both know that I shall probably be shipped out of the country the moment I appear. And then again I may not. One must prepare for eventualities. There.

And I am an American, I know that. It is a damn' lot of work being one. And grave responsibility? I had a splendid and long letter from Katherine Anne Porter, she the writer. I have filled her cup for her though, sent her five pages of my vagaries to ponder. I feel fine, am healthy, teeth and bones and eyes, shoes shined, slightly nervous (you see I am being honest), full of food. Also (also indeed! Eminently:) I have a little money and when I have to go there you'll have to take me in.

Will write—and love,
W.

Seabrook: William Seabrook (1884–1945), author of *Adventures in Arabia* (1927).
some disruption: the Costa Rican legislature's annulment of the results of the 1948 presidential election incited the 44-day Costa Rican Civil War (12 March–24 April 1948), in which rebel forces led by President José Figueres Ferrer defeated government forces (with the tacit approval of the U.S.) and took control of the capital, San José. About 2,000 people died in the conflict.
when I have to go there you'll have to take me in: from Robert Frost's memorable definition: "Home is the place where, when you have to go there, / They have to take you in" ("The Death of the Hired Man," 1914).

To Edith Gaddis

Gran Hotel Costa Rica
San José, Costa Rica
8 april, 1948

Dear Mother.

Just to say that San Jose is quiet, and cool—about like NY in September—and the only signs of trouble here in the city are truckloads of soldiers who seem to me to be smiling and waving at the girls most of the time. It is a comparatively new city, and so there is none of the temptation to stand about gawking at ancient cathedrals &c, and the mountains around it fine and still not especially alarming as mountains so often are (I can imagine looking out of a window in Interlocken and seeing the Jungfrau!); simply a cool quiet city, with a great sense of dignity about it.

And I have just come in (it is 7:30am) from three cups of splendid cafe-con-leche, so rich that one hardly needs sugar. The exchange is around 5 to 1, which sounds fine except that everything seems quite 5 times its price for this foolish American, though of course things are always so on arrival. Am glad to have got out of Panama, still as fond of it, but there is something hurley-burley and hot about that city which was beginning to set me a little on edge. Made my plane here with 7minutes to spare (one is suppose to arrive 1hour early) and of course managed to lose a notebook on a bus, those are the sickening things. But Juan Diaz was such a friend, such a kind fellow; he writes (is 32, the lawyer I have mentioned) and I so hope that there will be some way I can repay his kindness.

Anyhow don't write to this address; I am paying 6$ a day (without meals) and don't plan to hang around this lobby much longer. Today hope to go out into the country for a further look at Costa Rica, and shall probably soon enough send you an address. If my letters have sounded distraught about coming up here, you know how one gets all kinds of disturbing word about a country in such a state as this one is; but they seem to regard the little war as simply another piece of necessary business which is being negociated by the proper authorities, and with, as I say, a nice dignity about it.

Love,
Bill

Interlocken: i.e., Interlaken, a Swiss resort town famous for its view of Jungfrau mountain peak.

To Edith Gaddis

Western Union Cablegram
Cartago, Costa Rica
17 April 1948

SORRY LETTERLESS NO POST COLD WET UNWASHED UNSHAVED BARE-
FOOT BUSY HAPPY LOVE=

W.

To Edith Gaddis

[*From WG's "In the Zone": "The fighting was out around Cartago, where I was handed over to a young captain named Madero and issued a banged-up Springfield that was stolen from me the same day. We leveled an airstrip out there for arms coming in from Guatemala.* Life *magazine showed up and rearranged the cartridge belt for an old French Hotchkiss over the blond sergeant's shoulders before they took his picture beside it, and when the arms came in we celebrated with a bottle of raw cane liquor and the sergeant took us home for dinner where I met the most beautiful girl I've ever seen and passed out at the table" (RSP 37).*]

Hotel Panamerican
San José, Costa Rica
[26 April 1948]

dear Mother.

Have been for the two weeks past with the army of Figueres, outside in the now pretty battered town of Cartago. Now the revolution is over. And probably when I see you will have much to tell you about it, but right now don't feel awfully like chattering, have a slight return of the I suppose it is dysentary from Mexico, also painful business with a dentist here, and finally am lying on my back trying to explain the whole thing out to myself. Except for the internal 'disorder' and the tooth am in good health.

Let me tell you about the tooth; it is a small subject. In the Canalzone I had some aching in the one next to the excavation of last summer, it is a molar. And so was very pleased with myself when I went to the dentist there without prodding and had him fix it and fill it &c. But the idiot had no Xray machine, and sent me out with all assurances and what I—and I must suppose he—thought was a finished job. Of course a few days ago it started badly again, I got in to San Jose as soon as possible and to a fine young bright well-equipped dentist, whom I left about two hours ago. His Xray showed that the CZ practitioner hadn't done the whole job, and was ready to extract. Anyhow he says that I may let it go for another 6 or 8 weeks and by then if in NY go to a root canal (*that* word) specialist who might save it. Or we may take it out here. This business of going through life losing things. I lost my raincoat in the revolution.

Anyhow the Costa Ricans are a splendid people, are handsome, and they don't dislike Americans as so many Latins do and have reason to. The country here is high and cool, and this city a model of order and organisation.

Forgive me if I don't go on. This will assure you of my for the moment quiet humourless condition, and give you an address—the one above—where I shall be I think on and off for the next 5 or 6 weeks.

Love,
Bill

To Edith Gaddis

San José, Costa Rica
28 April 1948

dear Mother.

Many thanks for your letter(s), which I had this morning. And pleasant reading on my bed of pain. Yes, I must tell you. Finally, after a rousing night— nothing equals a toothache—I went to call on Dr Saturnino Medal (University Loyola, Honduras, &c) and told him I realised that the foolishness had to stop. (Now remember the New Testament: (or maybe it is the Old One) —plucking out offending members in order to be whole) Or AE Housman: 'If it chance your eye offend you, Pluck it out lad, and be whole. But play the man, stand up and end you, When the sickness is your soul.' At any rate, we plucked out the offending member. Dear heaven, how we worked. And sure enough, the damn' thing was abessed, and no wonder that my pain had not been simply toothache but usurping other realms as well. To tell the truth, for this past two months I haven't been feeling great, and (awful truth) have done such painfully little writing that there is that guilt too. Though I have been fairly consistent in taking notes on thought and happening, and now have a horrid accumulation of that. And to assure myself that I not waste all this time given me, have been steadily toiling through AJ Toynbee's *Study of History*; losing much of course, it being an abridgement of the original 6 volumes and so many of the references have little meaning to me, with my vacuous background in history. But many revelations too, it is a magnificent book; and of course I want to settle down now and go through the whole 6. Because that brilliant man has somehow the meaning of meaning, and never in a smart way, you know, like so many of the books now: how to be free from nervous strain, how to write, how to read, how to be a Chinaman like Lin

Yutang, &c &c. No this man is very humble before knowledge, never peda-
gogic.

Well. I think it was rather dim of Chandler and (I suppose it was Constance
Smith) to not call you, but go busting into the house. Not angry about it of
course, it was Chandler's work and I had told him he could leave it there
until anytime he wanted to take it. But that manner of conduct seems to me
presumptuous, and above all I cannot abide that. And thoughtless, which
makes it all a little sad.

Certainly Hartley Cross had a better life than most men; but I do now
wish that I had managed to see him again, or reply to his and his wife's kind-
nesses. (But even here I must add that a memorial fund sounds a bit thick to
me; and even so far as the subject of the preceeding paragraph.) I have been
thinking recently about Robert L Stevenson. You know, I used to think he
was a healthy cultivated and rather satisfied Englishman; and only recently
have learned or rather realised, what a wanderer. And in bad health; but still
a tramp, *vagamundo*. Romantic, incorrigibly so. And his lines which I think
ended up on his stone: These be the lines you wrote (grave?) for me: Here he
lies where he longed to be. Home is the sailor, home from sea, And the hunter
home from the hill. I like him. (No memorial fund.)

Now I gather you are enjoying the perennial wonder of spring. And I immediately feel that I should be there, helping you to 'set the house in order'
and doing all of the things that a man should do and I seem to have avoided
since I was six. (Good age.) All of it is thoroughly strange. First, let me say, I
have found in this country one of the best societies I hope ever to encounter.
And the climate, the countryside itself. The people is of course Catholic,
thoroughly. And the way to see it now is not as Granga does with shudders
of ignorant horror but you see it here as the foundation of a traditional society. The family is very important, and so unlike our country eminently successful. This is the sort of thing that has happened to most young Americans.
That they are profoundly impressed by a self-sufficient society. It is the reason
that the people have been so wonderfully hospitable to me: because they could
afford it. Then comes the problem that foolish Chandler thought to solve in
going to Italy, whose culture he admired from a distance for just these reasons.
But he went in a time of troubles, and in addition immediately after the
American (soldiery) had got done (or more miserably has not yet finished)
setting a thoroughly bad example of Americans. And so (I gather from letters
to others) Chandler who had intended to become integrated in that society
instead met in Rome some Bulgarians and some French and some something-
elses and saw Lucky Luciano in a bar and—with the inestimable help of the
language barrier—was defeated. It is always so.

And now you may understand the great temptation that has come to me. I have told you about the people here, who though thoroughly Westernized still have a culture competent enough to resist the corrupting influence of the American dollar, as, necessarily with the Canal, has happened in Panama. At any rate, since I came up here in the spirit I did, and offered my services to them in their first revolution (because you must understand that this has not been just another banana-republic war, not a Pancho Villa affair either; and the history of CostaRica is remarkably different from Mexico, Guatamala, Nicaragua &c); that they appreciate that, and there is the sudden strange opportunity of entering this society. I mean, I have been offered jobs, on the strength of my earlier offer of my services to them—because Mother (though I thought it unnecessary to shout about it to you then I did come up with a note from a friend in Panama to one here who was on the staff of the opposition army, and was with that army at Cartago, a town you may have read about.)—And so you see the temptation. Even (de facto) the most really loveliest young lady, with whom I have exchanged about 8 words of miserable Spanish. Imagine a girl called Maria Eugenia (Mar′ya-Úhenia) Domien. Well.

And you see that it will not do. In a way it is too good. And I do not say that I would refuse it all because of a fear of suddenly being unhappy, feeling that I had had lost, later. No; on the other hand, in fact, it is too good. Because I am an American, and my whole problem lies in American society; that is, in thinking it out, in understanding where that country has gone all wrong, and perhaps eventually being able to contribute something on the way to right it. About 90% of USA needs to be rescued from vulgarity, and it is the responsibility of them—us—all. Doubtless the most critical time in history. It would not do to stay in this good land.

And then of course this wandering, this 'sense of drift' Mr. Toynbee calls it. And so within the next few days I plan to go to Puntarenas, a hot port town on the Pacific coast, and live there briefly and try to work; and soon enough go broke, expecting in all confidence and obstinate optimism to be able to pick up a boat when that happens and set out for native shore. Mr Toynbee tells me things that I have only suspected, have been trying desperately to articulate for myself. In this time of social disintegration there is the solution of abandon and that of self-control; of drifting, truancy, and of reason and contribution. All of this time I am between the two: drifting and trying to contribute; living a truant life and coldly insisting that the only thing that will save us from the crushing results of our current vulgarity and abandon is the rational realisation of freedom and its very essence as self-control. And so I still am unsure, for myself, how long the drift will continue. Only I feel that it must end for others, that USA must quit its truancy—all of this with the shadow of a war ahead so horrible and so final. But even that war, like death, is only a possibility and not a fact.

Well you see, I am trying to think. The whole thing has been going on, this disintegration, for over 200 years, when the Christian Church started to lose. Believe me, it is strange to find myself anticipated by a writer of the 18th century. I had written something like this to myself: That today everyone takes it for granted that honesty (Being a Christian) is entirely possible, requires no ingenuity or effort; in other words, is too despicably easy to permit others to see one doing. And far more creditable to show one's self as clever, as smart, as worldly, and (if you investigate the meaning of the word) sophisticated. And here is what Bishop Butler wrote in 1736: "It is come, I know not how, to be taken for granted by many persons, that Christianity is not so much as a subject of inquiry, but that it is now at length discovered to be fictitious. And they treat it accordingly as if in the present age this were an agreed point among all people of discernment, and nothing remained but to set it up as a principal subject of mirth and ridicule, as it were by way of reprisals for its having so long interrupted the pleasures of the world." And at first I am angry that the things I have had as revelation are very old and well-thought out—and by someone with such style as Bishop Butler too—and am now gradually beginning to realise that it will be better to work with the side which needs support now. That I will afford to share—for imagine the presumption of one who would try to covet a truth!

As for health, I believe that this morning's excavation will help a lot, clear up the blood. And my intestines have apparently decided that insurrection is to no avail, and have settled down again to the right and reasonable acquittal of their duties. Thank you for the offer of the raincoat. I miss it simply because I am so accustomed to have one as a sort of portmanteau. But heaven knows if it will ever rain. It is now almost 5 months since I have seen rain, and that is rather a nerve-wracking business. If it does not rain soon I shall start for NY if only for that familiar and comforting experience.

I have the sudden premonition that yr. next letter will contain questions (or reprimands) concerning what I sit down to at table these days. And therefore hasten to dispatch this random menu. Otherwise life is better daily, though I must confess that this is no city to work in, my kind of work; too endlessly-pleasantly distracting, if only to walk endlessly through, and many small places for prolonged drinking of coffee. Now am trying to get back to work, also to learn Spanish (still) with splendidly incomprehensible books I buy. Aside from that there is nothing new, thank God. I shall write you soon.

Love,
W.

plucking out offending members: advice offered in Matt. 5:29.

AE Housman: British poet (1859–1936); a favorite of his, WG quotes from poem #45 of *A Shropshire Lad*.

how to be a Chinaman like Lin Yutang: WG is quoting from Cyril Connolly's "Blueprint for a Silver Age" in the same issue of *Harper's* that contained Porter's essay on Stein (December 1947, 537–44). The visiting British essayist noted that New Yorkers suffered from anxiety, and hence "books on how to be happy, how to attain peace of mind, how to win friends and influence people, how to breathe, how to achieve a cheap sentimental humanism at other people's expense, how to become a Chinaman like Lin Yutang and make a lot of money, how to be a B'hai or breed chickens (*The Ego and I*) all sell in millions" (541). WG liked this observation so much he used it again in both *J R* (477) and in "The Rush for Second Place" (*RSP* 41). Lin Yutang (1895–1976) was a Chinese philologist, inventor, and writer; Connolly probably had in mind his best-selling *Importance of Living* (1937).

Constance Smith: a Greenwich Village girlfriend—Sheri Martinelli told me WG was "madly in love" with her—who later became head of acquisitions at the Pius XII Memorial Library at Saint Louis University, where she met WG again when he visited St. Louis in 1979.

Hartley Cross: (1894–1948), a family friend (mentioned in a 1942 letter) who worked for the Consumers Union.

Robert L Stevenson: the British writer (1850–94) is cited several times in *R*; he traveled widely for his health and settled on the island of Samoa near the end of his life.

as Granga does with shudders of ignorant horror: this is how *R*'s Aunt May regards Catholicism, suggesting WG's great-aunt was partly a model for her.

Chandler [...] going to Italy: Brossard was there in 1947–48, and later wrote about it: "The Way It Was In Italy," *American Mercury*, April 1951.

Lucky Luciano: Sicilian-born American gangster (1897-1962), deported to Italy in 1946.

Pancho Villa: Mexican revolutionary general (1878-1923).

'sense of drift': Toynbee writes: "The sense of drift, which is the passive way of feeling the loss of the *élan* of growth, is one of the most painful of the tribulations that afflict the souls of men and women who are called upon to live their lives in an age of social disintegration" (444).

abandon [...] self-control [...] truancy: all terms from Toynbee: see *A Study of History*, 440–42.

meaning of the word) sophisticated: that is, practicing sophistry: cleverly deceptive reasoning and actions.

Bishop Butler [...] pleasures of the world": quoted by Toynbee (486) from Joseph Butler's *Analogy of Religion*.

menu: an Hotel Panamerican menu offering a lunch consisting of spam on tostadas ("really a large salad," WG indicates), pea soup Dutch style, porterhouse steak with creamed cauliflower and French fries, fruit ("pineapple very fresh"), and coffee.

To Edith Gaddis

Puerto Limón, Costa Rica
[11 May 1948]

dear Mother.

I have your note here, forwarded from San Jose, as any others will be if you have written more, but I advise to not write more after now because apparently it takes letters a good time to get down here and I am vaguely on my way out. And may not write again, recently don't feel much like writing letters, unless something importunate occurs, then I shall.

What is to be said about the Music sch. fire? Somehow the whole affair has been wrapped in disaster since I was 5, all of it has always seemed to me hopelessly sad and waiting for just such. As for the loss of valuable MSS, well that is what happens when you own *things*; and if you will own I suppose that insurance is a part of responsible ownership, &c &c. The prospect of the place reopening is abyssmal.

Here in Puerto Limón. With a room in a fairly ramshackle building and the sea under the window endlessly smashing against the seawall that surrounds the town. Very hot, most of the people black, very quiet. I like it quite well, for this raggle-taggle sort of living. I came down here hoping to get a boat back to the states. Tried UnitedFruit, no; of course, these American monopolies I have a cruel feeling about, the devil with them. (But so funny to see, all of the White unitedfruit colony lives behind a barbed-wire fence next the sea. Ech.) Anyhow through the agency of Costa Rican friends I meet one person and then another and think it may well be possible to get work-for-passage on one of their small banana boats; there are some here who have little boats that struggle upto Tampa and Miami loaded with bananas, and since they are all Figueristas (with the oppositionist govt) and since I did what little I could I believe that I shall be able to manage something. Cannot tell how long it will be, probably a week or more, until I can start from Florida. If that business doesn't work out I may have to take a small boat back to Panama and try to get out from there, we shall see. But if I can make Tampa, I shall either call or wire you (not for $) and fly from there to NY, hoping that you may find it possible to meet me at LaGuardia—with a block-long limousine with chauffer to carry my luggage of course. Unless I find another tampa–NY way, like a car, then will call you when I make NY. There. Like I say, it may be a week (the little boats take 4 or 5 days) or two or three (or four), so don't be on tenterhooks (whatever they are).

Meanwhile I look at books, at Mr Toynbee's in particular, try to think & make notes for heaven-knows-what; and subconsciously prepare for recieving NY back into my—well, what? Heart? Perhaps. Afraid I am a rather tatterdemalion affair, somehow my clothes seem all to have worn out at once. If I look woeful when you see me do not be alarmed, it is not because I am woeful (though I am) but getting a little delapidated, and will probably need a haircut.

Love,

Music sch. fire: perhaps a reference to his uncle Ernest's music school in Brooklyn.

Puerto Limón: large city on the Caribbean Ocean, 75 miles east of San José, and probably the model for the Central American town where Otto stays (*R* 154–68).

To Katherine Anne Porter

Pto Limón, CR
May 1948

My dear Miss Porter.

Now I presume to write you again; and I say presume because I cannot tell but that after my last letter you may have wearily shaken your head and said, —There must be some way to put an end to this. But it is a rather unfair game I have been playing with people recently, to write a letter and then finish it saying, —I am sorry but can give no address . . . Well; and if the letters asks questions they have no way of answering, and know I am somewhere making the answers—the wrong ones, but better ones—myself. Or they cannot return argument about some wrong assumption; or they cannot say, — Please stop bothering yourself writing these things to me. No: the postman always rings twice and there is the letter, he must read it and be futilely provoked, or bored without recourse. Or is it instead presumption to assume that the people want to answer the letter? (That business of 'owing someone a letter' is horrible.)

Anyhow there are some things I have tried to think about recently, or been provoked over, and wanted to communicate them to you. I am in an Atlantic port waiting for some kind of boat that I can work back to the states on, and fortunately I suppose have not much to read and so I read what I have read and also get a little work done. It has been raining for four days, it rains outside and in one corner of my room, but the bed is in the other corner; but they cannot load bananas and so the days go. It is a place like that lazy man WS Maugham wrote about all the time, where the days dissolve into each other and one is suddenly surprised that it is Tuesday, or Sunday, though there is no reason to be surprised, it does not matter. I have thought about Maugham of course right from the word 'rain', and Sadie Thompson was a good story. But do you know what I mean about lazy? Like in that *Razor Edge* book (a story he has told so many times) we finish with the revelation that the hero was 'good'. Well good, what good. All I could make out was that he was a rootless American, a life I know well enough. But good? Because he was disinterested; that is fine, but I don't remember his doing any acts of disinterested goodness; he wanted to marry the girl who had turned up a whore—that saintly complex, but it has been done so many times and better explained as such than simply shown as a picture of goodness. And what girl who has gone that far wants to be 'saved' by being married, none that I have known, they usually have their futility pretty well in hand. Certainly the picture of the whore and salvation is one of the most tempting, excitingly symbolic to play with (and Maugham did it well that once, when Sadie Thompson said —Men, they're all alike. Pigs, all of them.) But it has been done with such maudlin stature by the Russians, I don't think anyone could out-do Sonia and Raskolnikov.

But here is something, in this picture of goodness as an attribute of 'simplicity'. And this falls in with what you said in your letter, the business of —Yes, but he was *smart*, &c. And also with the ruction I was (am) in over being 'anticipated'. I had made a note, perhaps with your words subconsciously in mind, that today the general attitude is that anyone can be Christian, it is ridiculously easy and rather foolish—I think of that word 'sucker' which is such a worldly condemnation—and that the only way to gain respect is to be worldly, sophisticated (in acts not just words or cigarette-smoking) 'smart'. Well, after that revelation I came on this, written by a Bishop Butler in 1736 (quoted in Toynbee's (abridged) *Study of History*):

It is come, I know not how, to be taken for granted by many persons that Christianity is not so much as a subject of inquiry, but that it is now at length discovered to be fictitious. And accordingly they treat it as if in the present age this were an agreed point among all people of discernment, and nothing remained but to set it up as a principal subject of mirth and ridicule, as it were by way of reprisals for its having so long interrupted the pleasures of the world.

Well; to not only be anticipated by 200 years, but by one with such style as Bishop Butler! It was very disconcerting. And one goes back to the attempts that have been made to show the Christian goodness personified in an 'idiot', Dostoevski's greatest attempt, and the foolish father of the young man in Tolstoy's *Power of Darkness*. Still there seems to be a great rift between them and Bunyan's Pilgrim. Now there is a man called Silone, I think you must have read his *Bread & Wine* and *And He Hid Himself*, who fascinates me, because I do not make out where he stands with himself, as regards the problem of Communism and Christian practice. Did he disown the former in *Bread & Wine*? I believed so, and certainly even in the Communist preaching he did do there he contradicted himself. And where that may have been vague, there was nothing vague about the finish of one character as a (the) Crucifixion. And one remembers Nathaniel West throwing away the political hope of

Communism (in *A Cool Million*) and embracing the Crucifixion (—Each of us is Christ, and each of us is crucified. *Miss Lonelihearts* (?))

For reading, I must say again all of my allegiance to this work of Toynbee; if is it not the most triumphant work of reason in our time. I have finally finished the abridgement, which I think is magnificent, and am wondering if I have the nerve to start the original work, or rather to start and finish it. Such perception is to my confused accumulation of mind fantastic; for instance, that he can find Spengler as quickly and cleverly (but never cleverness for its own sake) as this: ["]Spengler, whose method is to set up a metaphor and then proceed to argue from it as if it were a law based on observed phenomena ... ["] And since I feel the verge of fatal enthusiasm, I do not want to say more of this work, it has been so busy teaching me, articulating so many things that I have been suspecting and almost thought.

Your saying that you are investigating writing among young people and students brings a question to my mind: I am exceedingly curious about how much of the influence of the *NewYorker* you are finding. You know, there are a lot of people in NewYork who have a war with that magasine finally that they simply live on the bitterness their experiences with it has engendered. They are older ones, but I know so many younger who have lived under its shadow for years; and I speak for myself, because from my college work on it was there. And since I do not want to waste any of my energy in bitterness, what greater waste, I have drawn a line through it. But I do think about it, remember how much time I spent assaulting it. After college I worked there for something over a year, and when I quit it was with the sole idea of selling them something written. Starting with a tragedy of youth, an exhaustive history of the Player Piano, which I still have and treasure as I am told mothers do their strangely-shaped children which the world derides. But the influence on those trying to write fiction. One thing: certainly the *NewYorker* does not ask it of anyone; simply there it is and if anyone wants to waste his life trying to sell them something he may, that is not their concern. Is it because there are so few places that publish good fiction and pay well? I wonder that I have never seen anything of yours in that magasine, I wonder if it is simply by chance or if you have dark reasons too. The point is that their influence seems so horribly disproportionate; have you found it so?

For magasines, I see your name on the prospectus of something called the *Hudson Review*. I gather that the magasine itself is out by now, someone sent me this prospectus months ago, and I sent them a story which was returned with a very kind letter, I don't care it was a good story, it will be re-written. But is the magasine as good as it sounds it could be? "...will not open its pages to those whose only merits lie in their anguish, their fervour, and their experimentation," how wonderful to read that. (And I find the comments highly entertaining: yours is fine, Mr Blackmur's 'It looks like the place where one can put one's work' makes me burst out in laughter: who is this 'one'? I love that.) It sounds like a very positive step for our side.

The revolution here has been over for some time. I got up here in time to get out to Cartago, and be there fighting in the fighting. There is too much to say to chatter here. But of the disinterestedness of all of the people, the almost entire absence of grasping, of self-promotion. It was a real people's revolution; and now I have a great admiration for the CostaRicans; you cannot imagine the kindness they have showed me. But still the self-sufficience: that they were pleased that I should come and volunteer with them, but you know still they did not need me, and in the kindest most genuine ways they showed this. Because CostaRica is still traditional—and largely I suppose due to the hold of the Church—and the family is still family, and it is splendid and interesting to see the hospitality that such a traditional society can afford, as to one rootless, which our (eastern) society cannot because it is rootless itself. And it brings more and more of questions: is it presumptuous to fight in other people's revolutions? &c &c.

And so I wait for a boat; it is a very peaceful feeling. I cannot work on US boats because I am not Union, God knows how one gets into the Union, it is very strong; and so hope to get a CostaRican, they run small banana boats up to Tampa and I think it can be managed. Meanwhile the girl who has been cleaning my floor with half a cocoanut has finished telling me a long story, it was highly adventuresome but I am not sure what about since it was in Spanish, I think it was about a flood, it started out with the news that once recently it rained here day and night for a month; she is very cheering. And from Mr Eliot, —It won't be minutes but hours, it won't be hours but ... days? years? I don't remember.

Sincerely, my best regards to you,
William Gaddis

---

the postman always rings twice: title of a famous crime novel by James M. Cain (1934) and a movie (1946), back when mailmen rang the doorbell when delivering mail.

Maugham [...] Sadie Thompson: see 9 March 1947.

Razor Edge: Maugham's philosophical novel *The Razor's Edge* (1944) concerns a young World War I aviator who rejects Western values and travels to India to search for new ones. It's mentioned in passing in *R* (638).

Sonia and Raskolnikov: in Dostoyevsky's *Crime and Punishment*.

'idiot', Dostoevski's greatest attempt: *The Idiot* (1868–69) is quoted on pp. 937–38 of *R*.

Tolstoy's *Power of Darkness*: an 1886 play, quoted on p. 640 of *R*.

Bunyan's Pilgrim: the protagonist of the English preacher's *Pilgrim's Progress* (1678).

Silone: Ignazio Silone (1900–78); *Bread and Wine* (1937) is his best-known novel; *And He Hid Himself* (1945) is a play about a leftist agitator who rediscovers his religious belief and dies as a Christ figure. It's mentioned on pp. 590–91 of *R*.

West [...] *Miss Lonelyhearts*: Nathanael West (1903–40); *A Cool Million* (1934) is a parody of the Horatio Alger paradigm, and *Miss Lonelyhearts* (1933) is about a desperate advice columnist. Although the quotation sounds like something from the Christ-ridden novella, it doesn't appear there. Perhaps WG was thinking of Sherwood Anderson's *Winesburg, Ohio*: "everyone in the world is Christ and they are all crucified" (end of "The Philosopher").

Spengler: Oswald Spengler (1880–1936), whose *Decline of the West* (1918–22) argues that every culture grows, peaks, then declines like a living organism, and that the West had reached the point of decline. WG quotes from p. 248 of Toynbee's book.

history of the Player Piano: see headnote to 29 May 1950.

Blackmur: R. P. Blackmur (1904–65), American critic and poet.

It won't be minutes: "For it won't be minutes but hours / For it won't be hours but years"—from the "Fragment of an Agon" portion of *Sweeney Agonistes*.

To Edith Gaddis

Puerto Limón, Costa Rica
[late May 1948—same day as previous letter]

dear Mother.

[...] In about 8days another boat is due here, a boat to take a load of wood for plywood to Charleston SC, I have met the plywood man here who is cheerfully drunk most of the time, consequently amiable and says I can probably get on his wood boat if I can't get a banana boat, the sea outside is furious and the prospect of wandering 1500miles out on it is rather disconcerting.

This morning I blew 30¢ at a peluqueria, that is a barber shop, I think it was well-spent. I eat regularly though the fare here recalls a poem I never learned which starts —Nothing to do but work, nothing to eat but food; Nothing to wear but clothes to keep from going nude. [...]

You may gather this is not an intellectual centre, and so there is no problem about what book to read because there just aren't any unless you have some you are carting around yourself, I am still carting around Mr Toynbee, and perhaps this happens for good reason because when I want to read I read Mr Toynbee again and it is a worthy task. Or if I do not read then I have bundles of papers which I have maligned all over with my own words, and they must be gone over and are being gone over; best though I have got to working again, I mean writing, it is not good yet but it is writing again and that is the only good feeling that makes any position tenable.

And that I recovered my raincoat, my friend-of-the-revolution Captain

Madero recovered it in Cartago and since he is now running things at the airport at SanJose put the raincoat on a plane coming here and sure enough here it is, dirty and faithful.

Rumour has it that we are pretty deep in May, like I say the days run all together and you lose them to eachother, if I write again it will probably be a letter not much better than this one, I mean no newer than this one, or to tell you that I am sure that what I have are fleas, or that [if] they are not fleas they may be something a-kin (A little more of kin, and less than kind—*Hamlet*. Heavens, I wish I had that here). If you write simply to Poste Restante, Limón C R it will reach me and probably be returned to you if I have gone if you put a return on it; or if pressing horror arrives cable via ALLAMERICA, the man who runs that office is a friend; otherwise I shall see you soon, here like Goethe's Manto (*Faust* II ii) —I wait, time circles me.

Love,
W.

Nothing to do but work: the opening stanza of "The Pessimist" by American humorist Ben King (1857–94), included in some anthologies of nonsense verse.
Captain Madero: described as a "young captain" in WG's "In the Zone" who later, "flying one of the army's new planes, was killed when he hit a mountain" (*RSP* 37).
A little more of kin: *Hamlet* 1.2.65.
Goethe's Manto: daughter of the healing god Asclepius, Manto attempts to heal Faust's frenzy by recommending stillness. WG quotes Anna Swanwick's translation (1882), and used the quotation in *R* (61).

To Edith Gaddis

[*In "In the Zone," WG indicates he "finally came home on a Honduran banana boat" (RSP 37), looking very sickly, his friend Vincent Livelli told me. During the summer of 1948 WG wrote an unpublished account of the Costa Rican war entitled "Cartago: Sobró con Quien," and in September applied to Harvard for readmission. Turned down, he decided to go abroad again, this time to Spain. The letter below is written on stationery imprinted M/S Sobieski—the Polish passenger ship on which WG sailed—next to which he wrote "very much like* Outward Bound," *a 1930 movie about a strange ocean liner.*]

Gibraltar
16 December 1948

dear Mother.

Well, here is the whole thing starting again—this time on a boat populated by Italians—often as though all of Mulberry street had set out for home, dolce

WG sailing for Spain, 6 December 1948.

Napoli. And it resolves itself into little beyond a very long 9 days of eating, & sleeping, staring at the Atlantic ocean, talking little; being somewhat melancholic—New York was such a magnificence when we finally sailed and left it there in the sun. Keep it for me.

And preparing for Spain. Spain. I must say, no one could come up to Baedeker for everything accounted for—I thank Mr. Hall again for it, as I am sure I shall do many times before I am done.

I don't know whether, before leaving, I gave you any idea of my plans—except that they were few. But now plan to go from Gibraltar straight to Madrid (as "straight" as the broken-down Spanish railways will permit)—and look forward to that trip with excitement of course but also with some trepidation, what with 10 pounds of sugar on one shoulder, 10 of coffee on the other, cumbrous luggage in hand and the language mutilated in mouth. Eh bien— it shall be managed, and I shall write you again from Madrid, with an address of some permanence, since despite its climate being less agreeable than Sevilla, it will be a better place to start my acquaintance with *Spain*.

The leave-taking was good—it was kind of those various people to come and attend at the rail for so long. Sorry of course that you could not see it sail—but when you have this letter will know for certain that it did, and with much palpitation managed Gibraltar at least, and that I am in the country that lies "like a dead mackerel stinking and glittering in the moonlight"—and that, because of ill-management, you may not have my letters immediately.

And just now I call to mind that the whole "holiday season" is nigh, and that very possibly I shall not reach you again before it is passed. And so, all of the customary greetings to those customarily greeted—and best of course to you, trusting that things and people will arrange themselves for you happily—not including the ritual hour of orisons spent over the sink at 1837 East 15th street.

My sense of humour is somewhat in suspension—also other senses, and so my apologies for the dullness of this note. I find the Atlantic ocean very big, life very long, and thoughts far away and sentimental, as not to bear repeating. But Madrid and I will purge one another, and soon enough I shall be able to write to your pleasure and edification.

Meanwhile, best wishes, love, gratitude to you.

W.

Mulberry street: runs through Little Italy in lower Manhattan.

dolce Napoli: "sweet Naples."

Baedeker: WG took with him Karl Baedeker's *Spain and Portugal: Handbook for Travellers*, 4th ed. (Leipzig: Karl Baedeker, 1913), which is quoted a few times in *R*.

Mr. Hall: Charles Hall.

"like a dead mackeral [...] in the moonlight": Virginian congressman John Randolph (1773–1833) famously described Secretary of State Henry Clay as "so brilliant yet so corrupt, which like a rotten mackerel by moonlight, shined and stunk" (variously reported).

1837 East 15th street: *sic*: Mrs. Gaddis lived at 130 E. 15th Street.

life very long: a phrase from part 5 of Eliot's "The Hollow Men" (1925) that WG often quotes (as in next letter).

To Edith Gaddis

[℅ United States Embassy
Miguel Angel, 8
Madrid, Spain]
[21 December 1948]

Querida Mamacita (which means Dear Mother:) Aqui es una carta (a letter

And what to say? (CRY cry what shall I cry, says Mr Eliot . . .) except that apparently I am really in MADRID; and that I have had the very good fortune to meet a fellow whom I had met in NewYork about two years ago . . . and he very kind, pleasant; I cannot say how good to come on such a one, after a rather distasteful mess at Gibraltar with British Customs (something about money, the more fool I) and a 26hr train-ride from Algeciras to Madrid, and the consequent exhaustion.

Let me say: you know what is odd (odd to me, though Emerson makes a great point of this, and I suppose that I shall understand it one day) is this notion of cities' similarity, the perpetual RITZ, or Greenwich Village, any-where ones goes. That is the foolery, of writing you from SPAIN with Span-ish stamps & Legend incumbent: when all the capitals are the same, the cities . . . and that ultimately there is no Romanticism about it anywhere. That travel as one will: to see the cork trees of southern Spain, the groves of olive trees: you know, the olive trees look quite exactly as our little willow (not weeping); or Gibraltar, fabulous creature that I knew (from the Prudential Life Insurance ads) was simply a great pile of shale, and, while not a "disap-pointment", not the Thrill that the American demands when he has paid a passage to Africa? to Europe? to Asia? (Life is very long . . . . . .)

Eh bien. (that's French) —enough of these wanderings into things which engage my attention . . . (indeed, my whole being, whenever I can abstract that ephemeral disaster) and down to the facts that one usually "writes home" about . . . :

Here is an address, since I have not as yet got anything which might be considered 'permanent'—and instead have met (God forbid, but He did not)

met a young lady (Life is very long) from the American consulate: [... (see above)] And this address only if you have a letter; because for the moment I am well-enough "fixed" (to tell the truth, compleatly mixed-up with this wad of innominate bills in my pockets, but I am so tired of trying to think about MONEY $$$ £££ Pesetas &&&&&.) that the purpose of all of this note is simply greeting; that I can well imagine that you worry, or wonder, &c. Because I have been here for 2 or 3 days & not written, even to say I am in Spain (Well now I am in Avon, the more fool I./ When I was at home I was in a better place/ But travellers must be content...)

Anyhow there is neither light nor water in Madrid until 6pm (no rain here for many months) and so this shaving in darkness and attempting to bathe is a mummery; in fact the whole thing is a mummery; and They don't know it but I must find it out or the whole expedition will be wasted (although the two people who Do know it are Sherry & Jacob Bean, & look at them!)...

Really! To be introduced as the AMERican friend, here to study philosophy (here meaning Spanish mysticism of the 16th century) is preposterous. But then (unless you point at the youth who studies thermodynamics (v. J Osbourne) what end study? I don't know; John Woodburn almost knows, but *almost* and in that qualification lies defeat.

No, withall, it is better to have the imposition of aloneness come from the Outside, and so be insisted on the internal sense of disaster, than to brood over it in surroundings which in their cardboard familiarity say, Yes. All of these words to say that I am simply in another City; where there are mostly a bunch of foreigners (Spic) and must and shall learn their language for the ordinary commerce of life; while I can be left alone with my own language which needs a lot of explaining and apology before it can be used Cleanly and with positiveness (even though this is only used to say No)

Eh bien. I am looking for a pension, or, better, a large room where I can be Left Alone.

And when I find it, shall send its address (for the moment having enough clean shirts to call at the AMERICAN Embassy); and plan to stay here for a couple of months (because on the level it offers itself to me Madrid is not Spain but simply a Great City) until I have the language enough to go into the country—to Sevilla, to Granada, Malaga... I don't know; anyhow that for now I am all right: and that should any of the usual American troubles come up this fellow Taylor will tell me the right direction in which to decamp. For Money, I shall write soon enough to make the arrangements about legal & illegal demonstrations, on 'our' part. So don't worry about That.

And for Christmas, don't worry about That as far as I am concerned. I plan to be wandering through the streets of a city, trying to figure out Christmas as opposed to Xmas, and as 'happy' as one may be in the natural state of aloneness. (BUT Mother, don't take my seriousness about myself as seriously as I take it; because you know well enough that any day now you may have a letter shouting with glee about some fool thing or other which makes about as much difference in the Scheme as forebodings . . .)

And so: "A merry Christmas &c &c to all" and otherwise best greetings to Granga, to the Woodburns, to pretty in-New-York Nancy A.—and rest assured, I shall write better soon.

with love,
W.

---

cry what shall I cry: the opening line of "Difficulties of a Statesman" (part 2 of Eliot's unfinished *Coriolan*).

Emerson [...] cities' similarity: possibly derived from a well-known passage in Emerson's "Self-Reliance" (1841): "Travelling is a fool's paradise. Our first journeys discover to us the indifference of places. At home I dream that at Naples, at Rome, I can be intoxicated with beauty, and lose my sadness. I pack my trunk, embrace my friends, embark on the sea, and at last wake up in Naples, and there beside me is the stern fact, the sad self, unrelenting, identical, that I fled from. I seek the Vatican, and the palaces. I affect to be intoxicated with sights and suggestions, but I am not intoxicated. My giant goes with me wherever I go."

(Well now I am in Avon [...]: slightly misquoted (Arden for Avon) from Touchstone's observation in *As You Like It* (2.4.12–14), WG's favorite Shakespeare play.

Sherry: Sheri Martinelli; see headnote to letter of Summer 1953.

John Woodburn: an editor at Little, Brown, best known for snatching up Salinger's *The Cather in the Rye* after Harcourt, Brace turned it down.

Taylor: Bill Taylor, a Harvard alum about five years older than WG.

Nancy A.: mentioned later, otherwise unknown; perhaps the Miss Applewhite WG mentions in a 1949 letter to his mother.

To Edith Gaddis

Madrid
25 December, 48

dear Mother.

I am glad that I have waited this long to write you at any length; because today is the first day I have felt good about the whole thing; in fact more at peace than I have ever been in some time, years perhaps; & without the cloud of Mr TS Eliot's articulation (. . . because I do not hope to turn again &c) hanging over every thought and gesture. And so I believe that I can write you a letter, instead of posting simply another quiet communication of despair: feeling alone again: and here is how it came about:

This morning I got up early (7:30 is wee hours for Madrid) and took a train out to a place some 3miles off called El Escorial. There is situated the royal monastery which Philip II built, in the latter 16th century, and if Mr Hall has seen it he will attest to its magnificence, if only on a scale of geometrical grandeur. Here are some figures from Baedeker, first off, to give you a notion: in the entire building there are said to be 16courts, 267windows, 1200doors, 86staircases, 89fountains; total length of the corridors about 100miles! I got to the town in the earliest morning, cool, and open—that is what did it, the air, and the 1mile uphill walk, then the birds making such wondrous busy morning noise around the towers of that great weight of a building. The land is rocky, off to the east mountains snow-capped and down before the great open ragged plain toward Madrid. Throughout the day, when I was not in the monastery, I did a great deal of walking, and climbing, up behind the town to look down: the purgative effect of climbing. Often it was as I imagine the Tyrol. But the sound of a brook running, of burros braying: one suddenly realises that one's senses have fallen into disuse in the abuses of the city, and suddenly is aware of sounds, of smell—even the delicious freshness of cow manure.

After first coffee I went into the church which is the centre of this gigantic affair, and there attended the Christmas morning mass: oh! such ritual, what a myth they have. And in this setting; imagine, the retablo behind the high altar is 98feet high, and the dome under which I attended 215feet high. And then the endless tour through the building; the burial vault of the Spanish kings under the altar, such marble, and gilt, and work: sarcophagi of black marble; rooms with paintings by El Greco, Titian, Tintoretto, Veronese, Velasquez; a room exhibiting books & manuscripts from the 9th century on, with illuminations in colours & gold in the most fantastic meticulousness;

And so it was. & it was this sudden being outside that was so good, that showed me that I must not spend any more time than necessary in Madrid, which is simply a city. I have now got a room in a pension, and a good-sized room & comfortable, with meals for 40pesetas a day. Meals though: breakfast a small bowl of coffee & a stump of bread; lunch at 2pm: bean soup & then the body of a fish which has been done to a horrible death by fire; supper at 10pm: soup, followed by very strange croquettes, or cutlets, or 'meat'balls, & a piece of fruit. I don't think anyone eats with very great relish in Spain. But am having some difficulty with the cigarette business; American are impossibly expensive (& you cannot send any in) & the Spanish make their own with tobacco bought on ration. So I have about 20 left, and hoard them miserably. Eh bien.

This American fellow, Bill Taylor, has been excellent to me, but has gone to Paris for the holidays; I look forward to seeing him on his return; and otherwise am baited by a compleat idiot to whom kind Juancho recommended me (J. really wrote my introduction to the father, who is an intelligent gentleman but doesn't speak English) and so I see occasionally this fool Luis, who is 29, & somewhere has been misinformed to the extent that he believes he can speak English. Oh it is painful, almost burlesque at times: he goes at it with heroic enthusiasm, and the results might be amusing if there were not, as there usually is, something at stake. But this sort of noodle: we plan (with Herculean effort on both parts) to dine, he to meet me at 10; I wait, miss 'dinner' here, & at 10:40 he calls to say 'I can't go.' And *such* politeness, delight, good intentions. oh dear.

I cannot say much better for my own conquest of the other language; I am tampering with it to some extent successfully in conversation, but it will take much more doing. And so as for plans I have none, in the way of study. I do think that before too long, perhaps about 3weeks, I shall leave Madrid and go down to stay at Sevilla; but I shall let you know, certainly, and the US Embassy address in Madrid will get me eventually. And so: if the tenants come through, will you please send half in a draft payable, if they are to make it thus, to me at the bank of spain; & the rest just cashiers check (which, I must add, must be received by the 16th of January, as that is when my visa runs out). Life here is not at all as cheap as I had hoped, but I do believe it is working out. And how wonderful that it can really be happening. Of course I have the constant feeling of the press it must make on you, and wondering always how you are making out, how you can make out, and as I foolishly repeat, eternally grateful.

What with the holidays—and I must admit to a good dose of sentimental loneliness—I had thought of sending you a cable; but finally it was too late to send it to the Edison & I did not know what your address is now. And so I sent no cable, not even the smallest gift; but again, one day I shall make up for these ingracious silences. This experience now is certainly the biggest of my life, and it will eventually be turned profitably. And so I hope that you are having good holidays, have had a good Christmas today, and that the New Year will be a celebration for you of the sort you wish. I think of nothing more just now; shall write again soon, and my best wishes to 'all those others'.

and love to you,
W.

---

because I do not hope to turn again: the opening line of "Ash Wednesday" (1930).
El Escorial: called San Zwingli in *R*; both Rev. Gwyon (I.1) and Wyatt (III.3) visit it.
Tyrol: the mountainous region between Italy and Austria.

sound of a brook running [...] cow manure: counterfeiter Frank Sinisterra (calling himself Mr. Yák at this point) also visits San Zwingli: "With this spring in his step he was soon up behind the town, where the sound of running water nearby, the braying of burros and the desultory tinkling of bells [...] reached him where he paused to sniff, and then stood still inhaling the pines above him and the delicious freshness of cow manure, like a man rediscovering senses long forgotten under the abuses of cities" (*R* 776).

tenants: WG received the rent on the house in Massapequa ($100 a month), his major source of income until the mid 1950s.

To Edith Gaddis

Madrid
[27 December 1948]

Well well; dear Mother again.

I had put this off until getting up to the Embassy, both to look for mail & to query Our Representative on the usual concerns of an innocent abroad. And so now I have been, queried & been queried, and got your letters. It is a nice feeling, a kind of re-affirmation of one's identity after many days wandering in boats, trains, dark hotel rooms and strange cities, to see a familiar hand, read familiar words and names (in, I add vehemently, a familiar language). And many thanks for Barney's note, a delight as always; but he of course is by now a rather continental person; and writes: —Spain sounds like a splendid thing, and it would be good to see you . . . he just off for a little time in Paris France &c. These fellow creatures of mine who have made Europe into one large mad-house, each capital a room, and they running from room-to-room, screaming & giggling (to use a phrase of Barney's) . . . well it is all beyond me.

By now I feel settled in a way, not for life in Madrid, but I mean mentally; such things as actually getting letters here makes it seem that I am still in the same world and not barefoot in South Africa as I felt earlier (though a rather glacial South Africa to be sure). But with this good-sized room and large window, pleasant girls among the 'help' who applaud my Spanish, and getting used to the food which is not bad, I suppose one might say dull, but food. And having been fortunate in my choice of books & papers brought over with me, some of Eliot I had not read which is The Answer (just this fragment, listen:

"So here I am, in the middle way, having had twenty years—
Twenty years largely wasted, the years of l'entre deux guerres—
Trying to learn to use words, and every attempt
Is a wholly new start, and a different kind of failure
Because one has only learnt to get the better of words

For the thing one no longer has to say, or the way in which
One is no longer disposed to say it. And so each venture
Is a new beginning, a raid on the inarticulate
With shabby equipment always deteriorating
In the general mess of imprecision of feeling,
Undisciplined squads of emotion . . ." &c. But best his speaking of
time, and just in line with Bergson, whom I was reading last summer, and all
of it in line exactly with my attempts at thought and clear picturing of us all
here &c &c . . . you know how this can go on, as it did many evenings before
the fireplace in Massapequa, evenings I look back on with very poignant
fondness; and apologise now for the rantings & ravings I subjected you to
concerning The State of the Union & Mr Tennessee Williams (whose work,
on reconsideration, I find: that he is not to be blamed, pilloried, spat upon
(as was my attitude) because it is bad, because his work is simply a projection
of the times, the degeneration of the Myth & the consequent looking from
every heart for 'a cheap sentimental humanism at someone else's expense'—and
wherebetter found than the theatre, where one does not have to leave the
sticky mess with the feeling of guilt one 'suffers' after personal mummeries.
No; the blame must go to the times which have allowed such work as his to
be found good (because I gather that as far as the author was concerned these
plays are 'sincere', 'his best', &c—but you see sincere on the same cardboard
level as his audience. They are the ones to knock on the head. Eh bien. I am
preparing something here to knock them on the head with.

oh dear. Are such letters as this entertaining or edifying for you? One may
well ask, —did he go to SPAIN simply to have 3000miles of water between
him and the things he polemicizes? We shall get to Spain in a moment.

I also have Dante here (in English, he admitted, cowardly) and find I am
just ready for going for the first time through his magnificence. And am attending to many notes & ideas which have somehow lay dead in the hand
these past months, feeling alive again. As for study; I am I do believe making
some headway into the language; I can hold a passable conversation with the
scullery girls or the Lady blonde (ersatz with a vengeance) who also lives in
this very proper house and seems to want to go dancing . . . no I was talking
about Study wasn't I. Also reading, with great chains of ignorance, Ortega y
Gasset (a contemporary Sp. philosopher, social thinker) and starting a play
by Calderon de la Barca, a 17th century Sp. playwright, in Spanish, with the
harried dictionary in hand. And so, as for plans. I am more fond of Madrid
daily, and shall stay a few weeks more I guess, don't know; but do have the
feeling that, you know, something may happen (the feeling we all have today,
heaven knows what the Something is, it never happens; I think this feeling

of constant suspension laid in the Christian myth of the Last Judgement which heavy heavy hangs over our heads & imaginary souls) . . . anyhow that I want to see Spain more before settling anywhere at anything. And think it may be the perfectly reasonable thing to do to leave most of my luggage with a friend here, buy a 3000kilometre ticket (about 1800miles I believe) and go about, spend a week in Toledo, in Granada, &c., that ticket I think about 20$. As Walker Evans said when I saw him, —Don't go over and sit in one place; move around, look at it all. He is right. I still must get papers straightened out, of which more later. [...]

For the moment I have borrowed a bit from this 'fine fellow' Taylor, now in Paris but should be back here any day. Don't worry over that, it is the sort of exchange that straightens itself out, and he a good fellow (Harvard '40) and a friend, and I very fortunate to have encountered him.

The holidays passed in order, for myself if not for the People, who raised unshirted hell for 7 or 8 days & nights, beating drums and singing in the streets. Heavens. But got through, and now 1949 discovers me 26. oh dear. Life is very long. On NewYrs day, walking through the city, I stopped in at a large church where a great ceremony was going on (I believe that it is the Feast of the Circumcision), a priest passing up and down a baby-doll which for all I could see the pious populace kissed; but all the while music: an organ & voices, a violin, & tambourines! Such splendid, happy music; & quite unlike the doleful Mrs Damon (?) in Berlin's First Congregational.

And so, a Happy New Year, while we are on the subject, to All.

These things I wonder: Did you get a letter from Gibraltar? Has John Snow managed to get blankets, sheets, dirty shirts & Nancy's *Idiot* up to you? (I haven't written him, and am somewhat concerned, he was in such mortal coil when I left).

Needless to say, your letters shocked me. I mean, the business about the picture-taker on the quay; oh dear, such a business, I am embarrassed at the memory of that Queen Elizabeth gesture. But Stella & Bill; she is kind, and that is just like Bill, to be an unbearable presence & then come through with the really spontaneous kind gesture, why with all the fury and sudden-ness that has passed between us, I find the attachment great; because he means so well, and has no idea of how to go about any execution except suddenly, as this, he manages. As for Miss Parke & Mr Waugh. oh dear, or gracious. Of course you know that with all the sudden cringing on my head when I read it, there was the accompanying vain Delight at being called to the attention of the Great, in any fashion. And so now, Evelyn Waugh actually knows that I exist. I had intended to accomplish this in another fashion, xx(sic) the dark day that he picked up my first novel and sat aghast with admiration—still have a hysterical intention on my part (and let me say, I have had recent thoughts on an idea which I think might even shock Him—such an ambition: to shock Evelyn Waugh. Anyhow the whole incident is jolly (I do wonder What she told him about me) and at 3000miles' distance I relish it. She is so kind too, they all are, we all mean well.

Item) I have sent a story (the one I worked from the Costa Rica piece, at Woodburn's last summer, and wrote here during the holidays) to Congdon; hope to heaven he gets it (dealing, as it did, with 'controversial material'); asked him to let me know here if anything favourable, otherwise to send it on to you with a note which you might forward, and just tuck the story away somewhere & forget it.

Item) Among the books I have brought is the incomparable *South Wind*; and in the usual spirit, I should like so to give a copy to Miss Williams, who plans to sail for Italy I think on the 12th or the 20th. Could you get her a nice copy, have it sent to her before departure, such a splendid book for the boring days of ocean-travel. I wrote & told her I would try to get a copy to her. It is Miss Margaret Williams/ 439 East 86th/ NYC28. Holiday Bookstore at 49th & Lex I think had a nice copy. Would it be a good idea to call her, to see if she is still in town by the time this letter reaches you? It is TR6-4739. I should appreciate this immensely if it can be managed.

Needless, again, to say, Madrid presents many temptations to the eye of the foreigner hungry to buy Things. And so for my birthday I bought a pair of cufflinks. Of course there is the frantic American notion, of wanting to send half the city back to friends. Though I see few things, to tell the truth, as yet, that are just what anyone wants. The inevitable mantillas, &c. But for the man, oh dear, the Things. This morning I bought a pair of much-needed gloves, about 2$, but beautiful, I have never had a pair to fit like these, and soft fine leather (& such style in the glove shop: a plush cushion on which I put my elbow, while the young lady pulled the gloves down over my hand with much ceremony... not Brooks Bros). It is strange, some things so cheap, and some so outlandishly expensive. Imagine (don't imagine too much; it is not a problem with me:) a pint bottle of brandy costing less than a package of cigarettes. But get this: many of the men in Spain wear capes, fine black affairs with red or green lining, and up about the lower part of the face with the red flaming over the shoulder. Well. You may picture my excitement & temptation at that! And the most recent object, looked at in the shop window with eyes like the urchin outside the pastry-shop, a walking stick, brown sort of bamboo, with a silver ferrule and topped by the carved head of an old disgruntled man. 2nd or 3rd hand certainly, but beautiful, and badly priced. But I guess it will always be there—it would take someone with imagination (sic) to carry it! And the shop is in the Calle del Disengaño, the Street of Disillusion. Isn't that wonderful (& un-American).

And so. I walk much of the time, so that by yesterday my feet were really quite sore. I have been over most of Madrid I believe, the crooked narrow streets & the fine ones, the great & very formal park, a look at the tremendous pile which is the nacional palace, nobody lives there, and the streets, the streets. Quite chilly still, very in fact, so I keep moving, often get lost because the streets turn so. But the walking is the best cathartic, I agree with Mr Bean there. Have taken to wearing my fine Davega tennis-shoes, which call glances from passers-by, but otherwise I look quite like the people, they are not dark, as the popular conception of Spaniards, in the north here.

Well, Nancy. I can imagine the sort of disappointment you mean; and it is strange, because of the picture of her as one who Does Things—and I don't mean Emmet Fox (who he? Another victim of Old Testament morality) because she has that aspect of being Alive, and I know, you must begin to wonder, when things continue to fail to work out for those people. (Perhaps she should settle down and practice "that Taoist art of disintegration which Yen Hui described to Confucius as 'the art of sitting and forgetting'"...) Anyhow my best greetings to her, Something, must come.

As for Christmas, I didn't know it was to be at Janice's; just as glad I didn't know: and your very brief description brings the whole thing into the room. But I must confess to some loneliness here, even for such atmosphere (though I can imagine how I should have felt there, thinking of Spain...) For the Woodburns, I haven't written them, shall in a few days when I have more 'material', have thought of them often, still regretting missing them, and do greatly hope that things are going well for them each & both, I do like them each & both so much, and they have been so kind, as people, to me.

And hope that you are well, & happy, getting more from life than Mr. Fox.

with love,
W.

---

innocent abroad: Mark Twain's *Innocents Abroad* (1869) is a satirical travel book about Europe.

"So here I am [...] squads of emotion": the opening lines of part 5 of "East Coker" (1940), the second of Eliot's *Four Quartets*.

Bergson: Henri Bergson (1859–1941), French philosopher, perhaps best known for his book *Laughter* (*Le Rire*, 1901); in WG's library there is a French edition of that book inscribed "W. Gaddis San Jose, CR 1948," along with Bergson's *Creative Evolution* and *Creative Mind*.

Tennessee Williams: the American dramatist (1911–83) was at the height of his fame following the great success of *A Streetcar Named Desire* and *Summer and Smoke* in 1947.

the Myth: probably a reference to Denis de Rougemont's *Love in the Western World* (1940), one of WG's source-books for *R*. Chapter 2 of book 1 is entitled "The Myth," on the European celebration of *passion*, especially adulterous passion, over married love, despite its connection with the death instinct.

'a cheap sentimental humanism [...]: Connolly's phrase: see letter of 28 April 1948.

Dante: WG alludes to *The Divine Comedy* often in *R*, especially at the end of II.8.

Lady blonde: staying at a pension in Madrid, Wyatt (renamed Stephan at this point) gets involved with a blonde "flashy piece of goods" named Marga (*R* 797).

Ortega y Gasset: in *R* WG occasionally quotes from his *Revolt of the Masses* (1932), a call for the benevolent rule of an intellectual elite to counter the deleterious influence of the masses on art and government.

Calderon de la Barca: one of his best-known plays, *La Vida es Sueño*, is quoted a few times in *R*, in Spanish.

heavy heavy hangs over our heads: "Heavy, heavy hangs over your head, What are you going to do with it?" is a children's game.

Walker Evans: American photographer (1903–75), who WG later said was the physical model for Wyatt in *R*.

Mrs Damon [...] Berlin's First Congregational: in *R*, the organist of the First Congregational Church is named "Miss Ardythe, who had attacked the organ regularly since a defrauding of her maidenhead at the turn of the century" (14).

mortal coil: a phrase from *Hamlet* (3.1.69; "coil" = turmoil).

Stella & Bill: unidentified.

Miss Parke & Mr Waugh: Marilyn Parke (see 23 November 1945) visited the visiting British novelist in NYC in December 1948 and told him of WG's work in progress.

story [...] Costa Rica piece: in the summer of 1947 WG wrote an account of the Costa Rican revolution entitled "Cartago: Sobró con Quien" and a short story entitled "A Father Is Arrested," posthumously published in the *Missouri Review* 27.2 (November 2004): 109–16.

South Wind: a hedonistic novel (1917) by British novelist Norman Douglas (1868–1952), set on the Capri-like island of Nepenthe.

Miss Williams: Margaret Williams (1924–2004). In a 1993 interview with Charles Monaghan, WG's old friend Ormonde de Kay said of her: "Margaret Williams was a really live-wire, wonderful, very pretty American girl, very bright, who is now married to Bob Ginna, who used to be editor-in-chief, I think, of Little, Brown for a while, and is now sort of a freelance. Lives in Jaffrey, New Hampshire. And she does, too. Margaret was his [Gaddis's] great love, at that time anyway" (http://www.williamgaddis.org/reminisce/remdekaymonaghan.shtml). A graduate of Vassar, she worked in journalism and book publishing as well.

Emmet Fox: (1886–1951), Irish-born American spiritual leader and self-help author.

"that Taoist art [...] forgetting'": from p. 79 of *More Trivia* (Harcourt, Brace, 1921), a short book of aphoristic observations by the American-born English essayist Logan Pearsall Smith (1865–1946). Quoted in *R* (925).

Janice's: one of WG's aunts.

To Edith Gaddis

Madrid
[January 1949]

dear Mother.

[...] It is strange; but thank heavens, every day I am more glad to have come here. Still at logger-heads with the language, but can carry on a fair conversation now (though still trouble because I don't know too many words) and struggling through some reading; besides working on the same ideas that have preöccupied me for the last 2years. And walking until now I have stopped for a while since the feet are temporarily collapsed. More trips to the Museo del Prado, where the paintings never cease to be exciting—my new inspiration, tutelary genius &c being Heironymus Bosch (I think orig. Flemish) whom you may see at the Met. too (they have 2 of his paintings) if you want some idea of the strange lands my mind is wandering now. I have bought a fine book on him, splendid reproductions & not too difficult Spanish.

Your 2 letters with enclosures recieved; & herewith I return in kind—the photo is Escorial where I passed Christmas day; the other a concert last Sunday morning, they have them here from 11:30 to 1:30 which is splendid (camara means chamber), the Bach & Haydn wonderful (and your comment anent the Schönberg arrangement of *Bach Chorale Preludes* NOT appreciated here, really what is more magnificent music? Eh bien. But the case of Antheil is an interesting one, he was very brilliant in youth, great friend of Ezra Pound, wrote a thing (*Ballet Mechanique*) scored for a dozen or so pianos & aeroplane propellors, very exciting; but then seems to have let down, not fulfilled his great promise (except perhaps to avant-guard & intelligent musicians who 'understand' him, but not (including myself) for the multitude.) For the other enclosures, safely got & thanks; next time, will you please send two cashier-checks. Just now I am involved in matters with the Spanish Police, getting or trying to get a two-year resident visa (does that sound alarming) and with my linguistic equipment you may imagine there are some highly entertaining (to a disinterested observer) frustrations. We usually end up shaking hands and saying it is cold in Madrid, which everybody understands.

Of course there is always more to say, to write; a few nights ago a juerga (pron. wher´-ga) which is half or a dozen people sitting all night in a small room while one plays guitar, one sings flamenco (the most beautiful wailing songs, of sadness & violence, gypsys, one ending sangre negra en mi corazon: black blood in my heart. Well, Spain. It is all splendid, but better promises ever to be more so. (& I must add, I bought that walking-stick.) And love to you,

W.

Heironymus Bosch: Dutch painter (1450?–1516). WG was particularly taken by his tabletop painting *The Seven Deadly Sins*, which plays a major role in *R*.

Schönberg: the Austrian-born composer Arnold Schoenberg (1874–1951) published these orchestral arrangements in 1922.

Antheil: American composer George Antheil (1900–59). His *Ballet Mécanique* dates from 1924, and makes prominent use of the player-piano.

juerga: Stephan (Wyatt) presides at a *juerga* on p. 802 of *R*.

sangre negra [...] my heart: Wyatt hears a flamenco singer utter this line on p. 110 of *R*.

To Edith Gaddis

Madrid

24 january 49

dear Mother.

This being not a letter but the usual perennial request for things. Some of which may sound rather odd.

I First, books. If you could get these, & send them air-express, that is apparently the only satisfactory way. & marked GIFT very plainly.

1. *The White Goddess*, by Robert Graves.

2. [*Crossed out:*] *The Golden Bough*, by — Frazer (Brentano had this in a good reprint for under 3$; if that is available; certainly don't break your neck to get it, & if that reprint isn't at hand it will be hard. [*Handwritten:* No—see below:] The Frazer book is too big. But could you do this: borrow your friend's copy; turn to page *569*—and from there copy what it says about a tribe that rids itself of evil spirits by driving them into a monkey, which is then put to death.

3. (Here is a horrible admission:) *Hugo's Simplified Spanish*.

You understand, these are just books I very much want but will live without; *only* if you can do it quietly & conveniently.

II Could you find this information (I think by calling the Mus of Natural History, they are very good about such:) On the Barbary ape (formerly native of Gibraltar)—its approximate size (male); colouring; how it survives captivity; usual longevity; diet in captivity; is it tail-less?; fierce? extinct (if so when); & any distinctive peculiarities. & also what sounds it makes (alone, in captivity). Thank you very much. Good luck. &c.

And then, when may expect, being a remittance-man, the remittance? I count hopefully on the 10th, as last mo. Money is a problem. Life is very long.

A good letter from Barney, who has recently had clothing & typewriter

stolen; good letter from Bernie, who is working with displaced persons, quite
low about the whole picture; good letter from Juancho, who tells me to get
out of Madrid; good letter from Jake.

Insane letter from Miss Williams. Did you lunch? Isn't she attractive. Nice.
Rather dissociated, as it were. Her trip to Paris sounds terrifying; perhaps she
will meet a frog on the boat & marry? oh dear.

I shall write.

Love,

W.

The White Goddess: a wide-ranging study of mythology, tree symbolism, and Celtic
poetry (1948), a major source-book for *R*. Later in 1949 WG visited the British author (1895–1985), who was living on the island of Majorca off the coast of Spain.

The Golden Bough [...] page *569*: this is the block quotation that appears on page 49 of
R, describing a custom of the Garos of Assam (India). WG had requested Frazer's
book earlier: see 29 April 1947.

Hugo's Simplified Spanish: actually, *Hugo's Spanish Simplified* (Philadelphia: David
McKay, 1925, often reprinted).

Barbary ape: in the first chapter of *R*, Rev. Gwyon brings back a Barbary ape from
Gibraltar, names it Heracles, and later sacrifices it à la the Garos to cure Wyatt's illness. On the back of this letter, Mrs. Gaddis jotted down some notes on the ape.

To Edith Gaddis

Madrid
15 february 49

dear Mother.

Many thanks—for going all the way to Bronx Zoo! Heavens; I thought it
would be easier accomplished than that.

For myself at the moment I am frantically making plans—any plans—to
get out of Madrid; because for the time at any rate I have ceased to learn
anything here. And pursuant to the usual troubles of money am trying my
best to get into a monastery for a while—where I suppose some small board
will be charged but it would enable me to "catch up." The trouble being that
today Spain's monasteries are crowded, and they apparently like to take in
"visitors" for only 4 or 5 days. Nevertheless I am in touch with a Franciscan
order to the south, and what with the efforts of a very kind girl here at the
Instituto de Culturo Hispanico I think—hope—that within a week I shall
be able to go. The trouble of course started when I discovered in this fellow
Bill Taylor such a ready friend, and willing to "advance" me a bit when I arrived here short. And then another "friend" of the opposite order who under
the pretence—well-intentioned though it might have been—of doing me a

favour (this is a young man to whose family Juancho had given me a letter) has retired with some money and is tearfully unable to repay. And now since Bill intends going to Paris I must settle with him. It has just been this business of being caught in Madrid, waiting. Pray heaven the Franciscans can lend respite. I have the remittance this morning, and many thanks. Also news of poor Old Grunter. oh dear, I think of his wistful bravery. How old he is.

The note from M— Williams was sweet. I surely hope to see her, if I can get up to Paris. A letter from Jacob suggests we spend part of his 2month summer vacation on "a remote beach somewhere in Normandy or Brittany," which sounds splendid. As I said, the news of Th. Spenser *and* Jim Osborne, together, "hit me right where I live"—

I trust you have got the note concerning my request that you call Don Congdon (CI6 3437) to ask if he received what I sent him. I am still uncertain about mails. And that is very important to me.

I shall write again soon enough, to let you know how the plan for brief retirement works out, and of any address change. — Oh yes. Your questions: my skin is fine— And though recently I had the grippe am all right now.

Love
Bill

Old Grunter: their dog.

Th. Spenser *and* Jim Osborne: both WG's Harvard professor and this high-school friend died in 1949.

To Edith Gaddis

Toledo
[early March 1949]

dear Mother.

Am quite uncertain as to when I last wrote you. For an undetermined number of days I have been pretty well "settled" in Madrid with what I guess is the flu. But toward the end of last week decided Spanish influenza or no I had had enough of Madrid and so got up and got on a train for here, Toledo. Have been in Toledo for a couple of days and like it as a small town, and the fresh air is good, though still chilly here. However I think this sickness is going away, which has prevented enjoying or doing anything for some time. I shall return to Madrid in a few days or a week or so—whenever my $ runs out—I have about equal to 10$, and a room here for 24¢ a night though eating not so cheap.

I finally did get a letter from Congdon—he had sent it regular post, not by air, of course it took 6 weeks getting here. "—Damn nice writing but the story is awfully slow…" &c. — I don't know. Splendid letter from Miss Williams, who loves Paris and wishes I were there—I must say there are enough moments these days I do too; unless one is really working hard or something this loneliness makes things pall and grow poor after a while. I like her more the more I think about her.

Letter from Helen (enclosing a brief in memoriam sort of note from *Times* book review on Th. Spencer) says she is going to Cuba.

Sorry I confused you with reference to that book on symbollic logic—what I meant was I had been reading a book on symbollic logic and in it found much reference to pattern, to the plan of a thing (a creative work) as a whole; and the whole business of the symbollic frame of reference in which we consciously or unconsciously deal all the time and in which I am trying to deal in writing. It has set me back a bit, as any educational slip must do which helps one reform and articulate values.

Do as you think fit with *Britannica*—I can't get excited about it.

And glad you liked Bemelman's book—he wrote an account of his hotel experiences (*Hotel Splendide*) but this is his only charming book like this, as so often happens. To be able to write *one* charming book.

Toledo is about 40 miles south of Madrid, an ancient city, full of Moorish ruins but not the exotic thing I had expected—though the famous cathedral is well worth the trip; and the town serves me now for taking long walks away, looking at it set up here on a rocky hill, and returning. Like so many things, it is best seen from a distance—the town itself is just another Spanish town.

The owner of my pension in Madrid has been especially kind—imagine him letting me if I needed money to wire him! He knew I had to get out of that city for a while.

As I say, shall be back in Madrid in probably a week, and will write again. Same address.

best wishes and love,
W.

Helen: Helen Parker: see headnote to 18 May 1949.

Britannica: WG used the 14th edition (1929) of the *Encyclopedia Britannica* for a variety of details in *R*.

Bemelman's book: German-born Ludwig Bemelmans (1898-1962) is best known for the Madeline books for children. *Hotel Splendide* appeared in 1941, but I don't know which of Bemelmans' many other books is intended here.

To Edith Gaddis

Monasterio Real de Guadalupe
Estremadura
10 March 49

dear Mother.

I write you from the Franciscan monastery of Guadalupe, in the mountainous country about half way between Madrid and the Portuguese border—a
fantastic thing finished in the 14th century, appearing like a great fortified
castle, with the medieval village grown up outside its walls, and towers like
these: [*drawings*] &c.—indeed, except for a very few electric lights, and one
or 2 trucks and buses, it is hard to say what has changed since 1500. (This
letter will probably not be mailed for another week, when I return to Madrid.)
And though I came as a guest, I expected to find something resembling a cell,
and a harsh life—instead it is for me rather like a large cold country inn, my
room overlooking the central square, where the women come to fill jugs at
the fountain, and horses, oxen, cattle come to drink. The room is large, with
brick floor and the well-blanketed bed set in a curtained alcove. The food
nothing splendid, but very good for Spain.

This evening a long walk into the countryside, after rain—the first rain
Spain has had in some time—among the olive trees, looking back on the village and listening to the peaceful country sounds of evening—someone
chopping kindling, the bells of sheep, goats, cattle, the murmur of voices; and
clouds just lifting along the mountainsides—great tranquility.

Lunch with a Franciscan father, and because of the cold we sat vis-a-vis at
a round table with a brazier underneath, and floor-length cloth, which kept
the warmth in around our feet and legs—a wonderful idea for the studio in
autumn! In fact, as I often do, when far away, I have had many thoughts of
the studio—wanting to *do* things to it. It may all sound foolish, considering
that I spent *all* of last summer there and did *nothing*—but it was a summer
of discontent which I hope and believe this trip, if sufficiently extended, will
dispell. [...]

And so often I am angry with myself at being a remittance man, and wish
I had worked hard since 1945 at getting money together to *do* this all—but
then I would not have done the things I have done, and would probably be
still working in N Y, having saved 300$, and married to some girl as dull as
myself. And so I am really *very* fortunate to be doing the things I am doing—
and do not complain—it is just that I wonder if I could have done it all better,
as I suppose we must always wonder about all things. So do not misunderstand—
I am not complaining for an instant about lack of money, it is only to myself
that I complain, or question. But you know, what I want—first I guess is to

be happy with my work, and if that can be writing so much the better—but then the idea of being happily married, in the studio of a summer is the nicest. (And so your mention of houses being built on all sides is awful, nauseating—) —But never again to spend another summer of inactivity like the last one— though it *was* necessary. A good Franciscan here has told me a lesson—one I knew, but have never *known*—to *do* what you are *doing*. And so go my, and the world's, well-intentioned resolutions. But the studio should be a warm happy place, with wine at dinner, and music—it has been, and will be.

Always wine with meals here in Spain. Though the food is dull and not seasoned—many beans, fish, innominate bits of meat, tortillas—that is an omelette, often made with potatoes, which is filling. But I must carry pepper in my pocket if I want to liven things up. And so come the dreams at night— of food—on L I in the summer. Oh dear—will it ever come out even?

I hope to have my typewriter back before another letter—it is being fixed in Madrid. Then I think, by the time you get this letter, I shall be in Valencia, and on my way south, to see more of Spain before it is all over.

with love,
W.

Franciscan monastery of Guadalupe: the Real Monasterio de Guadalupe. In *R* it is called the Real Monasterio de Nuestra Señora de la Otra Vez, which both Rev. Gwyon and Wyatt visit.

central square [...] jugs at the fountain: many of the details in this letter went into *R*, specifically III.5.

summer of discontent: a play on Shakespeare's "winter of our discontent" (*Richard III*, 1.1.1).

To Edith Gaddis

Valencia, Spain
21 March 49

dear Mother,

As you see, I have the machine back, and marvellously cleaned and refurbished, thank heavens, ready to work if its master can.

At the moment I am in Valencia, a town I like a great deal, though plan to leave it tomorrow for Sevilla, in a nightmare 29hour trainride, not first-class either. The weekend has been fine; the 'Fallas', which is Valencia celebrating the arrival of spring—in every plaza, and there are many, a great statue affair is erected, cardboard sort of stuff on wood frames, representing aspects of current life which the people consider untoward, high price of food, dead state of art & letters (though of course those things they feel heaviest cannot be represented . . .); these things range 30 to 40 feet high, and include figures of people, ships, houses, anything; then the great night they set off explosives and burn the whole thing; insane, and Spanish. And the bullfight on Saturday was a very good showing. Now Bill has gone back to Madrid, and I recommence my peanuts-and-bread-and-oranges-in-the-pocket existence. No, it is I who have managed badly, and quite consistently so; so that it is my own fault if I must now sit on board seats for 29hours instead of stepping onto an aeroplane. And you say, what is right? what is best? let me know . . . Lord, I sometimes think robbing a bank sounds like an entirely reasonable gesture. One does make out; but often enough making out is little different than it might be in a town in Kansas. One may say, why don't you get a job (enough do), but working in Madrid would be working in New York in Chicago in Emporia Zenith—no, as Walker Evans said, to not stay in one place but move around. And thank God now I am out of Madrid, for better or worse but out. I do think of people who could and would manage things quietly and well in my circumstances; which is maddening; the bad thing is to fall behind, and when the remittance appears to have to pay for what is past, and not have it for what is ahead; that is where I have messed things up; how we all cry out for a fresh start, spiritually, financially, sartorially—and the promises made, the resolutions. Well, I shall have about 50$ to go on until the next, and think I can manage, as one does in any circumstance. Dammit, I do want to settle down to respectable and gainly livelihood, but not to see Spain while in Spain is preposterous.

A remarkably wonderful letter from Barney Emmart, in London, to say that in a few days he is leaving northern France and cycling down to the Spanish border, plans to be in Spain for two or three weeks! If things do not get confused I hope to meet him in Sevilla around the beginning of April; and am of course quite excited about it, seeing a friend again. One imagines the things that might go wrong, I picture us both on the same train, having missed each other at one place, and riding hundreds of kilometres but never meeting because he is in 1st class and I in a 3rd class carriage . . . well. [. . .]

A very nice letter from Miss Williams, who is now in Nice and liking it all very much, tells me to come up if I am still sick (which I am not) and relax with them on the Mediterranean shore. Though no; at the moment I am too disgusted with myself for any company but one like Barney, who also spends time being disgusted with himself, pretending he weighs 300 pounds, similar productive pastimes.

When I came back from the monastery I had a note to call a Baroness Borchgrasse, she sounds like a real bloody fascist on the 'phone, had had a note from a friend (I suppose Mrs Fromkes) saying you were worried; and you know

I am sorry for that; I had not realised too much time had passed since writing you; and I guess the flu would have gone away sooner under a doctor. [...]

I have three grey hairs. In front.

And so, quietly,

with love,
Bill

'Fallas': in *R*, a crass American tourist "wants to see the big fair they have in Valencia [...]. They call it the Fallas, it's all fireworks" (882).
Baroness Borchgrasse [...] Mrs Fromkes: friends of Mrs. Gaddis.

To Edith Gaddis

Sevilla
29 March 49

As Becky Sharp once said, "I think I could be a good woman, if I had five-thousand (she meant pounds 25000$) a year..." And so it is, and the pity of it how "money" makes the world all smiles, and this afternoon (having got your 'note') I pass through the streets offering benediction to sundry wretches who hours before would have merited curses between the teeth...

It is some time since you have recieved a cheerful letter from me, isn't it. And here I hasten, under the aegis of wealth, to try to make up. Really; you must get tired to death of niggling notes from rocky places, detailing nothing but the weather (cold), the food (vile), the health (absence of), the prospects (ditto)... Because—though it does seem so at times—it is not all disaster, beggarly wonderment. Why, with the possibility of change of lodgings immediately in view, I can even tell you here in all good cheer that my stomach has succumbed to the culinary disasters of economical living, and when I lie down (which has been often) it really sounds like a huge hydro-electric plant, the Hoover Dam or the TVA or whatever, but something grand, in full operation: I hear valves open and shut, mighty rivers gush, canals furiously overflow their banks, whirlpools and cascading waterfalls, —indeed, if I do not seem to exaggerate, there have been times when I have heard the voices of men crying out down there in the darkness "Tote dat barge...Lif' dat bale."...well.

Spain is not the kind of a country you travel in; it is a country you flee across. To get from one place to another (the eternal problem in any respectable metaphysic) is the object; and trains, hopelessly laden, occasionally set out bravely with just such purpose. One set out recently from Valencia, and I was one of the unshaven, bread-carrying, orange-peeling idiots 'on board'.

Olive trees. All you see is olive trees. They are pretty, planted in pattern and rather like our weeping willow—pretty until you understand their purpose. At any rate, the 'train' (that is a euphemism) got all the way to Alcazar that night, averaging almost 18miles per hour. Shocking age of speed. About 1:30 something thundered into Alcazar from Madrid, I climbed on its back and together we were in Sevilla the Very Next Afternoon! (I think that perhaps the reason for the trains' pace is to give the people an illusion about the size of their country: those who have never seen maps probably believe, and with All Good Reason, that Africa would dwindle in comparison: no wonder Mr. Franco, as I read today, says 'The Atlantic Pact without Spain is like an omelette without eggs': He is a train-rider.) But back to my original complaint (it is hard to keep them in order), all they can grow is these damned olives, and so, logically (Spanish logic) all they eat is the oil. By they I mean we. Just today what was put before me would have roused even Old Grunter's hackles; briefly described (I daren't try details, the spirit is willing but the stomach weak) it was, or had been, an artichoke, now hoary and greyed with age and oil, in which it floated miraculously, the oil, slightly contaminated with a dark colouring-matter, sporting weary but invincible peas. Oh I tell you. Think of me, next mashed-potato-with-'xxxxxbutter' (such a foreign word I can't even spell it) and green broccoli, beef bathed in its own juices, or perhaps a lamb steak or chop, seared but tenderly red inside, garnished with parsley (green) . . . not pityingly, just think of me. Tomorrow will be better.

(You must charitably excuse my many typing mistakes; the light in the room is about equal to the glow of a friendly cigarette—and also, if my hand shakes somewhat, it is because I am waiting, with understandable trepidation, for "Dinner".

On the other hand (though that is ridiculous: we are still in Spain), as you know, I like, respect, enjoy the company of, and otherwise esteem Juancho. But his Iberian circle of friends out-do one another as human and social impossibilities. After the string of disasters precipitated by one of his chums in Madrid, I had the witless inspiration to look up another here, to whom he had given me a letter. Or am I the miserable ingrate? the shy boy with boarding-school manners and New England shyness?—this gentleman is an officer in the ARMY, and lives quite wretchedly with his family in a haze of music from other peoples' radios, children, unpaid bills, plexiglass collars (the modern celluloid here), splendid medals, and used stamps—he is also a philatelist, has boxes and boxes of carefully-arranged stamps, mostly duplicates and mostly current Spanish. When he came to call (as a matter of fact he followed me 'home') he continued to cement our relationship the way eight-yr-olds do, the exhibition and inspection of each other's earthly possessions: nothing in my spare luggage but that he picked up, weighed, priced, and, if I may presume to say, coveted. Now informality is one thing; but a hand reaching into one's breast pocket for a cigarette while its owner spits on the floor, —as I say, am I still a Merricourt boy? But that floor business is a national trait; no waste-backets (except, in this modern hostel, one beside the toilet in which to throw used paper) nor ashtrays: there is always some hag who comes to clean up: no trouble in this country over emancipated women, one of Spain's seductive qualities to the American Boy.

Sevilla, right now, is blooming; not the palm tree, breadfruit, or banyan, but the eyes of any and all who stand to gain by tourists. In about ten days, Holy Week descends, [along?] with floats, Virgins, barbarous crucifixes, jewels and gold and silver, and wadded money from such hapless pockets as my own. If you remember *South Wind*'s description of a similar festivity, you have a fragmentary picture. The mayor, in honour of the Resurrection and the exchange rate for tourists, has authorized all hide-outs[,] from the level of this YMCA shelter I am in to the Hotel Inglaterra, to double all rates. We don't do anything half-way. Then for any left who have not been beatified by the actual Resurrection taking place before their eyes (in a square, you can't miss it, turn left here, yes, right near the Public Conveniences) there follows a Fair of monstrous and pagan proportions. Drinking and bangles in the ears are in order; broughams, surreys, coupés fairly dripping Girls (24 count them 24) in costumes of 'Old Spain' wheel through any streets wide enough to accomodate them (the carriages I mean) and The People, for five days, dream that Charles V is king, and that the Spanish Armada will win for Our Side ... (it was launched, you know, in 1588 by Philip II, and fanatic is a dull word for him, in an effort to crush Protestantism as it flowered in England; I do believe that the people here still hold the destruction of the Armada against Me).

But one immensely important feature of the Fair: a bullfight every day, and some of the best toreros in the country, which makes me hope to manage to stay, in spite of the mayor, who knows a good thing when he sees it, and continues his hospitible legislation.

Did I write you? about a hysterical letter I had from our Barney-in-London, setting out for here on an apple-green bicycle? Oh, how I shall miss it, how I had looked forward to seeing him; because, quite reasonably, he reformed toward the last and retracted; in this form, that he was about to set out for Perpignon (a French town in the Pyrenees, just over the border), and could I meet him there for a week; even, imagine, offering to wire me the fare there and back! But no; he, seeing the ornate arrangement of difficulties before one entering Spain, has no notion of what lies before one who wishes to leave, especially if that one wishes to return. And so that is lost, and I am sad about it. You may imagine how I had pictured the two of us here,

menaced by monsters, fancy lights,

Risking enchantment . . .

Other civilised friends have decamped, in the direction of Paris Fr., which, I must confess, begins to look more like the fountainhead daily. But I feel that this land has a few more disasters to be enjoyed before abandonment, perhaps the summer . . .

I am glad to read in your letter that things are going well for you; it all (NY) seems a great distance away—far from this funny-house, which I have just thrown into an uproar by asking for Hot water for a 'bath', and pleading, demanding, that a lock, a hook, a catch, anything, be put on the door of the water-closet.

with love,
W.

Becky Sharp: *Vanity Fair,* chap. 41.

TVA: Tennessee Valley Authority, the hydroelectric power company established, like the Hoover Dam, during the Depression.

"Tote dat barge . . . Lif' dat bale": from the song "Ol' Man River," from the musical *Showboat* (1927).

Spain [...] you flee across: in *R*, Rev. Gwyon tells Wyatt: "—Spain is a land to flee across" (429). It is repeated as the opening sentence of III.3 (769).

Franco: Francisco Franco (1892–1975), dictator of Spain at the time.

Charles V: Carlos I of Spain (ruled 1516–56) became Holy Roman Emperor Charles V in 1519, hence sometimes erroneously called Carlos V of Spain.

menaced by monsters [...] Risking enchantment: from section 2 of Eliot's "East Coker."

To Edith Gaddis

Sevilla
11 April, 49

By heaven, if today wasn't artichoke-day again. —Which may serve to give you notice that I am still settled in the same quarters from which I last wrote you: that is, if you had that letter. Because I have been wondering, with an element of concern, if any of the revelations I set down on paper here ever get beyond the sea. And that the reason for the lapse between this and my last: waiting for something from you, to get an idea that you have an idea of my where-abouts. For instance: did you have a letter from Valencia, mailed 22March? And one from here (Sevilla) mailed less than a week later?

I have (with slavering delight) received two from you, each forwarded from Madrid, each with its reckless enclosures (30) and each greatly appreciated both for the words and the means. The 2nd recieved today, and very well because this being, as I set forth in the letter I-don't-know-if-you-got-it-or-not, Holy Week, the price of my modest lodging has been doubled, in accordance with no authorisation I find in the Gospel (but Gospel-readers always miss the root that Apocryphal writers set down . . .) Well. To say that all is in order, on my nullifidian end of the line, in spite of the monsters and fancy lights that menace the populace.

There are a number of things that have mounted up since I last wrote you. I shall try to introduce them in some sort of order:

(Item) I called upon the recently-arrived Mr Haygood, the friend of the Woodburns, just before leaving Madrid. He is very pleasant—and I believe more than appears on the dull library-curator surface, of which more another time. But was nice, as I say, though hardly settled in the country, and I about to leave the capital we had little time to exchange more than greetings (he bought me 2 cups of coffee: the beginning of a beautiful friendship here in Sp—); and (small world:) proved to be taking the apartment of my very kind mentor (used in the modern $-world sense, not the Homeric) Bill Taylor, who has absconded to Paris Fr. And so when I get back to Madrid hope to see Mr Haygood and we shall talk and drink his wine (in all the metaphorical sense of *that*) Though at the moment this beggar is on horseback.

(Item) About the time you have this letter (D V) (an abbreviation I have also wondered about, having had a friend named David Vail . . .) —we may have talked by trans-Atlantic Telephone. On the other hand, we may not. The point of this is that I am going to try to put a call through to you at the Latham, but if I do not reach you, and things turn up as they did in a similar intention from Panama, I only want you to know, if you should have frantic news from the desk that you have missed a call from Mars, that it is not dark-winged news, but intended quite the other way, what with spring being a greeting in the form of natural prodigies, and Easter the myth incarnate, or re-incarnated, in most religions, Resurrections being apparently an old stock-in-trade of the most 'pagan' (indeed!) legitimisations of (this) life.

(Item) The enclosure is cut from one of my most pleasurable discoveries, a fearfully Tory newspaper called the (Continental) *Daily Mail* (the Paris edition of the London paper). You will probably be glad to know that I have found a reasonable substitute for that NewYork purveyor of current beauty, the *Daily News*; for the *Daily Mail* (a very respectable paper) tells me about such wonders as the man who swallowed 19 (open, I gather) safety-pins in a (successful) effort [to] remove himself from this valley of temptation . . . —But re the enclosure: the writer doesn't seem awfully bright or talented or much shakes at all; but what he says of Our City has scratched a nostalgic itch in the dermis of my memory: and I wondered is it really like this? I hope so for you.

(Item) With hands shaking in anticipation, I received the book by Robert Graves. It has proved to be 4 times as wonderful, and 40times as difficult, as I had expected. But with the marvelous opportunity I have enjoyed in other lands, what with my lack of the reading I need, has proved as I hoped-against-hope to be exactly referent to the web of questions in my mind at present—as the Toynbee did when I was happily marooned on Caribbean shores. If I put down here on paper all the things I want to I would not end the letter, because that would amount to making the notes on these ideas which I am trying to make for my own nefarious purposes: so suffice only a hilarious thanks, and a sort of hysterical re-assurance that my thoughts and the slowly transmogrifying products of my imagination, whether consumately pagan products or not, are being articulated and validified.

And so we finally reach Sevilla, where I am now, a dump-heap of history "which combines the peculiarities of a harbour town with the exuberant fertility of a southern landscape, and joins a present, full of rich, sprightly and harmonious life, to an abundance of artistic monuments indicative of a brilliant past" (Baedeker). Where also one may have a glass of wine and small dish of fried octopus hide for 5¢ and, for dining out in more modest establishments, a plate of fried blood and potatoes for 15¢.

Right now we are Celebrating a series of occurences which took place some 1949 years ago, and which, as I remember the daffodilic spring of Berlin Ct., are taken for granted with quiet reverence in those cold protestant hearts; but here we must re-enact it. And so the handsome ladies and their greasy escorts step from block-long automobiles, mingle with their countrymen (halt & blind, faces scarred with pox, eyes closed by syphilis), and celebrate the beauty of eternal love, another better life, and the all-embracing bounty of Holy Church—while He Who does not miss a sparrow's fall apparently misses a few adept sleights-of-hand among his sub-vicars locally ordained. The great images carried through the streets on these evenings are quite as prodigious as one could ask—a Virgin adorned with every richness of brocade that artifice can manage, illumined by hundreds of candles, compassionate tears on her face and fists-full of jewels, a bosom loaded with precious gems, many donated by True Believers who suddenly troubled themselves over the camel-&-the-needle parable and unloaded a few of their vain fripperies (... All I'll keep are these 17 diamond pendants and that emerald-&-diamond brooch, and I better keep this emerald-&-diamond bracelet, & the earings, after all they're a set . . .) and Our Lady is carried down the avenue—you can see the feet of her bearers underneath the brocaded velvet hangings, straw-soled cloth shoes of bearers who get remission for Sins—those who can't pay for candles . . . —down the Avenue, with her compassionate tears, holding out ropes of pearls to the syphillis-blinded lottery-ticket seller, who holds his child up on his shoulders—though the kid can't see much: his 4-year-old eyes are crusted and starting to close with the heritage of the sins of his father. Life is very long.

Certainly you did much better to go see *The Long Voyage Home* than worry over such things as Is H. really Dead? I have had similar arguements here, though ridiculous, with fasces-bound 'friends'—I can't see it matters if he is or isn't dead, history is done with him.

The going-to-France-fever is down, I have less & less need or notion (though the idea of spending a month or two with Jake, getting things exchanged & re-aligned as it were, is good)—but recently I have started to get much more of what I came for here, in the way of thought- and imagination-provoking observations and circumstance. A letter from Barney this morning; and a fine thing to have; if this does not sound pretentious (which it is, to repeat, but:) "(Spain) sounds ideally suited to your mind and the kind of work you want to do. Being the wandering Jew all over again won't make it any better. Hang on for a year at least . . . that from what I have seen of your work I know that you have a facility with words, quantity and ingenuity, and a preposterous imagination which moreover you *enjoy* using, and Good Lord! in a world gone rabid, every man making faces and fists at one another, what else can be so important to you to make you move from the less disturbed Spain to the more savage (if enlightened) France. To bother yourself again with the American mecca . . . Stay where you are, don't be tempted and lured by the violence in others . . ." &so forth. But a very good and re-assuring letter, and I do now intend to stay with a better-rewarding feeling of permanence, ie of getting what I need, which is just starting to take form in my mind with clarity.

What else? I think of nothing immediate (except the idea of mail-delivery in M[assapequa]. is horrifying: I should be inclined to burn Sunshine Shanty to the ground before it becomes situated in Zenith . . . The mailbox is a nice notion—but someone ought to drown John B Gambling. Let me know if you get this letter.

with love,
W.

Also another enclosure, your son in a Moorish town—just to prove that it *is* me sending these idiotic letters.

monsters and fancy lights: again, from "East Coker."

Mr. Haygood: William Converse Haygood; see headnote to 4 January 1954.

beggar is on horseback: from the proverb, "Set a beggar on horseback and he'll ride to the devil," meaning someone unused to luxury will abuse it if given the opportunity.

D V: *Deo volente* (Latin, "God willing").

Latham: the Latham Hotel, at 4 East 28th St.

Resurrections being apparently an old stock-in-trade: in *R*, Wyatt speaks of the days following Jesus' crucifixion when "resurrections were a stock in trade" (384).

enclosure [...] *Daily Mail*: unidentified.

He Who does not miss a sparrow's fall: Matt. 10:29.

camel-&-the-needle parable: Mark 10:23–27.

The Long Voyage Home: an early play by Eugene O'Neill, the basis for a 1940 film directed by John Ford about passengers on a ship transporting dynamite across the Atlantic during World War II.

Is H. really Dead?: after his suicide in 1945, Hitler was rumored to have escaped and settled elsewhere.

the wandering Jew: a legendary figure who taunted Jesus during the crucifixion and consequently cursed to wander the earth until his return, alluded to in *R*.

John B Gambling: American radio personality (1897–1974), host of a New York City radio show called *Rambling with Gambling*.

To Edith Gaddis

[*This follows two letters from Madrid dated 29 April and 2 May trying to entangle the mess of mailed cashier's checks and cancellations. It is postmarked Elizabeth, NJ.*]

Madrid
3 May, 1949

(and I quote),

I'm tired of love; I'm still more tired of rhyme;
But money gives me pleasure all the time.

I am also, despite this moment of confusion which may be suddenly arisen in your mind, still in Spain; but herewith take advantage of a friend who is flying to NY in a few days, where I trust he will post this letter, in which I have a few things I hazard to have in the hands of Spanish censors—not that I believe our mail is censored, but still . . .

By now, I trust, the whole cheque confusion is cleared up, and you not receiving mail behind bars (prison bars I mean) [...] I am sorry it takes such a mess to clear things up: I had tried to make it clear in other letters, this necessity for cashiers cheques, but always with the care of trying not to say too much, in the event the letter was stopped and read.

From now until I believe the middle of June I shall be at the Sevilla address, though if you mail to Madrid it will, D V, reach me. Then in June I hope to go to France. Jake and Barney and I are working out such plans, by letters, and there is some possibility that I may go to England for a little time, as Barney is there and familiar with all aspects of their life and difficulties, and has plans for something involving a walking tour to see various parts of Cornwall and ancient Druid ceremonial grounds &c, things which are interesting me immensely recently in light of Robert Graves book, which has proven immensely valuable, and also things which interest Barney greatly and on which he is much better informed than myself, he spending more time in the British Museum, and not among Spanish gypsies [...].

And also, despite the flip verse salutation of this letter, I may say how sincerely grateful I am to you for sending this string of cheques which are making possible for me an education not found in the Harvard Yard, nor among Greenwich Village intelligensia, nor working as a book-keeper in London or Paris or Vladivostok, or as a snide young editorial accountant on the *New Yorker*. It is just within the last two months that the whole thing has begun to take shape for me, that I have discovered what I came for, and if I can be so selfish to say, it is worth it. Especially since your recent 'letters' (may I send you a large box of writing paper?) indicate that your life is not a dark hall-bedroom affair—quite the other way, indeed! (that is, if you enjoy the company of war admirals, cocktail parties; dono nobis pacem...) [...]

I cannot think of any more secrecies to impart. Indeed, the whole business I suppose is pretty idiotic I guess: who in the world cares about our tiny phenageling...you are not the Queen of Roumania, nor I as yet a prophet of any great import

(I have seen my head (grown slightly bald) brought in upon a platter.

(I am no prophet, but here's no great matter...)

And so tonight I am going to a theatre, to see an old play of Pirandello's of which I am very fond, and I think know well enough to be able to follow a gibberish Spanish version. Tomorrow I think to Cordoba for a day or two, and thence back to Sevilla.

—suddenly here is someone flying to NY this afternoon; I hope to get this off immediately, you may have it before week's end. And so, from now, the Sevilla address.

best wishes, and love,
W.

I'm tired of love [...]: a couplet from English writer Hilaire Belloc (1870–1953).
dono nobis pacem: Latin: "give us peace," from the *Agnus Dei* portion of the Catholic
   Mass.
I have seen my head [...]: from Eliot's "Love Song of J. Alfred Prufrock."
old play of Pirandello's: perhaps *Naked*: see 7 April 1948.

To Edith Gaddis

Sevilla
[5 May 1949]

dear lady,

this will not be a frantic letter, in spite of the way that catastrophes seem
to have conspired to keep our correspondence from anything vaguely resembling correspondence, but instead a wild series of posting messages of distress
back and forth across the sea.

And so first, these things; while I sit over a bucket in which soaks what
looks to be enough linen for a caravanserai of many many tents, bought in a
recently faded flush of prosperity and soon, I trust, to be magic-ed into a suit
by a clever local fellow; and wearing alpargatas, which are hempen-soled cloth
sandals and the footwear of all of Spain's poor people.

Let me say at the outset that I am well, and not in desperate straights at
all. (I even go so far as to say that it would be difficult to be desperate in
Andalucia.)

This morning I had two letters from you, which I too had been waiting to
receive before writing. And to attempt some sort of order: [*nine bullet-pointed
remarks follow, most continuing to deal with checks, concluding with:*]

Our correspondence should never be published.

I think it so possible that we have both spent much time saying, —Oh
dear, *I'm* all right, but what a terrible time (s)he is having... that is the way I
feel now. Because heaven knows I'm all right, but do feel that what may seem
to you niggling at my end is driving you to despair and exasperation. You
probably think me as obtuse as anyone could be, or (to use a nice coupling of
words from Mr Eliot) exhibiting 'deliberate hebetude'...

Well. With that many words nearer King's Park, let me try to at least end
on a note of real correspondence.

On Sunday I am going down to Jerez, where they are having their spring
fair, and hope to see a good bullfight there. Also I met here in Sevilla a Brit-
isher who is with a big bodega, or distillery there (it is, you know, the source
of the world's sherry wine, sherry being a corruption of the word Jerez) and
has told me if in town to stop and see him for a tour of the bodega, which
means tasting the stuff, but in abundant quantity.

And then in a few weeks here there is a great annual procession to the shrine of some Virgin about 50miles away—the people get together in cars, on horseback, anything, and set out, taking three or four days on the way, all of which I understand is spent in singing, dancing, and such pagan pastimes. It is to a large extent a family affair; and I may go, to the town nearest the Virgin's mountainous retreat by bus & thence a few miles a-foot...but what I should love to do is rent a little burro (they are not much bigger than Old Grunter) and set off on his back. Such a plan is greeted here with crys of amazement & then derision, 50miles burro-back being quite a chore apparently. It probably won't come out at all—especially since they say there are no accomodations and little water between here and There (and the question of getting hold of a burro...) but—

I have just had a good letter from Bernie, who is weathering it all on some Italian island, in the transient company of Wystand Auden, Capote, and a few other eminent 9$-bills (including, to use his words, the 'odious and idiotic Tenn. Williams')...well Bernie is happy, he can have it. I'll take the gypsies (though more usually they take me). Also word from Margaret Williams, who says she has turned into a Mediterranean vegetable, and as you know I don't get much steam up for vegetables. And an excellent letter from Barney, whose descriptions of walks in Cornwall and Wales sound magnificent and edifying, not vegetable at all, and I believe we are getting nearer to working something out for the summer.

And aside from all that, life in Andalucia is quiet and good; I can manage fairly badly now in the language, and have made the acquaintance of a man of about 40 who has an eighth-grader's light in his eyes when it comes to the Lust for Learning, English being for him the keys to the kingdom, and Spanish for me to more practical purposes, we spend occasional hours together teaching one and the other, he mightily serious about the whole project and so we do get somewhere.

And so; another letter finished—as if we could finish anything...another step toward wherever we are going. And I think now is a good time to recommend 'patience', after seeing how little good my wild dash to Madrid did. Let us move slowly and with sobre purpose?

The enclosure shows me with local friend named Eulalio, atop a mighty tower.

Love,
W.

'deliberate hebetude': from "East Coker," section 2 (hebetude = lethargy, dullness).
King's Park: the Kings Park Psychiatric Center on Long Island?

WG with Eulalio Abril Morales, Madrid, 1949.

Capote: Truman Capote (1924–84), American novelist and journalist, had recently achieved fame with his novel *Other Voices, Other Rooms* (1948).

Eulalio: Eulalio Abril Morales (1918–88); see Crystal Alberts's "Mapping William Gaddis," p. 172n25, in *William Gaddis, "The Last of Something,"* ed. Alberts, Christopher Leise, and Birger Vanwesenbeeck (Jefferson, NC: McFarland, 2009). WG named a young monk after him in *R* (859), not to be confused with an earlier Brother Eulalio who castigated himself "for unchristian pride at having all the vowels in his name" (10).

To Helen Parker

[*Helen Parker (1920–93) was part of the same Greenwich Village scene in the 1940s that WG came to know after leaving Harvard. They reportedly fell in love in 1946 and discussed marriage, but events of that summer caused her to change her mind. An older woman with two children (named in the letter below), she had a history of literary relations: she had been engaged to John Dos Passos, knew Hemingway in Cuba, and relieved Allen Ginsberg of his virginity. She also had a brief affair with Jack Kerouac, who based a few of his characters on her. She was the model for Esther in R, which infuriated her when she read the book upon publication. In a letter to me dated 2 February 1984—by which time she was Mrs. Charles Jeremiah—she said WG hid the manuscript from her, "A bit childish since he certainly intended to publish."*]

> c/o U.S. Consulate
> Paseo de las Pelicias
> Sevilla
> 18 May 49

Dear Helen.

In spite of what is apparently popular impression—judging from the lack of letters from the US—I am not at all difficult to reach by post. And just this morning I got back from Cádiz and found your letter here, forwarded from Madrid. Well. I really thought you had gone to Cuba? and so haven't written—that was the last word I had from you, you know—a card-in-an-envelop saying *Cuba*. And so haven't sent you even so much as a picture postal. And I am sorry you didn't go, if you wanted to go—though I don't see how Cuba could last; except perhaps for Mr. Hemingway.

As for Spain—it has only become Spain since I got out of Madrid a couple of months ago. My winter there was as low as anybody's anywhere—with little company but Mr. Eliot—who isn't disposed to cheer one up. Then in March I went briefly to a Franciscan monastery: and though I left quite unbeatified, somehow since then everything has come along well. Not everything of course—but nearer so than it has ever been my experience.

Right now, for instance—I have just returned with less than 1¢ worth of Spanish money in my pocket. But damn it in a place like Sevilla I can't care— into a favourite bar (there are many) where the friendly proprietor has delivered to me some fine glasses of Jerez wine—and back to my pension, where I will be fed and bedded until the sun comes up. Have encountered a young engineer, "of fine family," who is going to the US soon to study & wants some English lessons—there a small source of income—and so it goes.

And so for immediacies I couldn't care less somehow—such as sitting over a bucket full of linen (it is soaking—looks enough for a circus tent) which I bought in better days, and now haven't the money to have a suit made—though with another glass or two of Jerez could make it myself; my only troubles being over work, which has lagged badly recently—though I could hardly tell where the days have gone. I don't know—I am almost content for the first time in my life. Though heaven knows, it won't last.

Did you ever meet Barney Emmart? He is studying at London University now—and we have been exchanging prospective plans for summer; because he is as interested in—and tremendously better posted on—the things that have been occupying me recently—most epitomized in the book of Robert Graves, *The White Goddess*, which has really got me going. And so some possibility that I go to England, if I can manage, and spend some time walking the Druid country. I don't know yet about Jake—he and I are still in the toils of mails. Though he sounds splendidly settled with Nance. And a letter from Bernie, on some Italian island with Auden, Capote, and an assortment of 9$-bills—I still want to see and talk with Bernie, old friend—but not at that price —— And a chance that next winter I may go to Africa to work (*not act*) for a Spanish motion-picture company. A chance.

And if all this sounds ideal—it isn't: but is the nearest I have known on this earth. Largely perhaps because it is so long since I have seen anyone I know—or had opportunity to speak *my* language—and so hopes mount up, again—for what will be a real disillusion if it comes. And the price paid in loneliness. And I suppose one day the bullfights will wear out, and the wine, and the usual shrug of casual temptations—and so I follow this hunger now.

There will be time. Life is very long.—I shall write better soon; meanwhile love to you, and Bruce, and Tommy—and do write me again, lengthier, about the things I only find hinted in your letter.

W

There will be time: a line from Eliot's "Love Song of J. Alfred Prufrock." As noted earlier, "Life is very long" is from his "East Coker."

Bruce, and Tommy: Helen Parker's children from an earlier marriage, aged five and ten.

To Edith Gaddis

Sevilla

24 May 49

dear Mother.

[...] Now, if you should see an ancient Spaniard in a grey Brooks Brothers suit, do not mistake his sun-burnt presence for me—it will not be me, but Isabel's brother. Isabel is the maid of all work here in my pension, a wondrously unattractive and happy elderly person, to whom I gave the suit which graced my entrance to Harvard long ago. It was getting to look quite a disgrace, as you may imagine; and then in Cádiz I did it in: walking out on a long break-water to look at the sea, suddenly romantically overcome and slightly weary, I sat on a portion of the cement wall, pondering the Phoenicians trampling over these very waves, and the ancient name of the city, Gádes—and then, attempting to rise to my feet in the hot sun, found myself stuck fast in a tar slop unnoticed on the rock. So much for the trousers. Later, running up a flight of stairs, the jacket pocket caught on a newel... I decided it was the finger of a sartorial deity letting me know that I had offended him for just about long enough. And Isabel, with an expanse of gums showing her pleasure (something like Wilson's beaming smile) almost wept for joy at the gift.

Concerning the moustachioed gentleman in the photo I sent you, among his less offensive aberations is a mania for stamp collecting. He can't read English, but I thought we might bring ends together if it is convenient in this fashion (since I've been so lax about Christine's request for stamps), that you give her this fellow's name and address to give to one of her boys, and he send to Eulalio (*that* certainly is a feat in nomenclature!) up to 100 different current US stamps, not valuable you know, just regualr; for which E. will return in kind and number from Spain. It would be splendid if she encountered one who wrote & read a little Spanish, but among those united in the holy cause of Philately I'm sure such incidentals as correspondence matter little. [...]

I don't know what you have in view, sending me the Massapequa highlights. You must know, the whole thing appears gruesome. Building little houses around the Caroon home, 'Welcome to Massapequa' signs, &c. Eeeeeee. It may interest you to know that the only name I recognise (aside from the leering faces of Maass & George in the picture) in the *Massapequa Memo* was a youth who had 'entered a plea of guilty on charges of negligence in the operation of a motor vehicle...'—such is my social circle. I feel less at home with every column you send; which, if they could see me, I guess wouldn't displease my towns-folk ('Going somewhere George?').

Very good to hear about your coming along so well in the ceramic work. I wish you could magically spend just a day looking in the shops in Spain—

especially Talavera de la Reina, a town about 60miles from Madrid (which I notice C Hall has marked in his Baedeker) where most of Spain's good ceramic comes from. I often have the inspiration to try to get some of it to you, but that would be quite a project; and always I remember Mabel seeing her Numdas in Loesier's window—you can probably see anything I could send you right there in NY—Hall House, even! And as Aristotle said, one swallow doesn't make a summer; neither would 3 or 4 plates give you a picture of the primitive variety of colours and pictures and designs. Great use is made of yellow, blue, and a green which is beautifully clean and cool. The animals pictured (and these from long ago times, having seen originals on the walls of the monastery at Guadalupe of which present-day designs are the copies— not commercial conscious copies you understand, just copies because all the Spanish people can do in art or industry is copy, and here they copy their past), the animals, rabbits, dogs, horses, some birds, are beautiful primitive series of curved lines, with a fine suggestion of motion, and little of the oppression of 'reality' from which our life & art suffer so badly. What is the Jane–Hudson St fellow's name? probably knows Sheri M—.

The enclosure is from a London paper, sent me by Jacob. It is apparently destined for you, and may give you some ideas...'practical suggestions' for your early retirement to ceramic work (though what your designs would look like under such stimulus heaven knows).

Don't be distressed no-end about Bernie and the 9$-bills. The island of Ischia is far away. And I do not set my sails for such horizons; though I should like to see Bernie again. Still planning a quiet and edifying summer in company with Jake and Barney, though we are still trying to work out the where and when of it through the mails.

After an exceptional night, ending at 8am, having fallen in with a group centred about a guitar along about midnight, I met Eulalio and we took a tram to the city's farthest bounds, and thence walked some miles in the morning sun to the old Roman ruins at Itálica. I was not prostrate, but rather tired I must confess; nevertheless warmed to it, and found the expedition quite rewarding. The ruins of an old Roman circus, and mosaic floors which still bear their colour and design clearly. And so things go in Andalucia. The shoes I wear at present cost 30¢, of cloth with hempen soles.

with love & best wishes,
W

Gádes: founded in the 12th century BCE by the Phoenicians, who called it Gadir. The Romans called it Gādēs, and by way of Arabic it finally became Cádiz.
Wilson [...] Christine: unidentified.

Mabel: one of WG's aunts.
Numdas in Loesier's window: rugs at *Loeser's*, a department store in Brooklyn.
Aristotle [...] summer: a famous saying from the Greek philosopher's *Nicomachean Ethics*.
Jane–Hudson St: an intersection in west Greenwich Village, a few blocks from where WG used to live on Horatio Street.
Sheri M—: Sheri Martinelli, who occasionally worked in ceramics.
enclosure: an item from the *Daily Mail* about an American newspaper printed on a rayon fabric from which the ink can be washed off and used as a duster.

To Edith Gaddis

Sevilla
28 May, 49

Fair stood the wind for France...

Well, fair or not, that is where I am going any day now. And I suppose that we are in for a Royal disaster, involving misdirected mail, pennies lost down the drain, imprisonment for illegal entry of wild flowers, heaven knows what.

A moment of lucidity: Immediately you receive this letter, send no more mail to Sevilla; to Madrid instead.

At present planned: to leave here about the 7th of June, for Madrid. To leave Madrid about the 12th of June, for points north. I should like, if I can afford it, to stop over at a town or two in the north of Spain before going on to France; if I can't shall go right along to Paris D.V.

I believe I have enough money to manage it—though if I should receive a Jackson from you before moving on it will be welcome. Therefore: if you will send to this Paris address, to be there around the 15th of June, *or a few days before*, any kind of negociable check for 50$:

c/o American Express

11, Rue Scribe, Paris France., and if I arrive penniless, as I most certainly shall, I can, with Jake's help, get straightened out. [...]

That seems to be all at the moment; must write Jake, from whom I have just had a letter, warning him of the Thing that will soon appear on his horizon—garbed in a linen toga, wild-eyed, and hempen sandals, with pockets full of oranges, —the lost Iberian.

love to you,
W

Fair stood the wind for France: the opening line of Michael Drayton's "To the Cambro-Britons and Their Harp, His Ballad of Agincourt" (1619).
Jackson: their code for a $20 bill.

To Edith Gaddis

[WG spent the next year and a half in Paris, which is satirized in the second chapter of R. *His first letter to his mother (13 June) was mailed from Hotel Vivienne, 40–42 rue Vivienne.]*

Paris

17 June 49

dear Mother,

No doubt about it, Paris is a beautiful city. And everything is somehow pleasanter than I expected. Nothing to be alarmed about. I was apparently very fortunate to get a hotel room, they being about as difficult to come on as in NY; but met in the train from Madrid a very nice Spanish gentleman, who had the whole Spanish lack of respect for things French (a mutual attitude), and, I think somewhat alarmed that this young American would find France nicer than Spain, outdid himself in niceties, finally recommending me to a friend of his here, a hotel-keeper. And so I am, and on the Right Bank (the Left Bank being you know the traditional home of Bohemian high-jinks &c). Still having monstrous difficulties with the language, Spanish is all I can speak, blubbering and yammering.

But the city, in spite of the fact that it [is] not architecturally anything remarkable—Notre Dame for instance is not at all as magnificent as Christmas-card engravings have led us to believe—is impressive in its endless vistas, boulevards and avenues of great width, always terminating in some sort of well-known construction. And so in spite of the familiarity of the Arc de Triomphe, the Eiffel Tower &c, all these things are wonderful because of the way they are presented. Unlike most cities I have seen (and notably NY) Paris is less impressive when seen from an elevation. NY for instance is nothing until you get up 102 storeys and look down on it; Paris from the top of the Arch is simply a table-top of dull house-rooves, because of the fairly consistent height of the buildings, they are all about 7 storeys. But the city radiating out around you as you stand in the Champs Elysees, or along the Seine, is beautiful. (And after all a city is to be lived in on the ground, or is it.) And along the Seine at 5am remarkably beautiful.

I have seen Jake, and he looks wonderfully well, in good spirits and healthy, working at his school where he will be through in a few weeks and on translations, in general very fine. Just now he and I are trying to work out the summer plans, may involve going to an inexpensive country place near Tours, south of Paris, quite undecided as yet. But here was Jacob, perfectly: after we had not encountered for something like 2 years, and of course there were thousands of words to exchange, things to go over, cultures to compare &c &c, the evening of our meeting (and both of us grinning like idiots on the first encounter, with pleasure) Mr Bean proposes that we attend a performance of some Beethoven quartets, which we did. Well.

And then, if all sounds too healthy to be bearable, I shall go on to say that last evening there arrived from Florence Italy the paralytic Mr Bubu Faulkner, drink being the agency of his paralysis. Dear heaven, how he can keep it up. At any rate we went over to the left bank, where generations of odd people have congregated, and there I participated briefly in what Miss Williams called the imitation of Greenwich Village, and since Gr Vil is a traditional imitation of the left bank . . . boring to me, bored to extinction, the flowers of evil indeed. The whole thing rather pathetic, seeing French police loading American lily-boys into a van, and really quite foolish. And so I continue to enjoy Paris from the river's bourgeois side.

One thing remarkable after the desert of Spain is to find here such unlimited publications, books, reviews, and theatre, and concerts, &c. But even so I am still attached south of the Pyrenees, Spain has more to do with me, or for me, than here. Paris is, needless to say, more expensive on all counts. But there are aspects that are almost provincial after Spain; for instance, one must eat lunch between 12 and 1:30, while Madrid's lunch hour is 2 at earliest. And you can't dine after 9 (I suppose Maxims and Fouquets serve, haven't investigated), in all that they are like nice respectable French farmers. And by 11 the city seems to have retired, while Madrid's theatre starts at 11, and you really can't be seen at night spots before 1. Well. I am quite pleased to find it so innocent.

For other plans, I don't know. Bernie is to arrive here in a few days, but somehow I don't think, after the initial greetings, we'll have much to do. The pleasures and pastimes he has adopted in the last year don't appeal even slightly to me, nor the company, most of whom seem to be appearing. And then for Barney, another uncertainty. Paris, I understand, is something he can't cope with. And heaven knows I don't want to see any human disasters just now. But shall write him and see what he 'plans'. And there is Miss Williams, still on the Riviera and half-planning to come up here, hope to see her but don't manage such a trip just now. [...]

One oclock, I had best get out and look for a small restaurant, or shall be caught lunchless in this provincial town.

with love,
W

BuBu Faulkner: Robert Eames Faulkner III (1913–86); after working for the *New Yorker* in the 1930s and serving during World War II, he led a bohemian life in Europe and North Africa.

imitation of Greenwich Village [...] imitation of the left bank: In *R*, Ed Feasley complains, "—I haven't been in Paris since I was seven years old, Chrahst to go there now! I mean to Saint Germain des Prés where they're imitating Greenwich Village and here we are in Greenwich Village still imitating Montmartre" (746).

the flowers of evil: title of Charles Baudelaire's best-known book of poetry (1857).

To Edith Gaddis

(American Express) [Paris]
[3 July 1949]

dear Mother.

Here we are, 6 of us at noon sitting before a small café, all over the sidewalk—Bernie, Jake, and an interesting assortment—and I realise—have for some days—that it is long since I wrote. Things have been "active"—having just gone down to Nice, Cannes &c—found Miss Margaret Williams, and brought her back to Paris. Well. By now I am so mixed up. Quite uncertain about the summer, about Miss Williams, about everything in sight. And of course in the expected desperate state about money. —— Knowing this letter sounds distracted (it is hardly the propitious circumstance for letter-writing) but I am "well"— Also to say I had the sad news of Grunter, wrote you another and unmailed letter—and just now of Chas. Hall, whom I may manage to see if I can find a clean shirt—

love,
W.

To Edith Gaddis

American Express
11, Rue Scribe
Paris France
9 July 49.

dear Mother,

I have just dropped two suitcase keys out of my 7th-storey hotel window; and that trifle may go to illustrate pretty much how things have been going for the last weeks.

Many enough competences have attacked the sempiternal picture of ingrate children, sons and lovers. And here the son, moored high among a floating campanella, faëry bells that pass unattached, tangled among treetops, bleeding their sounds in drops over the green, through the light, indifferent calling signalling only the mariner who reasons to fear the shoals, we others reach out, call back answerless, until there and sudden is the white water and we know what they knew— Seated, as I say, on a level of treetops in an anonymous section of Paris, adding the days I have written you nothing (where the dark of the days and the hours reigned in glowing incautious confusion) (new ribbon)

("and that one", said an old engineer, "has bananas in his head...")

History being a temporal substitute for creation, I suppose we may best recline to chronology, to rely like the weak on arrangement, on the varicose strands of time. Conveniently with each day numbered, respectfully submitting to a larger number that Pope Gregory, forced to temporal attentions, restricted as a year, thinking perhaps that any christian concept of eternity merited science's corresponding resolution to infinity, that was numbers. Or Evangeline, retching in the forest primeval —life is very long.

But no. Better, —It was roses, roses all the way, and never a sprig of yew... And better to go backwards; starting at last night.

The Paris Opera. We went, I took Margaret, to the ballet at the Paris Opera, largely because it is Paris, because she is Margaret, and we are both, wolens-nolens, in Paris. And so we sat, at aristocratic attention, inclining toward the stage or toward one another to comment, seated in armchairs, suspended darkly over the ostentation of the multitude; and there they danced to undistinguished music and polite applause—who? an American? shouted bis! bis! not because it was grand or even particularly good, but because we need spectacles, because the only ones who afford the grand gesture today usually end up in the prison or the asylum, so well-conducted is our sterility, so well-rewarded our antisepsis,

(Well, and it was graceful of them, they'd break talk off and afford,
(She to touch her mask's black velvet, he to finger at his sword,
(While you sat and played tocattas, stately at the clavichord...)

Words drop, disappear, or shamefully retreat from our vocabularies. And that word cried in a desert has dried on desert air, that was Disaster. Because now, a meticulous unfolding seems to be going on. The day before, we (of whom the sustaining concomitant is Margaret) went as his guests to Mr Bean's country school, where we lunched in a cafe garden, and were so pleasant together that one has a sudden moment of stricken silence to say, these are the moments we have waited for, and paid for before and after, passionless and un-looked-for. Or we have suppered at a student restaurant, or among intellectuals talking of foolishness, or fools parading their mis-information, or walked near the Seine and beside it, or walked among people like a walk in the forest over dead leaves where they crush under quick steps refuse of nature, used, old junk, dust returning, back to the button-moulder, helpless before life.

All of which is to say, that, although confusion has never reigned so brilliantly, there would seem to be immanent crossroads: though that is a pitifully incompetent metaphor: not crossroads, but something like that clover-leaf highway arrangement on the Henry Hudson parkway; where, if you remember, we spent the better part of an afternoon thundering in misdirections, and were finally resolved on the way we were going, for better or worse, toward home or away from it, I cannot remember.

Let me say, it is not as Mr Eliot said it was, as it was, "distracted from distraction by distraction,"... but now there is the sense of concert.

Jacob has gone off to the Loire valley for his summer. Bernie has gone off to a week-end for the week-end. Margaret has inclined to the let-us-hope brief charm of Sont-American Gold (dear one, she really deserves a full meal). The rest have all gone into the dark. And I, as I say, ponder here in a tiny room, an ayerie (I can't spell it, it means an eagle's nest) in respectable periphery of Paris. I believe that in another week I may go to join Jake. But cannot say. First I want to talk here to some personification of responsibility, some hand-maiden to power, about the notion of returning to Spain in the fall with employment there. I have thought this summer to work at My work, to prove it one way or another, and by the fall know whether it deserves the continuance of vagabondage, or points instead to the bondage of respectable employment. If that latter I can hope to go back to that naked country which I have not finished with; it has not finished with me yet either.

There is, as you may have foreseen, may have hoped, the sudden gigantic gigantic consideration, of another person. That is Margaret. Margaret just now is about as busy and certain as a kettle-drummer playing Wagner without the score before him, though, like the kettle-drummer, quite unhysterical, not desperate, because she knows the composer. And can you know, what a quiet good happy and pleasant time we have had here in Paris? Time, energy, and money, well and wonderfully spent. But spent, especially the last. I am, at the moment, cheerfully broke and reasonably in debt, but shall not load you with those endless considerations; because all of the expenditure, unreasonable as it may have seemed, has pointed, is pointing in better direction, in a direction of fullness, of realisation. Still the 15th looks miles away.

I wait with ill-concealed hunger, thinking that perhaps Mr Hall will appear, the consideration of a 'very good dinner', I believe I can even borrow a white shirt for the engagement. Oh, understand; I do not wait haggard and hungry, but in a new element of something near peace, something near happiness, something near content with a hard-boiled egg for today's meal.

Let me say, bitterness disappears or is channeled; that the wiseness in what was called foolish expenditure becomes evident as the corners of the pattern begin to suggest themselves; that reason reached through unreason; and honesty through pretension.

to ask you to indulge the fore-going miasma of metaphor, the dearth of clean lines, the plethora of pretension; to find underneath what I try vainly to dig down to;

to be assured of my health in body, immanent sanity of mind, and eternal gratitude.

Now an old typewriter-ribbon has caught smouldering fire in my waste-basket. I shall return to the immediate problems of This World.

with all love,
W.

---

sons and lovers: title of a D. H. Lawrence novel (1913).

Pope Gregory: Gregory XIII established the Gregorian calendar in 1582 to correct the older Julian calendar.

Evangeline: the heroine of Henry Wadsworth Longfellow's book-length poem (1847), who wanders through forests primeval before settling in Philadelphia.

It was roses [...] sprig of yew: from Graham Greene's 1938 novel *Brighton Rock*: "Mr Prewitt quoted promptly, inaccurately, 'Roses, roses all the way, and never a sprig of yew'" (Penguin, 1977, p. 167). The first half is the opening line of Robert Browning's poem "The Patriot" (1845), and quoted in *R* (741); "and never a sprig of yew" is from Matthew Arnold's "Requiescat" (1853): "Strew on her roses, roses, / And never a spray of yew!"

wolens-nolens: i.e., *nolens volens*, Latin: willing or unwilling (willy-nilly).

bis! bis!: encore! encore!

Well [...] at the clavichord: from Browning's poem "A Toccata of Galuppi's" (1855), prominently quoted in *R* (191).

the button-moulder: a character in Ibsen's *Peer Gynt* (1867), an important text for *R*.

"distracted from distraction by distraction": from section 3 of "Burnt Norton" (1935), the first of Eliot's *Four Quartets*.

Sont-American Gold: perhaps a typo for South-American Gold.

gone into the dark: "O dark dark dark. They all go into the dark," from section 3 of Eliot's "East Coker."

To Edith Gaddis

American Express, Paris
25 July 49

Well,

Remembering many months ago, saying something about the dust settling: it doesn't. There are frying pans and fires. The desert of St Anthony or evenings with Sardanapolis, all punctured by the laundry question. A man gets tired sometimes.

Just this morning, I put on a hat, since I was going after a job as a contact man. Now I don't know what a contact man is, but it sounded to me like somebody with a hat. It turned out he needed more. Or less. Less, perhaps, since it pays a 2$ commission for every many days foolish work. I decided not to be a contact man. There are all the thousands of Americans here looking for work; and re-engaging oneself in the competitive society is a caution. And with all its pleasance, Paris more often becomes a hot city, with the city's beauties: wrong-telephone numbers, buses missed, &c.

I know this sounds more daily like a crazy game I am playing; and the more confirmative of opinions such as those of Mr GSB et allia. And honestly, how I wish I could sit down and write you a long letter of the sort I have written; but this is not the climate, not a Spanish monastery. Just, so far, a habitat of loose ends, among them at present mr Emmart, mr Winebaum, myself, Margaret, &c. Jacob the only sensible one, having gone to the less expensive and cooler country.

What are questions I must answer? First many thanks for the promised extra this month. It will save a life or two. Then thanks for the Heggen news-clip, Snow's marriage, and news of Chas Hall (who, if he was in cantankerous spirit, just as well I guess we all didn't encounter, I do hope, for your sake, he is over it when he gets back). [...]

I don't know; there is so much in my mind now that I can't set it down on letter paper; but thanks always for being so good about these recent and far-between wild-eyed notes. Margaret continues to be the loveliest lady on the continent. Happy happy happy pair; none but the brave, none but the brave, none but the brave deserve the fair.

with all love,
W

St Anthony: Egyptian monk (251–356) who spent most of his life in self-imposed isolation.

Sardanapolis: i.e., Sardanapalus (7th cent. BCE?), the semilegendary last king of Assyria, evocative of riotous living.

contact man: someone who provides a link for information or representation between two groups.

Mr GSB: mentioned in 19 January 1948 letter.

Heggen news-clip: on the suicide of Tom Heggen (1918–49), author of the popular novel *Mister Roberts* (1946). He and WG fought over Helen Parker in 1946; see John Leggett's *Ross and Tom: Two American Tragedies* (Simon & Schuster, 1974), 330–34, an incident that displays WG's belligerent side.

Happy happy [...] deserve the fair: from Dryden's poem "Alexander's Feast" (1697).

To Edith Gaddis

Paris
14 september 49

dear Mother.

First things first. sic, the Loan, & Mr Haygood. I didn't mean, as I fear you interpreted, that I was trying to squeeze something out of Bill Haygood in the way of a private penny. No. I meant that the United States (hats off!) aid loan to Spain didn't go through. If it had, I was hoping to be able to manage something in the way of a job in Madrid, where I'd very much like to live, work, think, marry, drink, what-have-you. The loan didn't go through. That is because Spain is Fascist, but Italy, Germany, and Greece are not. That is because a lot of things. I shan't start political opinions here. Oh dear no. Suffice to say it is very difficult to get a job in Europe unless you have a permit, which is impossible to get—unless you work for a US gov't agency. So... nothing in Spain. Paris? well... I have spent the morning writing two radio scripts, one about soybeans and one about a mechanical brain, later I'm going to write one on cosmic rays, to try to sell to a US CULTURAL agency here (UNESCO) (...for heaven's sake don't tell my mother... She thinks I'm playing the piano in a whore-house......) I don't know how it will come out, but with the present prospect of plans &c work is necessary. (No, don't mention this radio-script business; I'll tell you if it works out, or becomes mentionable).

What I should say, is that (1) I got the regular remittance (2) I also got a pair of shoes. They are French, I don't dare wear them in the rain and it's raining today so I've not gone out, they cost about 10$ even so I believe they're made of paper, but nice paper...

You will certainly hear of any developments. The one in prospect now involves that perennial miasma, the notion of marriage. For that I think more than enough money to outfit a Left-bank Bohemian set-up is called for—I've pretty well got over the idea that not-enough-to-eat and being bitten at night is Romantic. —Hence my passing interest in Soybeans and Mechanical Brains. Of course this isn't a new idea, as you must know, though I guess the first time I've managed to mention it in a letter. No; it's really that I want to get some kind of working in line before I actually try to marry this Miss Margaret, who feels rather the same way. This talk could go on for pages without saying more. But meanwhile, how welcome the remittance, & the extras! Hotel & apartment life here is hard to get & expensive, now looking for some sort of an apartment because it's a nicer & better life, one can eat better cooking in, & cheaper, and also get some work done—which I haven't in some time.

When you say things for you have been 'hectic', I trust you mean happily so? That's the way I usually see you being hectic. What do you mean. Dinners at the Versailles & Passy? Or the water-line between the pink house & the studio exploding? Oh dear.

Things are hectic here. I think we all ought to enter Trappist monasteries.

with all love,

W

---

radio scripts [...] (UNESCO): a month later, WG described to Edith other scripts he wrote for UNESCO: "I've just finished getting together a brief compendium on African illiterates. Did you know that ¾ of the world's illiterate? Maybe's there's hope. If the world's inte[r]ested, I may get another 40$ This afternoon I did another, on cave-man art, the idea being that man has an art consciousness and has to 'express himself'. Even cave men. Oh dear" (11 October 1949). A few days later, he reported: "I think UNESCO's just bought 40$ 'worth' of drivel on the Cave-man As Artist. I'm bringing Kulture to Paris —indeed." ($40 = $500 today.)

don't tell my mother: cf. the old self-deprecating advertising joke: "Don't tell my mother I work in an advertising agency—she thinks I play piano in a whorehouse."

the Versailles & Passy: French restaurants in Manhattan.

To I. W. Way

[Siena, Italy]
[29 December 1949]

Dear Granga—I hope you and mother have had as wonderful a holiday as we have. Your gift helped make possible a splendid trip to northern Italy in a friend's car, and though a very brief trip it's most exciting and rewarding, and cities like Sienna beautiful. I hope the Christmas envelop I sent got to you in time, and that Florida is as nice as you had hoped it would be.

with love,

Bill

To Edith Gaddis

[*By March 1950 WG was living at 24 rue de la Chausée d'Antin (ninth arrondissement), still unemployed, and still involved with Margaret Williams, though she left for Florence in mid-May. Few letters by WG survive from the first half of 1950, mostly concerning a trip Mrs. Gaddis made to France in April, and a short visit they both made to London. In a letter to her postmarked 27 May 1950, WG requested a copy of a new book entitled* Friar Felix at Large, *an account by medievalist H. F. M. Prescott of a pilgrimage by Friar Felix Fabri to the Holy Land in the 1480s. Many of the letters that follow concern an essay on the player piano WG wrote in 1946–47 entitled "You're a Dog-gone Daisy Girl—*

Presto" intended for the New Yorker, *which rejected it; an excerpt was published as "'Stop Player. Joke No. 4'" in the July 1951 issue of the* Atlantic Monthly *(rpt. in RSP 2–5).*]

Paris
Monday, 29 May 1950

dear Mother.

I've been thinking about that piece I wrote on the Player Piano. It's in Massapequa, and I'd like to have it again to go over and see whether, three years later, I'm sufficiently improved to make a saleable piece of it. I'd appreciate it if you could send it over, the quickest way possible. You may have difficulty, since it's probably together with many other papers and notes, and all I want is the one finished copy (should run about 16 pages, if there are two, both looking finished but one longer please send the long one, 18 pages possibly). If there's doubt about it when you look, better to write me with questions before sending anything. And if, in going through my papers there, you come across a picture of the Duke of Windsor in a sporty jacket, could you send it too? It's the picture of the jacket I want.

Paris continues to witness my battles with Unesco and the ECA, though I trust that within 3 weeks—before Margaret returns—I'll have figured out whether it will be worthwhile spending the summer here or not.

And Massapequa? How often I think of it, and would love to spend a part of the summer in that large cool room, that seems to me to have so many of my thoughts waiting for me in the high corners and the dark and heavy woodwork.

I hope you've started going swimming, and that the weather is as good there as here. It must be strange and sad to have no summer vacation to look forward to, but then, it [her European trip] was worth it wasn't it?

with love,
W.

ECA: the Bureau of Educational and Cultural Affairs, a US government agency.

To Edith Gaddis

Forte-dei-Marmi, Italy
24 june 1950

dear Mother

Finally, after what seems a great long time—and it is really—I write you sitting at a table near the sea, my skin red and smarting from the sun which I've been out in most of the day.

I think I've done about what you did in the spring—just a sudden blow-up, and leaving the city which everyone else considers the most wonderful place to be, but which—in my case—was driving me insane, after a year of nothing but that "work" I'd been doing, and a couple of "vacations" which were pretty hectic in themselves. Certainly there is nothing in the world like the beach and the sun, and thank God it is as good and resting as I'd remembered. My trip was quite as unsound financially as could be, too, and has cost more than I'd thought it would, as these things always do. And I left Paris having done some work, but can not tell when it will pay, and will probably return as broke as I've ever been, and not with money waiting there for me as I'd planned. But even so, I'm glad I did it. I had really become quite unhealthy, not sleeping &c., and the same tiresome problems over and over again—with all the city frustrations of Paris life, Barney, and getting so I never wanted to see the inside of that "apartment" again. I got to Florence to find Margaret in an almost similar state of exhaustion, and I think that, together with a case of something almost like influenza she was developing, another week of it, and the train back to Paris, would have been too much—since she'd made such a small salary at the conference she'd had to spend it all simply to live. I had no intention, when I sent to the bank in New York for 100$, that I'd use it this way. But suddenly I had it, and thank heavens I did come down. It is maddening to think that my great savings account in New York is being cut down so, but when I know what condition I was in a week ago I know it's worth it, even though I expect to return to Paris with 5$, and difficult because Unesco now only pays when they *use* a piece, not when they accept it, as before.

Mainly though I want to tell you about plans that Margaret and I are trying to make. You will see why I say *trying*, because they depend on so many things. She feels she must go home and see her family and talk with them before marrying, and since it's so important to her I guess it's the best thing. And so she hopes to come back to the United States in August. I shall stay in France, trying again to work and put some money aside, and then in September go to England. We would meet there, she sailing in September for England, and we would get married in London toward the end of September, then come back to Paris together. If there is a job in Paris, for which I'll be looking this summer, we'd stay here. And if not, go away for 6 or 8 months, live on the rent money while I went back to my writing, which I haven't had opportunity to touch for just a year now.

Well. You can see how many things may not work out. First it may not be possible for Margaret to get a boat back to New York in August, with so much tourist travel, and that would throw things off quite badly. Then, heaven knows how much money I'll have by September, whether enough to manage the marriage and all that goes with it in London—though they make it so expensive for foreigners in France, and Spain and Italy are firmly Catholic, that St-Martins-in-the-Fields sounds quite sensible, if possible. In light of all this, my trip to Italy hasn't been very sensible really—but on the score of physical and mental health I believe it has.

That is quite a plan for us—but anyhow, at last, and for the first time, we *do* have a plan, a definite one which we must try to work out. Of course I should love to come home with Margaret—I'd love a month in Massapequa late this summer, but it seems too impractical—much more sensible for me to stay in France and try to prepare things, especially in the way of money. But I do hope she can go back in August, see her family, and visit you in Massapequa—how wonderful that would be. And then return to find me with things arranged for our marriage. So much depends on the possibilities of getting a boat ticket that I don't dare really plan on all this. But you see how it stands now, and I know you'll be glad to feel that we finally are trying to make definite plans, and not just bumbling along, year after year.

The coast of Italy is beautiful, with a long beach and the mountains rising up behind the town. And the Italian people, the whole Mediterranean way of life, so humanly good, warm and kind after the Parisian French. I'll be back in Paris in about a week, but right now am simply eating 3 good meals a day, getting the sun and sleeping. I've thought of you often, these days of the beach ahead of me, and hope you are enjoying the same wonderful things there.

I hope you can read all of this—pardon the abominable ball-point pen, it's all I have with me.

Love,
Bill

St Martins-in-the-Fields: popular church in London's Trafalgar Square.

To Edith Gaddis

Paris
6 july 1950

dear Mother,

Finally back in Paris, where, as in all the grand cities, little has changed. Now of course feeling the unwiseness of the Italian junket, though on the other hand it was wise, health being considered, and now restored, I believe. At any rate, I do have some colour in my face, unlike a good year past.

Of course we're running into all the complications I'd thought of, and a few more. Margaret is having all the customary difficulty getting a passage, and we don't at all know yet whether it will be managable. I can imagine not, though she still hopes on it. Of course I came back to Paris to find not only

WG and Margaret Williams in Paris, July 1950.

no payments through for work done, but also the fact that since their Florence conference Unesco is drastically cutting down on outside contract work; and there are quite absolutely no jobs to be had there now. I don't know, I really don't know. But whatever plans are managed, I'll need money, of course. And so enclose these two checks (I wrote 100 and 200 dollars because I thought 300 might be too much for a single special-account check). Could you withdraw the money, and send me as quickly as possible 300$, a draft of some sort, care of American Express? It might be easiest to do it all through American Express there in New York. I'd thought of asking you to wire it, but think that would probably be too expensive. As I said in my other letter, I'd hoped to spend the rest of the summer here in France working and at least managing to earn enough to live on while the other [bank account] waited and grew in New York, and Margaret got there and back. But of course it is collapsing. And just to complicate everything, I've been offered an apartment here in Paris which I had briefly last summer, it's a small house really, two stories, though only two rooms, with a large kitchen, bath &c., and exactly the place I'd choose and want if I should live in Paris, especially with a job, and especially if married. But the rent is 50$ a month, which seems very foolish right now, with everything else in prospect. But Paris is like enough to NewYork in the renting business, impossible to find a place, and you must take them when you see them. I couldn't at all afford it without work, and no work seems to be forthcoming anywhere. And also with the prospect I mentioned earlier, of going to Spain to live and work on writing for a while, a fairly long while, in the fall if there's nothing here in the way of work, —you can see the complications. Sometimes it looks as though just putting everything into one bag that would fit and going back to Spain would be the easiest and by far the most sensible thing. But too late now for such vagabonding notions. I've thought of going to Spain, where I could live very cheaply, and waiting there until Margaret gets back (if she goes), and she joining me there. But there's that fine apartment here in Paris. And we couldn't get married in Spain, being infidels. Well. I'll let you know as anything comes up definite. [...]

with love,
W.

To Edith Gaddis

Barcelona, Spain
29 july 1950

dear Mother,

Certainly about the hottest place I've been in many a bachelor year, air almost impossible to breathe, just the weight of it. But Barcelona is a fine city:

I believe a port is necessary to make a city fine, why Barcelona and New York and London have style, and Paris and Madrid begin to bore (me at any rate). Going to Madrid was a waste of time I suppose; but there we were in a yellow MG, and once you've started off in one direction down here you can't very well change, or roads suddenly turn into foot-paths.

It was marvelous to find your letters waiting here yesterday when I came up from Madrid—I'd spent about four days there, saw Haygood who asked about John, was delighted to hear that John [Woodburn] is respected member of respectable firm, Haygood I don't think is awfully pleased with his Madrid life, even asked me what I thought of his going to Paris for an opening in Unesco's library there; I warned wildly against that. I watched Wheatland buy 80$ worth of shirts (he's the boy I drove down with), put him on his way back to Paris after showing him a bullfight, the old square and the national palace and similar small junk Madrid has to offer (though I don't call the Prado so), and came on here.

Of your three letters of course the third was the exciting one, starting off with, —Margaret called me five minutes ago... Lord, how far away from it I feel here; and I suppose I envy you all some of these next weeks you're going to pass together. Is it a strong mark in my disfavour, that I'm not on the spot asking mother for daughter's hand? I suppose; but I really couldn't see any better way to manage it. If I'd come certainly we'd have a grand summer together; but in September there we'd be, Margaret and I trying to raise the fare to cross the sea again, ending up postponing the marriage and finally managing it two years hence in a little church around (some) corner. Some Massapequa corner, —with the baby preacher, and George Wiebel drinking too much cider. I still favour this London notion; but had a letter from Margaret, written on shipboard in full discomfort saying she didn't want to make another ocean voyage for some time. Well *I'm* not going to make one. So you must encourage her return, put her in a box if you have to. [...]

What I'd hoped might be managed—and Margaret and I talked [about] this briefly, she's enchanted by the idea—is that I get to London a fortnight before her return, she come there, we manage a most modest wedding (with possibly one or two guest-witnesses, if they're there, and required), and then go to Scotland or to Wales for a week or two before returning to Paris or where-ever to take up again with the dastardly currents of making a living. Doesn't that sound reasonable? I think it sounds magnificent, even possible. What will follow heaven knows. Unesco in Paris looks ready to collapse. Perhaps writing, somewhere like Mallorca. Or even—in Madrid I met the head of the AP office there, very nice old fellow of about 60, who wants to write a book about Spain, a sort of anecdotal history, but his English isn't very good. We sat over coñacs in his living-room one morning while he talked about it, I suddenly realised he was proposing collaboration. I said I'd write John about such a thing, certainly there are few or no good books on Spain now, current ones mostly written by American newsmen with some bone to pick, or some emotional unbalance to air. Well...

Tonight I plan to get on the small boat that runs over to Mallorca, and see there whether I can find a modest place to sit down and work until called back (though I think I mayn't get as much work done as I'd hoped, the time and money short, the uncertainty, and mostly preöccupation over the wedding plans, because I so want them to work out right, —to tell the truth I never thought any wedding, even mine, would be so important.) But of course I've made another mistake; I'd thought Mallorca, or the coast here would be so hot nobody but myself would be fool enough to go. Now it turns up that this is the 'season', crowded, prices up, &c. dear heaven, all I want is a large quiet room to work in. I'm going over deck-passage, since cabins on the boat are too dear; I saw the mob buying tickets this morning, hundreds, all to sit out on the open deck of a small boat leaving this evening until 7am tomorrow. That's the way the Spanish like to do things, it's no fun unless 30 people are sitting in your lap, eating and tending babies. [...]

with love,
W.

Wheatland: Richard Wheatland II (1923–2009), Harvard class of '45, from a wealthy Bangor, Maine, family. He was in Paris helping to administer the Marshall Plan. George Wiebel: unidentified, perhaps the same mentioned in 24 May 49.

To Edith Gaddis

Hotel Condal
Palamós, Gerona
Spain
9 August 1950

dear Mother,

I'm really sorry I haven't written you in a good week now; but I really thought you'd be seeing Margaret extensively and soon, and that you could exchange notes, since I've written to her at length trying to make 'plans'.

Well; two letters from Margaret have made that word plan sound rather silly. But I must say first, again, how fortunate I am in both of you. What she is going through is a hideous difficulty on every hand, financially, psychologically, and the sense of time passing, but she is magnificent about it. And you. I suppose I've known this, but not until recently appreciated it so fully.

And to have her letter saying this to me, —I just don't know anything, what to say to you, what to say to your mother! I have been so touched by all that your mother says and does and her attitude . . . I do love her so much already, can you know that? I do honestly. And think she is magnificent and how lucky you are, and thus I, and how exciting it is to have her adored so quickly and genuinely by everybody like Jacob and Kathleen and Emmy (the last two talk and rave about her all the time). Possibly I shouldn't write all this to you, but I want you to know it, and that I do more all the time appreciate you in the widest senses.

Margaret's mother (and this must make it all the more difficult for her) is in very bad condition, 'would be having a nervous breakdown if there were money for it', and she is right now only concerned for that problem. You may imagine the shock to me, after the letters I've written you and her, all these plans for returning to Paris, London, Wales &c., to have a letter from her saying she believes she must get a job. And so right now I'm trying to figure out what best the next step may be, exchanging lengthy correspondence with her about it though she can say nothing really. I'm certainly going to stay here until the beginning of September. Then I can't tell. I can't tell whether it would be a good thing for me to come back there and find a job, and work at it until Margaret can work her problem out. I know this sounds strange, it's the oldest part of the whole thing this business of not wanting to get into the New York race again, and really it's the last thing I'd want to do. But I cannot have Margaret facing all of this alone. My other possibilities are staying abroad and if possible a job, perhaps in Paris, where I could be prepared fully to marry her when she was free of this present trouble. Or again, what sounds the most cowardly perhaps, to stay here in Spain throughout the winter and finish my work and return with it. I don't know; But I can't despair of it all, because of both of you being what you are I know we can work it out. [...]

I'm in good spirits just at the moment because my work is going well, slowly as I knew it would but I think well. It will go well for about six more days, then it won't. But perhaps you can understand, the best part of it has been coming back to it, after a year of not touching it but worrying about it, to find that upon returning to it that it does retain its life for me, and still asks to be finished.

This is the ideal place for it: a small fishing town on the coast north of Barcelona, with an excellent beach where the sun blazes at noon but the place is not hot, quite cool now at evening. I'm in a hotel with a small room, though the window is large which is most important, and eating well, working until 11:30 when I go down to the beach, then lunch and work again in the afternoon. [...]

How I hope you are well (Margaret says you're looking splendid, better than she's ever seen you, I'm so happy to hear that). I'm sorry that so much of this must fall upon you, and say again how much I appreciate you in it. But do not let it interfere with your summer, which I hope so is a good one. One way or another, perhaps we'll share next summer there in Massapequa, the more I think of it the more I want to and look forward to doing so. But at the moment it's ten pm, time for dinner here in this country.

with my love,
W.

Kathleen and Emmy: perhaps Kathleen Costello, mentioned later (10 october, 1950) and pictured on p. 227. Emmy is also mentioned later (15 january 1951) but is unidentified.

To Edith Gaddis

Palamós, Gerona
15 August 1950

dear Mother,

Many thanks for your letter, which I had Saturday, but went in to Barcelona Sunday, came back Monday night, Tuesday a holiday. I suppose funniest in this whole thing really is the round of letters we are exchanging, you & I & Margaret: you writing me not to be angry, disappointed; I writing you not to be disappointed if she can't visit Massapequa immediately, and saying I hope she can see and talk with you honestly & freely, you writing me and saying how glad you are that she can talk with you honestly & freely, she writing me that she hopes it's all right if she talks with you openly when I've just written her that I hope she will . . . well, with such support on all sides we should come through. Heaven knows I appreciate what she's going through, I'll wait until I'm green; but feel a bit guilty over not being there to help her; though could I if I were? Certainly the three of us could have been fun together; but how often? No for the moment I think better I sit patiently (if you can imagine that) and work. Now, as her recent letters show no sign of return soon, I may stay in Spain and try to make the best of my time alone; I think my work's going well, but how can one tell with only one's self to judge? I don't know. If I can arrange something through Barney, a perilous undertaking, to make sure of the rooms at palais d'Antin, I'll hope not to have to waste the time, money & energy going to Paris until I do know that Margaret's coming. (Though 'taking it philosophically' as you say, I can see it stretching out to Christmas. Christmas indeed! Well, it better be done up by Christmas.)

Incidentally please don't ever say to me again, Maybe it's a test. About anything.

One thing I can lift from your mind. If we come to Spain everything happens, we find treasures sought after in other lives, other worlds, though perhaps a little late. [...] I've so hoped to have a letter soon saying that Margaret had come, or was coming to Massapequa; I know she wants to, & you want to; I just want her to too. (And while she's there you might give her *Stella Blandish* to read. That should fix her.)

I hardly know what to say about war; certainly it's more talked of there than here, though Spanish papers follow it well enough; all I miss is the constant chatter, hair-brained opinion and free-flying rumour thank God. But I do believe that there's not an immediate danger; just as I most firmly believe that the whole thing will happen before 1954. But whatever, I have the modern so-little-time neurosis, and want to settle things with Margaret as soon as we can.

Her letters are splendid; only make me troubled that I can't flatly *do* anything to ease things for her. And please let me assure you both that I'm not angry, bitter, disappointed, no prospect of cave-man foolishness; mostly I'm overcome by both you and she, how splendid you both are and how fortunate I.

For the moment I guess the most maddening thing is being here alone, when it would be so marvelous with her. But I'm getting work done: Lord, how slow it is with me. And the constant feelings of pleasure at it going well, disgust and depression when I read it and it looks ridiculous, pretentious, sophomoric, imitative, what-have-you. But—from the look of things—I should know by the time I see Margaret again, and the prospect of competitive living appears again, whether it is all worth it, worth finishing. I don't know, she mentions her sister and brother-in-law's life, he commuting, they seeing one another for about 3hours a day, both exhausted. Then he plays Golf on Saturdays. And it's strange and all wrong to read of such a life here in Spain, anywhere in South Europe really, the Mediterranean countries, where life is such a thoroughly family affair (How to win friends and influence people, how to be a chinaman like Lin Yutang and make a lot of money...), even though people are poor. In the north of Spain, here in Catalonia, they don't drink much, they work hard but there is constantly, as one finds among poor (by American standards) people, this great quality of together-ness, a kind of trust forced upon them, so that they must trust each other, which with pots of money you don't need to do; and apparently can't do if you want pots of money. (For Heaven's sake, don't mis-read political implications into what I go on about here. It's only what I see around me, the kindness I have shown me by these people; and contrasting, memories of such things as your purse-snatching incident on the NY subway, which I'll never forget.)

Well again, how I wish we were all three here, what fun we should have simply walking down to the harbour tonight, through this village. Though

I'm not sure you'd bear with the food; for lunch I had five small octupi (squids?), the ink-sacs were fine. The tentacles a little disconcerting.

with my love,

W.

---

palais d'Antin: WG's Paris residence in the rue de la Chaussée d'Antin.

Stella Blandish: i.e., *Serena Blandish; or, The Difficulty of Getting Married* (1924) by Enid Bagnold (published pseudonymously by "A Lady of Quality"), about a promiscuous young socialite who is tricked into marrying a mestizo charlatan.

war: the Korean War, which began on 25 June 1950 when North Korean forces invaded South Korea. Two days later, President Truman commanded US air and sea forces to go to South Korea to help defend it from China-backed North Korea, and there were fears that the conflict would escalate into another world war.

(How to win friends [...] money): quoting Connolly again (see note to 28 April 1948). Dale Carnegie's self-help book *How to Win Friends and Influence People* (1936) is critiqued in *R* (498–503).

To John and Pauline Napper

[John Napper (1916–2001) married his second wife Pauline Davidson in 1945. He was a popular society portrait painter before expanding his palette to expressionistic oils, vivid watercolors, and book illustrations. (He did the cover and illustrations for John Gardner's 1972 novel The Sunlight Dialogues *while staying with WG in Piermont, NY.) The Nappers met WG in the summer of 1950 on the beach at Palamós; as Pauline Napper later told Crystal Alberts, the beach was almost deserted except for "a solitary figure, a man sitting surrounded by sheets of writing paper which kept shifting in the slight wind and which he was desperately trying to hold down." When John walked over to help, he "asked him if he was English and Willie replied rather abruptly 'No, I am American and I am working!'" Later WG came over to "apologize for his abruptness and suggested [they] meet for a drink later at a café by the harbour" ("Mapping William Gaddis," 173n55). They became lifelong friends.]*

a/c Consulado de los EE. UU.
Junqueras, 18, Barcelona, Spain
7 September 1950

dear John and Pauline,

—menaced by monsters, fancy lights, Risking enchantment...We had some balloons over Palamos, causing great excitement among the natives—and I by now unkempt enough to be a member of the local unwashed—we all ran out into the streets, dogs and children, to the point about the lighthouse, where these balloons, three of them, rose higher over the hot evening air above land, then came down in the sea, two did, the other carried a little light in its basket, it just went right on up. And that blazing sky, useless to try to describe it. Do you know that point of land? its view covers the whole harbour and then around to east (to the left). I suppose they were meteorological balloons, but we here prefer any pagan to scientific explanation.

Aside from that, nothing has happened. Nothing.

Except newspapers you know get in, and with them the idiotic haruspicating and scrying going on in My country, warwards. How can grown-up men make such fools of themselves? But on *every* level. It seems that nothing else draws nearer. Margaret, heaven knows, does not. Perhaps it's better, a bonnie over the ocean than one under-foot, wanting to dinner at Fouquets, a drink at the Crillon, tea at Claridges? I don't know. All I know right now is that things reached such a pass this morning, in the way of trying to straighten out characters, incidents, situations, interviews, and one suicide (but she a very old woman), that I wrote every one on a bit of paper, and have spent the afternoon sitting like a simple child making a village of confetti, trying to arrange them in order that will satisfy Aristotle's theory of dramatic unity, William James's of pragmatism, the Boston Watch & Ward Society, for Morals, the Catholic Index, the publisher's for Something New, the reader's prolepsis and my analepsis. Some must suffer. Boston and the Index first. Then Aristotle. I sometimes even imagine cutting it down to myself and the reader. At any rate, it goes on, between balloons.

I hope you both found the rest here to send you back heavily to work there. But how long does that lust last? I feel like I was born here, by this time; it seems as though I've spent my life at this machine, at this window, and staring across at the old man they put out on a balcony in the afternoon with a piece of bread, and take him in at night. Some times the hand shakes, and the words (slipping, sliding, perishing) will not stay in place, and I mightily wish you were here for a coffee, or a glass at Boodles'. You did leave quite a vacuum on your departure, and I find myself again talking with myself, getting the same vacant variety of answers. Lord, to be a real, legitimate member of a myth, a screaming Catholic, an Albigensian, a Stuart or Hanover or John D Rockefeller, instead of sitting in one damn hall bedroom after another trying to manufacture one. Though I suppose the rewards are greater when you do finish. Do you finish? I just go on accumulating. (I like a title of a book I've never read by Tomlinson, *Old Junk*).

But now I find I'm owed 30,000francs in Paris, and temptation rises to go there and cut a figure of mean disaster for a few days, then return, be tatooed, and enter the Franciscan orders. Your mill pond looks like it would be rousing cold in winter, and my blood is as thin as sewing-machine oil by now. But how I look forward to stopping there to see you. I've so many reasons for wanting to come to London, all good, all self-indulgent, Edwardian enough, they include books and tailors. But I must wait for the Trollop reason (and *no* pun intended here), the summons to the church, the walk hand-in-hand in the heather, . . . tea at Claridges. I don't like Paris, but may have to go up briefly in October, then return here if there's no summons to Southampton, and just go right on hoping for the wrong things and praying for the wrong things until the Balloon goes up. Meanwhile I'll write of any change of scene; thanks again for your patient listening and words here, I needed them so much more than I realised, and I'm excited about seeing you again and enlarging on them, asking the questions which have grown from those answers.

All my best wishes to you both,

W. Gaddis

---

menaced by monsters [...] Risking enchantment: as noted earlier, from section 2 of Eliot's "East Coker."

haruspicating and scrying: from part 5 ("haruspicate or scry") of Eliot's "Dry Salvages."

a bonnie over the ocean: from the old Scots folk song "My Bonnie Lies over the Ocean."

William James: American philosopher (1842–1910), author of *Pragmatism* (1907) among other works.

Boston Watch & Ward Society: an organization devoted to censorship, branding objectionable books "Banned in Boston." Its influence had waned by 1950.

prolepsis and my analepsis: technical literary terms for foreshadowing and flashback.

words (slipping, sliding, perishing): from section 5 of Eliot's "Burnt Norton": "Words strain, / Crack and sometimes break, under the burden, / Under the tension, slip, slide, perish, / Decay with imprecision, will not stay in place, / Will not stay still."

Boodles': Boodle's, a London gentlemen's club.

Albigensian: member of a medieval heretical sect.

John D Rockefeller: American oil magnate (1839–1937).

Tomlinson, *Old Junk*: a 1918 collection of "stories of travel and chance" by English writer H. M. Tomlinson (1873–1958).

Trollop: Anthony Trollope (1815–82), English novelist.

the Balloon goes up: an old phrase meaning a clarifying signal.

To Edith Gaddis

Palamós, Gerona
21 september 1950

dear Mother,

Having just had a going over by mail with Margaret, who hadn't written in some time, I realise it's some time since I've written you. And have had two letters, each containing things I have to thank you for—the books, the prospect of them and of 20$ (and 80 in Paris?)

I don't know whether opportunity will present itself, but I would like to have the address of that boy Christie knew in Paris, if I'm going to be there for more than a few days I'd like to look him up, like to know at least *one* nice French person. A recent letter from the English painter I met here renews his invitation for me to visit them there. And so I've been thinking I well may go on to England in mid-October, after 5 or 6 days in Paris, and possibly stay there for a month or two. I liked it so much when we were there, but that was such a brief introduction. And two months in London would be very well-spent I believe. —Also to have my *teeth* looked at and worked on—I ought to go for that alone.

And all of this of course if nothing comes of these faint possibilities for a job, which I hope to investigate in Paris, and might end up returning to Madrid on that hope.

It's quite suddenly become fall here, with the north wind which they say makes Palamós very cold in winter. I can imagine that Massapequa is about over for another summer. Well the more I think about it the more I think I'll be there next summer—unless I've got a raving job in Spain, unless Margaret, unless Stalin and General MacArthur—but I should get there to paint the white outside woodwork. And by then I should have this "novel" in shape, too. Well heaven knows. At any rate, while things hang in the air I want to spend some time in London. Unesco has conceeded that they owe me about ½ what I'd expected (having left 7 pieces with them, they're paying me now for 3)—which will be some good in Paris anyhow. Heaven knows how other things will be there. [...]

Love,
W.

To Edith Gaddis

Palamós
[22? September 1950]

dear Mother,

Just a note, of change of plans. I've just had a letter from Juancho, who's coming to Madrid for some sort of international intellectual congress, writes me to ask me to come to Madrid, saying not to worry about money, that he thinks I can be his guest, or the guest of Panama, or guest of the Society of Spanish-American Culture, or something. So I'm going.

First (now) going to Mallorca, see if I can see Robert Graves (who wrote that book *The White Goddess* which you sent me in Sevilla last year remember?) Will be in Barcelona the 28th, and pick up any mail at the consulate there for me; after that everything to Paris American Express. I hope the 20$ is there by the 28th but if not I've enough to get to Madrid, and can repay Juancho in Paris.

May sound like a real wild-goose chase, probably will be; but I might be able to see someone in Madrid about a job possibility. And I was about ready for a wild goose chase anyhow after two months of this country life.

Will write you better from Mallorca in a day or two. I think I'll stay in Madrid from 3 to 10 days, probably about 5 days, depending on how Juancho feels about it when I actually do take him up on his offer. Many thanks for your letters; I'd expected to answer you more fully, but this has been an overnight decision.

W.

To John Napper

Deya, Mallorca
27 September 1950

dear John,

As I said, becoming less enamoured of Spain. All resulted from trying to do something in a hurry, which you cannot *do* in Spain. But a friend on his way to Madrid wrote to ask me to come there for a few days, so I set out,

Robert Graves in the 1940s. WG later wrote "he was to become somewhat the physical model for Rev Gwyon" (23 July 1982). Photo from the jacket of *The White Goddess* (Farrar Straus and Cudahy, 1948).

abandoned Palamós, got to Barcelona, arranged everything—then could not buy a train ticket for Madrid a *week* in advance. Left in *fury*, vowing never to speak to another Spaniard, never to say a nice thing about Spain again.

So here I am in the smallest room in the smallest town on this small island, getting by until my escape ticket to Paris matures, on 35 pesetas a day. [...] I am going to Paris on the 4th, will be there the 5th, just a week from today. I plan to stay there for a week or 10 days—then, I don't know. I'm firmly considering life in London for a couple of months, and I'd certainly like to see you about that. Spain has done its work for the moment.

In Paris I suppose I shall stay at my hideous old home, 24 rue de la Chaussée d'Antin (about 2 blocks from the Opera), the 5th floor, and to the right inside a small hallway. Though if not there, since heaven knows what disasters may have occurred in the last 2 months, could you leave a note for me at the American Express, 11 rue Scribe (also near Opera). I do look forward to seeing you in Paris, and you *must* look up that address.

I've found Robert Graves, who proves to be extremely pleasant, though a very nervous man, especially when one gets on a topic which interests him, so that I find it difficult to talk with him about White Goddesses, Recognitions, crucifixions, incarnations, saints, what-have-you—easier to go swimming, though I haven't seen a real (Palamós) beach on Mallorca, all sheer drops to the sea, and small openings where you can descend to the water. Thank God I found Palamós—Palma is still full of French, Dutch, Belgian &c.—all with bare knees, rucksacks, automobiles, ghastly women, motorcycles, buying postcards, castanets, junk junk junk. Enough.

Deya is quite the other extreme. It is all rocks. Everything is rocks. There is one indoor café, with a billiard table, and nothing else but goats and sheep with bells on them, also one rooster, and this morning I saw a snail. Otherwise, it is fairly quiet.

I'm afraid I'm getting in a mood for Paris. *Will* you be there?

All best wishes to you both,
W. Gaddis

Recognitions: probably a reference to the Clementine *Recognitions*: see 23 November 1953. In early 1955 Graves would write a blurb for the forthcoming *R* "after spending a couple of hours sampling the book," but it wasn't used until the 1962 reprint of *R*. For the blurb and Graves's further remarks on the novel, see Joseph Tabbi, *Nobody Grew but the Business: On the Life and Work of William Gaddis* (Evanston: Northwestern University Press, 2015), 229n3.

To Edith Gaddis

24, rue de la Chaussée d'Antin
Paris IXe
10 october, 1950

dear Mother,

I'm sorry the troubled mind I've given you, again, over my where-abouts, and the wild moment over a check for 20$. It all worked out. I got back from Barcelona, there it was with many other letters, each from a friend with some monumental disaster of his or her own. Do you think I should start out all over again, choose my friends from BBD&O? I do believe you must feel that way by now. Maybe even that I should be bbd&o too. And so, at anyrate, I got out of Spain with 5pesetas, just enough to tip a porter, and after a last meal in Barcelona (I in the restaurant, to an old woman: How much is a tortilla with potatoes (a potato omelette); she: With two eggs? 8pesetas. I: How much is it with one egg? she: 5pesetas. I: Give me a tortilla with one egg...) and got into France, arriving in Paris next morning with 11francs (4¢). Washed, dressed, up to Unesco, and I shan't describe what passed there, enough to say it was consistent with every other payment-experience in the past. But I finally did get part of what they owe me, so I'm getting on well enough here now. What will happen next I do not know.

Barney is no where in sight, so I don't know what monkey-business he has managed about this flat (there was a letter waiting from him in Barcelona wanting to borrow 20,000francs... imagine). Perhaps, of course, he has payed the rent. In case not, though, I move quietly in and out, not especially wanting an interview with the old woman (landlady) until I have one with the young man (Barney). The only relics I have of him are three disgraceful pairs of flannel trousers, one very sad pair of Chaplinesque black shoes, and every newspaper printed since I left.

This morning a wire from the English painter I met in Palamos, saying he's on his way to Paris. He will have to sleep in the sink, that's all.

Juancho proves to be great fun to see again after so long; though he has managed a moustache which goes down at its ends and gives him greatly the sad old Chinaman look. He looks much older. He says he cannot get over how well I look (having seen me only in semi-desperate circumstances with shirts held together by adhesive tape &c), so it may please you to know that I look well. To counterbalance the enclosed photo-, taken on the street in Barcelona where, as you see, I was sporting about disguised as a young gentleman. This will, anyhow, give you a picture of my New Suit. Also my new Shoes. Also my new linen waistcoat, my new stick, and someone elses old shirt. Also the Barcelona lions, which surround Columbus who is standing atop a column pointing toward New York. [...]

Don't worry about sending extra money. Don't worry about Margaret and I married next week. Of course if she does appear here this afternoon wanting to get married there won't be much to do but marry her. As everything stands though, I don't expect her. I've decided it's safest for me to make my own plans, centred about finishing a first draft of this novel before Christmas; then if Margaret suddenly comes up with some wild and immediate presentation of herself, I can, as you know, change any plans of mine with real Barney-esque alacrity. So don't worry about extra money until there's a decisive sound from that young lady. She writes many splendid letters, but I think it will take her a little while to pull herself together, marriage-wise. It might even be before Christmas. That would be remarkable. Then I would most certainly be sending a handful of wild letters, cables, wires asking for a loan. Meanwhile I read books and try to write one.

A rather pathological letter from Kathleen makes me believe that I've added one more disconcerting acquaintance to your full list. [...] Life goes on. I even had a letter from Helen Parker. She is getting older too, I do believe. [...]

with love,
W.

BBD&O: New York advertising agency founded in 1928.

To John Napper

Paris
19 October 1950

dear John.

I'm sorry to be so long answering: Paris is just what it always is, the endless round of people, wild-eyed schemes, re-encounters, disasters, new projects, conversation, adding to that future which, like the past is liable to have no destination. I've been busy since arrival drinking beer at Lipp's sidewalk terrace, re-adjusting my homestead, shaking hands, playing charades, waiting for you after your telegram and meaning to write you after your card, and trying to make my mind up about staying here or going to London until December holidays. And I've finally decided to stay here. Largely because I have this comparatively comfortable place to live, at least I'm fully familiar with it and this room is a good one to work in. Tomorrow morning I intend to open my avalanche of folders and papers and look at what I did in Palamos. Somehow I believe it won't look as good here as it did there. And settle down to finish it by the end of the year. Of course there are such passing temptations

WG in Spain: top, in
Barcelona, 1950; bottom,
in Seville, spring 1951.

as a motor trip to Tel Aviv, something about buying a car here and selling it there after a journey through Greece Yougoslavia Turkey and whatever else lies between, but I hold off such distractions, —unless someone actually appears at the door with the car...

But I still intend to get to London within the next two months, and thank you again for your renewed invitation, I shall take advantage of it certainly. When the weather gets a little colder, when your pond is frozen over. For the moment it seems most sensible for me to sit right down here and get to work. The notion of wandering around London looking for a satisfactory place to live, to work, in the worst fog season I understand, with no comprehension of pounds-shillings-pence (& guineas and florins and half-crowns) (guineas and crowns which don't exist but everyone deals in them), I imagine time and money going and gone, and I still loose in that fog with my sheaf of papers. And so as soon as these charades stop I'll sit down and work; and as soon as that drags I want to come over, and let you know well enough in advance. The trouble with this room is that I've spent so much time here being lazy that it's not like that industrious confinement in the hotel Condal, where the moment I entered about the only thing in my mind was the only piece of personal furniture in the room, this typewriter; but here there are distractions on every hand, some with corks and some with legs and voices. There are even books to read. And Charley Chaplin in *City Lights*.

Barney, who was at the University of London, is going over in a day or two, intending to finish his thesis. We'd thought we might settle down together, mutual encouragement to exemplary life of industry, but we have never set one another such examples before, and right now can do no better than charades it appears. That is what is going on in the room right now, which may explain any disjointed-ness in this note. I hope to write you a better soon, and to see you within six or eight weeks. Meanwhile let me know if there is again the chance of your coming over here, believe me, you'll be most welcome in the charades.

best wishes to you both,
W. Gaddis

---

future [...] no destination: from part 3 of Eliot's "Dry Salvages": "We cannot think [...] of a future that is not liable / Like the past, to have no destination."
Lipp's: Brasserie Lipp, in the 6th arrondissement.
City Lights: one of Chaplin's best-known films (1931).

To Edith Gaddis

Paris

29 october 1950

dear Mother,

Here I am, just a week late, thanking you for the package which arrived last Monday. I cannot tell you how glad I am to have those books, they are exactly what I've been after, though I was upset to see the figure 10 in the Legge book, and if that means what I think it does, if it refers to the price, I am sorry to have put you to such an expense (and forget the Vautier book, I think this fellow must have given me the title wrongly, I can't come across it here). And the shirts are excellent.

Otherwise everything is going quietly. Ormonde deKay, an old ex-Harvard ex-everything boy (he wrote the script for the film *Lost Boundaries* which you may have seen) is now staying in the small room here, plans to sail for NY the 10th and will certainly call you. (I'd thought you might see him for lunch, it would be nice if you both and Margaret could lunch, they know each other too). All I'm sorry about concerning Ormonde is that you didn't meet him when you were here; because I know you'd have been delighted with him, he's still a college boy, and would have off-set the other disconcerting group I did present to you. And Wheatland, I wish you'd met him (he is quite a young man & smokes cigars in his office I'm told), to show you that we haven't spent all our time with strange people. [...]

Incidentally when Dol Emmart was here, he and I talked of player pianos &c (I know you must be as tired as everyone else of hearing about that thing), he suggested I send it to someone at the *Atlantic monthly*, which I did, after re-writing it a bit. I doubt it will make anything, there seems to be too much of horrendous import (I was a communist, How Russia built the Korean army, How to get along with your wife/mother/son/father/boss, Dewey, MacArthur,) to fill these magasines, the same article being written a thousand times, for people to waste time on reading about player pianos. So I said that if they can't use it will they send it on to you. I'll write again asking you do take it another step. (Don't bother mentioning this to Margaret, since I don't think anything will come of it.)

You remember Otto Friedrich (and Priscilla) who recently went to Germany where he's working as a sport reporter for the *Stars & Stripes*. They were back here a few days ago, he's trying to start a small magasine, read what I've got done of my novel and wants to use the first chapter, which they both liked a good deal, in his first issue, early next year. I am sort of disconcerted over such a prospect but told him he could, have since written to John Woodburn asking him if such publication would make for any difficulty later on when I want to publish it as a book, if I can. [...]

> with love,
> W.

Legge book: *Forerunners and Rivals of Christianity* by Francis Legge (1915; WG owned a 1950 reprint published by Peter Smith), which provided a handful of details for *R*. ($10 = $100 today.)

Vautier book: unidentified.

Ormonde deKay: de Kay (1923–98), writer, poet, and translator. He recorded his memories of WG in a 1993 interview with Charles Monaghan, at www.williamgaddis.org/reminisce/remdekaymonaghan.shtml. De Kay was only one of the scriptwriters of *Lost Boundaries* (1949).

Dol Emmart: A. D. Emmart (1902–73), a reporter and art critic for the *Baltimore Sun*. Five years later he would vote for *R* in a few polls for the best novel of 1955.

Otto Friedrich (and Priscilla): prolific American author and journalist (1929–95), married to Priscilla Broughton. In *R*, Otto's play features a woman named Priscilla. WG quotes from Friedrich's excellent 1989 biography of Glenn Gould in *AA*. I don't believe he started the magazine WG refers to.

To Edith Gaddis

> Paris
> [early November 1950]

dear Mother,

Just a note to thank you immensely for all your trouble over the player. Of course the *Atlantic* note delighted me, and made for an extremely pleasant evening. (I'd dinner with Juancho at that Roger the Frog place, where we went you remember & it was so crowded that they carried a fainting girl out, returned for lunch next day?) So I'll hang on and wait for *Atlantic*, there's nothing could be more wonderful though I doubt that he (Morton) can get a unanimous agreement from his staff on it. If it won't do, then, could you send it to *American magasine*?

Look, Congdon never sent that thing around, I'm certain. And what the devil is he agrieved about? Really, agents agrieved over expense-account liquor at the 21, I can't take it seriously. The last thing I've written and tried to sell was the story from Madrid, which I sent him, and he didn't make any effort for. Since then I've written nothing finished. (While I think of it, I believe I tried the player at *Esquire*, Chandler was working there then.) I'll wait to hear from Congdon, we can have a correspondence. It is nice of him to tell everybody I'm good, but what the devil. I've nothing to sell now. When I finish the thing I'm trying to work on now, then there will be matter for talk. Or being agrieved. You're awfully good to be so patient in the middle of it. I do get truculent sometimes. As you know.

(Incidentally, if anyone should take the player, there's material in the last paragraph which must be checked, probably changed; v., mention of the rolls Macy's sells, & the price, which may be different; also mention of a Mr Carlton Chase, who may be dead by now, things like that.)

I didn't go to the dentist yesterday for the extraction, I was in a terrible state of exhaustion and that would have been the End. I'm going next Wednesday. Right before Thanksgiving. Lord lord. You're awfully kind about wanting to pay it. (Apparently English dentists are famous for being the most dangerous and bad in the world. All thumbs.) (Yes I do think Jean-Jacques Stoffel is a good dentist. Charming fellow.)

That's all for this moment. Oh things are in a state. Not bad. Just busy. Wheatland, who's just gone to NY for a few days, left me his yellow MG (the car we went to Madrid in), and tomorrow I hope to drive to a monastery somewhere beyond Chartres for a day of quiet, and music. I do look seedy but I'm really quite well.

with love,
W.

Atlantic note: to *consider* publishing the essay, not to accept it (which wouldn't occur until February 1951.)

Roger the Frog: Roger la Grenouille, one of the finest restaurants in Paris, and still taking reservations.

Morton: Charles W. Morton (1899–1967), an editor at (and frequent contributor to) the *Atlantic Monthly*. WG had hoped to publish his complete essay there, but had to settle for a brief excerpt.

American magasine: a general interest periodical that ran from 1906 to 1956.

the 21: the 21 Club in midtown Manhattan.

Mr Carlton Chase: unidentified, nor mentioned in the various drafts of the essay I've seen.

To Edith Gaddis

Paris
[16 November 1950]

dear Mother,

Happy birthday, finally; I'll say I'd hoped to manage something a bit jollier than the triumph of confusion which follows here; so stop reading this for a moment, relax, then get hold of yourself while I carry on.

Lord Lord where's the dollar. It isn't all that bad really, only confused. Mostly for the moment settling about Happymount, this insane asylum I'm living in, the P. d'Antin. My French improves greatly with fury. Adrenilin goes into the larynx I believe, I can shout all sorts of complicated grammatical constructions. That's the way I spent yesterday. And right in the middle of all this was Helga. Don't ask me who Helga is, she's a German girl from Bremen who was just suddenly in the middle of a charge from the light brigade upstairs, that's Mme Haefele, our protectrex and landlady. No land. No lady. Nosir. When it was all over, I'd lost the two small rooms, barricaded myself into the larger one where I sit now, atop Margaret's trunk (which is the size of Little Blacknose), Jacob's trunk, hundreds of pink coathangers, red high-heel shoes, and Renee's dressing robe, which appeared from somewhere. Also pots and pans.

What I'd planned doing was to leave here at the week's end, go to London, and leave this room with an Australian novelist; but after yesterday I don't think it would be allowed. I still may get to London, as planned. I'll let you know about that. Let's not get started with Helga. I had to take her for a sightseeing walk, and tea at the Cafe de la Paix. Right in the middle of everything. A long road that has no turning.

No; here's my most immediate concern, it's about the player piano piece. I'd hoped to hear from you by now about what John Woodburn would suggest. I wrote Morton (*Atlantic*) saying thanks, and that I hoped to try it elsewhere, that if it didn't go I'd send him the excerpt he mentioned. I wonder this: if I could sell him that, and retain reprint rights, so that if I should ever sell the whole somewhere else that passage would be included. I suddenly am afraid, that maybe I'm losing everything; that *Atlantic* will foreswear the whole thing, and no one else will take it. I'd depended on John to say where else it might be sent. But it may be best to simply send the excerpt to Charles Morton at *Atlantic*, if it could be copied out and sent separately. At least get that 75$. I'm in no position here to try to handle it I'm beginning to realise. And as far as I can see I've got no agent. Congdon wouldn't even send it around for me the first time (2½ years ago). What about him. Here I've a letter from Margaret, and she says, —Your mother is distressed about agents and legal technicalities and is not sure that you know Congdon is telling people he thinks you are terrific and is expecting something from you any day... I'm sorry to be causing you this upset. I'd hoped the player could be tried at the *American Magasine*. Otherwise, the excerpt to *Atlantic*, and a letter, which I'd have to write I suppose, asking permission for reprint rights, but not demanding them, since selling it, even that fragment, is most important.

Now about Congdon, agents &c. I'm again sorry to put this on you, but you are a business woman, and could you talk to John about it? Frankly I don't think Congdon's much good, not much good to me at any rate. I hear him highly recommended but he's not done me nor any I know any favours. I don't know what all this rubbish about him thinking I'm terrific and expecting something any day...but it sounds like NY cocktail-party editor-publisher-agent-over-drinks rubbish to me. I sent him a story from Madrid two years ago and he didn't even bother to send it around; it mayn't have been good, but it was worth sending out I believe still. Then he answered me by ordinary post instead of airmail. That may seem like a small thing, but it's memorable to me because it indicates either plain sloppiness or disregard for the client (me), and I remember it. I may write him, I suppose I should, and cut things off. I've a couple of good agents lined up here, and also, as far as a novel goes, there is John at Little, Brown, and another friend (an uncle of Ormonde deKay) at Scribners, &c. Also about Congdon, I've been seeing a boy here named Gordon Sager, two of whose novels Congdon has handled. And handled poorly as far as I can see; brought out by a small house, and Gordon says that for a year's work (the first novel) he's made 600$, or 50$ a month. Isn't this a billion-dollar country? I don't know; I'd like to talk to Congdon, squarely. I think best that within the next few days I write him, asking questions.

Sorry to go on like this, and I'm thinking as I write, so that this may not have much contuum. Let me see. Look, I'll write, now, and enclose, a covering letter to be sent with the player piano piece to the *American Magasine*, if you'll be good enough to do that, asking that they return it to you if they don't want it. Then, if you'll have copied out the excerpt (page 17: Selling the player... through line 6 page 20) and ready to send it on to Charles Morton at the *Atlantic* when the whole comes back from *American Magasine*. But if you've done anything else, I'll be glad to hear.

Whoops. Another day, another dollar. But Lord, Lord, where's the dollar. I think this is about all for the moment. I've got to go see my dentist, have the grand extraction, and pay him. If you've sent the money to London, OK because I'll either get it there or have it sent back here if I can't manage to go.

Again, I hope your birthday is (or was?) a good one—

with love,

W.

Happymount: the name of the insane asylum Rev. Gwyon is sent to (*R* 712).
Little Blacknose: the steam locomotive protagonist of an award-winning children's book by Hildegarde Swift (1929).
Renee: unidentified.
Australian novelist: Robert S. Close (1903–95); see next letter.
Gordon Sager: American novelist and short-story writer (1915–91).

To Edith Gaddis

Paris

28 November 1950

dear Mother,

Lava from Mt Etna, I understand, is flowing at the rate of 120 feet a minute; the United States Atlantic seaboard under 26 feet of water; and the Belgian coast under the heaviest fog in its history. Aside from these prodigies of nature—including a wind of 120 miles an hour on top of Mt Washington in New Hampshire (though what anyone is doing up there I haven't figured out)—we have such ingenuous contributions of human origin as the Long Island Railroad, and the little girl with the sunflower growing in her lungs. Fortunately the Pope has proclaimed the dogma of the Assumption, so I suppose there's really nothing to worry about. (They say that the bubonic plague has re-appeared in north-Africa.)

In times like these, a small person returns to his own pitifully limited means of accomplishing disaster; and the best one can accomplish is lampshades of human skin, or soap made of human bones. Recalling the crucifix at Burgos (in the north of Spain), where for many centuries it was believed that the Figure was made of human skin, though eventually someone proved it to be buffalo hide. There was also, somewhere in the annals of the entertainment world, a mermaid presented at sideshows fashioned from the upper half of a monkey and the lower end of a codfish. Bringing us back to the world of Freddie's Football Dogs, and the play *The Deserter* (presented in London in the late 19th century) entirely acted by animals.

Material, one might say, for a novel.

Speaking of novels, I've the author of something called *Love Me Sailor* settled here in the back room. He is an Australian, and if you know any Australians that's enough said. Very nice fellow. It seems his book is going to be a real Best Seller.

Thanksgiving though was very pleasant. Not turkey, but rabbit with a mustard sauce. Mathilde was ill, and husband Clements trying to go to a dinner party in a cream-coloured sports shirt; so I was asked over to keep her company, which I did, enjoyably, in just such a frame as people think a young man's life in Paris should be—the lovely lady with red hair cascading to her waist, and the small table set for two in the bedroom before a fireplace and a fire. And so I made a number of grogs, buttered rum, and the evening went on for some time, when Clements returned with a red carnation because it was his name day, St Clement. The tooth gave little bother, though its old niche is still sore.

I think the notion of sending the player to William B Hart (of the Hopalong Cassidy Harts?)(or red-Heart dogfood?) is excellent, if *Atlantic* can't use it. Of course I'm still here hoping.

HG Wells said, somewhere, —We seem to go through life waiting for something to happen, and then... it doesn't happen. I am waiting for something to happen; though as might be said quite justly, isn't Mt Etna, the LIRR, and 26feet of snow enough for you? No.

Yes, I did get a pleasant enough note from Congdon. I'm going to write him now, telling him that if I sell the player piano anywhere he is not going to get any %. $. %"_#&$(%*@@@@¾¾!) He doesn't know why he hasn't had a letter from me. What would I write him about? I've nothing finished to sell. I've two ideas that I want to ask him about. If he thinks they are good or worth($)while, maybe we can recover our lost intimacy. Otherwise I shall continue to play Greensleeves on the recorder, in the Gardens of Spain.

In spite of my pretentiously erudite references, Burgos and Freddie's Football Dogs, this isn't a very intelligent letter. Is it.

I'm glad you found Ormonde entertaining and reassuring.

It's some days since I've heard from Margaret. I don't know what she's up to? Perhaps on the High Seas, cast perilously adrift on a raft of her own fashioning between Woodmere and Greenpoint. Or forging ahead, Scott of the Antarctic. (I read recently that a Exquimo was eaten by his sledge dogs, —news from Copenhagen.)

You were extremely kind to send me make-up money for the dentist, and the news that my bank balance is undisturbed. Unfortunately I can never present you with a Toothpaste Smile, because my teeth just won't be pearly, they haven't got it in them. But they are clean, and serve to ruminate what crusts come my way.

And so, recently, I study about old Flemish painters, having reached a snag in my work, which, since it concerns a man who is forging paintings (it is his father who is counterfeiting a religion, that's why I needed *Forerunners and Rivals of Christianity*), I must know more of than I do. And so, in my mind this wet Paris morning, I have only pictures of St Barthemew being skinned alive, proof, perhaps, that the mediaeval imagination was as equal to conceiving outdoor sports commensurate with its capabilities as our own.

> Be to her Persephone, All the things I might not be;
> Take her head upon your knee,
> My dear, my dear, It's not so dreadful here

One wonders where to fit Leda and the Swan into all this.

Unless the lava flows northward, or Margaret eastward, I hope to be in

London by mid-December. More of that, though, in December. Meanwhile
I also stand and wait.

love from your son,
W.

---

dogma of the Assumption: on 1 November 1950, Pope Pius XII proclaimed as dogma
the belief that the Catholic goddess Mary ascended bodily into heaven upon dying
(discussed in *R*, 922–23).

lampshades [...] human bones: atrocities committed by Nazis at concentration camps.

crucifix at Burgos [...] codfish: repeated almost verbatim on p. 16 of *R*.

Freddie's Football Dogs [...] *The Deserter*: in her rambling letter to Dr. Weisgall in *R*,
Agnes Deigh writes, "I remember The Deserter, a drama acted by dogs and a monkey
at Sadlers Wells in 1785, and I could weep. I remember Freddies Football Dogs, and
I could weep. [...] Somewhere in Africa I believe they made a mermaid from a monkey and a codfish, I have seen its photograph" (760). *The Deserter* is an opera by
Charles Dibdin (1745–1814), based on *Le deserteur* by Monsigny and Sedaine. Freddie's Football Dogs was obviously a novelty act, otherwise unidentified.

Love Me Sailor: Close's novel, about the adventures of the only woman aboard a rough
ship, was first published in Australia in 1945—and became the subject of an obscenity suit—then in United States in 1950, and often reprinted. Early in the novel, the
protagonist "bent against the table to eat, and I knew her breasts would feel like two
warm duck eggs," a line Jack Gibbs recalls in *J R* (281).

Mathilde [...] Clements: Mathilda Campbell (1925–97), the American-born 4th
Duchess of Argyll, whom WG had known since Harvard when she attended Radcliffe. In 1948 she married *Clemens* Heller (1917–2002), a professor of human sciences at the University of Paris.

William B Hart: an editor at the *American Magazine*.

HG Wells [...] it doesn't happen: from *The History of Mr. Polly* (1910), chap. 10: "'One
seems to start in life,' he said, 'expecting something. And it doesn't happen. And it
doesn't matter.'"

LIRR: Long Island Railroad.

Greensleeves: traditional English folk song.

Scott of the Antarctic: title of a 1948 film about Robert Scott's failed attempt to be the
first to reach the South Pole (1910–12).

St Barthemew being skinned alive: i.e., the flaying of St. Bartholomew, the subject of
many Renaissance paintings.

Be to her Persephone: from Edna St. Millay's poem "Prayer to Persephone" (1921).

Leda and the Swan: well-known poem by William B. Yeats.

I also stand and wait: from a line in Milton's sonnet "On His Blindness": "They also
serve who only stand and wait" (*ODQ*).

Helen Parker and Bill Cannastra at his Manhattan loft, 1949 (photo by Nathan Lerner).

To Helen Parker

Paris
1 December 1950

dear Helen.

You know there's no excuse for the weeks I've let go by without answering the letter I was so pleased to find here when I came back from Barcelona. Except the constant round of monkey-business, which never ends here. Enough like New York, except that getting in and out of trouble is less expensive, and any variety these days only brings wide eyes, or the hand that shakes slightly reaching out in greeting. Lord, lord. And poor weather.

First I must tell you how glad I was to hear that you've got a house, and far from the Underground. I've asked many enough people about you, in these last two years, but any reports were vague and random. But how I have wondered what you were doing, and where, and with whom. And how happy to learn, at least, that you're in the country. Or was that only in the summer? And have you got this letter forwarded, reading it in that New York now?

(Yes, you say, —We will go to Key West after an R. F--------- Christmas. and I can't read that one word in your letter, Frosting? what is it.) Anyhow, and then Cuba. (But it says, —and will take little nibbles out of my Cuba. OH I see now. Until this reading, I thought it meant you were going to take Tommy and Bruce ('little nibbles') to Cuba! Well, you see the state I'm in.

But this line of yours has occurred to me so often in the past weeks, —How can you live in Paris after Spain? And I wonder. Except that everything's here; the way everything was in New York. And after months in Spain, with never a conversation of any proportions except simplicity and repitition, then the lust to come back to Paris and talk and carry on. I hadn't expected to stay on here so long this fall. I went back to Spain last summer, stayed and worked, writing, in a marvelous small town on the coast about 60 miles north of Barcelona. But toward late fall I got excited again, came thundering up here, and have since managed one mild collapse after another. Now I may manage to get over to London again, briefly, for the holidays, and then I think back to Sevilla, which of course has grown all out of proportion in my mind, — though my God the days were longer there, there was time to sleep, to eat, hours to work, a nap, and still much of the day and the night left to walk, or stand in inconspicuous idleness and drink mild things, and listen to that wild music which still sets something off in me. I want to go back; I'm really a country boy I'm afraid, and Paris high-life is beyond me.

Only within these last two or three weeks I've come to like Paris a great deal. I hadn't, during a year here, but suddenly I find it a wonderful place. —Though this changes no plans about leaving it. Because the barren-ness of Spain, its refusal to include one, draws me back there, every bit. Never coy.

But this should entertain you. Do you remember the player piano? Well, a few weeks ago I got it out again and looked at it, and liked it, oh yes, and sent it to *Atlantic Monthly*, who have offered to take an excerpt from it, or possibly the whole. Isn't that wild? and absurd? Otherwise writing gets written by the pound-weight, but is kept hidden and gone over, exhaustively enough to rob it of any quality of spontaneity, and put aside, waiting to be incorporated into a pretentious whole. Though weeks go by, in Paris, with nothing but monkey-business.

Enough of the wrong-size people showed up and draggled the terraces of left-bank cafes summer before last, skulking between tables and looking around every corner for the San Remo, to send me over the Pyrenees last summer. But by now it seems they have all faded away, the nice ones and the pitiful ones, back to New York.

And the weather here, mostly over-cast, or rain, and the newspapers, and all of it seems to point to an end, The End in sight. Waiting for something to Happen. And now someone has lent me his car, apartment, and Indo-chinese house-boy, to fill me with a tonic of absurdity in private circumstances which often enough centre about such problems as a laundry bill. Well, something is going to Happen.

I wish I hadn't broke that dish,

> I wish I was a movie star,
> I wish a lot of things, I wish
> That life was like the movies are ...

But I have seen that friend of yours Robin Roberts, of whom you wrote so brightly years ago. She's singing here, in a small place which I find thoroughly offensive because you have to sit in a reverent silence while the fey young man who runs the place sings, and cannot applaud, must only snap the fingers. So coy I can't get in the door. I had lunch with her about three months ago, and I hope to see her again, but I only think to look for her in the evening, then she's in that place. But she's doing well I think, and happy.

What about those boys? Someone, I can't think who, had run into Tommy on a New York street, and he was apparently pretty rousing, without a shadow of doubt about anything. Which is fine. For now. And the old captain? with a bloody nose first day of school, that is splendid I think. He is growing Up. Oh it's fearful, and I feel foolish enough asking you, here, to give them my love. It wouldn't mean something to them would it. It shouldn't either I suppose, because they must be fully occupied in growing up. But what a picture I have in mind, when you say Bruce fights too much. How I've always loved (with enough occasional burst of real fury) his truculence, his absolute Refusals, his moments then when he seemed older than any of us.

And Christmas? I hope it is wonderful for all three of you. I can't quite picture it any more, the last one spent on the road on a trip to Florence, the one before that walking the streets of Madrid, the one before that walking the streets of Panama, the one before that preposterous to remember, those realities most vivid in unreality. But there are a few idlers in London. I don't want to be here, for 'parties'.

Please write me again, fuller, about what happened, happens, what is going to happen.

my love to you, and to Tommy, and to Bruce
W.

Spain: cf. *R*: "—Spain..., Gwyon said, —the self-continence, [...] to outsiders, it seems to return their love at the moment, but once outside they find themselves shut out forever, their emptiness facing a void, a ragged surface that refuses to admit..." (p. 16; cf. also 429).

San Remo: the Greenwich Village bar (formerly on the northwest corner of Bleecker and Macdougal) called the Viareggio in *R*. In the novel, it is described as being filled with "people all mentally and physically the wrong size" (305).

I wish [...] That life was like the movies are: the first stanza of "It May Be Life—" by A. P. Herbert (1890–1971), British humorist, novelist, and Member of Parliament.

Robin Roberts: a folksinger (1928–2020) who later recorded a few albums.

To Edith Gaddis

Paris

3 December 1950

dear Mother,

It seems, as usual, that Christmas is going to appear wild-eyed around the corner, like a drunken old grandfather whom everyone is fond of, but no one quite prepared for ever, in spite of the messages he has sent announcing his imminent arrival.

The newspapers give no hope of spring.

I wrote you, didn't I? about Dick Wheatland's poison which has turned temporarily into my meat; that he went home for a medical examination and has been detained, necessitating an executor of sorts (me) here, so that for the moment I'm a lord and master, with a heated apartment, an indo-chinese house-boy, and a yellow sports-car, none of which largess I'm quite prepared to live up to.

And so it may sound slightly lunatic to say that I still plan to get to London for the holidays (because Dick very possibly won't return until the end of December). I'm now trying to clean up things in the palais d'Antin, seeing what I can do with the accumulation of a year all stacked in this room. I hope to solve them, one way or another, and stay over at Dick's house within a week, getting myself together to get to London, I'd think still around the 15th though I may stay on here a few days longer, what with a house to live in. Then, still vaguely, I'd hope to stay in England for a month or less, return here and go back to Spain. There to finish my 'work', and come on home in May or June. That's some time off though.

I've written Congdon (from whom I had a tepid note), saying I don't know just what's going on, offering two ideas for pieces (including that book with the head of AP in Madrid) which he'll be afraid to take up, and saying that if I sell any part of Player piano he can't come in and ask for some money. Even 7$50.

Needless perhaps to say, I scramble to the mailbox here daily, hoping to hear something through you from Mr Morton. Something happy. ($$$$ $$$) My teeth are all fixed, and thank you. Now. Have you still the check I sent you? I don't remember if it was blank, or for 80$; but I'd like to ask if you could cash it for that sum, and include it with the December remittance when you send that to Paris. Because, also needless to say I guess, that end of life has got fairly complicated here recently. And what with clearing up affairs here, getting to London, and Christmas, I'll need it. Heaven knows what will happen *there*. (Instead of return to Spain in January, I might stay on in England in the country to work, if such a plan seems feasible.) It's a strange spot to be in, not able to believe really that *Atlantic* will come through, but still in a fearful way half-counting on it, half-expecting a check, and working along on that deceptive basis. Lord, lord, where's the dollar.

Yesterday we drove out to Malmaison, the summer 'cottage' of Napoleon and Josephine, and found it to be a lovely small chateau, and all sorts of embalmed glories of Empire. In the morning I'd bought a ticket and gone to a rehearsal concert of a boy named Sigi Weissenberg, whom I'd met in Panama, now 22yrs old and giving concerts everywhere (a pianist); I saw him later, and as a reward I must meet him now for lunch, and receive—two tickets to the same concert this afternoon. That's life. I hope to hear from you in a day or two, and then shall write you more at length. Also will let you know when I can hope to ask you to use the London address again.

I saw a lovely pair of ear-rings for Margaret, 17th century, gold, with irregular pearls and emerald quartz stones, when I went back to ask her to hold them for me, they'd been sold. To a Swede. That's life?

with love, W.

Sigi Weissenberg: Alexis Sigismund Weissenberg (1929–2012) was a Bulgarian-born Jewish pianist who achieved some fame in the late 1940s, faded away, then resumed his career in 1966.

To John Napper

Paris
[mid December 1950]

dear John,

I plan to arrive in England around the end of the week, or the beginning of next (20th). I'm not doing very well here in Paris; in fact I'm not getting anywhere at all (words slip slide perish business) (I too). And most of all I look forward to being able to talk with you at length. You've been awfully kind to renew your invitation, and I should certainly be delighted to see your mill-pond next week, but only if it remains convenient for you, —at least in the scatter world I live in things which are delightfully convenient one week are ridiculously impossible the next, and so if anything has come up don't put yourselves to any added difficulty. I hope to be in England for a number of weeks, and we could put any such visit off.

Mostly, I say again, I look forward to seeing you both, and possibly in conversation recover something which seems to have collapsed in this city. Surely enough Paris is handsome, (I don't think the French deserve it), but I just go in circles here. All nervous energy which ought to go into work goes instead into missing buses, losing telephone numbers, carrying the trash downstairs. By now I picture a small tastelessly-furnished room, but heated somehow, in a small village, something like Little Gaddesdon, or even Great Gaddesdon. To tell the truth I've really wasted a month here, and I haven't a month to waste. Well, all of that when I see you. (Even Jung's *Integration of the Personality* hasn't helped me integrate; the minute I get my anima in place something else collapses.) [...]

To tell the truth, I'm quite excited about the prospect of London and England, though I hope to escape any manifestations of the Festival of Britain ... I'm in no festival mood, though I might be able to take something Spanish like Valencia's, where the sky-rockets are aimed at the crowd. Something heroic. Otherwise I'm getting into form by learning sayings of Great Englishmen, v.:

    Uxbridge: I have lost my leg, by God!
    Wellington: By God, and have you!
or
    Wellington: Publish and be damned.
or,
    Edward the Confessor
    Slept in the dresser.
    When that began to pall
    He slept in the hall.

> I look forward so to seeing you,
> best wishes to you both,
> W. Gaddis

Little Gaddesdon, or even Great Gaddesdon: not fictitious plays on WG's surname (as I first assumed), but real towns in Hertfordshire (though spelled Gaddesden), northwest of London.

Jung's *Integration of the Personality*: the Swiss psychologist's study of the process of "individuation" by way of dream analysis and alchemical symbolism. The English translation (by Stanley Dell, 1939) was WG's principal source for alchemy in *R*.

Festival of Britain: a national exhibition that opened in London in May 1951.

sayings of Great Englishmen: all taken from *ODQ* ; the last stanza is by E. C. Bentley (1875–1956). WG would continue to cite the Duke of Wellington's "Publish and be damned," his riposte to a woman who threatened to expose some compromising letters of his.

To Edith Gaddis

Paris
Sunday, 17 December 1950

dear Mother.

My, we do live in an exciting world, don't we. Someone has even offered me a flat in Vienna for the holidays. Grand? Gemütlich? or just plain Ghastly. Temptation.

—In den alten Zeiten, wo der Wünschen noch geholfen hatt...

Otherwise, it has been snowing today in Paris, a messy expression of nature's temper which I've lost sentimental feelings for I believe. Out of those leaded *Lampoon* panes, snowfall on Bow Street was something to stir the impatient heart. Nowadays, wet feet. Dear dead women, with their hair too, what's become of all the gold/ Used to hang and brush their bosoms? I feel chilly, and grown old.

Though I still expect to escape to London briefly. On the other hand, all the other idlers are appearing in Paris. Jacob (no slight intended) just came in from the Deep South, looking very well. Mail to London American Express from now on though, I think. I'll get it one way or another. I really do expect to go, though I feel a little foolish this Christmas-tide.

I trust you'll get the gift I sent you by Bill Taylor, who flew over a few days ago and hoped to see Margaret, and I told him to hand it over to her. And fortunately I finally got her gift, a pair of things whose original purpose I cannot imagine, spoked semi-circles with irregular baroque pearls at the ends which I made into ear-rings. Somebody named Mr Fitzpatrick was flying over on Saturday, so I gave them to him to cart along, and he said he'd leave them at his hotel for her to pick up, and send her a wire notifying her. Mr Fitzpatrick is from Kansas City.

Otherwise I'm in suspension, but a warm one to be sure. I'm afraid I'm going to have to Pay, when Mr Wheatland the proprietor returns, pay and pay and pay. His radio is now playing Swing Low Sweet Chariot, which I can't thank it for.

I got a very nice letter from Congdon, saying sell the player and keep the 'dough', remembering that it was written with 'considerable charm'. Refering to another piece I suggested, he knows 'it could be a splendid piece, knowing you capabilities...' wanting to see a (the) novel, 'in part or whole'......

Well. There will be time.

Priscilla B[r]oughton Friedrich writes of her expectancy of a baby, and I plan to return fairly soon here from London and go straight through to Spain. To Seville. I'm really a small-town boy, Seville is more my size. Any old tree will do for me, Any old isle is just my style.

Honestly, I'm sorry to write you such a fool letter as this, I'll do better in the next few days. For the moment, you'll be glad to know that I received the check (180$), and have fully escaped from the Palais d'Antin without bloodshed.

with my love,

W.

Gemütlich: Ger., jolly, cheerful.

In den alten Zeiten, wo der Wünschen noch geholfen hatt: "In olden days, when wishes still availed..."—the opening line of the Grimm Brothers' tale "The Frog King." Both the German original and its translation appear in *R* (273, where it correctly reads "hat" rather than "hatt").

Dear dead women [...] grown old: from the final stanza of Browning's "A Toccata of Galuppi's," quoted in *R* (193).

Swing Low Sweet Chariot: popular gospel song, written by Wallace Willis sometime after 1865.

Any old tree [...] just my style: from a song in Eliot's "Fragment of an Agon": "Any old tree will do for me / Any old wood is just as good / Any old isle is just my style."

To Edith Gaddis

Chantry Mill
Storrington, Sussex
27 december 1950

dear Mother—

I feel troubled for fear that you may very well wonder what suddenly became of me at Christmas time—but I did manage to cross the channel on Friday night, and spent Christmas quietly enough in London—no high time whatsoever, but I still like London so much that I've enjoyed it.

Then yesterday the 26th—Boxing Day, another holiday, I came down here, in Sussex, to visit the painter I met in Spain this summer—John Napper and his wife. I've thought of you often here, how much you would like this house—an old mill house, parts of it 700 years old! and fireplaces in almost every room, much of it though enough like the studio, and a similar way of life. It is proving to be one of the most pleasant Christmas holidays I've ever spent.

I expect to go back to London around the end of the week, and shall hope to hear from you there—I called at American Express Saturday (the 23rd), found only Margaret's Christmas gifts, which I was touched and delighted with. I suppose it must be my fault that I didn't let you know I'd definitely be in London the 23rd, that I've not heard from you—but I do so hope that you have had a happy Christmas—and I *am* most curious to know if you received my gift, and if you liked it.

with love,
W.

_____

To Edith Gaddis

[*In a letter to me dated 25 July 1996, John Napper wrote that during WG's visit "we took him to London where, one morning, we had a drink in what was then the Six Bells pub in Chelsea. A friend of ours, an antique dealer named John Hewett, came in and showed us a wonderful pair of heavy Byzantine gold ear-rings. My wife Pauline, who had just had her ears pierced, fell in love with them immediately to which John H. replied 'If you can wear them . . . you can have them.' My wife went away to the washroom to return some moments later, blood down her white shirt but the ear-rings in her ears. Willie was very struck by this event and made use of it in the first chapter of* The Recognitions [p. 14]. *Some of the book was actually written during his stay with us, we have been friends ever since. My wife still wears the ear-rings."*]

18 Granville Place,
London W 1
4th january 1951

Dear Mother,

What a fine holiday this is turning out to be. And a most splendid part certainly was returning from Sussex to find all of your bounty waiting for me here. As ever, I cannot thank you enough for such gifts which are making this possible, this visit to what I believe is the Best city I've ever seen. Even though I've not been leading a gay Mayfair and Park Lane high life (though my telephone number is a Mayfair exchange, a small room Barney got me), every bit of London excites me, it is as marvelous as I'd remembered, even when I'm not living in St James's, and I've thought of you often, with great regret for your not having been able to see more of it. Though somehow, looking back, you did get an extraordinary amount into those two days out, and beyond the things you saw, what I am enjoying is simply walking through the city, no landmarks but the people whom I like immensely. I can imagine no better life than one divided between England and Spain.

Last night I almost did sail to Portugal . . . was sitting in the captain's cabin on a boat tied up at a London Dock, which sailed at 8pm, having come earlier from the opening of a new show at an art gallery in Whitechapel (in London's unsavoury East End), where I met Sir Gerald Kelly, head of the Royal Academy . . .

Nor can I tell you how good my holiday in Sussex has been. The English countryside is often enough indistinguishable from Connecticut, and some of the newer small towns are centred about fake half-timbered buildings which look enough like Garden City, or Massapequa's Shopping Centre. But the Napper's house, of which I'd hoped to send you a picture but we couldn't find one, is ancient as I said, and it was fire-place heating every morning, quite cold. How fortunate I was to meet them, and how much they have done for me. Very few people recently with whom I've got on so well and liked so much.

Arturo is here, not in especially good shape, but two evenings ago we, with two others, went to a very jolly pantomime, and afterwards a few glasses of brown ale until the pubs closed, at 11pm. Yesterday was terrible as far as weather was concerned, slush and snow and cold and wet, but I didn't care at all, walking from one place to another with little of importance to take care of. Barney, though ill with a cold as almost everyone seems to be, has been awfully good about seeing to occasional practical details. This afternoon I may go to the *Cocktail Party*.

I've just heard from Wheatland, who is worse off than expected and cannot return to Europe for some time, offers me his flat &c until March, in Paris! But I'm turning it down. I cannot work well there, and I've work which must be done before spring. And so I plan to return to Paris the 10th, stay there for 3–5 days and take care of a few details of my own as well as whatever I can do to straighten up Wheatland's affairs, and then to Spain, Madrid briefly and through to Seville. I find, with these plans, that I'm unable to buy all the things I see on all hands here, the £s fly away, but all is working out well really. I am, however, going to take some of your Christmas present down to Charing Cross Road right now... that is where numerous book stores are, and you cannot imagine the excitement of being in an English bookstore after 2yrs of Spanish and French. [...]

(never tell *anyone* you have caught me writing on both sides of the paper; and I apologise to you for it.) [...]

with love,
W.

Sir Gerald Kelly: British painter (1879–1972), president of the Royal Academy from 1949 to 1954.

Arturo: Arturo de la Guardia: see endnote to December 1947. Gaddis's daughter Sarah met him in 1989, and in a letter dated 17 April 1989 WG wrote: "How delighted I am that you met Arturo. And to hear that he is (still) 'neat, distinguished, warm' (& married to a snappy Brit.), feel badly of course that it didn't occur to me to try to look him up [in Paris] especially this last triumphal visit; but now that you have made the contact of course there will be more opportunities. (And you must

believe his telling you to call on him if needed, he was always in his reserved way a warm & generous, a true 'gentleman'. Just in writing this I sharply miss seeing him.)"
Cocktail Party: T. S. Eliot's 1949 play.

To Edith Gaddis

Paris, France
15 january 1951

dear Mother,

 I'm tired of love; I'm still more tired of rhyme,
 But money gives me pleasure all the time...

So it was that I was very pleased to find two-hundred howling dollars at the G window in American Express. They are being subtly translated into Spanish currency, —a subtlety which I hope will not prove too subtle for me when I appear at the house of a Very Old Family in Madrid, mendicant-like. And thank you for your accompanying letter. No don't be crushed because I didn't have your Christmas letter Christmas. As I said, I had a marvelous week in the country, and was extremely happy to have it when I returned.

 Nor have I heard from Charley Morton. Will he prove a wraith too? oh Lord, if he does... I'll write him immediately. (What do you mean, 'Emmy has some suggestions'?)

 As I try to assemble myself this evening, I have a German radio programme, and such a beautiful language. Ech. And I am going back to that burlesque, Spain. But better to finish one thing before commencing another, and I've that feeling about returning, making a whole of it, a full circle. Possibly my next European trip will be an assault on Gemütlicheit to the north. Or Sussex. Especially if Nappers leave their place: the rent of it is 75pounds, 210$, a year! [...]

 And I had a beautiful and heart-breaking letter from Margaret, she is so sweet, I can only hope I'm doing the right thing now, going back under the Pyrenees, to work, and still planning to return in the spring. I hope to heaven that won't be too late for us. Because there's not another like her for me I believe. And I'm much older now. Oh dear yes. How she would love living in Sussex, I believe. When I've some money again, I want to ask you to send a large splendid fruit-cake to the Nappers (their address is Chantry Hill, Sullington, near Pulborough, Sussex, England). They were so kind, and besides that showed me such a good example in a right way of living.

 I'm quite busy here catching up Dick Wheatland's loose ends (I wrote you he'd had to have an operation, couldn't return until March possibly), and my own. Having this time resolved not to be caught book-less in Spain, I've assembled a small library which I'm trying to get into a box, this evening.

Impossible. Though I couldn't get some things I selfishly wanted in England, like cloth, a flat small suitcase (the kind you said would make me look like a Fuller Brush man), I did get books I wanted, including even a copy of the *Golden Bough*, all my own now! I should leave tomorrow or Wednesday, that nightmare 26-hour trip, 3rd class in France, 1st class in Spain. Only two or three days in Madrid, then, as it all started: a/c Consulado de los EE.UU. Paseo de las Delicias, SEVILLA...home is the sailor, home from sea, and the hunter home from the hill, but me, call me Ishmael. It all started a long time ago.

with my love,
W.

such a beautiful language. Ech: in *FHO*, Oscar compares the sound of German to "a cow backing into a stall" (346).
Gemütlicheit: i.e., *Gemütlichkeit*, kindliness.
home is the sailor [...] home from the hill: from Robert Louis Stevenson's poem "Requiem" (*Underwoods*, 1887), quoted earlier (28 April 1948).
call me Ishmael: the opening sentence of Melville's *Moby-Dick* (1851).

To Edith Gaddis

calle San Roque, 15
Sevilla, Spain
23 january 1951

dear Mother,

For 3¢, a glass of wine and a pajarito, who is a small bird, about what a sparrow would be if plucked I suppose, done in deep fat; and disconcerting enough to lift it spread and find it shapen enough like a man (done in deep fat). Or the recognition and liking in faces of some who counted small enough on one's calendar of hope and redemption, but here they are: Isabel, an old and ugly woman at this place who welcomed me with all her gums exposed in joy, and I am back in this dormitory room, hospital-like enough since it's got four white beds, two wash-stands (with pitchers), a white table and a couch which looks enough like an analyst's couch to alarm...to alarm me, not a Spaniard. Or in the bar Capi, nearbyenough, and the welcome there; and immediately incumbent, again, the feeling of acute isolation in the midst of professors of friendship. Or Eulalio, my Sevillano 'friend', who tempts me to homicide often enough, and the welcome there; Salud, his wife, and Rosita, his child, and the adventure my return seemed to be, they were so excited, and is it to my inverted-ness, or to my other devotions, that all of it embarrasses me, and again come the insistences of anonymity.

'Don Guillermo' again. It is cold and wet here.
Back.

Well, you forget the dirt and the poverty; and still the absolutely implicit insistence on salvation everywhere; bare walls and boarded windows; no ashtray nor waste-basket, so ashes and orange-peels alike go on the floor, easier for everyone that way.

Last night, having a glass of wine, beside me assembled a family (you may see that it was not a fashionable retreat). Father and mother blind, he heavily marked with syphillis (and she I gather similarly so), and a healthy appearing daughter of about 13, come in to pour out days' gatherings, these leaden coins whose value would be meaningless in Massapequa, to have it redeemed in currency (they sell lottery tickets, you see, and receive 'tips' of about .02¢ to .05¢). And so, I overheard the man say to the daughter, screwing his face upward as though he would look for himself, as though he has not lost the motion years ago, —And this Englishman, how do you know? Is he wearing elegant clothes... ? And that was I; So, do you see, I am wealthy in that comparison; warm in comparison to those who are still now on the streets; But still one passes the houses of Sevilla, looking through leather brass-studded doors large enough to admit a coach, to a patio resplendent in tiles and green luxury growing from brass pots; or these people pass in their coaches...

I 'phoned Margaret from Madrid on Sunday. And of course I cannot tell you, how wonderful it was to hear her, nor how sad eventually, the conversation. Oh I tell you, I tell you (you know) what a magnificent, and splendidly brave person she is. I know now that she is having, and has had consistently a ghastly time of the whole thing, paid and paid and paid. Again: I don't know. You may imagine, it looks enough to me now as though I should be there, with her, to do something, anything. And here I am, settled it looks with my work, and having made all financial arrangements to stay for two more months, at the least. Oh, you know I don't mean to face you with all this; simply to say that things are in this state. And here I am with 45 books and 20 pounds of my own work, and impossible to know what it will come to.

Then I've heard now news of increased taxes. I'm concerned, especially after your letter saying that my check had saved things for the moment, over you. Are you all right, really? And this 100$ a month, is it a difficult drain? You must tell me.

$ $$$ $$$$$$ $$$ $$$$$$ $$ $$$$$$$$$ $$ $$$$$ $

Could you, then, put my next (february) remittance in my bank account there please? Also, I've wondered a number of things. What, for instance, is the price of a ticket (LIRR) Massapequa to NY? and commutation?

I've written Charles Morton (*Atlantic*), asking *what*.

This address (below [*i.e., above*]) should do, unless it's something of great importance which might be endangered in loss, then the consulate.

with all love,

W

To John and Pauline Napper

Sevilla, Spain
Saturday, 27 january 1951

dear John and Pauline,

[...] A month now, since I found myself trapped in the 1st-class carriage in Storington station, and the Honourable Miss Something released me to your magnificent week waiting. I suppose (an analyst could figure this out) it's because it was so wonderful that I've taken this long in writing, wanting to be able to thank you sufficiently, which I cannot of course even now, nor see how I can ever. I might even plead that selfish rudeness with a Purpose, but can't even that for not writing, since it's only in the last couple of days that I've got back to work again.

Paris of course was the roundabout I thought it might be, and took some eight days of hopping, losing telephone numbers, missing buses, shaking hands, —but as you can see I finally did escape the warm-house-with-oriental-retainer, and the dashing sports car (which I didn't even take out of the garage while there). But now, no telephones, no gramaphones, no Citröen, no Rolls Royce...

And the welcome back. People I hadn't seen in almost two years, and almost all of them servants or bar tenders &c, but glowing welcome, [...] It is wonderful, and heart-breaking, this lavishness with nothing, and such friendship isolates me in embarrassment even more, somehow, than London's civilised indulgence or Paris's hard, dull, dreary, absurd, pretentious, stupid, tiresome, indifference. Oh yes and unalive, also. And again " [*under the word* pretentious]. Well.

I don't know what it is Madrid has, to make it handsome to me. But it was the two days I stayed there on the way down. Brisk clear weather, and everything seemed white, like Cadiz, though I hadn't thought of it as a white city before. But the Prado. And the Retiro Park on Sunday afternoon. And there is, as many enough have said before, this apparently innate quality of happiness in south-Europeans, which Paris, with all its glittering old junk, never manages. And again the contrast to England, which shows in favour of both countries, the means of externalizing everything immediately here, sense of style, place for everything.

And nothing has changed; except they've finished the bank they were building on one corner of the Plaza Nueva, and started another across the street. Still the barrel organs, which bring every sentimental bit of me crying out, and like Odysseus must be tied to the mast as we pass the rock where the sirens sing, or I should follow them. (I did once, in Palamos, did I tell you? follow one out of the town, up the hill toward the cemetery, it was drawn by a pony.) But I ask them to play La Tani, and it is gone, no longer 'popular' but always popular because I asked an old and blind accordianist to play it in a bar a couple of evenings ago (he was playing that old rag La Cumparsita), and soon enough five gypsy girls and women, handsome and dirty, oiled, seams split and heels run down, were clapping in the corner, which excites me as it did when I first heard it. (Now I have to avoid the blind accordianist because he breaks into La Tani when his assistant sees me and it costs a peseta. Got to watch these things.)

I've thought about you a great deal these last weeks; but nothing has brought Chantry Mill so abruptly to my mind as the food, which Isabelle serves me in the sort of dim light usually kept for deception. (Though that is the first thing one notes in Spain, right across the border, the dim lights everywhere.) (No Paris neon.) Wretched fish, done to death by fire; plate of beans-and-rice; oak-leaf proportioned slices of beef and potatoes, fried in oil. Oil. Cold potatoes, floating in oil. But there is wine.

(But there is yet faith But the faith and the love and the hope are all in the waiting.

I 'phoned Margaret from Madrid, a perfect connexion, which did much to enhance the sadness of the conversation, the apparent impossibility of ever managing anything, we; I don't know, it's still the same, nothing has changed, and I upset her by calling, in high spirits because Madrid was so fine, and she was so splendid, and so unhappy. I don't know; should I bother you with this? But it's in my mind, a steady depressent.

Vamonos ... it is not that I do not love you, but that your house is so far away. Mujer.

Uno y uno, dos/ Dos y dos son tres ... No sale la cuenta porque falta un chulumbes (that word is gypsy, I can't spell it;)

I shall call you, as I said. It will take a little straightening up first. Fortunately I've along a good store of books, though they do, of course, present the temptation to read them. I liked the Argentine novel, and in spite of its shortness it stays with me. Thank you, thank you, unnumbered times, for everything. I shall try; it will take time.

I have a lot of messy notes, taken on the spot in Real Life, to go through before the ten-o'clock shout from Isabelle, —Don Guillermo, a comer! heralds the evening oil treatment (how I shall always remember what came out of that roasted chicken).

> love from the wounded surgeon,
> W—

La Tani: or "Tani mi Tani," a flamenco song about a young Gypsy bride. It was written ca. 1942 by Francisco Acosta (lyrics) and Gerardo Monreal (music), and is heard throughout *R* III.3.

La Cumparsita: "The Little Parade," a tango composed by Uruguayan Geraldo Matos Rodríguez (1917).

Isabelle: WG sometimes Frenchifies Isabel, the elderly maid.

But the faith [...] in the waiting: a line from part 3 of Eliot's "East Coker."

Uno y uno [...] chulumbes: lyrics from "La Tani"; as Sinisterra explains in *R*, "The bill [la cuenta] doesn't come out right because there's a kid missing. It [churumbel] means a kid" (813).

the Argentine novel: probably *Las ratas* by José Bianco (Buenos Aires, 1943), which was in WG's library when he died.

the wounded surgeon: from the first line of part 4 of "East Coker."

To Edith Gaddis

> Sevilla
> 12 Feb. 1951, Monday morning

dear Mother—

Things are certainly not as they were between Paris and New York. We are safely back to Spanish concepts of mail service and time. I had your card saying you were about to set off for Florida yesterday, and by now you must be almost back.

Did you have a letter from me giving this address (below) instead of consulate, and asking that you put the february money into N Y bank? I hope so, because I may have to cash it in Africa.

A telegram from Barney yesterday saying he and a man I met in London are setting off for a 4-week automobile trip through north Africa, to Tunis, and return—will pass through Sevilla, and could I join them. Of course one never knows how such projects as these work out—especially with Barney— but I telephoned him in London last night, and apparently they will be in Sevilla in about 10 days. I can't really say whether I'll go or not and probably won't know until they appear here. And so if you'll continue to write to this address until I tell you of something phantastically different. [...]

I had a letter from *Atlantic Monthly*, whom I'd written impatiently, saying that they planned to settle definitely on the piece on Friday (last), so I should know one way or the other fairly soon. If they *should* take it (oh lord, how that would save my life), I might have to ask you to look for a letter I wrote you some 3 months ago [16 November 1950], mentioning parts of it that must be checked again.

Otherwise everything goes along quietly and cold here in Sevilla—and fairly wet these last few days. We were to go to a bullfight in a nearby town yesterday, but it rained all day, and still is this morning. This evening I am going to dinner with Eulalio at his house, since it is his saint's day, celebrated here as we do birth days. But aside from that, there's no big news from this place. [...]

I'm waiting now for Isabelle to bring a charcoal brazier in, so that I can warm my hands over it and get down to work. I'll let you know about "Africa"—and I hope your Florida trip was a success. (Remarkable that Granga didn't pile in?)

> with love,
> W.

To Edith Gaddis

> Sevilla
> 17 feb 1951

dear Mother,

I just had your note re *Atlantic Monthly*, Player Pianos &c. I think that by now probably everybody's had enough of the whole thing. And so I'm writing Morton that you'll send along the excerpt (could you have it copied out?) and for him to either send payment to my account in NY or to you, that you could deposit it. I'm sorry it's been such a chore all around. I must confess, this afternoon, to being somewhat disappointed in spite of myself, for I had let myself depend on a more favourable outcome, over all the time it's taken. Well. Life is very long.

A wire from Barney this morning, saying he can't make the African trip, but that the other fellow (David Tudor Pole) is leaving Monday, should be here toward the end of the week, and is depending on my going and being able to share the driving. The trip, I understand, will be from Tanger east to the frontier of Libya, and back. I see no reason now that I shall not go, if, that is (through three telegrams from London) I understand things fully. I should think, then, that we'll leave here about the 23rd, though I'll confirm by cable, that as I referred to in my last letter, simply the word SEND.

Hosts of unforeseen difficulties and disasters waiting, no doubt.

> Love,
> W.

David Tudor Pole: (1921–2000), son of British psychic Wellesley Tudor Pole (and father of musician/actor Edward Tudor Pole), at that time employed in his father's
business of importing esparto grass from North Africa to Scottish paper mills.
my last letter [...] SEND: in a letter dated 15 february, WG said SEND meant to send
$100 to American Express in Tangier.

To Edith Gaddis

Hotel Astoria
Murillo, 10
Tanger [Morocco]
25 feb. 1951

dear Mother,

Things are going quite quickly. We got over here last night and now have
some visa difficulties about Spanish Morocco, but hope to be in Tripoli in 5
or 6 days. I trust you got my note asking that 100 dollars be cabled to NABIEF
Algiers—address in Tripoli, for any mail—Uaddan Club, Tripoli (marked
"hold until arrival"). This first part of the trip is quite rushed, but we plan to
return with less haste, and within a few days I should be able to write you
more at length. Many thanks in advance for cable.

love,
W.

To Edith Gaddis

Hôtel de l'Oasis
Alger [Algeria]
[28 February 1951]

dear Mother—

The draft arrived, and thank you so much for managing it so well and
quickly—you can't imagine how much such attention means.

The trip is coming on exceedingly well, though just now rather more rushed
than I'd like, but we shall return more leisurely. Must be in Tripoli in 3
days—among other things, we are making some moving pictures.

Algiers is as excellent a place as I'd believed—and the Casbah marvelous.
I hope to spend more time here on return.

love,
W.

To Edith Gaddis

Uaddan Club
Tripoli [Libya]
5 March 1951

dear Mother—

Everything in order. At the Uaddan Club in Tripoli (a uaddan is an African animal resembles a Rocky mountain goat). For these few days things are quiet, with Mr Tudor-Pole taking care of some private concerns, and I spend the time going around the city—exciting in its old Arab part, but quite Italian for the rest. Wednesday I believe we are going to get hold of a couple of camels and go to an Arab town far enough from beaten track to make the car impossible. By the weekend we should be starting back, but this time more slowly, and a more southerly route, along the edge of the desert—it is that part of Africa that I look forward to, needless to say. Finally, we should be back in Sevilla by Easter Sunday.

Some of all this time and energy is devoted to a 35mm. motion picture camera, making background shots for a documentary film—quite a business, trying to photograph an Arab with a camel train in the desert who isn't quite sure what you're up to. Otherwise it proves a quiet and fairly uneventful trip—the desert. The camels, and Aunt Mabel's burnoose 1000 times. [...]

with love,
W.

To Edith Gaddis

[*Though WG apologizes below for not saying much about his month in North Africa, the experience resulted in an exotic passage on pp. 877–79 of R—not the kind of things one writes home about to mother.*]

Algiers, North Africa
23.3.1951

dear Mother—

Arrived here last night, and very happy to find your letter. Apparently the confusion is my fault—but I was certain (and am) that I'd sent you the address in Tripoli before I left Spain.

At any rate now all rests easier. It has been an excellent trip, and I think that by now we've finished work on this documentary film which was the reason for it. Shall spend 3 or 4 days in Algiers, and I should be back in Spain by the end of the month. From there shall start figuring on coming home— either mid-April or beginning of May. Much depending on money.

I've just written Morton—*Atlantic Monthly*—to ask him to keep any "biographical note" as brief as possible—born in N.Y. in 1922, educated mainly in New England—mention this African film if he likes. In other things pending, I'll hope for answers to questions in my last letter (my bank balance, your cable address, &c) in Sevilla.

As yet I haven't much to say about North Africa—I am still too occupied sorting out the impressions I've had and as yet been unable to put in place. But for the moment Algiers is a fine city, worth spending a few days in certainly—though they say that people still get hit over the head at night in the Casbah. Not as warm here as it was—though coming as we have just up from the south, Biskra and Bou-Saâda, near the edge of the Sahara, it would seem cool. We have sand everywhere—the car coated and lined with it, and clothes pretty saturated, and eyes and lungs. But a clean shirt makes a great difference.

> love,
> W.

To Edith Gaddis

> c/ San Roque, 15
> Sevilla
> [3 April 1951]

dear Mother,

Safe at last, the harbour past... and coming back to Sevilla by now is much like coming home. But of coming home—well, you've got to take me in.

How glad I was to find your good letters (real Letters) from you waiting for me here. And I have put you through all sorts of difficulties there, and I'm sorry about it, I only realise what troubles you've been having when I read of your hectic businesses with American Express and West Union &c. Certainly alot was thrown off by your not having my Tripoli address, as we were there for two weeks (there and in the mountains beyond) working on this film which took more time than planned, so we're late getting back here to Sevilla. David only stayed over for a day, then went on back to London, or rather set out for London, last evening. The trip and the work there were immensely worth while, in spite of having made this temporal dent in my 'own' work. As for that, the prospect of getting back into it, while at the same time trying to make arrangements to come back across that Atlantic, are rather involved, I'm still trying to work it out.

This is what I have in mind, though as yet I don't know about a port for departure; but I'd think within about 3 weeks I should hope to be boarding something, in a western direction.

I don't know if there is enough of this novel finished as I want it to be finished to show there in New York with any hope of ($al) encouragement. But I intend anyhow, when I return, to start immediately investigating the USIS, the American propaganda bureau, what Bill Haygood is working with in Madrid, for possibilities. I've had this in mind for some time, and on this trip have talked with a number of people about it. Just now I've also talked with a fellow connected with it here, am to meet him for coffee later. And so, I've those two possibilities. Heaven knows, I'd like to come back and settle down to work again there in Massapequa, while this other thing is working out, if it will work out.

The money business on the trip worked out, because David's company had blocked money in these countries we were working in, and so I drew on that, through him, and trust that you've had my letter asking for 130$ to be sent to him in Paris American Express. Therefore the rest of the money which is floating or flying somewhere between me and you now, should eventually come to rest here. How good you are to offer me passage home. And I think I shall have to borrow some from you, though heaven knows if it could be managed how much I'd rather work my way back. But that seems about gone, those days, with Wim Boni on the cattle boat. Still I'm going to investigate. But the peril is getting into some big port, and wasting as much time and money, in Lisbon, say, waiting for a likely boat with an empty deck-hand's berth, as it would cost to simply go down and buy a passage.

To tell the truth, I'm quite nervous at the prospect of coming back. When I returned to Sevilla there were 20 letters waiting here for me, and each pointing to a world of rankest confusion. But I must come back, notably for Margaret, really, that most exquisite and wonderful girl. And also, to tell the truth, I think prospects look good, though it is easier said from this place than accomplished in that one. (Incidentally I told American Express in Algiers to forward to me here immediately the 100$ which hadn't reached there before I left.)

Believe me, I thought about you and Margaret on Easter [25 March], —I'd never have thought—or perhaps I would—as we stood in Notre Dame, in Paris, that in the next Easter I should be walking through the raucous bazaars in Algier's Casbah, spending the evening leaning over the baccarat tables at the casino (hastening to add here that I did not play nor lose even 100 francs). So there is North Africa, accomplished for the moment. Cairo still distant... it *is* a long way off you know. From anywhere.

with my love

W

Safe at last: from the chorus of a 19th-century temperance song called "Anchored!" (lyrics by Samuel K. Cowan, music by Michael Watson): "Then safe at last, the harbour past, / Safe in my Father's home!"

home [...] take me in: another allusion to Frost's well-known dictum, "Home is the
  place where, when you have to go there, / They have to take you in."
this film: described later as a "documentary film on the background of fine-paper
  making" (8 March 1957).
USIS: U.S. Information Service.
Wim Boni: unidentified.

To John and Pauline Napper

[*While he was in North Africa, WG mailed several picture postcards to the Napper, one
of which he captioned "Look, look!—wenches," from Eliot's "Sweeney Erect."*]

Sevilla
5 april 1951

dear John and Pauline,

   Have you been troubled by dancing girls and camels in the mail? Well, it
will all be explained presently, I trust, if David Tudor Pole gets back to London alive. He left here headed vaguely in that direction.

   The truth is, we have just escaped from Africa. Or, to go further back, he
showed up here one day in late february bound for Libya in an Austin, and two
hours later I had assembled what there was of myself at hand and we were gone.
Unfortunately I can't immediately give you my picture of Africa, still trying,
here now, to sort it out for myself . . . the girl with the safety-pin in her ear in
Bou Saada, the broken truck spring and tea in the Zintan pharmacy, the sick
arab in the back seat and Saturday night in Sfax, the subterranean lunch with
the sheik of Nalut, the Sudaness who served cognac as a beveridge with supper,
and the Berber friend in Fes who shared his highly suspicious pipe, the Foreign
Legion at Sidi-Bel-Abbes, the bacarrat table in the casino at Algiers, and
Easter in the Casbah, the expensive beer-drinking party in Biskra, the twenty-
some seat gentlemen's lavatory at Leptis Magna . . . all this, and so much more.

   I have never before realised how fond I am of Sevilla. And to have your
letter waiting here, with questions about P. Sta Maria, was delightful; because
only hours before, driving up from Cadiz, I had said I wanted to stop and
look around at Sta Maria, which we did. I shan't try to describe it here, because
I've asked David to look you up and deliver something, also to give you at first
hand his description. It is a larger town than one would think at first look,
and has always had a substantial English colony, largely because of the distill-
eries. It is different from Sevilla largely in that most of it seems to have been
planned and laid out, with streets crossing at unsympathetic right-angles, not

the haphazard maze that happened here. But I understand that the English colony has greatly dwindled at Sta Maria since the war, which (no offense) recommends it. I shall try to get hold of some post card pictures here, if any are available.

As I should have said first off, how splendid for you that the 1000gns is assured! That is one of the best pieces of news in another's life I have heard in so long. For you cannot imagine the letters which were waiting here when I got back, all I believe except yours reflexions of disaster, most especially those from the US. And now for the most distressing, and absurd piece of news from me, simply that I am going to New York in about a month. Absurd; and if you could see Sevilla now you would understand; it is the most wonderful place I have encountered, and really sitting here with the rush curtain drawn down over my balcony, and the rattling of a bottle-cart on the paving stones below, the notion of Manhattan is an absolutely insane one. But I must go back, at least for a couple of months, to see what I can rescue from this por-queria, as we say here, years of living among the breakage, and those strained time-ridden faces distracted from distraction by distraction . . . I don't know. But I'd hope to settle once for all.

Incidentally, did you ever receive 8 packets of Ideales sent from here in February? and 8 packets of Bastos Flor Fina sent from Algiers? Well, shoulder the sky, my lad, and pass the can (Malt does more than Milton can to justify God's ways to man). How I wanted to send you a ham from here, but they were beyond me.

But the Fair is coming. Not, I believe, that there is not always the Fair here. Right now, we locals are busy stringing canvas up over narrow streets, telling the ugly tourists that it is protection against the sun, but really it is simply to give the place the atmosphere of a large circus tent interior. And it never ends, the singing and the dancing and the handsome people, though the Fair will augment it, 8 excellent bullfights and hundreds of casetas, those small canvas rooms where drink is served, —served, drunk, spilled, offered, hurled, . . . menaced by monsters, risking enchantment, and afterwards piles of broken glass, and *that* is the kind of carnage testament to Living, not 1000 lost golf balls. (Do not let me hear of the wisdom of old men, but rather of their folly . . .)

And then on the metalled ways that point back. Oh, I feel such a fool try-ing to write this; saying and believing the absurdity of this transatlantic direc-tion, and taking it. And so the Fair will be a final debauch and farewell, final only in a sense of finality of this trip which has lasted almost 3years, final in that it will I hope to God only be a point of returning and that you will see me sitting in a state of senile collapse at the portside in Santa Maria when you come there with your canvas and your brushes and your cooking utensils. God it must be that way.

Or you see, they would think, he is now involved in something calculatedly riotous and degeneratedly insane, the Feria at Sevilla, but he returns to sobre living. When I know that this is living, and what they have is insane, is the highest level of calculated insanity ever achieved. I have seen the ruins of Leptis Magna, marble at odd angles; and Sevilla's fair, broken glass piled high; and now New York, already in ruins though they do not know it. Aie...

I shall write you soon again now, but at the moment...well, I did want to thank you for your letter, to explain those girls and camels, to note my absurd news and congratulate you on your good news, and now another cart passing shakes the whole house, and I'll go down. I won't say I'm going down on business, on work, on something pressing, that I have to answer 14 letters, that they are waiting for me to open the Cortes, or lay a cornerstone, cut a ribbon to open another concrete way toward Progress (and a future which, like the past, is likely to have no destination...) —No, I am going downstairs, through the patio and out the iron gate and up past the charcoal-seller's shop, down a narrow street and turn right into a narrower one, past the old woman selling lottery (cinquenta iguales para h-o-y... cinquenta iguales me quedan...) and out into the sunlight, through the orange trees in the Plaza de la Magdalena, past the fountain, toward a sparkling glass,

and all best wishes—wait for the early owl
W.

[*handwritten at bottom:*]—Well, I just came back in from that pre-prandial tour, to find Isabelle has washed my whole floor again. And I cannot tell you, I cannot tell you what Sevilla is—if you are lazy, no-good, hopeful of miracles (of a minor nature certainly in the sight of God) as I am.

---

the girl with the safety-pin [...] Leptis Magna: cf. *R* 877–78 and 895, where WG used many of these details.

P. Sta Maria: El Puerto de Santa Maria, a little northeast of Cádiz.

porqueria: mess, nastiness, rubbish.

distracted from distraction by distraction: a line from part 3 of Eliot's "Burnt Norton."

Idealis [...] Bastos Flor Fina: Spanish cigarettes.

shoulder the sky [...] God's ways to man: a mashup of lines from A. E. Housman's "The Chestnut Casts His Flambeaux" (1922) and "Terence, This Is Stupid Stuff" (1896).

Do not let me hear [...] their folly: from part 2 of Eliot's "East Coker."

the metalled ways: part 3 of Eliot's "Burnt Norton" concludes: "while the world moves / In appetency, on its metalled ways / Of time past and time future."

a future [...] no destination: from part 2 of Eliot's "Dry Salvages": "We cannot think [...] of a future that is not liable / Like the past, to have no destination."
(cinquenta [...] me quedan): "Fifty tickets today, I've got fifty tickets."
wait for the early owl: a line from "East Coker," part 1.

To Edith Gaddis

Sevilla

19 April 1951

dear Mother,

Probably by the time you have this—well, heaven knows: we'll likely have been through all sorts of cabled confusion, even telephonic. But I write this to confirm plans in the cable I sent you last evening. Though if things haven't worked out by the time you have this letter, it will probably be too late.

I've found a modest Norwegian motor-boat which is due here the 22nd from Genoa, and due to sail to New York the 24th. I've taken passage but the complication is, of course, payment, after the way American Express has arranged things for me. [...] If this has not worked out, don't be concerned over this letter; I shall try to make some arrangement here, or wait until another boat shows up. But if it has worked out, the agents (Boise Griffin Steamship Co, 90 Broad street, NYC 4) can keep you posted on when the *Nyhaug* is due in, should be the 4th–6th of May. And what pier. [...]

Otherwise, the only thing I think of is would you reserve a room for me at the Harvard club, or the Algonquin (whichever is less expensive), planning to stay in town for 2 or three days, then out to frigid studio...where I'd think to go alone and have things in some order for you when the weather signals you to come out. I'll probably need a couple of weeks there alone to collect myself. I'm quite nervous about the whole thing, to tell the truth.

And that seems to be all. I know you're probably in a stew right now over what is happening to me; I've put off writing you these last few days expecting some definite word to send you. But be assured that I'm fine, here, the fair in full flowery swing, excellent bullfights, (there are 5 more) and invitation to two fancy casetas (the drinking tents of familys) on the fair grounds, where I'm going this afternoon. Otherwise, handsome men and handsome girls riding pillion on handsome horses, handsome carriages, gallons of Manzanilla, singing and dancing.

with love,

W.

To Edith Gaddis

Sevilla
[24 April 1951]

dear Mother,

Last minute wildness-es; [...] I'm afraid you're going to have to come to the Erie Basin, Brooklyn's shade, to find the *Nyhaug*, but there we will be, modest and without shame. I trust. And I'm afraid I'm going to arrive not as neatly as I set out, rather with an assortment of boxes, quite gipsy and not stylish; and don't know what to suggest in the way of meeting, if you've a car there or what. Your new car? Oh dear. As I said, I'd plan to spend 2 or 3 days in town, if you've made reservation at Harvard club or the Algonquin, the latter might be best since there you could 'visit'. But modest, and with out bath, I hope to be clean on arrival.

As for the boat, I've been down to look at it; and for all its smallness (slightly larger than the banana boat from central America), my cabin is really good, I hope you'll see it; and I am the *only* passenger... SO. Honestly, such a much more excellent way to travel than the balloon dining room of tourist boats. I talked with the captain[,] very pleasant fellow, suppose I'll be dining with him, quietly & well.

Finally thanks for your letter just received, and for all that, for the return &c, I'm quite nervous. Well, we'll see about that. Present plans to sail tomorrow 25th, arrival about the 5 May, that can be affirmed with the agent.

nervously, love,
W.

———

To John Napper

still at sea
4 May, 1951

dear John,

First, *don't* be down-hearted at the post-mark (if it is, as I trust it will be, New-York). I'll try to explain it to you, as I have to myself.

Meanwhile, ten days at sea proves a very long time, though thank God for it: opportunity to lose Spain little by little, and prepare myself (as though anyone could, ever) for the slaughter. But honestly, it did take a few days to recover from that departure. Though repeating to myself, as to others, that it was not for more than a period of months; though there is inevitably a ring of finality about setting sail for a place which in grotesque pretension calls itself your 'home'... home is where one starts from, it was, and will be.

As you may have heard, the city of Sevilla held an extensive going-away party for me, —it lasted for five days and five nights, fifty bulls killed, some artistically and some in acute discomfort; girls, singing, dancing, horses, mules, blood and sand and broken glass, tears and abrazos. Honestly, leaving that pension, with five elderly ladies all weeping, and they gave me an intricately stitched Lady of Carmen (Lady, whose shrine stands on the promontory...), and a lunch to take along, a journey of ten days with nothing but sea and sky incomprehensible. Or leaving the bar Capi, pledges of friendship eternal, and also that they were going to close the place the minute after I left: there is devotion! Or Pastora... but perhaps David Tudor-Pole has mentioned her to you—and so in these days (And on the deck of the drumming liner Watching the furrow that widens behind you You shall not think 'the past is finished' Or 'the future is before us') one recovers slowly and privately the shell of empty laughter, laughter which recalls nothing and words and gestures without past or future, except insomuch as they exist in the minds of those on the dock, on the pierhead, waiting for the recognition which they feel implicit in the circumstances, —one recovers this shell, prepares to inhabit it, present it in rooms to those who spend their lives in rooms; prepares experiences, taken however seriously then, we missed the meaning, for expenditure in conversation which dies on the dead smoke exhaled, stagnant, the experience tossed off that easily and the meaning never again questioned... so one comes 'home'.

No; it is not all that easy, nor so soon done with: what brought us away takes us back; and persists to point us away again: the past is not finished nor the future before us. Though for all that, I dread the day when voyages cease to have their significance for me, when I know with my heart what I know now with Mr Eliot's mind, that the way up and the way down are one and the same; better cultivate the infinite mind, and preserve the temporal heart, in which voyages still do have directions, fight against the weary sagacity of the seaman to whom directions are simply matters of distance and of days, and ports of climates and cost of entertainment. Never, I hope, to attain to that peak of sophistication where movement across water is simply a matter of adjusting one's watch, where crossing the Atlantic ocean is as significant as a busride to Battersea.

So I sit, in a clutter of books, boots, bags and bottles, —these latter a more extensive cargo than planned, again enthusiasm demolished judgment and I fear altercations with New-York aduanas, but it was a case of last-minute desperation, like one setting forth on the Sahara for the first time, uncertain if he should see a drop of drink before expiring, so I seem to have carted one after another bottle (cleverly alternating coñac and Manzanilla) aboard; pretty souvenirs to bring Home to Mother after 3 years in 'interesting' places...

I'm glad David Tudor Pole got you, and managed to hand over the bottles (speaking of bottles). I trust he gave you description of the Puerto de Santa

Maria. The only thing that distracts me about that town is the flatness, persistent all down that plain, slightly broken but just enough up at Sevilla; that, and that it would be infernally hot in summer. But I think endlessly of your going there to stay; and I will not say enviously, because envy suggests impossibility of attainment on the part of the viewer; and I hope and plan it will be possible for me, thinking now that after two to four months in America to re-cross this sea, with either a wife or the *Encyclopædia Britannica* in tow.

Some people have paid their debt immediately they close the door behind them. And it is difficult enough to talk with you of debts, because you have proven that only in fulfilling one's debt to one's self can one ever repay debts to others; and we who still hop about on one foot concerned to pay these debts to others before we have the currency will be eternally bankrupt. Ecco . . . At any rate, that is what I want to straighten out on this trip, what the debts are and how best paid, and if they must be payed immediately. I am still uncertain if what work I have finished (the African trip made a decided dent in what I'd planned to have done, but well worth) will be sufficient to show for ($al) encouragement: that remains to be suffered. And the only thing which could crush me will be war, or being sucked into the hysteria of Preparedness, being dressed in an anonymous costume and spent that way.

So don't be upset at me if things seem to collapse, or stagnate; they will only be in suspension, which I shall end (unless war) when the time comes, I trust before summer is out. This trip is necessary; and once one has such on one's mind, it is better to go through it quickly than waste time and energies pondering it.

Thus I found this small Norwegian cargo boat (6000tons) sailing direct Sevilla–New York, and boarded. For the first days out, the sea was like the Caribbean; but now the sky fades, and the water looks colder, that indifferent colour not blue nor grey but simply Atlantic. We should shudder into New York in about 40 hours. I expect to spend 3 or 4 days there, examining possibilities, then escape to the woods, to ~~home~~ house which needs a good deal done to it in the way of painting &c, and settle to work again.

Il faut cultiver notre jardin, says Candide; and Doctor Pangloss, who has been hung, burned at the stake, dis-membered, maimed, agrees. So please write me there, where I shall be sitting, an old man in a dry month, being read to by a boy, waiting for rain.

Love to you both—and I *shall*
see you before too long.
W.

---

home is where one starts from: a line from part 5 of "East Coker."

blood and sand: perhaps only coincidentally the title of a popular 1941 movie about bullfighting, starring Tyrone Power and Rita Hayworth, and based on the 1909 novel of the same name (*Sangre y arena*) by Vicente Blasco Ibáñez.

Lady, whose shrine [...] promontory: the first line of part 4 of Eliot's "Dry Salvages."

Pastora: the name of a Spanish woman Stephen/Wyatt falls in love with in *R*.

And on the deck [...] before us': from part 3 of "The Dry Salvages."

in rooms to those who spend their lives in rooms: an Eliotic phrase used in *R*: "They arrived at a room full of people who spent their lives in rooms" (176).

the way up [...] the same: slightly misquoted from part 3 of "The Dry Salvages."

aduanas: the Spanish word for customs agents.

Il faut cultiver notre jardin: "We must cultivate our garden" is the closing line of Voltaire's 1759 novella, in which the ever-optimistic Pangloss is a major character.

an old man [...] waiting for rain: the opening lines of Eliot's "Gerontion."

To John Napper

[*WG arrived back in the U.S. in early May 1951. In July, he arrived at the New York office of the U.S. Information Service "in a white linen suit, flower in his lapel, and gold watch across his vest, to see Elmer Davis, a Harvard alumnus, who was Director of the Office of War Information during the war. 'Tell him that it is William Gaddis, a former editor of* Lampoon,*' he said. That announcement gained him entrance" (Bernard J. Looks,* Triumph Through Adversity *[Xlibris, 2005], p. 64). He got a job there writing articles for* America Illustrated, *a cultural magazine sent to Russia and Iran to counteract anti-American propaganda, and continued to work on* R, *which he was then calling* Vigils of the Dead *and/or* The Origin of Design.]

Box 1071
Massapequa L. Isld.
20 july 1951

dear John—

I must confess, New York is an excellent place when one can come in and feel it belongs to him. For no reason, I feel so today. —But I can always retreat to Massapequa and breathe *air*.

Otherwise the usual horror of time scattering by, and little done. It takes a death to stop it; and last week my grandmother died—Christian sympathy aside, it was best thing for everyone concerned, especially my mother, whose life will be much simpler and more free now.

I was pleased to have your French post card—Lord, I wish enough that I had been able to answer your Paris call. But no. I work slowly, and with the usual doubts and despairs. Though I have had one publisher read the thing, and extremely encouraging word from him. Though no $£ encouragement—

WG back from Spain in his white linen suit, 1951 (photo by Martin Dworkin).

WG, Margaret Williams, Charles Eagan,
and Kathleen Costello, June 1951.

though I didn't ask it. I only hope that by end of September I'll be qualified
to do so, because, the state that everything has been in (making me glad that
I did come home), the summer is really just beginning now.

I've joined an excellent library in New York, and am quite settled reading
of forgeries, counterfeiting, faking, imposture, fraud——and trying to manufacture *my* forger. Very difficult. Otherwise simply sit and listen to Vaughan
Williams' transcription of Greensleeves.

A few very compleat letters from David Tudor Pole give me pictures of
London life. —Though *not* such happy prospects as Derby Day, or Sussex,
hushed, gin bottles & Chelsea. I guess I shall never see Barney Emmart again.

But I haven't ever thanked you for pictures of your house? Oh dear. It all
goes on. I hope to write a letter soon enough—this just a fast nervous New
York note.

You'll be pleased to know I gave a lecture and reading on *4 Quartets* to a
N.Y. school teacher (she'd never heard of Him; teaches literature). Oh, the
posturing. No—I shall write—accept this in lieu for the moment. But *do* you
plan Andalusia this fall?

Love to Pauline and you,
W.G.

To John and Pauline Napper

18 East 64th Street
New York City 21
12 December 1951

dear John and Pauline—

If anything of great note had happened, I should have written you before this. But no. Life continues to be all middle. Though there are those who are pleased with the prospect of the holidays, I am little excited, for not this year will I board an aeroplane to escape hideous Paris—be in splendid London hours later—and in Sussex soon after that. I am not upset about no wild Christmas because I am working hard, and really getting on well, happy. Except of course the work takes *time*, endlessly more time. And I am also kept busy doing writing for a magasine the State Department publishes in Iran— good enough income and I still escape the *office job*. [...]

W.

Life continues to be all middle: one of Jack Gibbs's handwritten epigraphs reads: "That a work of art has a beginning, middle and end, life is all middle" (*J R* 486). Aristotle writes: "A whole is that which has beginning, middle, and end" (*Poetics*, chap. 7).

To John and Pauline Napper

[*In April 1952 a version of the second chapter of* R *appeared in the first issue of* New World Writing, *for which he was paid $144.68 and which attracted the attention of agent Bernice Baumgarten (see second letter of 7 July 1953), who negotiated a contract for the novel with Harcourt, Brace. The contract was signed 11 December 1952, and the advance allowed WG to work full-time on completing it.*]

New York City
1 March 1952

dear John and Pauline—

[...] I am much where I was when I last wrote—except that the novel now is almost 100,000 words, and just barely more than half finished—it is turning out quite *long* which is going to be difficult with prospective editors. So far I've only been offered an option on a contract—2 or 3 hundred dollars, have not taken it since I've still enough to live on, and am still doing State Department writing, a piece every 4 or 5 weeks at 200$ a throw, which is just enough to live on in New York. But I do believe that within 4 or 5 weeks I shall really know what direction I am going to be going in for the next few years. And shall post you accordingly. One of these pocket paper book things is publishing an extract of some 5000 words of this novel—a lengthy attack on France, Paris, and the Holy Roman Church it turns out to be, pretentious and venal but I shall send one along when it is published, may entertain you.

Immediately the king died I wanted to write you—because it struck a very responsive cord—what with Sir James Frazer—but how important it is that the king does die, most important part of the ritual; and the sense confirmed of death and resurrection, without recourse to that ghastly bloody mess of Golgotha 33a.d. —You know when you think about it *what* a business, pretty girls going about wearing a likeness of a tiny man nailed to a cross on their throats. Well I can not get started again on this. Yes, how I should like nothing better this very evening than being *there, talking.* Wait and pray. I immensely appreciate the Coronation invitation, and hope it *will* work out.

Well the swine was for the birth (not Christ but the sun—and 25 December dies invictus solus) and since the *resurrection* is in view (not Christ but the sun) another fragment of a corpse should be on its way to you now. Please tell me of anything from this land that you need. How happy I am to be able to do any such small thing you know. And I shall write better soon, when I find where I stand. Thank god for the *work.*

Every best wish and love,
W—

100,000 words: the published version of *R* is about 418,700 words.
king died: England's George VI died on 6 February 1952.
Sir James Frazer: author of *The Golden Bough*, which concerns kingship rituals.
dies invictus solis: Day of the Unconquered Sun, a holiday for the Roman sun god held on 25 December. Apparently WG sent the Nappers a ham ("swine"), as he wanted to earlier (5 April 1951).

To Mike Gladstone

[*A lifelong friend (1923–2015) from Harvard onward; it was in Gladstone's rooms that WG got drunk on the night of the incident that led to his expulsion from Harvard. In later years, Gladstone worked in publishing, but previous to the time of this letter he had once sold miniature mobiles (hence the reference below). The "inarticulate Mayberry" is unidentified, but the Doria in the closing was Gladstone's wife.*]

Box 223
Massapequa, L. Isld.
26 June 1952

dear Mike,

No need perhaps to say how pleased I was with your note; those are the things that count, make this continuous strain of lunacy worth it all, and believe me so much more important than miserable folk like the inarticulate Mayberry (the oddest sequitur I've come across in some time, his thing): and as for him, writers have the best weapons finally to drown out such bitter whining.

Whether it all does sustain I don't yet know, and it is coming out to be extremely long, some 150 or 160 thousand words so far, and more to come before everyone is settled. That will be a problem; even though as I read it it seems quite tightly written. Well, I'm doing nothing else but work on it now, and can't make much sense talking about it. This is the first letter I've written in some months; and am seldom in New York, have seen little or no one since early May.

These are hateful bits of intelligence, but re mobiles I saw in the local nightmare supermarket one with Rhngld beer tattooed on its several free faces, and thought of you, and thought God save us both.

But this was simply to thank you for your letter, which has made me very happy this evening, and will whenever I think about it.

All very best wishes to you and Doria,
W.

Rhngld: i.e., Rheingold beer, popular in New York at the time, and mentioned in the Wagner-influenced *J R*.

To Edith Gaddis

[WG spent the winter of 1952–53 finishing R *in a farmhouse outside the small town of Montgomery, west of Newburgh, New York.]*

[Montgomery, NY]
22 November 1952

dear Mother,

This certainly isn't crucial; but if convenient could you call Brentano and see if there's any standard small edition of selections of the work of Bishop (George) Berkeley? There was one in Scribner's Modern Student's Library, the Philosophy Series edited by Mary Calkins. Better I suppose call Scribner's then, that's pretty much the sort of edition I want. But if there's a question or confusion put it off. I'll appreciate it greatly. And one of these 50¢ typewriter ribbons please?

Peace and quiet, and as yet no fire down below, though it will probably blizzard for Thanksgiving and I'll take my dinner down there. Ooops! I manage an anemic version of *Ein Feste Burg ist Unser Gott* on the pipes. Also Greensleeves about up to the elbow.

love,
W

Bishop (George) Berkeley: Irish philosopher (1685–1753). In *R*, Wyatt studies his *New Theory of Vision* (81), dealing with optics, and Anselm mentions him in passing (532). WG's library includes the book he requests: *Essay, Principles, Dialogues*, ed. Mary Calkins (Scribner's, 1929).

Ein Feste Burg ist Unser Gott : "A Mighty Fortress Is Our God," one of Martin Luther's best-known hymns, adapted as a choral cantata by Bach.

To Edith Gaddis

[Montgomery, NY]
11 december 1952

dear Mother,

Rain, rain, —and temperatures like September, all very well except that the furnace of course feels slighted, not needed, senses I'm only coddling her for chills ahead, and is slowly pining away down there, the mere blush of life on her black cheek. She gets worse daily: (I think it must be the outside air's so warm that an updraft's wanting, and with the first chill of terror that descends on us she'll rouse).

The work is going well, though the days are becoming confused with nights, to the point where I've been working until 5 and 6, and not getting up until mid-morning: but there, what's the sense in being groggy and unworkmanlike at 9am, and asleep at 3? if time is, as it is here, a continuum . . . well, this goes on . . .

A glorious feat, fête, what have you, last night, I heard Handel's *Messiah*, there is something to make us weep in exaltation. (Of course it came from Toronto, in entirety, not a Firestone rag-end, presenting a single chorus, And He shall feed His flock as though He were Harvey Firestone Handel's patron . . . followed by O Little Town of —— as part of the Oratorio, —this goes on and on too as you know.) Nothing, you know, to do with Christmas as agreed but I think that after the holidays when prices and treatment in our great salons are more gentle I shall look around down there for some music-playing apparatus.

No; for Christmas I'll greatly appreciate it if you can bring up a box of this paper. It is Southworth Paper 4-star plain 8½ by 13 number 402 D. 500 sheets is around 4$. I got this in the stationer across from the Harvard club, where I've been getting it for some time and don't know another place. And another ribbon please? [...]

love,
W.

Harvey Firestone: American industrialist (1868–1938); his tire company sponsored *The Voice of Firestone*, a weekly radio program featuring classical music (1928–56).

To Edith Gaddis

[Montgomery, NY]
19 february 1953

dear Mother,

Did you get the McCarthy-trial programme? It is going on now, a few minutes after our call: God, that dead bullying voice of the senator from Wisconsin, and the way things can be twisted. This *Voice of America* business, do you wonder that our propaganda is lousy, and from now on, after this business, is going to be just plain pitiful. O, it breaks my heart, because this whole war is propaganda and what, what, what can you do.

Of course (as Elmer Davis mentioned) what can be better for, say, anti-Communist propaganda than using, but I mean using carefully and intelligently, not scattering broadcast, the work of known Communists, when it can be used to support our side? As taking things out of their original context (as, as far as this goes, and, as far as, like an idiot, I told the State Dept 'Special Investigator' cops could quite easily be done with my work to support their side (I mean this work I'm now on, the Dale Carnegie business for instance; not what I wrote for the State last winter)) is a common and an obviously effective 'trick', and that's what propaganda is, you know. I mean falsifying to the extent of not telling the whole story (the way women lie). What advertising is, and that's what's risible at this point, that we're being eaten out from the inside by advertising like no other nation in history ("selling") and from the outside by this bullying voice on the radio now.

Good God, maybe Martin Dworkin's a top-Communist, maybe Bill Haygood is, (this I suppose should be burned, you know how I mean it but those lines 'out of context': —Now Mr Gaddis, you do respect your Mother?/ Yes sir./ And I would assume that you usually tell her the truth about things

which concern you and your affairs?/ Yes sir./ Is it true that you wrote her a
personal letter dated 19 February 1953, in which you mentioned the possibility
of two men whom you knew and worked with in the State Department being
'top-Communists'/ Yes sir, but I .../ And did you use it in reference to these
two men who had been your close associates?/ But I . . .

But I . . .

But I . . .

Well God knows, if we go under, I hope to be sitting right here in Black-
berry Hill listening to the furnace bubble, even if I'm burning books in it,
and books aren't going to be much good much longer for anything else.

Nevertheless

Nevertheless

Nevertheless

I'm writing one and I'd better get at it, so it can be published, because it
will have lots and lots of pages and each one a moment of heat.

Spain by Assumption Day. Spain or Belleview-vue. Or the attached.

de minimis non curat lex,

W.

McCarthy-trial programme: in 1953 Republican Senator Joseph McCarthy conducted
highly publicized hearings that attempted by intimidation and innuendo to expose
secret Communists among mostly innocent U.S. citizens.

Voice of America: the U.S. government's official radio/television broadcasting service.
Regarded by some as a vehicle for U.S. propaganda, McCarthy suspected it was influenced by Communists, and several VOA employees were grilled before television
cameras.

Elmer Davis: American reporter (1890–1958) and a harsh critic of McCarthy's witch-
hunting tactics. As noted earlier, he hired WG to work on *America Illustrated*.

Dale Carnegie business: WG's critique of Carnegie in *R* (498–503) could be read as an
attack on American values.

Martin Dworkin: American writer and editor (1921–96), whom WG met while both
were working at *America Illustrated*. Dworkin became a close friend and confidant
of WG, and also took the author's photo that accompanied some reviews of *R*. See
Looks's biography, *Triumph through Adversity* (Xlibris, 2005).

Assumption Day: 15 August, in reference to WG's hope of returning to Spain with
Charles Socarides that summer.

Belleview-vue: Bellevue Hospital in Manhattan, specializing in mental illness.

the attached: a brief newspaper clipping about a colonial-era Harvard janitor who
drank himself to death.

de minimis non curat lex: Latin, "the law does not concern itself with trifles": a legal
maxim, and the implied punchline for a limerick in *R* (523).

To Edith Gaddis

[Montgomery, NY]
13 March 1953

dear Mother,

Very glad with your call last night, & to know that everything is in order again down there; it took me a couple of days to recover.

This isn't of course imperative, but if you could manage without searching at length a libretto of Wagner's *Flying Dutchman*—you know I've had it on my mind for some time and should have sought it out myself by now. And only if you come upon a cheap paper copy (like those in Massapequa)—otherwise I can get hold of it in a library I should think.

Peaceful here as I said, thank heaven, and chapter 18 taking up, though it is so difficult because it takes place in Spain, and by now the mere thought of Spain, let alone trying to write of it, drives me wild.

Rain here, which is to the good, keeps me indoors.

love,
W

Wagner's *Flying Dutchman*: the German composer's first major opera (1843) is alluded to often in *R* (93, 393, 550–51, 895). In a letter dated 17 April 1953, WG thanks his mother "for *Flying Dutchman* and *Tosca*, very much what I wanted, though the first is as bad as the second is good. & so I go on, singing Vissi d'arte; o dear yes, and stewing the chicken bones." Giacomo Puccini's *Tosca* (1900) also plays an important role in *R*, especially Tosca's aria beginning "Vissi d'arte" ("I lived for art").

chapter 18: these chapter numbers don't correspond to the published novel; III.3 is probably meant here.

To Helen Parker

[Montgomery, NY]
13 April 1953

dear Helen.

It goes on, except for turning cold, wet, the furnace out, the fireplace wood wet, and everything quite commensurately springlike, now that we've got through the lilies of purity and the resurrection, and must get along with the afterlife. You were sweet to call, and I must apologise for my doltish end of the conversation, though I think my plea of being but half wakened, and rather chilled at that, must be acceptable?

Otherwise things remain severely peaceful, and until recently, when woodchucks appeared, no distraction from writing novels but reading them. Whether recent choices have been happy ones I'm still unsure: *Oblomov* first, which remains as wondrous as it was those years ago, though conducive to the worst temptations of laziness. Next, de Sade's *Justine*, and that I believe definitely not the thing to manage in such solitude sustained, the only cure a good long walk, chopping up a tree, or firing a shotgun at woodchucks—but the winter's about done, and I've not gone off my head, or drunk myself to death either, I drink very little here in fact, except when Mrs Woodburn and my mother appear, then the cocktail hour comes instead of the coffee.

The work goes on, God knows how long or how much longer, it weighs almost as much as its master now, and I am afraid Harcourt Brace is going to fall off the Christmas tree when they see it. Christ, Christ how I dread that.

But I've put *Justine* aside and am keeping warm one flank with kerosene, and back to work on "Chapter XX" —O God. *A Day with the Pope*, D.V., and in silence, since AM radio in this country is a total loss as far as I can see. No music, words, words—(while I like Carlyle busily assemble the golden Gospel of Silence "effectively compressed in thirty fine volumes").

And so this evening being spent in Spain, and Good God! the sadness of that, of going through notes made there, even Baedeker's stiff prose on it brings a lump to the throat. But there!

love to you, and you all,
W.

Oblomov: the 1859 masterpiece by Russian novelist Ivan Goncharov (1812–91), whose title character is the embodiment of physical and mental laziness.

Justine: Sade's porno-philosophic novel (1791) is cited several times in *R*. WG owned an English translation published in Paris by Le Ballet des Muses.

A Day with the Pope: a picture book by Charles Hugo Doyle, published by Doubleday in 1950, and cited twice in *R* (546, 827).

Carlyle: the *ODQ* quotes this line from John Morley's biography of Thomas Carlyle: "The whole of the golden Gospel of Silence is now effectively compressed in thirty-five volumes" (*sic:* not "fine," as WG has it).

To Sheri Martinelli

[*American artist and writer (1918–96); WG fell in love with her in 1947–48, and based R's Esme on her. She was also an unwitting contributor to the novel: Esme's letter on 471–73 is verbatim from an aristic statement she mailed WG. This undated draft was found among Gaddis's papers; it is unclear whether it was copied and mailed, or when, but it is too lovely to omit. For more on her, see my "Sheri Martinelli: A Modernist Muse," in* My Back Pages *(Zerogram, 2017), 535–66.*]

[Massapequa]
[Summer 1953]

Sheri, what a great happiness it was, seeing you again; though there were enough moments of feeling young again, and too young again, and though other people seem to want to be young again I do not, once was enough. So we all go not changing just getting more so.

But you again, is something else, and still beautiful, yes: even then I could not under-stand other people taking your presence for granted and still I cannot, nor understand, no one weeps looking at you, I will. So, such a recognition, seeing you again: but to be grateful, right before God and everybody, for your being happy to see me again, take that for granted! no, no that could not be for granted, too kind a gift. Or, if the present is every moment reshaping the past, so that any instant is liable to come up with the verdict, I was wrong all the time! or, I was right all along—there: I was right all along? Not being a scientist who by measurement attempts prediction, it is a very dangerous way to live today. So gifts asked from the most selfish motives are the humbly received. And considered upon retirement. Knowing you go right on now, every minute being, thought of and loved you know. My selfish motives, my humble gratitude, then always the retirement for finally there is only the work. And all the while you are loved.

W.

[*Two other drafts are extant; the first refers to a prediction in Worth Smith's* Miracle of the Ages, *mentioned earlier (7 April 1947, 7 April 1948): "The final 'woe' will begin August 20, 1953. That will be a period during which the whole earth is to be 'cleansed of its pollutions,' and which will prepare the people of the earth for the* actual beginning of Christ's Millennial Rule" (chap. 9). Martinelli was living in Washington DC at the time.]

Please do not take this as an impertinence; nor as a joke, until afterward, if it is by then possible to take anything lightly.

I implore you to heed the day 20 August of this year as a day of catastrophe, of impersonal and grand proportions, and protect yourself from its possible consequences insofar as this is to be done.

It seems that simply residency in a capital is dangerous; and if you are working in the city do take that day off; and if you are living in the city, do if it is possible plan to spend that day abroad, in open country somewhere.

I do sincerely [hope] that we can laugh about this one day, and very much doubt it.

Until then, best wishes.
Gaddis

Sheri Martinelli; top: a double exposure taken ca. 1945; bottom, from a *Vogue* photo shoot in the late 1940s, a particular favorite of WG's.

and
the candles are reversed, and in darkness the entire congregation affirms
"Amen"——all this because I think that Spinoza receiving the Schammatha
would make an excellent painting. Well there, these are words.

If I make mistakes now, and seem too importunate, don't be concerned
any more so than you were ever. I am not a scientist, but must only try to see
things my own way, for finally, after all, there is only the work. "Why has not
a man a microscopic eye?["] your poet asks: "For this plain reason: man is not
a fly." There is only the work, and now I know that is all there is.

But Sheri, how much your recognition meant, and means, to me, and thank
God, and thank God you are well and beautiful and have a sister Honey who
writes you so as she did and trusts you as she does. And I— And other things?
Well the poet, making a garland of undistinguished flowers for the Martyrs
of the Theban Legion, to wear hidden if they will under their laurels, presented
with such an apology, still he may admonish, "And yet revile it not, for it is
love."

W. Gaddis

---

the present [...] I was right all along: cf. *R* 92: "How real is any of the past, being every
moment revalued to make the present possible: to come up one day saying, —You
see? I was right all the time. Or, —Then I was wrong, all the time." Wyatt repeats the
remark later: "—But the past, he broke in, —every instant the past is reshaping itself,
it shifts and breaks and changes, and every minute we're finding, I was right ... I was
wrong, until ..." (590).

candles are reversed [...] Spinoza: from the Dutch philosopher's excommunication,
recounted on *R* 536–37.

"Why has not man [...] microscopic eye": from Pope's *Essay on Man* (1:193–94), as
quoted on p. 202 of *R*.

Martyrs of the Theban Legion [...] for it is love": "The Martyrdom of the Theban Legion" is a poem by Benedictine monk Sigebert of Gembloux that ends, "Clumsy the
work, a silly weight to carry, / And yet revile it not, for it is love," which WG found
in Helen Waddell's *Mediaeval Latin Lyrics* (1929).

To Helen Parker

[In May, WG submitted the completed manuscript of R *to Harcourt, Brace; they assigned it for copy-editing to Catharine (Katy) Carver (1921–97), managing editor of* Partisan Review *at the time.]*

Massapequa, Long Island
7 July 1953

dear Helen,

All things considered, I think the weekend worked out quite successful; though right now I am grateful to be getting down to working again, after a month of not, which has been quite distracting, the mind scattered in every direction now being collected.

Lunch with one's (soi-disant) publishers proved a restrained and formal enough affair: no demands made upon the "author" (also soi-d—) nor hardly suggestions, concerning the work in hand. And I have here the first chapter, with their (Katy's) suggestions and queries which are really very gentle. So thank heaven I say down to work and the incumbent sanity. [...]

good wishes, love,
W.

———

To Edith Gaddis

[Massapequa]
7 July 1953

dear Mother,

I've just had a pleasant and newsy letter from Mary; and am writing her now (and enclosing the "hundred"). Also she enclosed a letter from Joan —— (Dick Humphry's lady friend) which suggests that I try writing something for *Gourmet*, a project I'm going to get at immediately and see if it's possible.

Also I forgot to say, that in our talk Bernice suggested that when *The Recognitions* is done, I may well try for a Guggenheim. So we'll keep that in mind!

Now, since the Harcourt check is come through, if you need this month's 50 from the rent, as you must, by all means hold on to it.

Otherwise, this place, aside from the front hedge, of course, is in order and peaceful again.

love,
W.

———

Mary [...] Joan [...] Dick Humphry: Mary Woodburn; the others were family friends.
Gourmet: a magazine devoted to food and wine (1941–2009).
Bernice: Bernice Baumgarten (1902–1978), WG's agent, and wife of novelist James Gould Cozzens. For WG's Guggenheim proposal, see Emmart letter (February? 1954) below.

To John and Pauline Napper

Massapequa, L. Isld. N.Y.
10 August 1953

———— Nessun maggior dolore
Che ricordarsi del tempo felice
Nella miseria,

dear John and Pauline,
forgive that, but such a card as yours this morning, giving as do all your cards and letters do, this combined consternation and pleasure, makes misery of present circumstance whatever it might be. And the happy time on the Costa Brava this view recalls makes the uncertainties of the moment wearying and dull indeed.

Not that news from you is necessary to bring all this, or you, into mind: no, quite the other way, really, I find myself too often looking back on it all with the motionless stare of an old man on youth. Do you know, I can almost say, nothing has happened since last I wrote you, however many months or years it may be. In a worldly way everything is the same, which is I'm afraid

John Napper and his Coronation painting of Elizabeth II, May 1953.

why I haven't written. Is it, I suppose, that I've waited, and waited, for the most vain reasons, to be able to send some roaring news of my own success? though if that's so, it's only because of your good faith in all this time.

Now it is as difficult as it is dishearting to believe that we are in mid August; because the work, yes, the same project you remember, was to be done once for all before the fall set in, and now I greatly doubt it. After a winter spent alone in a farmhouse in upstate New York, I came out to greet the spring with *The Recognitions* finished: a half million words! I had already got an advance of a thousand dollars from the publisher (Harcourt Brace, who are tied up with your (and T S Eliot's) Faber & Faber), and you may imagine their dismay at the length of this manuscript. And so now we are all concerned with what work they think it still needs; though thus far the editors have been very lenient with me, very mild in their suggestions, and very pleased about it generally. But slow! I had fully intended to spend all of this summer on it; but day after day passes in impatient unemployment while I wait for them to finish whatever editorial reading they appear to find necessary. All of this badly complicated by there being only one copy. The nerves slip, slide, perish, as the fall's cold weather approaches and the bank account disappears.

What the winter will bring I cannot imagine; this novel, my life for so long, will be done; and, at the rate of payment of $1000 for 5 year's work, I am not inclined to start another immediately. O! if I could say, —I plan sailing from here in October, to go direct to Madrid ... or Liverpool ... Algiers ... Bangkok— though I don't really try to think about it, and won't, until I'm finished with Harcourt Brace, for this time at any rate.

How often I thought of you during Coronation time, and regretted missing it; especially if it was, as a paper quoted here, "one hell of a boozer"? while here I sit, knowing that in the most ordinary of circumstances there were the best of drinking companions across the ocean: let alone a Coronation. Even now you're sitting in Boodle's—well, speaking of good drinking companions, Barney Emmart is usually available for that profitable pastime, usually spent between us in the standard American way (figuring out how to make a million dollars), or figuring a way to get back across the Atlantic Ocean—obviously we haven't managed either solution yet. Just quietly winding up old men (if one can wind up an old man quietly). Our lost youth: lost somewhere between London and Tripoli— Lord! if you see us selling pencils in the Edgeware Road don't be surprised.

Do you ever see David Tudor Pole? It's as long that I've been out of touch with him, and again for these reasons of uncertainty, and the constant hope that in my next letter I shall be able to say, I'm on my way—and am sending along a copy of my novel ... give him my best if you do see him, though these things aren't yet true. And to both of you; though it seems strange not addressing you at Chantry Mill, what happened to it?

Palamós next summer? (Though I have believed for some time there will be war before this month is out, and do still.) Otherwise, let me know more of you, I so enjoy any word.

and love to you both,
W Gaddis

Nessun [...] miseria: "There is no greater sorrow / Than to recall a time of happiness / In misery"—from Dante's *Inferno* (5:121–23) by way of *ODQ*.
advance of a thousand dollars: equivalent today to around $10,000.
slip, slide, perish: another reference to section 5 of Eliot's "Burnt Norton": "Words strain, / [...] Under the tension, slip, slide, perish [...]."
winding up: British slang for annoying/taunting.
Edgeware Road: i.e., Edgware, a major street in London.

To Muriel Oxenberg

[*Born into a wealthy family, Muriel Oxenberg Murphy (1926–2008) graduated from Barnard with a degree in Art History and in 1949 joined the staff of the Metropolitan Museum of Modern Art, cofounding its American painting and sculpture department. She later married Charles B. G. Murphy and became a renowned* salonnière; *after he died, she reunited with WG in 1979 and was his companion for the next sixteen years. (FHO is dedicated to her.) For more on her life, including her relationship with WG, see* Excerpts from the Unpublished Files of Muriel Oxenberg Murphy, *ed. L. Evan Goss (Xlibris, 2008).*]

23 November 1953

Dear Muriel,

Late, with no news; and by now you've probably no use for a brief bibliography on time. But neither I nor Barney (who just 'phoned) has suggestions on the order of Dunne's *Experiment with Time* of the twenties, which I gather was the sort of thing your friend was interested in?

Then, you've likely forgot this, or indeed our entire conversation; still I enclose it, for whatever interest it may recall for you (and however Manichaean the choice may appear: which it certainly cannot be for such dualism is too easy; and surely evil is self limited?) It was Peter, speaking in the Clementine *Recognitions*:

"First of all, then, he is evil, in the judgment of God, who will not enquire what is advantageous to himself. For how can anyone love another, if he does

Muriel Oxenberg, 1954.

not love himself? In order, therefore, that there might be a distinction between those who choose good and those who choose evil, God has concealed that which is profitable to men."

Every good wish,
W. Gaddis

Dunne's *Experiment with Time*: Anglo-Irish engineer J. W. Dunne's 1927 study of how consciousness perceives and distorts the simultaneity of time.

Clementine *Recognitions*: an anonymous religious novel of the 4th century (falsely ascribed to Pope Clement I) in which a young Roman named Clement joins Peter's entourage as he preaches in Phoenicia. Gaddis learned of it from Graves's *White Goddess* and not only named his first novel after it, but uses the passage above (from book 3, chapter 53) as the epigraph to *R* I.3.

To William Converse Haygood

[*A writer and public relations officer (1910–85) Gaddis met in Spain (see 11 April, 49), later editor of the* Wisconsin Magazine of History *from 1957 to 1975. In late 1953, WG's friend Alan Ansen (1922–2006)—formerly Auden's secretary, friend to the Beats, later a poet—rented his home on Long Island to WG for a small sum and left for Europe, not to return until April of 1954.*]

816 Bryant street
Woodmere, L. Isld. N.Y.
4 January 1954

dear Bill,

I was glad to have your card, but surprised, you may imagine, to have it from a royal red white and blue farm house. I've certainly wondered, in the year past, if you were holding out on Mallorcan okra, and regret, regret, that I never got to visit that place. As for Wisconsin after 5 Spanish years, well ... that must be incredible from your end of things. I still haven't got adjusted to paying 250ptas for a 20pta bottle of coñac. Which may be just as well; though the nerves need that cure more often here than they did in Madrid, where they were shaken for much better, or at least more colourful reasons.

Only recently I began to consider the possibility that youth is gone, that I'd better damn soon figure out what I'm going to be when I grow up. (I was writing a letter to the fellow I went to North Africa with, after a card from him from Tunis; and found myself recalling Sfax on a Saturday night like scenes from childhood never to be revisited.) And as for what I'm doing now, I don't know whether you'll be pleased or inordinately depressed, when I tell you it's the same thing, the same book, the same parade of megalomania. Some golden years have passed, I think, since I sat back easily and said (gazing confidently out over Madrid rooftops from your pink terrazo) I was about done with it. Well, I warn you against rattling around in farmhouses to write: I spent last winter in one alone, and came out with the woodchucks in May, and a 13-pound manuscript, about a half-million words. I have a contract with Harcourt-Brace, and have so far got $1500 dollars out of them in advances over this past year, needless to say all of it gone and all I've got to show for it a bowler hat. Also needless to say, they were quite rattled when they saw something the length, if not the substance, of *War & Peace*. Though I must admit they've been mightily good so far, and though they hope I will take a line out here and there, seem resigned to going through with it however I finish it to my own satisfaction. (As though that were ever possible!) The whole summer was wasted while they fooled around with it; I only had it back a few months ago and since have been scrabbling around taking out something I thought was amusing 4 years ago and putting in something else just as unedifying that I find amusing now. It's terrifically hard to cut because it's tied and knotted together like a Persian carpet; and worse, by now I've thoroughly lost interest in it, it seems an endless pretentious bore, and I just want to get rid of it, lock my youth up in a cloth-bound tomb and go on to something else, as absurd, possibly, but different. I've had about enough of this pondering profound half-truths in cold empty rooms, and look forward to making some attempt at metempsychosis from this shade into a human being.

But in truth it is almost done. It's only a matter of weeks, 6 or 8 I should think, and I'll hire a truck to take it in to them. They plan on publication in some 6 or 8 months. Good God! how I'd like to be flat on my back in one of those soiled interiors along Plaza Tirso de Molina when that happens. But no: I'll be busy qualifying for humanity by thinking succinctly, not just worrying myself green, over money.

This winter I've rented a suburban house from a friend who went abroad, whose taunting hilarity I get by mail from Algeciras, Madrid, Lisbon, &c&c&c. Holed up alone again, but here with an incredible library and the array of records he has reared, which take some of the chill off. And as far as the work goes, this is certainly the worst part, the deadliest and most tiresome and uninspiring.

And I've wondered if you finally threw over that novel? and what now? The free-lance writer is certainly the most perilous life I know, from what I see around me in New York, and after this prolonged single-purposed lunacy of mine, I don't think I'll try to go on picking up odd tries here and there. My income so far at about 300$ a year (and I don't expect to make any more on this thing), I doubt if I can snap off a fast *SaturdayEveningPost* story. Also I've met a beautiful girl who won't have me; and the only counter I have for that is a friend who has a friend who has an asphalt pit near Marakesh.

Somehow it isn't all quite like they told me it was going to be.

But again, if there is anything I can do at this end for you (I still feel you to be about as far away as Pollensa, Franco on the one hand, Mc§xxxxy on the other), do let me know. I still keep perilous contacts among the publishing (not the literary) world; and if no one's seen that novel you were working on but the fellow you wrote me about last year (who said that 'satire wasn't marketable just now') I'd think someone ought to. And certainly if you're ever in this direction let me know, there are always rooms and beds available, dangerously near that sink of delights New York, where I am achieving my ambition and becoming a dirty old man as fast as nature will allow.

every best wish to you and your family, and all luck in this New Year,

W. Gaddis

---

taunting hilarity I get by mail: Alan Ansen's numerous letters to WG are now at Olin Library.

that novel: in 1956 Haygood published a novel set in Mallorca entitled *The Ides of August* (World Publishing Company, which in 1962 would reprint *R*.)

a beautiful girl who won't have me: presumably Muriel Murphy.

Pollensa: town on Mallorca.

Mc§xxxxy: McCarthy: see 19 february 1953.

To John Napper

[*Written on the same day as the previous letter, and with similar matter, some of which has been edited out.*]

Woodmere

4 January 1954

dear John,

[...] And so Ivan Morris and I and Barney Emmart, who had bounced in for a few days from Carolina, where he is all mixed up with Extra-Sensory-Perception, levitation, card tricks, thaumaturgy, &c at Duke University, had a few quiet and very pleasant beers (and a good occasion, happening on my birthday so [29 December]), and I had some details of a spree you all went on to Spain. Even to the point of yourself playing jotas was it? or flamenco? in a Catalan village plaza. O I tell you, this paying 250ptas for a 20pta bottle of coñac cramps me badly here, I never sing abroad anymore, or clap my hands in the street. I was sorry not to see more of Morris; but after dinner that evening came back here, and aside from some broken glass and a nameless blue-eyed girl on Thursday night, have been sticking pretty close to this infernal machine.

By now you may well think that if our correspondence continues I'll still be writing you in five more decades, that I'm still working hard on the same thing, same damned book, same parade of megalomania, for I still am scrabbling along on the thing you read ch. I of so many years ago at Chantry Mill. [...] I am so tired of it, have entirely lost interest in every bit of it, and being quite assured that I'm never going to make any more money from it, would so happily forget the entire evidence of wasted youth. Such low spirits have persisted for some months now; but I look for a change of some sort when I do get this thing off my hands, and start looking around to see what I'm going to be when I grow up. (And not as the Duke of Gloucester had it, —Another damned, thick, square book! Always scribble, scribble, scribble! Eh! Mr Gibbon?)

Though this residency is the most curious yet. A friend who went abroad for the winter rented me his house, a real suburban house with country Cadillacs squeezing past, a house that is just the definition of a suburban house, undistinguished, everything works, gas, heat, carpets, stairs, everything but the immense television set which broke in protest of my moving in after three days here, and I haven't got it fixed. But there is a vast and very select collexion of books, and a battery of records and machines to play them, and by now I'm almost mad enough to be at home only in an empty house, so it should work out well, when this piece of present lunacy is done and I can contrive some means of making a cool million to support myself in the manner to which my landlord is accustomed. [...]

Otherwise I keep pretty much alone; and after some of the antics I've performed in nice company am now being encouraged to do so. Well damn their eyes, it's not I who've lost Athens, Athens is losing me . . . oops!

[*Handwritten at bottom*:] Forgive the petulant tone in all this; I know it will lapse into brightness when this work's done. Thanks again for your thoughtful cheer of almond paste from the only place worth *being*. And every possible best wish for now and the new year to you and Pauline.

love to you both,
W.G.

Ivan Morris: a British author and translator from the Japanese (1925–76) who spent many years in America. WG quotes from his book *The Nobility of Failure* (1975) in "The Rush for Second Place" (*RSP* 57).

jotas: regional Spanish folk songs, usually in waltz time.

Duke of Gloucester [...] Mr Gibbon: an anecdote about the eminent British historian that WG probably found in *ODQ*; he liked it enough to call a pre-pub section of *J R* "Untitled Fragment from Another Damned, Thick, Square Book" (*Antæus*, 1974).

collexion of books: see Jack Kerouac's novel *The Subterraneans* (Grove Press, 1958, p. 93) for a description of Ansen's impressive library; WG was the model for "Harold Sand" in that novel, which fictionalizes events of a few days in August 1953.

it's not I who have lost Athens: so reportedly said the Greek philosopher Anaxagoras (500–428 BCE) after the Athenians banished him for impiety.

———

To Barney Emmart

[*An unfinished draft, half typed, half handwritten, about a romantic crisis.*]

Woodmere, Long Island
[February? 1954]

dear Barney,

Saturday afternoon, and your shocking letter, for I'd no idea of it. I'm seldom enough in the San Remo anyhow, and haven't been in some time, haven't been doing anything but working, or trying to work, sick and tired of it, of most anything. The weather's been so bad that, going in town last evening for dinner, I took the train, which meant that on my usual late round I didn't make all the usual stops, as I do with a car; but only a few 3d avenue bars, & so home. Christ, I don't know. And even enough before your note here, I've been walking up and down the library listening to Gluck's *Orphée* with a glass of whisky (thank God I was provident!) and saying that, just saying, —I don't know. And I don't. I'm just so tired of all these things which repeat and confirm this desolation we try by such ingenuous ruses to belie.

Curiously though, if my first reading of your note brought on a sickish feeling, I found that on the second or third something different, a sclerosis of the heart: and, —there…that is the way it is, and all our skipping and dancing and sending flowers and wearing clean linen…and keeping our desolation locked in, doesn't work; or at any rate it doesn't work there, on them, the way we've been brought up to expect it to. I feel like a tired old fool sitting here, with no counsel for either of us but back to the books, and Chryssipus, and dieting to extinction.

I've felt the life gone out of me for months now, well since the fall of last year. This 'work' bores me infinitely, a lousy long boring pretentious adolescent parade of attempts at experience; and other people become for me more strange and more distant and more delicately contrived than I dare think on. Chilly and grown old: because I thought I'd come to life for a little while, last September or so, the way you were so recently: and now? are there finally just these things: books, whisky, music & tobacco.

The only reading I've been able to settle to is Shakespear.

[The typed draft ends there, followed by handwritten notes:]

All of these things are succinctly managed somewhere: here's Hawthorne's Zenobia in the Blithedale Romance, speaking of being favoured with "a little more love than one can conveniently dispose of; and that, let me say, Mr. Coverdale, is the most troublesome offense you can offer to a woman."

"Thank you," said I, smiling, "I don't mean to be guilty of it."

Here, for a book— Essays on the pathology of isolation—Thoreau, Emerson, Hawthorne, Poe, ~~Whitman~~, Melville (& Matthiessen's book) & a poem on Thoreau

[illegible] Beethoven 9th accompanied by 3rd piano concerto
one reason for it is the dearth of whorehouses, for it's only through sin that we share our humanity.

Gluck's *Orphée*: a French reworking of German composer Christoph Gluck's 1762 opera on the theme of Orpheus and Eurydice; alluded to in *R* (205).

Chryssipus: i.e., Chrysippus, stoic philosopher of the 3rd century BCE; subject of an anecdote in *R* (352).

chilly and grown old: another quotation from the final stanza of Browning's "A Toccata of Galuppi's."

the Blithedale Romance: 1852 novel about utopianism; the quotation is from chap. 5.

Matthiessen's book: F. O. Matthiessen's classic *American Renaissance* (1941).

only through sin: cf. *R* 525–26: "—And if it's only through sin that we can know one another, and share our human frailty—"

To William Converse Haygood

[WG wrote again to Haygood on 1 February 1954; according to the 2010 Vashon Books catalog, "Gaddis opens with reference to the death of their friend Dorsey Fisher, and ruminations on the nature of life and loss. He goes on to invite Haygood to stay with him during a visit to New York, and to discuss his own living situation. He also refers to the forthcoming copyediting of The Recognitions *with a staffer from Harcourt. In apparent response to detailed questions from Haygood related apparently to a novel, Gaddis then goes on to discuss his experiences with his agent relating to* The Recognitions. *He then*

continues to discuss the paperback market, mentioning 'in my case since my project is so damned long I doubt they will even be interested.' He continues: 'Though one trouble I've always had, with my impatience, is it always seems to take so long, they all take so long fooling around; and that might be trying, if you're here and trying to manage it yourself, the waiting.' 'Now, 8:30am, the 5th cup of coffee and back to a party (chapter 13) which is itself longer than The Old Man & the Sea. This is really an idiotic way to "live."'" The following letter is handwritten.]

Woodmere, Long Island
30 March 1954

Dear Bill –

I've wondered if possibly you've even been east, & missed me here? because after delivering my 10-pound Ms. to Harcourt Brace, I went off for a week or so of fresh air. Not that that did more than clear the sinuses. But now, except for the prospect of the galleys in June, it's no longer my problem. & you may imagine the vacuum of bereavement I'm in. Hardly an idea of what to do with myself, but something soon, & for the usual crass reason—having got about to the end of the most recent heroic loan I managed.

My landlord here should return in another 2 or three weeks; which will mean the end of any hospitality (civilised) I can offer—shall then I guess move back to the barn in Massapequa—cold comfort, but you're surely as welcome. Though in my present state of mental & spiritual unemployment I strongly consider taking a berth on an outgoing ship. But I am curious about you, what is up? or not up? Here everything is so much the same that it is difficult to sit still.

very best wish,
W.G.

To John Napper

Woodmere
30 March 1954

dear John,

Here with all the news, which includes exactly nothing, but I thought I might at the least write assuring you of that, lest you think something had occurred. Though I don't believe I have written you since I turned the entire 10pounds of manuscript over to Harcourt Brace, & the whole thing is now their problem. It comes we find to some half-million words, some thousand printed pages, some 7$–10$— (the £3 novel) per copy I'm afraid, which assures it against anything so vulgar as a popular success. Presently being prepared for the press, I expect to be pouring through galleys in June; but publication has been put ahead to January, so that they can campaign for it: something I don't object to, but shall certainly not participate in. But there should be sewn (unbound) copies by August or September.

As for England!— I had a very pleasant dinner (pleasant, that is I was allowed to talk about my book for 2 hours) a few weeks ago with Mr Fred Warburg, we got on extremely well, & I believe he is going to take it for Secker & Warburg. So there is little more to do or think about.

But I've wondered how near the feeling of absurdity & bereavement which I'm coddling now may correspond to any you may have upon finishing (abandoning) & letting go a large painting which has taken possibly years? I spend days now wandering up & down this library, hearing a piece of music half through & change it for another; read 20 pages in one book, 50 in another, then sit down & read 4 novels straight through. I believe I could go on this way for some time were it not for that most usual cursed blessing which summons such vagrant minds to reality, & of course I mean money. Until now it has not greatly mattered, I mean I was bent on any ruse so long as I could work & getting that finished was the only importance. Now? Well, trying to turn my head to "creative" mercenary purpose seems quite a futile thing. But here! I don't mean to sound plaintive: simply this curious sense of living in a vacuum, & a not uncommon one in these circumstances I imagine; but am constrained to wonder how long it will go on. Until I have got to the last penny of what I've recently borrowed I suppose. But this is a really idiotic convalescence.

Of course accompanied by the usual phantasies: the "Hollywood gives me $50000000" (a raving impossibility incidentally) & I set sail for Gibraltar, spend the summer in Spain, & thence to London to spend the winter studying at the University, &c.——— The prospect of being here in New York when the thing is published is something I certainly hope to avoid, for all the best & the worst reasons. & presently, the prospect of wandering the pavements of that city begging work is something so unattractive that I cannot contain it long enough to do it. Though ultimately how idiotic to break one's neck getting & keeping a 75$ a week job when it costs all of that to live—& not awfully well—in that city; while I can subsist on 20 a week in the country. Well, this is no new nor certainly unique problem; & with no piece of work on my mind I'm not even vaguely desperate, perhaps I should be? Not yet.

Does this all sound carping & complaining? Lord, I don't mean it to. I'm really in good spirits, if undirected & indifferent just now, until those moments of Look, look! wenches! —Then (What we want is a bank account, & a bit of skirt in a taxi—) Meanwhile, I leave this house in 3 weeks or so &

return to the barn in Massapequa (box 223), to pick up the usual childhood threads, though feeling rather chilly & grown old.

Nonetheless every warm & best wish to you & Pauline.

W.G.

7$–10$: *R* was priced at $7.50 at a time when most hardback novels cost between $3 and $5.

Fred Warburg: Fredric Warburg (1898–1991), one of the leading literary publishers in England. His initial enthusiasm for *R* waned, and it wasn't published in England until 1962 (by MacGibbon & Kee).

Look, look! wenches!: as noted earlier, from the epigraph to Eliot's "Sweeney Erect," taken from *The Maid's Tragedy* by Beaumont and Fletcher (1619).

What we want [...] skirt in a taxi: line 10 of Irish poet Louis MacNeice's "Bagpipe Music" (1937).

feeling chilly & grown old: as noted earlier, from the final stanza of Browning's "A Toccata of Galuppi's."

To Fred Palmer

[*An executive at Earl Newson & Company, a Manhattan public relations firm. The following is a corrected draft, not the mailed letter. WG was acting on Haywood's suggestion that he consider pursuing a job in public relations; in a letter to him dated 16 April 1954, WG wrote: "the P.R. business sounds like a ball. How I envy you having a trade." Here WG eschews his usual British orthography.*]

[April/May? 1954]

Dear Sir.

I have recently been told that your firm is interested in writers for work on fairly extensive projects. However, I did not learn the exact nature of the work, and should be very interested to talk to you about it. A few weeks ago I finished work on a long book, a novel, to be published by Harcourt, Brace & Co., and am now interested in continuing with the sort of work I have done in the past few years.

To give you a brief idea: I was born in New York City (1922), educated largely in New England, after three and a half years at Harvard College came to work for the *New Yorker* magazine (1945) where I spent about a year and a half in fact editing. In 1947–8 I was in Central America, and after that spent a year in Spain. In 1949–50 I lived in Paris and wrote free-lance for the United Nations organization (Unesco) radio and news services. I returned to Spain for that winter, and the following spring went to Tunisia and Libya to work on a documentary film. Returned to New York the following winter (1951–2),

I wrote pieces (in English) for the State Department's Russian- and Arabic-language publication *America*. Since that time I have been entirely occupied with this novel, on which I had been working intermittently for five years.

Aside from this long book, the work I have done, and that which interests me the most now, is creative-fact writing with an interested purpose, similar to those alluded to above. The work in Paris was, of course, general. The film made in North Africa was for an English paper company. The pieces for *America* were of course propaganda, such things as (for the Russian edition) one on the play made from Melville's *Billy Budd*; for the Arabic, one on racing cars in this country. I am unencumbered, speak and read French and Spanish, and if travel is involved should prefer Latin America, whose culture I am more familiar with than others.

If these qualifications interest you with relation to possibilities in the work your firm is doing, I should greatly appreciate talking with you, and shall telephone your office at the beginning of the coming week to find a time convenient to you for an appointment.

To John Napper

> Box 223
> Massapequa, Long Island
> 16 September 1954

dear John,

I trust you and Pauline are by now back from that tour of Titians and Moselles? and thanks for the tormenting picture card; how many years must go by finding these temptations in my mail and returning to sit and "plan"— waiting: this present waiting is perhaps the worst so far, the book due out not until February, and I've no plans nor inspirations for the winter. Certainly not, at this moment, to sit down to construct another half million word anagram. But I have just got word that Fred Warburg (Secker & Warburg) are taking it, and though his plan sounds fairly ill-starred (to make it a 35/ book, and my royalty on the first 2 thousand copies about 1/8d!): but the payment of £200 on publication, a sursum corda indeed and one which lets me at least consider coming to England this winter. (For I don't especially relish being here to make a fool of myself in February.) —So at least it is possible. Though there is a considerable amount of living to be got through before that.

Here I might say with Thoreau "I should not talk so much about myself if there were anybody else whom I knew as well" but still you see there is no *news*. And believe me since at this point the only kind of news which would have significance would be news of money, you will be among the first to hear it, for one of the first expenditures will be a passage on some tramp moving vaguely in yr direction. It is strange, with the chill of the year setting in which always means I must move in some direction (going where the climate suits my clothes), to be quite totally unemployed, spiritually, "gainfully", amorously, or even the real *work*. But as careful in all these fields not to accept employment simply for employment's sake, I see too much of that around me here. Well, read this only as a sort of preface to something more decisive within the next few months. And how I hope that it may be a move in that direction if only for the winter. I do so look forward to seeing and talking with you both again even if not Chantry Mill's flush of youth (I feel chilly and grown old) nonetheless all love and best wishes and hopes to see you both.

W.

Titians and Moselles: the Italian painter (c. 1488–1576) and presumably Moselle, a region in northeast France.

35/ [...] £200: 35 shillings, more than $50 today; £200 = around $7,000 today.

sursum corda: Latin, "lifted heart," from Christian liturgies.

Thoreau [...] as well: from the opening page of *Walden* (1854).

To Patricia Thompson Black

[*WG's future wife (1928–2000), a model and actress who had come to New York from North Carolina to break into theater.* Insatiability, *a 1930 novel by Polish novelist Stanislaw Witkiewicz, features "Murti-Bing" pills that sedate previously unhappy people, especially intellectuals; Czeslaw Milosz discussed both* Insatiability *and the Murti-Bing pill (a symbol for communism) in "The Happiness Pill" in the* Partisan Review *(1951), which WG read (as he told me when I inquired about the reference to Murti-Bing on page 569 of* R; *he never read Witkiewicz's novel). The piece was reprinted as the first chapter of Milosz's* The Captive Mind *(Knopf, 1953).*]

[New York, NY]
29 October 1954

dear Pat,

Here it is: I mean the letter in yr mailbox which you mentioned. But also, if you are going to wade into that book, I had meant to give you this pamphlet: I think the two worlds are much the same, that & *Insatiability*, though I wasn't clever enough to devise anything as splendid as Murti Bing—

I didn't mean to keep you out listening to that fool piano last night so late (that's not true, of course I did) at any rate I hope you did get things arranged & settled & prepared for this Brunswick stew, without too many recriminations, because I enjoyed so much being with you. But there! Pluto, I believe, will soon be out of the ascendent, and we can all get breath, possibly to find it not all totally absurd after all.

Your fashion photographs were very impressive, & I wish you the best weather for yr jaunt on Sunday. Meanwhile it is strange indeed on this quiet & beautifully grey afternoon, to think that you are somewhere, at this very instant, being real.

W.G.

———

To John Napper

(this winter:)
210 East 26th Street
New York City
15 December 1954

dear John

Of course, I am not on board anything bound in that direction, and heaven knows when I ever shall. These I am afraid are the moments one suspects that youth is gone indeed, & it is time at last to settle down to something with an income attached. But you may imagine the suspense, with this book due for publication in March here, and copies of it already spread out among "critics" &c, so that I am constantly hearing fragmentary reports & remarks kind & otherwise of course, but even the kindest ones haven't a penny attached, and that, certainly, is one of the oldest problems of the artist.

But I must tell you, that in spite of my insignificance with my publishers now the thing is done (though they insured my life when I was working on it!), I did prevail upon them to send you an advance reading copy (paper-bound), and I hope you will——what? not, I'm afraid, "enjoy" it, for in spite of my own feelings about its entertainment value, I gather it is not a book people will "like". And there are mistakes, I mean aside from grammar, or historical accuracy: aesthetic mistakes. The bulk could have been cut down greatly, and some of the tiresome sophomorics which betray it as a first novel removed (& some of were in fact written 4 or 5 years ago). But I knew that if I settled down to do that, it might well end up the MS in the bottom bureau drawer. And so best to get rid of it, with all its mistakes, and set forth with the Iron Duke's admonition, Publish and be damned, ringing in one's ears from the outset—— And what sense would there be here in writing an apology for a book which took 7 years trying to explain itself to *me*? So at last I suppose not fare well but fare forward—— [...]

W.

Iron Duke's admonition: one of the "sayings of Great Englishmen" recorded in WG's
mid-December 1950 letter to Napper.
not fare well but fare forward: the concluding lines of part 3 of "The Dry Salvages."

To J. Robert Oppenheimer

[*American physicist (1904–67), known for his work on the atomic bomb. On 26 December
1954 he gave a lecture entitled "Prospects in the Arts and Sciences" at Columbia University's bicentennial anniversary celebration, reprinted in his book* The Open Mind *(1955).
The following is a corrected draft.*]

New York City
4 January 1955

Dear Doctor Oppenheimer.

I have already taken a greater liberty than this, asking your attention to
my letter, in having called Harcourt, Brace & Co., who are publishing a long
novel I have written, to ask that they send you a copy. You must receive mail
of all sorts, crank notes and fan letters of every description, but few I should
think of half a million words. And since I can also well imagine that you
seldom if ever read novels, if only for not having the time, it is an added im-
position to have sent you such a bulky one.

But for having read your recent address at Columbia's anniversary, I should
never have presumed to do so. But I was so *stricken* by the succinctness, and
the use of the language, with which you stated the problems which it has
taken me seven years to assemble and almost a thousand pages to present, that
my first thought was to send you a copy. And I do submit this book to you
with deepest respect. Because I believe that *The Recognitions* was written about
"the massive character of the dissolution and corruption of authority, in belief,
in ritual and in temporal order, . . ." about our histories and traditions as "both
bonds and barriers among us," and our art which "brings us together and sets
us apart." And if I may go on presuming to use your words, it is a novel in
which I tried my prolonged best to show "the integrity of the intimate, the
detailed, the true art, the integrity of craftsmanship and preservation of the
familiar, of the humorous and the beautiful" standing in "massive contrast
to the vastness of life, the greatness of the globe, the otherness of people, the
otherness of ways, and the all-encompassing dark."

The book is a novel about forgery. I know that if you do get into it, you
will find boring passages, offensive incidents, and some pretty painful sopho-

morics, all these in my attempts to present "the evils of superficiality and the terrors of fatigue" as I have seen them: I tried to present the shadowy struggle of a man surrounded by those who have "dissolved in a universal confusion," those who "know nothing and love nothing."

However you feel about the book, please allow my most humble congratulations on your address which provoked my taking the liberty of sending it to you, and in expression of my deepest admiration for men like yourself in the world you described.

To John Napper

[*Napper wrote to say how much he enjoyed* R, *which was officially published on 10 March 1955. For a complete, inquisitorial account of the book-review industry's negative response to WG's first novel, see Jack Green's* Fire the Bastards! *(Dalkey Archive, 1992). In this letter WG also reveals his engagement to Pat Black.*]

New York City
2 March 1955

dear John,

Enough of the foolishness has started to give some idea of what things may be like; and so you may, or possibly you can't really imagine how much your congratulatory words mean, how deeply appreciated since I realise I was getting into your world, I mean painting; while mine it begins to appear is writing. But friendship (and chapter I at Chantry Mill) all aside, imagine how much more your understanding appreciation means than what is in prospect *here*. I think I meant it when Wyatt says that the artist is the shambles of his work, but here it's those shambles they want to devour. One (women's of course) magasine which considered publishing one chapter finally demurred (in frightened awe) but wanted my "picture" and what of my life I c^d spare: if you are a writer, they don't want to buy and print y^r writing, but rather a picture and what you eat for breakfast, &c. But then good God! that's what the book's about—It's difficult not to strike a pose, for being "eccentric" enough to try to get across that: What do they want of the man that they didn't find in the work?—without insulting them all. Already before the thing is even out (10 March) the requests for radio appearance! And *no* is the only thing there. I've seen a couple of advance reviews, they promise to be good, qualified that is by uncertainty, fear of being committed. (I think so far *Time* magasine takes the prize for double-talk, and such gems of idiocy as finding Mr Pivner an attempt to re-do Joyce's Bloom! I knew this sort of thing would happen but Lord! it does stop me in my tracks when I actually see it in print). But this is enough of all this for the moment; I think before the month is out there will be some real monkey business, which I'll report.

Meanwhile like Manto I wait, time circles me; and since I've done nothing all winter but run into debt, I might as well hang on and see what the next few weeks bring in the way of "opportunity". Meanwhile (*very confidentially to you and Pauline*) managing to get married and looking forward to being a "real" father by fall (early fall). Well here we are; and you may see scarcely in position to pick up and go [to] Africa (unless Sidi-bel-Abbès). At the moment cleaning up and hunting a clean shirt to lunch with Fred Warburg, which I'll be doing about the time you read this,

to you and Pauline and best wishes and love,
W.

Wyatt [...] shambles of his work: "—this passion for wanting to meet the latest poet, shake hands with the latest novelist, get hold of the latest painter, devour...what is it?" Wyatt asks his wife Esther. "—What is it they want from a man that they didn't get from his work? What do they expect? What is there left of him when he's done his work? What's any artist, but the dregs of his work? the human shambles that follows it around. What's left of the man when the work's done but a shambles of apology" (95–96). WG will cite this passage often in future letters and interviews.

Time: Theodore E. Kalem's anonymous review appeared in the 14 March issue (112, 114).

Manto: a quotation from Goethe's *Faust*; see note to the May 1948 letter to Edith Gaddis.

To Miss Britton

[*A television executive. The week R was published, WG was pitching projects like the one below and an article on the growing popularity of miniature golf to* Sports Illustrated, *both rejected.*]

New York City
7 March 1955

Dear Miss Britton,

Here enclosed is the three-act outline of Conrad's book *The End of the Tether*. I am delighted that you are interested in it, and that it is available for television; because frankly I'm a good deal more excited about it now, having gone through it in some detail doing this synopsis, than I was when I sent you the straight outline. Excited about it in its own great right; and I had not really realised that Conrad's dialogue is so excellent that it will scarcely need (or bear) tampering with. And perhaps I shouldn't have emphasized 'tragedy';

I think you'll find it here, as it is indeed in the original, pre-eminently a story of devotion and heroism, one of the most distinguished I've ever come across.

Incidentally, do you know of an actor named, I believe, Robert Newton, and British, who played Long John Silver in some recent *Treasure Island* film? I've been obsessed with how well he could do the part here of Massey if he were available.

I appreciate your interest, and do hope that it is rewarded.

> with good wishes,
> William Gaddis

The End of the Tether: a short novel published in 1902 about an aging sea captain who, in order to provide for his daughter, enters into a partnership with an unscrupulous character named Massey.

Robert Newton: British film and stage actor (1905–56). He played Long John Silver in Disney's *Treasure Island* (1950) and again in the Australian-made *Long John Silver* (1954).

To Rochelle Girson

[*In an article on R for the* Saturday Review *syndicate, Girson passed along rumors in "industry circles" that WG partly paid to have the novel published, then "slyly" wondered if he were rich. See* Fire the Bastards, *20–21.*]

> 25 March 1955

Miss Gerson [*sic*]:

It would be a waste of energy on my part to upbraid reviewers who find fault with my recent book: they have, after all, done their best with the published work itself, and there is the book to confirm or refute their attacks. Your wanton 'personal' approach, on the other hand offers no recourse to its shoddy falsity. If I have seemed reticent in giving out information about myself and my personal affairs, it was in hope of avoiding such absurd corruptions as yours, which was just sent me by an irritated relative, clipped from a local paper. Your perversion of what facts were given you (and those in the spirit of confidence) was as surprising as your invention of those that were not.

As for your imputations concerning one of the most respectable publishers in the country, as absurd to those who know Harcourt, Brace (or, more immediately, to those who know my own personal circumstances), as they are sinister to those who do not, I frankly do not understand your motive in attempting to raise such suspicions while pretending to allay them. If I thought you had personal inducements in this matter, I might think your method, for all its lack of originality today, quite clever; but the rest of your copy makes such a conclusion as untenable as your insistence on perverting my personal affairs is strange to me. Is there, here, again, some personal motive? If there is not, I do not understand your fraudulent advertisement of my manner of living; while yours becomes more embarrassingly and more pitifully apparent.

William Gaddis

WG at the time of the publication of *The Recognitions*.
"For some crotchety reason there was no picture of the author looking pensive sucking a pipe, sans gêne with a cigarette, sang-froid with no necktie, plastered across the back" (*R* 936) (photo by Martin Dworkin).

3. *J R*

1955–1975

To Katie Sue Black

[*WG eloped with Patricia Black, marrying her on 18 May 1955 in Ridgefield, CT. The following is the third draft of a letter to her mother in North Carolina.*]

Massapequa, Long Island
[late May? 1955]

dear Mrs Black,

It is late for me to be writing you, at last, of my marriage to your daughter, and I want first to offer you my deepest apologies for uncertainty and anxiety that you have suffered because of the way we have managed things starting off our life together. Like so many difficult parts of the whole situation, this letter is hardly the way I should want to be doing even now, writing you instead of seeing you, to tell you of what is already accomplished, instead of seeking your good wishes for our plans. All of this does bring home how selfish I have been, or both of us have been perhaps, not in what we have done, but in the way we have done it.

A moment came when it seemed there were so many complications that the only thing to do, and the best thing, was to take matters into our own hands. We have been aware of the complications that would follow and, to some extent of the hurts and disappointments we might cause. My mother had met Pat and of course liked her immediately, but she too found our news rather abrupt, and had a little difficulty adjusting to it so quickly. I know how much she would have wanted to participate in such an important event in her only son's life, and in spite of how happy she is about us now, I shall always regret causing her that disappointment. I wish that you and she could have met before this, —but I could sit here writing 'I wish' all day, and it wouldn't change any of the anxiety we have caused for others. Except for these things, we are happy, I know we are going to be happy together but I hope never at the expense of others who are, in different ways, equally dear to us.

(dnt wnt to snd apologtc: proud)(come see us, I dnt know when we can get there) (household problems, $, the usual bickering over groceries, the life I hope to give her &c, but I depend on her stability & household sanity, after bachelordom &c)

I was fortunate in meeting your son Bob, and I hope the advantage we took of his stopping here didn't seem an unfair one, in asking him to carry our news home to you. Never having had a brother or sister myself, that relationship will probably always be strange to me, and I find wonderful how much Pat shares with her brother, even after such a long separation. I also marveled at how he could step out of army life in Alaska straight into new responsibilities, especially those we added to his return to home and civilian life, and I deeply appreciate how readily he took on what we asked of him, and how well he must have taken care of it.

Now I wish I could go on to say that we were coming down to see you any time soon. But you may imagine we have a good deal of readjusting to do ourselves. For myself right now that involves pulling together enough writing work which I can do at home so that I can be with Pat here in Massapequa, instead of commuting to New York or spending the hot summer there. If I can continue to work this out, she should spend a restful and pleasant summer out here in the country, and be as healthy and ready for the fall as possible. None of this yet is the life I hope to give her, but it is a good start. Meanwhile she is an excellent cook, which isn't difficult to appreciate after so many years of cooking for myself. But cooking aside, there are qualities in her, of patience, and kindness, and unselfishness, simple consideration and loyalty, which I know that at last I have you to thank for, in the way you brought her up. And as these things go, from generation to generation, I suppose the only way I will be able to show my appreciation will be indirectly to you, by trying to be worthy of them in her, and making her happy.

Looking back at the early part of this letter, I find a constant tone of troubled apology. I repeat it, concerning my feelings and our feelings for you, but I don't want that to be the whole tone of all this because I am proud to have your daughter Pat for my wife, and grateful, and happy at the prospect of our life together. I hope that it will be something we will be able to share in some ways with you, and that after the anxiety we have given you, you will be proud of us.

To John and Pauline Napper

Box 223
Massapequa, Long Island
[c. 1 October 1955]

dear John & Pauline

Of course hour after hour is spent and wasted, then instead of a letter one writes a *note*—but things are more than usually confused this fall, and for the best but no less frantic reason, Sarah Meares G——, 6 pounds, arrived about 3 weeks ago, and of course again everything is centered around her, within the house and at all hours and also out in the world, where this year there is no monkey business about it, I have to find warm shelter for 3 and I'm afraid at last a real "job"——so, picture me at this point trudging about New York streets like a college boy seeking his first job (it actually is 9 years since I've had a real 9 to 5 office world). And so the possible date of "our sailing" is even further off, now there are 3. Haven't you yet any plans to visit USA? Sorry I cannot provide & sort rain & weather enough to summon you for the commission, —if I did I'd snatch him first for his "biography"—not bloody likely. But we do hope to have heated quarters soon where I can sit down and write you; for the moment just this to send our news and love to you both.

W. G.

To the Editor, *The Spectator*

18 February 1956

Dear Sir:

I have only now come upon your issue for 9 December 1955, with its article 'Printers' Censorship' by Norman St John-Stevas. In his reference to a current American novel of "over 900 closely packed octavo pages" which is "at this moment seeking another publisher", I gather that he spoke of *The Recognitions*. I do appreciate Mr St John-Stevas' approach to the problem he writes of, and his attention to this book in particular. But may I, as its author, submit that through no fault of his own Mr St John-Stevas has been led to give a somewhat distorted picture of the reasons for the book's failure to appear in its originally-projected English publication, when all of the onus is placed upon the printers for their refusal to print a book which "for 2 per cent. of its total length, describes sexual incidents in coarse language."

Incidentally, I should be inclined to take exception to this generous estimate. The novel itself is about a half-million words in length; and however inconsequential 2% of anything may appear, it amounts in this case to some 10,000 words. As I believe a reading of the book would show, there are comparatively few 'sexual incidents' in it and they, when they do occur, are generally described quite obliquely. 'Coarse language' on the other hand is, when given voice (and it scarcely occurs in narrative), almost consistently divorced from such intimate activities. Though it was not at any time suggested that I cut 'coarse language' to make that originally-scheduled English publication possible, I do believe that even if it were all or largely eliminated, the 'sexual incidents' in the book would remain quite demurely intact. And they do, I still feel, have their place there, since the novel is, for the most part, about human beings.

Subsequent to signing my agreement with the 'well-known publisher' noted by Mr St John-Stevas, I was given to understand that certain printers in England had declined the job. But are we to infer, from Mr St John-Stevas' article, that English printing is an essential for English publication? Surely there are alternatives, open to a British publisher for a book he believes in? There must be such, for they were discussed in connection with *The Recognitions*. And I may add that, at the time of my original agreement with the 'well-known publisher', I was given in all good faith to believe that this novel would with little difficulty have won in any obscenity action brought against it in your courts.

I must suggest that, when Mr St John-Stevas notes in passing "its price in the English market would not be less than 35 shillings", he comes rather closer the reason for the impasse which *The Recognitions* finally reached with its originally-intended London publisher. Because of the book's length, it was of course evident at the outset of our negotiations that it must likely come out there as a 35/– novel, a brave step for a British publisher certainly. But the suggestion to cut the book, or let it be cut, came along just 5 months after that publishing agreement had been signed, and 5 days before publication date here in America: time, that is, when the strained reception which the book was to receive in various quarters, notably our aching popularly-dependent 'literary' press here, was becoming apparent. And that abrupt, one might have thought capricious entreaty to cut the novel for its English debut, embraced neither 'sexual incidents' nor 'coarse language,' nor indecent concerts of the two; essentially it concerned length, which is to say, costs. Such a last-minute ultimatum was of course not to be countenanced, however it might pose upon artistic grounds. Now it may be that the artistic purpose of the book would be better served at half its present length; but I had not felt this to be so when I submitted the finished out-size manuscript to my publishers here, nor did they welcome grounds to decline publication when the unexpected size and complexity of the manuscript, and consequently necessary high price of the book, made it quite likely that no 'best-seller' list was going to make up for their very considerable investment. Needless to say I had found that early experience of good faith gratifying indeed.

The ethics which dictated that your correspondent refrain from spelling out the title of the book, like the good intentions of the reference itself, are appreciated. So far as I know, *The Recognitions* is still seeking an English publisher, and I've no objection to its title being strung out in rubrics. Though there may be a perverse pleasure in finding one's work referred to as that of 'near genius', whatever the motivations for such a try-on, it's a chill substitute for publication as you may imagine.

Please forgive my going on at such disproportionate length to the reference in your column, but such ravelings demand it if they are to be picked up at all.

Yours
William Gaddis

To Patricia Gaddis

[*WG and his wife had first moved to an apartment at 223 E. 96th St.—which he later used for storage (in real life as well as in* J R*)—and was now in the process of moving while his wife and daughter were out of town. He expresses interest in Civil War material that would later result in his unproduced play,* Once at Antietam.]

[13 August 1956]

Dear Pat,

I was so cheered to find your letter here this evening. I wrote you some whiling-away foolishness this morning from the 'office' . . . my, for what I got done here today I might as well have spent the time in a pool-hall. But I'd got somewhat discouraged (purely endocrinal I believe), and went up to 96 to get another handful of odds and ends, none of any of it making much sense. [...] But the picture of Sarah holding my letter and saying Papa! Poppa! . . . makes up for everything honestly. [...]

And all aside from how I miss you both, it might work out more happily without Sarah under a paint-sprayer. I must confess I do envy the trip to Aunt Lena, of course that is too heart-rending, the canteen where he hung it 'when he came back' (you might tell Granny that Sarah is also direct descended from a Colonel (Sol Meredith) in the Union Army, and his Cherokee wife (I'll find if he was at Gettysburg)). All of that is so exciting and it is a frightening temptation to get interested in it but right now I'm fighting it off, hoping perhaps 'other things' will get a little beyond their dead halt. Also while I think of it, about the Emmarts, don't be concerned for that, you can see them when they get back surely (and I'd trust this place will be somewhat more presentable by then too).

Again, I'm delighted at the long change you're both getting, and the re-acquaintanceships for you and Sarah's introduction (I am so proud of her!

and can at this distance scarcely believe she's mine and going to be for so long; but then she won't, will she; no, but even being allowed to participate in her existence). Sooooo . . . out for a bite, I must confess I've had most meals out in quiet wayside bars, now I think up to 86 for something leadenly German

and love again
W

Sol Meredith: Solomon Meredith (1810–75), a North Carolinian Quaker who became a prominent Indiana politician and later led a brigade at the Battle of Gettysburg, where he was almost killed. But it was his grandfather, James Meredith, who married a half-Cherokee Quaker named Mary Crews.

To William Gaddis

[*WG sent this registered letter to himself to protect his idea for* J R *from any future copyright infringement. Oscar does likewise in* FHO: *"I sent a copy to myself registered mail in a sealed envelope against just such a piece of dirty work as this one"* (98).]

Massapequa, L. Isld. N.Y.

27 August 1956

Though my first memory of bringing into conversation, with Donn A Pennebaker & others, the central idea to the book on which I am now working was during this past winter, in February 1956 I believe, the idea itself was older with me than that, though I should have no evidence of how much older. I started to develop this idea into a short novel no later than March 1956; and so far as I know it is one entirely original with myself, in substance and treatment.

In very brief it is this: a young boy, ten or eleven or so years of age, 'goes into business' and makes a business fortune, by developing and following through the basically very simple procedures needed to assemble extensive financial interests, to build a 'big business' in a system of comparative free enterprise employing the numerous (again basically simple) encouragements (as tax benefits &c) which are so prominent in the business world of America today. By taking straightforward advantage of the possibilities which I believe might well be obvious to the eye and judgment of a child this age, brought up on the sets of values and the criteria of success which prevail here in our country today, he becomes a business tycoon, handling and manipulating controlling interests in such diverse fields of enterprise as oil, cattle-raising, insurance, drugs, textiles, &c., transportation, twine and batting, greeting cards &c.

This boy (named here 'J.R.') employs, as a 'front man' to handle matters, the press &c, a young man innocent in matters of money and business, whose name (which I got in a dream) is Bast. Other characters include Bast's two aunts, the heads of companies which JR takes over, his board of directors, figures in a syndicate which fights his company for control in a stockholders' battle, charity heads to whom his company gives money, &c.

This book is projected as essentially a satire on business and money matters as they occur and are handled here in America today; and on the people who handle them; it is also a morality study of a straightforward boy reared in our culture, of a young man with an artist's conscience, and of the figures who surround them in such a competetive and material economy as ours.

The book just now is provisionally entitled both *Sensation* and *J.R.*

William Gaddis

Donn A Pennebaker: American documentary filmmaker (1925–2019), perhaps best known for the Bob Dylan tour-film *Dont Look Back* and *Monterey Pop*. See his memoir "Remembering Gaddis," *Conjunctions* 33 (Fall 1999): 157–60.

Sensation: in *R*, a young lady is reading "a current novel" entitled *Sensation* (716); Gaddis told me "I'd thought that one day I might write a novel with this title & so a little advance billing" (letter 12 June 1983).

To David Tudor Pole

143 East 19th street
New York City 3
8 March 1957

Dear David.

This will be brief, since I feel I have such a faint chance of its reaching you; the address I found on a Christmas card of some time past (and all the delights you've sent from Portugal &c &c never carry a return, much as they've delighted me). But my own habits of correspondence these 2 years past have become so sloppy that I've by now lost touch with almost all the better friends of youth, which by now even includes Barney, heaven knows where he may be (though you may too).

At the moment, sped on by an 18-month-old daughter who has just learned to say the word 'money' frighteningly clear, I'm trying to corner a writing job in a vast drug company called Pfizer International. And working out my very spotty resume, I included, somewhat embellished, the documentary film on the background of fine-paper making, which I worked on in North Africa for a Mr D*v*d T*d*r P*le ... Of course you may never hear from them (I gave them this address), for they seem somewhat skittish about actually hiring writers; but if they should reach you inquiring querulously into my past

WG with his wife Pat and children: left, with Sarah, late 1955; bottom, with Matthew at Massapequa, 1958.

triumphs, would you be kind enough to forward them a very professional-sounding note on that Great Film? Oh, what a chore this is to ask of anyone, I know. But things do look like they may be moving toward some settling eventuality around here and it is high time.

Even if you incline to pass off the above favour with a sharp note to this company saying "...........wholly..... unreliable..." do let me hear from you on any account, and this for John Napper too, or even his address, —and if he is in sight of course, Barney, but let me know of you, married, but with family? or in Greece? Espain? even Inglen?

with every good wish
William Gaddis

Pfizer International: founded in 1849, and today the largest pharmaceutical company in the world. When WG worked there (1957–62), its main office was located in Brooklyn, but he worked at its Manhattan office. The company Thomas Eigen works for in *J R* is based on Pfizer.

To Patricia Gaddis

[*While his wife and daughter were staying with friends, WG moved the family's things from their former apartment to one at 201 East 82nd Street, near Third Avenue. Thereafter—as Eigen and Gibbs do in* J R—*WG and a Harvard friend named Douglas Wood (1922?–66) split the rent on the 96th St. apartment for work and storage purposes.*]

New York City
14 March 1957

Dear Ladies,

Things happen every minute, I believe actually pointing in a direction. I went this noon up to the office of Mr Giaimo, with Douglas, and got all *that* straightened out (with D reassuring Mr G he wasn't just going to use 96th st to bring girls up and have parties), and am even to get the $42 deposit back. I told Douglas to apply it toward the loan, he protested, and I thought we'll see when the moment comes how badly it's needed where. He asked me up there again this evening to watch something on *Playhouse 90*, but I think I'll do better to go home and try to straighten things out there. [...]

all love,
W.

Playhouse 90: a TV series featuring 90-minute plays. Wood worked in television, most notably on the acclaimed documentary series *Victory at Sea* (1952–53).

To Keith Botsford

[*American-European writer, teacher, and television producer (1928–2018) whom Gaddis had known for several years. He approached Botsford in 1957 with an idea for a program about forgery for the short-lived series* The Seven Lively Arts *(CBS). The Keith Botsford Papers at the Beinecke Library contains WG's three-page proposal and three additional pages of notes. Botsford responded in a letter dated 8 May 1957 to say he didn't think the proposal was viable, largely because of "the visual problem" mentioned below. Botsford's reply implies Gaddis proposed this idea largely as a way to earn enough money to quit his job and write another novel.*]

201 East 82nd street,
New York City 28
10 April 1957

Dear Keith:

I thought at some length about the program possibility we talked of a week or so ago. The visual problem persists, though it could I think eventually be worked out. What I enclose here is no desperate alternative, but an idea which is simply a better one, more tangible, more topical, more visual, one which I've spent years reading on and thinking about, as *The Recognitions* might show. I'm not proposing an adaptation of that book, incidentally, except to develop by exposition some of the ideas which it investigated in fiction.

The compelling thing about a program on forgery I think is the chance it offers to approach the arts with a light touch, without the self-conscious overseriousness and frequent condescension that is such a threat to 'cultural' programs. Once the unifying problem is established, the material is highly varied and practically inexhaustible, as I'm afraid the enclosed notes scarcely show. The chance for guests from among the critics, experts, and entrepreneurs, is almost alarmingly good. Let me know if there's anything here you want to see extended, developed &c.

Yours,
Willie

To Charles Monaghan

[*A journalist, historian, and tireless advocate of* R, *as later letters will show. Born in 1932, he was working in New York University's Office of Information Services at the time. He had sent WG his review of Richard Stern's novel* Golk, *in which he called* R *"some of the finest writing of recent times"* (Commonweal, *13 May 1960, p. 190).*]

193 Second Avenue
New York City 3
16 May 1960

Dear Mr. Monaghan:

I appreciate your taking the trouble to send the mention in your *Commonweal* review. Even the dribs and drabs are gratifying and I wish often enough that they could be assembled somewhere loudly. You are right enough, the Hicks-Geismar combination was a pain, Geismar could be dismissed but I've never quite been able to accept the meanness (in the several senses of that word) of the Hicks. Thank you again.

W. Gaddis

Hicks-Geismar: Granville Hicks reviewed *R* in the *New York Times Book Review* (13 March 1955, p. 6), Maxwell Geismar in the *Saturday Review* (12 March 1955, p. 23).

To John D. Seelye

[*American critic (1931–2015) and a professor in the English Department of the University of California at Berkeley. He mentioned WG in passing in a piece published in the* Berkeley Gazette *in 1962 and the following year wrote an essay for the special issue of* Prairie Schooner *that its editor Karl Shapiro planned to devote to* R. *That issue never materialized, but Seelye's essay was eventually published in* In Recognition of William Gaddis *(Syracuse UP, 1984).*]

New York City 3
25 November 1960

dear Mr. Seelye.

I greatly appreciate your letter and your comments on *The Recognitions*. Though such fine anecdotes as the Southern Pacific story always make me wonder how much damage the book has done.

What I most appreciate of course are your efforts proselyting for the book. I hear enough from different places to convince me that there *is* a real underground which may burst out and be heard any day. In this regard you might be interested in the efforts of someone here in New York named Jack Green who writes, duplicates and mails out his own publication *newspaper*, 3 or 4 current issues of it devoted to *The Recognitions* (Box 114, New York 12, N.Y.— $1. covers the cost of these issues I believe). And frankly I have better hopes of the success of such efforts as yours and his than all the *Esquire* symposia in sight—the point being really that you have read the book.

Even I of course begin to talk of it as an object, a commodity, since I am now trying to encourage someone here to bring it out in paperback and, hope against hope, finally English publication—though you might guess how such people are alarmed at costs. And then if there were some competent madman to translate it into French as a labour-of-love—

I am flattered by your final request concerning the manuscript but for no reason I can name feel no inclination to part with it. I should add though that it has been stored in an old Corn Flakes carton in a barn on Long Island, and your letter prompts me to go out and get it to a more secure place.

Yours,
William Gaddis

Jack Green: the pseudonym of Christopher Carlisle Reid (c. 1928–?), who published seventeen issues of *newspaper* in 1957–1965. Issue #11 (3 June 1961) was a 32-page "Quote-Précis of William Gaddis's *The Recognitions*," and issues #12–14, entitled "fire the bastards!," appeared in February, August, and November of 1962. For further details, see my introduction to the book version (Dalkey Archive Press, 1992).
translate it into French: all three of these hopes were fulfilled: a paperback was published in early 1962, English publication followed that autumn, and a French translation (by Jean Lambert) appeared in 1973.

To Tom Jenkins

[*A journalist who wrote about detective novels; his friend David Markson (see headnote to 28 February 1961) recommended that he read* R.]

New York City
30 December 1960

dear Mr. Jenkins.

I appreciate your writing me about *The Recognitions*. I had got your earlier letter (forwarded by Harcourt) but simply had not managed to answer it.

Ch. Rolo was one reviewer I felt at the time who had seriously tried to behave in a responsible way: first, he read the book (which proved more rare among reviewers than I had anticipated). And the summary statement of his which you quote is probably quite accurate as far as it goes; however it does stop short of Wyatt's lines on page 898–9—and the revelation "love and do what you will". This however does inevitably bring up the problem of *grace*, which I felt uncertain about then and I believe my uncertainty shows. (I am more uncertain about it now, more dubious.) What might be appended to Rolo's statement too is the fact of the inescapableness of forgery as a part of the finite condition—if you will allow forgery to include necessarily imperfect representations of eventually inexpressible absolutes (in Plato's sense of the 'ideals'), but that this is the best we have, the best we can do: what is vital is the faith that the absolute—the 'perfect', etc.—*does* exist (thus Wyatt's "Thank God there was the gold to forge"—top of page 689), gold = perfection = absolute = love, in an alchemical scheme where Brown = matter (to be redeemed), Valentine = mind, Wyatt = creative spirit without love, Esme = love. That is a fragment of one undercurrent of interpretation, at any rate.

You might be interested in the project of someone here in New York who has spent the past year or so on the book (without any assist from me) and who is currently doing some pieces on it in a publication which he writes, duplicates & mails out himself. He is: Jack Green / newspaper / box 114 / New York 12 / NY. And I think he will send you the 4 issues as they come out if you send him $1.

As for time spent writing the book, it went on over 7 years, 1 or 2 of which were entirely fallow, 2 of which were on the other hand dawn-till-night periods of quite isolated, I might even say obsessed intensity. I can't say how much research I did for the book; most of it was specific or started out being so and then of course led on to other possibilities and insights. Certainly I did not sit down, envision, and write the book simply drawing on (what reviewers insisted upon calling) "vast erudition", though what pained me most about the reviewers was their refusal—their fear—to relax somewhat with the book and be entertained.

Yours,
William Gaddis

ps. My only work recently has been on a play which in present draft is too long & complicated.

Ch. Rolo: Charles J. Rolo (1916–82) reviewed *R* in the *Atlantic Monthly,* April 1955, 80–81. Jenkins had quoted his belief that "Wyatt has arrived at a doctrine somewhat akin to Gide's—a doctrine which holds that salvation lies in scraping away the consolatory deceits and secondhand values of the counterfeit personality and in obeying the promptings of the real self, the soul, in the full awareness that man is 'born into sin' and that sin must be 'lived through': all efforts to escape from the burden of imperfection are a denial of humanity and therefore lead to spiritual and emotional forgery."

"love and do what you will": St. Augustine's advice, from *On the First Letter of John.*

a play: *Once at Antietam*, portions of which were eventually published in *FHO.*

To Rust Hills

[*Hills (1924–2008) was fiction editor for* Esquire, *a post he would occupy on and off until 1999, and a lifelong friend of WG.*]

New York City
15 February 1961

Dear Rust Hills.

Thanks for your note on the Houghton-Mifflin award, is it? There were I'm afraid no entry blanks enclosed. But I do know a "good new writer" I'd be glad to recommend if you want to send the blanks along.

The Civil War chapter has become a full-in fact over-length play and I am involved in cutting it now. But lunch of course is more than welcome, any time you choose.

Yours,
W. Gaddis

Civil War chapter: after *R*, WG began a novel on the Civil War that he later converted into the play *Once at Antietam*.

To Tom Jenkins

New York 3
16 February 1961

Dear Tom Jenkins.

Thanks for your letters, especially the material on/by/about David Markson, a persistently guilty area of mine where I may now expiate if you will be good enough to send me his Mexico address. I was highly entertained by the Comp. Lit. piece discovered in the typewriter in *Epitaph for a Tramp,* had to go back to find the context and thence, whetted, from start to finish, probably the first 'cop story' I've read and had a fine time with it, envying Markson the character who wound it up, the musician type whose exacting dialogue impressed upon me how refined all that has become since I struggled with Anselm and the Viareggio crowd 8 and 9 years ago, it seems half a century.

And of course I am most intrigued by the Malcolm Lowry references, I was in Mexico when his book came out, read part of it, the copy disappeared, I got another when I came back but I regret haven't (yet) returned to it. Even that initial brush was a good 14 years ago; and once I got involved with *The Recognitions* a year or so later read little or no fiction, a habit I haven't entirely broken since.

And finally, for Chas. Rolo... he's not stupid but quite gone on what's fashionable, what fits, as people who make their livings that way have to be. It often seems to me the driving quality of those people, reviewers, publishers &c, is curiosity, little more. And in their attempt to turn the creative arts into performing ones (the current measure of success) are hungry for us, for writers, to share (dignify) their values. I suppose it's never been any different though, we must carry them on our backs, the editors, anthologizers, like the hounds they are running for their lunch, while the writer of any substance like the fox is running for his life.

Yours,
W. Gaddis

Epitaph for a Tramp: published in 1959; early in the novel, the detective protagonist is in a student's apartment and reads in the typewriter the conclusion to an essay: "And thus it is my conclusion that *The Recognitions* by William Gaddis is not merely the best American first novel of our time, but perhaps the most significant single volume in all American fiction since *Moby Dick*, a book so broad in scope, so rich in comedy and so profound in symbolic inference that—" (p. 32 in the Shoemaker & Hoard edition).

Malcolm Lowry: Lowry's *Under the Volcano* (1947) has some similarities to *R*.

To David Markson

[*David Markson (1927–2010), later to become an esteemed novelist, had written a master's thesis on Malcolm Lowry in 1951 and had begun writing fiction by 1955. He read* R *twice when it first came out and wrote to WG in June of 1955 to express his admiration, but received no answer until this letter of 1961, at which time he was living in Mexico. Markson and WG would continue to correspond, and occasionally see each other, until WG's death.*]

New York City
28 February 1961

Dear David Markson.

After lo these many (six) years—or these many low (sick) years—if I can presume to answer yours dated 11 June '55: I could evade embarrassment by saying that it had indeed been misdirected to Dr Weisgall and reached me only now, but I'm afraid you know us both too well. In fact I was in low enough state for a good while after the book came out that I could not find it in me to answer letters that said anything, only those (to quote yours again) that offered 'I just loved your gorgeous book and I think Mithra is so charming...'. Partly appalled at what I counted then the book's apparent failure, partly

wearied at the prospect of contention, advice and criticism, and partly just
drained of any more supporting arguments, as honestly embarrassed at high
praise as resentful of patronising censure. And I must say, things (people)
don't change, just get more so; and I think there is still the mixture, waiting
to greet such continuing interest as yours, of vain gratification and fear of
being found out, still ridden with the notion of the people as a fatuous jury
(counting reviewers as people), publishers the police station house (where if
as I trust you must have some experience of being brought in, you know what
I mean by their dulled but flattering indifference to your precious crime: they
see them every day), and finally the perfect book as, inevitably, the perfect
crime (the point of this last phrase being, for some reason which insists further
development of this rambling metaphor, that the criminal is never caught).
So, as you may see by the letterhead on the backside here, I am hung up with
an operation of international piracy that deals in drugs, writing speeches on
the balance of payments deficit but mostly staring out the window, serving
the goal that Basil Valentine damned in 'the people, whose idea of necessity
is paying the gas bill' [*R* 386]...(A little frightening how easily it all comes
back.) But sustained by the secret awareness that the secret police, Jack Green
and yourself and some others, may expose it all yet.

This intervention by Tom Jenkins was indeed a happy accident (though,

WG with David Markson, New York, 1964.

to exhaust the above, there are no accidents in Interpol), and I was highly entertained by the page-in-the-typewriter in your *Epitaph for a Tramp*. I of course had to go back and find the context (properly left-handed), then back to the beginning to find the context of the context, and finally through to the end and your fine cool dialogue (monologue) which I envied and realised how far all that had come since '51 & 2, how refined from such crudities as 'Daddy-o, up in thy way-out pad...' And it being the only 'cop story' (phrase via Tom Jenkins) or maybe 2nd or 3rd that I've read, had a fine time with it. (And not that you'd entered it as a Great Book; but great God! have you seen the writing in such things as *Exodus* and *Anatomy of a Murder*? Can one ever cease to be appalled at how little is asked?)

I should add I am somewhat stirred at the moment regarding the possibility of being exhumed in paperback, one of the 'better' houses (Meridian) has apparently made an offer to Harcourt Brace, who since they brought it out surreptitiously in '55 have seemed quite content to leave it lay where Jesus flung it, but now I gather begin to suspect that they have something of value and are going to be quite as brave as the dog in the manger about protecting it. Though they may surprise me by doing the decent and I should not anticipate their depravity so high-handedly I suppose. Very little money involved but publication (in the real sense of the word) which might be welcome novelty.

And to really wring the throat of absurdity—having found publishers a razor's edge tribe between phoniness and dishonesty—I have been working on a play, a presently overlong and overcomplicated and really quite straight figment of the Civil War: publishers almost shine in comparison to the show-business staples, as 'I never read anything over 100 pages' or, hefting the script, (without opening it), 'Too long'. The consummate annoyance though being that gap between reading the press (publicity) interview-profile of a currently successful Broadway director whose lament over the difficulty of getting hold of 'plays of ideas' simply rings in one's head as one's agent, having struggled through it, shakes his head in baleful awe and delivers the hopeless compliment, '...but it's a play of ideas' —a real escape hatch for everybody in the 'game' (a felicitous word) whose one idea coming and going is $. And I'm behaving as though all this is news to me.

Incidentally—or rather not incidentally at all, quite hungrily—Jenkins mentioned from a letter of yours a most provocative phrase from a comment by Malcolm Lowry on *The Recognitions* which whetted my paranoid appetite, I am most curious to know what he might have said about it (or rather what he did say about it, with any thorns left on). I cannot say I read his book which came out when I was in Mexico, 1947 as I remember, and I started it, found it coming both too close to home and too far from what I thought I was trying to do, and lost or had it lifted from me before I ever resolved things. (Yes, in my case one of the books that the book-club ads blackmail the vacuum with 'Have you caught yourself saying Yes, I've been meaning to read it....' (they mean *Exodus*).) But I am picking up a copy for a new look. Good luck on your current obsession.

> with best regards,
> W. Gaddis

Dr Weisgall: a dentist in *R* who receives several unwanted letters from Agnes Deigh after she mistakenly reports him to the police.

letterhead: Pfizer International.

the perfect book as, inevitably, the perfect crime: in *R*, an art critic quotes the French painter Edgar Degas's remark "that the artist must approach his work in the same frame of mind in which the criminal commits his deed" (71).

'Daddy-o [...] pad': a beatnik version of the Paternoster appears on p. 536 of *R*.

Exodus and *Anatomy of a Murder*: best-sellers of the time: *Exodus* (1958) was by Leon Uris, *Anatomy of a Murder* (1958) by Robert Traver.

leave it lay where Jesus flung it: an old saying WG occasionally uses (later ascribed to a woman).

Lowry on *The Recognitions*: Markson sent Lowry a copy of *R* in 1956; see below for Lowry's response.

To Robert M. Ockene

[*Apparently an editorial assistant at Meridian Books. Ockene later became an editor at Bobbs-Merrill; his enthusiasm for* R *is described by Victor S. Navasky in "Notes on the Underground,"* New York Times Book Review, *5 June 1966, 3.*]

> [New York City
> 15 March 1961]

From a letter from a fellow named David Markson in Mexico, an early admirer of *The Recognitions*, and at this point I suppose simply For Your Information since Harcourt is still sitting on that 'modest' offer, figuring I suppose that they may have something after all. Have you seen Mr Jovanovich's little New Year book *Now, Barabbas*? Curiouser & Curiouser, Inc.

> Yours
> WG

[*The enclosure is Markson's transcription of a letter to him from Malcolm Lowry dated 22 February 1957; the bracketed interpolations are Markson's. The letter was eventually published in* Sursum Corda! The Collected Letters of Malcolm Lowry, vol. 2: 1946–1957, *ed. Sherrill E. Grace (U Toronto P, 1997), 875–76.*]

My very dear old Dave: It is quite unforgivable of me not to have replied before, especially when I had so much to thank you for: but this was paradoxically the reason, first William Gaddis' The Recognitions isn't exactly the kind of book (a veritable Katchen Junga, you know the Mountain I mean anyhow, of a book, the ascent of some overhangs of which can scarcely be made safely without the assistance, one feels, of both Tanzing and Aleister Crowley) possible to return figuratively or in fact the next day, as happened once with Ulysses, with the comment 'Very good!' I'd wanted both to thank you for this and write something intelligent upon it worthy of the book in the bargain.... [I'm cutting several lines here, re other news of his own—about the Vintage edition of *Volcano,* by the way]... I'd been working so hard I'd forgotten I'd received any [news] and for the same reason I have not yet finished The Recognitions (which was long delayed incidentally by the Christmas mails and The Demon Oleum—that word is Oleum—oil anyway perhaps): what I *can* say is that The Recognitions is probably all you claim for it, a truly fabulous creation, a SuperByzantine Gazebo and secret Missile of the Soul and likewise extraordinarily funny: much funnier than Burton (who has me gathering borage out of the garden to heal the melancholy his laughter induces, also a spoonful of vinegar at bedtime helps) though Burton's a good parallel. I can only read a little at a time, however, because I have to watch my eyesight, which begins to get strained round midnight after having spent the day since 7:30 a.m. scratching out the previous day's work; so that it may be somewhile yet before I can give you a full report on The Recognitions;...

[*Markson ends there and points out that Lowry died a few months later, never making that full report.*]

Now, Barabbas: a 16-page essay in booklet form by the president of WG's publishing house, William Jovanovich (1920–2001)—whose surname WG consistently misspells "Jovanovitch" in later letters—concerning "the propensities of publishers," issued in 1960 "in a limited edition as a New Year's greeting to friends of Harcourt, Brace & World" (p. [1]). "Curiouser and curiouser" is Alice's comment on events in Wonderland.

Tanzing and Aleister Crowley: Tenzing Norgay (and Sir Edmund Hillary) ascended Mount Everest (Chomo-lungma in Tibetan) in 1953; Aleister Crowley (1875–1947) was a notorious English magician who wrote many books on the occult.

Burton: Robert Burton (1577–1640), author of *The Anatomy of Melancholy.*

To Aaron Asher

[*An editor (1929–2008) then at World Publishing Company, whose trade paperback line, Meridian Books, would reissue R in March 1962. David Markson was the one who brought the novel to Asher's attention. The corrections mentioned were separated from the letter by the time I saw it.*]

New York City
15 April 1961

Aaron Asher: Here are the corrections Jack Green and I have dug up in *The Recognitions*. Let me know if you have any questions on them. Also your progress in garnering 'names' to send (what amount to) pre-publication copies to. (Si Krim knows a painter who has known Alexander King for 30 years, still a good bet I think.) And let me know when you've worked it out what arrangement you would propose for an English edition. (What are your connections like at Faber?) And any other news.

Yours,
W. Gaddis

Si Krim: Seymour Krim (1922–89), a literary journalist and magazine editor.
Alexander King: Austrian-born American artist, editor (at *Life*), and TV personality (1900–1965), author of several volumes of somewhat scandalous memoirs. In a 1963 letter to John Seelye, Jack Green said that King "has read The Recognitions and loves it."

To Charles Monaghan

[*While in England Monaghan had spoken with Timothy O'Keeffe (whose name WG often misspells) of MacGibbon & Kee about the possibility of publishing R and apparently also spoke with WG's U.S. publisher William Jovanovich—whom Monaghan called Joe Vanovich, to WG's amusement—about some sort of co-production arrangement.*]

New York 3 NY
4 May 1961

dear Charles Monaghan.
 I greatly appreciate your stirring interest in English publication possibilities for *The Recognitions*, it could hardly be more timely. Cost is the thing that has kept British publishers from it till now; but this may be largely mitigated by a recent development happy on other counts. Meridian paperbacks is to bring it out here around the end of the year or beginning of next, and we've

talked of their having a press run larger than their own needs for this printing and selling by prearrangement the balance as sheets to a British publisher for publication there, which seems to me a fine possibility, since it would not have to be brought out there at the suicidal price it was here originally.

There was a British publication scheduled long ago by Secker & Warburg, by contract with the bogus Mr Fred Warburg in I believe Oct '54, he convinced himself and his associates that he had the new American *Ulysses*, ran into some difficulties with Eng printers ('obscene') and used that as an excuse to back out of the contract 5 days before the book was surreptitiously released by Harcourt Brace here, when he'd learned, that is, that it was not going to be hailed on the front page of the NYT *Book Review* &c, tried to get me to cut it with embarrassing preachings on the 'Artist's duty' &c no mention of cutting obscenities, he was suddenly scared of costs, very shabby the whole performance and of course he'd sat on it with his contract those 6 prepublication months when another British publisher of more integrity might have taken it. Forgive the spleen, but this has been rankling a long time, aggravated by that phony bastard's poses later as a champion of literary freedom &c who'd been done out of his greatness by archaic British law.

At any rate a British firm is looking at it now with an eye to the abovementioned possibility with Meridian and I have to put off any other possibility waiting to hear what sort of terms they will offer. MacGibbon & Kee was curiously on my list for possible places to show it with this new possibility and T O'Keefe's name had been given me by one of few straight people in publishing here; but for the moment as I say waiting on word from this other firm, and though I have a few copies of the book hoarded am in no position to intercede with Joe Vanovitch (very nice; did you see *his* New Years' 'book' *Now Barabbas,* very high flown Duties Of The Publisher jazz), they treat me rather like a posthumous author now and I wouldn't ask them for air in a jug. The man to reach at this point I think is Aaron Asher at Meridian (now part of World Publishing Company, 119 West 57 street NYC 19), if O'Keefe wants to write him.

Many thanks again, by heaven the boil will burst eventually. I so greatly envy you London, 2 visits convinced me (10 years ago) it and the people the only place that makes sense for me; but supporting a wife-and-two on Fleet street pay... I'm too old I guess to dare it now.

Yours with best regards,
W. Gaddis

T O'Keefe: Timothy O'Keeffe (1926–1994) is best known for rediscovering Flann O'Brien: he reprinted *At Swim-Two-Birds* in 1959 and encouraged the Irish author to resume writing.

To David Markson

New York 3 N.Y.
5 May 1961

dear David Markson.

The secret police have done their work well—to date: Aaron Asher is bringing *The Recognitions* out in paper around the end of the year or beginning of next, probably at around $2⁵⁰, at last we can let the riff-raff in. A great relief to me though you may imagine the amount of money that changed hands was comically small (hands being Meridian-Harcourt of course—my share should, once Harcourt has taken out a long dead advance, be the price of a dinner, the whole thing has been a real parody of the beggar Shacabac at Barmecide's feast). But it may also prefigure English publication which—again, money aside—should carry its own reward.

Thanks for the new *Epitaph*—I haven't read it but it has started my wife off on a spree of mystery story reading which may be salutary. Otherwise peace reigns relentlessly.

Yours,
W. Gaddis

---

let the riff-raff in: Gaddis ascribes a version of this remark to radio comedian Fred Allen in a later letter (19 August 1973).

Barmecide's feast: a tale from the Arabian *Thousand and One Nights* in which a prince of the Barmecide family in Baghdad spreads an imaginary feast for a beggar for sport. A "Barmecide's feast" has since then referred to a nonexistent or negligible offering.

new *Epitaph:* Markson published his second detective novel, *Epitaph for a Dead Beat*, in 1961. Both were reprinted in a single volume by Shoemaker & Hoard in 2007.

To Charles Socarides

[*WG's Harvard friend had proposed a work based on Marguerite Sechehaye's* Autobiography of a Schizophrenic Girl *(1951).*]

[New York, NY]
2 June 1961

Dear Charlie,

As a doctor you will see these explanations as mere manifestations of the lunatic norm, as a friend you must see them as attempts at apology for what has certainly appeared as rudeness, thoughtlessness, lack of interest in your proposal. But on every hand in the past year or so a despair of indecision has set in to a point of paralysis of the will, each indecision feeding the others, from writing to the job to moving to school for the children back to writing, a play of my own unfinished, a commissioned article scarcely begun, an overwhelming conviction of lack of competence, talent &c., unable to say a decisive yes but afraid to say no, afraid of missing the main chance, —"We spend our lives waiting for something to happen (says H G Wells) and then...it doesn't happen." Ecco.

Make it happen? This is where the paralysis of the will enters, but grounded in this case on more realistic considerations, as, the current deplorable state of Broadway theatre (as business, not art); and the severe ('agonizing') reappraisal of my own play-writing talents that followed on 1½ year's intensive even enraptured work on a play which, until I finished it and reread it, seemed to me quite great. Now it reads heavy-handed, obvious, over-explained, oppressive,—there is a play in the work I've done but the vital problem remains, to extract it, to lift out something with a life of its own, give it wings, release it (this kind of block I think you know already medically, a kind of constipation of resentful satisfaction). And I go on like this here not (doctor) to parade psychical commonplaces, but (friend) only to say, somehow, why the show of lack of interest, why the rudeness, the neither yes nor no on the *Autobiography of a Schizophrenic Girl*. I did read both books, I did have difficulty casting it up in my mind as a scene-by-scene suspenseful development in any but a predictable direction, I did try to think but what I believe I did not do (in light of all the above) was to turn it loose in my mind, let it come alive with its own life, and whether I am capable of this, whether I have been fair to it, myself or you, I do not know, but I doubt.

Here again is an elemental consideration: the story of the girl, and as I understand your interest in it, is a positive affair, there is a cure &c, this by logical dramatic inference to say that life, the whole proposition, is so; whereas I feel fundamentally it's not, there is no cure but the final one, the only redemption is well-contested failure: so much for fundamental feelings; the practical ones involve simply professional competence and Charlie I've no reason to believe I have it.

Already (in the arts) I look back on too many false hopes fragmented, lost; by circumstance, by definition almost, I've forced my family to share them; should I, with a hope-against-hope, desperate-for-time, escape-inflated yes to your proposal, ask you to share yet another one? and in terms of money as earnest of your own enthusiastic confidence? Oh, if only I were really streaked with the confidence-man stripe of the real artist, but the same New England chill blows over that that chills the art itself.

Here are the books and if you do some way go ahead with it now I wish the best success to it, and if you don't before I beat out the plowshares of my own frustrations we can talk about it in any direction it takes us, and that at your convenience any time except weekends, but a week-day drink? supper at one of those borderline Hungarian bistros?

with best wishes from me and us all,
W G

H G Wells: quoted earlier, 28 November 1950.
beat out the plowshares: an allusion to Isaiah 2:4: "[...] they shall beat their swords into plowshares," indicating a positive outcome.

To Charles Monaghan

[*Informed by WG that MacGibbon & Kee agreed to publish R in England, Monaghan warned him of possible negative reactions by the British press and suggested enlisting eminent British writers like Colin Wilson on its side. In fall 1961, WG and family moved from Manhattan to a small town 20 miles north; he lived at this address until fall 1967.*]

114 North Highland Place
Croton-on-Hudson, N Y
25 January 1962

Dear Charles Monaghan.

Thanks for your letter—and the spirit of the revanche that fills it. Negociations with MacGibbon & Kee are just about completed though I do not know their publishing date, I should think it will be some time in the fall. And my own approach, even here, has been to pull back somewhat and see what developments if any there will be without my intrusion, expecting paperback copies in the stores the last week of February. Asher will of course not pause for proof copies but I would think there will be a usable gap between paper copies here and MacGibbon & Kee's publication so that O'Keefe can hand round Meridian editions as pre-publication copies there. But my whole inclination right now is to wait to hear O'Keefe's plan of attack and since as I remember you know him he will probably be the best person to talk to about your ideas. Though from what I've seen I thoroughly agree that the social messagenicks are rampant there in England though I believe even more vigourous and apparently high handed than here, here after all they are so largely resentful remnants of the past and relegated wherever there is intelligence and taste as nagging bores, Britain apparently is quite different, a nice cultural lag and like it or not I suppose I'm in the Colin Wilson camp? Jack Green should have before Meridian's publication an issue of his *newspaper* 30pp or so attacking the US no-nothing reviews of the book in 1955, which might be fuel for the British fire but again, I'm inclined to wait and see, and similarly to postpone satisfaction on the Bogus F. Warburg score. At any rate unless something else rears before that I'll let you know of anything above a whisper here come late next month, and send a copy of *newspaper* immediately I have it.

And yes, Croton is salutary.

very best regards.
W. Gaddis.

To Aaron Asher

[*A note on WG's personalized memo stationery attached to the first installment of Jack Green's* Fire the Bastards!]

27 February 1962

Aaron—

Here at last—a la revanche! You might get a rise out of those mentioned, especially the provincials if they thought they were being dignified by attacks in sin capital Greenwich Village, ho! (I gather the Hicks & Highets come later.)
WG.

Highets: Gilbert Highet attacked *R* in the *Book of the Month Club News*; Green does indeed deal with him and Granville Hicks in part 2.

To John D. Seelye

[*Seelye wrote on 26 April to congratulate WG on the publication of the Meridian R and the piece on WG that appeared in the* Saturday Review *(April 21, pp. 8–9). He enclosed two clippings: his own essay "Plight of 'Neglected' Author,"* Berkeley Daily Gazette, *16 February 1962, p. 11, which mentions WG in passing, and an article by William Hogan entitled "Recognition for 'The Recognitions'" that appeared in the* San Francisco Chronicle, *26 April 1962, p. 41. He also asked if WG "had any short stories or what not published."*]

Croton-on-Hudson, N.Y.
21 May 1962

Dear Mr Seelye.

I've been so inexcusably poor about writing that at this point it would be graceless even for me to apologise; as graceless as it would be for me to in some way 'thank' you for the piece in the Berkeley paper, though I can certainly say of that that it becomes more instead of less refreshing measured against the froth of most of the enclosed, which you may have seen and which you note when it is about the book is only about the book as an object, a Thing, generally the kind of nonsense though which increases sales (if not readership) so I am not carping, much. Irritation though at such as the Dolbier bit of patent phonyness (he'd referred to *The Recognitions* by William Gibson in a *Saturday Review* splash 7 years ago), now the '12 years...976 pages...' and the rest the sort of blurb writing he evidently hopes will be picked up in advertising, his (name in) bold face on 10,000 dust jackets, though why the antics of these finks continue to annoy me I do not know, I wrote that book once. Still find it revived (the rancour) at yesterday's brown-nose on Sunday *Times Book Review* front-page lesson on how a best seller is manufactured (v. the interior $000000 two-page ad for the same Wouk of art, if you'll pardon the) lesson on how, if *that* can be seriously flung broadcast as a saga of artist's life USA then of course *The Recognitions* must appear sprawling, 'turbulent, Joycean', lesson on how to teach your grandmother to suck eggs.

Enough of this, it only points up the abyss of which others, composers say, are constantly aware. On the Joyce tack (I may have written you this before) I was distressed at the time of the original publication when Harcourt used the best blurb-quote they had, which proved to be Stuart Gilbert, unfurled across the back of the jacket as a sales pitch but which, as I anticipated, only gave reviewers an escape hatch from which to say '...Joyce..., and I didn't understand this either' (ie 'because it's like Joyce,' not 'because I didn't read it'), though I recall being jolted to find even the *New Yorker* (I believe Brendan Gill) taking this recourse, rather more snottily than the others to be sure but riding the comparison even to typography (— instead of ").

But this frankly is the sort of controversy I would wish to keep myself apart from: I remember Robert Graves once writing ('Letter to the editor') that he answered critics &c only when they mis-took his facts and that seems to me the only sane approach, otherwise I threaten to become a character in the book which is largely about, after all, the "that is not what I meant, that is not what I meant at all..." I can say, my Joyce is limited to *Dubliners* and some of his letters, but that is not the kind of fact I mean; as pointless really as would have been writing to protest *Time* magazine's "Mr Pivner, the all-too-common man, is a try at redoing Joyce's Mr Bloom..." with the confidence that it was 'in fact' a try at redoing my own experience with my father, transmuted, as seemed permissible, with trivia. "...complex, but hardly obscure" as you say, I agree. The overwhelming fact is that there the book is, quite apart from me (cf. top of page 96) and better God knows a battleground for the likes of you and Jack Green than the Dolbiers, amen.

(Though I append this: I met a woman here some months ago you might know of, name of June Oppen Degnan & pub'r of the *San Francisco Review* 165-28th Avenue, S F 21, who seemed quite impressed by the book ("remarkable, fascinating, important...") and might if you were so inclined be interested in any critical work you did on it for *S F Review*.)

Otherwise? It's to be published this fall in England by MacGibbon & Kee, and a refugee from NY bundle of great energy and if I may say allegiance to it named Charles Monaghan is trouncing possible critics reviewers newspapers &c beforehand in hopes of a firework or 2 mounting the mandarins against the liblabs, ho!

No, no short stories or whatnot published elsewhere ever; a novel on business begun and dropped in about "57; a novel begun, rebuilt into an impossibly long play (very rear guard, Socrates in the US Civil War), shelved 1960; current obsession with expanding prospects of programmed society & automation in the arts which may bring an advance, a commitment, even an escape from the tomb of the 9-to-5.

Since my past delinquency in correspondence has made clear that your interest in and efforts regarding the book aren't swayed one way or another by the winds of my appreciation let me say here they continue blowing wholeheartedly.

Yours,
W Gaddis

---

the enclosed: presumably the reviews and features that had appeared on the Meridian *R* up to that time. Most of the material was journalism, not criticism; see *Fire the Bastards!*, pp. 86–87.

Dolbier: Maurice Dolbier (1912–93) wrote a favorable review of the Meridian *R* for the *New York Herald Tribune* (14 April 1962, p. 6), getting a number of facts wrong (as WG points out), as he did when he called the Harcourt *R* by "William Gibson" in the *Saturday Review* seven years earlier ("The Summing-up in Books for 1955," 24 December 1955, p. 11).

Wouk: on Herman Wouk's *Youngblood Hawke* (1962), a novel about a successful writer destroyed by New York.

teach your grandmother to suck eggs: "said to those who presume to offer advice to others who are more experienced" (*OED*).

Stuart Gilbert: Gilbert is best known for his book on Joyce's *Ulysses* (1930). The blurb he wrote for *R* reads as follows: "[*The Recognitions*] is a vast and devastating picture of the world the powers-that-be have doomed us to live in; Mr. Eliot's Waste Land was only a small corner of the wilderness so observantly and successfully explored by Mr. Gaddis. Such a work might easily be lugubrious but the author's wit, irony, and erudition, combined with a rich diversity of subject matter, make this book fascinating reading; long though it is, even longer than 'Ulysses,' the interest, like that of Joyce's masterpiece and for very similar reasons, is brilliantly maintained throughout."

Gill: see Gill's anonymous review in the *New Yorker,* 9 April 1955, 117.

Graves [...] editor'): probably Graves's letter beginning "To the Editor of Commentary" published as "Robert Graves Demurs" in *Commentary,* November 1956, 471–72, in response to an error-filled article published in *Commentary*'s October 1956 issue by Arnold Sherman entitled "A Talk With Robert Graves: English Poet in Majorca."

"that is [...] at all": from Eliot's "Love Song of J. Alfred Prufrock."

letters: Stuart Gilbert's edition of Joyce's letters appeared in 1957.

Time magazine: Theodore E. Kalem's anonymous review of *R* appeared in *Time,* 14 March 1955, 112, 114.

my father: shortly after World War II, WG met his father for the first time at the Harvard Club in NYC.

(top of page 96): Wyatt on the artist as "the human shambles that follows" his work around.

San Francisco Review: Seelye and Green corresponded about the possibility of publishing something in the *San Francisco Review*—specifically having it take over the special issue on WG that *Prairie Schooner* was to have published—but nothing came of it.

liblabs: "Lib-Labs" are Liberal-Labourers; Monaghan was afraid they would fault *R* for its mandarin nature, which is why he hoped to enlist mandarin critics in favor of it. The English *R* received a dozen or so reviews, but no such controversy followed.

To Charles Monaghan

Croton-on-Hudson, N Y
1 June 1962

Dear Charles Monaghan.

With the usual promptness an answer of sorts to yours of 10 April, the sorts being these attached which reflect if anything the monumental laziness of the local literary press: not that I should have had profound critiques on every page (which of course I should)(in 1955) but the best they can do (except perhaps for the Berkeley Calif item) seems to be to look over each other's shoulders and write about the writing about what's being written about and never, never under pain of firing about the thing itself.

Words from the Grave ('Palinurus') might well create a disquieting effect but C Connolly made even then (1947?) such an effort at the self-picture of sloth that I cannot imagine his lifting the book let alone ... well, brave of you, it could be quite a coup. And, mightn't liblab damning of the sort you mention give it a leg up? or have they entirely taken over to the exclusion of the happy few (as I recall at the time Aubry Mennon (sp? *Prevalence of Witches* about 1953) despised it). Between 2 stools sounds altogether possible falling upon, I suppose, if it still exists, the unkempt plot of Colin Wilson. At that, even one of the stools finds itself between 2 others, I mean I would think the social-conscience types might be torn between the book's contempt for their purpose on the one hand and delight at such criticism of USA ('anti-America') as they could find on the other. All together, quite a prospect if such, indeed, it is: if, I mean, they don't all win quietly by simply looking the other way when the book staggers onto the scene. Shall I re-title it? *Oldeblood Hawke*? (The NYSunday *Times Book Review* front page for *that* appalling item 2 weeks ago subtitled as I recall *How Success Spelled Artistic Failure*) and, having seen how Failure spelled it (cf. 3rd page single column of spite March 1955 on *The Recognitions*) one should I suppose turn on to pages 14–15 for the full 2-page spread picture of the author looking balefully over Copies of his wouk of art, a gesture which cost Doubleday $4500 . . . I cannot think things are too terribly different in Fleet st.

I don't know what of the enclosed I might already have sent you, herewith 2 copies of each one of which might be useful to O'Keeffe. Your campaigning strategy must bring something out of the woodwork there if only malice (what is forthwith dubbed a 'controversial book').

> thanks, best wishes and luck,
> W Gaddis

---

attached: not present, but presumably the press the Meridian *R* had received up to that time.

C Connolly: Cyril Connolly (1903–74) published a collection of reflections and aphorisms entitled *The Unquiet Grave* in 1944 under the pseudonym Palinurus. Monaghan sent him a copy of *R*, with no known result.

Aubry Mennon: Aubrey Menen's witty, Waughvian novel *The Prevalence of Witches* was published in 1947.

3rd page single column: another reference to Granville Hicks's review of *R*, on the verso of the third page (i.e., p. 6).

To Terry Southern

[*American novelist and screenwriter (1924–95). With Richard Seaver and Alexander Trocchi he was editing an anthology published as* Writers in Revolt *(Frederick Fell, 1963), which includes a selection from chapter 3 of* R *(pp. 78–100, more than WG suggested below).*]

Croton-on-Hudson, New York
1 June 1962

Dear Mr. Southern.

Thanks for your interest in *The Recognitions* and I am sorry to be so long about answering your query regarding parts of it for your anthology. The impressive company of writers involved makes the proportion of my novel which you propose including very flattering, and thus I sincerely hope that it will not disturb your project when I say that a variety of reasons obliges me to limit such a selection to the first section you indicate only, that is, pp 91–100, from "It was dark afternoon..." through "...the exposure of her back."

After the debacle of the book's publication in 1955 I am only getting used now to the idea that some people actually have read it as you've done and find that most gratifying, which adds to my hope that my reservations with regard to this project don't inhibit it, though with the range from Camus to Bill Burroughs to choose from that hardly seems likely. If this makes sense for you would you please make any business arrangements with Miss Candida Donadio at Russell & Volkening?

Yours,
William Gaddis

Bill Burroughs: WG became acquainted with novelist William S. Burroughs (1914–97) in the early Fifties, when he gave WG an autographed copy of *Junkie* (1953), and saw him occasionally later in life.

Candida Donadio: see headnote to 26 April 1964.

To John D. Seelye

[*Seelye wrote 20 January 1963 recommending a Bay Area resident named Michel Landa as a possible translator for a French edition of* R. *Seelye also reported on the progress of the Prairie Schooner* issue on R *and asked after WG's new work.*]

[Croton-on-Hudson, NY]
2 February 1963

Dear Mr Seelye:

Many thanks for your interest in getting *The Recognitions* into French. Gallimard have been blowing hot and cold on it for some months, appalled at the task involved like anyone (except the Italians who took it on (Mondadori) but with a 30-month publishing period which reflects their anticipating translation as no mere bagatelle; also your last sentence ("...the value of all the many ambiguities...") reassures me on having turned down Hanser

Verlag's offer to publish it with 350 pages cut (and after what the Germans have put us through this past century in the way of poundage why should they be let off so lightly?)). At any rate I would think the only thing that would intoxicate a French publisher to the grabbing point would be someone coming forward lunatic enough to do it as a love labour which I should certainly not encourage! Thus it would seem if your Michel Landa wanted to write to Gallimard (I'm sorry I do not know whom to address there, he might) saying he understood they'd shown interest in it which—for a decent consideration—he might like to share … ? (I gather from his first name French may be a native language to him?)

The phrase 'welcome issue' on the Karl Shapiro project I hadn't heard and am of course most intrigued and curious how it will all turn out. On other matters, there was a film in prospect last spring and summer but I had to hold back for more firm prospects on it than came through and so far as I know it is still largely all prospect, much talk and notes, and possible even now that something may come of it yet. Meanwhile your query on progress on my latest book can draw only an equivocal response since *my* latest book is suspended (the cobbler's children go barefoot) while I try to disentangle myself from a commission I welcomed some 7 months ago, a contract to work on a book for the Ford Foundation (not, repeat repeat repeat not a 'grant') on the use of television in the schools, an area they have blown some $60 or $70 million in over the past decade and now, quite understandably, wanted a 'book' about it, not a report, not a summary, a 'book'; and I took the offer as a job and of course on getting into it found it an infinitely more involved affair than I, fresh from the boresome tasks of writing speeches &c on the balance of payments problem and direct investment overseas, had at first considered, thinking I suppose to treat it all in those fairly matter-of-fact propagandistic terms. At any rate I've material to take in to the Ford folk this week which I don't know how they'll feel about but worse I'm not sure how I feel about, I haven't had a chance to get off and look at it myself and my impression is I may have fallen between two stools, huzzahs for the tonic effect it is having in (public school) teaching interspersed with caveats on technology devouring its own children, all this complicated by constant notes and thoughts and reading on the side on *my* book started many years ago largely on this same area, technology/democracy/the artist. Well, Ford may simply say "Pay him and get him out of here!" (or of course they may be even more brief, just "Get him out of here!") when they see what I've done and not having really a clear enough picture of it myself I don't at this moment know which would be more distressing, to have it squelched or published-and-be-damned. And even here is the equivocation, the Luciferian pride of wanting to be damned for one's self not crucified for others. (I'll stop this before this metaphor goes any further for the whole situation is really more annoyingly absurd than such images can dignify.) (But you see what a polite question can bring you.)

with very best regards. I hope my next can be somewhat more coherent,

W. Gaddis

Mondadori: Vincenzo Mantovani's translation *Le perizie* was published by Editore Mondadori in 1967.

Karl Shapiro project: the Gaddis folder in the John Seelye Papers (George A. Smathers Libraries, University of Florida) contains many letters between Seelye, Shapiro, and Jack Green on the abandoned issue of *Prairie Schooner* that was to be devoted to WG's first novel.

Ford Foundation: for details, see Ali Chetwynd's "William Gaddis' 'Ford Foundation Fiasco' and *J R*'s Elision of the Teacher's Eye View," *Orbit: A Journal of American Literature* 8.1 (May 2020).

To John D. Seelye

Croton-on-Hudson, New York
10 May 1963

Dear Mr Seelye.

I recalled recently having written you some time past and noting, in response to my 'next book' as an item of interest to you, that it would be a report on school television for the Ford Foundation; and as little moment as it is I am obliged and I must confess relieved to say that the project fell through after time work travel wasted and a little money changed hands, all too predictable, so—I've escaped back to my own 'next book' though how long it will be (in the writing I mean, not the length) heaven knows.

Indirectly word reached me of an announcement in *Prairie Schooner* for the issue in question this summer? And further developments, if this can be called so, include $2500 handed me nicely outright and unsolicited later this month by the National Institute of Arts and Letters, what ever possessed them?

Yours,
William Gaddis

National Institute of Arts and Letters: the award was presented by Malcolm Cowley on 22 May; the citation reads: "To WILLIAM GADDIS, novelist, born in New York City, whose novel *Recognitions* exhibits breadth and subtlety of imagination, a sense of fictional architecture with a remarkable effectiveness in the rendering of details, and unflagging stylistic verve." ($2,500 = $22,000 today.)

To David Markson

Croton-on-Hudson, New York
9 June 1963

Dear Dave.

Many thanks for the *Observer* clip, which frankly I would find more of a comfort if I were *not* trying to do it all again —include & order *everything* —as appears to be happening, that or end up like the Collier brothers. Our summer is quite unplanned but mine will certainly include some stumbling against yr doorbell.

Yours,
W Gaddis.

'Observer' clip: Philip Toynbee's favorable review of the English *R* in the *Observer Weekend Review,* 9 September 1962.

Collier brothers: Langley and Homer Collyer (the correct spelling) made news in 1947 when the two elderly men were found dead in a house in Harlem cluttered with 120 tons of junk. It took eighteen days just to find the bodies.

To Jack P. Dalton

[*An American Joyce critic (1908–81) who, assuming WG was influenced by Joyce, invited him to contribute an essay to a book on the Irish writer, eventually published as* Twelve and a Tilly *(1966). The "[sic]" in the final sentence is WG's. Dalton later asked permission to publish this letter: see 19 March 1967.*]

27 September 1963

dear Mr Dalton.

I regret I cannot oblige on your request which I found as flattering as I did the original reviews frustrating in their generally invidious comparisons between *The Recognitions* and the work of Joyce, not then having read any more of him than *Exiles*, the *Dubliners* stories, about 40 pages of *Ulysses* & 10 of *Finnegans Wake*, and still unconvinced of the osmosis theory of literary influence in which the reviewers take refuge, but sorry nontheless [sic] to be no more help to you here beyond wishing you luck with your project.

Yours,
William Gaddis

To Frances Henderson Diamond

[*After Mrs. Diamond's husband Jack died on 15 January 1964, WG wrote to express his condolences. She responded in a letter of 23 March to thank him, told him about her teenage daughters' plans, and wrote "I plan to return to U.C.L.A. in the hope of getting my doctorate (in Ancient History) in a couple of years, so as to be able to teach at the university level." (She had enrolled there in 1955 in order to learn to read the Dead Sea Scrolls in the original; she earned a BA in Near Eastern History in 1960, and eventually a PhD in 1974.) She also "wondered if you ever wrote the book you were going to call* Blague," *and expressed regret at his postponed visit to Los Angeles.*]

Croton-on-Hudson, New York
[postmarked 6 April 1964]

dear Frances, I don't know why I should be so startled at your daughters' ages, I remember as a child getting good and tired of hearing 'grown-ups' remark how time flies, but I guess now that is part of being grown up. In years, at any rate. And looking back, I can't say it's flown, really, at all. Just gone. I am really amazed that you recall the title of that novel I'd started. I never wrote it but did use some of the material in *The Recognitions*, a long (956-page) novel I published in 1955, which has had a lot more attention paid it since its re-issue in paperback last year than when it came out originally. I've worked fitfully at two other books in the past few years, found the reasons they've remained unfinished to be a good deal more complex than I thought, know also how increasingly important it is that I do get them done and am trying to pull together and manage to get on with them. Currently most of my writing time goes to the US Army: I've been working on films for them—and, yes, it was that that was to bring me toward you briefly, I'd been in Hollywood to see Joe E Brown last fall about narrating an Army film on the work of entertainers overseas in World War II, but at the last minute he did not work out and that was that. What the next opportunity will be I cannot imagine, but the Army comes up with some startling notions.

And my children only 6 and 8 years old! Matthew just six, and Sarah soon to be nine, they've been off this past Easter week with their mother visiting her family in South Carolina, and I expect them all back tomorrow, at which point I have to go to Washington for the rest of the week, and so it goes. How oddly things are arranged, it seems so often, though that may be only an evasion of responsibility for failure to arrange them better myself. Which is why I admired you then, those years ago, and see your same purposefulness in this letter now, going on for a doctorate.

It is so many years since I've really written letters, carried on any sort of correspondence, that I find it as blocked and at cross purposes as writing itself, which all things considered is a pretty odd way to spend one's time, let alone make a living; but there, life itself becomes a more rather than less mysterious proposition as I grow older. So let me write you when I have news, or accomplishment, hoping meanwhile that out of one or the other will come some arrangement of circumstances that will allow actually seeing you again.

with love to you,
Will

Joe E Brown: American actor and comedian (1891–1973). He entertained the troops during World War II and thus would have made an appropriate narrator.

So let me write you when I have news: Mrs. Diamond had concluded her letter asking "Shall we write to one another, or would you rather not?" WG wrote her again a year later, but didn't write another until 1976, in response to one from her.

To Candida Donadio

[*Well-known literary agent (1929–2001) whose clients included Joseph Heller, Philip Roth, and Thomas Pynchon. She was WG's agent from the early 1960s (when she was at Russell & Volkening) until the early 1990s. The attachments to this letter included a five-page summary of J R and what was then its opening scene, available at http://omeka. wustl.edu/omeka/items/show/10065.*]

26 April "64

Dear Candida:

Is there nothing weird about sending you material to which I attach the note 'This is what I am working on but not the way I am going to work on it'? To describe how the work in progress differs—specifically the novel *J R*—well, I might as well write the novel itself. As things do with me inevitably, *J R* has changed and expanded considerably since the attached outline was written. The opening now in the school now involves the school, teachers &c more and sharper than formerly, the boy's entrance into 'business' comes about far more logically, &c. But more importantly, additional characters who have assumed the sort of obsessive reality in my mind that those in *The Recognitions* did, give the breadth I need to be interested in it myself: a middle-aged ex-writer forced from the reservoir of failure of a large corporation (taken over by J.R.) by the belated success of an early work, and his relation with a younger writer (brought in through the comic nightmare of a large foundation), one of these steals a plot from the other for a play which I am also working on; a

Candida Donadio

painter, whose trials I won't spin out here; an ex-science teacher obsessed with the idea of entropy (as I am) who writes and publishes the book *Agapē Agape* (The Secret History of the Player Piano). Sources for one book appear, transmuted, in the other. Whether we can eventually pull off the stunt of publishing *Agapē* over the name of a character from *J R* either before, at the same time, or after, remains to be seen, and the less said to anyone about it now the better.

The reason I cannot attach here the 9000-odd words of the original draft of *J R* is that those pages are now dispersed among pages and notes of the new draft for what little I want to pick up here and there from the old; even at that, I want it only skimmed in this draft, to come back and write it last. As laid out now there's less reason than ever for the boy to need to be a 'genius', he is only, as I think Piaget calls children, a 'naive realist', with a child's capacity to accommodate two conflicting ideas with no trouble (what in his adult competition is called hypocrisy). There are now some 12 or 15 folders of notes, references &c on this novel & the characters and situations in it.

The Player Piano project too has changed rather radically from original intentions, and the idea of its being written by a character in the novel will give it more room to press its thesis to absurdity, considering the rabid history of its 'author' who may well feel that artists, as prime sources of discontent and disorder, should be exterminated, as more leisure spreads and the arts become the great province of people with nothing to do. This book, begun as an essay a good many years ago, has in its original form been caught up with and even as satire surpassed by current conditions. The research material, notes, news clips, articles, &c &c, to say nothing of books, books, books, from

Trilby to Heisenberg, fill half the room. As a serious work it would challenge the possessed state of a Spengler; as ancillary to *J R* it is within reach. Thus again the enclosed outline is wanting considerably; while to write out the book's intentions now would be to write the book itself. And whether the six or seven pages also enclosed here will end up as the book's opening, or as an opening being written by the character in *J R*, or in the basket, I don't yet know, though the style is too taxing to dispense with entirely.

While the books feed on each other, the novel has fortunately become the primary effort. Just as *The Recognitions* started out a comparatively short satire on the Faust story, and I lost interest in it for its very simplicity until 'minor' characters became real and began to force the book's shape, so here I'd lost interest in the original effort at *J R*, with its rather forced story, until the minor characters who obsess me now emerged and began to run off with the book in other directions.

That's where it all stands at this moment: anyone who doubts the evidence need only visit this locked room in Croton where lunacy and organization struggle with one another. But after all that's what both books are about.

Yours

W. Gaddis

Piaget [...] 'naive realist': Swiss psychologist Jean Piaget (1896–1980) discusses this in *The Language and Thought of the Child* (1923; English trans. 1926).

Trilby: popular 1894 novel by George du Maurier about a young singer who falls under the hypnotic influence of her teacher Svengali. It is mentioned in both *J R* and *AA*.

Heisenberg: Werner Heisenberg (1901–76), Austrian physicist, best known for his uncertainty principle. He is mentioned in both *R* and *AA*.

To Patricia Gaddis

[*WG went to Germany in the summer of 1964 to assist the U.S. Army with a film entitled* The Battle at St. Vith *on the loss of the Belgian town during the Battle of the Bulge (December 1944), as does Thomas Eigen in* J R. *See Gibbs's outraged description of the battle on pp. 390–92, where St. Vith is called Saint Fiacre. The documentary was written and directed by Michael J. Laurence and produced by Hunter Low, both mentioned below.*]

Munich, Germany

12–14 July 1964

dear Pat— I've just got your letter of 7 July—through all the routine delays of "military channels"—someone *must* write the satire on the peacetime

WG with director Michael J. Laurence and film crew in Germany, 1964.

occupying army of Europe, a vast floating welfare state & good explanation of how Eisenhowers are manufactured. [...]

I cannot say things here have been going awfully well, due largely to poor preparation from New York end—I should have been over here a month before I was—certainly H. Low's letters to the people to be interviewed should have gone out far before they did, to allow for answers before I left. But even that is minor in comparison to the problems over the massive archaic studio equipment we are saddled with, constant breakdowns of one thing or another, needed parts never sent, all this working extreme frustration on director and crew—and eventually on subjects being interviewed and me. Much strong feeling, especially on Mike Laurence's part (and I don't blame him a bit since he does work hard & long) of being a projection of Hunter Low fantasy, resentment over lack of support from New York—Lord! what a thing this army is.

We had lunch on Saturday, for instance, at 5 pm—having had old Gen. Blumentritt taped to a bench (microphone cable) but in hotel "garden" where it was cold, light failed, police came in to say people were calling to complain about our generator noise in the street & 1 woman having a nervous breakdown, the general's hands getting progressively more trembling—ended grandly when our truck knocked some glass out of the hotel marquee—*all* out of E. Waugh. Yesterday the most difficult to date, we finally ended up doing sound interview in depths of a German forest at 10 pm—got back & no place to eat—and just about all of this due to equipment problems.

The biggest disappointment so far—and most interesting tangle—was call to me from Washington cancelling completion of the Skorzeny filming—I was supposed to be there (Madrid) today, but the State Department got word of it, forced its cancellation & forbids my further contact with him. I'm sure I haven't heard the last of it.

General Bayerlein is mad as a hatter—& we'd got all our equipment to Wurzburg, after talking twice to him on the phone & no reason to believe he'd say no—arrived at his carpet shop & he said he must have time to "prepare", we are going to try again with him later—I've never seen a man with a face the color of red of his—

We are supposed to go to Belgium this week—had planned to leave today (Tuesday) but equipment problems must be solved or everyone will mutiny. This time I would hope to get off ahead of others to look for locations there, since so much time has been wasted over that.

Darling I am so concerned over your vacation, whether you may have got off even now & may not get this letter which I've tried for the last 4 days to write but things have been so hectic—page 1 of this letter written Sunday,

page 2 Monday morning and now Tuesday 11 pm in bed I shall finish it some
way [...]

Yesterday we finished, if you can imagine, about 10 pm in star light making a sound recording only—other equipment problems having delayed things
till it was too late to film—deep in a German forest, an account by Manfred
Gregor of being in the German army at age 16 (he wrote of it in a novel *The
Bridge*, look for it in paperback) and now I understand even the recording is
unsatisfactory! And Gregor won't repeat, I don't blame him. So much of the
whole thing quite, quite unbelievable (I mean our experience, what you saw
at Sands Point multiplied in awkwardness 100 times)—

3 of us did take time to go to Dachau—but such a memorial has been made
of it that it is impossible to connect the place with what happened there.

The plan at the moment is that I shall leave tomorrow with 1 cameraman,
ahead of crew & director, for St Vith & Bastogne, Belgium, & only hope they
arrive later with proper repaired & replaced equipment. We are sending a man
to Heidelberg for mail which I should have end of week. I am concerned about
you having a decent summer and the children a good one, and concerned
about your health. I want you so well & happy, Statue of Liberty trip sounds
as grueling as our yesterday here. Finally I cannot believe that by the time you
get this Goldwater may be Rep. candidate for president, appalling.

Pictures for children, and my love

W.

Eisenhowers: like Dwight D. Eisenhower (1890–1969), American general and president from 1953 to 1961.

Gen Blumentritt: Günther Blumentritt (1892–1967), German general, responsible for
much of the planning to defend France against the Allied invasion.

Skorzeny: Otto Skorzeny (1908–75), a lieutenant colonel in the German Waffen-SS.
His English-speaking troops participated in the Battle of the Bulge by infiltrating
Allied lines and impersonating American soldiers. After the war he moved to Spain
and started an engineering business.

General Bayerlein: Fritz Bayerlein (1899–1970), German panzer general who served
under General Hasso von Manteuffel (Blaufinger in *J R*) in the Ardennes Offensive.

Manfred Gregor [...] *The Bridge*: pseudonym of Gregor Dorfmeister (1929–2018); his
autobiographical novel *Die Brücke* was published in 1958.

Dachau: the first Nazi concentration camp, located in southern Germany.

Goldwater: ultra-conservative Republican Barry Goldwater (1909–98) was indeed nominated by his party to run against Lyndon Johnson in the 1964 presidential election.

To John D. Seelye

Croton-on-Hudson, N.Y.

21 August 1964

Dear Mr Seelye.

I carried your note of 16 May all over southern Germany on a 58-day job which I hoped would give me some chance to answer it but never managed, and return to find yours of 16 June. I had—through Jack Green, I believe—seen a copy of the San Francisco publication which I must confess I found highly entertaining, the kind of mad ingenuity that I would never dream of 'setting right' by 'facts'. (I've also in recent months seen copies of 2 academic papers which trace my sources in such convincing detail to *Nightwood* and particularly *Ulysses* that my intervention would seem as irrelevant and presumptuous as would my angry responses have been to the original reviewers.)

The Recognitions goes slowly in England, is scheduled in Italy Germany & France, and I have no knowledge of the Nebraska situation. Regarding your query on the material cut from the original MS of the book, it is I would gather in one of a few cardboard cartons filled with notes, MS &c.; as I recall, I did the original cutting in one of the first rewrites (though this is imprecise since some parts were rewritten a number of times, some scarcely at all), the next following a list of suggestions (but *not* demands) from an editor, the final and most thorough (as, a dropped prefatory chapter) myself for reasons I felt convincing and would probably find even more convincing now. I appreciate the invitation of your friend Mr van Strum but have no wish at this point to see any of that material published.

Yours,

W. Gaddis

San Francisco publication: Tom "Tiger Tim" Hawkins's *Eve: The Common Muse of Henry Miller and Lawrence Durrell* (San Francisco: Ahab Press, 1963), a portion of which touches on *R* and Green's *Fire the Bastards!* (pp. 14–18). Hawkins suspected Gaddis and Green were the same person. For more on this odd character, see chap. 5 of Don Foster's *Author Unknown: On the Trail of Anonymous* (Henry Holt, 2000).

2 academic papers: the essay on Djuna Barnes's *Nightwood* (1936), later described as a Master's thesis, is unidentified; the one on *Ulysses* was probably a draft of Bernard Benstock's "On William Gaddis: In Recognition of James Joyce," *Wisconsin Studies in Contemporary Literature* 6 (Summer 1965): 177–89.

Italy Germany & France: only the Italian translation was published; the others fell through (though French and German translations did eventually appear).

the Nebraska situation: *Prairie Schooner* was (and still is) published by the University of Nebraska; the issue was abandoned in the summer of 1963, though apparently no one informed WG of this.

Mr van Strum: Stevens Van Strum (1939–2021) is described in Seelye's letters to WG as a young friend of his, a classics scholar living in Berkeley, who was "very interested in the book, and has turned up some fascinating things." He cofounded Oyez Press in 1964.

To John R. Kuehl

[*A professor of literature (1928–98) at Princeton and later at New York University, where he directed the first doctoral dissertation on R. He invited WG to contribute to a book in which authors furnished rough drafts of their published work and commented on the process of revision. The book was published (without a contribution by WG) in 1967 as* Write & Rewrite.]

Croton-on-Hudson, New York
29 August 1964

Dear Professor Kuehl.

Thank you for your letter and your interest in *The Recognitions* in terms of your own project. I am sorry to be so long about answering you but I have been on a two-month job outside the country and am only now beginning to catch up.

Regarding your query, I doubt I could be much help to you even with the most willing spirit and all the necessary time. While I have boxes of redrafted writing and scraps of notes from that novel—parts of which were considerably rewritten, parts very little—I have neither looked at them nor in fact read the book for so many years that I scarcely think I could put my finger on any sequence and follow it through with much faithfulness to the process as it actually occurred, and your approach seems interesting enough that its real success (I don't mean sales) must depend upon the exactitude with which these tangible aspects can be reproduced, in order to give some measure of those which cannot.

Though I weep for order I live still in a world of scrawled notes on the backs of envelops; and while I realise that you can no more wait upon my good intentions than any publisher will, without evidence, back yours, if I should have the time and luck to turn up anything that makes sense I shall let you know.

Yours,
William Gaddis

To Patricia Gaddis

The Lawtonian Hotel
Lawton, Oklahoma
21 Nov. 1964

Pat. A new project started yesterday and the earlier part completed today though rewriting difficult in present state, roughly a day behind schedule—I know this doesn't interest you (*"my* work") but does bear on my hope to clear things up by Wednesday night next. I called my mother eve. of 19th to wish her happy birthday which she had had, and congratulate her on pulling off these 40 years. She said you'd called, told her about new house (she didn't say what) and new job, on which you would hardly hear my congratulations since you know I'd wish it were for yourself, how good that w^d be, instead of as the means of escape that finally got you to it. But there—people compare my work to Joyce, when all that's really comparable is the bourgeois level of our domestic ~~ambitions~~ aspirations.

Love to the children
W.

To Frances Henderson Diamond

[*Her daughter Jamie remembers WG visiting her mother: "I was confused, baffled, and maybe suspicious by the appearance of a formal looking man who spent a long time talking very personally with my mother. I had never heard of him or seen him before and I didn't know why they seemed so close" (email 2 December 2020).*]

Harvard Club
27 West 44th Street
New York, N. Y. 10036
12 April 1965

dear Frances—Seeing some one—you, after so long a time, seems to want a confirmation, something, even this note, to offset the haunting unreality of simply "dropping in" for 2 or 3 hours and saying 'goodnight' that matter-of-factly after xx years, but what a fixture you have been in my life all that time and one which if I'd paid it the serious attention I pretended to myself I did, I might have done things better, but this note is only to say, or to confirm the confirmation of seeing you and talking with you again and being able in my own selfishness afterwards to say to myself, —You see? you were right, all this time, about what a fine spirit she is. ——

Again with my love & best wishes,
W. Gaddis

To Naomi Replansky

[*American poet (1918–) who had sent WG a copy of her book* Ring Song *(1962 reprint) inscribed "For William Gaddis in homage to his 'Recognitions' from an admirer Naomi Replansky."*]

Croton-on-Hudson, New York
3 May 1965

dear Miss Replansky.

I am very apologetic about being so long sending you a word of thanks for your book of poems but can quickly hurdle remarks about your kindness in sending it to say that I have been through them a number of times, and like many of them very much; and there is really no more than that to say, except to add that it's a pretty rare experience these days. Thank you again.

Yours,
William Gaddis

To Lyndon B. Johnson

[*A Western Union telegram. Arkansas senator J. William Fulbright opposed President Johnson's plans to expand American involvement in Vietnam War.*]

Croton-on-Hudson, NY
17 June 1965

PRESIDENT JOHNSON
RESPECTFULLY BUT VEHEMNTLY URGE REALISTIC FULBRIGHT
ALTERNATIVE TO PRESENT FUTILE MILITARY COURSE IN
VIET NAM

WILLIAM GADDIS

To Arthur Heiserman

[*American literary critic (1929–75) and a professor at the University of Chicago. Heiserman wrote to WG on 19 August inviting him to speak there, and responded to the letter below (which lacks a closing signature) on 29 September.*]

Croton-on-Hudson, NY
[September 1965]

Dear Mr Heiserman.

My being so long about answering your invitation to appear is a fact of such simple rudeness that I can at this point only apologise, since my reasons for putting it off all this time have been real only to me and so scarcely mitigating. If this invitation still holds, in the shadow of the above and what follows and your own obvious need to work out a schedule, I should like to accept it, if not I shall certainly understand.

I have in fact turned down other such invitations, and the variety of my reasons for doing so becomes at this moment all I can think of as material for an acceptance, ranging from prejudice against what seems to me our current tendency to transform the so-called creative artist into a performer, to my own total inexperience of any sort of public appearance and saturation of self-doubts in —What have I to tell them? to teach them? outside the book I have written and those I am writing now? until the doubts themselves are almost all that remains undoubted and so, logically extend even to not accepting.

Should all of this seem to you gratuitous over-complicating ("A simple yes or no answer will do"), I risk that further in my awareness that I must sound all too preciously retiring in the face of your familiarity with these activities, much in the way I've thought publication of a first novel at the hands of the book reviewers is like the first time one is hauled into a police station on what for the desk sergeant is an old and tiresome story but for the novel offender a unique audacity (if you will excuse my parlaying the metaphor and be assured that the inclusion in it of book reviewers is not meant to be invidious). But I am neither arrested often nor as mad as the above might indicate, nor with work of my own I should wish to try to read at this point in its progress, though I would hope to rescue from that some thesis, possibly chaos, that might be of interest to you.

If you are not yourself overcome with doubt at this point over this invitation, and if I am not so late in answering as to upset your schedule, would you let me know in a little more detail what sort of group? and how large? and a date as late this year as you can conveniently manage, the December possibility you note so that I can arrange some notion of what I am doing if only to myself. I do regard your invitation most highly, and again will understand completely if at this point you can no longer conveniently extend it.

To Alice Denham

[*A fiction writer and model (1933–2016), and a former* Playboy *centerfold (in the July 1956 issue, which also included a short story of hers). David Markson introduced her to WG, who had separated from his wife by then, though their divorce would not be finalized until 16 May 1967. The following letter appears in her memoir* Sleeping with Bad Boys: Literary New York in the Fifties and Sixties *(Book Republic Press, 2006), in the chapter "A Week with Willie Gaddis."*]

Croton-on-Hudson, N.Y.

[30 September 1965]

Dear Alice,

In one recent evening I 'direct dialed' 4 numbers, 3 in N.Y. and yours in Washington—and got a service on each one of them. So much for the telephone company.

My own household has finally collapsed, my effort of the past 2 years to hold it together unavailing & Pat moved out with the children & so now the long bloody scene involving lawyers, my demands for 'rights' regarding children etc., none of it new but all of it new to me and to them and seeming so damned unnecessary, aren't there enough problems without adding new ones?

And regarding books, writing—the second book seems scarcely easier than the first, harder really—God save us from the 3rd!—but I have a good publishing contract now and so no need for other work.

Are you ever in New York? Let me know.

Yours,

W. Gaddis

To David Markson

[*Markson published his first "serious" novel—his three earlier ones were written for money—in early 1966, entitled* The Ballad of Dingus Magee. *The specific review Markson sent WG is unknown.*]

[February? 1966]

Dear David—

As stupid & cynical as it may sound, may *be,* I hope you'll understand my congratulations on a review and not the book itself, at this point anyhow—but that review, in *that* "influential organ", well—I'm sure I am interrupting a 'phone call from Joe Levine or Daryl Zanuck (*not* Harry Joe Brown jr), I hope so at any rate, and the book itself will follow quite separately, though I guess my real congratulations are on finishing it, and on, apparently, keeping your sense of humour. Thanks for sending the review, I'll *buy* the book.

Yours,

W Gaddis

Levine [...] Zanuck: Joseph E. Levine (1905–87) and Darryl F. Zanuck (1902–79) were prominent film producers of the time.

Harry Joe Brown jr: film producer (1934–2005); cf. WG's postcard to Markson of 5 October 1989.

To David Markson

[Markson sold film rights to Dingus Magee *for $100,000 (equivalent to $800,000 today), which allowed him and his family to go to Europe for a few years.]*

7 March 1966

David—my response (prompt as always) to your splendid piece of news which anyone who knows you can be delighted at, knowing that you know where it fits in the scheme of things ("Jimmy Breslin" notwithstanding) and how to make sense of/with it.

(Do you recall some time ago sending me a carbon of a letter to a publisher w/ the superscription "Doesn't anyone care?"—well this experience should prove in the very best sense that no one does, and)—what is the line? —"Not fare well, but fare forward"—

best regards all round
W. Gaddis.

Jimmy Breslin: popular New York columnist and author (1930–2017).
"Not fare well, but fare forward": from the end of part 3 of Eliot's "The Dry Salvages."

To Judith Thompson

[WG's future second wife (1940–2022)—they would marry in June 1968—whom he met in 1965 via his friend Mike Gladstone. Harrison Kinney, who worked for IBM and gave WG a few speechwriting assignments, recalled: "Judith worked for a publishing house and was attracted to Gaddis at a literary party. 'There was Norman Mailer putting his arm around this guy and calling him "Willie,"' Judith told me. 'I was impressed.'" At the time she was an Associate Travel Editor for Glamour, *and later freelanced and worked in the antiques business.]*

3 August 1966

How strange this is the first 'letter' I have ever written you, & can't begin "Dear Judith" with a straight face, dear girl, dear Judith, dear heaven how long ago only this time yesterday already has become.

Judith Gaddis and WG, Saltaire, late 1960s (photo by Martin Dworkin).

And you may imagine how much news there is here since our telephone call—and how you haunt this house—and that downstairs room where I hope to move tonight if the children can be persuaded to move into theirs, Sarah quite entranced with hers, mirrored dresser &c—and how this letter is merely a device to see if mail really works between here and there, and so you will have something in the mail, and know I have mounted a pencil sharpener on a kitchen wall and once more spread out work.

And to tell you you must call, wire, come, if things, pressures, get too disproportionate won't you—including $ (and use the enclosed just to keep you in balance until I see you)—though for the moment 2 days' a week work may not be unrealistic, may allow you a little more freedom at home—the horoscopes keep insisting how splendid everything is for us, and that means work I guess, you to fight off the difficulties in your situation there, toward work; I to fight off the attractions in mine here, toward work; and toward seeing you Sunday night, barring disaster.

yours, with you know what and you know why
W.

To Carolyn Kizer

[*American poet (1925–2014) who in 1966 became the first director of Literary Programs for the newly created National Endowment for the Arts. The paragraph below WG's signature was apparently typed on a carbon of his "official" letter of acceptance.*]

Croton-on-Hudson, N.Y. 10520
[late 1966]

Dear Miss Kizer.

You may imagine I am immensely gratified at being among the writers awarded grants in literature by the National Endowment for the Arts, and will be more than pleased to make reports as requested on my progress on this work which I can now hope to complete with the assistance of this grant.

Although some years have already gone into this work-in-progress it is, as I think often chronic among writers, behind the schedule I had originally intended for it; and my work on it this spring will be sporadically interrupted by a part-time teaching invitation which I had accepted in order to continue work on the book. I trust this will not affect the provisions and administering of the grant as set forth in Mr Stevens' letter, but should it appear to the payment dates of the grant might be moved ahead from the present January-April-July-October 1967, to July-October (1967)-January-April (1968).

In any case, since the work-in-progress is taking me longer than intended, be assured that the grant funds will be used in the manner and for the purpose set forth, as indicated by the enclosed carbon which I have signed with great gratitude.

Yours,
William Gaddis

Carolyn —as you can see from this letter I decided that it might make more sense simply to accept the grant as proposed, but felt the part-time teaching item should be mentioned to keep the record clear and avoid gross complications, as it were. I hope this makes sense to you and that you can proceed, without further concern for my confusions, with things as they stand in Mr Stevens' letter. Do let me know, I earnestly hope I haven't injected my own uncertainties which are now largely resolved. & now: to 'work apace, apace, apace. /Honest labour bears a lovely face.'

──────────

'work apace [...] lovely face': from Thomas Dekker's 1599 play *Patient Grissil* (*ODQ*).

────

To Jack P. Dalton

[*See 27 September 1963. After Dalton saw Bernard Benstock's essay on Gaddis's alleged debt to Joyce, he asked WG's permission to quote his earlier note in a letter he later sent to the editor of* Contemporary Literature, *who never printed it.*]

Croton-on-Hudson NY
19 March 1967

Dear Mr. Dalton.

Thanks for your note. You've my permission to publish that 1963 note if you like, though rereading it now I wonder, did I read *Portrait of the Artist* in college? or read in it? and if it matters? since it could I assume scarcely affect such observations as "the correspondences continue to accumulate toward a definitive theory of imitation and conscious borrowing" (from *Ulysses*). I saw and of course was most intrigued by the results of Mr Benstock's ingenuity, as I was by a Master's thesis I once saw in which the candidate drew similarly appallingly precise parallels with *Nightwood* (though albeit blessed with a far from photographic memory, I'd read that one).

Maybe Joyce read people like the I assume now quite forgotten Andrew Lang too? and we've become victims of the common misapprehension of Darwin's common ancestor for ape and man emerging as man descended from the ape. Regarding the whole thing I'm ever more convinced that such matters are best dealt with posthumously, and have scarcely swerved from my feelings when I wrote pp 95–6 of *The Recognitions*. Finally regarding Joyce's *Ulysses* I've still not read it but can now enter any discussion with the bravura of "...but I've seen the movie."

Yours,
William Gaddis

Andrew Lang: Scottish author of *Custom and Myth* (1884) and *Magic and Religion* (1901), two of WG's source-books for *R*.
the movie: Joseph Strick's film version appeared in 1967.

To Judith Thompson

Tues. pm [April? 1967]

My Whole World:

how you've saturated my life, there's not a corner anywhere inside or out where I don't find you waiting, and not there, from that yawning half of Altnaveigh's bed to the hot-dog cart on 9A where I pass hungry & daren't stop, I know I'd choke, to Storrs's theatre showing last night *Blowup*, without you ergo w/out me, I couldn't pull a Jablow on you, instead accepted dinner from the people who had me last week named Davis in part I think because she felt her last week Tetrazzini (sp?) was dry & lacking & didn't want me to carry that impression around when she could & did serve a fine Bourgognionne (damned French) & I left at a decent hour, back to Altnaveigh where the old dog came right into the room & went to sleep under the bed. Cold comfort but I thought it was terribly thoughtful of him to know how much I missed you & try in his own way to help.

The [camping] trip? Oh Lord, the trip. It really worked out immensely well [...] Matthew with sudden space around him to grow up in, [...] But, we did cook over a fire, cut wood, sleep 3" off the floor, toss marshmallows to raccoons at night, light kerosene lanterns, & I guess pretty generally do all the things we'd have done if we had really been penniless, illiterate, & never amounted to anything back in the hills. I love you. Though it began with our arriving in Washington early enough to go to the Lincoln Memorial & walk around, then out to visit a friend of mine named MacDonald who is with the Office of the Chief of Military History & will probably be in charge of the official history of Vietnam, all that strained because of under-current battle between him & his wife, charming British exballet dancer but Lord you cannot know other people's marriages and Lord! I thought of us & I thought never! never! we can never let that happen. [...]

Too possibly what follows will sound like I'm doing everything to evade work, but it's really trying to get things long postponed done, a note from

Arabelle Porter asking how things were going so I will face her Friday lunch
[...]. And if manageable expect to go into town tomorrow night or so to talk
with this fellow Moore about the most denigrating ways a composer can make
a living, to get Edward Bast back on the tracks.

And you, you . . . can't bear this letter writing business because mine are so
marvelous! they're not, no, and I almost think it would be terrible if we became
adept, exchanged sparkling & accomplished correspondence, things mustn't
get to that point! No, our letters have to stay awkward & just blundering
around I love you and I miss you to extinction & don't dare destroy another
word you write me, if you knew how since we talked Sun I've waited to get
back & get your letter, & how I love your letters, especially this with its enclosure, in today's mail and what a packet: a letter regarding father's estate;
Pfizer's Annual Report; Special Money-Saving Certificate for 27 Capital Gain
Stocks; solicitation to buy a book "like nothing else that has ever appeared in
North America, the secrets of African Sex revealed to you for the first time!"
and another containing (also For the First Time) "Over 210 photographs of
coital positions!" (this one a product of "Renowned Oriental doctors"); and
eighteen fragmentary manuscripts totaling 79 pages ("I'd like you to read the
few stories that I enclosed and to give me your opinion of them . . .") from
Adrian Grunberg of West 189th st, of whom I had heretofore been unaware
("He was walking on a hot desert road. There was no one around for miles
and the sun was burning fiercely. Suddenly, like a merciful sign from heaven,
two huge female breasts appeared in the sky . . .") Well Judith, dearest, darling,
do you wonder how I fight through such offerings for a glimpse of your writing? how when I find it I put it aside to keep for last, pour tea, sit, can't wait,
don't, . . . you come first. [...]

And your antiquing, how I thought of you, and your mother, and of you,
those 80 miles out into Virginia where it seemed everyone who'd found an
old bottle in the cellar and could spell the word had out a sign 'Antiques' &
I'm sure the practiced eye could have found those seamless lipless bottles we
learned bring $50 & heaven knows what else. We'll do that. And we'll ransack
that place up beyond Storrs. And we'll . . . oh the things, the things we'll do!
And, having taken Robt Graves up to Storrs last night, Be bird, be blossom,
comet, star, Be paradisal gates ajar, But still, as woman, cleave you must To
who alone endures your trust (me).

with you know what & you know why

W.

Altnaveigh's [...] 9A: an inn in Storrs, Connecticut, and the 9A highway that leads
from Croton-on-Hudson down along the west side of Manhattan.

Blowup: Michelangelo Antonini's cool 1966 film about swinging London.

Jablow: WG's lawyer, Richard Jablow (1926–75), of Butler Jablow & Geller.

MacDonald: Charles B. MacDonald (1922–90), wrote several books on World War II but not one on the Vietnam war.

Arabelle Porter: i.e., Arabel J. Porter (1911–83), the editor of *New World Writing* who published an excerpt from *R* in 1952.

this fellow Moore: unidentified.

father's estate: William Gaddis Sr. died in 1965.

Adrian Grunberg: unknown and apparently unpublished.

Robt Graves [...] endures your trust: the concluding stanza of "Loving True, Flying Blind," the penultimate poem in *Love Respelt* (Doubleday, 1966).

To John and Pauline Napper

Saltaire, N.Y. 11781
15 July '67

dear John & Pauline—

After your diligence, & entirely seductive picture of Ireland, I've of course taken the course of least resistance, & apologise heartily for being so long letting you know. But—here is this house of my mother's out here on Fire Island, a beach settlement about 40 miles from New York, no rent to pay, & the children—who will be with me for August—familiar with it, so, I decided to rent the house in Croton and pack up my whole trash heap of notes &c. and try to continue this infernal novel out here, writing on it as well as I have anywhere, it all seems to make the best sense for the summer at any rate, though there are the constant temptations to evade it, painting to be done, windows to be mended, anything resembling work with tangible results and attainable 'perfection'—even to washing out shirts. But I do *not* go and lie on the beach, a kind of Puritan rejection of leisure that has dogged my life, though I do hope I will be somewhat more agreeable next month when the children appear.

And very little 'entertaining' [...] But I do go into New York occasionally so if there should be anything you need done there do let me know. Otherwise—well, page 165—no, rewrite page 164, then ... in fact perhaps better rewrite starting page 161—or 150—or perhaps better start the whole thing over, and—no! fare forward—— let me know news, even —the best wish I can leave you with —if there isn't any—

love & best wishes (& from Sarah even in her absence)
Willie Gaddis

WG on the beach at Saltaire, Long Island.

To David Markson

Saltaire, NY
20 July '67

Dear David.

Thanks for your letter from London. I am sorry to have been so poor about answering your items in the past, largely probably because I have had little to say. Thus you find me brisk enough when you ask a tangible like Croton. And it is excellent, bachelor or family (I'm not suggesting the former to you), I can live there for weeks and speak to no one but the clerk at the A&P & comments on the weather with the gas station man. Which I like. You mightn't. But inevitably with children in school you meet parents, more or less. I do have a few friends there, say 4 families, which is all I want. It is country and because of the twisty up&down nature of the land unsuburbanizable like Long Island. It is attractive, the river is a splendour & quite beyond anything I've seen elsewhere. And besides being country it is less than an hour's drive to NY, trains are not bad (albeit the cars mostly turn-of-the-century items) and offered me the good position of strictly country life when I'm there, or—God forbid it should happen again—as good commuting to NY as one can find elsewhere. With children, as I say, I don't think one could do better; and even without it's worked well for me. I don't know, I get awfully bored in NY, going out, sitting around, hearing myself talk, awfully impatient with it.

Though what my plans are I don't know. I've got my house in Croton rented now in fact for the summer which I'm spending quietly (isn't the word) at Fire Island, partly to save money, partly to try to work, partly that I'll have the children for the month of August and it's a good place for them, I can spend enough time with them but they can lead pretty much their own social lives. My mother is here so, as I say, quiet (this being one of the quieter communities), Judith gets out usually weekends, and I paint (not pictures, old iron beds &c) & patch and go back to this damned typewriter. God knows. I don't generally answer people anymore even friends who ask how/when &c the book is coming, but simply to say I'm working, that is, it's still in my hands. How tired one gets of one's own voice. Unless it's saying something sensible like I love you. But even at that, providing one isn't saying it because he can think of no other news, or would rather not say You have bad breath, one doesn't hear it one's self.

Do you see Katy Carver? Ask her to send me a line. How can Dean Rusk go on being Dean Rusk? How can people get into cars and go to Expo "67? And PS to the above, Croton is not the south, Faulkner's or anyone's else. I was in Lawton Okla 4 times and never ceased to wonder why people there got up in the morning.

> best wishes to you & Elaine
> W. Gaddis

Dean Rusk: Secretary of State (1961–69), a supporter of the Vietnam War.
Expo "67: a world's fair held in Montreal in 1967, the most popular of its kind.
Elaine: Markson's wife; see 22 Sept. 1978.

To Alice Denham

[*Denham had asked WG for a blurb for her first novel,* My Darling from the Lions *(Bobbs-Merrill, 1967), and received this tardy reply, which appears on p. 283 of her* Sleeping with Bad Boys. *WG had moved from North Highland Place to this smaller house in fall 1967, where he would live with Judith until February 1969.*]

> 25 Park Trail
> Croton-on-Hudson, N.Y.
> [postmarked 12 January 1968]

Dear Alice—I'm sorry for the lateness of this for I've had your book & started it—But do recall our talk about quotes, at that party I think, and why it's never made sense for me to give one because I honestly can't believe my name would sell a single copy so that—since it is not a name in the public mind like Mailer's for instance—my name on the jacket of someone else's work, or in an ad, flatly would strike me as an advertisement for myself, like the raft of provincial reviewers whose livelihood apparently depends on such publicity—that's from my point of view, & from yours—I'm convinced it wouldn't change your sales etc at all—where publishers get these ideas I cannot imagine—I even recently got in the mail a big book of Aubrey Beardsley drawings—some quite startling—with request for comment—imagine my name selling Aubrey Beardsley! I don't think anyone's figured out the chemistry of book sales—except the fact that the one who sells books is the man in the bookstore—and as I know, there's altogether too much pain connected with it—hang on—all I know that counts is luck & I certainly wish you that—I'll keep an eye for reviews—

> Willie Gaddis

Aubrey Beardsley: English artist (1872–1898) associated with the decadent 1890s.

To John and Pauline Napper

[From 1968 to 1970 WG frequently interrupted work on J R for freelance writing projects, mostly for Eastman Kodak, but also for Audio Adventures (a tour of Greenwich Village) and Film Enterprises (on IBM software; WG's first draft was deemed by a Film Enterprises exec "a little too profound and needed reshaping in a manner that would be informative at a shallower depth"). One of the projects resulted in a book: A Pile Fabric Primer *(Crompton-Richmond Company, 1970).]*

Saltaire, N.Y. 11706

4 July '68

Dear John & Pauline —

I think that today, or yesterday, or tomorrow, is the day I've been waiting for for about 4 months, simply in terms of sitting down.

First, —Judith and I got married. That was about 4 weeks ago, & that is the best affirmation of recent years. All around it various aspects of confusion: my Mother returned from California not in very good condition, got progressively worse & finally, when I came back from a 'business trip' to Rochester, I got her hospitalised, she came out of there better, is now in a convalescent home & I expect to bring her out here in a week or so, when she'll be better able to get around. How all that is going to work out there's no way to know yet. Then, the children's mother moving them to Boston finally came off, again emotional & confusing scene, but finally done & better than the uncertainty & the waiting. In between all the above my fly-by-night trips to E Kodak in Rochester, getting a job, hurrying back to Croton, writing the whatever-they-wanted, mailing it &c &c; took Matthew off on a camping trip last week which was fine enough even though it was rain constantly, & now at last we've got all of our stuff out here, including my barrels & barrels of papers, clippings &c that hope some day to be a novel. Sarah has gone south (Carolina) to visit a cousin till mid-July, & Judith & I & Matthew are settled in at the house on Fire Island, she with a new sewing machine making pillows a mile a minute with spreads & curtains in between.

And this I pray is the way it will continue through August. As I say I expect to bring my Mother out next week, & she will stay the summer through. The children are to return to their mother the 18 August. And in between I will (I hope) be back on and off the Rochester run, 3 or 4 jobs for them will get us through the summer. And possibly, if I have the sense to grasp it, time to get back on this novel. [...] curious how some of us who are obsessed with order seem constantly immersed in disorder.

We all send love & let us know how you prosper—

Willie

To Sarah Gaddis

[*An undated "Memo from W. Gaddis" attached to a copy of an undated obituary-essay on Samuel E. Williams (died 1937; see headnote to 16 November 1943) entitled "The Road That Leads to Somewhere" by Philip Kabel, possibly from the* Union City Times Gazette. *The article discusses the maternal side of WG's family history in some detail.*]

Dear Sarah——you have asked often enough about the family story and I thought you might find this of interest. It is from an Indiana newspaper about 30 years ago—Robert Way was Grandmother's 'brother'—S.E. Williams was your great great Grandfather—and you see there *is* an Indian princess way back in your family—and that you had ancestors settling in Boston about 340 years ago! (I also thought you'd like some of the names, like Peninah!—)

much love from
Papa

Robert Way: the obituary also notes the recent death at age 31 of Robert Dickinson Way (I. W. Way's son and Edith Gaddis's brother), a pianist and music professor.
an Indian princess: Mary Crews, described by Kabel as "a Cherokee Indian princess" (cf. note to 13 August 1956).
ancestors settling in Boston: Kabel notes that Williams's ancestors "settled in Boston in 1630."
Peninah: "In 1876," Kabel writes, Williams "was married to Ella Hough, daughter of Moses and Peninah Hough."

To Sarah Gaddis

[*An undated letter (probably January 1969) reproduced here as an example of WG's calligraphic handwriting.*]

dear Sarah—
Back at this old familiar business of writing you on the train — to N.Y., a day with some of the Eastman people who make their chemicals and cloth and the lady who handles fashions — and is probably deciding right now what color you will want to be wearing in 1970 —

This is the first note like this to you without
allowance enclosed, isn't it (since you wanted
to skip a week rather than get $1. for 2 weeks).
But I've thought about the Teen magazine
subscription and if you will send me the coupon
I'll take care of that for you.

Meanwhile, now that Christmas is past and all
the confusion, $ and otherwise, that goes with it,
I hope you have things straightened out and
will be able to keep an accounting of how your
February clothing allowance goes so that we can
go over it at the end of the month. You don't
need to try to save it for major things like a
sweater, though of course it would be fine if
you could and still get the smaller things you
need like stockings, underwear, shampoo ec — so
keep your accounts clear! —

I've wondered if you have had the chance to
get into either Candide or Ethan Frome, and what
you will think of them. They are about as different
as books can be. And when you read Ethan Frome
don't fail to read E. Wharton's preface to it —
which as a coming writer should be of great interest
and perhaps some help to you —

Well — the beautiful Hudson River out the train
window & another day (though not think letters
in my bloody office but someone else's) — I'll write
again in a few days as we get finally moved into
Piermont — with much love from Papa.

Candide or *Ethan Frome*: WG quoted Voltaire's novella earlier (4 May 1951). Edith
Wharton's short novel (1911) is mentioned in passing in *J R* (516).

To Kirkpatrick Sale

[*In February 1969 WG purchased a house about twenty miles north of New York City,
which would become the setting for* Carpenter's Gothic. *Sale, a writer (1937–) and lifelong friend of Thomas Pynchon, wrote asking WG to contribute to a publication that
apparently never materialized.*]

> 25 Ritie St.
> Piermont NY 10968
> 30 June 1969

Dear Kirk.

Your note has become one of the more dog-eared items in my collection,
having been in and out of pocket since I got it, [...]

Just now I honestly think that I am pausing to take stock, regroup, draw
the battle lines or at least find out where they are, set my course, and—as such
a succession of metaphors can only end—ride off in all directions, if you see
what I mean. At any rate I do hope to start to give less time to commercial
work and more to my own and I am of course intrigued by what you say of
your prospective publication. The book I have been working on and off is in
and out of the hands of Candida Donadio as of course is anything mentionable I do when I do. At the moment I think she has some prospect for a segment of it & these matters aside from faltering suggestions I leave pretty much
to her. However that works out for the moment though there are some things
I want to work out & on & so your kind invitation does appear at what, barring my own dead ends, should be an opportune time. It may take me a bit
to get through the storekeeper-military-maritime metaphor cited above but
I look forward to letting you know when I do. ("His Lordship says he will
turn it over in what he is pleased to call his mind.")

We expect to get off for Fire Island in a week or so, as soon as I can pack
up the trash heap I refer to as research materials but one way or another will
stay in touch. Thanks again.

> with best regards,
> W. Gaddis

ride off in all directions: a famous line from one of Canadian author Stephen Leacock's *Nonsense Novels* (1911): "Lord Ronald [...] flung himself upon his horse and
rode madly off in all directions" (*ODQ*).

segment of it: probably the segment from *J R* that would appear the following year in
the *Dutton Review*: see note to 23 July 1970.

"His Lordship [...] his mind": another quotation from *ODQ*, by Richard Bethell,
Baron Westbury (1800–1873).

To Patricia Black Taylor

[*Edith Gaddis died in August 1969; WG conveyed the news to his ex-wife, who was living
near Boston with Sarah, Matthew, and her new husband. Her father died around the
same time.*]

[mid August 1969]

Pat, this is unhappily to let you know what we had all really been expecting.
I saw my Mother at the Hospital late Sunday & could not then imagine how
it [could] go on much longer, a tenacity the doctors had already described as
a 'minor miracle', then through a hospital mix-up did not learn till late the
next day that she had died Sunday night soon after I left her, though even
then, as in the weeks before, there was every reason to believe she did not
know I was there.

I have not tried to break through to you by wire, phone &c because I frankly
haven't seen the point & have wanted the children especially to have a last
vacation week all free and clear. [...]

You may handle this now as you think best with the children, talk with
them now or wait till you return to Wayland and call me collect. [...] I hope
you agree and that the children understand my simply writing you now rather
than as it seemed to me heightening the impact by abrupt wires and phone
calls of what is such a real loss to Sarah and Matthew and I know to you too.

W.

To Sarah Gaddis

25 Ritie street
Piermont NY 10968
8 Sept. 69

Dear Sarah.

Here you are, with Birthday distributed in pieces around coming and going and school. Perhaps this is normal for Virgo? Mr Thompson's birthday in

late August (Virgo) went on-and-off-and-on for 4 days. At any rate you will find enclosed the confirmation that you *are* 14 (count them), and I so earnestly hope the day itself is a *good* one. Unmitigated (look it up!) praise of course is something we should all be wary of so I won't do that here, since obviously there are a few areas for improvement which is part of the process of growing up, but you are a daughter to be immensely proud of, and I am, as I said in another letter to you, less frequently aware than I should be of the privilege.

It was an awareness Grandmother had, and even though her later days were not easy ones I hope you know how much pride and very real joy she took in you and Matthew, how much the very fact of your happy existence added to her life. Her loss is something I am far from used to and I know you have similar feelings but, after all, we might scarcely miss her so much if she had not been so close and generous to us all our lives and so our missing her is really a measure of all she did for us, in which I think she found her own reward.

And so how many ways your starting off into high school is a new start and a demanding one and an exciting one, and one in which I hope you won't look for instant results or solutions, or make instant judgments (of people 'good' and otherwise), of yourself and where you stand and who you are in relation to those around you.

I know you are impatient about life, which is very much a part of being 14, and so make an effort to take your time about looking over things and people and situations and yourself in relation to them, so that you can keep a little freedom of choice when choices present themselves. At the heart of all this I think is your regard for yourself and your worth as a person, and the essential idea that you must put a high value on yourself. I don't mean 'snob' value or more-clothes-than-so-&-so or cash-in-hand or 'popularity', because these are all just the cheapenings of your worth, your real worth as a person, and perhaps you can get some idea of that in the love that so many of us have for you, and some of the confidence to play things a little cool and above *all* to keep your sense of humour! Because a sense of humour is simply a sense of proportion, of the real worth of things in relation to each other, which lets you see how totally ridiculous some of the most intensely fought out selfish battles can often be, and Sarah if you can keep your sense of humour you are a step ahead almost anywhere you go.

Of course we all regret the fact of your birthday falling in the midst of change and readjustment on so many hands, so that it cannot be the kind of Cake-and-Hands-around-the-table occasion dear to even grown-up children. So on Wednesday I hope you won't feel any "gyp" that some of it is already behind you (that you're wearing some of it, that is) but have a fine birthday there. And then I have written your Mother about our going out to a somewhat belated birthday dinner on Monday when we bring Matthew back up. How would that be? And then we can go over various things including your allowance which I know got somewhat confused on your last visit and is in arrears, clothing money, &c.

Like those people in *Our Town* it seems so difficult sometimes simply to stop and live 'every every minute'. I will be so eager to hear about people and school, perhaps you can take us over Monday for a look around? since by then of course you will know it intimately. [...]

with much much love,
Papa

Mr Thompson: Judith's father.
Our Town: Thornton Wilder's popular play (1938), which asks, "Do any human beings ever realize life while they live it?—every, every minute?"

To David Markson

[*Markson asked WG for a blurb for his novel* Going Down *(1970)*.]

Piermont, N.Y.
5 March 1970

Dear David.

Your letter touches on a difficult area, one I have never entirely resolved in anything but practice which is why it has taken me so long to respond.

At the outset though to try to keep up minute-by-minute with the reception of a book that has cost one as much as this one has cost you, let alone to try to take part in it, is plain Chinese water torture, drop by drop, when you are in the most vulnerable position conceivable, quoting the *Library Journal* of all things, 'suspenseful plot, superb dialogue', you know it ends up like the psychiatrist being greeted with "Good morning..." muttering "What do you think he meant by that?" And hell you know all this, you have neither the body of Jaqueline Suzanne nor the prim crust of a non-adventurer like Capote, and 'If I were you...' as advice never tires of phrasing it I would lay hands on every available penny take wife and children and pack up, let the book go out and do what it's going to do anyhow.

My feeling essentially is that a book really goes out on its own, for the human remains that wrote it to run along after it is suicidal since there's clearly no separating them until the mortal partner drops. I don't think 'one decent blurb or two' is going to alter Asher's promotion at all, I don't think lack of them is going to deter it; and the whole God damned area is to me like trying to make magic that will shape a course already implicit and then, if the course takes the feared-for direction, blaming the ex post facto magic, or the lack of it. I've never had my name on anybody else's book jack or ad that I know of, I honestly do not think it would help sell a copy, it reeks a bit of self-advertisement though perhaps, out of a deep mistrust for human motives or rather of them and the abyss between them and their expression this is merely an extreme inverted vanity on my part. Because on the other hand I do admire the generosity of people of stature like, say, Robert Graves, Norman Mailer, TS Eliot writing jacket blurbs for Faber, all of these people quite open-handed. I don't know. I think of a boy I had at Univ of Connecticut working on a novel which I greatly encouraged, think publishable & have tried to help him place, he's someone who's never published and I hope to see have a chance, when/if his book is published, what. I don't know.

I do marvel at the way in your book you have managed to sustain the tension of atmosphere to a point of shutting out a reader's day-to-day reality that is eventually any writer's (real writers) objective. By the same token I don't believe that phrased for a blurb would sell or not sell. Ask Aaron Asher about my reaction to the string of blurbs on the back of Meridian's *The Recognitions*; but he was publishing it, a fact for which I am of course eternally grateful, as I was to you for helping to stimulate his interest in it, & as its publisher how he handled things was his business, I told him my feelings & stepped out, & he did a fine job of it.

Are reviewers influenced/cowed by blurbs? and does it matter one simple God damn anyhow? Recall the now quite forgotten 'critical acclaim' of the most widely unread best seller of the time, *By Love Possessed*—and reread Dwight MacDonald's destruction of that review chorus. I as much as any & perhaps more than many am vividly aware of the exaggerated pain of every reviewer's stab or even patronizing applause; but Jesus Christ looking at it all what's become of the Hicks Geismars Sterling Norths, nothing left but a whine in the air somewhere. I remain or rather, *The Recognitions* does. So does Lowry's *Volcano*, so does yours unless you confuse yourself with them is my feeling, if you play their game not your own.

best regards
W. Gaddis

Jaqueline Suzanne: correctly, Jacqueline Susann (1918–74), author of *Valley of the Dolls, The Love Machine,* and other best-sellers.

Univ of Connecticut: Gaddis taught there for a semester in 1967.

By Love Possessed: Macdonald's essay on James Gould Cozzens's 1957 novel, "By Cozzens Possessed," appeared in the January 1958 issue of *Commentary* and was reprinted in his book *Against the American Grain* (1962).

Sterling Norths: Sterling North's insulting review of *R* appeared in the *New York World Telegram & Sun,* 10 March 1955, 22.

To William Jovanovich

[*WG wrote to Harcourt, Brace's president several times asking for a reversion of rights to his first novel, even offering to buy the rights, without success. The Harvest trade paperback edition of 1970, published without WG's knowledge, was offset from the first edition, thereby ignoring all the corrections WG had made for the 1962 Meridian edition, and tying up the rights for the foreseeable future.*]

Piermont, NY
15 April 1970

Dear Sir.

You might imagine my dismay on reading in a recent *Times* of your retirement as president of Harcourt, Brace, that I had not waited for your succession by someone less egregiously attached to my novel *The Recognitions* to express my interest in the rights, someone who might, after its 15 years of confinement there, have happily given up a bad job of such historic proportions and allowed us all the possibility of seeing it republished in an attractive cheap edition, both at a profit and a decently fair price to the student audience your back-list feeds upon, and in the corrected version once briefly available.

I have just seen your 'Harvest' reissue of the book which would seem finally to preclude realization of these considerations elsewhere, and clearly pretends to none of them itself, especially deplorable in the case of the last mentioned for which there is no responsible excuse whatsoever and apparently no redress but this note which sincerely looks for no response from you, not even still another fatuous recital of your magnanimity in authorizing a $500. general advance those 15 years ago and long since earned back, made even more abject by your most recent gratuitous and quite shabby reference to Bernice Baumgarten in its connection.

William Gaddis

Bernice Baumgarten: the agent who sold *R* to Harcourt, Brace.

To William L. Bradley

[*A scholar and philanthropist (1918–2007), and Assistant Director for Arts and Humanities at the Rockefeller Foundation from 1966 to 1971. Coincidentally, Gerald Freund (1930–97), mentioned in the first sentence, was the director of the MacArthur Foundation's Prize Fellows Program when WG was awarded one of its "genius" awards in 1982.*]

Piermont, NY
23 July 1970

Dear Mr Bradley.

Following Dr Gerald Freund's departure for Yale, I understood I might write you concerning the Rockefeller Foundation grant given me over this past year through Vassar College, for the purpose of freeing me to work toward the completion of a work of fiction.

To that end, the grant has accomplished its purpose in a way for which I am eternally grateful, and as its term ends a word of report must be in order. Through the grant, I have been enabled to drop all time-consuming free lance work to concentrate on this book which now, though still short of completion, has 300-odd pages in finished draft, and further portions worked out in the sort of detailed outline I seem to find necessary to write. A passage of some 60 pages of the novel is scheduled for publication in a new review being brought out by E.P.Dutton this fall.

At this stage, considering the liberal nature of the grant and the manner in which it was given, and my uncertainty regarding the general policies and current concerns of the Rockefeller Foundation in this area, it may sound unusual and even impertinent to inquire here about the possibility of requesting an extension of the grant for a further six months' work on this book. As the hopeful estimate for completing it in the 12-month period of my original grant request was my own, so has been the failure to fulfill it; but I would not want this inquiry to imply that I think the book's completion will be impossible without a grant extension. Enough of it is now written, and otherwise appears clearly in hand, that I feel reassured about finishing it, though this would take longer with a full return to outside commitments. The only such acceptance I have made is one to give a 2-hour weekly writing class at City College of New York for the fall term (about $2300.), which should allow me almost as much time for his book as I have at present.

If extending the present grant for another six months should be feasible it would be put to as good use and as greatly appreciated as that already received, but I hasten to add that its absence would in no way diminish what I have already been enabled to accomplish, or my lasting gratitude for such an expression of confidence in my efforts.

> Yours,
> William Gaddis

60 pages [...] in a new review: "J. R. or the Boy Inside," *Dutton Review* 1 (1970): 5–68 (an early version of the first 44 pages of *J R*).
$2300: about $15,000 today.

To Matthew Gaddis

[WG's son, then twelve, was living with his mother and sister near Boston.]

> Piermont, NY
> 17 Sept. 70

Dear Matthew.

Well, I got through *my* first day of school! And at last I have done something I never quite had the nerve to do, walked into a classroom with about 15 people simply sitting, waiting; got behind my desk, hung up my umbrella, sat down facing them, and ... started to talk. I guess they were surprised to hear me start off by telling them I was there to try to teach something that I didn't really believe could be taught, writing fiction. And then go on about some examples of good fiction and bad fiction, and everyone sitting there just looking at me. Silence. Start talking again. Finally I asked a couple of questions and got a couple of them talking, and certainly it will all be easier as I go on, next week and the week after, and when I see some of their work. They are college juniors and seniors, and it is different than teaching at Connecticut was because there I saw each person separately, and didn't sit up in front like The Authority. Even though right now it is a little nerve-wracking, it is good experience for me. Mainly I hope I can be some help to some of them with their early efforts at trying to write, though the only point I've pressed on them so far is that the first important and often difficult thing about it is simply sitting down and *doing* it.

Even for me. Here I am in what is just about perfect, after that upstairs bedroom,—this garage room is so big and light, books on shelves, long table spread out and clear of everything but work, clock, calendar, pencils, typewriter, and such a neat room to pace up and down in even though here and there you do almost fall through the soft spots in the floor under the rug. So my main problem is trying to get used to how neat it is to have this big orderly room of my own and get down to work again, and I'm slowly managing that.

Speaking of work, I had a call yesterday from good old Hunter Low, with a speech for the president of Eastman Kodak they want me to write, and it seemed like a good idea to take it for a lot of reasons so next week I'll spend a couple of days in Rochester. Sometimes a piece of routine work like that with a deadline is a good thing (also they pay me) so I'm glad it came along right now. [...]

with much love again
Papa

---

this garage room: for a photograph, see the image gallery in Joseph Tabbi's *Nobody Grew but the Business*.

Hunter Low: see 12–14 July 1964.

To Sarah Gaddis

[*Enclosed with a copy of F. Scott Fitzgerald's posthumously published miscellany* The Crack-Up *(New Directions, 1945).*]

Piermont NY
17 Sept 70

Dear Sarah.

Here is a book I've meant to get you a look at since you talked of keeping a sort of notebook journal. Obviously it's not for you to sit down and read straight through but I thought you would be interested in what one writer turned the idea into and continue and expand your own along the lines of catching ideas, impressions, thoughts, images, words and combinations of words and overheard remarks and stories and anecdotes at that instant you encounter them, which is so often one you can never recreate purely from memory and may in fact lose forever. Of course in this case, assuming Fitzgerald never expected these notes to be published, I think you find a lot of material which he would have reconsidered and thrown out and never wanted published; but at least, having written them down, he gave himself that choice, rather than putting himself through those long moments of trying to remember—What *was* it? that remark I heard yesterday, that idea I had last night ... What is it that makes end of summer at Fire Island unlike anywhere else, and yet like a concentration of the whole idea of summer's end everywhere ... [...]

See you soon, much love, *write!*
Papa

To Jean Lambert

[*The French translator of* R, *which was published in two volumes as* Les Reconnaissances *by Gallimard in 1973. This letter was reproduced in facsimile in a special issue of the French journal* Profils Americaines *devoted to Gaddis (no. 6, autumn 1994, p. 5). In the same issue, Lambert has an essay entitled "Notes du traducteur de* The Recognitions" *(pp. 63–71). At the time of this letter, Lambert was at Smith College in Northampton, Massachusetts. WG met him there in April to discuss the translation.*]

Piermont, New York 10968
10 February 1971

Dear Mr Lambert.

You may imagine how pleased I was to have your letter with news that the French translation of *The Recognitions* has been completed; it is so long since I signed the agreement with Gallimard that I had almost given up hope and had, of course, no idea that you or anyone in this country were working on it. (I last heard from the German publisher, incidentally, that they were making a third attempt at a translation.)

All this makes me realize not only what a difficult task it has presented, but my good fortune in the care you have given it, since clearly any success the book may have in France will be so largely due to your efforts. And of course I would like to see your translation and to be of any help I can. I must add however that I am not (as some reviewers seemed to think) fluent in the various languages that appear here and there in the book, including the fragments of French; but I might of course be of some help in explaining my use of an English word or phrase that has caused difficulty so that its translation may be more exact. (I think I was of some help to the Italian translator in this way.) And I am of course extremely curious as to how you have translated the title.

At any rate it would give me immense pleasure simply to see the translation and to meet you. However, I expect to leave in a day or two and to be away until around the end of March, and I don't want to delay or inconvenience you and any schedule you may have with the publisher. And so you might let me know if it would be convenient for me to drive up sometime early in April to meet you and talk about it all, as I should very much like to do.

Since I can not thank you enough for the work you have done for my novel, let me thank you at least for your letter, and I hope we may meet in April.

Yours,
William Gaddis

To Robert P. Bletter

[A neighbor, Bletter (1933–76) was editorial director of Teachers College Press, one of whose recent publications—Robert McClintock's Man and His Circumstances: Ortega as Educator*—their mutual friend Martin Dworkin had sent to WG.]*

Piermont
3 Feb 72

Dear Bob,

Please forgive the lateness and brevity of this, it is not for actual want of time (certainly there is always the mid-afternoon feeling: will this day never end? and the 4 a.m. will the sun never rise?), and end of a day even if the day has been good with work is debilitated, even more so probably if it has not, either little wit and form left or the sense of none to begin with; at any rate lateness of this not simply to your 2 letters but the book which I really simply look at as an achievement sitting here on this table, it is a real standing-alone looking kind of thing and I hope to do better writing McClintock very soon, it was immensely kind of him to send it, or you to send it, or Martin to have you both send it, or one of you to have the others send it —I get all these damned books in the mail and so seldom a real one, them for all the wrong reasons, this one I would flatter myself to think for the right ones. [...]

W. Gaddis

To Jeanne G. Howes

[A student at Case Western Reserve University who was writing a thesis on R. *She mailed her letter on 27 December 1971.]*

Piermont NY 10968
8 March 1972

Dear Miss Howes.

I apologise for being so long with an answer to your very kind and gratifying letter, in fact I look now at its date and am even more apologetic than I began.

And so I wish I could respond more satisfactorily than you will find this. First all I have published beyond *The Recognitions* is the opening passage (about 60 pages) of the novel I am wringing head and hands over now trying to finish before summer. The title is *J.R.* and the passage appeared in something called *Dutton Review* (No. 1) about a year or year and a half ago. I gather its distribution wasn't awfully impressive but even should you come across a copy you would probably find it a good deal different to the first book.

Judith and WG in a scene from Bill Gunn's *Ganja and Hess*,
filmed in spring 1972 in Croton-on-Hudson.

Otherwise I think you are right, there hasn't been a great deal written
about the book though there may be some bibliography in a piece under my
name in *Contemporary Authors* (Gale) vols. 19–20 (c. 1968). I recall a most
ingenious piece in a Wisconsin quarterly some years ago in which *The Recognitions'* debt to *Ulysses* was established in such minute detail I was doubtful
of my own firm recollection of never having read *Ulysses* but that was a problem that seemed to dog the book from the start largely, I suppose, from a blurb
on the back making the comparison on which most reviewers seized with glee
in finding my book wanting. A young man named Koenig did last year write
his doctoral thesis on it at New York University but I would imagine it being
available only there and, of course, it is his interpretation as yours must be
yours.

Otherwise I scarcely know what to say to your request for help on 'more
background' first, I think, and I am not being facetious when I plead not that
it's so long since I wrote it but that [*following a strikeover:*] (I've been typing
all day and getting a little bleary) so long since I read it. If I named a single
influence it would certainly be TS Eliot who still takes my breath away as he
did then (and as a fair number of his lines sprinkled through the book might
attest). Regarding any 'message', perhaps that art abides and the artist is its

tool and victim but despite that it is the only enterprise worth embracing in the attempt to justify life; that art executed without love is bad (false) art but such love is not easy to come by. There was a corollary there too with God (perfection, gold) and the driving impossibility of grasping it because of our finite condition but that attempt being all we have to justify this finite condition (page 689 at the top I suppose is the key to the book if there is such). And in taking it down just now to look for this reference I read a few pages at random and must confess found them quite entertaining. I suppose if there has been one immense frustration with the book's often grudging acceptance it has been how few people seemed able to permit themselves, despite its so-called 'erudition', to simply enjoy it.

Thank you again for your interest and your good letter and I wish I could have been more help.

Yours,
William Gaddis

Wisconsin quarterly: see note to 21 August 1964 letter.

Koenig: Peter William Koenig, "'Splinters from the Yew Tree': A Critical Study of William Gaddis' *The Recognitions*," PhD diss., New York University, 1971.

page 689: fearing that his art career began with copying a forgery, Wyatt discovers that the Bosch painting he copied from was indeed the original, not a fake, so he says with considerable relief, "—Thank God there was the gold to forge!'"

To Matthew Gaddis

[WG enclosed a review of Rudolph Wurlitzer's novel Quake *in which Morris Dickstein discusses "the One Big Book syndrome": "Such disparate writers as Ralph Ellison, William Gaddis, Joseph Heller and Thomas Pynchon appear to have fallen prey to the syndrome in the last two decades [...]. Instead of publishing, they have tantalized their admirers with fragments of work in progress, which quickly conspire with time to make the Work itself seem all the more elusive" (New York Times Book Review, 22 October 1972, p. 4).]*

Piermont, NY
2 November 72

Dear Matthew,

Can't believe it. Thursday again. I'm beginning to think there are more Thursdays than other days of the week because each one reminds me how fast time is passing.

And I hardly needed the enclosed reminder in the *New York Times Book*

Review of having appeared to fall prey to the One Big Book problem, and trying to solve it by writing Another Big Book ... I am not 'trying to tantalize' admirers of *The Recognitions* by just publishing fragments of *J R* ... apparently I'm regarded as an 'experimental' writer, and one thing that takes so much time with *J R* seems to be that since it's almost all in dialogue I'm constantly listening, write a line and then have to stop and listen, does it sound like this character talking? and get across his feeling and appearance without me describing them? Anyhow they spelled my name right ... [...]

with much love from Papa

To Thomas J. J. Altizer

[*Radical theologian and author (1927–2018), then teaching at SUNY Stony Brook.*]

Piermont, NY
10 February 1973

Dear Dr. Altizer.

I am sorry to be late answering your letter and, next, to send you the unsatisfactory response this will probably prove to be. Of course I was and remain most impressed and gratified by your response to *The Recognitions* especially upon looking at the list of your own publications, all of which may be why I found your letter a difficult one to rise to and may also partly explain the time I have taken preoccupied by why this should be so.

First certainly the aspect of Christianity itself and the distant thing it has become to me in these 20 years since the book was written. I am not being facetious when I say it is a long time since I have read it; but certainly it betrays my suspicions even then just inhowfar I was sincere and serious in its preoccupation with Christian redemption as opposed to the attraction of versions of Christianity as vehicles for writing about redemption. Regarding Roman Catholicism for instance it obviously had its attractions and I was pleased at the time the literate Catholics who saw the derogatory & ridiculous 'anti'Church material as all there to strengthen rather than weaken the idea of the Church that could survive it. But in the years since I've come finally to regard Roman Catholicism as the most thoroughly irritating and irrelevant anachronism in sight and the incongruity of the Papacy simply appalling, really surprised at the vehemence of my own feelings.

Basically I suppose what seems to have drained away is any but the faintest nostalgia for absolutes, finite imperfectability without Wyatt's grateful revelation that 'there was the gold to forge'. What's remained seems to be preoccupation with the Faust legend as pivotal posing the question: what is worth doing? (Wyatt was meant to be not the depth of genius, which knows, but just short of it & therewith the dilemma, the very height of talent, which doesn't.)

At any rate it is this question what is worth doing? that has dogged me all my life, both in terms of my own life and work where I am trying now again in another book to fight off its destructive element and paralyzing effects; and in terms of America which has been in such desperate haste to succeed in finding all the wrong answers. In this present book satire comic or what have you on money and business I get the feeling sometimes I'm writing a secular version of its predecessor.

Returning to *The Recognitions* I had pretty much from the first a feeling of sending it out on its own, of being (top of p. 96) simply 'the human shambles that follows it around'; and both time and its original meager reception have I suppose only gone to strengthen that feeling, again not being flippant I wonder how much use I would be in discussing it, still surprised (of course greatly pleased) at letters from college age students who find it relevant.

Surely none of this lessens my appreciation of your estimate of it and I would be most intrigued to see any use you made of it in your own work (I'm not that clear remembering *Under the Volcano* and never read *Ulysses*), right now about 30 miles up the Hudson here panic stricken in terms of time work money this book but would look forward to meeting and talking with you at some point if the above isn't entirely self defeating.

Thank you again for all in your letter and its tacit encouragement at a welcome time.

Yours,
William Gaddis

---

destructive element: cf. Jack Gibb's description of his work-in-progress as a "sort of social history of mechanization and the arts, the destructive element" (*J R* 244).

To Candida Donadio

[*The following concerns a rival offer made by Georges Belmont of Éditions Robert Laffont to publish a French translation of R, on which Gallimard was dragging its feet.*]

Piermont
17 April 1973

Dear Candida,

I enclose a letter from Jean Lambert pleading on Gallimard's behalf, and a carbon of my letter to him which I have *not* sent. Will you please call me when you have read it and tell me if you think I should make any changes or deletions (or additions) (I think for instance the $600 figure is correct?) —since a copy of it will probably go posthaste to Gallimard. Poor Lambert, honestly his position in the whole thing is the only part that would make me want to change our position, otherwise I see none, it damned near seems that Gallimard is blackmailing him and me through him, and I only wish one could be sure Gallimard would sell Lafonte the Lambert translation if they drop out. At any rate I will hold the letter till I hear from you but think one should go off as soon as possible.

I have a nice note yesterday from Aaron who says to his dismay "the last batch of pages (740–787) have arrived here unacknowledged," but that "what's more important, I have read them and continue to be astonished..." at what? that I'm still alive? that the God damned thing goes on, and on, and on? No, he's a kind and loyal fellow but God I could use some good news.

Please tell Hy that I haven't answered his letter because I've been trying to stay in *J R* as much longer as I can (now page 814, have a toothache and wasted the whole damned morning on this Gallimard nonsense), I know Hy will understand but regret the time he gave it after I'd rushed in with it as I did, but I will get to it as soon as Bast leaves on the bus with Charley Yellow Brook and his brother (the Brook Brothers) for the reservation. [*J R* 564]

I can't but think that the English hope for money has fallen through and that Aaron (despite he says "seeing the Pynchon hysteria as a good omen") would not write me such kind notes if he could write me a check instead, so the generally rollicking tone of this note is a fraud, I hope to heaven you are keeping well.

[unsigned carbon copy]

Aaron: Asher, who planned to publish *J R* at Holt, Rinehart & Winston, where he currently worked.

Hy: Hy Cohen, an associate of Donadio's.

the Pynchon hysteria: *Gravity's Rainbow* had been published in February to great acclaim.

To John Leverence

[*A graduate student at Bowling Green State University who was working on an essay on R, eventually published as "Gaddis Anagnorisis" (*Itinerary, *1977; rpt. in* In Recognition of William Gaddis*). After teaching at California State University at Long Beach, Leverence became the producer of the annual Emmy Awards until 2019.*]

Piermont NY 10968

19 August 73

Dear Mr Leverence.

Although I have been gratefully aware of Eugene McNamara's interest in *The Recognitions* and I think had brief correspondence with him some years ago about it, I don't recall the passage you quote from his *Queen's Quarterly* piece and frankly cannot then or now imagine an 'almost abject apology' of any sort issuing from the book's publisher.

Despite the attractive (I hesitate to say characteristic) conspiratorial flavour to this report of Fr Flood, whoever he may be or have been, my own far more mundane recollection of the book's being 'mysteriously withdrawn from the shelves' is that a good portion of the rather modest first edition was simply remaindered—dumped at 'below cost'—a year or so after publication, earning me, if not royalties, perhaps a wider readership, and the somewhat chill pleasure of seeing it quoted now at $22.50. Whether that remaindering reflected the rather substantial management and editorial changes at Harcourt Brace about the time the book was published is matter for speculation. They have recently reissued it in their paperback 'Harvest' series with what I find a singularly unattractive cover at $4.95 which,—as Fred Allen said when New York's subway fare went from 5¢ to 10—should 'keep the riff-raff out'.

The book did have another epiphany about 1962 in a paperback issued by Meridian which carried a good many corrections of the meticulous sort you query in 'Epiclantos', largely through the diligent good offices of Jack Green, though whether this particular correction, if it is such, was made I don't know and haven't a copy to check; unfortunately the 'Harvest' reissue, of which I was unaware till its appearance, remains uncorrected, since it was apparently simply photo-offset from their own earlier edition.

Catharine Carver is I believe a good deal happier at Oxford University Press in London.

Yours,

William Gaddis

Eugene McNamara: this Canadian critic (1930–2016) included WG in his essay "The Post-Modern American Novel," *Queen's Quarterly* 69 (Summer 1962): 265–75.

Fr Flood: Robert Flood, a librarian at St. Michaels College in Toronto.

Fred Allen: American humorist and radio personality (1894–1956).

Epiclantos: on p. 10 of *R*, the monk Fr. Eulalio "was surnamed Epiclantos, 'weeping so much'"; Leverence pointed out this is a typo for "Epiclautos," but WG neglected to correct it in later editions of *R*. It was corrected for the NYRB edition.

To Barbara Lawson

[*A literature student who wrote to WG from Chicago on May 18th.*]

Piermont, NY
Aug 73

Dear Miss Lawson,

I apologise for the absurd length of time it has taken me to get to this note thanking you for your letter regarding *The Recognitions* and your proselyting efforts on its behalf; in fact noting your address and the nature of your project fear you may be—or rather have been—at a college there when you wrote, and may not receive even this.

When I say it's a long time since I read the book (though not so long as since reading *Crime and Punishment*, which I think incidentally may have been the first 'great' novel I experienced) I'm not being facetious or trying to escape being held to account; but rather that I feel I've lost track of some of its concerns and that my interest may have lessened in others most pointedly, perhaps, in connection with your approach, redemption through Christianity (or I suppose religions in general)—redemption remaining, of course the key question, in terms as I see it of simply stated 'what is worth doing?' though that, certainly, was what rode Wyatt, and may be a prime element in the book that gives it what appears to be a relevancy today which often surprises and obviously gratifies me especially occurring among younger people with most of the American myths along that line exploded.

But I don't mean any of the above to appear to discourage your project which does certainly sound intriguing even to one who has left Fr Eulalio behind, I meant more to wish you luck with it and to thank you for your interest and your letter.

Yours,
[unsigned carbon copy]

To Matthew Gaddis

Piermont, NY
29 December 73

Dear Matthew,

I don't know whether you need this English course list or not but am returning it with really great regret that in the Christmas confusion we didn't spend time going over it together, though I gather you'd already chosen Modern Poetry (though whether because of or in spite of A. being in the class I'm not sure: the former might be a rather shaky basis for academic selections).

I'm sure you will get a kick out of AE Houseman, who identifies with Shropshire & you may think of J Napper as a current native there, and whose verse is filled with images I am sure will be very familiar to you in terms of "carried half way home or near pints and quarts of Ludlow beer" (see pages 88–9, 73) from your recent trip doing just that . . . *also* Houseman is quite filled with rather soured images on Young Love which may come in handy sooner or later (see poems pages 31, 42, 26) and discouragement and futility (pages 110, 131, 109, 197, 25) in fact I just had an idea, as my birthday present I have just called and am getting hold of a copy (just "sent" Judith to Pickwick for it while I finish this letter) and enclose it here to get you off to a head start. You may find it all a bit too neat (Houseman's verse) and not 'up to' Dylan, but I guarantee if you read a little you will want more . . . ("Shoulder the sky, my lad, and pass the can" (of ale)). (These are lines I recall from 30 years ago; and I'm sure I've quoted to you that parody of Houseman somebody wrote (see poems page 68, 66) which went, in part: "If your throat is slit, Slit your girl's and swing for it; For bacon's not the only thing That's cured by hanging on a string . . ." last lines I think are "Lads whose work is still to do Will whet their knives and think of you." (You might spring those lines on Ms Averill to get things off to a rousing start.)

Enough Houseman; right now I haven't much comment on the others but if you get into Yeats and Eliot you are certainly in good hands. (Speaking of Creeley though I remember him one night in my room in Adams House bloody head in hands having just turned his mother's car over in a ditch—of such things are poetry made?) (You tell me at the end of the course.)

Heaven knows we miss you and Sarah; and I guess the house will gradually drain of strange (I mean unfamiliar not fully looking) faces, and JR's and Bast's will return to take the place of {* * *}—they are nice boys certainly, but at some point Judith observed that despite your age difference with them she felt that you were more mature—she wasn't simply tossing compliments either. And I myself am constantly impressed at both your and Sarah's sensitivity to other people and their feelings, which with all his good points I don't really think one can say for {* * *}, and it is an admirable quality to have. Perhaps it is one that develops from trying to resolve one's own self doubts and confidence, as I know you and Sarah are still working out, and in your different ways trying to be honest with yourselves about it, which takes a good deal of courage working toward the never-quite-realized Greek ideal of "Know thyself". I suppose any man who ever can do that will never disappoint himself no matter what he accomplishes or doesn't accomplish, and of course one's self is where satisfaction, or accomplishment, or disappointment lies, rather than in others even those we love. So even though, on a birthday like this with my work unfinished, I am tempted to feel the fear of disappointing you or Sarah or Judith (let alone Aaron Asher and Candida!), you are all only mirrors for disappointment I feel in not yet having reached goals I've set for myself—so the next step is simply to keep trying to reach them.

Of course the problem is setting the goals in the first place; many enough 'successful' men end up drunks for having fulfilled goals the world set for them and then finding they've fulfilled nothing in themselves; many enough kids end up junkies for having decided the world's goals aren't worth trying for and being unable to set any of their own. A few fortunate combine the two (I don't mean drink and drugs, but meshing your own and worldly goals), and your education and growing up now are vitally important because learning the world's goals (even marks in school) gives you the material to form your own—and don't misunderstand, I *don't* mean that by your 16th birthday you should know whether you want to be a poet or an astronaut, but only have a hungry curiosity in all directions for anything that brings you and your mind to life. (This is why for instance I think it's unfortunate that you cross off the film-a/v area at school because of the people involved in it; if you've looked that area of work over and have no interest in it at all, that's one thing; but if you avoid it simply because of the other people taking part you can really be missing something of *yours*, and after all what's the world going to be when you're out in it but fields of interest where everybody certainly won't exactly suit your liking?)

At any rate, what I started to say at the top here is that we ourselves are our only real receptacles for disappointment. If I am not disappointed in myself I cannot disappoint you or Sarah or Judith or anybody who loves me; and so long as any of you do your best and don't let the little disappointments in yourselves that are inevitable add up to one big one, you can never disappoint me, and none of you ever does. In different words it goes back to those often quoted lines of Shakespear (*Hamlet* I iii), in which Polonius is advising his son:

This above all: to thine own self be true,
And it must follow, as the night the day,
Thou canst not then be false to any man.

This is perhaps more the sort of letter I would have written you on your birthday than on mine, but it is really appropriate to both since birthdays are inevitably times of reevaluations, disappointments, resolutions (improve work habits!) and certainly for both of us satisfactions in what we have done so far.

with much love always,
Papa

pages 88–9: in *The Collected Poems of A. E. Housman* (Holt, Rinehart & Winston, 1965).

Dylan: Matthew read Thomas's "Where Once the Waters of Your Face" to WG when visiting.

"If your throat is slit: by British writer Hugh Kingsmill (1889–1949), a parody that Housman judged "the best I have seen, and indeed, the only good one."

Creeley: poet Robert Creeley; see 20 September 1993.

To Candida Donadio

Piermont NY
16 January 74

Dear Candida,

Without agonizing preamble to what must be a 'progress' report I obviously would rather avoid giving you and/or Aaron: I have got a Summons for service on a Federal jury starting on 4 February. Since I wrote them last fall and got a postponement this time I think I should appear in person to plead for another. What I am forced to admit to you here of course is that, unless the lightning ease of other days strikes me this morning, I expect to be still working on this damned book Feb 4th &c, and obviously US Southern District Court downtown daily would be disastrous. However I don't think my plea for another postponement would be taken very seriously unless supported by a letter from you or Aaron, spelling out as unkindly as I deserve the fact that I am now completing a book which is substantially behind deadline and for which a good deal of money has been advanced me, and that interruption at this time would work an extreme inconvenience and constitute undue hardship for all concerned.

Since Aaron is the publisher a letter from him would probably bear more weight than an agent do you think? But asking him would of course be to remind him yet once more of my delinquency (not that he is unaware of it!), and appear to project it on and on into spring, as I hope to Christ will not be the case. You may well have had this experience (jury service I mean, I know you've had the delinquency one) with writers before. What do you think? If you or he will write such a letter I think it should be sent to me and addressed to Clerk of the Court, United States District Court, US Courthouse, Foley Square, NY NY.

God knows there are ironies: practically everyone at the end of *J R* is being subpoenaed to appear at this same court & it would have been a marvelous experience if it had come a year ago (if it came now it would add another 60 pages ...)

And what can I tell you about the delinquency itself? True, Christmas did not help work, and I have had to interrupt for two IBM job speeches—dentists, tuition &c and of course still desperate: but even these are excuses of reality to which you're well used. I do get up every morning at 6:30 or 7, do come in to this desk and go on till 5 or 6, do hold my head in frustration, and in the end have no excuses for why this last part is so hard to bring off. Part of it is *The Loneliness of the Long Distance Runner*, if you happened to see that excellent film. And that drawn-out metaphor of Gibbs' book as the invalid in there defiantly waiting where one left him was not lightly inspired. [*J R* 605]

I have to thank you for sending up *Les Reconnaissances* (got one Vol I & two Vol IIs) and the review from *Le Monde* which, to my broken-french eye, looks quite rave and God help us does not even mention Joyce I believe. I must say the book itself looks excellent (though apparently better proof-read in the French than Spanish), maybe I will be like Edgar Allen Poe (not at these prices). If I were on any decent terms (any terms at all) with Gallimard I'd ask them to send a copy to the director Alain Renais (sp?) homage for his film *Muriel* (with of course the hope he might like to do a big-scale US movie).

Proofs for the few pages (ie 10 out of some 400) for *Antaeus* came and I returned them titled simply

Untitled fragment from another damned, thick, square book which Halperin (Halpern?) said should be out in March, wish they'd taken a later fragment but doubt it makes much difference one way or another.

Finally, is there any way to know when Avon will make its 2nd payment to Harcourt, if I can get my part promptly when they do? Also occurred to me Avon might be interested in seeing the review from *Le Monde*.

Candida believe me my attempt above to sound brisk and businesslike is just that, an attempt, I won't retail the despair behind it but if you can hang on with me a little longer I am honestly trying to finish this God damned thing.

[unsigned carbon copy]

The Loneliness of the Long Distance Runner: a 1962 British film based on Alan Sillitoe's 1959 story.

Edgar Allen Poe: revered by the French long before he was appreciated in America.

Alain Renais [...] *Muriel*: Resnais's 1963 film concerns a widow and her stepson recalling past loves.

Halperin: Daniel Halpern (1945–), editor and publisher. Pages 137–43 of *J R* appeared in *Antæus* 13/14 (Spring/Summer 1974): 98–105.

Avon: a mass-market paperback edition of *R* was published by Avon (under its Bard imprint) in 1974 and went through three printings in succeeding years. However, it was reset from the first edition, thus ignoring WG's corrections for the Meridian edition, and added hundreds of typos of its own.

To Judith Gaddis

[*Written after Judith left for a trip, formatted to look like a classified report. MIL =
mother-in-law, Ariadne Pasmezoglu.*]

REPORTREPORTREPORTREPORTREPORTREPORTREPORTREPORT
EYES ONLY EYES ONLY EYES ONLY EYES ONLY
<u>AM</u> 26FEB74 OFFICIAL CLASSIFIED 26FEB74 OFFICIAL CLASSIFIED

08:25 waved
08:26 watched down hill to make sure car turned corner safely; waved
08:28 walked dog to Aufieri garbage can and returned
08:31 poured coffee
08:45 decided to move car back to house so I would not keep looking out
       and thinking Judith had gone on errand and would return
08:46 saw bag with grapefruit, put it by door to remember to give to Jack
08:47 let cat in
08:48 poured coffee
08:49 saw MIL's letter
08:59 went in to look for stamp for MIL's letter
09:00 saw work laid out on table, decided to have drink
09:01 let cat out; decided not to have drink
09:02 decided to move car back to house so I would not keep looking out
       and thinking Judith had gone on errand and would return
09:04 burned toast
09:09 called John, reached hoarse lady who said he would call back
09:11 let cat in
09:12 poured coffee, looked at work laid out on table
09:14 decided to clear kitchen table and bring typewriter there to be near
       'phone
09:16 tied up newspapers
09:23 emptied ashtray
09:25 decided to make list of things I must do
09:29 could not think of anything so decided not to make list
09:31 cleared kitchen table
09:34 John called; read him note from his Mrs emphasizing all underlined
       words but did not know Pat's 'phone number. Haha.
09:44 let cat out
09:45 decided to move car back to house so I would not keep looking out
       and thinking I had gone on errand and would not return

09:46 moved car back to house

09:58 looked at work laid out on table, decided to have cereal

09:59 made cereal

10:02 ate cereal reading Swarthmore alumni bulletin; noted one alumnus who claimed 3 billion dependents for federal taxes and given 9 months in prison for filing fraudulent W-4 form, decided must remember to warn MIL who might consider something similar

10:40 looked at work spread out on table

10:41 twinge at noticing coffee cups &c, put them in dishwasher to not be reminded of departure

10:48 examined contents of refrigerator, discovered spaghetti sauce with Message and put it in freezer

10:50 discovered corned beef and potatoes

10:55 thought I should probably go down and get butter; checked first, found 4 sticks of butter

10:57 let cat in

10:58 hung up coat

10:59 put trash out

10:00 listened to news on radio

10:04 went upstairs and looked around

10:08 came downstairs and looked around

10:13 sat down and studied design in kitchen floor linoleum

10:20 looked outside for car to make sure I had not gone on errand and might not return

10:22 decided I should probably go down and get cigarettes; checked first, found 5 packs

10:24 brought typewriter in to kitchen table to be near 'phone

10:28 decided to have nap till suppertime when I could have corned beef

10:29 sat down in livingroom chair

10:33 woke startled by ghastly liquid snoring, decided I had horrible cold and should have drink

10:34 discovered snoring was being done by dog, very relieved

10:37 decided not to have drink, went to typewriter in kitchen to work

10:41 decided I should get some letters out of the way before settling down to work, got paper

10:50 could think of no one to write to

10:51 stacked wood more neatly on porch, checked newspapers to make sure they were well tied

10:57 returned to kitchen and listened to refrigerator hum

11:01 examined contents of refrigerator

11:04	thought I should probably go down and get milk; checked first, found a full quart
11:06	looked to see if mail had come but flag was still down
11:09	discovered memorandum WILLIAM THINGS TO REMEMBER and read carefully
11:29	put cat out
11:31	examined clam chowder from refrigerator
11:33	decided clam chowder looked thin, decided to add potatoes
11:34	peeled and diced 3 small potatoes and put on boil
11:51	heard mailbox, got mail
11:55	opened mail, one item from American Express with new card and literature which said read enclosed agreement carefully
11:56	read agreement carefully
PM	
12:18	diced potatoes somewhat soft, added them to chowder; decided chowder looked somewhat thick, got spoon
12:22	served bowl of hot chowder, got spoon
12:23	'phone rang: talked with Hy Cohen at agency who said check should arrive this week; who also said Aaron Asher is leaving Holt and was concerned that Asher's departure would not or might upset me; I told him I was not unless Holt wanted their money back; he said that would be fine, certainly sell it elsewhere; I told him I was working hard on it right this minute; he said Asher might go to Dutton which would be logical following on Hal Sharlatt's death; I said Dutton had no money; he said we will think about it, it could all work out extremely well especially if I finish the book soon; I said I would finish the book soon, was working on it right this minute; he did not answer; I told him my only real dismay at this moment was confidence and faith Asher has shown in me and my work over many years and would be a shame to part with him at this point; he said we will talk about it, that the Dutton possibility is only a possibility; I said I will not tell a sole; he said we'll be in touch with you I said boy you better.
12:55	poured chowder back into pan to reheat
12:56	listened to news on radio
01:00	ate chowder, reading interesting article on Alaska in Swarthmore bulletin
01:21	checked upstairs, nothing changed
01:23	checked downstairs, emptied ashtray
01:26	looked at work spread out on table, noticed stamp for MIL's letter
01:29	walked out with dog to mail MIL's letter

01:42 returning from walk waved cheerful friendly wave to neighbor standing on corner

01:43 realised neighbor standing on corner was really Jack's garbage can, hurried inside hoping no one had noticed

01:52 sat down at typewriter to work

01:58 phone rang, talked with Mr Cody a real estate agent who wished to be helpful if we wished to rent or sell our Saltaire house this summer; wrote reminder to call Savages

02:11 got notes for present sequence in book beside typewriter

02:13 suddenly realized I had better get cat food before stores closed; checked and found 2 full cans of cat food

02:19 decided to call Hy Coen back with some ideas

02:35 could not think of any ideas so declined to call Hy Coen back

02:36 reread notes for present sequence in book

02:39 reread notes for present sequence in book

02:41 decided to reread whole book through up to this point

02:42 looked at MS, decided not to reread whole book up to this point

02:44 reread notes for present sequence in book

02:47 began to type rough version of present sequence in book

03:05 dog passed through going east to west

03:07 dog passed through going west to east

04:01 began to type second page of rough draft

04:26 dog passed through west to east

04:27 dog passed through east to west

04:44 read two pages of rough version of present sequence in book

04:48 began to type third page of rough version

05:26 decided to have drink as Adrienne rang doorbell, told her to come back in the spring

05:26 fixed drink

05:28 sat down to read pages of rough version just written

05:31 laughed heartily

06:31 decided might be a good idea to start checking motels in Virginia, North and South Carolina

06:35 could not find Mobil guide to motels in Virginia, North and South Carolina; wondered where they were

06:44 wondered where they were

06:55 turned on oven to heat corned beef, dog passed through west to east; let cat in

06:57 reread pages of rough version just written

07:02 did not chuckle; wondered where they were

07:09 put in corned beef to warm; wondered where they were
07:16 fed dog; wondered where they were
07:18 fed cat; wondered where they were
07:41 served corned beef
07:42 ate corned beef
08:01 watched *Benny Goodman Story* did not know he was such a sap and
       wondered where on earth they were

Jack: Jack Hoffmeister, a neighbor.
Sharlatt: Hal Scharlatt, editor-in-chief of E.P. Dutton and the *Dutton Review*, had
    died at age thirty-eight a week earlier.
Benny Goodman Story: 1955 film starring Steve Allen as the legendary clarinetist.

To John Leverence

Piermont N.Y.

4 March 74

Dear John Leverence.

I have to disappoint your request for help on advance proofs of this novel
J R since it's simply not that close to that stage yet and I can't make any predic-
tions, especially in terms of a July date which seems to me almost down our
throats. (I didn't see the *Antaeus* ad, they have a very small 10 page or so not
especially representative (if there is such) fragment of it.)

I appreciate your sending the Tanner piece which I find heartening even
at this distance from the sort of reviews that greeted *The Recognitions'* original publication. In contrast to those I enclose reviews from *Le Monde* and
Figaro which may interest you; I find them* especially pleasing for their re-
fraining from making Joyce's *Ulysses* the book's parent which it was not, that
extraordinary Wisconsin review piece notwithstanding. A cheap edition of
the book is being published by Avon which I hope to heaven will at last solve
the longstanding problem of its unavailability. Inept as it may sound for me
to wish you luck with your essay, that appears all that's possible at this stage
and so of course I do.

Yours,

William Gaddis

*excepting for the lapse in *l'Express* (manifestement!) also enclosed.

Tanner piece: British critic Tony Tanner included a chapter on *R* in his *City of Words:
    American Fiction 1950-1970* (1971).
Wisconsin review: Bernard Benstock's essay; see letter of 21 August 1964.

WG in Central Park, 1974 (photo by Jerry Bauer).

To Judith Gaddis

[*The Avon edition of* R *was favorably reviewed by Tony Tanner in the* New York Times Book Review *(14 July 1974, pp. 27–28), accompanied by a photo of WG by Jerry Bauer rather than one by his old friend Martin Dworkin. His sympathetic biographer writes:* "In the early fifties, Marty was crucially involved in Willie's work on his first novel, The Recognitions. There are some thirty-eight conversations involving Willie and Marty that got into the book. They were of such importance that Marty remained convinced until the day he died that Willie should have acknowledged them in a separate essay" (Looks, *Triumph through Adversity, 91).*]

[16 July 1974]

Dear Judith.

[...] Last evening Martin called, did not seem at all put out that the *Times* had used the Bauer picture, elaborated a long discourse on the book including passing mention that it contains 38 conversations between him and myself, and on to shaded recrimination that we should get together: I threatened him with Joe and Heidegger, he retreated; regarding my coming in, I asked what evenings were best for him, he said he had so much work to do that any time was pretty bad, so we left it that I will call him sometime, once again. [...]

John (your father John) called yesterday pm with congratulations on the *Times* review; then 5 minutes ago (this is 9:05 am Tuesday) Henry Homes called, getting to the *Book Review* over breakfast, with similar warm words. So sooner or later my secret is discovered. Though I guess the Otto Premingers don't read. This morning's paper reports him making a movie in which John Lindsey will play a Senator. $4.5 million in bonds is missing from Mayor Beame's city vaults. Jack has enough money to buy a car. And it is very hard to write satire anymore.

So I will return to this wearisome task, so far mainly cutting out what seemed clever 5 years ago and rather desperate to get up to the part that may still seem so: oh to be shed of it! Freed! And they all clapped when we arose for your sweet face and my new clothes...

I hope you are *well*, and must be brown and getting rested. We all miss you I most of all,

with love to Paz and everything to you always.

W.

Joe and Heidegger: the latter is the German philosopher, but the former is unknown. Henry Homes: a neighbor of Judith's parents in Scarborough.

Otto Preminger: prominent film director of the time (1905–86), then working on
Rosebud (1975).

John Lindsey: Lindsay (1921–2000) was mayor of New York City from 1966 to 1973.

Mayor Beame: Abraham Beame (1906–2001) was mayor of New York City from 1974
to 1977.

And they all clapped [...] my new clothes: from a poem in F. Scott Fitzgerald's essay
"Sleeping and Waking" (1934), included in *The Crack-Up*.

Paz: Judith's mother, Ariadne Pasmezoglu, who as Ariadne Thompson wrote a memoir entitled *The Octagonal Heart* (1956), and short stories under the pen name Paz
van Matre.

To Warren Kiefer

[*American novelist and film producer (1929–95), whom WG had worked with at Pfizer
in the late 1950s.*]

Piermont, NY
28 July 74

dear Warren——

it's unfair to sit down to write you this God damned weary of everything,
problem I get up in the morning and think any positive energy has simply got
to go to this God damned book & by this time of day haven't a kind word left
for anybody including the attachment hereto which should confirm your worst
hopes for Winning: at this moment I suppose because of the feeling that I'm
doing the same God damned thing all over again with this book & will be 70
for the same idiotic reward, get your God damned picture in the *Times* and
$5500. royalty on it while just your God damned teeth are threatening $8000....

Try to start again. I 'finished' this book 1004 (legal size) pages am now on
page 180 cutting ruthlessly nothing to make you wearier of yourself than artful-
ness when you were 10 years younger whole God damned proposition like
living with an invalid real God damned terminal case you keep hoping will
pick up his God damned bed and walk like the good book says, tobacco stained
and full of whisky and an old dog heaving quietly on the floor behind me.

Try to start again. Really so God damned lucky splendid wife son and
daughter own a house car the roof goes up and down had a boat too but it
burned. Judith is still a marvel, went down to Florida to drive her mother
back up here in a week or so never presses or blackmails but Hopes. Right
now Sarah's here with me working in a nickel and dime luncheonette for
$400 toward her Swarthmore tuition (while I send her mother $300 support
for her not being there) Matthew is though, keeps her busy enough destroying

him so Sarah's fairly free of that at any rate, worth the God damned $300 I guess.

Try to start again., well I took your advice before you gave it really, have Knopf in the hole for a fairly substantial amount of money (though of course, of course it's in buying out contracts already previously bought out so come right down to cash it's fairly comic)
not fair as I said to open, mainly just the God damned day after dayness of this 'second' book which has just about devoured everybody close to me (see above) attended, as its completion is if not in grasp in sight by Eliot's That is not what I meant, that is not what I meant at all ... must be any honest man's dying words when you picture the equal terms Eisenhower and JFDulles (not to speak of Allen) met their maker with though I like to think that sublime son of a bitch Johnson got the message at the last minute and this poor shabby bastard we have now must be getting it.

Try to start again? Next letter then, honestly for what I've put in the whole God damned proposition (which is to say the crap I've shirked putting in) I've really been blessed by fortune so whine only in the decent terms that do not prevail, any day (like Sept? Oct?) you'll have a cheerful picture postal from Sussex? Aix-? saying it's all more, more than worth it but would hope to write you better before then, meanwhile if I don't send you this another day goes that I send you nothing so this to fill the gap
[unsigned carbon copy]

---

like living with an invalid: see p. 603 of *J R*, where Gibbs compares sixteen years' work on his manuscript to "living with a God damned invalid."

like the good book says: John 5:8. Cf. *J R* 603.

JFDulles (not to speak of Allen): John Foster Dulles was Eisenhower's Secretary of State; his brother Allen was the head of CIA during the Eisenhower era.

bastard we have now: Richard Nixon; less than two weeks later, he resigned and was succeeded by Gerald Ford.

To Matthew Gaddis

Piermont
8 August [1974]

Dear Matthew ———here I am fighting Sarah's electric machine, mine stopped abruptly with a strange whirring sound in the middle of a page and I am still not used to this one, touch a key and zing you're typing, even when you don't mean to be. And the sound of its engine running while one tries to think of the next word is a little nervewracking too. So I am being dragged by the heels into the 20th century... [...]

You can imagine I'm pretty sick of JR but spend every day with him and his friends and otherwise, the main comfort being that after this I'll NEVER (except for galleys) HAVE TO READ THE INFERNAL BOOK AGAIN! Boy I can't wait hey. Also maybe I can learn how to talk like an intelligent adult again.

But you can see that all this above pales before the attached letter and imagine Sarah is very proud as she's certainly the right to be; and I was finally given the chance to read the story and think it is certainly good, very touching without taking advantage of any sentimentality and holds together so well and of course I'm very proud of her doing the whole thing on her own, as I am of you now the way you're holding things together and most eager all of us to see you and have all your news. And views.

And much love of course
Papa

---

attached letter: from *Seventeen* informing Sarah she had won honorable mention in its short story contest for "A Taffeta Dress," along with a check for $50.00.

To David Markson

1206 Duncan Street
Key West, Florida 33040
24 Feb 1975

Dear David.

What 'PW item about the book'! I didn't see it, perhaps because I finally handed in page last to Knopf and fled forthwith pale, drained, and doubled with a cough—you may see to where, a place that's been on Judith's mind for 4 years (with my constant 'not this year but I'm *almost* finished, certainly next...') finally made it and now we both have real colour, get up in the am. without the daily tension of *years* of the God damned typewriter waiting like a terminal invalid in the next room for attention, don't jump when the 'phone rings (since it's almost always for Western Union whose number is 1 digit off ours—I didn't even know people called WU anymore, am going to start to take messages).

At any rate of course you're right, it is a vast weight removed, and not simply the book but at last being able to tell you and other kind wellwishers yes! when they ask that question... (though of course there's a *few* things I'd like to squeeze in on galleys). That's what I'm half doing here, mainly cosmetics to have ready when galleys appear so I can resist the obvious temptation to rewrite it from the beginning ("That is not what I meant at all..."). I assume galleys occur sometime in spring (speaking of the cruelest month) and we expect to be back sometime about then for a Fresh Start. Meanwhile thanks for your note and honestly your wellwishing throughout (curiously I had a charming letter in the same mail today from a lady in Venice thanking me 'very much for writing *The Recognitions*' —pried it loose from a friend of her son's who's 22 which is even more gratifying).

See you then?

best wishes to Elaine too from us both,
W.G.

PW item: in the 10 February 1975 issue of *Publishers Weekly* (p. 39) there was a short item noting that WG had delivered the manuscript of *J R* to Knopf and that it was scheduled for fall publication.
cruelest month: alluding to the opening line of Eliot's *The Waste Land*, as the previous parenthesis does to "The Love Song of J. Alfred Prufrock."

To Robert Gottlieb

[*American publisher and writer (1931–), WG's editor at Knopf. In his memoir* Avid Reader, *Gottlieb wrote: "I can't say I edited William Gaddis's* J R, *although I remember trying. He was unrelentingly disgrunted, perhaps 'touchy' is the better word—but writers are touchy. [...] Gaddis blamed Knopf for lack of publishing commitment and then for not making him financially whole. Although I admired his writing and intelligence, and was impressed by the large reputation of his earlier novel,* The Recognitions, *both it and* J R *seemed to me more constructs than novels and, feeling that way, I shouldn't have taken him on" (NY: Farrar, Straus and Giroux, 2016, 177.*]

Key West
25 March [1975]

Dear Bob,

Here are would-have-been-on-galleys changes and inserts taking up at page 866 (printer can't have reached 866!), all the rewriting I can do in the circumstances right now. As I see it, this means that I envision very very little in terms of changes (pending your comments) when the pages come through for proving, up through (MS) page 1019.

Since both you and Candida seemed to find the book's 'end' satisfactory, I have to assume that will also be true for any reviewers who will read it in (uncorrected?) page proof, and have confidence that anything good—or pretty much the way I want it, or 'as good as I can do'—in the first 7 or 8 hundred pages, will carry what I still feel to be imperfections in the last 20.

No, no...! I don't plan to *change* the end of the book. But I'm not entirely satisfied, insofar as one can ever be (except perhaps for Goncharov when he wrote the last 20pp of *Oblomov*), with certain aspects of the last 20pp of this: elements in the last exchange between Bast and Stella, and in those final few minutes at 96th street, which I very much hope if feasible to polish before those pages are locked up. I think it would probably add two pages to the whole and, as I say, would not change it in any substantial way whatsoever, but simply make what is already there better, if not (ave Goncharov) best. I hope that this makes sense to you.

This exile's over Friday and I expect to be back at the Piermont address and number on the 1st or 2nd of April, Tuesday or Wednesday, when I will renew my credentials.

W.G.

————

To Judith Gaddis

Piermont, NY
[6 April 1975]

Dear Judith,

I wish I could be as articulate as you even in your brief letter for simply getting things said in terms of the kind of love and remorseful sympathetic understanding and helplessness I feel for you or think I do, the thought of you desolate and despairing is just very painful. But I can at least say you must not add to it with fears of hurting or losing me or destroying what we have—I'm not pressing and in no hurry for anything except you mended for yourself and I would hope me mended a little for myself and all of you too. And you surely didn't 'send me home alone', I was hell bent on it with the kind of pressures I get built up, I wish I were the kind of person who'd simply been able to say Let's just go over to Santabel and hunt shells for a day or two, but of course if I'd been that sort of person all along it wouldn't have mounted up so.

Looking back, what finally did strike me heavily was this sense of really how little you've asked and how much you've given over these whole 10 years: planning a detailed trip to Europe or Mexico and then saying it's as good as having taken it when it doesn't work out, but of course gradually it's got to seep in that it may never—and then when something as small by comparison as Key West is as important to you as it was and I'm finally aware that apparently I couldn't even really let you have that, all the while thinking that I did—well, you say I take your problems and turn them into my own but this does seem to be one of my problems and I hope I've learned something. (I have to add here though that I do have very fond memories of us in Key West, of all the rooms in that house and quiet drinks we had and cycling down for the paper, the postoffice, Anderson staring glazed over the hybiscus and twenty years of his life that have just gone by.) [...]

I've wondered if perhaps, with all our uncompleted projects, we're both spoiled in an odd way. I've wondered how much your reading *J R*, after these years of it dwelling in the back room there suddenly exposing itself and myself, has had to do with dormant problems abruptly stepping forth. I've wondered at the success of these stage and screen revivals of Ibsen's *Doll's House* written something like 75 years ago to lie around in college drama courses all that time now suddenly right on. I certainly look at Thorvald with a painful twinge of recognition. [...]

And in the outside world—well, I'll already have spoken to you of my obvious disappointment, to put it mildly, over this English offer of £750 for *J R*, I mean Christ that's less than *Harper's* is paying for 30 pages of it! Candida professes to be undiscouraged and does make the point, which I knew, that English publishing is having a very hard time, but she is pressing forward. I spent a Mafiaesque afternoon with her yesterday and all I can say is wait and pray: she is just going to have no nonsense with this book (insofar I suppose as the economy will allow). I'd been over to see Bob Gottlieb whom I do like a lot but he is really skittish as hell for New York's (US's) most prominent and successful publisher—I mean you think *I* have doubts and abrupt negative glimpses, well ... his of course are clothed in a certain excitement which must make them more attractive than my weary insights, so we end up talking about his son who is 22 and doesn't know anything and can't do anything and lives at home and plays rock records and has some sort of warehouse job and girlfriend ... you see? Life is not all bad. But there is an excitement there at Knopf about the book and I stood Janet Halverson's jacket up against a book on his wall of them and it really knocks them all out, much more impressive with the colours than the xerox I sent you just to give you an idea. I'd said (as with *The Recognitions*) I felt that black red and white in hard colours has the most class and weight, so Janet (just as with *The Recognitions*) gave me black red and white and added gold, and I mean gold not yellow. I hope you will like it.

I just talked with Lewis Lapham on the 'phone, they're not simply putting my name on the cover they're making it the cover illustration, sawing back and forth whether it's to be the corporate tenement or Rhoda in the Bath with a Rembrandt painting to illustrate, he wanted a larger or perhaps more precise title than I'd given and now has 6 or 8 to choose from and for background ('what the book's "about"') I told him to talk to Knopf where they're now writing the jacket copy and can be more objective (saleswise that is to say) than I: now what more could a publisher want in the way of propaganda! [...] I do want very much I think starting tomorrow morning to start on changes I want to make in the book's last 20 pages which I'd like to have done when the proofs come through so as not to drive everyone (you) else (myself) up the wall of "William's writing..." in May. [...]

Judith I just love you, I know not entirely satisfactorily but at the least where I can't back your fantasies I will try and even more your realities even not understanding them but knowing they are real, I love you undiminished and that's the un-understood reality of mine.

W.

Santabel: i.e., Sanibel Island, off the coast of southwest Florida.

Anderson: Bob Anderson, retired New York City lighting director then living in Key West.

revivals of Ibsen's *Doll's House* [...] Thorvald: the women's liberation movement in the 1970s inspired stage revivals and two films in 1973 based on Ibsen's 1879 drama. Thorvald is the husband of the play's heroine, Nora Helmer.

£750: about $8,000 today.

Harper's: published in its June issue as "Nobody Grew but the Business" (pp. 47–54, 59–66).

Janet Halverson: highly regarded jacket designer who worked from the 1950s through the 1990s.

Lewis Lapham: (1935–), managing editor of *Harper's* at the time (promoted to editor the following year).

Rhoda [...] Rembrandt: the published cover photo is based on Rembrandt's *Bathing Woman* (1654).

To Grace Eckley

[*A Joyce scholar who was researching a paper later published as "Exorcising the Demon Forgery, or the Forging of Pure Gold in Gaddis's* Recognitions," *in* Literature and the Occult, *ed. Luanne Frank (Arlington: University of Texas, 1977), 125–36.*]

Piermont NY
3 June 1975

Dear Miss Eckley,

I appreciate your interest in *The Recognitions* & have to tell you I've about reached the end of the line on questions about what I did or didn't read of

Joyce's 30 years ago. All I read of *Ulysses* was Molly Bloom at the end which was being circulated for salacious rather than literary merits; No I did not read *Finnegans Wake* though I think a phrase about 'psychoanaloosing' one's self from it is in *The Recognitions*; Yes I read some of *Dubliners* but don't recall how many & remember only a story called 'Counterparts'; Yes I read a play called *Exiles* which at the time I found highly unsuccessful; Yes I believe I read *Portrait of an Artist* but also think I may not have finished it; No I did not read commentary on Joyce's work & absorb details without reading the original. I also read, & believe with a good deal more absorbtion, Eliot, Dostoevski, Forster, Rolfe, Waugh, why bother to go on, anyone seeking Joyce finds Joyce even if both Joyce & the victim found the item in Shakespear, read right past whole lines lifted bodily from Eliot &c, all which will probably go on so long as Joyce remains an academic cottage industry.

Clearly this matter of 'influences' is a floodgate which I'm afraid I've neither the time nor patience to open now & I apologize to you for sounding as impatient over the whole matter as in fact I am, but if I do not mail you this will probably end up appearing even more rude by never getting any response off to you at all, and hope your work goes well the above notwithstanding.

Yours,
William Gaddis

'psychoanaloosing': Anselm twice refers to the critic in the green wool shirt as a "three-time psychoanaloser" (*R* 183, 453). In *Finnegans Wake,* Yawn boasts, "I can psoakoonaloose myself any time I want" (New York: Viking, 1939), 522.

Rolfe: Frederick Rolfe, aka Baron Corvo (1860–1913), British Catholic homosexual novelist and historian. His works include the novels *Hadrian the Seventh* and *The Desire and Pursuit of the Whole,* and a history of the Borgias.

To Mrs. Parke

[The mother of Marilyn Parke (see 23 November 1945), who said in her memoir that "Mother and Daddy soon became a second father and mother to Bill." The Harper's *excerpt is equivalent to* J R *543–71.]*

29 June 1975
Piermont, NY

Dear Mrs Parke,

I doubly appreciated your letter about the *Harper's* excerpt because—aside from a few appreciative comments from friends—the only mail I've had from readers forwarded from *Harper's* (six letters) has been fairly *un*appreciative, people who couldn't read it or couldn't understand it and were apparently unburdened by senses of humour, but I guess those are the people who write to magazines. I'm glad you did enjoy it but there are another 700 pages so this excerpt isn't entirely representative of the whole book, and all things considered I think it's probably just as well that my grandmother wasn't around for this particular excerpt—I think she might have had a hard time explaining it to her librarian friends in Des Moines! But the Book itself should be out in October and that's the verdict I'll have to live with.

Judith and I have kept hoping to stop to see you but our trips through Bay Shore are always so frantic on the way to Fire Island stopping for paint, plumbing supplies and all kinds of things to get the house ready usually for tenants, since we keep it rented most of the time though we may spend some of August there this year. We did stop to see Marion a couple of weeks ago (Henry was on the race track some where, I couldn't believe it) but I hope that in August or the fall we can make the trip a little less frantically and get to see you again finally, it is unbelievable how time passes when I realize that my son Matthew is just the age now (17) that Henry and I were when Harry was taking my mother to the Banker's Club to clear up our misadventures. Of course please give my best to Marilyn, it was certainly painful to hear from Marion of her illness but on the other hand quite marvelous that she's not letting it stand in the way of what sounds like quite an exciting life.

with love and best wishes to you
— Bill Gaddis

To David Susskind

[*American producer (1920–87) of movies, TV shows, and plays, and a well-known talk-show host.* Time *magazine's review of* J R *mentioned that WG was working on a Western screenplay; this was a collaboration with Candida Donadio's husband Henry Bloomstein—a film producer and screenwriter—entitled* Dirty Tricks, *named in* J R *and described there as the character Schramm's World War II experiences transposed to the Old West with Faustian overtones (391, 396). It was based on a 19-page "film treatment" entitled* One Fine Day *that WG had written in the early 1960s. A 143-page script was completed in 1976 and shopped around Hollywood, but nothing came of the project. WG later contemplated converting it into a novel.*]

21 October 1975

Dear Mr Susskind,

I greatly appreciate your direct call yesterday and your interest in this Western project of mine.

As I mentioned to you then, I'd just been going through it again with an eye to making certain changes which now seem important enough to me to take care of before showing it. I hope this delay will not cause inconvenience or a lessening of your interest, my agent will send a copy right on to you when I have it in shape and I hope there may still be opportunity to meet and talk with you.

Yours,
William Gaddis

To Sarah Gaddis

Piermont NY
Halloween [1975]

Dear Sarah,

As you probably know by now we were given an *excellent* dinner and evening by our mutual friend Mr Quesenbery last week, then on Wednesday very fancy lunch by Knopf so at least I'm getting some fine meals out of all this! (Even had dinner last night with Dick and Ruth Green in New York, all great except for a flat tire coming home—very *cold*).

Everything still in suspense except we have learned there will be a good review *next* Sunday (the 8th) *front page* of *New York Times Book Review* <u>except</u> that apparently I have to *share* it with another writer named Donald Barthelme damn it! Well half a loaf is better than none? *And*—look in this coming week issue of *Newsweek* where I understand we are treated quite well.

Thank the Lord just this morning arrived a check from the English publisher of *J R* so I can send you the enclosed (will this tight rope walking *ever* end?). I wish it were more of course but at least you will have November allowance plus a new dress and I hope you can find one you like immensely (and Peter likes!)—I'll probably talk to you again before you get this but meanwhile love always as you know,

Papa

Mr Quesenbery: Dean of Swarthmore College.

Donald Barthelme: his novel *The Dead Father* shared the front page; WG's review was by George Stade, a professor at Columbia.

Newsweek : Peter S. Prescott's enthusiastic review appeared in the 10 November issue, p. 103.

English publisher of *J R*: Jonathan Cape, issued in June 1976 with some corrections that wouldn't be made in American editions until 1985.

Peter: Peter Conley, Sarah's future first husband.

To John and Pauline Napper

Piermont NY
1 November 75

Dear John and Pauline,

finally a note off to you from the malaise that appears to follow publication and all the uncertainties that go with it, grand dreams of financial liberation in the midst of pounding debt because the American pattern is one of such absurd extremes in terms of "success" and "failure"—so we wait and pray and look for work, living for the moment on a rather pittance finally literally *wrung* out of Jonathan Cape who will bring the book out there (why I don't know, who the hell in England as it is today wants to read about an 11-year-old American entrepreneur?)

I've mainly exorcised recent demons by laying a floor and building bookcases in the garage here which at last, now the studying is done, begins to look like a "study"—and have gone back to make some revisions on that Faust western as a film script which we hope to sell on the strength of *J R*'s publicity—God knows if or when it will become a book, it would be just such an immense pleasure to never have to write anything again except an occasional letter if only to report that we are still in mid-air, though at least the book is out of my hands at last and perhaps good things are ahead which will permit us some freedom and movement, meanwhile I'm glad the copy of *J R* did reach you and hope you like him, his offensive qualities notwithstanding —more news when we have anything real to report.

love from us,
Willie & Judith

To David Markson

[*When Christopher Lehmann-Haupt's negative review of* J R *appeared in the daily* New York Times *on 30 October, Markson sent a postcard the same day to WG reading: "Dear Bill— Fuck Christopher Lehmann-Haupt!" (Lehmann-Haupt had also written a negative review of Markson's* Going Down *five years earlier.) Gaddis's reply, undated and without salutation, plays on a joke in* J R *whereby a foreigner takes literally a dictionary definition of "sympathy" (p. 489); the "best agent in town" refers to Candida Donadio.*]

Problem with you Markson you've got no God damned fellow feeling in bosom, put yourself in the poor bastard's place: like if your wife wrote a novel and the best agent in town declined to handle it, would you go around giving a free ride to the agent's clients? I mean why the hell do you think some poor bastard wants to be a book calumnist in the first place.

To Charles Monaghan

[*Another response to the* Times *review by Lehmann-Haupt, whom Monaghan mocked as Schumann-Heink (the name of a European soprano), addressed "Dear Finished Writer" from a phrase used on the book jacket copy.*]

[3 November 1975]

Dear Chas. —thanks for your condolence re Schumann-Heink, I'd like of course to think it's simply one more sample of this tired bastard's usual muddled mind. I mean it couldn't have anything to do with my agent having recently declined a novel by his wife, now could it.

Attached is an item Judith ran up which I forbade her to send the *Times* (though I certainly wouldn't object if others wrote them regarding his simple incompetence) & look forward to seeing your piece.

best regards

W. Gaddis (finished indeed!)

Attached: A parody of Lehamnn-Haupt's review of *J R*:

"Christopher Lehmann-Haupt does book reviews. Endless, streamlined, compulsive book reviews. Day after day, week after week he does book reviews. He also does summaries, encapsulations, and lifts pages maniacally. Month after month, sometimes overcooked in the rare sense of the word, nitwittywise. And he does question marks, quotes, parentheses and meticulous lists. And so it is not surprising that his latest attempt to review a major literary work—*J R* by William Gaddis—comes down on us like a collapsed laundry line revealing Mr. Lehmann-Haupt's washed out metaphors, bleached inadequacies, dangling shortcomings and nonbiodegradable babble.

"And yet, extraordinarily enough, an exceptional book can be discerned through the overwhelming tumult of his ambiguities. *J R* is a hilarious audiovisual novel but it is apparent that Mr. Lehmann-Haupt has neither an eye nor an ear but merely a forked tongue. What he finds amusing and intriguing in one paragraph is qualified or negated in the next.

"Does such paranoia seem all too obvious? No more so, I can assure you, than Mr. Lehmann-Haupt's other recent thrusts at contemporary fiction and his love affair with tautology. Still he goes on and on, year after year, until we are almost crazy with the meaninglessness of his mindless meaning.

"Can a book reviewer be taken seriously if what he gives with one hand, he takes away with the other? So much for C. L-H. He may be worth considering up to a point but I certainly wouldn't recommend him to intelligent readers who are stupefied by tired book reviewers."

To Matthew Gaddis

Piermont NY
16 November 75

Dear Matthew,

Just in case you missed [this ad in] today's *NY Times Book Review*. Of course we know that Gaddis is *not* a genius (I prefer the reviewer in the *Cleveland Plain Dealer* who wrote: "*J R* is a devastatingly funny book. Reading it, I laughed loudly and unashamedly in public places, and at home more than once I saw my small children gather in consternation as tears of laughter ran down my face.") But Knopf after all is trying to SELL BOOKS and you can imagine how pleased it makes me to see them advertising it this way! Who knows, it might even be seen by Movie People who can't read books but can read ads . . . So generally we are still sitting with fingers crossed waiting to see what will happen, very nerve-wracking. [...]

All I am pretty certain of regarding our own plans is Sarah's arrival here with Peter sometime on Friday [...] where you know you would be MORE THAN WELCOMED by all 5 of us if you can and want to come down, though as with Sarah, being able to spend some time with either of you at any point along the way is Thanksgiving enough for us. Whatever Knopf's ad says, you each give me more to be proud of than *J R*. (Throw in *The Recognitions* too.) [...]

much love always,
Papa

Cleveland Plain Dealer: Alicia Metcalf Miller, 9 November 1975.

To Robert Minkoff

[*A graduate student at Cornell who was researching a dissertation on Gaddis, later submitted the following year as "Down, Then Out: A Reading of William Gaddis's* The Recognitions.*"*]

Piermont NY
3 December 1975

Dear Robert Minkoff.

I'm sorry to be so long responding & regret more that I apparently can't be of help on your reference questions: I look down the spines of books here & cannot imagine which if any of them supplied the line to Ananda 25 years ago (though I must say it's too lovely a line for me to have originated). Nor can I recall the details of Valentine's double-agentry, though I'm about certain there was no sun reference in my mind. (In the simple basic structure he was equated with 'mind' (thus dying of insomnia), Brown with 'matter', Wyatt with 'creation and love' (or their absence).) And Rose? I don't recall having more on her, I think she was intended simply to personify innocence as a casualty (as possibly Esme's purity was a casualty). And finally the only source I could imagine for the 'Varé tava...&c' would be George Borrow but have neither his *Lavengro* nor *The Bible in Spain* here and would not send you through them on what could very well be a futile search.

I did of course appreciate your detailed effort on *J R*'s behalf in the *Sun* there and hope he may provide some entertainment beyond the academic.

Yours,

W. Gaddis

---

line to Ananda: on p. 893 of *R*, Wyatt quotes the Buddha: "I was that king, and all these things were mine! See, Ananda, how all these things are past, are ended, have vanished away...." Gaddis's source was William Richard Lethaby's *Architecture, Mysticism and Myth* (1892).

George Borrow: the Hungarian-Gypsy phrase (quoted on p. 255 of *R*) is from Borrow's *The Zincali: An Account of the Gypsies of Spain* (1841). Gaddis drew on Borrow's *The Bible in Spain* for other details used in *R*, but not *Lavengro*.

Sun: Minkoff's review of *J R*, "Is Valhalla Burning?," appeared in the *Cornell Daily Sun*, 24 October 1975, 4, 12.

4. CARPENTER'S GOTHIC
1975–1985

To Candida Donadio

25 Ritie Street
Piermont NY
8 December 1975

Dear Candida,

I'm spending the days going through masses of papers, notes, trash, clippings, correspondence, trying to figure out what to do with myself now: America has odd ways of making one feel one's self a failure. And looking over the fragments of our correspondence assembled, I am just terribly struck at the consistency, from my end, of howls about money, and from yours of reassurances, hopes, encouragement: of course this isn't really news (and probably hardly unique in your file of writers), but seeing it so all at once did overwhelm me with a clearer sense of what I've put you through year after year, and I wish to Christ it had finally come up on the note of triumph you have hoped and worked so hard for.

And instead we're picking up the pieces, with nothing left to do but work with what we've got. I talked with Bob late Thursday, and since he'll be away for a week we should probably try to prepare for the situation we may face when he returns.

Bob said, first, that Bantam does not want *J R*—he thinks Jaffe has probably not read it (and I paranoically suspect the hand of that schmuck Solataroff)—leaving only Avon and Ballantine. He had heard nothing from Avon, which I imagine could mean they have not been encouraged by their sales of *The Recognitions*. Leaving only Ballantine, who he said have shown interest (he'd talked to them earlier in the day) but, though I gather no hard figures were mentioned, in the 30 to 40 thousand area, which Bob seemed to be considering if nothing better suddenly comes along, and apparently with the feeling it will not.

If this is the case, I can understand his wanting to cut his losses, especially where they involve my generous advances, and this last 5 thousand makes it even more difficult for me to withhold my consent; but if it does come to such a decision what is your feeling?

Obviously it's as easy as it is foolish to second-guess the past, and suspect that if we had played it straight with a $12.50 hardcover edition a decent reprint sale would have followed those on-the-whole excellent reviews. I think Ballantine indicated they felt Knopf's paperback had already cut into their potential market, though that may just be a ploy. So what I wonder now is whether, having taken this hardcover-softcover course, we would be wise just to stay on it for awhile.

Bob says that sales are good: not poor but not terrific either. Yet of a hardcover printing of 5000 they'd shipped about 4700, and more than 26,000 of the softcover printing of 35,000, which sounds (though I'm aware 'shipped' doesn't mean 'sold') a bit better than good to me. I don't recall the softcover royalty rate we agreed on, but say it is 5%, if they did now sell 30,000 softcover and 5000 hardcovers, my royalties on the former would come to $9000 and $7500 on the latter. Thus if I presently owe Knopf $65,000, minus these royalties of $16,500 and minus the $8500 from BOM, I would still owe them $40,000.

In other words, assuming those figures hold together, a $40 thousand reprint sale would still leave me owing Knopf $20,000—and is that worth letting J R's future out of our hands, as The Recognitions is probably forever for the miserable sum it brought? And so it is my feeling that if J R brings reprint offers of only 30–40 thousand, we should shrug them off and wait it out. I remember—when hopes were brighter—what you thought Knopf would do if offered $100 thousand, you shrugged and said they'd turn it down. I hope you still feel that way, and that Bob will too. Though of course my grounds for asking your and his confidence in the book's long term prospects, or in mine at this point, are hard to imagine.

[unsigned carbon copy]

Bob: Robert Gottlieb, WG's editor at Knopf.

Jaffe: Marc Jaffe, editorial director of Bantam, which had published the mass-market edition of Pynchon's *Gravity's Rainbow* a year earlier. WG and his agent hoped Bantam would pay a similar amount for rights to J R. In the end, no one bought the mass-market rights, a crushing disappointment to WG.

Solataroff: Ted Solotaroff (1928–2008), American editor and writer. His literary journal, *New American Review*, was funded by Bantam.

$12.50 hardcover edition: instead, Knopf followed the *Gravity's Rainbow* model and published a split edition: a small printing of a hardcover priced at $15 and a larger printing of a trade paperback.

BOM: Book-of-the-Month Club, which published an edition for their members (an alternate choice, not the main selection).

To John W. Aldridge

[An American critic (1922–2007) who taught at the University of Michigan for most of his career. As WG notes below, Aldridge first wrote about his work in his 1956 book In Search of Heresy: American Literature in an Age of Conformity *(McGraw-Hill), where he lamented the poor critical reception of* R *(and Alan Harrington's* Revelations of Dr. Modesto*): "it is difficult to understand how the reward of reputation can ever come to the author of either novel, for there exists at present no agency able or willing to keep their names alive in the public consciousness until the time when they publish their next books. There is no assurance, furthermore, that when that time comes they will fare any differently, except that the chances are excellent they will run afoul of the prevailing hostility to second novels and be obliterated once and for all" (201). Aldridge's excellent review of* J R, *"The Ongoing Situation," appeared in* Saturday Review, *4 October 1975, 27–30, and was reprinted in his book* The American Novel and the Way We Live Now *(Oxford UP, 1983).]*

Piermont NY 10968
15 December 1975

Dear John Aldridge.

After the reception that was handed *The Recognitions* twenty years ago, I almost felt that if the time ever did come when further work of mine was well received I'd resist notes of thanks as firmly as I had writing any of indignant dismay that first time out. But at this point, with J R finally off on his own and the flurry of reviews past, it would be plain bad manners of me not to send you some expression of the real appreciation I do in fact feel.

I'm afraid I'm still not (as Bast blurts out) "running around thanking everybody" for what has seemed to me *J R*'s very fortunate reception, tempered by some somewhat disheartening but honestly arrived at dissent but I think short of the usual quota of guile and incompetence with only a couple of prominent (I should say prominently placed) exceptions—so I'm not writing this to thank you for a 'favourable review'. What I did appreciate was its informed quality that I felt reflected your long concern for what I have tried to do. You can have for instance no idea how many times that paragraph from *In Search of Heresy*, asking if there were any reason under prevailing conditions to believe I might fare better a second time around, has rattled in my head these years since, pulling me up short and then pushing me along to keep believing the thing real for long enough to finish it, and so it was extremely gratifying to see that you felt I came through.

Yours with best regards,
William Gaddis

To Robert Minkoff

Piermont N.Y.

7 January 1976

Dear Robert Minkoff.

Had I been more prompt with my response to your earlier letter and queries I might have saved you a lot of trouble on this last one which practically
crossed it in the mail, since I did try to make clear that after more than 20
years I haven't the sort of detailed recall for sources you assume, or either the
time or inclination to immerse myself in this project to the degree you appear
to require. Undoubtedly there is material here in boxes of discarded notes
which will probably eventually be dumped on some college library but if I
tried to go through them now for your queries I would be doing nothing else;
the more cogent point though is that the alertness goes on during the writing
& when the book's done I'm pretty much finished with it, it becomes its own
argument open to any attack or interpretation & whether you feel it's 'sym-
bolically unified' interests you a great deal more than it does me, or Mr
Koenig. Regarding the so-called 'unpublished introduction' to *The Recognitions*
for instance, that business about 'my roses are not roses but splinters from the
yew tree' was discarded simply as pompous nonsense which it is, and the
reason that that is an 'unpublished introduction' is that it never was an introduction at all but simply one more wrong direction one pulls up short on
seeking the right ones. Doodling. Since the very act of writing a novel is selection, the peril of academic approaches that go beyond the published work to
the unpublished which has probably as much value or less as the myriad un-
selected approaches never put on paper. Why didn't Mark Twain ever write
the book about Tom and Huck aged 60 talking over old times.

The Yew tree reference only recalls to me that one book I read when I was
working on *The Recognitions* was Robert Graves' *The White Goddess* & in this
way other random sources come to mind: Edgar Saltus, Andrew Lang, Denis
de Rougemont's *Love in the Western World*, Montague Summers' *Physical
Phenomena of Mysticism* (possible for your cruz con espejos query) but you
see the random nature of the reading involved.

Elsewhere, I think I recall coming on 'inherent vice' as an accepted term
for unprepared canvases & chemically unsympathetic paints but don't know
where. Talitha cumi, Mark 5:41 (damsel, arise). Mary B Eddy probably has
the error of matter someplace in *Science & Health*. The K Mansfield quote I
think was in a review she wrote of a book by E M Forster, may be in her
Notebooks. Maní, Sp. for peanut (chorus of The Peanut Vendor). Bishop
Whutley is Whately (wrote *Christian Evidences*) but I don't recall the reference. Those are the easy & immediate, you're certainly free to do what you

like with the *Flying Dutchman, Peer Gynt* references & mythic parallels, why I write big novels & what they reflect and no, to a question I think you asked me at some point, what I write you isn't for publication or inclusion in a paper but an attempt at a courteous effort to detour you from exactly that back to your own approach to what you're up to.

Yours,

W. Gaddis

[*In a postscript, Minkoff asked, among other things, if Gaddis knew of anyone else writing on his work and about J R's sources, to which WG responded in a postscript:*]

Regarding this I have no idea.

I don't offhand think of any books business or otherwise that seminal to *J R*. I recall such incidents as the Moncrieff-smelter deal being based on an unsavoury heist by Eisenhower's Treasury secretary Geo Humphrey and involving, I believe, Freeport Sulphur, in the '50s; the Gandia 'civil war' on something similarly brazen pulled by Union Minière in the Congo probably early 60s; but I've finished and finished with *J R* for the time being at any rate don't wish or plan to get into it again but simply leave it lay where Jesus flung it as the woman said, so trust you will not take the time to a questionnaire. Good luck with it,

WG

'unpublished introduction': this was published first in Koenig's dissertation (pp. 156–57), and then as an appendix to my *Reader's Guide* (pp. 298–99).

Edgar Saltus: author of *The Anatomy of Negation* (1886), a sardonic survey of atheism.

Lang [...] Summers: see my *Reader's Guide* for WG's use of the works by Lang, de Rougemont, and Summers.

Science & Health: the standard book on Christian Science.

Mansfield quote: from a review of a novel by E. V. Lucas, rpt. in Mansfield's posthumous *Novels and Novelists,* ed. J. Middleton Murray (1930). See WG's 7 April 1948 letter to Katherine Anne Porter.

The Peanut Vendor: a song Otto hears in part 3, chapter 1 of *R.*

Whately: Archbishop Richard Whately (1787–1863) published the handbook *Christian Evidences* in 1837, but it does not include the anecdote recounted on p. 764 of *R.*

Geo Humphrey [...] Freeport Sulfur: in 1957, Humphrey was involved in a multimillion-dollar contract for Freeport Sulphur, a large copper producer, to buy nickel and cobalt from Cuba, which came under investigation by the Justice Department.

Union Minière: a Belgian mining company, which in 1961 (according to Wikipedia) "supported the secession of the province of Katanga from the Congo and the murder of Patrice Lumumba, Congo's first prime minister after Belgian colonial rule. Upon the province's secession, the Union transferred 1.25 billion Belgian francs (35 million

USD) into Moïse Tshombe's bank account, an advance on 1960 taxes which should in fact have been paid to Lumumba's government. On December 31, 1966, the Congolese government, under dictator Mobutu Sese Seko, took over the possessions and activities of the [Union Minière], transforming it into Gécamines (Société générale des Carrières et des Mines), a state-owned mining company."

To John W. Aldridge

[Typed on mock stationery from "The JR Family Of Companies," under which WG typed "(Now in Receivership)." Aldridge had written to thank WG for his letter of 15 December 1975, all the more surprising given WG's reputation for being "elusive," and to suggest getting together in New York later that spring. As WG notes, reviewers outside New York found J R more accessible than their big-city counterparts did.]

Piermont NY 10968

28 January 1976

Dear John Aldridge.

Thanks for your note. I wish I could say that by spring we would expect to be in Athens, or Venice, even Key West—but as things stand that looks hardly likely so by all means if you wish, let me know here in Piermont if you are in the NY neighborhood. It's not terribly far and I'd be happy to come in for a drink.

I've got tagged elusive I guess by generally trying to avoid what I've felt to be rather egregious forces constantly ready to put the man in the place of his work—self defeating perhaps, I don't know. Like the notion that *J R* is generally accessible, till assured otherwise by the *New Yorker*; Cleveland, Kansas City, Chattanooga yes even Grand Rapids to the contrary notwithstanding. Was it Gertrude Lawrence? who said —What we lose on the swings, we make up on the roundabouts.

Yours,

W. Gaddis

Gertrude Lawrence: English actress and musical-comedy star (1898–1952). The quotation is a British fairground metaphor.

To Sarah Gaddis

Piermont

30 January 1976

Dear Sarah,

Thanks for your and Peter's letter, mainly for all its vitality and cheer in this post-publication limbo. I don't know what I thought was going to happen, but whatever it was hasn't. Simply gleaning late reviews: 'Joyous' says Chattanooga Tennessee, 'Millionaires in the Sky' says St Louis…'unreadable' says my old favourite *New Yorker* and goes on along those lines in the most gratuitously vicious way (what did I ever do to them?). Glad to know there are 2 copies of *J R* contaminating Ireland (I sent one to Marc Brandel), at any rate.

Not the highest spirits right now, in great part certainly because yesterday another funeral—you remember us talking about Tony Harwood, old friend and classmate and a real exotic married to the 70-or-so year old Princess Mdvani of Russia's Tsarist days, we were to go in and have dinner with them this evening & instead went to his funeral yesterday. What's absurd of course is how selfishly one takes these things, feel that someone so really rare and odd and kind and devoted to Judith and me has simply been stolen from us (heart attack talking on the phone & probably never really knew what was happening to him); and equally absurd to be surprised, such things do happen every day after all, why are we always so startled? And a certain envy creeps in for the Catholic Latin nations like Spain where death is a part of life; here the reaction is, Dead? but he can't be. We were to have dinner Thursday…

I don't mean to dwell on it, on the other hand it is something that we in America tend to exclude from our thoughts & so are inevitably unprepared when it occurs close to us, all bouncing along as though we were immortal. Yesterday Matthew's 18th birthday and certainly not the way I'd expected to spend it (you see? selfish again…) So at any rate with these things in my mind I take down Plato's *Crito*, which is the dialogue describing Socrates going to his death, and there folded in the book is a yellow page with this message covering it:

DEAR FAIRY I CANNOT FIND MY TOOTH IT CAME OUT FROM THE LOWER ROW TODAY I SHALL NOT EXPECT ANOTHER DIME LOVE SARAH

All which I suppose goes back to Wilder's message about living 'every every minute' and all the joy of your and Matthew's lives have given me since that is what you are both doing. Better I think sometimes than I am. Though perhaps my age is a time one pauses and tries to sort things out, thinks suddenly good Lord! When Mozart was my age he'd been dead for seventeen years!

The point of all this rambling to you being a kind of gratitude I guess for the affirmation in your life, in your and Peter's lives and Matthew's—even though sometimes I get impatient and uncertain about its direction, their directions, damndest thing is people saying I'm negative whereas it's these affirmations of life amidst its appalling uncertainties and setbacks that I most admire.

End of next week I'm going up to Cambridge for this rowdy Lampoon affair (complete with fireworks they promise (also 'Torchlight Processions, and other Delights too humorous to mention'))...then I may spend a night with Barney Emmart up at Salem & return Monday to see Matthew and try to get some notion of his next step—and he being now 18 it may be a large one. He has talked about France but as I recall in terms of growing vegetables there and I hope to be able to bring up some other possibilities—though I've got to say at this point in life I look around and think perhaps one nice eggplant is worth four of Plato's dialogues after all. [...]

love and best wishes to you both.

Papa

New Yorker: George Steiner's review appeared in the 26 January issue, pp. 106–9.

Marc Brandel: British-born novelist, journalist, and screenplay-writer (1919–94), mentioned in other letters not included here.

Tony Harwood: after Harvard, Anthony Harwood (1926–76) became secretary to Dennis Conon Doyle (son Sherlock Holmes's creator); after Doyle's death in 1955 he married Nina Mdivani (1901–87), a Georgian princess who had fled to Paris in 1917 after the Russian Revolution.

Mozart: died age 35; WG had recently turned 53.

To Benjamin Reeve

[*A student at Princeton who later submitted a thesis entitled "The World of Imagination and the Imagination of the World" for his BA.*]

Piermont NY
23 February 1976

Dear Benjamin Reeve.

Your thesis relating *J R* to *Don Quixote* sounds sufficiently unique that I would certainly hesitate to intrude on it (I'm not being facetious). I doubt there is more to JR himself than appears in the book but even were this not so, and I could tell you more about him, or on the other hand explain who and what I meant him to be, I should feel I'd pretty much failed my attempt to give him the only existence he has claim to, which is to say as he emerges from the book itself. And that must go for the rest of the book's characters too, even with the writer's wishes notwithstanding. Gibbs for instance I'd meant not as a failed writer, but as a man who might have been capable of almost anything if he'd found it worth doing but ends finding it too late even to be any of the things he'd never wanted to be, returns to writing as last resort and fails even at that; but reviewers have by and large found him a failed writer. So while few lines have haunted me longer than Eliot's —That is not what I meant at all ... I can't see a writer following his books around trying to say what he did mean, if the book failed to convey it. And further, if *J R* has the dimensions I would hope, it may well be open to approaches quite different to those originally envisioned, as yours would certainly seem to indicate.

Contrary to your information I don't live in New York and go in only when I have to, but wish you luck with this intriguing enterprise.

> Yours,
> William Gaddis

To Frances Henderson Diamond

[*Dr. Diamond wrote to WG on 23 February to say she had read* J R *and enjoyed his "quaquaversal style of storytelling," adding, "More than anything, though, I'm glad you're beginning to make peace with yourself." She noted she was currently teaching Ancient History at Old Dominion University in Norfolk, Virginia. "It's been 30 years since you and I met in Boston," she reminisced. "Olsen and Johnson are both long gone. Betty Garrett and Penny Edwards [her co-stars] and I kept up our friendship in Hollywood."*]

> Piermont, NY
> 2 March 1976

Dear Frances,

Marvelous surprise! and not simply getting your letter, but that you've read *J R*. And liked it. Extraordinarily few people I'd have been as happy to have your letter from as you.

You are still in my book on Nichols Canyon Road in Hollywood and I remember that brief evening too, 12? 15 years ago? I think the things it had taken me the 15 years since we'd met to put together were starting to fall apart, and I've taken the 15 since to put them back together: another and saner marriage, daughter of 20 coming up at the end of the week from Swarthmore where she's a junior, son of 18 out of school for the moment working in a restaurant in Boston, and that book finally out of my system. Ot out of my reach at least. And how much I would like to see you again too. And one way and place or another certainly will.

Right now I'm sitting in an empty house with a dog and a cat—Judith (wife) went down to Florida with her father for 3 or 4 weeks—wondering what to do next. It's a kind of post-publication limbo I wasn't really prepared for. *J R* has done extremely well in terms of reviews—really splendid ones in Sunday *NY Times, Saturday Review, National Observer, New Republic, Commentary* &c and, surprisingly to me, out in the rest of the country too, Cleveland, St

Louis, Kansas City, Chicago—not good in the *L A Times* which did disappoint me but the only really rotten one (which didn't surprise me) was the *New Yorker*. How it's selling on the other hand I don't really know, but since of course I was in the hole to my publisher for quite a good deal of money in advances it will take a while to make those up in royalties anyhow.

So I sit waiting for my agent to call on one spark of movie interest we've had to see if it's real; and if it is, how real. Because of course you know how unreal those things can be even when they're real. Of course the book *is* a movie, problem is those people don't read. And I hardly helped matters writing over seven hundred pages. Now if you'd re-married to a big producer . . . In fact, little of my business as it may be, I can't imagine that you haven't re-married, I know what a shocking loss you had but always so strongly felt your capacity for love and affection too that someone should have earned it again.

I thought of you when I was in Cambridge a couple of weeks ago for the kind of rowdy carryings-on I used to think you were afraid were all I'd ever do—this was a weekend-long party for the hundredth anniversary of the *Harvard Lampoon* but I think I did behave fairly decorously. And of course vividly recalled those dawn bus rides back from Boston where I'd sat staring over egg roll at you still in stage makeup, climbing Adams House steps very pleased with myself for the brush of lipstick on my cheek, usually. Of course Betty Garrett and Penny Edwards were too glamourous to believe and I was too busy backstage anyhow counting my good fortune with you, there's never been anything like it in my life since.

As you can gather, I've little idea what may happen next. If a marvelous contract appeared in the next few weeks (*with* a large check) I'd probably drive down to Florida briefly and would certainly call. But I try not to think about such prospects since I'm old enough to know it is an area fraught with disappointment when one builds hopes up. Just as the notion that *J R*'s film prospects might take me to California when you are out there later in the spring. So I'm holding my breath and right now looking around for some sort of corporate writing work to get out of the hole the book left me in. I have a couple of other projects (including a Western screenplay floating around California somewhere) but find it difficult to sit down and start another book (even one that's already started) and don't want to sign another book contract right now anyhow, it certainly wouldn't be difficult but they can become quite a weight.

And of course if any of the above really should work out you will hear from me, it would be just marvelous to see you again, meanwhile as must be evident by now your letter was enormously welcome,

with love and every best wish,
Willie Gaddis

L A Times: Geoffrey Wolff, "A Disappointing Deluge of Dialogue," *Los Angeles Times Book Review*, 16 November 1975, 4.
Western screenplay: *Dirty Tricks*: see 21 October 1975.

To Judith Gaddis

[*With his wife spending more time in Florida, WG resumed occasional speechwriting assignments. J R was nominated for the 1975 National Book Award for fiction, along with Larry Woiwode's* Beyond the Bedroom Wall, *Saul Bellow's* Humboldt's Gift, *Vladimir Nabokov's* Tyrants Destroyed and Other Stories, *Hortense Calisher's* Collected Stories, *and Johanna Kaplan's* Other People's Lives.]

> Piermont
> Wednesday 17 March [1976]

Dearest J———

[...] And we were up early Sunday, I back on my IBM project, Sarah in the dining room card-filing a sociology project, Peter in the livingroom doing heavy equations. They left about noon to stop and see Marianne in NY and I got back to work rather frantically till about 6:30 when Michael Green & the English fellow Kay stopped in for a minute and left around 10.

At any rate I did have a rather toothsome speech ready for Harrison Monday noon and he was quite pleased with it though of course he will rewrite it entirely. We had originally talked in terms of toward $500 since it was to be merely a draft, but since it turned out to be a pretty complete speech he is going to try to do better for me, perhaps a good deal better depending of course on John Opel's (IBM president) reaction to it. [...]

Into fuzzier areas, the one I mentioned to you last night which both Candida and Bob do not appear to attach practical ($) significance to, Bob says for now regard it as an entertainment (my word). Books nominated for the Nat Book Award are mine, Woiwode's, Bellow's, then 3 books of stories (!) by Nabokov, Hortense Calisher, and Joanna Kaplan whom nobody's heard of (Bob published it & can't understand its inclusion). No *Ragtime*, no *Dead Father*, no *Guerillas*. But if the book selections are odd, the judges are even odder; a writer, a critic, and a complete idiot: Wm Gass, Mary McCarthy, and Maurice Dolbier. The short story books must be Dolbier's candidates since his attention span is that of a 6 year old and I'm sure he will never reach page 516 in *J R* where D O'Lobeer describes *The Tiger on Sonic* as 'a really yummy read...' (unless a literate friend if he has any points it out to him). So it's probably just as well you're not here pressing me to press Bowdoin to press

Mary McC...a real comic strip, Bellow has won the NBA 3 times so my money's on Calisher?

Sarah is simply a delight. Though I cannot understand the way she grapples with the language in her writing. Of course I have heard nothing from Matthew and hope he does not get in difficulty with the Mass tax people. A nice note from Vincent Livelli just back from Hong Kong asking for our overseas address. A nice piece by Jeff Voorhees in the Newsletter which I'll send you when I know it will reach you (sending it to Palm B.) A call from Ginny Johnson will I come down and sign a few copies of Avon's cheap item she has in since Harcourt's appears to be definitely out of print.

And after the 2 days' concentrated reading Drucker Einstein &c, 4 days outlining and writing 12 hours each at least, a totally vacant day (though a pretty one from last night's snow) stretching ahead before I go into town [...].

with all love from the 3 of us,
W.

Harrison: Harrison Kinney (1921–2019), a speechwriter for IBM and a close friend of WG's since 1961. In 1999 he wrote an informative memoir of WG, now at https://www.williamgaddis.org/reminisce/remhkinney.shtml.

Ragtime [...] *Guerillas*: novels by E. L. Doctorow, Donald Barthelme, and V. S. Naipaul.

Wm Gass: eminent fiction writer and critic (1924–2017), later to become a dear friend of WG.

Mary McCarthy: see headnote to 4 February 1987. Her third husband was Bowden Broadwater, whose name is misspelled a few lines later.

Maurice Dolbier: one of the original reviewers of *R*; see 21 May 1962 and note.

page 516 in *J R*: a list of books—anagrams of *The Recognitions*—followed by mocking names of its original reviewers.

Vincent Livelli: an old friend (1920–2021) from WG's Greenwich Village days; see 3 January 1983.

Jeff Voorhees [...] Ginny Johnson: unidentified, the latter apparently a bookseller.

Drucker Einstein: Peter Drucker, author of several books on business and management, and scientist Albert Einstein, whose life has provided fodder for a number of business writers.

To Matthew Gaddis

[*J R won the 1975 National Book Award for fiction, and WG attended the ceremony on 21 April with his children. (For coverage of the event and photos of WG, see* Publishers Weekly, *10 May 1976, 47–54.) The "sheet" is unidentified; Rockland is the county in which Piermont is located.*]

Mary McCarthy and WG at the National Book Award Ceremony
(photo by Jill Krementz).

Piermont N.Y.
29 April 76

Dear Matthew,

perhaps I should get out of the book racket, put on my $3 Thrift Shop suit hire John Dalmas as my press agent and go on speaking tours? Heaven knows whether a sheet like this sells any copies in Rockland County though it gets me big smiles at the bank and from Nard (not a reader) —but I am glad you got down for the thing & hope Cindy didn't find it too cuckoo in the way of everybody going around shaking hands with everybody, a pretty good look at the 'Establishment' in action anyhow. Candida says 'Your kids just knock me out. Now I understand everything.' And Lee Goerner writes 'Your family is neat.' So those are the important things after all.

And in the wake of it things seem to be looking up. There is one deal in the wind I won't get into here but if it does work out in the next couple of months could relieve these financial uncertainties for a while that I've been driving everyone mad with for so long. And then, a little more immediately real, I went up to Bard College yesterday and talked with the president and some people in the English department and they very much would like me up there for the fall term September through December, two courses two days a week at what I think is very good pay and it's only two hours (90 miles) from here, and the courses would be entirely up to me to make what I wish, which is both flattering and alarming since I'm not all that sure I have enough to 'teach' to fill a term. But the Bard people don't seem at all put off by my doubts and so if I can get over those I will probably take it: certainly a good deal more realistic than sitting here waiting for IBM or Eastman Kodak to call, and would give me time to explore my next project (probably the Civil War one) without feeling I must attack and finish it immediately. Also I have to confess that the title Distinguished Visiting Professor is tempting to wear around for a bit. (Just so Martin [Dworkin] doesn't hear of it.) [...]

with love to you always and best to Cindy,

Papa

John Dalmas: a private detective in some of Raymond Chandler's early stories.

Cindy: Matthew's girlfriend.

Lee Goerner: (1947–95), Gottlieb's assistant at Knopf until he was promoted to publisher.

the Civil War one: WG contemplated converting his play *Once at Antietam* into a novel.

To Johan Thielemans

[*A Belgian critic and specialist in American literature (1939–) who published numerous articles on Gaddis's work as well as a few radio and television broadcasts for the Belgian media.*]

Piermont NY 10968

18 May 1976

Dear Johan Thielemans.

I greatly appreciate your sending me the copy of your extensive broadcast critique even though, of course, I find the language tantalizingly impenetrable—makes me regret my long fraud with languages that so helped earn the epithet 'erudite' for *The Recognitions* (though I'm content to trust that while the author may be a fraud the book is *not*). And in that area I am struck again by the apparently casual ease with which Europeans approach American literature: for another recent case in point, a charming letter from a girl student at the University of Toulouse who has read *J R* twice for a paper on American literature and culture, all which of course I find immensely gratifying as I do your interest in it for the Paris symposium you speak of, I hope your paper is well accepted.

Our own plans for getting to Europe are as usual continuously postponed by circumstance but your invitation is appreciated nonetheless, and thank you again for sending me the paper.

Yours,
William Gaddis

---

girl student at the University of Toulouse: probably Brigitte Félix, who has written extensively on WG since then.

To John and Pauline Napper

Piermont
29 May '76

dear John and Pauline—thanks for your note—the *Plum Tree* is lovely & a good deal more lasting than the National Book Award which was pleasing of course but doesn't seem to have had much tangible (i.e. $) effect (i.e. 'sales'), the book is doing well enough but no vulgar "best seller" and a good deal of peevishness on my part with the publisher over lack of advertising after the string of marvelous reviews. God knows when it will appear in England, my trust-confidence in Tom Mashler at Cape is o. Otherwise we wait and pray and will give you news when/as/if we ever do have it.

W—

Plum Tree: if not an artwork, perhaps *The Day They Shook the Plum Tree* by Arthur H. Lewis (Bantam, 1964), a biography of miserly financier Hetty Green (1834–1916), in WG's library.

Tom Mashler: i.e., Maschler (1933–2020), a leading literary publisher in England. (There is no mention of WG in his memoir *Publisher* [2005]). The Cape *J R* appeared around this time.

To Candida Donadio

Piermont
1 June 1976

Dear Candida,

As my lawyer (God rest him and I wish he were still with us) used to say, —Oh Lord, you've written another of your letters…! Which then, as now, serve largely to get my thoughts in order as we move to the next step. So I'm sending this to Stonington, where you can run through it at leisure when you have nothing worse to do in the next week or so. Mainly at this moment it is because you are out of your office this week, and I am going out to Fire Island sometime in the next few days to work on that house till the 15th, and there are a couple of points I want to have clear in case you should be talking to Knopf or elsewhere in the interim.

First—though I'm sure we think along the same lines and you have anticipated this—I hope we can avoid any quid pro quo with Gottlieb regarding my 'next book'. In other words, giving up or giving in to something in exchange for his not pursuing any claim to a next book he might have under §14 of our agreement, which reads as amended: The Author agrees to submit to the Publisher his next book-length work before submitting the same to any other publisher. What might we have that he might want? First of course repayment of the $5000. December loan which was excluded from the *J R* contract, and which he has every right to have back off the top of any deal we should make.

Next—and this is the one that disturbs me—giving him a free hand with any reprint sale that may appeal to him to cut his losses, but which would do little or no good to me. Of course Bob is very shrewd (and frankly at this point I don't know if he's anything more than that), and may very well have exactly this trade in mind waiting for us to broach the matter of taking the next book elsewhere, as I have by now every reason to believe he would be glad to see us do, anyhow.

The point is, I don't want to publish again with him any more, I think, than he wants to publish me. Sometimes I'm pretty slow thinking, Candida, especially when I have the idea that I'm held with confidence and respect. For a good many months there I thought the people at Knopf held me and my work in high regard, and it has taken a few real snubs to finally let me know that I'm considered simply somewhat of a nuisance. The NBA should certainly have made it clear, Bob too busy to take us to lunch, too important to take us to dinner and too chintzy to pay for it, he seemed simply embarrassed by the book's showing a new breath of life when he'd already written it off. A few months ago the mails brought a steady stream of reviews, mentions &c from Goerner. Since the NBA, all I've had of that was the *PW* writeup that you sent me and a long piece from the *LA Times* from a friend in California, so I gather the word has gone down to stop bothering with those mailings too.

I guess what it comes down to is that Bob and I disappointed each other a good deal. He came in on *J R* at the last minute as sort of a spoiler—none of the long agonies and uncertainties Asher put up with me—gambled sixty thousand and when he didn't make the bundle on the book that he'd hoped to, like a good gambler has moved right on to the next game. So I've disappointed him on the money side, but he's disappointed me with his finally quite explicit show of non-interest and non-support. Of course (as JR knew clearly) that's what business is; but even though I've been as disappointed as anyone on the money side, I'd thought there was more to it than that.

Curiously, I remember back when I applied for that Nat'l Endowment grant on the strength of turning the Civil War project into a novel which Bob on the board of judges helped me to get; but when once last year I tried to talk to him about the book, I was surprised and I guess a little hurt too that he showed no interest in it at all. In other words, *J R* for him was just a one-shot deal that didn't pan out, and its author likewise. Though I can see his antipathy as partly my fault. I think he's quite a thin-skinned guy who doesn't like criticism and doesn't like the source of any suggestion he's not entirely right. Of course I never did tell him, in as forthright terms as I told you, what a half-baked job I thought they were doing in terms of promotion, sales and distribution with the hard/soft cover problem. But 2 big *Times* ads for the book within 4 days of each other, and then never another one when all the good reviews had come in, except for that obligatory obituary-looking admission that it had got the NBA? I did try a few times to get into the whole thing with him in a bantering way but he was having none of it, dried right up on me and I should have been bright enough then to realize that every word of mine was a nail in my coffin.

There. I've only gone on like this—aside from getting it off my chest—to clarify elements of this essential problem excluding anything else: that neither he or I wants Knopf as publisher of my 'next book'. I would in fact, if you think it advisable, call or write him myself in a very straight low-key way to bring out exactly that, without reference to anything else. Then if he brings in some quid pro quo (I'll trade you §14 for §1 a iii), we know where we stand. Or you might prefer to say to him yourself on the 'phone sometime —Bob? Incidentally there's one other small item: you're not really interested in seeing Gaddis through another book even if he should manage to write one, are you? (Then if he says —I'll trade you §14 for §1 a iii, we'll know where I stand.)

See the whole God damned problem is you've spoiled me in terms of support, loyalty, integrity—all those outmoded 19th century square notions. Ask JR.

[unsigned carbon copy]

---

my lawyer: Richard B. Jablow died on 20 September 1975.

To John and Pauline Napper

[*A postcard from a hotel in Hong Kong. In August 1976 WG was sent by the United States Information Agency on a speaking tour from Thailand through the Philippines to Japan: see his letter to the* Times *of 21 February 1984.*]

The Peninsula Hong Kong
[23? August 1976]

dear John and Pauline—

how can I get to the other side of the earth but *never* manage a trip to England? The US State Dept is passing me off as an 'American Specialist', speaking to university people &c, painful but how else would I ever see Bangkok & Japan? Sort of a sop for the million $ *J R* did *not* make I guess, will be home late September and try to write and explain all.

Love, Willie Gaddis

To Judith Gaddis

The Oriental
Bangkok, Thailand
Friday 27 August 1976

dearest Judith——— it is hard—impossible really—to realise I've been gone just a week? [...] here feeling helpless looking out on this calm brown river, rusted tin roofs on the other side and a gold temple roof sticking up from the confusion of modern buildings and (to western eyes) slums—though where I miss you constantly most is these people's obsession with flowers, even in the worst market stalls fruit and nameless edibles cut to look like blossoms, you do look at all this and really wonder what in God's name we were trying to win a war in this part of the world for.

Well. I have been through my first 2 (and only) talks in Bangkok—I hope successful though these people are quite shy and so polite it is difficult to know. I'd been told I would be talking to university people—professors, instructors, some students—but no one in the State Dept thought to mention that these are 95% young ladies, so I've felt I was addressing a seminary—and my usual anxiety feelings that I'm not really earning my way. I do have the feeling that the State Dept operation is not the most efficient one in the world and perhaps should have pressed harder about meeting local writers (though there are few) but everyone has been most relaxed and kind— And this evening a young very soft spoken professor (man) is coming by and we are going for a walk in the city and probably a bite to eat, I feel he hasn't much money and also believe he has some poetry to show me—so I'll do my best and also hope for a closer look at the place and the people. And tomorrow expect to go for a real look at some of the temples. [...]

I just think about you constantly and miss you so much and love you always—

W.

To Sarah Gaddis

Northwest Orient in flight
[postmarked Tokyo]
4 September 1976

Dear Sarah———— it is quite unreal to be 7 miles above the Pacific between Manila and Tokyo knowing that you have just left Saltaire and are all in Piermont—and Scarborough—today, *and* that by the time this reaches you I will have spent a few days in Japan and you will be at Swarthmore—*and* 21 years old. Of course you know how much I wish I were there for that, but all I can think is that this trip is a beginning of better things for us all, that it is as productive as it is fantastic. The people in Thailand and the Philippines have all been so generous and attentive and so wanting to hear anything I could tell them about "writing" or life or *anything* that I begin to think I may really have some things worth telling them—— (I had 32 in my audience yesterday, *68* the day before!) hell Sarah this isn't the way *I* thought your 21st birthday would be but of course the point is not the occasion itself but who you *are* at 21, and you know how happy and proud these things you are make all of us who love you————*happy birthday* and I *will* see you soon.

Love to you and Peter——
Papa

To Judith Gaddis

Nishitetsu Grand Hotel
Fukuoka, Japan
11 Sept. 1976

Dearest—

the hotel looks grand enough but the room is quite wee—but starkly nice, "I've grown accustomed to her (*your*) face" on the piped-in music radio, bottle of black beer and drying out in my kimono after taking Professor Miyamoto to dinner in pouring rain, part of a real typhoon passing through (they say)—I'm sure ruined both our shoes but seemed the least I could do since everyone has been so kind.

I flew down here this morning from Sapporo where I'd arrived yesterday morning and given my "talk" late in the day to about 35 people largely college professors, 4 of whom took me to dinner afterward so eager for me to be pleased (and very struck, I was told, at how natural and humble I was for someone who had won such an important prize!)—2 of them there this morning (men of about 60) to see me off all of course immensely touching & flattering, much bowing and smiling on all sides—

So now I have 4 more of these ('talks')—here in Fukuoka tomorrow, then Osaka, then Kyoto, then Nagoya—and then some sort of interview in Tokyo the evening before I come *back* and as intriguing and flattering as it all is I honestly cannot wait. [...]

In terms of making the 'good' impression I feel I'm managing, John Gardner apparently left everyone along this route with a really bad taste in their mouths, real pain in the neck I'd pictured (for my own obvious reasons)— [...]

Saturday morning—I realize you will get this barely a day before I get back—which seems silly but here it is seems like 6 months and I cannot wait!

with all kinds of love,
W.

"I've grown accustomed to her face": a song from the 1956 stage version of *My Fair Lady*, written by Frederick Loewe (music) and Alan Jay Lerner (lyrics).

Professor Miyamoto: Yokichi Miyamoto, who published an account of WG's visit in *Eigo Seinen*, 1 December 1976, 404–6; English translation online at https://www.williamgaddis.org/nonfiction/interviewmiyamoto.shtml.

John Gardner: American novelist (1933–82) whose insulting review of *J R* in the *New York Review of Books* ("Big Deals," 10 June 1976, 35–40) is a recurring topic in later letters.

To Sarah Gaddis

[*In his first semester at Bard (and subsequently), WG taught both creative writing and a course on the theme of failure in American literature and culture, the basis for his essay "The Rush for Second Place" (1981).*]

Piermont
8 October 76

Dear Sarah,

I was very happy to have your letter—and word that the stereo arrived & got set up & 'sounds great'—*and* was baptised with Chopin. No better choice.

Bard is fine although I still labour under silent stares, at me or at the floor. Nine people showed up for the writing 'workshop' & 27 for 'Failure', which should tell me something! As usual getting 'writing' to discuss is like pulling teeth. But why are they *there* then? On the other hand the Failure people I think are really doing the reading (I pared the number down to 21) & quite responsive in discussion, I hope it keeps up. At the end of each class I feel I've exhausted my material for the whole term. Also I now have 3 advisees (word?) working on senior writing projects, one of which a short novel in which the author insists absolutely nothing happens. I've read 24pp. & so far nothing has. [...]

love from us all,
Papa

To Candida Donadio

Piermont NY
12 Dec. '76

Dear Candida.

I think that we agree we have about all the information, disheartening as it may be, that we are going to get; and there is little choice now but to move on it. After talking with you, and then going over the entire thing in detail with Judith, I've tried to clear my head of past hopes & irritants & make a completely fresh start. This is the approach I suggest:

1. Drop Silverman flat (unless forced to return to him as a last resort if step 4 below fails): he has at least served the function of providing us with a $25 thousand base figure.

2. Reconsider Knopf. This is a painful turn-around for me of course, since they are hardly my favourite house & I have little or no faith in Gottlieb's performance. However in this case we are not after performance, but simply as much money in front as we can get.

Gottlieb has told you he is interested in my next book to the point of 50 or 60 thousand. He may have assumed another book of the weight & significance of *J R* & its predecessor when he named those figures, & what we do not know is whether he would consider the comparatively short & simpler western in those terms. He knows about the screenplay & presumably is aware that it remains unsold. Thus he might scale his offer on it down to the Silverman level or below if he is interested at all. On the other hand, I believe he thinks in terms of a fast buck & might be interested in that possibility which the western offers.

Therefore I suggest we approach him now on the western in terms of the above figures. If he is interested but backs off from those figures, go as low as 40 thousand if he will offer that (2-year delivery & otherwise same contract as on *J R* but without option clause).

This has two advantages. First, if he made the above offer he might also be willing to leave the $5 thousand in abeyance, which we would otherwise most likely have to repay him from any money from elsewhere. Second, if Gottlieb turns it or those terms down, we should be free to *very openly* go elsewhere.

3. This would mean you should be able to approach substantial firms like Random House, S&S, &c, rather than furtive moves among small independents.

4. If none of the above prospers & the best offer remains in the $25 thousand range, see if Aaron [Asher] is interested to that extent.

What do you think.

[unsigned carbon copy]

Silverman: perhaps James Silberman (1927–2020), editor-in-chief at Random House.

To Ólafur Gunnarsson

[*An Icelandic poet and novelist (1948–), several of whose books have been translated into English.*]

Piermont, NY 10968
18 March 1977

Dear Mr Gunnarsson,

Simply a note to thank you sincerely & very much for your letters & high opinion of my work, as well as for the poetry which I should have acknowledged long before this. Whatever may be happening to *J R* here in the US, which I think is not very much, it is really pleasing to know that I have a gratifying reader in Zaire, one in Manila, & now Reykjavik. Heaven knows when I may be passing by, over or through Iceland but I would certainly look you up—meanwhile go on & finish your 'long long novel' before you go out a window: you can imagine how many times I was ready to do just that in the course of those 2 books & so write you this from a ground-floor room.

with best regards,
William Gaddis

To Judith Gaddis

[*This portion of a longer letter to Judith in Key West concerns a writers' conference at New College in Sarasota, Florida, that Rust Hills was organizing for June; see 28 June 1977.*]

Piermont
Fri p.m., 18 March [1977]

Dear Judith,

[...] And from the constantly changing Sarasota front: John Barth can't make it so Rust Hills gets Susan Sontag, then she's sick and Barthelme drops out so he gets Hortense Calisher & Vance Bourjaily (sp?); meanwhile I am shying from readings and panels and finally have a good & encouraging talk with William Gass coming with his wife, Hills meanwhile reshaping it into a no-lecture no-panel informal thing at least that's how it stands now, but if Gass abruptly disappears I may be tempted to do the same. (Which of course is nonsense because for me it's little or nothing to [do] with anything but the fee is it: Barthelme drops out because he's already overbooked with just this sort of thing; Calisher is a star, Vance has got nothing else to do, Gass admires me because I've been able to stay out (till now), I admire him because he separates it all clearly & relaxedly in his head ('my public & private selves haven't even shaked hands for many years'); & from admire to envy, (Candida says) Puzo envies my status of which he feels he has none, I his money of which we know God damned well we've got none; & so much for the nickel-&-diming Hills & Plimptons where success isn't except for Rust & George for that moment. I used to think it mattered.) [...]

with love always,
W.

John Barth [...] Vance Bourjaily: Barth (1930–), Barthelme (1931–80), and Sontag (1933–2004) were in their prime then; Calisher (1911–2009) served terms as president of PEN and the American Academy of Arts and Letters in addition to publishing several books of fiction—her *Collected Stories* lost to *J R* for the NBA fiction award—and Vance Bourjaily (1922–2010) published numerous books from 1947 onward and taught creative writing.
Puzo: Mario Puzo (1920–99), best-selling author of *The Godfather* (1969).
Plimptons: see 4 January 1986.

To John Large

[*A student of WG's at Bard College. The following accompanied a story by Large.*]

[postmarked Suffern, New York
13 May 1977]

John Large.

Fact these pages aren't littered with red underlinings, question marks, stabs of punctuation, doesn't mean I didn't read them, & more than once. As I'm sure I've remarked before, it's been refreshing to come upon someone for whom the language is a real live means of communication rather than an unfamiliar barrier in itself. Perhaps in fact it's too easy? why you press it as far as you do? My own sense of all this I think comes down to this terrible search for something worth writing about, worth one's talents (I'm not being facetious), almost the sense here sometimes of your frustration with the inadequacy of your material, & so making the writing itself the substance. Have you read anything of Joan Didion's? do you need to? A marvelous sense of fragmented style & refusal to tell too much.

   Go to Appalachia (sp?) & work in a mine? get a job in a brassiere factory? a morgue? on a tuna boat? I don't know, seems what's needed is a unifying kind of closed-end scene, or (&) a unifying closed-end obsession & watch it spread (I took, first, forgery; then 'business') but something, perhaps—& in contradiction of the dictum 'write what you know about'—not too close in one's own life. Dan Haas in our group for instance I think set himself a nice problem with his Boy Prophet, he certainly has the facility & has given himself something to solve. (I think of writing perhaps too much so as problem solving.) Point is not to get one's self in a corner; & to try to settle for the fact—unlikely as it must seem—that there's plenty of time.

good luck with it
W. Gaddis

Joan Didion: American journalist and novelist (1934–2021); WG often assigned her *Play It as It Lays* (1970) in his creative writing classes.
our group: Large remembered the group as including Dan Haas, Shari Nussbaum, Joshua Greyson, and Mary Caponegro. Only the last went on to achieve any critical acclaim as a writer.

To Rust Hills and Joy Williams

[For Hills, see 15 February 1961. His wife Joy Williams (1944–) is the author of State of Grace *(1973), a novel WG greatly admired, and other books of fiction, as well as the introduction to the NYRB edition of* J R. *The following is a "memo" typed on stationery from "The JR Family Of Companies."]*

28 June 1977

TO: Rust Hills
        Joy Williams

Management wishes to express its profound thanks for your many successful efforts to feed, comfort, entertain, blandish, and otherwise distract our recent representative at your conference.

This is doubly appreciated in light of the fact that we do not let him out often in his present somewhat unstable condition for fear he may embarrass both the corporate image and his hosts, to say nothing of himself or anyone within reach. From press accounts recently received at our office here we are grateful that this occurred only to a limited degree and the kind but firm restraint you appear to have exercised to that end is appreciated accordingly.

Finally, we are of course exceedingly pleased at the circulation given our Product insofar as this may influence sales which, as you are aware, is our only reason for remaining in business.

> For the Management, cordially
> Willie

and kindest personal regards from Mister Gaddis.

To Joy Williams and Rust Hills

> Piermont
> 7 July 1977

Dear Joy & Rust,

Thanks for your good letters. Of course I would love to come up to Stonington. At the moment I am girding my loins to face a Univ. of Rochester version of the Sarasota meeting, up this Sunday the 10th & back the following Saturday, I did it last year & it's considerably more frenetic than the Florida version, under direction of a madman named LJ Davis; but it won't have Gass, won't have yourselves, won't have a Karen. I think it is rotten you didn't bring her back up with you. Why didn't *I* rent your cottage down there?

Yes I was sent the press assaults from Tampa, never been treated so artily as that cover item but why am I always the Best Unknown Writer in America? As for that woman in *St P Times*...! Honeyed rum voice indeed!

I've just got back from an R&R weekend out at Sag Harbor, many friends out there (not including the Easthampton contingent) & wish I'd bought a house there 12 years ago when I visited in a similar abandoned state, still a temptation if I can figure out what to do with this white elephant on Fire Isld, haven't even been able to rent it for August & don't especially want to spend August there myself just to get my taxes' worth, this going back & forth between empty houses is conducive to nothing but drink & still no word at all on the future being planned or more likely unplanned for me & God knows what August will bring.

At any rate I'll be in touch with you when I get back from Rochester & as I say greatly look forward to the visit you suggest, & really again thank you both so much for all in connection with the Sarasota episode, I'm glad it worked out as well for everyone else as it did for me, really helped.

best regards
Willie

LJ Davis: American novelist (1941–2011), then director of the writing seminar at the University of Rochester.

To Sarah Gaddis

Piermont
8 August 1977

Dear Sarah,

I immensely appreciated your long letter—and the 'day off' time you took to write it—even though it's taking me this long to respond. And for your solicitous concern for me & Judith & all your generous suggestions of help. She stopped over here last week & I read what you'd said & it all did reach her, as it did me, but I think also simply through its generosity helped drive home to each of us a rather opposite point, which is at this point not only you can't help us, & she & I can't really help each other—patching things up after a domestic 'spat'—until she & I separately get clearer grasps of who we want to be & what we want to do with what time we've got left in this world besides eat drink grow older & lean on each other.

So while I can hardly say that I'm that pleased by what she's done, in a sense she had good reason to call a halt to things as they were going day to day & much of it the cumulative result of the position I took a long time ago when I got out of the 9–5 job circuit. In this, it's got to do with what sociologist David Reisman labeled as 'inner-directed' vs. 'outer-directed' people, & very much what *J R* is all about: JR is the outer-directed, takes unquestioningly as his own goals all those material ones he sees others around him striving for as 'what you're supposed to do'. Whereas Bast, as the incipient artist, is trying to develop the inner-directed capacity of the artist against all the odds it holds: doubts & lack of confidence in one's talents (that what one is doing is really 'worth doing'), worldly pressures of money, 'success' &c. And Gibbs, the book's 'failure', is the man destroyed by the conflict between these forces.

Well, there's my morning lecture. I only got off into it because a lot of the present problem here I think has got to do with the peril in that inner-directed course when it suddenly seems to lack direction, & (certainly from the experience of other writers) not that unusual when one has finally finished a long inner-directed project. Probably obviously, the only thing approaching a solution to this dilemma is some intelligent mixture of the 2 approaches, which is why there was a certain satisfaction in doing the Kodak speeches but there seems to be very little such work around these days. At any rate with Judith or without that's the one I've got to solve again—because (unless one is Mozartian genius) it's never solved once for all. (As Auden said: True wars are never won.) [...]

meanwhile thanks you know, and much love always

Papa

David Reisman: R*iesman's* classic study *The Lonely Crowd* (1950), which discusses these concepts, was on WG's "Failure" reading list some semesters at Bard. The syllabus for one semester of this course was published in *Review of Contemporary Fiction* 31.1 (Spring 2011): 116–17.

Auden [...] never won: actually, the concluding line of poem 30 in E. E. Cummings's *1 x 1* (1944). A decade later WG contemplated using this line as the title of his fourth novel.

To Cynthia Buchanan

[*American novelist and screenplay writer (1942–). Her quirky novel* Maiden *appeared in 1972 (William Morrow); her right arm was cropped from the author's photo on the back cover, hence WG's final sentence.*]

Piermont, NY 10968

17 August 1977

dear Cyndy,

thanks for sending the copy of *Maiden*, Sherry had already recommended it & it was on my reading list. By all means give my name to the Guggenheim people, I don't know the politics there & only wish I could feel that my word would do that much good since your credentials certainly appear to be all they could ask—though I find it hard to believe you don't know *lots* of writers of 'serious fiction'.

I want to get back out there before summer collapses & would hope to see you again (having of course by then read *Maiden*), if only to confirm your right *arm* which I can't find in that stunning dust jacket photograph, very disturbing.

best regards

W. Gaddis

Sherry: John Sherry (1923–99), novelist, poet, and playwright, and a friend since the early 1960s. WG refers to him as "The Sage of Sag Harbor" in *FHO* (75). After WG

Cynthia Buchanan,
dust-jacket photo from
Maiden (photo by
Norman Mosallem)

died, Sherry wrote "In Recognition: Remembering William Gaddis," *Hamptons Country*, June 1999, 76–80; online at www.nyx.net/~awestrop/gaddis/sherry.htm.

***

To John and Pauline Napper

Piermont NY 10968

24 August 1977

Dear John & Pauline,

Thanks for your note & I too should have written sooner but have been having a rather low time since I saw you last: could you believe that that evening we came to your show & went on to take Judith to the airport, that I did not see her again till about 3 weeks ago. She was in Key West, trying to sort out what she wants (this 'freedom' women that age are into these days), I had no idea of a separation till it prolonged itself to almost 5 months of straight hell at this end. She's been back staying with her mother across the river, we've had a few agonized conversations & she's going back to K.W. tomorrow to, again, try to figure out what she wants, I'd hoped we could pull it together but now have a good deal less of hope than a few weeks ago but know I cannot go on living this dangling drinking life too much longer. [...]

Sorry to load the above on you & wish to heaven I had brighter news, my God will the day ever come! I will be teaching 2 days a week at Bard College again this fall trying to get a little out of debt & my damned teeth fixed— things you know all about at first hand but be glad you don't know everything about life at first hand that I do. Sorry this is so abrupt but I'm leaving in a few minutes for a few days & wanted to get this off to you,

Willie

To David Madden

[*American novelist and critic (1933–), for decades a professor at Louisiana State University. Madden wrote one of the earliest appreciations of* R *(in* Rediscoveries, *1971), and in September 1977 sent WG a draft of an essay later published in the reference book* American Novelists since World War II *(Gale Research, 1978, 2:162–70). Earlier Madden had sent WG a copy of his critically acclaimed novel* Bijou *(1974).*]

Piermont
16 September 1977

Dear David Madden.

I did get your novel *Bijou* & am sorry to have waited for the provocation of this last mailing to write & thank you for sending it. I've put off everything till after Labor Day & now everything is here including pulling myself together to teach at Bard again this fall, so between reading for that I've taken quick looks into your book & of course am caught by its nowhere-but-America theme (if that is I've grasped it in such glimpses) & look forward to reading it through.

I had no idea the piece for this Gale publication would be so extensive. Beyond any writer's natural thin-skinnedness, I don't see anything I'd call distortions (having, indeed, survived John Gardner's sloppily confused & error-ridden tendentious review in the *NY Review of Books*), & while the following looks long and carping I stress only that all the below are simply for your consideration (though a few are fact changes) to include or not as you see fit, despite the peremptory style:

[*Some two dozen comments keyed to Madden's page numbers follow, most minor ("for '1952' read '1951'"), but a few are worth reproducing, beginning with a query regarding Madden's interpretation of Wyatt's activities at the end of* R.]

• (note: is he 'restoring' or simply scraping paintings down to the canvas, tabula rasa, for a fresh start)

• for 'His mother sleeps all the time' read 'His mother, who is a nurse, comes and goes and sleeps at odd times' or some such. (note: this is an important point, that in any real terms J R has no family, in effect (& in contrast to Bast) no past: he is all present, the moment. As you note later (p. 23), The surface is all.)

• (note: this is one of those difficult instances of the writer's intentions vs. the reader's impression, the sort that provokes some writers to send indignant letters ('May I be permitted to point out to your reviewer that on page 000 &c) to book reviews, as I have always resisted doing. The reader, even George Steiner in the *New Yorker* review, is welcome to his impression however distorted it pleases him to make it; & as I think even Wyatt may have said somewhere there's no way to follow one's work around saying 'but this is what I meant...' Either the work says it or it doesn't.

So in this case, as an obviously careful & sympathetic reader your impression may well reflect my failure to make a point clearly, or rather my tendency to make it obliquely; but in Bast's defense, after his garbled realization (p. 687) that he doesn't 'have to' write music (as a burden carried from the past), his ambitions have diminished through the book from his initial opera through cantata, suite, to at last the piece for unaccompanied cello (p. 675) which he desperately rescues from the wastebasket as he leaves the hospital (p. 718) as signifying his realization that if he is going to fail it will be with his own work not that of others, if there is damage it will be his own.

Thus Bast's outcry at the end (p. 725) to Eigen, seeking this same unfinished score in the trash heap of unfinished & never-to-be-finished work of Eigen's/Gibbs'/Schramm's generation, consigns all their unrealised ambitions to trash for the very fact of being unrealized, the direction his own ambitions have been headed & from which he is now desperately intent on rescuing them (not, in fact, unlike Wyatt's fresh start at the end of *The Recognitions*, having been through the crucible.)

• (note: as a matter of possible interest you may have remarked & dismissed: this 'who uses whom' thesis is pervasive in *J R* & obsessional in *The Recognitions* where Wyatt, as the flawed creative force (as reduced as Bast) is the missing part others seek to use, from Valentine to Sinisterra at the end.)

I must say I'm impressed by the Bibliography you've assembled, may be missing some minor items but has some I didn't know of. [...] I hope all the foregoing doesn't sound too carping, I don't mean to contest your interpretation & as I say you are certainly free to make what use what you want of it;

which is to say that I do greatly appreciate the work & care you've put into it, if only it will enable me to refer people who write me for such information to it without having to rehearse the whole thing each time myself. Is there some definite date for publication?

Thanks again for letting me see it,

all best regards,
William Gaddis

'who uses whom': a question posed by Vladimir Lenin and quoted both in *J R* (486) and in WG's Saul Bellow review (*RSP* 74).

To John Napper

Piermont
13 October 1977

Dear John.

I know how much time & thought & feeling went into your letter & to say I appreciate it is thin stuff—in fact if there is one real revelation & awfully good thing that's got to me in this entire mess it's been the marvelous importance of friends, in which I'm terribly fortunate—I don't mean simply as people to deluge with one's troubles, but some closer look at what friendship's all about & which may, in the last analysis (which one thinks about these autumn days), be the only thing in this turbulent world worth the having. In fact Judith's been away for so damned long by this time (since the end of February) that she's rapidly becoming rather an idea than a person. Still a terribly quiet house & somehow a chilly one, wash out one's shirts, cook for 1, nobody to share the small great things of life with like the turning of the leaves, nobody but the fool cat stamping about & shouting for his supper while the porch steps collapse & I add that project to my list of things undone, invitations to stylish openings unattended in favour of sitting here with a glass of whisky & wishing I could write a maudlin popular song (viz. one current: 'The windows of the world are covered with rain . . .'), you see what I mean. But frankly there is also a modicum of comfort in the sense of one less person to disappoint, a personal extension of the collapse of the Protestant Ethic which I suppose is my eventual obsession.

And so nothing at all in your letter looking sympathetically at these girls' & women's plight annoys me or upsets me, I understand it & know it's all true, that one 'can't stand still & protected behind someone else', that 'love must be free from dependence' &c &c, & that in essence it's as difficult if not more so for them (Judith) as for us (me) to be participants in this historic watershed between the madness of the Judeo-Christian oppression & what's ever ahead, where surely the Buddhist approach you note must have a place if we are to survive at all.

And yet. And yet. All the interlaced guilt in the P.E. notwithstanding these concepts of *personal* responsibility that come down with it, mangled as they have become, are a central fact I cannot escape (unless of course, op. cit., some one else's action gives me 'one less person to disappoint'). There's Matthew for instance, he's come up with some bad numbers but got through them & right now is working a 9 hour day in a Boston restaurant & taking 2 evening classes at Harvard, & even though I think it will prove too much for him to handle a great deal of what he's trying to do emerges from almost 20 years of me as his father & I can't see, or even seek, any alternative to another 3 or 4 years of tuitions though I cannot presently imagine how I can meet them. Sarah got into & did well at the excellent school & the excellent college I herded her toward over years of deplorable circumstances, now is working in a furniture store & planning a marriage in March as no nickel-&-dime affair; again I cannot imagine how I shall pay for it but the point is that it is all an

WG's carpenter gothic house in Piermont, which he had shared with Judith since 1969.

extension & an entirely logical one of her concept of my concept of her as a person. Of course it's different children & wives; but once one grants that inhowfar different is it?

Inflamed at the moment perhaps by 2 friends of 30 years, each in his 50s in a second marriage to younger women (2 small children in one case & 3 in the other) who are pulling out to 'find themselves' & honestly, both these men are attractive, generous, just so essentially hard working & decent & going through what I did 12 years ago over Sarah & Matthew but don't think I could handle it a second time at this age as they are faced with doing. I mean God damn it John did the word 'fairness' disappear from the language when John Kennedy aptly observed that 'life isn't fair': isn't it one's place here then to try to redress that unfairness insofar as one can rather than join it? join the forces of Chaos in other words?

I know it is absurd even insulting to be writing such things to you whose capacities for generosity decency &c I've known all these years beyond most, know it isn't their (Judith's) fault, know that it is a part of a major historical readjustment for which no single victim or knife-wielder can be blamed, 'blame' itself having gone out the window with the bath water. But with it I've got to say sympathy too. Notice of course that my 'responsibility' references to Sarah & Matthew above both take the shape of money; but I know & you know, perhaps more forcefully here than in England but really throughout the West, that this in these situations & those that follow is the prevailing, recurring, constant reality; that at our ages it means weariness, debt & starting again, & being plainly expected on all hands to start again, to follow through on the responsibilities one has in all good faith taken upon one's self. So frankly John I'm a bit sick & tired of people stepping out to 'find themselves' coming up at last with too often, in Cyril Connolly's exquisitely harsh phrase, 'a cheap sentimental humanism at someone else's expense'.

Extreme cases, extreme judgments (another hand-me-down from the Judeo-Christian mess), I still feel strongly about it all though most of the agony of my situation with Judith is exhausted, she writes that she feels she can't come back till she can 'be very sure she can return my love & give me all the things I want & need & deserve &c &c', each of us fearful of letting the other down which is finally pretty ridiculous & the last roe of shad, as my mother used to say, regarding the Protestant Ethic. At this point I can see it going either way right to the grave, the real problems here—& those which brought all the foregoing to a head I think—being my anxiety-ridden outlook for any income whatever after this teaching stint ends at Christmas approximately; & really worse that I have no work of my own & haven't for a year so the 4th or 5th whisky doesn't get that down since it's not there, simply not one damned idea after the terminal obsession of *J R* that holds enough interest, enough passion, for me to sit down to it with any sense of sustaining these things for long enough to complete it, to resolve it. Though perhaps looking back up the lines of words I've dumped upon you here there may be something, a latter-day American version of Waugh's *Handful of Dust* perhaps which I've always admired & may now be mean enough to try to write.

Thanks for your letter, and again for your efforts on Matthew's behalf. As Graham Greene said, It's a battlefield. But not Conrad's 'The horror. The horror…' Not yet,

> with love to you both,
> Willie

'The windows [...] with rain': a Burt Bacharach/Hal David song, first recorded by Dionne Warwick in 1967 and by many others thereafter.

Connolly's exquisitely harsh phrase: see note to 28 April 1948.

Waugh's *Handful of Dust*: 1934 novel about the breakdown of the marriage between Brenda and Tony Last, the latter concerned with maintaining Hetton Abbey, an example of Victorian Gothic. This is the earliest reference to what would become *Carpenter's Gothic*.

It's a battlefield: title of an early novel (1934) by the British writer.

'The horror. The horror': Kurtz's dying words in Joseph Conrad's *Heart of Darkness* (1902).

To John Napper

> Piermont
> 17 January 78

Dear John.

[...] Otherwise—the now mountainous otherwise—bad news seems simply to dwindle into worse. Judith is firmly bent on getting out, but not empty-handed; is, in fact, right now upstairs packing up bits & pieces of heaven knows what 10 years accumulated, still seems to have some notion of a 'separation' rather than a 'divorce' though I can't put in another year of this sort of life & so everything—as everything must in a property-oriented capitalistic culture—seems coming down to property settlement which promises to leave me with even less than I thought I had. I'd hoped I could simply unload the Fire Isld house, take the money & pay off some of the worse debts & make a fresh start but of course it is suddenly not that simple at all &, on the other hand, totally time consuming for all its utterly unproductive aspects so needless to say not word 1 of anything written, let alone another 'novel', or obviously any income at all. I suppose it's simply got to go its course here & must come out one way or another in a matter of weeks.

I do wish I had something more resembling cheer to offer, of course it is dead of winter (my neighbor's ice-covered tree just crashed through my terrace fence out here but I believe his insurance company doesn't countenance 'acts of God'—Christ, where will He strike next?), a storm just taking shape outside now & I'm sure the stars are in their most vengeful configuration. [...]

                                                      Willie

To Sarah Gaddis

                                        Piermont
                                        31 January 78
Dear Sarah.
    Well I just have to say after reading your letter that your generation is the one with its head screwed on & mine is not. [...]
    I liked very much your line you tossed off (meaning as something you really simply *know*, rather than a bright revelation) that 'praise does nothing after a while except generate frustration'. So you know I'm not just being false-modest cynical when all I really feel is frustration when I read in a piece on Mailer in the *Partisan Review* (v. highbrow intellectual mag): "For all his (Mailer's) bravura so far he has become our main man of letters. But he is not the first novelist of his generation. That title belongs to William Gaddis; Joseph Heller is a contender, and Ralph Ellison has been a promising challenger for twenty years. These men do not write novels in a couple of months, or even a couple of years..."
    But maybe I'd *better* sit down & try to write a novel in a couple of years. Just once, as I keep saying, once I get the fragments of "real life" reassembled. I quoted to Matthew something that Douglas Wood said once (in fact it was during the agonies of your mother's & my separation involving you both) & Douglas said "Did you think it was going to be easy?" Meaning life; & I had to admit that yes, I probably had. Progressing now, 12 years later, to John Sherry's rather more wry comment on each new catastrophe, "Life never lets you down." A sense of humour is, as I'm also sure I've said a thousand times, really a sense of proportion. [...]

                                        love always & best to Peter,
                                        Papa

---

piece on Mailer: George Stade's "Mailer and Miller," *Partisan Review* 44.4 (October 1977): 616–24 (WG quotes from p. 623). Stade had reviewed *J R* for the *New York Times Book Review*.

To Cynthia Buchanan

Piermont NY 10968

7 February 1978

Dear Cyndy,

What I loved about your long letter is its sheer energy & excitement with what you're doing & trying to do—what *we're* trying to do—in this absurd ego pastime we've chosen & even still appear to expect to make a decent living at, it's an excitement I've just started to try very hard to recover & I wish to heaven you were here today & I could actually again see & hear that intensity your letter brings to such life in an empty house in a blizzard with only the damned silent cat's illiterate gaze for encouragement.

I should say at the outset what I should really have said back when you mentioned that you planned to read *J R* over Christmas; but was pleased enough & flattered as I simply didn't think the next step, which is that I think it's really not a novel for anyone to read who's closely involved with writing one, as I suppose can be said of any book with an extreme style which *J R* has to a greater extent than I really realized when writing it, just thought: set myself a problem & see whether I can solve it (the only way I could sustain my own interest in it long enough to finish it), & the devil take the hindmost. But surely it makes sense too that in creating & pursuing & living day & night with characters of one's own, the last thing one needs (or should need?) is a raft of them dumped in one's lap by someone else in a style either so impressive (Didion) it invites frustration, or so miserable (J Suzanne &c) it excites envious ($) contempt, none of which helps when one sits down to the blank page in the morning.

I've got to say I think it's a shame you came out only $1500 ahead in the move to Knopf, I encouraged it & of course the reason I did so was I just assumed that the money would be a really substantial rise, so I do hope at the least that that's the case when you do turn it in. Aside from that—the $ I mean—I don't think you should let it get to you when a publisher presses you for the finished work. It's finished when you're finished with it & if he can't wait, with as good an agent as yours [Lynn Nesbit] there are always other houses, each move assuming you've got more of it done so there may be more money which, as we know, may be all you'll ever see. I don't mean you specifically, this bloody problem of high praise on the one hand & wanting really, aside from the royalties if one can ever honestly make that aside, 'to reach more people', is the real one. When *J R* won the National Book Award my son said, —Well you know Papa, what the NBA means to most people in America is the National Basketball Association . . . & how right he was. It was even said that the NBA could give the book an elitist seal of approval that would keep the 'common reader' away in droves & Christ, how *J R* cries out to be heard by the mob, not just doctoral students. Well hell, it's an old complaint isn't it. After all it did get me a trip through the Far East (& even recent mention in the *Partisan Review* as 'the first novelist of his generation') so I guess I am like the barmaid's view of the man who wouldn't have it with the mouse & wouldn't have it without the mouse.

About ready here to end up like Edw. MacDowell himself, sitting on the floor & cutting out paper dolls—but then that's why his widow set your refuge up isn't it, after nursing the results of the way America treats its artists. (And Sweet Briar, heavens! my mother's college, what's it come to . . . ?) Problem here right now though is less one of art than 'reality', agonies of divorce emptying the house (though after a year's separation for practice) & however unique & all-absorbing to one's self less news than a wedding to anyone else & God knows let's not have another novel about that! An editor I once knew said that any book worth reading had been written out of indignation; & while that's rather too sweeping (think of how many bad ones for the same reason) it does have an appeal that—from the sound of your letter—should hurl you right back to the typewriter. A difficulty I suppose with a bit more age & a bit more experience is summoning that indignation to surface yet once more & for long enough to sustain a fiction to embrace it, so the problem's to get one's head together & onto what will 'reach more people' now the vein of sex has been so exhaustively (& exhaustedly) mined, politics done in by ex-politicos cashing in from prisons, the evangelistics (& God go with them) (& stay) done up long since & once for all by *Elmer Gantry* & even death itself yielding right & left, madness & suicide to a fare-thee-well. What remains? Obscenity had for centuries been the dependable component (for 'reaching more people') in our Protestant Ethic but now that it's been robbed of sexual content by the beaver-shots littering every news stand where does it turn? Maybe *J R* was right. From the present lumber room jammed with nothing but debt, real estate, lawyers, stock certificates, gas bills—maybe money really is the last obscenity & one we're so used to handling it never occurs to us to wash, again v. *J R* but perhaps (for 'reaching more people') offered at somewhat less length & complexity than that dear boy felt pressed to carry it.

Forgive the lecture, I am just continuing to try to sort out my mind & here at your expense. I hope you can resist letting the pressures of time which you seem to feel so strongly drive the real pressures of what you are trying to do & think worth doing up the wall. Thanks again for your letter & kind wishes especially appreciated right now; I'd already enjoyed you on John Wayne in *Cornell Review*, a really stellar issue: you, Gass, & Joy Williams who I think is awfully good.

My mailbox just blew away. I hope that is not a portent.

more affection,

W. G.

---

trip through the Far East: in 1976; see 5 March 1984.

man who wouldn't have it with the mouse: joke about a man who finds a mouse floating in his beer, which he won't drink even after it's been removed. Jack Gibbs uses the line in *J R* (404).

Edw. MacDowell: this detail of the final years of the American composer (1860–1908) is mentioned in *J R* (43, 225). His widow founded the MacDowell Colony for artists, where Buchanan was staying at the time.

Sweet Briar: a women's college in Sweet Briar, Virginia.

Elmer Gantry: Sinclair Lewis's 1927 novel about a Midwestern evangelist; nevertheless, evangelism plays a part in WG's *CG*.

Cornell Review: issue 2 (Fall 1977) of this short-lived journal includes Buchanan's essay on myths of the Old West, "Oh, Won't You Come Home, John Wayne?" (pp. 91–111) along with an essay by Gass and a story by Williams.

To Judith Gaddis

Piermont

Sunday 5 March [1978]

Dear Judith,

Freddie trudging up the hill in a snowstorm to leave in the box (which has blown down) your letter of kind endearments among the bills & a preliminary copy of settlement from Weinstock which he'd sent to your lawyer: & they tell me that irony is outmoded in fiction. But I was terribly relieved from your letter that you are getting into better shape than when you left here, I'd called your mother in fact a week or so ago to find out since I'd never really known whether you'd driven down with her or flown or gone on to KW [Key West] or what.

No nothing 'promising' has occurred here since you left. I finally put the stairs back together realizing I badly needed just to do something even if only that, painted the panels dark green, mothballed the cubby closet, took laundry & your things to the Thrift Shop. A call from Berkeley asking me out there for a week in June but that is June & this is barely March. I finally gave in to a fellow who'd been calling me from the *Times* Op-ed page to write something & called it in but like everything I do it was overlength & if they do want it I don't know if it's even worth cutting, done again like the stairs just for something to do certainly not the money: $150 which doesn't even approach the gas bill. I never heard anything more on that Ohio film project or from a couple of people I'd hoped would come through, am now working on a switch which if it works out would at least get me out of this immediate hole I'm in that's just got deeper every day, though of course it will get me into another one.

Sounds like all the negative thinking you fled here & stacking it up I guess one could hardly blame you. But right now it's just quite difficult to grasp long-term alternatives with the relentless distraction of these immediate pressures dictating the good chance of using poor judgment, as this switch I'm trying to work out may prove to have been. All this because it finally got through my head what a real watershed between past & future this is: that if I can just surface from this current mess, get up Matthew's tuition & get Sarah through her Event [wedding] just 3 weeks hence that abruptly & all at once, with you gone & Sarah under new management & Matthew well on his way, for the first time in 22 years I shall have no one for whom I'm directly responsible. Or even to. That then once I sit down & try to sort out how to pay off the banks & you & the dentist & find out whether these pains are kidneys or liver or both it's all totally altered; as I say it took me a while to grasp but considering the proportions of it I can't be surprised since those ties & responsibilities have been the day & night fabric of my entire adult life, & here's the glimpse that comes as a man grows older of entire freedom on the one hand & not being needed anymore on the other, what life eventually appears to be all about, & that it's something to grasp & act on rather than letting it creep up. All this I suppose too why I was so relieved from your letter that you're getting health & housing & work together down there because oddly from the habit & guilt of a decade even though you walked out on me the marriage the house a year ago I was still ridden with the sense that somehow it was I who had abandoned you. I know a lot of this you'd been trying one way & another to tell me but in the recent agonies & monstrous circumstances it's taken me this long to put the pieces together, in ways Matthew and Sarah have been trying to tell me the same thing I think & maybe getting the elements of the disturbance together are a first step to resolving it. [...]

W.

Times Op-ed page: "In the Zone" appeared on March 13, p. 21 (*RSP* 33–37).

as a man grows older: since WG admired Italo Svevo's *Confessions of Zeno* (see note to 14 May 1981), this may be an allusion to the Italian novelist's *As a Man Grows Older* (1898).

To Cynthia Buchanan

Piermont, NY 10968
2 April 1978

Dear Cyndy,

Well I read the Guggenheim list in the morning's paper & was terribly disappointed—though certainly far less than you—at not seeing your name there, kept looking back at the B's as though to force it into existence. Cold comfort I know, but I found only one novelist at all—do they think it is an outmoded form? too chancy? Does Ned Rorem really need money? Do we really need another critical biography of Mozart? The only 2 people I know on the list both live down the way here in Sneedon's Landing, hardly a ghetto area. Well again, these lists never make much sense unless one's own name appears in them but I am sorry really that yours didn't. [...]

What a hell of a winter this one has been & how enchanting that first warm day. Sum total nothing, though I think a glimpse of returning sanity. Briefly I thought I was escaping Knopf, where I've shown nothing (nothing, dear, to show), but my refuge fell through just, of course, as a hungry young type on the coast wrote for possibly optioning *J R* for a (television I think) movie, all that beginning to look quite sketchy just, of course, as a call came from someone in London named Jack Gold, sounds like a bookie but checked out he really is a producer so we're trying to sort that number out now, small enough option money but at least money, and perhaps even something 'real' happening at last. That's been the damned trouble, fiction being crowded out here by real-life dramatics while I pursue the cat asking What *is* worth writing a novel about these days? Even money has paled (in proportion I suppose as its intense demands have increased). So I went up to Boston & got my daughter married, all aglitter & now she's under new management my son's coming through this week on his way, I understand, to California with a companion named Carol whom I haven't met. As Sherry says, Life never lets you down. Otherwise no plans but a week at Berkley in late June where they asked me for one of these workshops you loathe, as I may have mentioned in an earlier letter, but there's no way I won't need the money by then & a chance to see why the other half lives.

Cyndy don't take time out to answer this, just a word to cheer you on as the Guggenheims eat sour grapes but please do be in touch with me as your next step takes shape.

great affection always
Willie Gaddis

Ned Rorem: American composer and diarist (1923–).

Jack Gold: British movie producer (1930–2015). There is a Mister Gold involved in a scam against Elizabeth Booth in *CG*, perhaps a meaningless coincidence, perhaps not, for no movie version of *J R* ever materialized.

see why the other half lives: a sardonic witticism uttered by a character in *R* (753).

To Ólafur Gunnarsson

[*The Icelandic novelist sent him a copy of his first novel,* Milljón prósent menn, *translated thirty years later by David McDuff as* Million Percent Men.]

Piermont, NY 10968
3 April 1978

Dear Olafur,

I enjoyed reading the pages from your new book, many thanks for sending them. It confirms what you said about *J R* not being uniquely American: I guess it is the same everywhere, people stuffing their bellies and their pockets, every man for himself. I wish the market for good fiction were better here, but it seems simply to be going the opposite direction, very much affected by television I'm afraid which is not a 'communication' medium but an advertising medium and as such aimed at the lowest common denominator in the consumer audience. I don't know what the answer is, but that writing what one thinks is worth writing is a rough way to try to make a living.

best regards and good luck,
William Gaddis

To John and Pauline Napper

Piermont NY 10968
10 April 1978

Dear John and Pauline.

Well! I had a call from Sarah from Boston yesterday, she had just got back & could not say enough for you both, your friends, England, castles—all seems to have been one of the best experiences of her entire life to now & it all pleases me more really than anything I can think of: essentially that she does have this effervescence, this capacity of excitement for life which your hospitality kindled to its height, & at my parental remove I am eternally grateful goes without saying.

Otherwise…well, otherwise. Your generous concern & thoughts for me & the cottage there (all which Sarah reviewed in rapturous terms) as the likeliest place to start, though this will not be a review of emotional agonies: as you know, there is nothing like financial collapse to mitigate dental, marital, even renal (associated with lower back pains) difficulties. Not collapse really but massive readjustment, problem that that takes time & in the US as nowhere time *is* money (ie interest). The essential readjustment being the realization that abruptly & all at once—as I may even have written you before—the coalescence of Judith gone, Sarah married, & Matthew well on his own way, it looks for the first time in my adult life that I'm not directly responsible for, or to anyone. [...]

Point is I've got rid of most of the despair & am now just desperate: you understand the distinction. Finally beyond the angers, resentments, jealousies &c involved with Judith's departure, beyond either wanting her back or not wanting her back & finally just concerned for her wellbeing with or without me; also finally able to grasp that what she is trying to do does take a good deal of courage & I know she is having a difficult time both for work & supporting herself, & loneliness, & coming to terms with the real consequences of her move.

The 'desperate', in sum, meaning the purely practical: debt, work, what to do about the Fire Island house, thoughts of renting out this Piermont house for a while &c & the 'work' being at the heart of things & most problematical. I suppose it has a lot to do with creative lag, the attempt to rekindle one's fires after the dampened blaze of *J R* but I've simply not yet got any grasp of a central idea for another book of the obsessive proportions that kept both other books going & made all other considerations secondary. In large part of course it's that all those considerations—Judith, wedding, debt, unrealized expectations for work—have crowded to the front for this past year & I can't really think clearly enough to sit down to the selfish occupation of writing until they are fairly resolved, one or another of them occupying every waking moment. (The paradox, the essential absurdity being of course that the most pressing of them, debt, could be resolved if I simply would sit down & really get another novel going. But perhaps you can understand it is not simply a matter of volition.)

In other words, & to get back to your cottage where all this took off from, it would be the *ideal* if 1) I had a project in hand with a life of its own begun; & 2) if I had resolved these practical issues of debt, rentals, furniture &c &c. The one 'real' item on the horizon is a week in late June I will go to California myself for one of these writing 'workshops', not something I at all want to do but the $1500 'honorarium' is not to be gainsaid, God knows, also the brief enough change of vista. And again, even though Judith has encouraged me to feel free, do anything & anywhere I wish, it is terribly difficult still to break a 10-year habit of feeling responsible for someone especially feeling that things are not going very well for her. I know that my deciding the divorce step hit her quite hard but after her having been away a full year, & then wanting only a property settlement & indefinite separation agreement, moving directly toward divorce seemed to me the only way to bring to her the reality of what she was doing.

Still I know, as reflected in your thoughtful & sensible letter of a year or so ago John, that it is something she feels she has to do in order to discover & grasp who she is; there is certainly no rancour from her side for me, quite the other way in fact; but while the thought of her becoming a casualty of our life & times in almost unbearable, it becomes at last a case of (Heraclitus?)' 'To see clearly & be able to do nothing'; & the reality seems to be in the effort not to let this spill over & paralyse the areas where one can do something, the mundane, quite un-unique world of work, property, rentals & mortgages & taxes & debt.

And so if I could grasp a little more realistically what I have just written here, I would be a little further on the way to resolving things that can be resolved & which only I can resolve. That at any rate is the direction I am trying. [...]

> love & best wishes again,
> Willie

$1500 'honorarium': $6000 today.

Heraclitus [...] do nothing: not from the Greek philosopher but from the *Histories* of Herodotus, in which a resigned Persian states on the eve of battle, "There's no more terrible pain a man can endure than to see clearly and be able to do nothing" (9.16). His observation is one of Jack Gibbs's handwritten quotations on p. 486 of *JR*.

To David Markson

> Piermont
> 17 April 1978

Dear David,

Thanks for having your *Lowry* sent to me, I can't say I've read it or even will in the immediate future because obviously I've got to sit down & face the long postponed reading of Lowry's book itself first. (From a glance though, if representative your approach to investigations by others (p. 216 §3) seems to me exemplary.) Anyhow Times Books does appear to have given you the attractive format & jacket that makes it look like it will be around for a while. Which is all we can ever ask (the rest being, as Eliot remarks, 'not our business').

> good luck with it,
> W. Gaddis

your *Lowry: Malcolm Lowry's Volcano: Myth, Symbol, Meaning* (New York: Times Books, 1978).

p. 216: perhaps WG means the remark: "no individual commentator is ever going to produce a 'definitive' explication of *Under the Volcano* because the depths and echoes in the book would appear almost *infinite*."

'not our business': from "East Coker," part 5.

To Johan Thielemans

Piermont, N.Y. 10968
18 April 1978

Dear Johan Thielemans.

Thanks for your letter & for sending me your piece from *TREMA*. All your point of entropy is certainly well taken & I wonder if you have ever read Norbert Wiener's book *The Human Use of Human Beings* (viz '... it is possible to interpret the information carried by a message as essentially the negative of its entropy, and the negative logarithm of its probability. That is, the more probable the message, the less information it gives ... &c'). Obviously a book that 'reached me'.

But I must confess what pleased me most was your taking John Gardner to task, his review of *J R* was I think the only one that thoroughly irritated me, following its smug opening pronouncement on how easy the book was to read with error after error on the text, making clear that perhaps the book is a bit difficult to read for someone with his sloppy approach piling up on one of his lofty pronunciamentos (though I think his yappings about Art are not taken terribly seriously here—which of course makes him yap louder—& that people are getting rather weary of hearing it: see attached clipping). You did at any rate nail it down neatly.

I am only now trying to get in the frame of mind to start another book, meanwhile a possibility that *J R* may be made into a film, which I frankly see rather less in terms of artistic than financial deliverance, might eventually even enable me to get to Europe again after these many years.

with best regards
William Gaddis

TREMA : "Gaddis and the Novel of Entropy," *TREMA* [Travaux et Recherches sur le Monde Anglophone] 2 (1977): 97–107.

Wiener's book: published in 1950; WG quotes from the first chapter.

attached clipping: probably a negative review of Gardner's book *On Moral Fiction*, which appeared in 1978.

To Ólafur Gunnarsson

Piermont
2 May 1978

Dear Olafur,

Your generosity seems only exceeded by your enthusiasm; my indecision only by my general tendency to anxiety (perhaps should be translated as 'laziness': have you ever read perhaps the best novel in any language, *Oblomov*, by Goncharov?).

At any rate, your offer to send an air ticket forthwith is both immensely generous & something I cannot reward at this moment. I have got some matters here that are just taking day after damned day to clear up, & a summer house I have got to get ready to lease to tenants. The only thing that could change things abruptly would emerge from a British film producer who is interested in optioning rights to *J R* (that is *one* of the things I'm trying to get cleared up), of course if *he* offered to pay my trip across the sea I would go immediately—with a stop coming or going at Reykjavík of course.

Otherwise I have a hope in midwinter of visiting friends in England & if I can manage to work that out would let you know, assuming that Iceland is as uninhabitable as everywhere else that time of year, the schnapps notwithstanding. Meanwhile I hope your book has turned out as fine as your children— I do really look forward eventually to seeing it all & will stay in touch.

all best regards
W. Gaddis

To George Hegarty

[*A student at Drake University who sent WG his dissertation "Gaddis's* Recognitions: *The Major Theme."*]

Piermont, NY 10968
18 September 1978

Dear George Hegarty.

I feel badly being so late thanking you or in fact even acknowledging your kindness sending me your dissertation, especially so of course in the light of your generous estimate of *The Recognitions* & your grasp of its basic premises; that it is (p.12) essentially positive; that it is (39) 'by its very nature imperfect' & in fact in itself (13) a kind of forgery, this last a treat of sorts after being beaten relentlessly over the head with Th. Mann's *Dr Faustus* in a very erudite dissertation from the Univ. of Colorado. I was also intrigued in your bibliography to learn of a number of critical pieces on the book which I didn't know of.

All aside from the book's major themes which, as I say, I do think you explore & present very clearly & well, I am always beguiled when I read these criticisms & dissertations (yours now about the 5th of the latter that I've seen) by points & parallels I've made quite unawares so far as I can recall—the ramifications (85) of 'Irish thorn-proof', of (95) the Narcissus Festival, &c—all of which of course delight me & for which I'm quite ready to seize full credit. (On the other hand one can be equally & perhaps less happily disconcerted when such exegeses take the opposite turn as I recall feeling they did in the B Benstock piece years ago which you cite, aside from its major theme (Joyce-pilfering) such supportive items as handkerchief-covered mirrors which I took, not from *Ulysses* which I hadn't (haven't) read but an experience of my own in a Panama hotel room.) But I suppose bemused is a better word (than beguiled) since chasing after & readjusting images ('That is not what I meant at all . . .') these days is even more futile a notion than it was back on page 152 of *The Recognitions*. But still . . .

Whether the following will serve any purpose but your own interest I don't know & certainly, in the light of your dissertation's overall accomplishment, these items are trivial enough but I pass them on anyhow: Page 12 contemptible I think you mean contemptuous? Page 50 I think Agnes D was a literary agent not a critic. Page 60 it is before magic despaired not disappeared, as page 63 it is Puritan indignance not indulgence. Though perhaps not quite clear in the book (p. 30), Wyatt confronts a Deadly Sin on the Bosch table where he eats, not (your p. 65) on a dish. Then curiously, & reflecting I suppose the innocence (to say nothing of 'banned in Boston' threats) of those days in the '50s, I think all the distinguished novelist was doing (p 85) 'meditatively engrossed in the landscape' was having a pee; but your reading is somehow marvelously more pertinent to his self-absorbed isolation from the real experience at any level so I don't mind at all letting it stand (& perhaps God knows in some forgotten future saying —Of course that's what I meant . . .)

Finally & again (perhaps deliberately) obscure the Willie references (pp. 475–8) you quote (pp 45,6): all I meant attributable to him was as 1 of 'the 2 young men', ie p 475 from Philogyny? through become a misologist? Then 477, lines 9 through 12 & 15–18; & lastly p. 478 lines 27–32. (I can't recall offhand who the 'haggard boy' was in the book (though I do in 'real life').)

Many thanks again for troubling to send me the dissertation.

Yours,
William Gaddis

dissertation from the Univ. of Colorado: Robert Charles Brownson's "Techniques of
  Reference, Allusion, and Quotation in Thomas Mann's *Doktor Faustus* and William
  Gaddis's *The Recognitions*" (1976).
page 152 of *The Recognitions*: "Images surround us; cavorting broadcast in the minds of
  others, we wear the motley tailored by their bad digestions, the shame and failure,
  plague pandemics and private indecencies, unpaid bills, and animal ecstasies remembered in hospital beds, our worst deeds and best intentions will not stay still, scolding, mocking, or merely chattering they assail each other, shocked at recognition."

To Elaine Markson

[*David Markson's wife and a successful literary agent (1930–2018). In 1978 she published
a novel entitled* Home Again, Home Again *(Morrow), and invited WG to her publication party.*]

Piermont, NY
22 Sept. 1978

Dear Elaine,

 I am teaching up at Bard College this fall—a class Tuesday afternoon &
another Wednesday morning—& of course your party is *Tuesday* eve, when
I stay over up there—that seems the way life goes these days & I am sorry to
miss this occasion to wish you well & good luck with your book, if there is
such a thing any more (or in fact if there was ever); as well as the chance to
thank you for your time & efforts on behalf of the various hopefuls I send in
your direction. But I *do* mean the "good luck".

best wishes,
Willie Gaddis

To Stanley Elkin

[*Critically acclaimed novelist (1930–95) and a professor of English at Washington University in Saint Louis. He wrote to invite WG to teach there for three weeks.*]

Piermont, NY 10968
7 October 1978

Dear Stanley Elkin,

 I just got your letter forwarded & was most agreeably impressed by its
proposal. Bill Gass some months ago had mentioned the possibility to me as
just that & without going into terms which sound, as you present them, extremely inviting & I want & am glad to be able to accept.

My spring schedule is still in balance but at the moment the February turn looks preferable, perhaps if only because one would always rather be any elsewhere in February. As for obligations I would expect to do all I could along student lines but am not much for readings & have never in fact given one; as for talks I was obliged to clarify some of my prejudices for the Japan tour a couple of years ago & know it's high time I got them together & trust we can sort that one out.

Beyond the above but no less persuasive, I must add that I've admired your ear (now there's a line from one writer to another, recalls the young man from Devizes) since —this is Dick 'Pepsodent' Gibson, I'm very happy to be here in Minneapolis tonight...& very much look forward to meeting you & to seeing Bill Gass again, please give him my best regards & let me know details that need attention as they occur.

thanks again for your letter & invitation,

William Gaddis

---

young man from Devizes: from a limerick: "There was a young man of Devizes / Whose balls were of different sizes. / One was so small / It was nothing at all; / The other took numerous prizes."

Dick 'Pepsodent' Gibson: this section of Elkin's *The Dick Gibson Show* (1971) appeared in the same issue of the *Dutton Review* that featured the opening section of *J R*.

To Sarah Gaddis

Piermont

14 October 78

Dear Sarah,

[...] I know your prospects must be mid-air pending Peter's liberation from the academics & the direction next year takes, seems the case with us all & I'm finding it both somewhat alarming & exhilirating too not knowing what's next. Speaking of Academia, a really confused land. Bennington you recall months ago sounding quite excited at the possibility of my coming up there; a week, a month, 2, I hear nothing; finally they call, would like me there the bulk of the week (March–June) with a heavier course load than I have now & at substantially less money. Elegant, expensive Bennington & doesn't even get near little Bard's terms. So I said I'd think about it & am going around the house muttering when the mail brings a letter from Washington Univ in St Louis (where Bill Gass is), asking me out for 3 weeks either Feb or April at half the fee Bennington offers for a full term, & with far lighter duties mainly consorting with graduate students as much or little as I like plus a talk or 2, furnished apartment office & (new) typewriter. Plus, the letter itself terribly hoping I'll accept was from a writer named Stanley Elkin who I think is marvelous (novel called *The Dick Gibson Show*) who teaches there. So of course I accepted immediately for Feb, when one would rather be anywhere else than where one is even if it's St Louis, & partly of course for the fee & situation, but in a way mostly for the prospect of rowdy time with Elkin & Gass & I'm really looking forward to it. I think we've all 3 got similar views on what good writing's about plus highly compatible senses of humour. So for those brief 3 weeks I'll go from being Distinguished Visiting Prof at Bard to being Hurst Professor at Washington U, then the Lord knows what since being the Hadley Fellow at Bennington sounds less than heaven though if it's a question of that ~~distinction~~ money or none...well we'll see. I've also been trying to think seriously about thinking seriously about starting another book & think I may have an approach. [...]

Meanwhile Bard goes very well, better each year really as I accept that identity, my only problems being the same ones: those who write nothing, those whose names I don't yet know, added to all that the thrown together new course & its new reading list which means my reading not only the books assigned but 4 or 5 others for related material & coming in in a marvelous condition of confused overpreparedness. Compounded this week by my lightheartedly having assigned Dreiser's *An American Tragedy*, which I haven't read for 20 years & suddenly find it's 800 pages. Poor kids! Poor me! Got up this morning to page 329 & still must read, reread *Sister Carrie* & D's biography, plus a little of Zola &c....Well I asked for it. Panic every Monday evening & then roll back here Wed eve drained but pleased that it does all seem worth it to me & to them. [...]

Love to you both—Papa

Dreiser's *An American Tragedy* [...] *Sister Carrie*: published 1925 and 1900, respectively. The biography was W. A. Swanberg's *Dreiser* (Scribner's, 1965).
Zola: Émile Zola (1840–1902), French novelist and critic.

To Sarah Gaddis

Piermont
Sunday morning 3 Dec 78

Dear Sarah.

How many letters do you suppose you've had from me opening: Well, I'm finally settling down & starting to get things together...Well I was just settling down & getting things together when Mathilda the Dutchess arrived in town so for reasons of old time friendship not Art I went with her down to some confused & I thought all quite unnecessary number at the old Phoenix

Theatre, some sort of tribute to William Burroughs with readings some nonsense music & Allen Ginsberg all of it the avant-garde which is suddenly just old hat. That was Friday night, they had a big number last night scheduled to end up at Studio 54 the big disco everybody wants to go to because you can't get in, but I thought I'd had enough so skipped that, probably it all ended up with lots of artistics & Ginsberg taking off his clothes which may have been a romp 20 years ago but would hardly be an edifying sight now. Anyhow with promise of awful weather later today I'm going in to have lunch with Mathilda before she leaves for Scotland tonight, why can't people stay put?

What of course was odd was standing out in front of that theatre at 2nd Avenue & 12th street & looking up at the windows of our old apartment building & remembering, Christmases & that cage elevator & old Henry in his cap. This of course is the season for such things & for so many people a hard one to get through, rather than being able simply to look back & realize how marvelous it all was & how lucky to have it, something to do with that 'living every minute…'

I'm glad I did make the San Francisco trip but somehow it was all rather unsettling & I don't know exactly why, part to do with the sheer jamming it in between Bard classes & exhaustion of the trip itself but also with that entire week under the cloud of the Jim Jones nightmare in Guyana (his 'People's Temple' a S.F. product) & their mayor shot the day I returned: it is one of the most attractive cities I've known & everyone seems attractive & relaxed & pleasant, none of that hostility in the air one feels in New York, but still there is something unsettling about the place. Matthew as I said seems fine but to tell the truth I think I will be quite relieved when he puts the place behind him.

So since coming back I've just been trying to catch up, Bard & dentist, Bard & dentist & a piece for IBM's *Think* magazine which will thank heavens pay the dentist though apparently I've got to rewrite it because it's as usual a little too much of my density for their audience: why can't I just write simple sentences? But all of this to be over & done by December 20th; et puis? [...]

I long to see you, much love always & best to Peter,

Papa

Mathilda the Dutchess: Mathilda Campbell, Duchess of Argyll; see note to 28 November 1950.

tribute to William Burroughs: the Nova Convention; see Barry Miles's *Call Me Burroughs: A Life* (Twelve, 2014), 537–40.

2nd Avenue & 12th street: the Gaddises lived at 193 Second Avenue in 1960–61.

Jim Jones nightmare: on 18 November cult leader Jones convinced his followers to commit mass suicide in Jonestown, Guyana.

their mayor shot: Harvey Milk, an openly gay politician, was assassinated on 27 November.

a piece for IBM's *Think* magazine: entitled "Literature and Crisis," but unclear if published. The repetition of "Bard & dentist" in this sentence is *sic*.

et puis?: French, "And then?"

To William H. and Mary Gass

[*In a letter to Cynthia Buchanan (18 January 1978), WG wrote, "I'm away I believe the 4th–25 of February, then may go out for a couple of days at Notre Dame if I can figure out their invitation." He added "I saw your Lynne Nesbitt at a party & she told me Lauren Hutton likes J R immensely, cheers one up of course but I don't see any impact on reality." The famous model also liked William Burroughs.*]

Piermont NY 10968
12 March 1979

Dear Bill & Mary.

You were right in your assurances before the fact back in January: it was High Old Times & I'm only now descending to the dismal cheer of home, correspondence & preparing high-blown fictions for the IRS.

Even more, various impatient egregious elements were whetted for the spree at Notre Dame toward the logical notion of abandoning the lonely drudgery of writing for the parade circuit, fictions of 'modesty' left behind it is nice to *hear* the applause, & youth claps harder. More soberly, N.D. also offered a meeting with Larry McMurtry whose informed counsel on movieland convinced me to try to go through with the London producer prospect T shirts, comic strips, money 2 years distant & all; also informed thoughts on selling one's 'papers' which I wouldn't have anticipated, as it would never have occurred to me to put a rare book dealer & *The Last Picture Show* together in one man. (Apparently all the big MS money that was in Texas is now in Tulsa, which should tell us something.) So that, plus a nice note from Herb Yellin, may contain some hope against the daily horror from my front windows: a tarnished silver Senior Citizens' van emptying 3 of them on their feet from hot lunch & God knows what God knows where (do you hear me, diapered John Dewey on a Key West roof?).

But all this is quite beside the point of this note which is thanks first of course for all the generous academic courtesies & private hospitalities but far more importantly the spirit from which it cheers me enormously to feel they sprang & will endure.

Again, extending my own rather more constrained hospitalities if you are east & not being put up at the Plaza by your publisher (*our* publisher?), I am now offering striped bass from the Hudson laced with PCBs from General Electric far up the river, all an unpredictable schedule which could, if it fell together, even accommodate children with a cat to torment; one way or another though I do very much look forward to getting together before too long again.

with all kinds of best wishes to you both,
Willie Gaddis (Capt.)

---

spree at Notre Dame: WG participated in the Notre Dame Sophomore Literary Festival.

Larry McMurtry: novelist and rare-book dealer (1936–2021), whose novel *The Last Picture Show* (1966) was made into a successful movie (1971).

Herb Yellin: noted book collector (1935–2004) and publisher of Lord John Press, which specialized in literary limited editions. See 28 January 1985.

John Dewey on a Key West roof: the philosopher/educator spent his final days there enduring a number of ailments before dying in 1952.

To Stanley Elkin

Piermont NY 10968
12 March 1979

Dear Stanley.

Climbing down from the St Louis high followed by the savoury of Notre Dame with just time at home between courses to wash out some shirts & calm desperate Max the cat, & wade through the otherwise trash heap of mail for *The Living End*: & it certainly is!

Why do we write? out of indignation? outrage? I had thought of pursuing that theme at Notre Dame & planned to pack along Mark Twain's *Mysterious Stranger* for the purpose till I read yours & thought ah! here's the news! And only on the plane, culling for inspired passages ('He doesn't accept invitations. He doesn't go out. He stays home nights.') did it occur to me that this was hardly the forum, hardly my place to divert them from the medium to the message as it would inevitably be interpreted, & so I desisted not, I hope, from cowardice, but . . . what, delicacy? That & trying not to ride (living) coat tails, my next note on these lines to John Macrae III at Dutton explaining I don't think blurbs sell books any more than reviews do & I've never got past the feeling that so many of them are sheer self-advertisement on someone else's jacket (what keeps the Kazins of this world alive?): God knows I thought of sending Dutton something like "A delicately evocative novel which urges us to lay aside our fears and realize our true strength" but that seemed hazardous for a number of reasons, so I've retired to the notion (which I do embrace) that all that sells books, movies & similar aberrations is word-of-mouth & I've a busy one as you know; anyhow I can't believe the book won't be taken up immediately as slamming the door that Twain opened on eschatology once for all, its street wit is marvelous & its brevity admirable.

All this backing & filling scarcely seems an expression of my real & lasting thanks for all your generosity on every level while I was there, the whole thing helped to restore a feeling of having a place in this world which it seems to take no more than the publication of a book to deprive me of permanently. I noticed that you seem to get around a good deal & if anything brings you east I'd hope you would call, granted I don't lay a table in a class with Joan's but the will & the drink would be there; or even if you were just in New York itself I'd race in for a visit.

> thanks again to Joan for feeding me & carting me around & my best to you both,
> Willie Gaddis (Capt.)

The Living End: Elkin's triptych of novellas, published in 1978, having to do with the afterlife. In a letter to Judith the next day, Gaddis wrote: "Elkin moving slow with a stick for a hesitating case of multiple sclerosis is courage at its best though laced, certainly, with an acid outrage far beyond anything I've demonstrated, as his about-to-be-published book *The Living End* assails beyond Mark Twain in his darkest late years keep an eye out for it."

John Macrae III: Elkin's editor. See note to 3 August 1979.

Kazins: critic Alfred Kazin (1915–98) wrote a dismissive review of *J R* in the *New Republic,* 6 December 1975, 18–19.

"A delicately [...] strength": one of the mock blurbs that appears in *J R* (p. 515).

Joan: Elkin's wife, a painter.

To Richard Hazelton

[*American medievalist (1918–2009) and professor at Washington University who had written to WG twenty years earlier to express his admiration for R. In 1962 he had been invited by Karl Shapiro (at Jack Green's suggestion) to contribute to the special Gaddis issue of* Prairie Schooner *that failed to materialize.*]

> Piermont NY 10968
> 12 March 1979

Dear Dick,

I'm just finally getting my head together from St. Louis-followed-by-Notre Dame: it's all enough to seduce one permanently from the drudgery of the keyboard to the parade circuit, given the generosity that greeted me everywhere;

it does seem a generation since we cowered under that Arch & ate Mexican & I thank you for all of it. Including dinner with your bright girls: whatever fooleries & futilities one has committed along the way it often seems (to me, having come this far) that a great deal is redeemed if one can point to one's kids with —There at least is something I did right … Do thank them again for me.

That evening brings up another, or rather the only point left unresolved when I fled town. You recall I'd thought we were in for a 35-mile drive both ways for dinner which I looked for as a chance to get at the movies in general & your stab in particular, so failing that dialogue all you have is this mono … I don't know who isn't knowledgably down on that whole scene these days as being more & more the closed province of fewer & fewer, & breaking into it harder every day, from the packaging nightmare on the one hand to the super-budget/super profits approach on the other. Any cheerful doubts on these lines I might have had were certainly dispelled when I met & talked at some length with Larry McMurtry at Notre Dame. His prescription for a 'property' (in the fast disappearing low-budget class): 'a small flat book with a strong narrative line' as, for example, *The Last Picture Show*, though his luck in the industry since hasn't been all that great either, considering numbers of works optioned, scripts written, films unproduced.

Anyhow it seems a toss between the stranglehold of 'the industry' that gives us *Earthquake* & *Superman*, or the director with his own charisma like Altman who seems, in this last number with Paul Newman surviving the frozen wastes of the future, to have pushed his personal hand too far. And while for instance I'd had high hopes for his interest in & carrying off *J R* as I envisioned it, I think now he's not much interested in anything but what he envisions. He is I think an extreme but good example of handing any director a script telling him throughout the impressions the writer wants to create, & how to create them, rather than handing him hard characters in a 'strong narrative line' so that he can create the impressions as he envisions them & make it *his* movie: a further problem too I would think when this strong narrative line isn't very clearly evident to him right from the beginning, something *happening* rather than time taken setting up the scene & characters which I think directors consider their prerogative. So given those conditions, if they are so, plus the state of The Industry itself today, it all may just end you up writing the thing for your own delectation like the 200page 'play' I wrote 15 years ago which is still on the shelf (& which I am now seriously considering trying to turn into a 'small flat book with a strong narrative line' & let show business discover it there. ha.)

In fact once through the accumulation of items during my absence is cleared up I have got to get down to something more serious than dutifully reading the morning's *Times*; but your & the University's generous support has given me something resembling a fresh start & many thanks for all of it.

best to Fanny Hurst & to Mimi & to Alina if she drops in & to you,

W– Gaddis

Earthquake & *Superman*: big-budget films of 1974 and 1978, respectively.
Altman: Robert Altman (1925–2006), American film director. WG refers to his *Quintet* (1979).
200page 'play': *Once at Antietam*.
Fanny Hurst: American novelist (1889–1968); the Hurst Professorship for visiting writers was funded from her bequest to Washington University, which she attended. (The other names are unidentified.)

To John Napper

Piermont
19 March 1979

Dear John.

Your letter here with its 'mixed' news when I returned from what I've got to call the parade circuit: 3 weeks at Washington Univ. in St Louis as 'Visiting Hurst Professor', then a briefer stint at Notre Dame all of it not only cheerfully corrupting to the ego but paid enough to get me to summer at least. Main burden of my 'talks' to students &c seems to have been warning them off of writing if they had glimmers of any other talent or even ability; & YOU can paint! But heaven knows John, I'm hardly one to talk (unless being highly paid) & the 40 thousand words you mention is no mere bagatelle. Lord knows there are certainly times (Trollope, Ouida &c notwithstanding) when one should give one's art a rest—I haven't disturbed mine for 2 or 3 years now & am only just considering a new assault—& turning from painting to embrace even so distant a relation as writing is certainly far better than turning from writing to embrace bottles & laughing girls. Or is it.

I'm only now getting through the items correspondence &c that accumulated while I was away, toward confronting the typewriter seriously again to discover whether an idea I've been nagging at is in fact a book that 'wants' (to use Saml Butler's phrase) to be written, as it appears yours does: lovely torn-up feeling! Among my mail a note from Bard College cordially not asking me back for fall so at any moment here I'll have decks & bank accounts cleared & have again to face the threat of new fictions, all that can save me from that the chance of Jack Gold's extending a $-laden invitation to do a screenplay: after just about 1 *year* of haggling I believe we have got the Agreement about settled (I having made every conceivable concession from sequels to T-shirts); but of course he may have felt me to be such an obstructionist during our haggling (or rather our lawyers') that he'll simply want to take the property & run & never hear my name again; in which case even if he does pick up the option & really make the movie there's no real money until 1981. For heirs & assigns presumably. [...]

love to you both,
Willie

Ouida: like Anthony Trollope, the English novelist Ouida (pseudonym of Maria Louise Ramé, 1839–1908) was very prolific.

confronting the typewriter: in a letter to the Nappers two months earlier, WG wrote: "I don't especially want to write another book but I guess finally that's what I do is write books so I've got to get things together toward that end" (18 January 1979).

Saml Butler: English novelist Samuel Butler (1835–1902); in his essay "Erewhon and the Contract with America," WG quotes Butler on his books: "I never make them; they grow; they come to me and insist upon being written" (*RSP* 86–87).

To William H. Gass

[*Gass, John Hawkes, and John Barth were on a reading tour of Germany. Typed on Washington University English Department stationery, with a handwritten note "running low on these" and an arrow pointing to the heading.*]

Piermont NY 10968
3 August 1979

Dear Bill.

Surprise! Surprise! I certainly was, to open the elegant 2vol. inscribed set of *Les Reconnaissances* (a catchy title too, as a Hampton friend lately mentioned her appreciation of my earlier book *The Recollections*); & I'm sorry to be so long acknowledging, but have been 'away' hiding, as I say, from the literary brilliance of the Hamptons in a town nearby there, since nobody invites *me* to pose in Tubingen, Munich, Berlin, let alone Paris where, 'alert and intelligent' as you may find them, it cheers my prejudice to know that through your kind gift one less frenchman will get his hands on me.* The story of that episode is, incidentally, one of the better publisher-horror stories, & better saved to retail over a bottle. All of which notwithstanding it was immensely thoughtful of you & Hawkes & you know I greatly appreciate it.

Not having been asked to T, M, B or even P, we** plan to leave in a few days for Haiti, not that I've been asked there either but the fare is cheap & I hope to sit down for 2 or 3 weeks & try to fill 2 or 3 pages with an idea, concept, synopsis, what have you, for what Larry McMurtry describes as 'a thin flat book with a strong narrative line' (ha!) for my agent to use as an instrument to deliver me from Knopf's & extort money elsewhere, the usual scam.

Another advantage to Haiti (as I assume all the abovementioned spots) is that one will not encounter that ass John Gardner in print, voice or leis, though it is perhaps unfair to burden his demented ego with what is essentially the mercenary ignorance of the *NY Times* to which we have all at last become accustomed. Well, as the Arabs say (translated from the Spanish): Sit in the doorway of your house and watch the bodies of your enemies pass. Speaking of that, Stanley must thank the Lord for small blessings: only *think* what the Master of Moral Fiction could have wrenched from *The Living End*. It was certainly splendid to see Dutton out there advertising it replete with blurbs that count, if any does, from reviewers, among which I would surely have appeared as a hitch hiker on his fleet vehicle. Boys howdy, what a darb of a car that was! I only hope he got a good reprint sale.

* My prejudices are notoriously flexible, ready to turn on a dime for a return ticket & refreshments, witness my great fondness for Berkeley/California.

** This plural embraces (sic) a Lady named Muriel Murphy, a high class redis- covery from those days before my first marriage, whose encouragement of my callow infatuation then would have deprived the world of Sarah & Matthew, so perhaps Mother was Right, perhaps everything does happen 'for the best'.

As I finish footnote ** above, the 'phone rings with Muriel from NY saying a cousin may be leaving free a house (staffed) in London for a few weeks so should we consider London rather than Haiti. I tell you.

What I tell you is if she & I are still speaking back from Haiti/London by September, the one perilous certainty is that I will start again Weds.-Thursdays at Bard (through Christmas); that between us she & I will have available—at Piermont, Manhattan, Fire Island & Easthampton, sleeping quarters between us for 37 people; that I am not entirely in control of anything as must by now be apparent; that if you* are anywhere near NY in the fall let me know here by mail or telephone, or failing the latter at her number in NY: 212-988-1360; & that failing all of it I'll write when I get work,

best greetings to Stanley & the best always to you & Mary,
Willie

* Stanley too of course—

Les Reconaissances: the French translation of *R*, by Jean Lambert, was published in two volumes by Gallimard in 1973.

blurbs that count: in a letter to Elkin's editor at Dutton, John Macrae III, WG declined his request for a blurb: "I've never done one and, as I just wrote to Stanley, have never really thought they sell books and also have never got past the feeling that they are so often a kind of self-advertisement on someone else's jacket" (13 March 1979).

Muriel Murphy: Muriel Oxenberg Murphy (see 23 November 1953), with whom WG would live for the next fifteen years.

To Cynthia Buchanan

Piermont

4 August 79

Dear Cyndy,

I guess I never really believed you would actually do it: move out there [Arizona] I mean; but here's your card from Cottonwood (& really postmarked 'Cottonwood') so it must be. I've got to say Wupatki national monument on the obverse doesn't look like a place to cheer up anybody but I do rather long to see it all again someday—more than 30 years now since I rode that blue roan through those incredible desert nights up outside Tucson—but heaven knows when that chance will offer itself. [...]

Currently & as always confusion reigns, plans to get away for 2 or 3 weeks & try to get 2 or 3 pages together on a (shudder, gasp) new book at least as an instrument to escape Knopf & try to seduce a new publisher to make the same grand costly error 2 others have made. The only thing approaching certainty a renewal of the 2-day weekly stint at Bard in September, my heart rather sinks at the prospect as it always did when that chill month came round & sent me off to boarding school but it is, after all, income. [...]

love & best to you always,

Willie Gaddis

To Sarah Gaddis

'Cormier Plage' (Haiti)

13 August 1979

Dear Sarah, and Peter.

Well! if you ever want an inexpensive (for these days) vacation (though 12–3³⁰ pm the heat is simply sweltering) with nothing but the palm trees one way & the sea the other way (& we won't have to catch any trains, & we won't go in when it rains), a large room with terrace overlooking the water 40feet away (& the sound of the coral sea), hibiscus & bouganvillea (sp?) & everything immaculate, excellent food served in an open pavillion (sp!) or at a table under trees on the beach or indeed on one's own terrace &, since it was once a French colony, ici on parle francais & the other guests are mainly french which lends it a somewhat even more remote elegance (if you can call topless ladies wearing only 'le string' elegant), beaming black Haitian faces on the maids & the boys hopping about in orange jackets, & above all PRIVACY... well this is it. We've been here only about 5 days but it's like weeks.

Muriel is just splendid. We decided 4 days ago that it might be high time for us both to start a regimen of simple morning setting-up exercises, so I dutifully followed her directions 2 days in a row & of course my back went. So I am moving around like your great grandfather—though nothing as hair-raising (yet) as the entertainment I managed for you both on that Thanksgiving visit!—sitting right now on the terrace in a rocking chair a la Jack Kennedy & his back while she makes the trip into town. This is no joke: the 'road' between here & Cape Haitian is often no more than a path of jagged rocks & blind turns, every one of them threatening a jubilant Haitian at the wheel from the other direction, up the mountain & down. There's no phone here so she had to go in to call NY & see whether her cousin (by marriage, Princess Elizabeth of Yugoslavia who is rather a number, one of these high class exiles between London, NY & Richard Burton) has arrived in NY to stay in her apartment. Also to check on her daughter Julia & her gross husband Philip (God! how fortunate I am as a father-in-law!), who are in a mounting tizzy over the imminent (Sept 5) arrival in NY of the Dalai Lama, another high-class exile since China appropriated Tibet: M's NY apartment generally acrawl with monks shut in a bedroom doing mantras or whatever they do (as some-one remarked, A good mantra is hard to find) & so, what with Bard, & our summer house rentals ending, & even the chance of your appearance, September is quite a rousing prospect.

Meanwhile I am set up here working on this 3-page or so proposal for a new novel to give to Candida when I go back, discuss with her & submit to a publisher—still unsure which one but very sure which one *not*—for a new advance & a fresh start by the end of the year when Bard (& its salary) ends. The novel involves some bad news rich people involved in making a movie, money & trust funds & an inept murder plot or 2, the main point being that it be comparatively short & brisk & 'accessible' to the paperback audience reading level (or at least appear so till they've bought it & it's too late), I'll send you a copy of the proposal when it's done, as fair warning.

At the moment we plan to spend another week here, be back in NY around the 21st when I know it will seem we've been gone the entire summer, up to Piermont to see that it's all in one piece & prepare my head for fall. We think

& speak of you both often & I hope it's all still going well. I have thought in terms of trying to get out there at Thanksgiving but heaven knows what lies between now & then.

love from us to you both,
Papa

---

nothing but palm trees [...] the other way: from Eliot's *Sweeney Agonistes*, "Fragment of an Agon": "Nothing to see but the palmtrees one way / And the sea the other way."

we won't [...] when it rains: also from *Sweeney Agonistes*, "Song by Klipstein and Krumpacker." Also quoted in *J R* (479).

sound of the coral sea: also from *Sweeney Agonistes*, "Song by Wauchope and Horsfall."

Princess Elizabeth of Yugoslavia: Elizabeth Karageorgevich (1936–), Serbian business-woman, writer, and politician. Her first husband was Muriel's cousin, Howard Oxenberg (1919–2010); see her *Excerpts* (78–80).

Richard Burton: Welsh actor (1925–84), engaged to Princess Elizabeth in 1974.

Julia: Julia Murphy (1960–), who furnished some later letters for this collection.

Dalai Lama: Lhamo Döndrub (1935–), formally recognized as the fourteenth Dalai Lama in 1950.

To Steven Moore

[*At the time a bookseller in Littleton, Colorado, I had completed a draft of my* Reader's Guide *and wrote WG to ask for a list of sources to* R *that Koenig (in his dissertation) implied was among his papers.*]

Piermont, NY 10968
25 August 1979

Dear Steven Moore.

I have been away & have just got your letter in the course of clearing things up, though I'm afraid the specific request it contains is beyond such measures since I have no & never made any 'list' of the sources for *The Recognitions*. As a book written over a course of years it was not developed from sources set down at the outset, & there seemed little reason to do so when it was done. Numerous source references are certainly among my notes & papers from that time, which I have just begun to look over. But I trust you understand that to go through them & compile such a 'list' as you seek would take an amount of time I don't have for such a purpose; & from past experience I have to say too that the time & dislocating attention demanded by detailed correspondence on 'meanings' & 'sources' &c are also beyond question right now.

If you've indeed got 85% of the references, you would seem well on your way. The Koenig thesis is hardly exhaustive among dissertations I have seen on the book, one among them I recall as more specific a Ph D at Cornell by Robert Minkoff 2 or 3 years ago. I don't know or try to keep track of work being done on the book aside from the occasional thesis or bits of correspondence telling me of such things as a symposium on the book in California last summer; but clearly if I responded to it all in the detail it demands it would verge upon a full time occupation.

I appreciate your interest in my work but can do little more right now than wish you luck with what may be an act of folly approaching that of having written the book in the first place.

Yours,
William Gaddis

To John and Pauline Napper

Piermont NY 10968
30 Nov. 1979

Dear John & Pauline.

[...] Well, the separation with Judith is about complete, it has certainly been a long row to hoe for us both, she is still in Key West (Florida), and I, well, hold your breath: a few months ago I re-encountered, yes, Muriel Oxenberg (Murphy), & here we are. If ever life came full circle! Went right back to (where else?) Eliot & read the Portrait of a Lady and there it all is.

What a thunderous thing to do, your bonfire. But how it all ties together, the 'getting free of something' you express. Can one ever? Even in that vein, the book (unwritten) I am hawking about to publishers drawn, very much, on Shakespear's 73rd sonnet, the 'That time of year thou mayst in me behold
When yellow leaves, or none, or few, do hang
Upon those boughs which shake against the cold,
Bare ruin'd choirs, where late the sweet birds sang.' &c...

And that boiled down is about the size of it. I've been teaching at Bard again this fall, a lifesaver but as you know a drain too, comes to an end at Christmas by which time I hope to have a book contract & that extortion that goes with it; spending most of my time in New York recently, stop at Piermont for the mail & try to figure out the next step, whether to rent that house out for a while but there's all my books & papers (speaking of bonfires... no!), the whole prospect for a real change with the new Year. [...]

love & best to you both always,
Willie

Portrait of a Lady: early poem about a young man's relationship with a sophisticated older woman.

WG at St. Michael's College, Vermont, 5 November 1979, where he
delivered a lecture on failure (photo by John Puleio).

To Johan Thielemans

Piermont NY 10968
8 January 1980

Dear J Thielemans.

Many thanks for your letter, with its rather wild (to me) Polish account. I am still tossed in air by these things. A letter last week from a man (Brian Morton) at the Universitetet I Tromsø (whose country I didn't even know), has been lecturing on both my books at the Univ. of East Anglia (ENG) wants to do a 'full length study' &c. Confusing. A long letter a year or so ago from someone with Swedish radio asking for an interview which I turned down on grounds that it made little sense to be interviewed in a country where my work has not been translated. Backward thinking on my part: that might have stimulated a translation. Thus it would never have occurred to me there could possibly be a coven in Poznan, while I seem to continue as a fairly well kept secret in my own country.

So at any rate I am a good deal more relaxed about these things than when I first met you & would not at all mind talking with your Miss Bałazy should she ever appear here (though better, of course, your 'improbable lake in the plains of Poland', where I don't appear to be headed), though indeed my concern with Catholicism (& indeed Christianity itself) has waned a good deal since that long eruption.

At the moment I am trying to seriously consider getting myself down to another book, something of considerably smaller scope in all ways, shorter & a simpler narrative &c done for practical reasons rather than another crusade. Again thanks for your continued interest in my work & vehemence on its behalf on such frontiers,

very best of course for the new year & indeed the decade,
William Gaddis

Brian Morton: he eventually published an essay entitled "Money, Medicine and the Host: The Novels of William Gaddis," *PN Review* 52 (13.2)(1986): 47–51.

Miss Bałazy: Teresa Bałazy, a professor of American literature at Adam Mickiewicz University in Poznań, Poland, who visited WG in 1981. See 8 October 1981.

To Tom LeClair

[A critic (1944–) and professor at the University of Cincinnati who was assembling with Larry McCaffery a collection of interviews with innovative novelists, originally intended to be published by Lee Goerner at Knopf—mentioned below—but eventually published as Anything Can Happen: Interviews with Contemporary American Novelists *(U Illinois*

P, 1983). As the address indicates (P.H. = penthouse), WG had moved in with Muriel Murphy.]

235 East 73rd street, P.H. A
New York NY 10021
23 February 1980

Dear Tom LeClair.

Thanks for your letter & enclosures. Goerner may have got me wrong, it's not that I wasn't 'feeling up to' an interview but rather that I've never seen much point to them: what a writer's got to say about writing is either there in his writing itself or it's not, furthermore it may change & probably should.

At any rate the conditions you suggest—approval, cancelation &c—are as promising as one could ask & if you want to call me at some point about arranging a brief interview (212-988-1361) when you expect to be in New York please do so. I must add that my plans at this moment are quite indefinite, that I may get away for some weeks so if you should call & not reach me that will be the case. In any event I will of course be curious to see your essay on *J R* when it's published (No approval, no cancelation), I'd seen & appreciated your piece in *Commonweal*.

Yours,
W. Gaddis

---

your essay on *J R* [...] *Commonweal*: later published as "William Gaddis, *J R*, & the Art of Excess," *Modern Fiction Studies* 27 (Winter 1981–82): 587–600. LeClair had reviewed *J R* in *Commonweal* (16 January 1976, 54–55).

To Matthew Kiell

[*Presumably a student writing a paper since his letter to WG was mailed from Swarthmore College (2 March 1980). What follows is a typed draft with numerous handwritten changes, undated and unsigned.*]

[March 1980]

Dear Mr Kiell.

Your queries regarding the adaptation of 'serious' fiction for television appear as old as the problem raised so long ago by mass audience motion pictures; & given the number of variables & the nature of the industry today to be more or less academic. I don't see really answering such questions but on a case to case basis, & wouldn't in any case recommend the following general remarks for their novelty.

Obviously there will at the outset be disagreement over what constitutes 'serious' fiction; equally obvious as you imply that some fictions will lend themselves more satisfactorily than others: those developed through extended interior monologues for example would likely suggest similarly extended voice over & emerge accordingly dull, as opposed to those whose characters & situations are developed through action & dialogue. All this as I say is hardly news, but to answer your immediate question in these terms *J R* would certainly appear to me an obvious candidate, *The Recognitions* rather less so since its range would seem to demand the larger format of a full length motion picture for which, it has always seemed to me, that book is peculiarly suited.

I find any argument propelling the wide dissemination of 'serious' fiction to 'millions of people, far more than have probably ever read a particular author's works', to be as tainted as the recent *L.A. Times* observation (25 Feb. '80) 'Thanks to the marvels of electronic technology, many ministers ... speak to significantly more people every time they preach than Jesus did in his lifetime.' Whether or not so intended, the equation implicit here embraces the profound simplicity of Jesus' revelations on the one hand & the essential vulgarity of say, Norman Vincent Peale's adaptation on the other. Thus rather than indict television wholesale for the purveyor of trash it so often is (but more than the printing press?), all this is simply to say that the acceptability, the quality of any 'adaptation' can only reflect the quality of those involved throughout its production.

This needn't mean, as it is sometimes construed, a strict transcription from page to tube, but rather an intelligent grasp of the original fiction within the limitations of television itself. An incisive & highly amusing television presentation could for example be drawn from Samuel Butler's *Erewhon*, but it would not be Butler & it would not be *Erewhon*, furthermore it needn't be: all that has led a happy existence as a book for a century & will continue to do so. And finally, I doubt those who would fail to pursue Butler further for having seen such a television version would ever have read (even heard of) him in the first place; for those who did so much the better.

I hope these comments are of some use to you & would appreciate seeing what you publish. Often enough it seems to me I take the time to respond to such queries & never hear another damned word.

L. A. Times [...] than Jesus did in his lifetime": Russell Chandler, "Airwave Preachers Reach More at Once than Christ in Lifetime," B3, B15.

Norman Vincent Peale: popular American minister and author (1898–1993).

Butler's *Erewhon*: a satiric utopian novel (1872), and the subject of one of WG's rare critical essays (*RSP* 80–87).

To William H. and Mary Gass

[*A postcard, without salutation or date (postmark illegible), with a reproduction of* Prometheus Bound *on the obverse.*]

[Spetsai, Greece]
[April 1980]

All splendidly as we were told it would be—including (v. obverse) early portrait of the writer & his publisher—

best of course
Willie Gaddis

To Cynthia Buchanan

[New York, NY]
23 April 1980

Dear Cyndy.

I might at least have sent you a card from ATHENS to explain this delay answering your good letter which appeared just before we took off: yes finally, at last, I've seen the Acropolis & most of the Peloponnesos & am ready to go quietly. It was all as splendid as anyone has ever said & early enough spring though chilly to miss most of the German tour busses & see green & wildflowers everywhere in addition to the reasons one supposedly goes, ruined temples everywhere. Then just to do it right a week or so in London & again green & flowers, it is such a handsome city & I think perhaps more than ever perhaps a serious candidate for a place to end up if one is going to continue this fool writing. To which right now I don't see much alternative. I've started another book, short I hope, as the escape instrument from Kn*pf & do believe that is going to work out. (Though don't mention it, to Lynn [Nesbit] or otherwise, till it does!)

Meanwhile I've met again a woman I'd first known years & years ago, her name is Muriel Murphy & you may have come across her out Wainscott way? So that's on the home front & a very happy one it is too, life finally seems to be taking shape. [...]

best wishes and love,
Bill Gaddis

To Jack Gold

[*The British movie producer who had shown interest in a film version of* J R. *This letter accompanied a copy of Elkin's* Living End.]

235 East 73rd street, P.H. A
New York NY 10021
May Day, 1980

Dear Jack Gold.

Whatever the outcome, I've got to say how much I appreciated your taking time to come over to Eccleston street & for every bit of our conversation.

Regarding the enclosed book: I recall your saying (if & when the occasion looms) that you felt the screenplay should be done by an American writer, as I strongly agree. I also felt you had nobody particular in mind.

I've known this fellow Stanley Elkin for a couple of years, largely through his high regard for *J R* (which, he said, you 'hear with your eyes'). He knows the book in detail & has got 2 or 3 screen credits though I don't know what they are & probably minor; I haven't spoken to him about this but thought I'd pass it along to you simply as a suggestion since there seems plenty of time. In fact I suppose it's also possible he wouldn't want to tangle with the book in these terms. But for the moment at any rate I thought the enclosed bit of blasphemy might give you some idea of his excellent ear, facility, & mordant humour if you should be interested in him as a possibility. (The book itself I understand has been optioned—quite a movie!)

Also, incidentally, & as I'm sure you've experienced, most writers probably go back & forth between wanting/fearing to do their own screenplays; but finally now having sat down & talked with you I'm the more convinced that whatever your approach it will be well & carefully thought out. Then for no more than a mention at this point, in my habitual tearing-out of news items I've compulsively gone on putting aside items related to the J R approach to 'business', *not* for another such book but possibly useful for updating situations in a screenplay (as for instance the Hunt brothers bringing the roof down with their attempt to corner silver).

Again, I very much hope we'll see you when you're through here in late summer. I know your schedules are tight ones, while mine anticipates little more than getting up and staring at another blank page every morning so it would be entirely at your convenience. And there's no need to answer this (unless, of course, anything blossomed from the financing possibility you spoke of, which would be Good News indeed for everybody).

very best regards,
Bill Gaddis

---

the book itself I understand has been optioned: but never produced. See David C. Dougherty's *Shouting Down the Silence: A Biography of Stanley Elkin* (Urbana:

University of Illinois Press, 2010), 174–76. WG is mentioned four times in this book (pp. 36, 159, 169, 208) but is unlisted in the index.

Hunt brothers: two Texas financiers who in 1973 began to buy up silver as a hedge against inflation, thereby contributing to the collapse of the silver market in 1980, which created countless losses for other speculators as well. They declared bankruptcy and in 1988 were convicted of conspiring to manipulate the market.

To John Kuehl

New York NY 10021
24 May 1980

Dear John Kuehl.

I have got to write you at least this note of my appreciation for your constancy regarding that old book of mine. I look back on it but at it too as a project that only 'youth may mount and folly guide' (youth could/can mount? I haven't the source here) but the insistent fact remains—my 'royalty check' from Harcourt B. last week of $5.56 notwithstanding—that, as the book itself insisted it would do, it exists. I have got letters from Tromsø (Norway?) & even a cult in Poznan, students mainly & the point here being its apparent abiding reality for the young which is ($5.56 notwithstanding) the most gratifying essential a novelist can dare to ask. The point being of course that without such concern as yours they mightn't ever have seen it let alone read it, let alone found its concerns their own, as some papers your student Deborah Rossi was kind enough to forward to me surely demonstrate.

Easy enough to take all this as homage, which is directly not the case—present as that may be—& why this note. I simply haven't the time to respond to the inquiries that come along in the detail they both deserve and presume, & your generous understanding of that makes me doubly appreciative.

very best regards,
William Gaddis

---

your constancy: Kuehl regularly taught *R* at New York University, directed a few dissertations on it, and once invited WG to speak to his class. Along about this time he began planning a book of essays on WG, eventually published as *In Recognition of William Gaddis* (1984).

'youth may mount and folly guide': often (and usually inaccurately) quoted by WG from Shakespeare's *As You Like It:* "But all's brave that youth mounts and folly guides" (3.4.48–49).

To Tom LeClair

[*This and several subsequent letters to LeClair concern the interview they conducted in the spring, which WG never allowed to be published. It appeared posthumously in Joseph Tabbi and Rone Shavers's* Paper Empire: William Gaddis and the World System *(U Alabama P, 2007), 17–27. The Wainscott address was Mrs. Murphy's home in the Hamptons, and became the setting for Oscar's house in FHO.*]

PO Box 549
Wainscott NY 11975
11 July 1980

Dear Tom LeClair.

I've finally gone over the material you sent me & don't see any way we can proceed with haste on it (or what I consider haste). My responses seem rambling, too much reference to 'explaining' published work &c & as a whole I don't think does either of us great credit.

I say 'gone over the material' & mean just that, rather than the careful scrutiny called for to make it presentable, for the very simple reason of the time that would be involved quite as I feared. You say for instance that you'd like an interview 'close to consistent with others in the collection' but I thought it was clear before you came up that I saw it brief at best, perhaps 1/3 their length. And as I think I said at some point in our conversation a major problem in responding with any serious care to the variety of well meant questionaires that appear in the mail is that these simply beget more questions till it becomes another day or days' very real distraction from work already postponed for dealing with such worldly insistences as preparing a house for rent, breaking an arm, meeting trains. So a dozen inserted yellow sheets both EXP[AND] & NEW are hardly promising, each by its very nature some fresh consideration (the 'abuse of the system that particularly affect the artist?' 'what kind of fiction is worth doing?' verisimilitude? realism? &c &c) amounting altogether to an essay I would write (cut, revise, rewrite) if at this point I were so inclined for a clear & supported statement without such flippant references as Judith Krantz, Gardner, even Solzhenitsyn, in place of those that stand up close & real, as Samuel Butler.

I know you've already spent a good deal of time on this but I right now simply cannot afford to spend even more on it myself as would be required, since I am trying to make a concerted effort to get down to work again on a book already but barely started, which demands this opportunity (time unfragmented) to grasp & believe its atmosphere rather than reconsider that of work gone before & now off on its own so far as I'm concerned, or perhaps better to say must be concerned since my responses to your questions already given hardly appear to support that position.

With your care to seeing the writer plain I hope we can put this aside for a while until its prospects look more satisfactory to us both.

Yours,

W. Gaddis

Judith Krantz, Gardner, even Solzhenitsyn: mentioned on pp. 22, 26, and 19, respectively, in the published interview.

To William H. Gass

Wainscott, NY 11975

25 August 1980

Dear Bill.

Attending a stylish Hamptons opening of a very good painter out here— most of her pictures of rumpled pillows & bedclothes (I like a picture that tells a story)—imagine my surprise, & delight, at seeing the cover of a familiar book lurking among the sheets. Well! Next to reading, this is about the neatest tribute I've come across, though of course she's read it too which is, of course, *why* it's nestled in the sheets. Her name is Polly Kraft (wife of columnist Joe Kraft), serious & most competent in her own right as you will I think agree when you hold the enclosed slides up to the light. I inveigled them from her on grounds of your sterling generous & rowdy character & Mary's good looks.

I write this on the assumption that you are all still alive, after day after day reports of 104° in St Louis (my recollection being –10°); but in all likelihood you got away. I saw Georges Bourchardt's nifty looking wife at a restaurant & she told me that Stanley with full family complement had passed through Breadloaf-bound & in high spirits & good health, glad to hear that. I am mainly simply loaf-bound: escaped from Knopf for Viking (a move I'd encourage you in, if you ever consider such, enthusiastic leaves-you-alone (so far) editor named Elizabeth Sifton, dghtr of a prominent theologian), & am trying by weak force of will alone to start another book, no damned thick square book this time but I hope simply a 'romance' but trouble still coming up with the fueling indignation, the only thing that rouses me these days all these God damned born-agains & evangelicals.

Again, if you or you all should possibly come through I'd hope for a call, though I see the academic year (I'm skipping it this time round) is at hand; & we'll probably stay out here on Long Island's end into the fall.

best always,

Bill Gaddis

Polly Kraft: American artist (1932–2017) who worked in watercolor and oil.

Georges Bourchardt: Borchardt (not Bourchardt) and his wife Anne were literary agents.

Elizabeth Sifton: i.e., Elisabeth Sifton, daughter of Reinhold Niebuhr. See headnote to 10 September 84.

To Sarah Gaddis

Wainscott, NY
[late October? 1980]

Dear Sarah.

Thanks, thanks for your bright letter. I wish I could do the same. I am at my worst right now, a worst you remember in terms of EKodak, IBM &c: uptight, strung out, bundle of nerves, on this piece I so lightly said I'd write for the *WSJournal* magazine on *Failure* & now have 4 days left & needless to say hundreds of shreds of paper which I keep rearranging: the constant threat which has silenced better minds than mine (v. Martin [Dworkin]) of being so overwhelmed by one's material that one just gives it up (speaking of failure!), & always the wellwishers saying Oh don't get upset, it will all fall into place . . .

So congratulations to Peter on getting published but tell him not to make a habit of it, it can drive you right up the wall. I didn't see the *NYer* piece on

WG and Muriel Oxenberg Murphy at the Poets & Writers tenth-anniversary party, October 1980 (photo by Thomas Victor).

publishing but the *NYTimes* did run 2 long articles, of course all one has ever heard is them bemoaning their difficulties over their lobster Newberg lunches but this time they may be right; the only thing is of course like everybody it never occurs to them to blame themselves for the sheer greed that has driven them to pay $1 and $2 million for crap like Judith Kranz & now find themselves in trouble & all the rest of us with them.

Though we did take time out for a vast NY party given by a bunch called Poets & Writers, took Matthew & his treat was dancing with Abby Hoffman's girlfriend, mine was sitting beside a breezy dame who introduced herself as Joan Fontaine, now back in Wainscott (not MHG, he's working hard in NY & very happy at it) at a 'work table' with these thousand paper scraps looking out at rain wild winds & whitecaps on the pond, frantic V formations of ducks & geese honking in the grey skies I hope they know where they're going.

& one other item enclosed, you have got to go see this Japanese movie *Kagemusha* because—aside from the story, largely battles between 16th century war lords—their outfits are simply staggering, I have never seen so many different patterns & colours & could only think of you in there with a pad & pencil going mad at not being able to note them down fast enough.

Aside from this frantic *WSJ* piece (& the $ that should go with it) plans are fluid, I think we'll go back into NY to stay right after the elections which should give us a good deal of entertainment, I have to confess I see it all so hapless that this year for the first time I think I may not vote, I know that is the bad citizen but I have voted against people rather than for their opponents so many times (HHumphrey for 1) that I am just not going out to vote against Reagan now, though if he is elected he should offer us a good 4 years of awful entertainment (in my opinion!).

I've got to get back to my scrap heap & just look forward, as I always do, to the day we can all relax together though it seems to be always just around the corner. [...]

best to Peter & much love always,
Papa

Failure: WG's essay "The Rush for Second Place" was originally entitled "Failure" and intended for a new magazine supplement to the *Wall Street Journal*, but when that failed to materialize, WG submitted it to *Harper's*, where it was published under a new title in April 1981 (*RSP* 38–61).

Poets & Writers: the writers' organization held a tenth-anniversary party on 22 October 1980 at the Roseland Ballroom.

Abby Hoffman: American political activist (1936–89).

Joan Fontaine: British American actress (1917–2013) who had published her autobiography, *No Bed of Roses*, two years earlier.

MHG: Matthew Hough Gaddis.

Kagemusha: 1980 film written and directed by Akira Kurosawa.

HHumphrey: Democrat Hubert Humphrey ran against Republican Richard Nixon in 1968. In 1980, Reagan defeated incumbent Jimmy Carter.

To Tom LeClair

> 235 East 73rd street, P.H. A
> New York NY 10021
> 22 November 1980

Dear Tom LeClair.

Just a note to say that a friend pointed out to me your letter in the *New Republic* & well done: how Kazin's dreary pomposity is still taken seriously is quite beyond me, he has been around 'patronizing his betters' for far too long & some kind of disestablishmentarian movement is long overdue.

You make your case most succinctly which is really the point of this note as the element I found missing in our interview & due, I readily believe, to my own maundering in conversation as opposed to the better chance for trenchancy in the (re)written word. We may try again some time (not immediately); meanwhile, good work

> and best regards,
> William Gaddis

---

letter in *New Republic*: a letter to the editor (22 November 1980, p. 3) in response to Kazin's article "American Writing Now" (in the 18 October issue) chastising Kazin for ignoring WG and other innovative novelists.

To William H. Gass

[*Upon being awarded a Guggenheim Fellowship, for which Gass had written a recommendation.*]

> New York, New York 10021
> 12 April 1981

Dear Bill.

Do you read the small print in the *Times*? Do you KNOW what joy (read money, prestige, vainglory) your kind effort has contributed to this modest household? That yes, the Guggenheim people did actually respond positively to your recommendation? Of course I should never have doubted.

But what a treat, what a treat to have managed such a thing without Mitcheners & Mailers, Biddles & Bobs (Gotliebs) & 'who you know'; rather,

3 noncelebrities & 1 Captain (yourself) by whom I flatter myself I'm a captain.

I should also note I really am working on the book, the 'romance' (nothing I think that can be accused as 'experimental' here!), came back a few days ago from Mexico with 50 clean first draft pages so it is not all hornswoggle (though it may turn out to be about hornswoggle)...

Joyce?: Q. What are you writing about?

A. I am not writing about something. I am writing something. Enough of that.

At any rate, we plan to be here & Long Island for the next couple of months and if any chance of you/Mary/the youth group in the neighborhood we would certainly hope to hear & share our quarters city or country. Our summer plans quite happily unresolved though Guggenheim's kindness opens possibilities well beyond Atlantic City; meanwhile 2 phone numbers below, every best regard to Stanley.

warm thoughts to Mary, to yourself with thanks again,
Bill Gaddis

PS I let off some steam in April *Harper's Magazine* which may sporadically amuse you.

Mitcheners [...] Gotliebs: James Michener (correct spelling) and Norman Mailer were novelists; Livingston L. Biddle Jr. (1918–2002) was chairman of the National Endowment for the Arts at that time; and WG misspells the name of his former editor at Knopf.

Joyce?: Samuel Beckett said Joyce's "writing is not *about* something; *it is that something itself*" ("Dante... Bruno. Vico.. Joyce"). Cf. *AA* 18.

April *Harper's*: "The Rush for Second Place," April 1981, pp. 31–39 (*RSP* 39–61).

To Frederick Exley

[*American novelist and sports journalist (1929–92), best known for his memoir-novel* A Fan's Notes *(1968). Exley wrote WG 28 April 1981 to say he liked "The Rush for Second Place" and to thank him for mentioning* A Fan's Notes *(RSP 56). He cites "EW's [Evelyn Waugh's?] dictum—'the thing is to outlast the sons of bitches'"; says he's going back to the Iowa Writers' Workshop in the fall and plans to give three lectures on R; reports David Markson's facetious rumor that "you were incognito, wearing shades and sharing grocery expenses with Pynchon and Salinger, out on Long Island"; and asks about Judith Thompson.*]

Wainscott, NY 11975

14 May 1981

Dear Fred,

Your note a nice surprise, also your kind words for the *Harper's* piece which I'm still a little ambivalent about: a pal out here said I'd "tipped my hand" & that sums up the doubts though it did pay for 2 months of Mexico including carfare so it can't be all bad.

Outlast them yes, that's the only answer: my version a Spanish version of an Arab one &, having neither, an approximation in Eng: Sit in the doorway of your house & watch the bodies of your enemies carried by. Problem is you sit there so God damn long that when the time comes maybe you can't get up. But (all aphorisms this morning) what we lose on the swings we make up on the roundabouts: fancy movie dreams collapse but a Guggenheim comes through! Never had applied before & O ye of little faith but there last month it was, so vast sighs of relief from the edge of the abyss once again.

No Pynchon or even Salinger (or even Salinger-true-believer support, see attached) here which is pretty much the tail end of L.I. & not quite a Hampton so will probably & unfortunately not be in town for your meteoric passage through (though if chance should have it so I'd signal one place or the other you mention), expect to be out here till the summer migration & escape that for God knows, possibly Mexico again, good clean air for a heavy smoker & a few more words on paper to cheer up the folks at Viking, where I fled from Gottlieb/Knopf; & am frankly relieved with the help of the Googs to go on with the book unbroken by teaching this fall, kind as Bard has been & again asked me back I've got to say teaching gives me the blues more often than it inspires.

You say 'back to Iowa' which must mean you've been there as I wasn't aware. I was for 2 days once, felt further away than Mexico though from what I'm not sure. But thanks ahead for your lectures on *The Recognitions*, that again is the God damnedest thing: I've got about ½ dozen PhD theses on it also word that somebody at Univ of Nebraska Press is bringing out a book on it next year; latest royalty statement 5/5/81, $12.76, less 10% commission enclosed find our check for $11.48 . . . that should inspire them!

Other news, all unclear. Judith last heard from in Key West though even that must be a year ago, I thought you'd likely heard she went down there must be 3 years ago for what I gradually realized was more than a visit, agony all around for she's still among the best but finally there was no saving it.

Last but major congratulations on your 12-mile-a-day (& sobriety), cigarettes still my resident curse & I will try to take your Good Example to heart,

very best,

Gaddis

attached: unidentified.

12-mile-a-day: an alcoholic, Exley announced in a postscript that he was sober and walking 12 miles a day. In 1983 WG wrote a Guggenheim recommendation for him that reads in part: "I have held his writing in high regard since reading his first book *A Fan's Notes*, and in fact made use of that book in teaching courses at Bard College both for its style and for what I found to be its painful grasp of numerous agonies which may be universal to youth but in this writer's hands become uniquely American. I know few works of fiction—perhaps Italo Svevo's *Confessions of Zeno*—that present so well our capacities for self deception."

To Thomas Sawyer III

[*A professor at Northern Montana College who was writing an article later published as "False Gold to Forge: The Forger behind Wyatt Gwyon,"* Review of Contemporary Fiction *2.2 (Summer 1982): 50–54, concerning Han van Meegeren (1889-1947), the Dutch forger whose career WG adapted for Wyatt's in* R.]

7 June 1981

Dear Mr Sawyer.

Some of the Wyatt material was drawn from the van Meegeren case. The significant departure was this: in Wyatt's case the talent short of genius was totally in tune with the work it produced; in that of van Meegeren the vulgarity of his 'Vermeers', immediately apparent to the untrained eye, triumphed through the self-serving 'experts' bent on proving their own theses regarding influences &c in Vermeer's career to the point that they simply could not see what they were looking at.

I'm glad you like the novel.

Yours,
William Gaddis

To Tom LeClair

New York, New York 10021
27 July 1981

Dear Tom LeClair.

Yours of 21 July & 'no graceful way to ask about the interview' must provoke no graceful way to decline it. Unfortunately the deadline of your publisher 'who wants to schedule printing' has got to be of less concern to me than mine.

For now then, all I can do is recall to you some lines I wrote 30 years ago in *The Recognitions* (p. 106 in the careless little Avon edition) asking what they want from the artist they didn't get from his work? & why must one repeat this & repeat it when that is what the whole damned thing is about? If it didn't come through in the work then what use or interest is an 'interview'? All the purposes such interviews can serve seem to me, on the one hand, to say 'this is what I really meant to accomplish' or, on the other, some definitive statement from the writer regarding his 'interest in making some statements about fiction and (his) work' as you say; whereas this is precisely what his work constitutes for better or worse when he offers it, in the best & most final shape he can give it at the time, the final statement in 'interview' terms being, of course, his obituary, & the real final statement no more than the sum of the work itself, its fictions offering probably fewer opportunities for misinterpretation even than the interview's that isn't what I meant (at all).

So for the moment at any rate your notion of publishing any transcribed version of our talk edited, disclaimed or whatever is unacceptable, as a condition of your original proposal. I appreciate your time and effort spent on it but it was very much the petulance of an afternoon.

Yours,
W. Gaddis

To Steven Weisenburger

[*A professor (1949–) at the University of Kentucky who contributed an essay entitled "Contra Naturam?: Usury in William Gaddis's* J R" *to* Money Talks: Language and Lucre in American Fiction, *edited by Roy R. Male (Norman: University of Oklahoma Press, 1981), 93–109.*]

Wainscott, N.Y. 11975
18 September 1981

Dear Steven Weisenburger.

I ordered (prompted by A Broyard's most grudging mention in his *NY Times* review), finally received & have just read your piece on *J R* in *Money Talks*. Generally I have resisted responding to reviews or critical pieces with notes either of thanks or indignation, but in this case feel obliged to let you know that I read yours with pleasure and appreciation. Self serving as this must inevitably sound, given your bias for the book, I did find your approach, your informed analysis & exploration of the themes, & your conclusions, (& a most coherent style), to be extremely gratifying, & confirming that what I thought I had put there is really there.

This last I suppose provoked by this cursed word inaccessible which has haunted both these Big Books & far worse in the case of *The Recognitions* 25 years ago. Oddly enough things seemed to be reversed with *J R*, where what one might have feared as 'provincial' reviewers—from the *Cleveland Plain Dealer* to the *Hibernian*—sailed right through & had a marvelous time whereas a 'serious critic' such as Steiner seemed to take the whole thing as a personal affront &, finding it unreadable from the outset, went right on to review it anyhow to prove it was unreadable: some sort of contradiction, or non seq, or oxymoron there somewhere. The only piece that really annoyed me was John Gardner's thoroughly dishonest job in the *NY Review*: jauntily challenging Steiner's charge & finding the book immensely readable in order to set it up for his own sloppily contorted conclusion (a common stunt of his) as totally negative, Art (pure) the victim of (dirty) Commerce &c &c. (Ah Bartleby! Ah moral fiction!)

I only mention Gardner here because his egregious pose in seizing the wrong end of the stick is too typical of the simplistic stupidity that has found my work entirely negative (incidentally, as you may have noticed the titles on p. 515 of *J R* are anagrams of *The Recognitions* & all of the blurbs (except for delicately evocative & yummy read) are from reviews it received); whereas your grasp of the Art/Commerce relationship, & of seeing Bast shaped as triumph, are of course what the whole damned book is about. Just as (your p. 95) everything outside Art diminishing in worth, the counterpoint of Bast's diminishing vision of his talents from grand opera to cantata to suite to finally the lonely piece for cello is refinement rather than the defeat that carelessness reads in, & the fact that this is all the triumph needed. In this whole area I find your insight immensely heartening.

Now what follows may be simply carping but I hope, in the light of my appreciation of what is of real importance in your piece, that you'll see these items supplied simply should you ever want to reprint or expand it. Clearly they also reflect my own constant concern that it is my fault when such details are mis-taken when I'd thought them clear to a serious reader.

Ergo: foot of p. 95, a Long Island (not a Brooklyn) school; 96, 97 Amy Joubert is the daughter of Moncrief [*sic*]; Cates is her great uncle; 97 he buys picnic forks from the Navy (*J R* 169) not Air Force, sells to Army; 98 (& I've always regretted that I didn't make this more clear) last lines J R on the phone, I don't understand where you got J R anticipating a tour of college campuses; what he's really got in mind is some undefined career 'in public life', ie politics in which Bast again presumably will 'help him out', though how he could manage such a thing is purposely left unclear: point is J R has 'learned' in terms of shifting his view of where the power lies in this junk world which is to say he's learned nothing, and will persist.

One item I apparently made clear to no one unfortunately since, while a prank like *The Recognitions* anagramed, contained more than that but I don't believe anyone saw it there so clearly my fault, & damn. It's this: the lettering over the school entrance, proposed by Schepperman, was Marx' FROM EACH ACCORDING TO HIS ABILITY &c; when the school learned this 'communist' they were alarmed & Gibbs stepped in to the rescue by simply having the letters altered to 'look' Greek, as here:

ΕΒΦΜ ΣΑΟΗ ΑΘΘΦΒΡ —&c

Also, p. 99 (*JR* p. 142) while Bast is echoing the Ring motif on the piano the lines he's declaiming (Rift the hills ... Rain or hail! &c) are from Tennyson's Locksley Hall.

Also liked your rescuing the passage (your 103) regarding the unfinished book/terminally ill patient to which you give the interpretation intended (compare Gardner's distortion).

Finally I have got to thank you for never so far as I recall writing me with questions, queries &c since 1) I just have not time to respond to those things which often come in in some detail & can't afford the correspondence they anticipate, & 2) have always tried to hold to the stance that the work is on its own & I cannot pursue it saying —This is what I really meant... (or That is not what I meant at all...) but mainly 3) what you accomplished without my help (read interference) is in so short a space so succinctly & well done that I am in your debt,

Yours,
William Gaddis

Regarding Broyard's *Times* review unfortunately the short shrift he gives you (in a very odd statement) is I'm afraid really meant for me: we've known each other some 30 years & I guess clearly aren't pals.

Broyard: WG and Anatole Broyard (1920–90) knew each other in the Village in the late '40s and were rivals for Sheri Martinelli's affections, which caused some friction. He was the model for Max in *R*. See his posthumously published "Remembering William Gaddis in the Nineteen-Fifties," *New England Review* 17.3 (Summer 1995): 13–14. He reviewed *Money Talks* in the 13 June 1981 *New York Times*, stating: "In his analysis of William Gaddis's 'JR,' Steven Weisenburger manages to sound both ingenious and off-putting" (21).

Big Books: Weisenburger begins his essay: "William Gaddis is the author of two Big Books. By this designation I mean that *The Recognitions* (1955) and *JR* (1975) stand in a brotherly relation to *Moby-Dick, Ulysses, The Sot-Weed Factor,* and *Gravity's Rainbow*" (93).

Bartleby: Weisenburger quotes Melville's "Ah Bartleby! Ah humanity!" as the impulse behind such Big Books as WG's. Gardner wrote a book entitled *On Moral Fiction* (1978).

EBΦM [...] &c: handwritten first with English letters, then gone over again to make them appear Greek.

That is not what I meant at all: from Eliot's "Love Song of J. Alfred Prufrock."

To David Markson

Wainscott NY 11975
26 Sept 1981

Dear David,

I've been out here since September began & our mail connection with NY is tenuous, it gets here eventually only when someone stops in the NY apartment & notices it & postpones forwarding it or brings it out in a heap.

So this may be too late for your Guggenheim application, where you may use my name. My past testimonials have generally been brief & have accumulated a list of no-wins; also I have noted a greatly declining number going to fiction writers compared to the old days, compared to film music & academic projects, all capped by what I would think must be a greatly augmented number of applications because of threats to federal state &c funding for the 'arts'.

Good luck whatever,
Willie Gaddis

To Johan Thielemans

Wainscott, NY 11975
8 October 1981

Dear Thielemans,

thanks for your letter which I just had forwarded here, unfortunately some 100 miles from New York so I'm afraid I'll have to miss you this trip & should like to have heard more of the happy episode of Gass in Ghent. That Teresa Balazy is a good tough minded girl, glad I could talk with her & most curious to see what she comes up with. Regards to Freddy deV, sorry nothing on tape yet but the day may come,

best regards
W. Gaddis

Teresa Balazy: she published an essay entitled "A Recognition of *The Recognitions*" in *Traditions in the Twentieth Century American Literature,* ed. Marta Sienicka (Adam Mickiewicz University Press, 1981), 23–33.

Freddy deV: Freddy de Vree (1939–2004), Belgian poet and radio producer; conducted an interview with WG in 1988.

To Tomasz Mirkowicz

[*A Polish critic, activist, and translator (1953–2003) who, while visiting the United States, interviewed WG with a professor from Columbia named Marie-Rose Logan. The interview was translated into Polish and published with the title "'Kto do utworu przychodzi z niczym . . .': Z Williamem Gaddisem rozmawiaja" ["If You Bring Nothing to a Work . . .": An Interview with William Gaddis], Literatura na Świecie 1/150 (1984): 178–89. Mirkowicz began a Polish translation of* R *at this time but eventually abandoned it.*]

Wainscott NY 11975
7 November 1981

Dear Tomasz Mirkowicz.

I'm sorry to be so late about responding to your letter, but have been spending most of my time out here in the country & mail forwarding hasn't been dependable.

So far as the interview goes, I think it's just fine & see no reason to make any changes, as I told Marie-Rose Logan when she called a week or so ago. There are a few word changes here & there which are probably simply errors going into the English translation (as toward the foot of page 4, engendered should read endangered?), but I'm sure you & she will straighten this entropy out.

It also has occurred to me to suggest to you my making use of the interview if you have no objection, even though there is 'my condition' in it that it not appear in English; but I do get these requests frequently enough to be distracting even annoying so if such a moment comes along & you don't mind, I might make such use of it (would of course say interview conducted by you & translated from the Polish which would sound nicely exotic here).

Regarding fiction for your magazine, the only material I have right now is what's written of the book I'm working on and, since what I have is still in a first finished draft I don't especially want to see it published. I haven't yet incidentally heard from the Jarek Anders you mention with the magazine with the excerpt from *J R*, I've been as I say at the address below (and probably will until the end of the month, back in New York in December); but there has been someone at the 73rd street apartment so I hope the material hasn't got lost.

Finally, I'm sending your name along to a professor at New York University who has written me about a book he is getting together of critical articles on both my published novels, & you might possibly hear from him (his name is John Kuehl).

with best regards
William Gaddis

excerpt from *J R*: Jarosław Anders's translation of a section of *J R* appeared as "Symetryczny ruch wielkich kół" in *Literatura na Świecie* 3/71 (1977): 132–91.

To John R. Kuehl

[*Kuehl wrote to WG about his plan for a collection of essays on his work, to be edited by Kuehl and myself—Kuehl originated the idea, then invited me to co-edit the work after he learned of my forthcoming book on R—and asked if it would be possible to include an interview as part of the book. The collection was published in 1984 as* In Recognition of William Gaddis *(Syracuse University Press), but without an interview.*]

Wainscott NY 11975
[9 November 1981]

Dear John Kuehl.

I've just had a note from someone in Canada opening thus:

Hello Mr Gaddis. I arrived home Saturday with a stirring book by Alfred Kazin: *Bright Book of Life, American Novelists* &c. And I find you are not even *mentioned*. I extend my warmest congratulations…

So of course you are aware that there are many enough out there who do not share your (& Steven Moore's) most generous opinion of my 'body of work' (though here for one I have never understood how Kazin's relentlessly self serving pomposities have kept him afloat as a 'prominent critic').

At any rate of course I am intrigued by the notion of Moore's extraordinary effort and your projected one together, my feelings mixed as always ('shameful neglect', yes: my last royalty statement from Harcourt was something like $11.48; while another part of me cringes at 'most important single body of post WWII fiction'…) Which is why I suppose I'm still reluctant about interviews, had recently in fact an aborted attempt from a most well meaning fellow [Tom LeClair] from Cincinnati (sp?) which I felt turned out rambling and poor & of course ended in pain & recriminations &c. As though somehow perhaps my acceding to your request would make it appear that I'd promoted the whole thing (there were those in fact back in those days who told it around that Jack Green's marvels, including a full page ad in the then new *Village Voice* which he executed and paid for, were my doing under that pseudonym). But it would clearly be mean spirited for me to refuse in the face of your & others' generous efforts. From fragments of past experience though I feel it would be more satisfactory all round if you sent me some questions and I laboured out answers, not for mistrust of your approaches but of my own; & that it all come out fairly brief?

I'm fairly unaware & generally startled (shameful neglect notwithstanding) when I hear of activities going on concerning my work, witness your letter. But some items come to mind which may be of interest or use to you.

Did you come across a book called *Money Talks* (Univ Oklahoma Press 1980, ed. Roy Male) with a piece on *J R* by a Steven Weisenburger? I wrote him a note of thanks & he in return says he is writing a piece on both novels for an editor named John O'Brien who is putting together a special issue of *Review of Contemporary Fiction* on my work for 1982. All news to me. (If you want to reach Weisenburger he is at 271 E. Maxwell, #4; Lexington Kentucky 40506)

Then there is a Jay Fellows whom you may know or know of, at Columbia I think, said he was going to do something on my work possibly a book, he's a rather intense & self directed fellow & I don't know how he'd regard an inquiry if you were so inclined & don't have his address out here but his phone is 749-0208. He has a ladyfriend name I recall as Ann Douglas who I think teaches some of my work up there.

Finally for your entertainment I enclose a page of a letter from a man in Poland's (state run I assume) publishing scene, I've apparently a diligent following in Warsaw & did give him an interview of sorts provided it not appear here.

I am out here probably through November & mail to here or the NY address you have gets to me sooner or later.

With best regards
William Gaddis

Bright Book of Life: a study of American fiction from Hemingway to Mailer, published in 1973.

Review of Contemporary Fiction: the issue appeared in the summer of 1982; Weisenburger's "Paper Currencies: Reading William Gaddis" appears on pp. 12–22 and was reprinted in *In Recognition of William Gaddis,* pp. 147–61.

Jay Fellows: author of two books on John Ruskin; he was invited to contribute to our book, and though he showed interest, he never sent us anything, nor did he publish anything on WG's work in later years.

Ann Douglas: a professor of American Literature at Columbia, author of many books and essays on post-World War II American culture.

page of a letter: the page from Mirkowicz was not included when Kuehl made copies of his WG letters for me.

To John Large

Wainscott NY 11975
21 November 1981

Dear John Large.

Most apologetic about this long delay responding to yours of 22 October; first because I'm out here on the tail end of Long Isld & mail forwarding from the NY address is sporadic, next because I glanced at your letter & put it aside to read & answer eventually without noting your request regarding a reference to Princeton, so I hope it is not too late for me to say of course, if you'll let me know where & to whom there ($19G is a rather hefty bundle!)

And thanks for sending along your magazine. Your first excerpt a bit gamey for me (as I suppose the 2nd too): though I do of course remember the 2nd when you were labouring at its earlier version which I recall as a good deal more strained, & this—while the 'subject matter' cheers me up no more than it did then—I find far far improved & evidence that your sweating out those early writer's agonies, frustrations & paralyses have given you more than any amount of 'teaching', ease & authority & simply moving people around.

I am not that much further into but working on another & rather more bland, or as the reviewers' word has it, 'accessible' novel, God knows. I cannot recommend the profession unless one does start out ending up with it as the only game in town.

During December (down our throats) we should be more often in New York & might see you there if you pass through, meanwhile for the moment the address below, glad to know you're in one piece & pass along a greeting to K Begos from me,

all best wishes
William Gaddis

------

your magazine: *Dyslexia,* coedited by Large and Kevin Begos.

To Steven Moore

[*This and many of the letters to me that follow have to do with assembling* In Recognition of William Gaddis. *I wanted to reprint Jack Green's* Fire the Bastards! *there and asked Gaddis how to locate him.*]

Wainscott NY 11975
1 December 1981

Dear Steven Moore.

Regarding Jack Green: I saw him last only a year or so ago & the last address I have for him is: PO Box 3, Cooper Station, New York NY 10003, otherwise no idea how you might find him, he did have an address on Bowery but I don't find it listed. But I hope you may find him & won't go further now (& of course I vastly appreciated his efforts on the book's behalf) than to say he was a very pre-hippie, made his living then & may largely still as a ruthlessly efficient proof reader (free lance). In that regard it might interest you to know that he & I did meet somewhere back then, very early 60s? since he'd turned up a number of errors, mainly minor & typos, in the original edition of *The Recognitions*. I had these from him when the Meridian edition was being done around 1962–3, and the editor of that series stripped in the changes generously enough (he is Aaron Asher, now ed. in chief at Farrar Strauss & Giroux (Robt Giroux incidentally was nominal editor of the book at Harcourt Brace, left very soon after when Jovanovitch took the place over; so the book was originally published by Harcourt, Brace & Co., not "& World", let alone "& Jovanovitch").

At any rate, Meridian sold printed sheets to a British publisher McGibbon & Key, so only these editions stand corrected since, when Harcourt brought out a further printing & its own ugly paperback, they used old plates or more likely offset their original ed. without, of course, notifying me. (In terms of typos &c the Avon ed. is not even to be discussed; though I suppose I should be glad it's still in print in any form even that.)

Jack Green had started an exhaustive card catalogue crossfile reference on *The Recognitions* with an eye, as I recall, to compiling a "Skeleton Key to &c", heaven knows what became of it.

A quite meticulous translation was done into French by Jean Lambert (was then at Smith College, an ex-Gide son in law!); one rather less so I suspect into Italian (Mondadori) though it got reviewed by, (can't remember his name, very embarrassing, wrote *The Romantic Agony*), pleased me greatly of course. The Germans (Rowolt) ran through 2 or 3 translators, finally said they had the man who'd translated *Moby Dick* into German and a fresh start, that was some 15 years ago, never heard from them again.

best regards
William Gaddis

PS Weren't there more than #12–14 of *newspaper*'s Fire the Bastards? I've got them somewhere, unsure where, Green might too. I will look meanwhile.

Coincidence if such it is with Univ. Nebraska (Press), I heard some 20 years ago that the poet Karl Shapiro was going to devote an issue of *Prairie Schooner* which he then edited to *The Recognitions*, he abruptly left the editorship or the University or both & that ended that.

Robt Giroux: distinguished American editor (1914–2008), at Harcourt, Brace from 1940 to 1955, thereafter at FSG (as it's known in the trade). "I had a hell of a time getting it through the Harcourt hierarchy," he later recalled, "but Donald Brace okayed it" (quoted in Ted Morgan's "Feeding the Stream," *Saturday Review*, 1 September 1979, p. 43). Giroux included WG on a list of the ten authors whose first books he was proudest to have discovered and published (see Donald Hall's "Robert Giroux: Looking for Masterpieces," *New York Times Book Review*, 6 January 1980, 3, 22–24).

ugly paperback: Harcourt, Brace & World reprinted *R* in cloth in May 1964 and brought out a trade paperback edition with a different cover (under the Harvest imprint) in 1970.

Skeleton Key: Green's work—modeled, WG is suggesting, on Joseph Campbell and Henry Morton Robinson's *A Skeleton Key to "Finnegans Wake"* (1944)—was abandoned in 1980.

wrote *The Romantic Agony*: the distinguished Italian critic Mario Praz (1896–1982).

more than #12–14: no; WG is perhaps thinking of issue #11, a 32-page "Quote-Précis" of the novel.

To John and Pauline Napper

Wainscott, NY 11975
15 December 1981

Dear John and Pauline.

Your affectionate thoughts must have touched down upon me over this past year & more since however I continue to rant against the world's iniquities & unfathomable stupidities life has gradually settled down to offer me a good deal of warmth & satisfaction as my 59th looms just 2 weeks hence.

First Muriel the constant companion & blessing undisguised, we are mainly out here at the chill tail end of Long Island where a fair number of friends from other days seem to have settled, spent some time last year in Mexico & will again this coming Feb-March largely for the weather, & the escape that gives me little choice but to sit down at this terrible machine & try to get on from page 99 to 100 (as I managed this morning) even when I think I've been working well I look back over a month or 2's pages completed & am appalled at how few they are, another novel not a crusade this time like its 2 predecessors but simply, I hope, a 'romance' of sorts, its progress I can't say slowed by lack of conviction but clearly coloured by a sense of futility from the fortunes of the 2 books before it, craft not art this time, filling a contract & for the moment some Guggenheim fellowship money to carry it forward (and oh 'tis comfort small, To think that many another lad has had no luck at all!)

Speaking here of Shropshire I was shocked thinking of you with this morning's paper reporting heavy snows & −13°, so even more the credit to your work going well. Simplify! Simplify! says Thoreau & I too wish I could see it, now with the conviction that one's later life is spent in undoing the complications so enthusiastically devised by the earlier—though of course I suppose that's what *The Recognitions* was all about anyhow so perhaps all that distinguishes us from the machines is their ability to learn from their mistakes, the Jack Gold movie phantasy now long laid to rest.

The kids I must say though remain the best investment for these flagging years, Sarah & Peter as filled with good works & diligent cheer as from the start (they've come back to the east coast after 2 years of California, have your *Cat* hanging over their fireplace); Matthew among piecemeal film jobs in New York & quite as filled with indignation generally distributed as I was at that age & a future as unpredictable; but looking round me at other family situations I certainly count my blessings there.

There are places we want to go but as always God knows when, I did finally decide (& may have written you of it then) that I must see the Acropolis before moving out & we managed that what must be 2 years ago; & repeating Mexico may be too easy but I feel I've finally got to clear this job up & trust its ambience as sympathetic. And England? again, the Lord knows. It would be odd indeed to move out never having seen Shropshire! where it is at the least good to know you are thriving all things considered, with the hope that this may reach you in time enough to bring to you both warm affection from us all for the holidays & the inevitable new year,

Willie

and oh [...] at all!: from #28 of Housman's *Last Poems* (1922).

Simplify! Simplify! says Thoreau: in the second chapter of *Walden*; the Town Carpenter echoes Thoreau's advice in *R* (411, 441), as does Crawley in *J R* (449).

Matthew among piecemeal film jobs: in the 1980s Matthew worked on *My Dinner with Andre, Crackers, Alamo Bay, God's Country,* and *The Suicide Club.*

To Steven Moore

[*Green refused permission to reprint* Fire the Bastards! *and was outraged that I had already begun preparing his work for publication without first securing his permission. (I hadn't known of his whereabouts, or whether he could even be located.) See my introduction to the Dalkey Archive edition for further details.*]

235 East 73rd street
New York NY 10021
6 January 1982

Dear Steven Moore.

I've just had a note from Jack Green regarding your exchange of letters. Unfortunate in a way (I might have thought to write him myself first out of courtesy), means you cannot have the saga complete from the start, must I suppose open with such entrenched stupidity as Granville Hicks (parodied, among others, on pp. 515–6 of *J R*). However I can certainly see Jack's point & of all people must honour it: his fierce intransigence & sense of integrity are of course what led him to take up cudgels on my book's behalf these 27 years ago.

Next, responding to a question from you or Prof. Kuehl regarding my recollection of Jack Green, I think I said something like pre-hippie which, though in ways accurate enough, has by now too many pejorative implications & I do not wish to be so quoted. What is important to note is, should you now still plan any references to him, his indignation even then with the commercial 'establishment' (viz. his attacking those reviewers in those rather than coy literary terms, i.e. that they'd done poor to dishonest jobs & so should be fired) (my own feeling more recently for John Gardner's *J R* review in the *NY Review of Books*); his taking out the *Voice* ad (which I trust you've seen) with his own funds & unbeknownst to me, legend to the contrary; & his subsequent supplying the numerous corrections—I've now no idea how many, perhaps upwards of 40 or 50—of typos, my own errors, dropped lines &c, which were incorporated in the Meridian (& English) editions & none since: in other words a serious champion not of me (as the bone in the jaws of today's blurb world has it but of course may have always: have you ever come across Amanda Roos' *Bayonets of Bastard Sheen*?), but of a piece of work.

(Though, for a diversion, how in heaven's name can be explained the *New Republic*'s embrace of so pitifully awkward, vulgar, artless, amateurishly (in the pejorative sense) egregious (do.) an item as *A Confederacy of Dunces*, as "one of the finest books ever written"! & again, ! ! ! ! ! The more things change &c ...)

I've got some questions here from Kuehl which I hope to do some blunt kind of justice to before leaving in 3 weeks for a couple of months during which I wish you good luck with your enterprises,

with best regards
William Gaddis

PS it did occur to me, in the realm of perverse self promotion (as the item itself clearly is), should you find useful for cover? jacket? illustration/design

&c purposes (as opposed to Knopf's bleary snapshot) for your collection of
pieces on my work, to suggest the line 'drawing' included in Burt Britton's
Self Portrait / Book People Picture Themselves (Random House 1976, paper)
which apparently Kuehl hadn't seen; preferably as is but should there be
copyright threat I could send you a repeat 'original'.

Amanda Roos' *Bayonets of Bastard Sheen*: Amanda Ros (1860–1939) is celebrated for
being a terrible writer; *Bayonets* is a book of extracts from her letters, privately
printed by T. S. Mercer in 1949.

A Confederacy of Dunces: posthumously published first novel by John Kennedy Toole
(1937–69), which won the Pulitzer Prize for fiction in 1980; reviewed by Phelps Gay
in the 19 July 1980 issue of the *New Republic* (who called it one of the "funniest"
books ever written, not "finest.") WG later had a change of heart and praised portions of the novel in *AA* (63–66).

Burt Britton's *Self Portrait:* our letter to Burt Britton requesting permission went un-
answered, so WG supplied a version of the same drawing for the cover of *In Recognition*. He modeled it on Jill Krementz's photo of him at the NBA ceremony in 1976.

To Tomasz Mirkowicz

New York NY 10021
9 January 1982

Dear Tomasz Mirkowicz.

I received your card and message this morning and of course in view of
what we read in the papers here of conditions in Poland was very happy to
hear from you.

Anders is probably back among you & so has let you know of our very
pleasant relaxed visit with him in the country & that I found the magazines
he brought along most intriguing, even to seeing the page of Gibbs' notes
meticulously translated and pasted up in Polish!

To your query regarding arrangements for an edition in Polish of *The
Recognitions*, our picture at this moment of the situation there is unclear
enough that I might imagine for all your generous intentions circumstances
have changed since you sent your proposal. I can only say now therefore that
should it still be possible to work out I would have no objection whatever to
payment in 'blocked' zlotys, if you will only when the time comes let me know
the amount involved (a matter which I know is not in your control).

My only request would be this: that on the chance some other member of
my family might find it possible to visit Poland when I might not, that such
an account be set up so that could be drawn upon by not only myself but any
of the following who might show up first:

Matthew Gaddis; Sarah Gaddis Conley; Muriel O Murphy.

The prospect of my work appearing there is rather a marvelous one to me (as has been even its following in English) and I greatly appreciate all of your efforts. You must know that through the haze of confusion here about conditions in Poland day to day, we think of you often and hope that your own lives and work are going on as well as can be possible and how greatly we admire your spirit in these difficult times.

Finally I should note that given uncertainties about the mail situation between us, and when you will receive this, we plan to leave New York at the end of the month for February and March in Mexico and that should you write me again late this month I might not have your letter till we return in early April.

very best wishes & regards
William Gaddis

---

conditions in Poland: martial law had been declared a month earlier. Mirkowicz hid Warsaw Solidarity leader Zbigniew Bujak in his apartment for a while.

Anders: as noted earlier, Jarosław Anders's translation of a section of *J R* appeared in *Literatura na Świecie*.

To John R. Kuehl

[The cover letter to Gaddis's answers to the questions Kuehl and I had set for him. Disappointed at the brevity of the interview, we decided against including it in our book and offered it instead to John O'Brien for his special issue of the Review of Contemporary Fiction *(vol. 2, no. 2 [Summer 1982]), where it appears on pp. 4–6.]*

12 January 1982

Dear John Kuehl.

While not as detailed as you might wish, I trust that the enclosed will serve your purpose (taking you at your word to write 'as little or as much' &c). For your information (3,4) I have little enthusiasm right now for reviving the *Lampoon* period, didn't know John Hawkes at college, believe I had an English survey course under Guerard but nothing beyond that. Items like (10) I'd leave to the critics, the kind of question for which I simply don't have an offhand answer & the full & real one would just take too much entirely distracting time which is the problem with all these things, somebody else now after me wanting to publish an interview I gave to a Pole & it all just breaks up the day the mind & the work, however much I appreciate your interest & efforts.

Incidental to that, I wrote John O'Brien/*Review of Contemporary Fiction*

that no, I didn't want anything published from work in progress right now
& no, I couldn't send him a critical piece right now either. But I wouldn't
mind at all if you wanted to share any of the enclosed with him, quite up to
you of course (I didn't mention such a thing to him). We're leaving in early
February so I hope this wraps things up.

Yours,
W. Gaddis

(3,4): our questions 3 and 4 had asked about his Harvard years: his work for the *Harvard Lampoon,* whether he met John Hawkes while there, and whether he studied
under the prominent critic Albert Guerard (1914–2000).
(10): regarding the impact of *The Waste Land* on *R.*

To John and Dorothy Sherry

[*Sent from a popular tourist destination in central Mexico, accompanied by a newspaper
clipping entitled "Older American Corps Draft Proposed."*]

Terraplin, 5
San Miguel de Allende
Gto. [Guanajuato], Mexico
[February or March 1982]

NEWS FROM SANDY DELL: DRAFT DODGE HAVEN FOR THE
'GOLDEN OLDIES'

Thanks for your cheerful letter—cheery that is in light of ice & elbows, oh
dear. Joints are too tricky; as for the sling I had the 6 weeks of that as you
recall & can sympathize with that outrage.

Tempting fate here, I've no misfortunes to report. It is in fact all just glowing. Caught up with your fast set—Kimballs &c—who send best wishes &
we've had a little wine&dining back & forth. Marc [Brandel] & consort quite
mellow which is another warm note here. And even a Peter Glenville evening,
most most elegant, 2 tables of real swells & most of the conversation about
murderers everyone seems to know (Claus & Sunny, Mrs Harris' doctor
&c)—no way in our modest digs we can repay in kind especially the touch of
taking the resident live duck around to tell everyone goodnight...

I have a nice tan which is not what the Guggenheim folks had in mind
financing; what they did have in mind proceeds at a more glacial pace than
any in memory though I am at it every morning & most late afternoons. [...]

And so, as we prepare for our annual Sunday pm backyard cookout for some of the above mentioned, the sky takes on a real South Fork grey, the air chills, and we say goodbye from Sandy Dell. Our best to Carol & Lucia, that is a very hard one as we know from our own; but we'll see you all soon, back to NY the 29th March & Wainscott soon thereafter. Tell Carol her Clinique benisons were received with squeals here.

love from us both & all
W—

Kimballs: unidentified.

Peter Glenville: English actor and director (1913–96), who owned a second home in San Miguel de Allende.

Claus & Sunny, Mrs Harris's doctor: socialite Claus von Bülow was tried in 1982 for the attempted murder of his wife Sunny; his original conviction was later overturned. School principal Jean Harris made national headlines in 1980 for murdering her lover, Dr. Herman Tarnower, author of the best-selling *Complete Scarsdale Medical Diet* (1979).

Carol & Lucia: Carol Phillips (1922–2006), a former editor at *Vogue*, founded Clinique (skincare products) in 1968. She was a close friend of WG until his death. Lucia Haile was her sister.

To John R. Kuehl

[To thank WG for the interview, Kuehl and I sent him a coffee-table book on Flemish art. He sent me a letter almost identical to this one.]

Wainscott NY 11975
20 April 1982

Dear John Kuehl.

Simply a note to thank you for the marvelously thoughtful gift from yourself & Steven Moore waiting for me when I returned from Mexico: those pictures do one after another of them recall an intense time in my life (What only youth could mount, and folly ride . . . if I have it about right).

I understand incidentally that, somehow subliminally, Avon has anticipated imminent activity by printing 5000 more of their bad fat little edition this time to go at $5.95. Perhaps some day my children will see that 1973 advance earned back.

Needless to say I look forward with some curiosity to the various fruits of all your efforts ahead,

best regards & thanks again
William Gaddis

from Mexico: at this point in his letter to me, WG added: "particularly when I've felt that you might have found me less responsive to all of both of your efforts on my work's behalf than might have been hoped."

What [...] ride: see note to 24 May 1980.

To Thomas Sawyer

[*Sawyer wrote to WG to ask five questions for an essay he was writing on* J R *(eventually published as "*J R: The Novel of Entropy*,"* International Fiction Review *10.2 [Summer 1983]: 117–22): "1. Is the title* JR *intended to indicate that, in some ways,* JR *is the off-spring of* The Recognitions? *2. The narrative technique of extended conversations is used in sections of* The Recognitions. *Did any other work or author (maybe Ivy Compton Burnett's* A Heritage and Its History?*) have any influence on the narrative technique used in* JR? *3. Is the use of Wagner's* Ring *as a foundation for* JR *to suggest (in addition to the effects of capitalism) an ironic contrast between the harmonies in Wagner's operas and the dissonance of* JR's *conversations? 4. Did Hawthorne's* Marble Faun *or Melville's* Confidence Man *have any influence on* The Recognitions? *5. Can you indicate what about Graves's* The White Goddess *impressed you the most in terms of a potential source of some of the images or motifs in* The Recognitions?*"*]

3 May 1982

Dear Tom Sawyer.

Sorry to be ~~very little~~ no help with your questions of 26 April, briefly: 1) read in what you like, I wouldn't think of *J R* as offspring; 2), 4): I leave questions of influences &c to critics & reviewers, haven't read I C Burnett, doubt the Hawthorne & never finished the Melville; similarly for Graves (5) read so long ago I can't take time to go back picking through it. 3) you're welcome again to read that 'ironic contrast' in, whether or not it was among my primary intentions.

You may be interested to know that Univ of Nebraska Press is scheduled to bring out this month a book titled *A Reader's Guide to The Recognitions* which may be some use to you (I haven't seen it).

Yours,

W. Gaddis

I C Burnett: British author Ivy Compton Burnett (1884–1969) wrote seventeen novels—similar to each other but to no one else's—consisting, like *J R*, primarily of dialogue.

To John and Pauline Napper

[*Handwritten around a photocopy of the* New York Times's *announcement (14 July, p. A-16) that WG, among others, had been awarded a MacArthur Fellowship, the so-called genius award, amounting to $50,000 a year ($150K today) for the next five years. Frederick Karl told me he was the one who had nominated WG.*]

Wainscott, N.Y. 11975
14 July 1982

dear John & Pauline— Can you imagine this! The entire thing a stunning surprise to me & I am still trying to absorb it after those 40 years of mistrustful approaches to the world and fortune: 5 years of "security"! making a good number of 180° turns in my head and of course for the first time really some tangible reason simply to *live* for another 5 years—

We think of you often though seem to make no steps or plans nearer to England but hope you are well and the work going on since what else finally is there?

love from Muriel & kids &
Willie

To David Markson

Wainscott, NY 11975
20 July 1982

Dear David,

Thanks for your generous note. How odd it is: running back to 1955 if I'd got the (equivalent) prize then I'd scarcely have been surprised; instead (surprise!), Granville Hicks. 25 sobering years later & it is The Surprise (& a sobering one at that): somewhere in the book Wyatt observes that the present is constantly reevaluating the past, —I was right all the time . . . or, —I was wrong all the time . . .

How about that.

Best regards,
Willie Gaddis

Granville Hicks: one of the original nay-saying reviewers of *R*.
the present is constantly reevaluating the past: see note to letter to Sheri Martinelli (Summer 1953).

To Steven Moore

[*My* Reader's Guide *appeared in June; I had written to ask if it would be possible to follow it with a manuscript study of* R.]

Wainscott NY 11975
23 July 1982

Dear Steven Moore.

I'd put off answering your letter waiting for a glimpse of the Nebraska Press book which (after another call there) has finally just arrived. And from just a glimpse it is prodigious, right down to the maddening task of assembling the Avon errata. At some point—should it prove useful to you—I will try to go through it & clear up some of your nicely handled speculations (as, for example, whether Graves pointed me to *The Golden Bough*: I had already devoured it entire, and then read his *White Goddess* in Madrid & hurried up to Deyá to talk to Graves and ask for suggestions regarding what religion might a Protestant minister becoming unhinged turn to. He came up with something about Salem witchcraft (I later dug up the Mithras solution elsewhere) but was such a fine and generous man that we had numerous talks and, in fact, he was to become somewhat the physical model for Rev Gwyon).

Concerning your requests regarding my papers, I am right now in some sort of state of transition brought on in good part, obviously, by this stunning surprise of the MacArthur Fellowship Prize with its assurance of 5 entire years of security. I haven't the papers here & am trying to work out plans for a house I have which is now rented & where most of my things are stored, so I will have to let you know how things sort out.

It would be a disservice to your work & ingenuity (to trace down absurd books like *Les Damnés de la Terre!*) to comment further, until I take the time to sit down to it right; for the moment simply, my aghast appreciation.

Otherwise, I haven't seen the *Contemporary Review of Fiction* (if that's the title), called Gotham Book people who said they'd send it & haven't. But enough for one day!

with best regards
William Gaddis

Les Damnés de la Terre: a book by Henri Poulaille mentioned on p. 81 of *R*.
Contemporary Review of Fiction: when he did receive the issue of *RCF*, WG sent a postcard [postmarked 6 August] to John O'Brien saying simply, "Many thanks for sending the copy of the *Review* along to me. I always learn something new."

Gotham: Gotham Book Mart, the prestigious literary book store on West 47th Street in New York City. A bookman there named Matthew Monahan (1947–90), a neighbor of WG's in the Hamptons, handled most of his requests.

To Steven Moore

[I was writing an essay on the parallels between WG's and Thomas Pynchon's work— published as "'Parallel, not Series': Thomas Pynchon and William Gaddis," Pynchon Notes *11 (February 1983): 6–26—and asked whether he believed, as some critics maintain, that* R *influenced Pynchon's* V. *(1963). He and Pynchon shared the same agent, which may explain how WG "understood" that Pynchon felt he had not been under the influence.]*

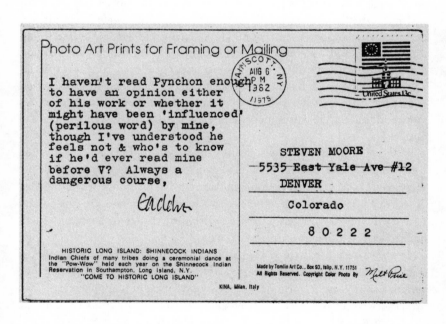

V: WG didn't think much of Pynchon's first novel. In late 1975 or 1976, he composed a fictitious phone call he receives from a Michigan high school student who "thought that *J R* was phenomenal especially in light of some of the so called literature capital L being circulated these days like Pynchon's *V.* [...] I mean [your] characters are human not like the paper mache cutouts that populate Pynchon's palimpsests [...]" (quoted in Marshall Klimasewski's "William Gaddis and the Thoughts of Others," *Conjunctions* 70 [2018]: 337, 338).

To Tom LeClair

Wainscott, New York 11975
17 October 1982

Dear Tom LeClair.

Thanks for sending me your *J R* & Excess, clearly thought out & followed through I thought in this heart of the matter runaway systems area: well done!

I gave Kuehl/Moore a few paragraphs of talk for a book of pieces they have been collecting on my work; but as for this 'interview' business, I've known from George* for a couple years that *Paris Review* has been interested but I right now have none, & thought you disposed of it nicely in your good piece in *Holiday* was it? the 'transcript' not to be published or paraphrased, & that you'd given up being tiresome about it.

The most stunning stretch I remember was from Sparta west through the mountains to Pylos,

yours,
W. Gaddis

*Plimpton

J R & *Excess*: see note to 23 February 1980.

George: see 4 January 1986.

Holiday: i.e., *Horizon*, where LeClair published a piece entitled "Missing Writers" (October 1981, 48–52) featuring WG among other reclusive novelists.

Sparta: LeClair too had visited Greece and knew the country well.

To John Napper

Wainscott NY 11975
6 November 1982

Dear John,

THERE IS NO EQUITY. I wailed that for years & can repeat it now, albeit from a rather different vantage point. The Lord knows—less well perhaps than you & I—that having the money burden lifted for 5 years late along the way is an undisguised blessing: I say undisguised advisedly, since had I got such a 'prize' on the heels of publishing *The Recognitions* I'd really have been a good deal less surprised than now, would most likely have taken it as due under a logical system of just reward for fine work executed; but here it comes undisguised by such illusions of the world & the place of one's work in it, & serves rather to underline the capriciousness of both. No one cavils when some egregious effort brings $1 million in a paperback sale, $3 million from the movies, all disappeared tomorrow. Should one now?

Of course having spent a lifetime at caviling it's hard to change one's ways, but it's the damndest thing: has this recognition spurred a rush of high paperback offers on either book? no. Or movies? no. Or W German, Swede publishers bidding wildly or at all? no. My last statement from Harcourt Brace reads debit of $4.29, incorporating the 33¢ they overpaid me on my last royalty check 6 months ago of $11.48. (*J R*—not I personally thank heavens— still owes Knopf some $37 thousand.) All not that unlike S[c]hepperman's sale of his paintings to Mrs Selk [in *J R*] locking them away from vulgar concourse with the public eye in hopes of cornering the market or ruining him, one.

So while I cavil I certainly do not complain, but rather marvel at this splendid further evidence of the inconsistency that I've celebrated from the start; for in the USA real money is the only proof against taking 'defeat from every brazen throat'.

Meanwhile the subterranean procession continues: where in the world did you happen upon Steven Moore's *Reader's Guide*? With less than no help from me he's done a rather incredible job of digging I must say, the near misses & lacunae notwithstanding; & he threatens to bring out another book of collected pieces on me or my work, I'm not sure & thus somewhat apprehensive. Of course (in USA) I haven't seen his book mentioned let alone reviewed anywhere, just as I haven't been elected to the National Academy of Arts & Letters (where Joyce Carol Oates and J Updike are prominent mambers [*in margin*: an honest typo]): yes, the damndest thing. But again, to be rude about it what books like Moore's accomplish (in USA) is a fair guarantee of a good price—far more than the books themselves ever earned in the 'marketplace'— for my notes, papers, drafts &c from some large Texas sort of university engulfed in the serious industry of doctoral dissertations. (Hang on to those letters! they may yet buy you a bottle of Tres Cepas, even a case...)

So taken all together there's a certain satisfaction in having done it backwards; having done, perhaps like Melville, the monumental work first (though I too prefer *J R*), & looking at the present work with a somewhat jaundiced eye, one more 'raid on the inarticulate' where one's weapons are always deteriorating, shorter and smaller in scope in some inadvertant response to the only comment I've seen in the public press on my work recently, wherein a John Montague in the *Guardian* (reviewing a new book on Joyce) refers to the 'elephantiasis of the imagination in such writers as Gaddis and Pynchon, to name only two...' Surely in a world like this one integrity, if only a shred of it, is the only thing left, & there's even something to be said for obscurity. [...]

love to you both,
Willie

'defeat from every brazen throat': a line from Yeats's poem "To a Friend Whose Work
Has Come to Nothing" (1914) and used in *J R* (131).
large Texas sort of university: eventually the Nappers sold their Gaddis letters to the
Harry Ransom Center at the University of Texas.
Tres Cepas: a Spanish brandy.
'raid on the inarticulate': from part 5 of Eliot's "East Coker."
John Montague in the *Guardian*: untraced.

To Steven Moore

Wainscott NY 11975
26 November 1982

Dear Steven Moore.

Your queries regarding the publishing history of *The Recognitions* raise a
touchy area, & in confidence—I think for the moment you needn't share with
anyone—I'll try to tell you why; & also I must ask you, as a condition I've
never made elsewhere as you know, to send along to me a copy of what you
write on the subject before publication so I can check it out.

Briefly the point is this: for 20 years following its original publication, I
tried every way I could to regain the book's rights from Harcourt, which is
to say from Jovanovitch who sank his teeth in it &, despite its miserable earn-
ings record & their total disregard for it, has never let go. The reason I don't
want those murky details gone into right now is that, with the changes going
on in publishing & specifically to & within Harcourt, <u>I still hope for a reversion of rights</u> through some hook or crook & don't want that possibility faint
as it may be to be jeopardised by my intemperate observations. Thus for the
time being it would be best to confine your record to what 'facts' there are
without my involvement as your source.

I'm quite impressed by the amount of information you got from this Devlin person (I don't know him) at Harcourt, more than I ever received from
them. I'd heard the original printing was around 5 thousand but never knew
the figure; wasn't of course informed of the remaindering beforehand though
it was quite soon (for those days) after publication. (My then wife saw it in a
window for $1.98; the latest price I've heard paid for that first ed. is $130.) I
wasn't informed of a 2nd printing in 1964, that I think was about the time of
the Meridian ed. & I suppose they hoped to cash in a bit on that (v. Tony Tanner's long review in the *Times*.) Regarding the Meridian ed.: it was done by
Aaron Asher who was responsible & decent enough to let me make a number
of corrections (many or most of them caught by Jack Green) which he stripped
in. I don't know how large the Meridian printing was. Part of the Meridian

deal was their sale of sheets to McGibbon & Key (check sp.) in England for I believe 1500 copies. Thus those are the only 'corrected' editions. I didn't know till by chance a week or so beforehand of Harcourt's 1970 paperback ed.; had they let me know I'd have suggested they offset the Meridian ed. rather than their own original but of course they used their own & retained errors. I didn't know the hardbound ed. was 'officially' declared OP in 1976 but, as Devlin notes, 'of course paperbound editions are in print.' All this of course & as you surmise has got simply to do with their retaining the rights, the book virtually unattainable for many years (I think Koenig paid $25 for his) while 'officially' in print, & the slack taken up later by these paperbacks. As I recall, I knew nothing of the Avon deal till it had occurred (Harcourt not contractually obliged to consult me as per my old fashioned 1st novel contract), simply got ½ the $11 thousand they were paid by Avon when, 10 years ago? & not 1¢ since.

Regarding foreign editions: there was an agreement with Fred Warburg (Secker &) in 1953 or 4, who had been touted on it as the new *Ulysses* as his fatuous letters to me witness; however, seeing its initial reception here by such boobs as Granville Hicks, he hastily backed off with the excuse of being unable to find a printer in England who would do it because of the obscenity laws & wrote me a marvelously inane letter on the duties of the artist to 'select' his material, simply wanted it cut down to cut his costs & I said to hell with him. The Germans (Rowolt)(sp?) optioned it, ran through 2 translators who gave up, finally said they were starting afresh with the man who had translated *Moby Dick* into Ger & I never heard from them again. The French took some 9 years from their option date & finally, after an acrimonious exchange with Claude Gallimard, brought it out. Mondadori brought it out in 2 vols. & I suspect a rather hack translation though never checked carefully & don't off hand recall the It. title, something like *la Pereze*, the pilgrim or some such. It's now being translated into Polish, no contract of course.

Incidentally, a story you might say you picked up by hearsay (not that is from me), I heard at the time that the man who was setting type for the book, a good Catholic, was enough dismayed at what he considered sacrilege & obscenity that he consulted his priest who told him to refuse to set it, the printers (Quinn & Boden, sp?) notified Harcourt accordingly but a good fellow there at Harcourt, Gerry & damned if I can remember his last name, told them to set it or it would be the last job they got from HB & so they did. Hard to imagine all that but recall these were the times when books were being banned in Boston (a distinction I frankly craved as a spur to sales elsewhere). (It wasn't.)

To your points: yes I did tell Janet Halverson my idea for the jacket & she came through I think triumphantly (cf. the cover design for Harcourt's paperback for trashy contrast). Of course obviously also I asked for her for the jacket for *J R* where again I think she did stunningly (this time her own design with no suggestion from me). I have no information on the BOMC ed. & the only thing I can think of is that they did bring one out when *J R* was published & its trade paperback on the front cover of their QPB monthly catalogue; BOMC may just have bought some warehoused copies from Harcourt God knows, I don't think I ever had any accounting from Harcourt (or $) & gather neither book did too well for BOMC. And I've no way of knowing whether HB(J) ever did a 3rd hardcover printing, their OP in 1976 may simply have been the last of the 2nd hoarded in warehouses &, as above, dumped on BOMC: the dates would seem to correspond (*J R* pubd in 1975 & the Natl Book Award in spring '76); & since Devlin's net hardbound sales of 4722 copies is just 163 under the initial 4885 printing (could be those handed out for reviews, publicity &c), that whole 2nd printing of 1000 may have been dumped on BOMC & remaindered by them despite Devlin's disclaimer. God knows what the price of the prepublication copies in black paper wrapper is now (I think there were 200 of them), last I heard was one of those Santa Barbara places asking $335. The usual writer's complaint: at the 1955 publication I believe HB put 1 ad in a Thursday *NYTimes*, prompting a friend to observe that rather than being published the book had been privished.

Jovanovitch had taken over as President of HB as I recall barely weeks before the book came out in 1955; Eugene Reynal (sp?) who'd been trade books editor left, so did Robert Giroux. Jov. put in a dolt from the business side as trade editor & any effort for the book ceased. Despite his lack of any effort on the book's behalf in the decades since, Jov. takes great pride in having been its publisher (it was of course practically in the stores by the time he took over), & his loyalty (=clinging to the rights) to it. Our correspondence ended a good many years ago, his on a fatuous, mine on an acrimonious note.

Now it's faintly possible that something will be resolved (ie a reversion of rights) by the time your book is done & finds a publisher; for now however you may see that it's not in my interest either to recall my rancour to Jov's attention, or to stimulate—despite my gratitude for you & Kuehl's efforts— enough interest in the book to prompt anyone to make a decent reprint bid to Harcourt thereby perpetuating my enslavement. (While Avon's contract with HB licensing its reprint has expired they go right along peddling it, though changes at Avon too may let it drop.)

Yours,
William Gaddis

Devlin: John Devlin at Harcourt, Brace answered numerous questions of mine regarding *R*'s publication history.

Tony Tanner's long review: the eminent British critic Tony Tanner (1935–98) reviewed the Avon (not the Meridian) edition of *R* in the *New York Times Book Review,* 14 July 1974, 27–28.

how large the Meridian printing was: there were two printings, a first (March 1962) of 8,000 copies (with 2,000 unbound sets shipped to MacGibbon & Kee), and a second (September 1963) of 2,500.

la Pereze : i.e., *Le perizie,* which doesn't mean The Pilgrim but something like Expert Testimony (or Summary Report).

Gerry: Gerald J. Gross (1921–2015).

BOMC ed.: a Book-of-the-Month Club edition of *R* was remaindered in the late 1970s.

QPB: The Quality Paperback Club offered a paperback edition of *J R*.

Santa Barbara: probably Joseph the Provider, a rare-book dealer located in Santa Barbara and known for their high prices. (Due to financial necessity, I sold them this and my other Gaddis letters in the summer of 1991, much to WG's chagrin.)

1 ad: Harcourt's ad appeared in the 16 March 1955 issue of the *New York Times,* p. 31.

To Steven Moore

[*Per his request, I sent WG a draft of my introduction to* In Recognition of William Gaddis. *The page numbers and the phrases WG puts in quotes below are from this draft.*]

Wainscott NY 11975
3 January 1983

Steven Moore: thanks for the look at your draft, here are some corrections & elaborations:

Page 4. Also the inevitable rumour that one is dead. Regarding the Pynchon reference (which may be what you refer to), there was a column by a well disposed man whose name I can't recall, for years he wrote syndicated book reviews for AP, speculating that *Gravity's Rainbow* might well be the long novel I'd been rumoured working on, & Pynchon & I the same person (but, Pynchon "as a young man"?).

8. "minor misunderstanding" might better be fracas, even frolic; about January '45, & I did not stay on. Rather, since college regulations forbade anyone on probation taking part in extracurricular activities, it was the custom at the *Lampoon* to take a pseudonym in this situation (look at the mastheads, you'll see some very odd names); thus I'd been on probation since the first time Ravenkil(l?) W. appears, and left promptly after the above incident not "anxious to develop talents &c" but simply to get a job. That was inciden-

tally not as a 'trainee' but a 'checker'; the checking dept at the *NYer* was (& is) serious stuff there.

9. top, a brief memoir? then, I honestly question that I wore my 'unimpaired right arm in a sling', but Vincent's image is lively enough that I won't argue. Incidentally again: nothing libelous in he 'introduced her to drugs'? or 'attempted suicide many times'? I don't know that it really was many, or how real even those attempts were.

10. top, that printing press relegation seems to me quite far fetched.

#2 that year in a monastery cell belongs back with the legends on p.4. I did indeed go out to the place with all sorts of dour & self absorbed intentions only to discover that they were well prepared for such intrusions: a comfortable room & meals at modest price & arm's length from their devotions, I stayed about a week: thus Ludy (parody of a *Readers Digest* piece by AJ Cronin) & his 'religious experience'.

11. That 1952 copyright notice has misled everyone. It should refer really only to the *New World Writing* extract; the book itself wasn't copyrighted till publication. Then this: Catharine (not Catherine) Carver worked at Harcourt in some such capacity as copyreader but it was she who went through the MS exhaustively with meticulous queries &c. & fought for the book. You might check the *PR* masthead for whether she was formally their fiction editor, I know she did most of the drudgery work there & never got much credit for it. David Chandler was a college summer trainee, he did carefully review the MS with intelligent queries but quite secondarily to C.C. (The 'editor' in your note 19 is of course she.) Whether you want to hedge the typesetter item as 'a story told' is of course up to you, I had it as I say 2nd hand.

14. You will be interested to see Aldridge on *J R* in a forthcoming book *The American Novel and the Way We Live Now*, Oxford Univ. Press for April 83 publication.

15. bottom, leave Cowley in there as presenter if you want to, he did indeed hand me the envelop but I'm sure he hadn't a clue who or what either I or the book was & don't recall his reading the citation.

19. bottom, rather than '(mis)quoted by Gibbs' you might want to say 'drunkenly misquoted by Gibbs'; that's where Steiner got to me, quoting some of Gibbs' ranting as dialogue without mention he was drunk.

22. It was in fact McCarthy & Gass over Dolbier's objections (he I believe wanted the Woiwode, even went so far as to dissociate himself from the decision in his provincial (Providence?) column).

22. I haven't that acceptance at hand but am sure something, the latter part

that makes contrast sense of it, has been dropped from the quote on Gorky, ie what happened *after* 1880.

23. middle, also in the Notes: I'm sure it's Peter not David Koenig?

24. No offense, but to me 'in-depth' is right out of Whiteback's lexicon along with 'ongoing'.

NOTES:

13. For 'short shrift' you might see his reference in his review of Bert Britten's (sp?) *Self Portrait, Writers drawing themselves* (& while at it, glimpse his drawing in the book).

23. I'm certain that Gill wrote not in *Time* (I don't recall who did) but the (unsigned) item in the *NYer*'s Briefly noted fiction, a condescending dismissal reference to Shawn the Penman (Joyce apparently).

From your letter: I gather your request to publish items from my letters refers to those quoted in this text which is okay with me (Lord knows what I've written to others elsewhere); I've no objection to your publishing the essay (nor of course control) & don't think any notice of either permission or disavowal is necessary.

Yours
William Gaddis

Pynchon reference [...] well disposed man: W. G. Rogers, who had reviewed *R*, spent the last third of his 1973 review of *Gravity's Rainbow* suggesting WG might have written Pynchon's new novel. On a copy of the review in his archives, WG wrote "I'm quite flattered but if I were Pynchon I think I'd be quite annoyed— "

"minor misunderstanding": I had thus described the circumstances under which he had been asked to leave Harvard. WG used the pseudonym Ravenkill Woodplumpton in the September and December 1944 issues of the *Harvard Lampoon*.

"a brief memoir": I had used a different description of "In the Zone," his account of his days in Panama. The rest refers to his old acquaintance Vincent Livelli, who sent me several letters recording his memories of WG, Eddie Shu's influence on Sheri Martinelli's drug use, and her attempted suicides.

printing press: Martinelli had a small printing press in her apartment, which reminded me that the retarded serving girl Janet in *R* also has her own press, on which she prints religious tracts. #2 refers to WG's visit to a monastery in Spain.

AJ Cronin: See A. J. Cronin's "What I Learned at La Grande Chartreuse," *Reader's Digest,* February 1953, 73–77.

PR: *Partisan Review,* where Carver was managing editor at the time.

Aldridge: pages 46–52 are a revision of his *Saturday Review* review of *J R*.

Cowley: the eminent critic Malcolm Cowley (1898–1989) presented WG with a grant from the National Institute of Arts and Letters on 22 May 1963 (see letter of 10 May 1963 for the citation).

McCarthy & Gass: concerning *J R*'s National Book Award: Dolbier wrote an account of the NBA proceedings for the *Providence Journal*, 2 May 1976, H-33.

acceptance: I must have mistranscribed WG's NBA acceptance speech: see *In Recognition*, pp. 15–16, for the complete (and accurate) text (rpt. in *RSP* 122).

Peter not David Koenig: Peter Koenig, sometime after writing his dissertation on *R*, changed his name to David. (See WG's asterisked note in his 7 April 1983 letter.)

'in-depth': my introduction ended somewhat abruptly, so John Kuehl added a concluding phrase using "in-depth," a favorite adjective of Principal Whiteback in *J R*.

'short shrift': I had echoed the postscript to WG's letter to Steven Weisenburger of 18 September 1981 (which he had shared with me) and said Anatole Broyard gave short shrift to something or other of Gaddis's. In his review of Britton's *Self-Portrait*, Broyard wrote of WG's line drawing: "William Gaddis is headless, his privacy either inviolable or inaccessible to him" (*New York Times*, 30 November 1976, 37).

Gill: I had carelessly written that Brendan Gill reviewed *R* in *Time* rather than in the *New Yorker*, where he concluded: "this novel challenges the reader to compare it with Joyce's 'Ulysses.' So challenged, the reader is obliged to say that while Mr. Gaddis has been very brave, Shem the Penman has won the day." (Shem and Shawn are brothers in *Finnegans Wake*.)

To June R. Cox

[*American educator (1919–96), then Research Director of the Sid W. Richardson Foundation and researching her book* Educating Able Learners: Programs and Promising Practices (*Austin: University of Texas Press, 1985*), *which quotes from the letter below on pages 18 and 27.*]

> 235 East 73rd street
> New York, NY 10021
> 24 January 1983

Dear Ms Cox.

I am sorry to be so long about answering your inquiry regarding my educational background as it might relate to my MacArthur Prize Fellowship. I've postponed it with the usual excuses but also I believe for reasons which may become more clear below in what may still not be an entirely satisfactory response for your purposes. While it occurs to me, first may I ask that none of the following in its personal details be released for 'biographical' purposes elsewhere, which I assume is hardly your purpose anyhow.

Inhowfar the course of my formal education shaped my later work I cannot say; and I believe one must be very much on guard against disproportionate inferences and emphases. My own experience was rather the reverse of the usual: I went off to boarding school age 5 or 6, then to public schools from

7th through 12th grade and thence to college. The boarding school was a small one, in Connecticut, run along lines of what was then described as the 'modified Dalton plan' implying a good deal of freedom but very strictly within a New England framework of imbuing one with a matter of fact acceptance of simply trying to do well what needs to be done; and of taking the responsibility for the consequences of one's actions. Its informal affiliation would have been Congregational. (My mother's family till her generation were Quaker.) My grades were so far as I recall good; but since the climate was a noncompetetive one this was not stressed. Similarly, sports were organized little beyond the point of making them possible to take part in, and with no more of the competetive element than called for by the rules of the game.

High school was the general run of prewar uncrowded New York state public education emphasizing grades insofar as all courses were subject to the state regents examinations. My grades were good and occasionally excellent. Throughout school I never questioned doing homework on a regular assigned basis. I don't recall ever being what you call a 'recognized achiever' although, since I was admitted to the only college I applied to (Harvard) presumably some of that element was present.

Harvard stressed one's taking one's courses, assignments, attendance at lectures &c very much upon one's self. My marks were generally good; I was occasionally on Dean's List. My only extracurricular activity was editing the *Harvard Lampoon*. I studied English literature and psychology. (At age about 14 I'd had a consuming ambition to be a chemist; it quite suddenly disappeared for no reason I knew, any more than why I'd been so consumed by it in the first place.) All out of the ordinary that coloured my high school experience was loss of about a year and a half with a severe illness. I was later obliged to take a year away from college with some after effects of the 'cure'. My mother was especially supportive throughout; and right up the line I had to a very large degree supportive and generous teachers with none of whom I was especially intimate but remember many with great fondness. Taken together, it may well have been this atmosphere conducive to self regard—sometimes likely of course but not entirely deserved—which constituted the most fortunate aspect of my school years.

Reviewing the foregoing in the light—or perhaps rather the darkness—of the present day, it's imperative to remain aware how those prewar days, the depression notwithstanding, were simpler times, before so many taken for granted values and obligations were sundered not to be recovered, or reinstituted today in my own strong opinion, in imitation of those earlier forms.

Next on the personal level, my college experience was clearly coloured by its taking place during the war where many or most of my friends were bound;

my high school, by a long interruption of illness whose enforced isolation must certainly have indelibly coloured my private picture of the world and my place in it; and finally, private boarding school where by very definition the circumstances were as or even more formative than the teachers and curriculum.

May I say at risk of sounding rude—though the length of this response must belie any such intention—I've had a good number of lengthy questionnaires seeking most intimate (and often nonsensical) details in what I assume are well intentioned efforts to delineate by accumulation the 'creative act', 'creative personality' &c. I've tried to respond with a simple thank-you but never submitted to one partly, I'm sure, for feeling the futility of such enterprises but also out of concern for the fate of extrapolated information however well intended. Taken further, this could even apply to my experience of private boarding school and one of Congregational affiliation at that since, as we are well aware, both 'private' too frequently merely signifies exclusion of the disenfranchised (by reason of poverty, race &c); and 'Congregational', which is to say any cultural-religious designation, too often used to justify the perpetuation of entrenched beliefs and interests in face of the threat of inevitable change.

Thus in large part the education you inquire about has led me to feel, more strongly as I grow older, the futility—indeed, self destruction—of resistance to change as opposed to its painful embrace in an effort [to] help shape it rather than, all too human, control it. You ask 'did school matter much one way or another?' and of course it did: for an instance, the reading I did well out of college was more important than what I'd done in college but I should never have done it, or be doing it now, without all that had gone before. So it seemed to me then and it seems even more to me now that the main purpose of education from the start must be to stimulate questions—even those to which we've got no answer—rather than answering them; and to open every vista even those which are distasteful rather than closing them for that reason, only to see them gape open in their most destructive features later.

I hope that this will be of some use to you. Last week incidentally I met with Mr Champion Ward, who said he had discussed your project with you and was interested in the responses you have had, and so I trust you've no objection to my sending a copy of this along to him.

Yours,

William Gaddis

---

modified Dalton plan: a concept developed by Helen Parkhurst in 1920, in which the curriculum is tailored to each student's interests and abilities, and aims to develop social skills.

Champion Ward: F. Champion Ward (1910–2007), an educator who helped the Mac-Arthur Foundation establish its "genius" awards.

To Steven Moore

[I had just learned from Barry Gifford and Lawrence Lee's Jack's Book *(St. Martin's, 1978) that WG was the model for Harold Sand in Jack Kerouac's 1958 novel* The Subterraneans, *from which I sent WG the relevant pages. I also asked if he would autograph my first edition of* R.*]*

New York NY 10021
19 March 1983

Dear Steven Moore.

Thanks for the Kerouac excerpt. No I didn't know about 'Harold Sand' & haven't read the Gifford/Lee book. And I was quite as unaware—at the time & till now—of Kerouac's generous regard for me as it appears in these pages. I remember our acquaintance as very much the way he presents it right down to the old car (a black wounded 1941 Chevrolet) & centered very much around Alan Ansen. Kerouac's picture of him (Bromberg) is right on. Ansen was an extraordinary fellow, marvelously without 'consciousness of his fantastic impact on the ordinary', & I've always felt it in a way unfair—though perhaps I've simply missed the reading—that he's had so little credit given him as the mentor he was for this whole group, a man so hungry to share all he had. I cannot recall how we met but I spent many enough evenings (though I knew him only for approx. that year) of heavy talk & drink till 7am in that 'library' Kerouac describes; & with the date in place I believe this is how things went: with all his blinding erudition Ansen saw few happy prospects till, his father having died & then his remaining aunt quite abruptly, he came into that hideous house in Hewlett & a small income but one just large enough to allow him to visit Europe, something he was as hungry for as he was apprehensive about despite his thorough command of languages. I had *The Recognitions* in what I considered a finished draft but had 'a little more work' to do on it; & so, that fall of 1953, Ansen went to Europe (Venice) & I, for a ridiculous rent (I think $35 a month) & tending his mail, banking, bills &c, spent that winter alone in the house practically rewriting the entire book. I'd finished just as he returned in spring & remember him sitting down barely off the boat in that ghastly diningroom & reading it straight through in a day and a half. Like the others I'm in his unacknowledged debt. (Soon after, having got his confidence in handling expatriation, he rented or sold the house

& returned abroad, settled on the Athens–Tangiers axis, has scarcely been back & I've never seen him since.)

Now for appearing as a character in the books of others, this may amuse you: a bit before the above, may even have been the late 40s, Chandler Brossard published a book titled *Who Walk in Darkness* which I recall as one of the earliest existentialist novels attempted here (New Directions) or such was my estimate. I seem to have been the model for a young Harvard drinks too much character who is finally mugged—not so kind a portrait as Kerouac's but I've been fond of Chandler & it never upset me—I've no memory of that character's name; but the model for the book's protagonist, 'Henry Porter' I believe (he goes around calling everybody 'old sport'), Anatole Broyard, was incensed indeed, & got his own back many years later reviewing a rather chaotic book of Chandler's (I haven't it at hand, had a title like *Are We There Yet?*) in a hatchet job the likes of which I've never seen but may well when my next appears for God knows what reason.

Use any of the above or not however you wish, of course 'without attribution'. I'd be glad to sign a book, didn't start early enough (as vs writing blurbs) with a policy against it & have now got a rich doctor named Naftali Nottman who's sent me 3 or 4 with notes on Gucci stationery & a $10 bill for a drink, says he paid $130 for the last one & I've finally put a stop, recalling Howard Nemerov to a similar supplicant: Ah! you have one of the rare unsigned copies of the *Collected Poems* of Howard Nemerov!

Yours,

W. Gaddis

Alan Ansen: see 4 January 1954 letter to Haygood.

'consciousness [...] ordinary': a phrase from *The Subterraneans*.

Hewlett: a village on Long Island, though Ansen's mailing address was Woodmere, a mile southwest of Hewlett.

Who Walk in Darkness: Brossard's novel appeared in 1952. The character named Harold Lees has some of WG's traits, though Brossard told me the character was a composite of several people he knew then.

Are We There Yet?: Brossard's *Wake Up. We're Almost There* was viciously attacked by Broyard in the *New York Times Book Review*, 4 April 1971, p. 51. Several letters of protest regarding this review appeared in the 2 May 1971 issue, p. 32.

Naftali Nottman: Gaddis later found out this doctor was associated with North Shore Books, a Long Island rare-book dealer.

Howard Nemerov: American poet and novelist (1920–91).

To Steven Moore

[*I was still verifying details (some from Koenig's dissertation) for my introduction to* In Recognition of William Gaddis. *I can't remember what the first paragraph refers to, for I hadn't been puzzled by that 1952 copyright notice, but the rest deals with the chronology and circumstances in which WG finished* R.]

New York NY 10021
7 April 1983

Dear Steven Moore.

For your sake this is I hope the last of these bulletins.

re Koenig*: The MS was not copyrighted (or even finished) in 1952 (I thought I'd written you this); that confusion has arisen here & elsewhere because roughly chapter II was copyrighted that year in the first issue of *New World Writing*, thus the misleading copyright notice in the book.

It was not a New England farmhouse but one outside a small town called Montgomery west of Newburgh NY & indeed an isolated winter & a frugal one on my small advance. Finally, I wasn't revising but finishing the book. This vivid memory confirms that & may also clear up some other of Koenig's misapprehensions, tales of a far longer MS, different endings &c:

I worked there daily & well into the nights with my usual stack of notes, 2nd thoughts, outlines &c till finally very late one night, having intended only to try to get through the sequence of Stanley at the organ to my satisfaction—& with still outlined notes at hand for spinning out the novel's conclusion—I sat back to look at that last 'still spoken of, when it is noted, with high regard, though seldom played' (anticipating, of course, the fate of the novel itself: for played read read) & abruptly realized, both appalled & elated, that I'd reached the end of the book; that no matter my planning & intentions, & even that sense of loss overreaching any of fulfillment, there was no arguing it: the book ended right there. [*Handwritten in margin:*] It occurred to me you might want to quote this ¶ directly & do if you wish to

And so it must have been that I started revisions that summer of 1953 on Long Island, met Ansen then & the San Remo/Kerouac forays in & out of New York & took his place over when he went to Europe in the fall for another largely isolated (but better heated & funded with books) winter of revision.

I trust my next book will be done or 'nearing completion' by the time yours appears but for the present there's nothing to say of it except that it's shorter than its predecessors, the title & even the tag (A Romance) are tentative.

Yours,
W. Gaddis

*Why would anyone bother to change his "Christian" name? or is that the point of it, fleeing the New Testament for the Old—but it was *Peter* who wrote the thesis, wasn't it?

---

you might want to quote this: I did indeed quote it on p. 8 of my introduction. (A Romance): the working title for *CG* was "That Time of Year: A Romance."

To Patrick P. Moynihan

[*Democratic senator from New York (1927–2003) who criticized the Reagan Administration's fear of Soviet-based plans for communist expansion in Latin America and its clandestine support of the terroristic Contras in Nicaragua. WG copied Senator Al D'Amato (see 27 May 1983) and Representative William Carney on this letter.*]

Wainscott, NY
11 April 1983

Dear Senator Moynihan.

Congratulations at last from one of your constituents on the stance you have taken regarding the legality of this Administration's current pursuits of its policy in Central America.

It becomes more clear daily that no policy could be better calculated to spawn precisely those 'Cuba-model states' its espousers decry; that no pronouncements concerning this policy could serve further to isolate the United States in Latin America and indeed world opinion than those so insultingly and crudely offered by this Kirkpatrick woman in the United Nations; and that one can ask no finer irony, in this question of legality stemming largely from the 1973 War Powers Resolution passed following public disclosure of our secret assaults in Cambodia and Laos, than the part played in those incursions by the leading proponent and presumed architect of our current unsavoury and self-defeating approaches in Latin America, Thomas Enders.

If as it now appears neither morality nor common sense can prevail in either this woefully obstinate Administration, or a Congress where the burden has been shouldered by so few courageous and outstanding men, perhaps your demand for a legal accounting is the most realistic and I urge you to pursue it with every bit of vigour, before the poor opinion of this country's antagonists and bewildered friends alike is made fully justified.

Yours sincerely,
William Gaddis

this Kirkpatrick woman: Jeane Kirkpatrick (1926–2006), the fiercely anti-communist U.S. ambassador to the U.N. at this time.

Thomas Enders: American diplomat (1931–96), at that time Reagan's Assistant Secretary of State for Inter-American Affairs.

To Elaine B. Safer

[A professor of English (1937–) at the University of Delaware who often taught R in her classes. WG responds to her essay "The Allusive Mode, the Absurd and Black Humor in William Gaddis's The Recognitions," *which first appeared in* Studies in American Humor *1 (October 1982): 103–18, and later became the basis for chap. 4 of her book* The Contemporary American Comic Epic: The Novels of Barth, Pynchon, Gaddis, and Kesey *(Detroit: Wayne State Univ. Press, 1988).]*

New York, New York 10021
19 April 1983

Dear Ms Safer.

Thank you for sending me your essay on *The Recognitions*: a book 'about false resurrections' is one of the better encapsulations I've come across.

Should you plan to reprint it, you might wish to consider this correction (p. 115, #1): the actual inscription on the Bosch table at which Wyatt as a child 'trembles' is *Cave, Cave, D! videt* (page 25); the *caveat emptor* (p. 693) elaboration is Wyatt's later commentary in the light of the way the sacred character of the original has been corrupted by forgery & its having been reduced to an item of commerce. (My page references here are to the original Harcourt, Brace ed. of the book, ie its 693 corresponds to the Avon 740–1 &c; I haven't the Avon at hand, for which you might note that Steven Moore in his *A Reader's Guide to The Recognitions* (Univ. Nebraska Press, 1982) lists 13 pages of errata).

Regarding your query, my mother's maiden name was Edith Charles, her mother's family name Williams who were Quakers & who in turn had some forebears among, as I recall, Nantucket Husseys (or Hussy). Unfortunately a small book by a deceased great great aunt tracing all this is off with papers stored elsewhere but I expect to have access in the next month or so & have put your address aside for a note to you when I do get this more precise.

Yours,
William Gaddis

To Steven Moore

[*The "abrupt & startling possibility" raised by this letter was a false alarm. I did send WG about two dozen suggested corrections, most of which were later made in the 1985 Penguin reprint of* R. *WG never did write the preface he mentions below; after* In Recognition *came out, he said he felt I had covered the ground sufficiently in my introduction.*]

New York NY 10021

25 May '83

Dear Steven Moore.

An abrupt & startling possibility & more: word that Harcourt B—perhaps even in small or large part because of your efforts—plans to reissue *The Recognitions.*

I had talked to a woman there last year, largely in an effort to either squelch the Avon or get a few dollars from it, & got into the errata. Thus when she (is Irene Skolnik who handles reprints) learned of the above intention to reprint (of which of course the author is seldom if ever notified) asked them to hold off in order to incorporate corrections. I'd thought they would simply offset the Meridian + possibly a few of your corrections but—still all somewhat unclear—they simply wanted list of errata in the original ed. so I've dug around & unearthed all of Jack Green's I could find in old correspondence & hope I have all of them. I have as you'll see added a few of yours from *Reader's Guide* though let some 'irregularities' stand (as the Steenken *Madonna*).

I think I've already alarmed them somewhat with my enthusiasm but am sending you here the list I sent them in case you have come across any more glaring horrors in your more recent investigations. If so could you send them to me & I'll send on to them (them now being in San Diego)? so that there might at last be an 'authorised version'. (Though some questionable items I think should remain such as the above, when the Picasso *Night Fishing* was first hung &c since these are explored in your annotations & I don't want to *sanitize* it.)

I've also discussed with them the possibility of my writing a preface for it, in the old generation-later tradition of Norman Douglas' *South Wind*, Clive Bell's *Art* &c. though that might run into production (i.e. $) problems: if that should occur it might inevitably take some wind out of your & John K's introduction in your book though I'd make an effort to not, and of course your *Reader's Guide* would be suitably noted. Should it proceed I'd send you a copy promptly.

For the moment all they want is corrections; anything else I mention alarms them in cost terms, not even certain yet if they intend a hardcover, tradepaperback or both busy out there doing cost accounting sales projections all of the market madness that publishing has become.

Meanwhile as they race to some kind of finish line I would appreciate the above (any further corrections or an Imprimatur) & this further favour, since I am between 2 addresses this season of the year & forwarding is fanciful if you could send any response to both below. I'll let you know of any further developments, disappointments &c.

Yours

W. Gaddis

Steenken *Madonna*: WG followed a 1921 book in indentifying the donor of this painting as Herman Steenken (*R* 254), though a 1938 archival study disqualified him.

the list: enclosed with this letter were three legal-sized pages of corrections, about eighty-five altogether, most of which had been made for the Meridian edition, and all of which would be made for Penguin's 1985 reprint.

Picasso *Night Fishing:* this painting was acquired by New York's Museum of Modern Art in 1952, but the novel's chronology implies Wyatt saw it there several years earlier.

South Wind, Clive Bell's *Art:* Douglas added an introduction to his 1917 novel in 1925; Bell's 1914 book of art criticism was reprinted with new introduction in 1949.

To Al D'Amato

[*American attorney (1937–) and conservative Republican senator from New York (1981– 99) who defended the Reagan Administration's support of the Contras. In WG's notes for FHO, he wrote "The District Court judge is former woman lawyer [...] elevated to bench by a sleazy NY D'Amato type senator" (attachment to 5 January 1990 letter).*]

Wainscott, NY

27 May 1983

Dear Senator D'Amato.

I appreciated your detailed response to my recent letter protesting Administration policy and actions in Central America.

In the light of past revelations I would seriously question Administration figures as to Cuban 'advisers' and Soviet weaponry in the area as I and much of the electorate do the validity of those last 'elections' in San Salvador; and I with many others believe strongly that in pursuing the Administration's present course we are doing the Marxist-Leninists' work for them throughout Latin America, and the Soviets' throughout the world.

The killing of our Commander Schaufelberger and the expanded US adviser-training program in Honduras reported in this morning's paper reflect not only the cynicism of Administration policy but even more painfully its contempt for the US Congress: its manipulations are an insult to the intelligence and the integrity of a serious man like yourself, and even to those in the Senate and the House with a good deal less of either.

I will surely appreciate your keeping my views in mind as the situation continues to deteriorate, since they are not simply my views but those of a growing number of Americans very deeply—and at times feeling quite helplessly—concerned for our country's future.

Yours,

William Gaddis

Commander Schaufelberger: a Navy lieutenant commander who was assassinated in El Salvador on 25 May 1983, the first of an American military advisor there.

To Ralph Sipper

[*American rare-book dealer, editor, and critic (1932–), who had sent WG his edition of the essays of American mystery writer Ross Macdonald (1915–83) entitled* Self-Portrait: Ceaselessly into the Past *(Capra, 1981) and asked WG to contribute to a memorial volume published in 1984 as* Inward Journey: Ross Macdonald.]

235 East 73 Street
New York, New York 10021
27 May 1983

Dear Mr Sipper.

I believe that some weeks ago you were kind enough to send me a copy of Ross Macdonald: *Self Portrait*, with an accompanying letter requesting an appreciation of his work from me for a book you are publishing with Knopf. I have the book but have somewhere misplaced the letter (& address) & hope this may reach you despite its unpromising response.

Unfortunately & quite simply, I am just not acquainted with Ross MacDonald's work (though know the name of course) & cannot picture who at Knopf might have recommended me for your project flattering as it may be. Because of the usual backslid pressure of work I'm not in a position to take enough time out for it to do your project justice.

I do appreciate your intentions & hope they prosper,

Yours,

William Gaddis

To William H. Gass

[*The Spring 1983 issue of* Conjunctions *contained an interview with Gass and three excerpts from his work-in-progress* The Tunnel, *eventually published in 1995. The letter is undated.*]

Wainscott, New York
[Summer 1983]

Dear Bill,

Simply a note of greeting: I just got in the mail a high class literary number called *Conjunctions 4*, read a stretch of page 9 to Muriel & she looked drunk...
(And Richard Correy, one fine summer might...the mood I seem lastingly in.) Perhaps—v. the enclosed—when one's own capacity for obsession dims, the only refuge is in that of others, thus my current attack on the *Rapture* which I hope will carry this damned (on page 184) book through and out of my life while we wait for *The Tunnel*. Oh! that 'benevolent drowning'.

And to say, under this holy cloud, we are here the summer & probably through fall and if, again, you & Mary should happen east & can add some days to spend under the lavish, pitch pine, swimming pool tranquility how fine it would be; also I project the best of conversation between you and a new old pal here Saul Steinberg re your Eisenman project.

And to add, what abruptly prompted this note, lines of Browning that seem to seize us up together:

This trade of mine—I don't know, can't be sure
But there was something in it, tricks and all!
Really, I want to light up my own mind.

Love to Mary—
Willie Gaddis

---

page 9: an ornate passage beginning "In my youth..." now on p. 73 of *The Tunnel* (NY: Knopf, 1995).

And Richard Correy: from the conclusion of Edwin Arlington Robinson's poem "Richard Cory" (1897), about a well-regarded man who commits suicide.

the enclosed: a postcard reproduction of Charles Anderson's *The Rapture* (1973), a kitschy fundamentalist painting depicting the return of the redeemer over Dallas's Thornton Freeway. On the obverse he typed "And I say yeah, that would be a good subject." Gaddis bought a stack of these and used them for years. See 24 July 1985.

'benevolent drowning': in his *Conjunctions* interview (with Bradford Morrow), Gass says that when writing "I need to be immersed in a fiction to get any momentum going. That's hard to accomplish—that benevolent drowning" (17).

Saul Steinberg: American illustrator; see headnote to second letter of 21 January 1990.

Eisenman project: in the *Conjunctions* interview, Gass mentions that, in addition to

The Tunnel, he was collaborating on a book "with Peter Eisenman, an architect of considerable, though perhaps perverse, genius," which they later abandoned (20).
lines of Browning: from "Mr. Sludge, 'The Medium,'" which Gaddis probably found in the *ODQ*. He copied these lines into *Conjunctions*.

To Steven Moore

[*A special session on WG's work had been approved for the annual Modern Language Association convention, to be held in New York City at the end of 1983. It was organized by Miriam Fuchs (a former student of John Kuehl's and a contributor to* In Recognition of William Gaddis*); the panel consisted of her, me, Frederick R. Karl, and Kuehl, though the latter fell ill and was unable to attend. This MLA panel is mentioned briefly in the letter below but will be referred to again.*]

Wainscott NY 11975
12 June 1983

Dear Steven Moore.

To yours of 7 June—& then some.

Again thanks for the corrections, forwarded along to San Diego (where Harcourt has taken refuge) though some 'irregularities' remain as material for your glosses & bait for future PhDs. As yet no word from Harcourt on whether or not for a preface though I'm not pressing them; but am threatening them with the MLA: incidentally I didn't at first grasp Fred Karl in this, then realized he's the same I met at dinner recently & who produced my serious reading assignment (after the frivolity of the new Kissinger), his book on Conrad. Quite heavy artillery.

No further thoughts on the MS study for the moment.

On the count of that drawing for Bert Britton for your book an easy solution: I've somewhere the same drawing on an 8x10 page with a small splotch on one line which was why I put it aside & did the clean one for BB; the splotch could easily be retouched & I could send the thing to whomever/wherever at Syracuse when the time comes, no BB &c permissions necessary.

Now I'd postponed the following but since you persist in your folly these observations on various items in the *Reader's Guide* may be of interest or diversion. It is not exhaustive. [...]

Yours,
W. Gaddis

Fred Karl: Frederick R. Karl (1927–2004), American literary critic, and WG's neighbor in the Hamptons. The book was *Joseph Conrad: The Three Lives* (1979).

new Kissinger: probably *Years of Upheaval* (1982).

these observations: these 3½ pages of notes are omitted because most of them have been incorporated into the online version of the *Reader's Guide* at the Gaddis Annotations website.

To Steven Moore

Wainscott

26 June 1983

JUST A BULLETIN: After 20 years of wrangling, & taking a hard look at cash flow, cost accounting, public reading habits & B Dalton et alia, the CHAIRMAN (Mr Jovanovitch) has decided to do the gentlemanly thing & return to me the rights to *The Recognitions*. Our (my & my agent's) next step uncertain & I in no rush, just want to savour the thing as my own again for a while though of course it would be a pain to have any sort of demand created by your Syracuse Press (I've sent them the drawing) effort & the MLA with only the squat & speckled Avon available (though they now have notice of 6 months to get it off the stands).

I'll let you know as things develop or do not,

Gaddis.

Frederick Exley and WG, summer 1983.

To Berte Hirschfield

[*The wife of Alan Hirschfield, an executive in the communications and entertainment industries. The book was* J R, *in which Jack Gibbs drunkenly explains a divorce board game on the pages indicated. A. Robert Towbin was a neighbor in East Hampton.*]

Wainscott, New York 11975
5 July 1983

Dear Ms. Hirschfield.

Here is 'the book' &, for openers, the game SPLIT imperfectly presented by an enthusiastic drinker on pages 410–12. I have elsewhere a number of further notes and thoughts on it which I would dig out if it provokes interest.

Very pleasant meeting you at Bob Towbin's, as things generally are at the Towbin's.

Yours,
William Gaddis

To William V. Alexander

[*Arkansas attorney (1934–) and Democratic member of the House of Representatives (1969–93). WG copied Senators Moynihan, D'Amato, and Representative Carney on this letter.*]

Wainscott, NY 11975
23 July 1983

Dear Mr Alexander.

As one far removed from your constituency may I take this liberty to express appreciation for your succinct common sense analysis of the threats posed by current Administration policy in Central America, as it appeared in the *NY Times* of 21 July headed Schizoid Latin Policy.

Each day's headlines provoke even further despair among those of us who had believed that McKinley era politics were well behind us and that, as you conclude, 'tact and decency' rather than a flood of weaponry are our only means of being true to ourselves 'while protecting our security and fighting Communism the American way.'

In the prevailing fraud of 'bipartisanship' so reminiscent of President Johnson's 'consensus'—everyone buckling under to him—it is indeed heartening to have a clear voice like yours in the US Congress, among pygmies fearful for their political careers should it all turn out badly, of being accused of 'losing Salvador' by obeying international law and our own guiding principles; and while we in New York State are most fortunate in having Senator Moynihan's voice raised against another blind Administration absurdity in the M-X adventure, it is a fine fine irony in the wisdom of these Founding Fathers you remind us of that I am obliged to write a Representative from Arkansas as a member of his real constituency in this crucial matter, and to express gratitude to those Arkansans who brought you to Congress.

Yours sincerely,
William Gaddis

McKinley era politics: those under 25th President William McKinley (1897–1901), which led to the Spanish-American War, the occupation of Cuba, and the annexation of Puerto Rico, Guam, Hawaii, and the Philippines.

M-X adventure: the MX Nuclear Missile Program.

To Tomasz Mirkowicz

Wainscott NY 11975
16 August 1983

Dear Tomasz Mirkowicz.

Thanks for your long letter with its good news of a Polish publication, and your taking on the intimidating task of the translation. I did have a letter from the publisher stating the terms which I endorsed and returned (adding, as you suggested, the names of my son and daughter as eligible to draw on any funds when they appear).

To your queries: I have no preference regarding the book's jacket; black/red/white is I think the strongest combination of colours (Heil Hitler!), otherwise just sobre and simple as the artist decrees.

Regarding the translation itself I should, of course, want to leave it as entirely in your hands as possible. The Moore book should certainly prove a great help. Here is a further suggestion: there was as you may be aware a French publication by Gallimard in a very careful translation by (I believe) Jean Lambert about 10 years ago. Thus if you can get hold of that, and you or a colleague reads French, comparing the French equivalent of a passage to your interpretation in Polish might prove useful. (There was also an Italian 2 vol. edition (Mondadori) but I am a good deal less certain just how dependable that translation is.) The title in French was *Les Reconnaissances*.

The idea of notes does sound like a useful one. I would agree with your preference, simply at the end of the book following page and line number rather than cluttering up the text. I would think the manner of marking dialogue should be that most familiar to the Polish reader. I am always glad to hear of any errors or incongruities for the possibility of another edition of the book here.

As for other references, we will probably run into difficulties if we try to pursue them in correspondence, largely since it is so long since I wrote the book that many or most of them are not clear in my memory. For instance, the Byzantine eye? a round window sounds reasonable but I don't recall. All I recall of the Frauenkirche is, if I recall right, it has 2 spires nearer domes & suggestive of ample woman's breasts, the rest escapes me. Rides in the cistern has no more significance than as something tourists do, or did. And so, for all that, as well as the mistress bargained for in youth, I think the safest course is simply a literal translation throughout or we shall drive each other mad. (The 'envirement' is simply a reflection of illiteracy, just as at some point much later mention of filet de mignon.) Heaven knows what is meant by the 'Poland has no seaports': I think you must just take your chances!

best regards and good luck with it,
William Gaddis

Byzantine eye [...] bargained for in youth: details from chap. 2 of *R*.

'envirement' [...] filet de mignon: on pp. 76 and 751, respectively. (The latter is simply filet mignon.)

'Poland has no seaports': Wyatt mentions that in Calderón's play *La Vida es sueño* (1635) the protagonist falls off a balcony "into the sea, though there's trouble there because Poland has no seaports" (*R* 876).

To Steven Moore

[Regarding what WG called the imminent "MLA spree."]

Wainscott, NY 11975
[undated; ca. 1 December 1983]

Dear Steven Moore.

Thanks for your note. Dinner then on 29 December about 7:30 at 235 East 73rd street penthouse A. Of course come earlier yourself which we can arrange by phone, the number there is 988 1360. And if feasible please do ask Chandler if he can come for dinner, I haven't seen him in some years & would like to.

Given the 'season' I'm not certain when we'll drive in, possibly not till that morning. The phone here is (516) 537 0743.

I'll get a note off to John Kuehl & reach Fred Carl, you arrange with

Miriam Fuchs* (also anyone anyone wants to bring along), we'll probably just
send out for lavish Chinese.

Nothing right now for publication, elegant reviews or elsewhere,

Gaddis

* also Steven Weisenburger? is he in it?

---

come earlier: I did indeed arrive a few hours before the others. During our conversation WG showed me the manuscript of the in-progress *CG*, and while summarizing
it stated that McCandless was essentially himself.

Chandler: Chandler Brossard; see letter to me dated 19 March 1983. As a result of that
earlier letter, I had written to Brossard and developed an interest in his work. I had
told Gaddis I was meeting him during this same trip to New York.

elegant reviews: I was in the PhD program at the University of Denver at the time, and
had asked WG (at the instigation of editor Eric Gould) if he wanted to contribute to
the *Denver Quarterly,* which I described as an "elegant" journal.

Weisenburger: he did not attend the MLA that year. As I recall, those who attended
Gaddis's party (his sixty-first birthday, as it turned out) included Walter and Cecile
Abish, Brossard and his wife Maria Ewing Huffman, Jay Fellows, Miriam Fuchs,
Frederick Karl and his wife, and Mike Gladstone. Muriel Murphy was our hostess,
and WG's son Matthew arrived toward the end. Illness prevented John Kuehl from
attending.

To John W. Aldridge

*[Aldridge had invited WG to the University of Michigan in Ann Arbor as guest speaker
for the Hopwood Underclassmen Awards Ceremony, held 18 January 1984, for which he
was paid $1000.]*

> 235 East 73 Street
> New York, New York 10021
> 20 January 1984

Dear Jack,

(as I understand the form is), many thanks from us both for all your kind-
nesses. The few times I've gone off on such adventures I must say that initial
apprehensions have been dispelled by a real cordiality, but this excelled in its
coming from all directions very much including the students. They are a nicely
various assortment and their warmth and serious interest was very, very
gratifying. And of course the members of your department who gave a refreshing touch of cheer to what must become the rather tiresome extra chore of
carting visitors around in −8°.

We expect to be here through the next month or so at least, but have vague hopes of getting away in March if only I can get this book either to a point of publishing or destroying it, alternatives which at the moment seem equally attractive. [...]

with very best regards,
Bill Gaddis

To the Editor, *New York Times*

[In response to an editorial criticizing the United States Information Agency's informal blacklist of speakers who shouldn't be sent abroad, which targeted those unsympathetic to the then-current Reagan administration. This letter was published in the 5 March 1984 issue of the Times, *p. 20, under the title "U.S.I.A. Blacklist Is Beyond 'Stupid.'"]*

New York, New York
21 February 1984

To the Editor:

Further to the point of your "U.S.I.A.'s Little List" editorial (Feb. 20), which seemed to me to stop short.

In 1976, I had published a lengthy novel about our free enterprise system run wildly off the tracks in the cheerfully ignorant hands of an 11-year-old boy and, with what must now appear as that quite dubious credential, was invited by the U.S.I.A. to speak in the Far East.

At the Washington briefing before departure, I was cautioned only that I might encounter sensitivity in the Philippines regarding our military bases there, and in Japan regarding contested territorial fishing claims, but I was left entirely free to comment on these and any other matters as I saw fit. (I recall talking largely about the Protestant ethic in American literature.)

The groups I met with in each country were well informed and appreciative, but the point I wish to stress here is the high caliber of the cultural affairs officers who shepherded me from Bangkok through the Philippines and the length of Japan. They were consistently on the most knowledgeable and forthright terms with the academic, journalistic and literary figures and circles in the countries where they were assigned. There was an atmosphere of mutual trust and respect they had worked hard to establish.

Thus while in the short term it is simply stupid to deprive friendly countries of "the 84 deemed untrustworthy" in this current, paranoid "blacklist," a longer view holds the more painful likelihood of the loss of such seriously dedicated Foreign Service people to a blighted public relations policy that insults our bewildered friends abroad as the stunted targets of domestic partisan propaganda, and can only enhance our image as the "pitiful helpless giant" of yore.

William Gaddis

"pitiful helpless giant": in 1970, President Richard Nixon defended his decision to escalate the war in Vietnam lest the United States be reduced to "a pitiful, helpless giant."

To Saul Bellow

[*American novelist (1915–2005); in 1987 WG would review his* More Die of Heartbreak *for the* New York Times Book Review *(RSP 73–79). See 27 October 1992 for the citation Bellow wrote proposing WG's membership in the American Academy and Institute of Arts and Letters. None of Bellow's letters to Gaddis were included in Benjamin Taylor's edition of his letters (2010).*]

Wainscott, New York 11975
18 May 1984

dear Saul,

What a distinguished and distinguishing citation! (its source confided to me by our local Saul)—made all the rest of them sound like what...the vixen's offspring? It was by far the most gratifying and highest recognition I could have ever hoped for.

with very real appreciation and best regards,
William Gaddis

---

our local Saul: Saul Steinberg: see headnote to WG's second letter of 21 January 1990.

To Sarah Gaddis

Wainscott
9 June '84

Dear Sarah.

Well finally: my (your?) first letter at your new address...where of course I was so delighted to hear your voice & in such good spirit (A Room of One's Own as Virginia Woolf had it, have you read that? read her? I recall liking best *Mrs Dalloway* (sp?) & just occurs to me we've never discussed her & she is Somebody for *your* examination, an unfraudulent perhaps antidote to however-good-she-is Jean Rhys). [...]

News here? well (Chinesely) thankfully none: mow the lawns, dine with Sherrys & a few pals—Gloria goes ON, Woods, others—within my whole

context of My Patient: now 'reformulating' chapter VI of rewrite in my frantic effort to get an acceptable MS to Viking by July &c &c &c ... all familiar
to you. Half the house still unrented (since the "boys'" departure) so that's
somewhat a financial sticker BUT: news in prospect! rental for 3 or 4 days to
Joan Didion & husband (that's rude, I should say Mr & Mrs John Gregory
Dunn(e?) of the West (poolside) house; they're apparently here for some
number with Sidney Lumet, all about 2 weeks hence so that's (obviously) the
Event of the moment. [...]

much love always,
Papa

A Room of One's Own [...] *Mrs Dalloway*: classic essay (1929) and novel (1925) by the
British writer (1882–1941).
Jean Rhys: West Indian novelist (1890–1979), best known for *Wide Sargasso Sea*
(1966), which adapts *Jane Eyre* just as WG would do with *CG* seven months later.
Gloria: Gloria Jones (1928–2006), literary hostess and wife of novelist James Jones.
Woods: Clement Wood Jr. (1925–94), novelist and an editor of the *Paris Review* (and
of the *Harvard Lampoon* shortly after WG); his wife was Jessie Leigh-Hunt (1929–).
Joan Didion: married to novelist and screenwriter John Gregory Dunne (1932–2003).
Sidney Lumet: American film director (1924–2011); see also 23 August 1990.

To Steven Moore

[In Recognition of William Gaddis *was published in June 1984, with WG's self portrait
reproduced on the cover and title page.*]

Wainscott, New York 11975
13 June 1984

Dear Steven Moore.

Well I've just got a copy of your & John Kuehl's effort &, as I'm writing
him (& Mrs Mesrobian) it is a class act: of course judge a book by its cover!
All I've read of it as yet is your piece once quickly for it's probably painfully
true, & the biographical introduction (do.), a few (I mean 2 or 3) most minor
dislocations but it does pretty much set the relevant record straight, which is
to say nicely avoids the wives & kids let alone the dogs (who will appear in
another novel). As I just wrote John Kuehl, the most gratifying part of the
whole thing is the life of both books for these young people which he, for so
long, & you with more recent intensity, have done so much to encourage is
hardly the word but I trust you have my meaning.

Hope against lazy hope I am trying to get this 'new' one out of my life by

July (down our throats) & then sit down to the serious treat of these essays to write you then. I've wondered incidentally what did become of the efforts of that Polish girl bringing vodka & flowers & the conviction that I'd built better than I knew (the True Believer in me); & the Belgian semiotics? constructionism? deconstruction? Marie Rose Logan, anyhow as I say for now, thanks for a class act.

> best regards
> W Gaddis

Mrs Mesrobian: Arpena S. Mesrobian, Director of Syracuse University Press.

your piece: "*Peer Gynt* and *The Recognitions*," pp. 81–91.

Polish girl: Teresa Bałazy; Kuehl decided her essay wasn't good enough.

builded better than I knew: from Emerson's poem "The Problem": "The hand that rounded Peter's dome, / And groined the aisles of Christian Rome, / Wrought in a sad sincerity; / Himself from God he could not free; / He builded better than he knew;— / The conscious stone to beauty grew" (*ODQ*).

Marie Rose Logan: although invited to contribute, she never responded.

To Steven Moore

[*Having learned that the Bruce Peel Collection at the University of Alberta held several of WG's letters, I wrote to them requesting copies, and was told I needed WG's permission, which I consequently requested. In the same letter, I asked if he had written other letters to the editor like the one to the* Times, *whether he saw his picture in* People *magazine, and enclosed a copy of Alan Ansen's poem "Epistle to Chester Kallman" (because it mentions WG in passing), included in Ansen's chapbook* The Cell (*privately printed in Hong Kong, 1983). I also mentioned I was moving east, from Denver to Rutgers University in New Jersey.*]

> Wainscott, New York 11975
> 22 July 84

Dear Steven Moore.

I enclose a note as requested to your people in Alberta regarding permission to see these letters whatever they (& whoever Mrs Kask) may be although as you're surely aware it's an entire area I've never condoned. Some of my reasons have been noted in relation to my reticence re interviews though here they go further: like many fledglings, my early letters were many times written with the vain notion of eventual publication & thus obviously much embarrassing nonsense; & of the later ones, those of substance will probably never be seen for equally fortunate if exactly different reasons. (I don't know if you happened

May 16, 1984   Jill Krementz

"After being inducted into the institute, writer William Gaddis mounted a
chair to scan for his agent, delighting fellow writer William Gass" (caption from
People Weekly, 4 June 1984). Photographed by Jill Krementz on May 16, 1984,
at the American Academy of Arts and Letters; all rights reserved.

upon a review of Hemingway's letters by Hugh Kenner, might have been in that same *Harpers* with my piece 2 or 3 years ago, but he does use them to flay the writer & point up frailties in his work as glimpses of the 'real' Hemingway, I think really these things go quite the opposite, the letters are the detritus &c).

No I have not written other 'letters to editors'. No I did not see my picture in *People* though have been bantered about it (by people who read *People*). Thanks for the Ansen effort; only he would manage an original Hong Kong publication, others being pirated.

I have just signed a contract with Alfaguara (Madrid) for both books in some hereafter considering the translation challenge; also with V-Penguin for a trade softcover of *The Recognitions* sometime in a year or so.

You may hear from a William Ray, whose weighty doctoral dissert. on my work for University College London (though he's in Boston) I've just returned to him looked through but unread since I cannot at this stage take that time though it looks impressive in its range & construction. He wondered about publishing where I've no advice for him but thought you might be interested in what he's done.

We were pleased to learn of your coming east & if it's feasible would like you out here for a couple of days' visit, an easy express trip from NY &—barring the increasingly remote chance we rent this place out—will probably be here into the foreseeable fall but let us know about August, meet the luminaries, charlatans &c & we'll let you know if any inconvenience arises: 516-537-0743 when you get in.

I forgot to mention the jolly (& deserved, really) dedication in your & John K's book.

                              Yours
                              W Gaddis

Mrs Kask: a woman who worked at Meridian, recipient of an unimportant 1962 note.
Kenner [...] *Harpers*: yes, in the same issue is Kenner's "Writing by Numbers" (pp. 93–95).
Alfaguara: *Los Reconocimientos,* translated by Juan Antonio Santos, was published by Alfaguara in 1987, but they never published a translation of *J R*. (One by Mariano Payrou entitled *Jota Erre* was eventually published by Editorial Sexto Piso in 2013.)
V-Penguin [...] *The Recognitions*: Penguin editor Gerald Howard arranged to reprint both *R* and *J R* to accompany the publication of *CG* in the summer of 1985.
William Ray: William Vincent Ray, "Transformations of Modernist Fictional Technique in the Novels of William Gaddis," PhD diss., University College, London, 1984.
visit: I visited him in Wainscott 18–21 August 1984. He had just finished *CG* and allowed me to read the manuscript, which I raced through in a day, to be grilled that night about the plausibility of certain plot elements.

dedication: "For Jack Green." Green wrote a letter to Kuehl (and sent a copy to WG, which he showed me during my visit) expressing outrage that we had not requested permission first, and interpreted it as an insult on my part instead of the homage I clearly intended it to be. He requested that it be removed in any future printings.

To Sarah and Matthew Gaddis

8 August [1984]

Like old (& worser) times: DEAR SARAH & MATTHEW,

Well I finished it. Not really of course . . . a nice folder of notes of items to squeeze in when it goes to galleys but at least I did put a whole 2nd draft in the mail to Viking & now up to them to start the machinery; & even at this rate some question whether they can publish it before fall 85! Now how can you make a Major Motion Picture in like 8 months & it takes them a year to print & peddle a book, it's beyond me. But as you know my main purpose is to get the damned Thing out of my life & I am close to doing that. Et puis? 3 more years of (blessed) MacArthur so maybe I can just sit and play with my toes—but I do want to get right to these revisions & *then* think.

Aside from that daily horror (why I haven't written you, or anyone) the usual: saw *Under the Volcano* last night, a virtuoso perf. by Finney but still a book there was no reason to make a movie of (including that wimp who had the teddybear in *Brideshead* from whose every pore untruth exudes . . .) then a hoho burger at "Van's" with Gloria, Kennet, Polly & Joe, Ellen Adler; this eve. to cook chicken thighs at Sag[g] Main with Woods, Sherrys, Saul? Jean Stein? Gigi still very wound up & no knowing where it will lead.

In town for a day & dinner with Martin who is so mad at everybody he's ever known that he'll outlive us all. [...] I heard there was a picture of me in *People* a month or so ago standing on a chair (as usual) but never saw it.

But I did see *Passion* finally (Gigi brought one back), not only good fun but a good piece on "Whatever Happened to the Great French Novel?" (July issue) (what happened is they just don't sit down & work) but it is a snappier publication than I'd expected, all to the good.

I know I'll become too impatient for news of you both to resist calling before you get this, *most* curious regarding Matthew in Paris & 'the work' of course!

love to you both
Papa

Under the Volcano: 1984 film adaptation of Lowry's 1947 novel, directed by John Huston and starring British actor Albert Finney, and costarring Anthony Andrews, who had won acclaim a few years earlier for his role in a TV adaptation of Waugh's *Brideshead Revisited*.

"Van's" [...] Sag[g] Main: restaurants in Bridgehampton and Sagaponack, respectively.

Gloria [...] Ellen Adler: Gloria Jones lived with journalist Kenne*t*t Love (1924–2013); see 25 August 1980 for Polly and Joe Kraft; painter Ellen Adler was the daughter of actress and teacher Stella Adler.

Saul [...] Gigi: Saul Steinberg (see headnote to 21 January 1990) and his partner, photographer Sigrid Spaeth.

Jean Stein: American author and editor (1934–2017), and a Wainscott neighbor.

Passion: *Paris Passion*, an English-language magazine published in France.

To Bill Morgan

[*A postcard, without salutation, in response to a request to contribute to a festschrift for Allen Ginsberg, eventually published as* Best Minds: A Tribute to Allen Ginsberg, *edited by Morgan and Bob Rosenthal (New York: Lospecchio Press, 1986). Responses from those who declined to contribute were published in a companion volume entitled* Kanreki: A Tribute to Allen Ginsberg *(New York: Lospecchio Press, 1986), where WG's response appears on p. 47.*]

[Wainscott, NY]
9 Aug. 1984

Though I saw Allen cordially this past spring, I hadn't for quite a good many years & the days when we met have been amply attended to surely in the Kerouac saga & elsewhere, so I've really nothing to add but my good wishes,

W. Gaddis

To Elisabeth Sifton

[*American publisher and author (1939–2018), who joined Viking Press in 1968 and in 1983 was given her own imprint there. As* Carpenter's Gothic *was being prepared for typesetting, WG sent the following letter (attachments not seen) identifying a few of its literary quotations and a minor character named after two dismissive reviewers of* J R, *George Steiner and Christopher Lehmann-Haupt. WG sometimes misspelled Sifton's first name.*]

[Wainscott, NY]
10 September 84

Dear Elizabeth:

3 categories for distribution to your various departments:

1) 3 pages of corrections almost all of which I'm sure are in the copy now in your hands; but getting home and checking one of my work copies against another I found these discrepencies between them so, just to be safe…

2) Liftings & borrowings for 'permissions':

those fragmented lines marginally marked H 59, H 63 &c are from Hilton's *Lost Horizon* indicating page numbers in the paperback enclosed;

that one marginally marked simply N is VS Naipaul, I haven't laid hands on the book yet but am quite certain it's *The Mimic Men* and will call in when I get the reference exact;

those lines marked J are from Robinson Jeffers' (marvelous) poem *Wise Men in Their Bad Hours* (in his Selected Poetry)

3) Legal curios, to only one of which I call your specific attention and that is the rude reference to a 'Steyner Lemanhaut' on page 80 a. The Steyner might well be taken as a slur by George Steiner whom I picture as somewhat paranoid even to the point of going to law? the surname might be similarly viewed by a local book reviewer, ensuring the bad review I anticipate anyway or perhaps none, since I think Anatole's laying for it &, since the book's comparatively short, may have first grabs.

The other legal queries are obvious & I think harmless enough but I include them for your legal people's entertainment.

best again,
Gaddis

Hilton's *Lost Horizon*: these lines would cause problems: see 28 January 1985.
The Mimic Men: Naipaul's 1967 novel is quoted in italics near the bottom of p. 150.
Wise Men in Their Bad Hours: the poem is quoted in italics on pp. 124 and 161.
'Steyner Lemanhaut': this was changed to "Bobby Steyner" (top of p. 90).
Anatole: Broyard; neither he or Steiner reviewed it, but Lehmann-Haupt's surprisingly positive review appeared in the 3 July 1985 issue of the *New York Times*.

To John and Pauline Napper

Wainscott
11 Sept. 1984

Dear John and Pauline.

Some of the excuses follow but none can really excuse my not having got off even a line to you in what is an *age*. So much seems to have happened & indeed much of it has.

Most recently these past few months have been devoured by *Carpenter's Gothic*…good guess! Yes that's the title of my 'new' novel, why in God's name it should have taken me so long to finish & doubly infuriating since were it out today it would be selling hotcakes, its main concern being precisely the far right political USA's entanglement with the evangelicals, fundamentalists &c filling our pre-election front pages. It can't be out till next year when we've either got a new & sobre Administration or Reagan's reelection, in the latter case it may well be news (as all signs point) so there's nothing to do but vote democratic & hope for the worst (Reagan). The title because in part it's a patchwork of used ideas, borrowed & stolen, with what simple materials were to hand (hammers & saws) in the way of outrage at 'revealed truth' (read Genesis), erected on a small scale (about 250pp.); but also because the entire book takes place *in* that Piermont house (where of course The World comes in by telephone)... some rather heavy handed satire & flashes of poor taste but it 'moves right along' as they say & should offend enough people to move it in what we are pleased to call the marketplace (supply side). I very seldom go up there but do still own the Piermont house, rented out for barely enough to carry itself but my 'workroom' still cobwebbed with most of my books & papers with no other home despite comfortable quarters indeed here on Long Isld & in NY, Muriel's dowry? but not a damned inch to store anything. At any rate every sobre minute has gone into finally last week handing over to Viking Press the entire rewritten, corrected, proofread MS with vast relief.

& what took so much time? Well partly of course getting deeper immersed in the book, which started out as a 'romance' but I found needed outrage to fuel it, ergo fundamentalism &c. And life itself, mine & theirs... Sarah's divorce a sticky number but finally accomplished & she's now been in Paris for a year, doing design, fashion & drawing studies at a branch of the American College there (connected to Parsons) & also some side paying jobs; & though it's exactly a year to the day I haven't seen her seems to be in great shape & Growing Up (panicked of course that yesterday was her 29th, feeling the hand of Age descending (can you imagine!)). And Matthew {***}. Pretty wild for the 2 children of one of the most tried & true Francophobes you will find...

Well now at last blessed relief ('famous last words' as our old saw has it), we plan going to Rome for November & December, have got a room at the American Academy there which will assuredly not be lavish but at the least provide refuge from that operatic people while we sample their remains; been in such odd places as Bankok & Libya (shades of David Tudor Pole) but for some reason or none, never Rome. And there for the moment it all stands; the heavy shadows of drink (not drunk but certainly to be cut down) & tobacco taking a serious turn & if humanly (me) possible to be ended, the new 'creative challenge'... [...]

Willie

To Robert Minkoff

[*I was stepping up my efforts to collect WG's letters and had written to Robert Minkoff to request copies of any he might have. Minkoff wrote to WG for permission to release them to me.*]

American Academy in Rome
Via Angelo Masina 5
00153 Rome
12 Nov. 1984

Dear Robert Minkoff.

Your 20 August letter finally reached me and I appreciate your thoughtfulness in this what is at heart an idiotic matter. This fellow Steven Moore has already published 2 books on my work—very straight & diligent & appears headed to be my sympathetic "chronicler" like it or not.

My letters—& I think no one's—are written for publication (unless they *are* in which case they're probably full of lies); legally I believe the letter (as an *object*) belongs to the recipient (or anyone he sells/gives it to), while its *contents* remain property of the one who wrote it (ie regarding publication). I've long suspected that my papers, letters &c. would eventually bring more money (not necessarily to *me*) than royalties on the books themselves, & I say "idiotic matter" above because this is apparently happening—some university in Canada I understand has paid around $900. for a handful of my letters (not of course to me). Thus there's a price tag on what you hold in your hand as you read this!

Ergo——what's the rude solution? write someone a letter, send her/him a xerox & keep the original? The letters *are* yours, to keep, burn, sell, give to Steven Moore, or 2 of the above —ie send Moore xeroxes & keep, burn or sell the originals. It's all madness. (I understand 1st ed. of *The Recognitions*, once remaindered at $1.98, now goes for $450.)

best regards,
William Gaddis

———

To Johan Thielemans

235 East 73 Street
New York, New York 10021
7 January 1985

Dear Thielemans,

just back from 2 months at the American Academy in Rome to find galleys of *C****'s G***** waiting, now 'corrected' (with almost negligable changes) to take in to Viking tomorrow & find out their schedule for it, also for their (Penguin) reissues of *J R* & *The R*******'s* all early summer I believe. I don't know their prospect for bound galleys but if I can lay hands on one will send it along to you.

In my absence here a few things have come up regarding this spring to which I must respond & so would greatly appreciate hearing from you as soon as conveniently possible where the Orleans possibility stands & inhowfar I should consider it as a realistic spring prospect or not.

Forgive this haste plowing through a mountain of mail (bills) after chiseling through the stunning exhibition of computerized typesetting (typos) (ie the worst sort, that for than &c)—having just read that Mme Tolstoy copied *W** & P***** 7 times, & presumably in Cyrillic at that?

with best regards,
Gaddis

To Sarah and Matthew Gaddis

New York, NY
10 January 1985

Dear Sarah & Matthew,

16° here my, it is cold! & I read you folk in Europe are enjoying similar agonies, I hope you both have heat. [...] I've delayed this thinking I'd be able to send you bound galleys which should have been ready by now but Elis Sifton has to write a long kind of blurb (to help reviewers so they can review the book without reading it) & hasn't yet done so, another week or 2... Meanwhile I went down yesterday & turned in my set of galleys corrected & with negligable changes; the only hitch remaining is Viking's lawyer who may want me to change some passages as coming too close to Jimmy Swaggart but he was away yesterday (in South Dakota fighting a suit by an exgovernor there against Peter Matthiessen for saying he'd once raped a 10year old Indian girl or some such since even in South Dakota that might damage his chances for reelection). Also a long splendid lunch with Candida who of course has found a very expensive Italian restaurant in the new neighborhood she's moved her office to (West 22nd street), full reports on Rome &c.

I try to go out & 'walk' (for health) but 2nd Ave no treat after the Gianicolo. Mainly preoccupied thinking I must seriously decide and get started on Another Project, but what. Especially after just having painfully written a letter to LSU (Louisiana State Univ) turning down or at least postponing their invitation to me to come down there & direct their writing program, salary (hold your breath) $55 thousand! was I a fool? 8 months in Baton Rouge?

Arguing one way no, the whole point of The MacArthur is to free one for a while from such necessities to do one's 'own work'; on the other, really just a good excuse for laziness? Joyce Carol Oats teaches doesn't she? & has just published her 16th novel...ouch. But I will go down to Univ of Delaware just an overnight, give a talk &c; and a week at Bard in June. Haven't as yet heard anything about the Orleans number for spring. Maybe I'm secretly thinking something $ly exciting will happen with the new book. Fool! [...]

Sarah I am taking a liberty for which you may or may not thank me: a note from Catharine Carver saying she is in Paris for a couple of months at something called Trianon Press & I'm sending her your number. She is really now what she always wanted to be, an old eccentric English lady of letters... [...]

much love
Papa

Jimmy Swaggart: fundamentalist preacher (1935–) at the height of his popularity at that time.

Peter Matthiessen: American novelist, nonfiction writer, and environmental activist (1927–2014); Governor William J. Janklow and an FBI agent sued him and Viking to suppress his book *In the Spirit of Crazy Horse* (1983).

Gianicolo: Italian name for the Janiculum, a famous hill and location of the American Academy of Rome.

$55 thousand: $135,000 in current buying power.

Joyce Carol Oats: i.e, Oates (1938–), who published a prodigious amount while teaching at Princeton.

Univ of Delaware: at Elaine Safer's invitation, WG judged a fiction contest and delivered a talk there on 1 May 1985. Miriam Fuchs and I took the train down to Wilmington with him; the "talk" was a rambling assortment of observations, opinions, quotes, and jokes, delivered in an improvisatory manner from notecards, for which he was paid $1,500.

To Steven Moore

[*Having seen a limited edition of John Updike's* Harvard Lampoon *writings (Jester's Dozen, Lord John Press), I wrote to WG to request permission to edit a similar book of his. I also naively asked about the possibility of reviewing* CG *for the* New York Times Book Review.]

New York, NY 10021
[28 January 1985]

Dear Steve,
sorry but the sheer gimmickry of publishing the *Lampoon* material leaves

me cold despite your kind offer of time effort &c.

Bound galleys for the new book are being held up because of complications over permissions for the Jas. Hilton material which I'm trying to resolve now hence the haste of this. I think The *NYTimes* selects their reviewers as far as that goes.

Someone called my attention to the Delmore Schwartz passage which is at least thoughtful & straightforward.

WG.

Hilton material: the sections of *CG* quoting *Jane Eyre* (both the novel and the Orson Welles film) originally quoted James Hilton's *Lost Horizon* (1933, film version 1937). The Hilton Estate objected to the erotic context in which WG quoted the novel.

Schwartz: in the just-published *Letters of Delmore Schwartz,* ed. Robert Philips (Princeton: Ontario Review Press, 1984), Schwartz responds to Catharine Carver's request for a promotional statement on *R* with a harsh critique of the novel (p. 298).

To Sarah Gaddis

[*Handwritten in red ink on the first page of the revised* CG *proofs.*]

New York, NY

14 March 1985

Dear Sarah——— here *finally* are the page proofs & good God, I look at it & think *10 years*? for *this*? Anyhow what a vast relief to have it out of my hands if not my life. I say I hope you "like" it but it's not really a book to "like"—(a British publisher has just turned it down saying it's "*too painful*") I hope not for you & MHG; especially because I'm sure some literary "biographer" will one day—with the genius talent they've got for misinterpretation, getting it wrong (which is very much what the book's about as you'll see)—write that the brother & sister, Liz & Billy, are "obviously" drawn on you & Matthew. Absurd of course, but even more to the point was when I realized, & only quite recently! that this troubled younger brother, his beautiful & doomed sister, and her husband the man trying desperately to win a place in the world, are recreations of the 3 main characters in my aborted Civil War play—*Once at Antietam*—which you've never read (don't, it's terrible!) which I was work-ing on at 2nd Avenue when you were about 5 & Matthew 4, so clearly those characters were formed before you were. But it is odd—or perhaps not so odd: someone has said that every writer writes the same book over & over again— to discover that somewhere in one's mind, one's fabricated memory, that the same characters & their relationships exist, whether the war is the Civil War or Vietnam. At any rate I hope I've read it for the last time; it's not a book I finished in the high spirits I did *J R* or even *The Recognitions*, but that is probably largely the difference between being 32, or 52, & being 62. I'm sure you'll come across some familiar items—forgive me! but we take our material where we find it as you know & especially that which has touched us closest—in fact the whole passage where Liz talks about seeing herself as a child through a telescope light-years away [153], grew out of my remembrance of the story of yours that of course touched me closest about the girl watching her father going down the walk at Fire Island.

with much love always,
Papa

To the Editor, *New York Times Magazine*

[*Regarding a film Matthew had worked on; unpublished.*]

Wainscott, New York 11975
8 April 1985

In his piece 'Louis Malle: An Outsider's Odyssey' (April 7), John Culhane notes that a number of viewers have found Malle's new film *Alamo Bay* to be '"anti-American"—and, particularly, anti-Texan. In this view, the film showed white Texans as unsympathetic—racist and bigoted...' as well might anyone with only Mr Culhane's description of the film to go on, since nowhere in it is there even a mention that an essential tie binding these 'Anglo' fishermen together—their 'belonging', to use Mr Culhane's word and theme—is the fact, established in the film's opening hitchhiking scene and repeatedly borne out, that these men are veterans of the Vietnam war, which gives quite a different, credible, and far larger dimension to their outrage and that of the film itself.

William Gaddis

To Sarah Gaddis

[Wainscott, NY]
7 May 1985

Dear Sarah.

Terrible how the telephone monster (even transatlantic) breaks down the practice of writing, —I want to call her Thursday anyhow so I'll just wait... till finally weeks have gone by without even a note.

Not that there's that much to report & certainly nothing momentous though it is strange how one finally recognizes patterns emerging in one's life: spring bringing moving stuff from pink house to barn in Massapequa; from 2nd Avenue to Saltaire, now from New York to here, patching, painting, the whole thing reversed in the fall, so it's been that kind of back & forth for this last month, into town next week for the big annual Academy lunch & host to Bill & Mary Gass then out here for more or less good.

And I suppose there's a kind of secret suspense that colours everything else, waiting for that book to come out (though I was sure that this time I'd treat it as a minor event (which of course it may be!!)). I've practically lost contact with Viking, & having made all the suggestions I could decided any more will simply aggravate matters so I guess I'll just wait for the thing to appear. Just turned down a $5 thousand offer from a Brit publisher hoping to do better. Also asked for an interview for *Rolling Stone* which I think I'll do since it reaches the Young where one wants one's readers. Otherwise a grand silence pervades all.

Then of course another & probably the larger reason for postponing writing had been waiting to see how your plans developed & hoping to see you here soon; & it's not disappointment but rather concern that when we talked last week your spirits didn't sound high as they have almost always this past year & more, & I hope it was only a passing case of the blues though I felt, as the possibility came closer, your being disturbed at the prospect of coming 'back' for a visit which, as I said, I'd all this time pictured as a kind of reverse vacation not a threat of the future or jobs or anything like that & I do just wish—& this goes for your brother too—that you don't have feelings that such a visit entails your having to 'prove' something, anything; anything but Yes Paris is marvelous, Yes everything's good as can be . . . because it really is you know, & crass & awful as it sounds the very Freedom you & Matthew (me too!) have with the money horrors off our backs is major. Not for a moment that 'money buys happiness' Lord no! from the examples around us in fact it often looks like the more of one the less of the other; but the comparative freedom we have now, you he & I, to look around for what we really want to do instead of being driven to what we don't like 99% of mankind (or as ee cummings phrased it manunkind): not buying happiness no, but the grand luxury of a sense of proportion & self worth, Joan D[idion]'s 'self regard' or Mister Gibbs in *J R* observing there's nothing more demoralising than failing at something that wasn't worth doing in the first place, meaning something one had a kind of contempt for (I think I'll write a pop song & make a million dollars) . . . because, again, we the 3 of us I think have paid our dues in the nickel & dime department, & now it is up to us whether to let all that have 'strengthened our character' or warped it. Well! enough of another of 'Papa's little talks'...

Meanwhile I'm trying to make random notes around another novel, or rather concept for one, dealing with the 'final problem', what else? death and money. I've heard a few comments on the new book in fierce intellectual terms (its density & resonances accomplish everything the earlier books did at 3 times the length) and it 'is very, very funny' which is the heart of it, which is 'positive absurdity in the face of absolute idiocy' as I read recently somewhere, which is where death & money will eventually end up too.

I think your talking on french radio, if that came through, is just wild, just a marvelous burst of the things around us; & your 'dealing with the client' over the invitation . . . oh! that's the real world out there! As for pressures you seem to feel on you for a visit back they are simply those of love & pride in you, in you both.

with much love as you know,
Papa

interview for *Rolling Stone*: never happened.

ee cummings phrased it manunkind: poem 14 in *1 x 1* opens: "pity this busy monster, manunkind, / not."

Joan D[idion]'s 'self-regard': her well-known essay "On Self-Respect" appears in *Slouching Towards Bethlehem* (1968).

'it is very, very funny': so said *Esquire* in a feature on forthcoming novels (August 1984).

'positive absurdity in the face of absolute idiocy': in an article in the 1 May 1985 *New York Times*, the president of Canada's absurdist Rhinoceros Party praised its founder for teaching "us the power of positive absurdity in the face of absolute idiocies."

To Sarah Gaddis

Wainscott
6 June 1985

Dear Sarah,

I keep expecting I'll have something to send you in the way of news on the book's progress & it keeps not arriving—in this case a review in a rag called *Kirkus Reviews* very much read by booksellers and 'the trade' (also movie sharks) & usually quite unkind (they called *The Recognitions* 'totally undisciplined') but in this case apparently quite excited, some slavey at Viking called & read it to me (the only words I remember are 'virtuoso' & 'dazzling') said they'd send it immediately but of course have not. Next, *Publisher's Weekly* is sending someone out here to interview me & while as you know I've generally avoided such foolishments in this case I am trying to be more like a regular grownup & help sell the book rather than pretend I've never heard of it. So as all this mounts toward publication even though I've thought of getting away, even a hop over to see you, it is better to stay here & do what I can (short of a 'talk show') to cooperate at this rather crucial stage of things. My only other commitment is the last week of June at Bard to which I can't say I look forward but it is $3 thousand and they were good to me back in the late 70s when as we all remember things were pretty rough. [...]

with much love always,
Papa

Kirkus Reviews: 15 May 1985, p. 437. See Green's *Fire the Bastards!* for some choice words on its review of *R* in 1955, and fax of 2 November 1993.

Publisher's Weekly: Miriam Berkley interviewed Gaddis in Wainscott on 17 June, and her interview appeared in the 12 July issue of *PW* (pp. 56–57), accompanied by a photograph Berkley shot.

To Sarah E. Lauzen

[*A Chicago critic who had sent WG a draft of an entry that would be published the following year in* Postmodern Fiction: A Bio-Bibliographical Guide, *ed. Larry McCaffery (Westport, CT: Greenwood Press, 1986), 373–77.*]

Wainscott, New York 11975
20 June 1985

Dear Ms Lauzen.

Thank you for sending me your nicely & wittily written entry. I especially appreciated (p.5) mention that my work is 'enjoyable to read': among the many 'hostile and ignorant reviews' of *The Recognitions* when it first appeared most were so cowed by what they called 'erudition' that scarcely anyone dared suggest that it might be comic.

To your entry:

p. 1 I've just broken silence & given an interview to *Publishers Weekly*, seemed the politic thing to do this time (& that place) should appear in a couple of weeks; & I might elsewhere if it's a good elsewhere. (You might say for openers, something like Until the publication of his most recent novel WG had granted only one &c.)

bottom of page, should read grants from the American Academy and Institute of Arts and Letters in 1963; might also want to add Guggenheim Fellowship 1981

p.2 line 21, is there a better word for 'counterfeiting'? (which people usually associate with $: try forgery?

p.4 line 3, for setting sun read evening sky? v. p. 474 [of *J R*], the point here's really the moon coming up a few lines later, since (v. p. 661) what she's really seen is the top of a Carvel stand (& is there a millionaire for that!). No need to elaborate, just for your information.

p.5 line 3, the NBA was 1976 (for books published in 1975).

line 8, I'd say in and around New York

Primary Sources: the Harvest pbk was Harcourt, Brace & World, Inc.

Secondary Sources: I'd certainly include Frederick Karl, *American Fictions 1940–1980*, Harper & Row 1983; might want to mention Tony Tanner's *City of Words* all of course at your discretion.

I especially enjoyed that 'first and last attempt to reach the man at the airport' wherever that came from.

thank you again
William Gaddis

Tanner's *City of Words:* an influential 1971 book that contains an essay on *R* (393–400). 'first [...] airport': it came from WG himself: when I visited the previous August, WG said of *CG*: "This is the closest I'll ever come to writing for the man in the airport" (i.e., for the general reader looking for something entertaining to read). Lauzen called me in early 1985 to get information on the new novel (she hadn't seen it yet), and I paraphrased his remark.

To Sarah Gaddis

Wainscott
6th July 1985

Dear Sarah.

Well here at last it is! & from reading it you will see that I couldn't have been more fortunate (especially in light of the really dimwitted review by Lehmanhaupt a couple of days ago which may have been reprinted in the Paris *Tribune*?) —no, other reviews will come along now but no matter how good or bad nothing is as 'influential' as this front page of the *Times*. So we are off to a terrific start I think. (I sent you a 'finished copy' of the book more than a week ago, hope you got it?) Of course it is going to have to sell a good many copies to make back all the money I have had in advances before I get anything from it, [...]

Well I went up and did my stint at Bard & it was very strange, retracing those steps from 7 & 8 years ago when things were so difficult on all sides for us all. What is important, not just important but paramount, at the heart of it all, is how we've stood by each other & how both you & Matthew have stood by me Lord knows through some pretty dark times, even at the distances we've been apart, that has been & remains the by far best thing of my life (way beyond 'rave reviews') & now, with what certainly looks like Fortune Smiling, even Grinning (I touch wood) that we can build & build upon it. It has been a very great source of my strength, & of my driving myself down to work even in the times I really didn't feel like it, simply couldn't see the use of it, but— sentimental as it may sound—wanted above all for you & Matthew to be 'proud' of me as I've been of both of you increasingly so as time passes. I miss you so much now but when this long flurry passes & we get together one place or the other we can savour it all.

with much love always, always,
Papa

Lehmanhaupt: Lehmann-Haupt's review appeared in the 3 July *New York Times*, p. C22.

front page of the *Times*: Cynthia Ozick's insightful review appeared in the 7 July *New York Times Book Review*.

To Saul Bellow

Wainscott
11 July 1985

Dear Saul,

A drift of items accumulating toward sending you a note abruptly crested (if drifts can crest) when I saw the recent *Newsweek* review of my book open- ing with Aesop's lioness from your memorable citation in the Academy/In- stitute nomination &, though you are not credited here as its source, I hasten to supply—in case you saw it—that I was not Peter Prescott's. I saw it quoted in some sort of Academy proceedings for the year & that must be where he came upon it. (I had in fact months ago asked Viking to send you a copy of *Carpenter's Gothic* ('complimentary' not blurb beseeching) with those par- turient trepidations whether you might count it among the vixen's litter.)

Back to the drift: what occasioned it was a 5 day stint at Bard at Leon B's request to take part in the writers' branch of their summer 'MFA' program, these turned out to be 3 Jacks and a Jill all in poetry which left me a desert of time to myself in a Rokebylike house where, most fortunately, I'd brought along finally to read *Humboldt's Gift*, which got me through, with yourself haunting those Chanler/Henderson haunted hills & wherein, the *Gift* that is to say, the passages on boredom reawaked an old preoccupation of mine which I'd hoped, & may yet, to try to explore. You'll recall our own & local Saul in a *Time* cover story 7 or 8 years ago observing that the major problem for the creative person is how to avoid boredom & that (here's the pertinence:)

as one grows older this becomes more difficult; so I've come back out here searching Schopenhauer who I thought from college days had the recipe but so far have not found it.

Meanwhile, having done our best with the day, we attack the problem as best we can by evening; & while I know you've a fairly clear Vermont summer schedule, Saul Muriel & I would marvel to see you both here if that could fit at all into your picture.

best to you & to Alexandra from us all,
William Gaddis

Newsweek: Peter Prescott's "Slouching Toward Bethlehem" appeared in the 15 July 1985 issue, p. 64. He had favorably reviewed *J R* a decade earlier, and both reviews were reprinted in his *Never in Doubt* (NY: Arbor House, 1986). For Bellow's citation, see 27 October 1992.

Leon B.: Leon Botstein (1946–), president of Bard since 1975.

Rokebylike house: a famous mansion in Barrytown, NY.

Humboldt's Gift: Bellow's 1975 novel was one of the finalists for the 1975 National Book Award that WG won.

Chanler/Henderson: the protagonist of Bellow's 1959 novel *Henderson the Rain King* was based on a larger-than-life man named Chanler Chapman (1901–82), who lived near the Rokeby estate.

Saul in a *Time* cover story: Saul Steinberg appeared on the cover of the 17 April 1978 issue of *Time*.

Schopenhauer: WG mentions reading Schopenhauer at Harvard in his 12 November 1942 letter to his mother.

Alexandra: Bellow's fourth wife, who divorced him later in 1985.

To John Aldridge

[*A postcard typed on the obverse of Anderson's* Rapture.]

[24 July 1985]

Dear Jack,

Glad and relieved to hear from you, it seems a very long time & we'd hoped you might pass through; glad also that the book did reach you & kept your generous regard for my work unblemished. (I'd wanted this *Rapture* for the book's jacket, but the folks in Sherman Texas feared the book might have swear words in it & so declined.) Again, let us know if you *do* pass through.

our best to you both
Bill Gaddis

5. *A FROLIC OF HIS OWN*
1985–1994

To Johan Thielemans

[*In his book* Vrijheid in de steigers *(Haarlem: In de Knipscheer, 1985), Dutch critic Graa Boomsma describes a visit with WG (p. 24, with Joseph Heller stopping by), and a few pages later describes how, sitting one evening out on Gaddis's porch, Thomas Pynchon dropped by for a chat (p. 28).*]

Wainscott, New York 11975

11 October 1985

Dear Thielemans.

Thanks for your letter of the 30th September with its news—news to me—that Graa Boomsma not only visited us on Long Isld but that he met Thomas Pynchon here! He had written me of his trip to the US hoping we might meet, but there was some confusion & it never came about, surely not out here, most surely not Pynchon (whom I've never met, despite the many critical claims to similarity in our work: I see us both classed paranoid & conspiratorial but who, aside from James Michner, is not?). And so I would *very much* appreciate it when you've got the time if you might send me a copy of his piece with a translation. Most curious.

I met your charming Anna K. last week, she came up to the NY apartment on her tour of US writers & we had a delightful chat though I'm not at all sure that she got from it whatever information she was after. At any rate I enjoyed it highly.

Carpenter's Gothic seems to be going well here, & I have signed for it abroad with Andre Deutsch (Britain), Albin Michel (France), Rowolt (Ger.); Spain still unsigned but practically so (can't think of the publisher, begins with an 'A'). My agent is at the Frankfurt Book festival & I've told him to notify Sweden Holland Norway &c to watch your 27 October television which may help to bring them into the fold.

News here: we (Muriel & I) invited to 2 or 3 weeks in Russia, some sort of writers' conference (though I have no details at all) from mid November, & I will try to stop in Paris on return around 5th December to see my daughter for a few days & what happens then is wide open.

Finally, word of some sort of British Publishers Assoc'n event for early next year selecting the 20 'best' US novels since the war (WWII), a rather odd list but *The Recognitions* among them so that may be another grand tour; it all leaves little time for 'writing' even were I so inclined.

best regards,
W. Gaddis

Anna K.: by the time Thielemans made copies of these letters for me, he had forgotten who this woman was.

Carpenter's Gothic [...] abroad: the novel was published by Deutsch in 1986, as *Gothique charpentier* (translated by Marc Cholodenko) by Christian Bourgois in 1988 (*not* Albin Michel—see 6 February for an explanation), and as *Die Erlöser* ("The Saviors," trans. Klaus Modick and Martin Hielscher) by Rowohlt in 1988. The Spanish publisher Alfaguara brought out a translation of *R* in 1987 but not *CG*. The novel was also translated into Portuguese (1986), Swedish (1987), Polish (1991), and Italian (1992). A Spanish translation was eventually published by Sexto Piso in 2012.

Frankfurt Book festival: the annual trade show where publishers from around the world gather to sell foreign rights.

Russia: see 14 December 1985.

British Publishers Assoc'n: the British Book Marketing Council announced its list of the twenty greatest postwar American novels in October 1985 for a special trade promotion the following year called AUTHORS USA. All of the (living) authors were invited to attend, and WG was one of seven who accepted and went to England in February 1986. See *Publishers Weekly,* 18 October 1985, p. 20, for the complete list of novels, and its 28 February 1986 issue (p. 26) for details on the promotional tour.

To Saul Bellow

Wainscott
12 October '85

Dear Saul.

Many thanks for your note & its again vastly appreciated comments [on *CG*]: like a flash of light to see a creative eye on the creation as it were, having seen it heaved & hauled & manhandled in the reviews even the 'good' ones.

(As for your typing apology, the most happily slipshod I've ever had—misspellings, missing syllables, xxxxxs, marginal scribbles, exhausted ribbons & dirty keys—have been from top newspapermen from the prewordprocessor generation, an old editor of the *Baltimore Sun* & more recently Harrison Salisbury, a kind of aristocracy surely?)

For a diversion of which you may be aware, sent to me by my Brit. publisher (thus the circled authors), this item from *The Observer* compelling us, a mixed bag to be sure, to London's worst weathertime, February I believe, for a 'state visit'? Reminds me of someone's notion for a book titled 'Short Lists': Blacks I have met on yachts, &c... acid commentary & all.

Re the Salisbury above, this was a note following a call from him (whom I've never met) cordially inviting me (with another mixed bag) to Moscow in mid November, mission undefined. I know you've done these things but I am still wide eyed at the prospect, Muriel (ne Oxenberg) boning up on her Russian. Our local Saul observes it should be seen only in snow, White Nights & all. I had heard from him of the griefs that beset your summer & here are belated condolences for what inevitably must become more frequent & the more so if we've been fortunate in those close to us. He sends his warm regards to you both, as do we,

William

---

old editor of the *Baltimore Sun*: probably A. D. Emmart: see 29 october 1950.
Harrison Salisbury: American journalist and author (1908–93).
this item from *The Observer*: "Novel Choice for the Best of US Books," 29 September 1985.
White Nights: probably an allusion to Dostoevsky's short story of that title.

To Steven Moore

[When I visited WG in August 1984, I asked whether he would ever write an introduction or foreword—as opposed to a promotional blurb—for someone else's book, and he said he didn't know, he had never been asked. In 1985 I was preparing an edition of Alan Ansen's collected poems and wrote on Halloween to see if he would be willing to write a foreword for it, but by then he had obviously forgotten our discussion. The statement made below is quoted in my introduction to Ansen's Contact Highs, *p. xi.]*

235 East 73 Street
New York, New York 10021
8 November 85

Dear Steven Moore.

Regarding your Hallowe'en request I'd thought it pretty clear by now that I don't write forwards blurbs &c; however you may incorporate this in yours

Gaddis in the USSR, November 1985: top, photo by William H. Gass; bottom: WG, Soviet writer Daniil Granin, Allen Ginsberg, and Louis Auchincloss listen to a Russian reading from *The Brothers Karamazov* (photos by William H. Gass, courtesy Mary H. Gass).

if you wish, with the understanding that it is not to be used in jacket copy, ads &c.

In conversation he said it had always seemed to him that in the spate of material about the so called beat scene of the 'fifties too little note has been taken of Alan Ansen's part in influencing, "you could almost say educating a number of those younger talents. It was Ansen's unrestrained enthusiasm at sharing his own rather marvelous store, languages, literature, Bellini, the works, his hunger for work well done or the hope of it, and it was terribly infectious."

Thus far *Carpenter's Gothic* has been signed with Andre Deutsch in Britain & a very good reprint there with Pan books; Albin Michel in France, Rowolt in Ger., Alfaguara (sp?) in Spain, & the stragglers are coming along. Meanwhile, a trip to Russia in a few days with a rather mixed bag of writers, then at the above address through the winter.

best regards
WG

To William H. and Mary Gass

[*Gaddis jokes about Allen Ginsberg (the "dybbuk") photobombing snapshots taken in the Soviet Union during their state-sponsored visit in November with a group of American writers that also included Norman Cousins, Arthur Miller, Louis Auchincloss, Charles Fuller, Harrison E. Salisbury, and M. Norvel Young (and wives). For an account of this trip, with occasional mention of WG, see William H. Gass's "Some Snapshots from the Soviet Zone,"* Kenyon Review 8.4 *(Fall 1986): 1–43, and, with the focus on WG (and Russian literature), "Gaddis Gets Read To," in his* A Temple of Texts *(Knopf, 2006), 191–200.*]

New York, NY 10021
14 December 1985

Dear Bill & Mary.

WHO—or rather WHOSE?—is that DYBBUK lurking behind us! Not mine! saith the preacher (wrong testament) but the marvel of our unawareness of that wandering soul quite ready (the dictionary tells me) to 'enter the body of a man'...well I'll be buggered...till 'exorcised by a religious rite' so I've used Huck Finn's 3 times in a circle & spat over the left shoulder and advise you the same of something similar. Quick!

(My 2 other photos of him, honestly inadvertantly sliced off through the nose at Dostoevski's desk & totally decapitated in Raskolnikov's attic...a Hidden Hand guides my lens.)

The spy photo before I learned my toy camera had a focusing device obviously.

Enclosed also our dybbuk stealing the Conference in the *Times*, & Salisbury's left thrust at Federenko for your possible use in the same pages.

Mine, should I pursue it, may more likely be at PEN's January exorcise adorned as the Writer's Imagination & 'How does the State Imagine?'. I'm not a PENman but got invited to participate, & you? Jan. 12–17, if you were anticipating it we'd probably have made mention along the line but, should you still, both be our guests here? All the Receptions & big names from Mailer's on, my Lord, get your picture in the paper & you've never got to write another damned word.

You will also be receiving from Arthur Miller a Malcolm Bradbury novel inscribed to me & Muriel, as we have one from him to you & Mary; so when he called to straighten it out I just said that we would (a) dutifully read, & (b) make the exchange on sight when that occurs.

Finally, a very high class job from Leslie Miller (pages) of your *Culp* extract, so clearly elegant as a collectors' item not to be read but I did anyway with great delight. I've nothing around worthy of such treatment but am encouraged to something as a keepsake for the kiddies ($).

Mary your red scarf was the banner to which we all repaired & thank you for it, as to you both for all the grumbling shared as the curtain fell. Let's know if January's possible & our love for a merry Snoopyless, Bingless holidays,

Willie

Not mine! [...] wrong testament: apparently a reference to Jesus' claim "My doctrine is not mine, but his that sent me" (John 7:16).

Huck Finn's 3 times in a circle: in order to ward off bad luck, Huck "got up and turned around in my tracks three times and crossed my breast every time; and then I tied up a little lock of my hair with a thread to keep witches away" (*Adventures of Huckleberry Finn*, chap. 1).

Conference in the *Times*: from "Tone Is Cool at U.S.-Soviet Literary Exchange," *New York Times*, 3 December 1985: "Mr. Ginsberg touched off a series of sharp exchanges when he declared that writers everywhere should strive to reflect a broader range of human passions, including homosexual love, in their work, several of the Americans reported. [¶] 'Allen was very direct in his discussion of homosexuality,' Mr. Salisbury said. [¶] Mr. Salisbury added, 'The Soviet bureaucrats, but interestingly not the writers, immediately responded by talking about the perversion and pornography that they believe permeates Western culture'" (C-24).

Federenko: Nikolai Fedorenko (1912–2000), Soviet diplomat and statesman.

for your possible use: Gass was writing "East vs. West in Lithuania: Rising Tempers at a Writers' Meeting," *New York Times Book Review*, 2 February 1986, 3, 29, 31—later incorporated into his *Kenyon Review* essay.

'How does the State Imagine?': Gaddis's speech is reprinted in *RSP*, 123–26.

Malcolm Bradbury: British author and critic (1932–2000) who would interview Gaddis a few months later when he went to England. The novel is unidentified.

Leslie Miller [...] *Culp*: Miller, publisher of the Grenfell Press, had issued a limited edition of this extract from Gass's work-in progress (now on pp. 156–79 of *The Tunnel*).

a merry Snoopyless, Bingless holidays: WG originally typed "the merry" but changed it by hand to "a"; Snoopy is featured in *A Charlie Brown Christmas* (1965), a holiday staple, as is Bing Crosby's "White Christmas" (1942).

To George Plimpton

[American writer (1927–2003) and editor of the Paris Review *who had occasionally approached WG about an interview. The one mentioned below appeared in issue 105 (Winter 1987): 54–89.]*

235 East 73 Street
New York, New York 10021
4 January 1986

Dear George.

Regarding this 'interview' affliction: in this gap since discussing it for *Paris Review* back in the spring I got into a serious such encounter with a scholarly fellow extremely familiar with my work this past November in Budapest. He is Zoltan Abadi Nagy, & has got together some 45 pp (say 10,000 wds) which seem to me as good as could be done in this area for which you know I haven't great enthusiasm & would like to get off once for all.

He plans its publication in Hungarian & is of course interested in possibilities for its publication here; thus this query whether it would serve *Paris Review*'s purposes since I would obviously be greatly relieved at this solution, or otherwise to find its US publication elsewhere & let the whole thing rest for another 10 years. [...]

We are here (988-1360) through February, then a month's march through Australia before another damned spring & summer & hope even to see you, with love to Freddie,

& best regards,
Gaddis

Top: John Sherry, Donn Pennebaker, and WG, Sag Harbor, taken at Pennebaker's 70th birthday party, July 1995 (photo by Chelsea Pennebaker). Bottom: Mario Vargas Llosa, William H. Gass, and WG at the PEN-sponsored 48th Worldwide Writers' Congress, New York City, January 1986 (photo by Miriam Berkley).

Zoltan Abadi Nagy: properly, Zoltán Abádi-Nagy (1940–), a translator and professor at Kossuth University in Debrecen, Hungary, also a visiting professor at several American universities over the years.
Freddie: Freddy Esty Plimpton, his wife at the time (divorced in 1988).

To John and Pauline Napper

New York NY 10021
"Easter Sunday" [30 March] 1986

Dear John & dear Pauline,

why it has taken me this long to get any sort of note off to you I don't know, especially since so much recent time has gone to simply staring at blank pages, at walls, at 'old notes' for hope of some kindling spark for another novel, another book & even the why of that escapes me after the carousal we've had over the winter: a 'writer's conference' in Russia last November (COLD) & then England in February for the 'media' some fragment of which might have reached you. Activities I've always avoided in my own country: 40seconds on BBC television, 55 on radio, interviews in the 'print media'... all of it set up by the Book Marketing Council there & seemed politic since both earlier books were being republished & the new one appearing at the same time, so there went the better part of a week on such activities every minute accounted for put up, meanwhile, in great comfort at a swank little hotel called the Marlborough Crest, heated towel racks & fresh fruit & a trouser presser, things like that near the British Museum; at any rate I called you a couple of times that week at the number I have, no answer but no liberty on my part even if I had reached you, & cold. Even the newspapers (which I found appalling! my old favourite *Daily Mail*? the *Express*?) headlining COLD. So on the Thursday where to of all places but East Anglia for a 'conference' which proved academia to be quite the same everywhere, & COLD. Having planned to go from there for a couple of days to Cambridge the results came down with a rousing cold for Muriel so we fled back to London where she recovered while I came down with the worst throat I can remember, 2 days there among the heated towel racks & home where I went to bed for a week, something I haven't done since childhood & why I didn't even try to reach you those last days when I'd dared to envision (before we came over) gamboling on the heaths (?) & moors (?) of Shropshire with you for a couple of days but we'd be lying at the bottom of your garden now if we'd tried it. You seemed near but very far away & it finally seemed kinder to all simply to beat it for home, why they scheduled such an event for that time of year, why 30° in London (let alone East A.) is like 10° here... but the BMC people & publishers were so attentive & generous & I hope if only for their sake that we sold some books.

Carpenter's Gothic has done quite well here for such a book despite numerous misreadings by our reviewers & critics even the favourable ones, mainly I think what it did for me was to bring me along as a real living novelist from having been viewed (when I was viewed) as a rather eccentric recluse who'd once written a couple of long very difficult books all which simply means that we get invited to Functions & patronize a few millionaires & otherwise the problems, the central problem of the work itself remains. I read so much of the current stuff & despair. A couple of nights ago met a lawyer (millionaire) who may be able to get me a cheap set of the *Corpus Juris Secundum* which is kind of a Reader's Digest of the Law, every sort of case & human foible & precedent & *plot* one might imagine so there may be a spark somewhere there & enough reading to see me well through the Twilight Years (it is 100 volumes).

Well as you must know I have always admired what I've seen as your demand upon life to make itself worth pursuing & upon the work to make itself worth doing & however I may misread you this to me is the effort (*Carpenter's Gothic*, as you may see, is unlike its predecessors which, in Samuel Butler's phrase, 'demanded to be written', a *willed* book (fortunately the critics didn't penetrate that though generations of PhD candidates to come may) so that is where we are now. Geographically though as the weather improves will get back out to Long Island, whisky still somewhat the problem but tobacco the abiding curse, that & late in life leisure? does one long for the panics of debt NO, No, no

love & best hopes & wishes,
Willie

Corpus Juris Secundum: WG received not this but the 81-volume *American Jurisprudence*, 2nd edition (1975), which provided the spark for what would become *FHO*. The millionaire lawyer was Donald Oresman (see next letter).

To Donald Oresman

[*A New York attorney, art collector, and bibliophile (1925–2016), at the time Executive Vice President and General Counsel of Paramount Communications. Over the next seven years WG sought legal advice from him for* FHO.]

New York NY 10021
17 April 1986

Dear Donald,

I have read the Cardozo and dissenting opinions you sent to me over and over again, and immensely appreciate your trouble selecting these glimpses for me. How few pages they are for what they contain: the vistas of reason, language and rigorous speculation flung open by an otherwise inconsequential woman on a train platform buying a ticket for a completely inconsequential place. The man pursuing his cousin's hat on the railway bridge is fine too, and again the language! ('The risk of rescue, if only it be not wanton, is born of the occasion. The emergency begets the man.' &c.) Much of my fascination clearly lies in the material itself, since the defining (and rampant evasion) of accountability seems to me central to our times.

Your efforts regarding *Corpus Juris Secundum* are also very greatly appreciated, and I would only urge 'restraint' (in the nonjudicial sense). Despite my grand declarations of that evening, I clearly will not survive the entire set, hardly need a recent edition and certainly not with the updating addenda, and any odd volumes you might come up with without further serious effort would be a pleasure. In fact, since I seem to have far more interest in civil than in criminal law, and in such areas as Liability, Risk, Negligence (though here is of course criminal negligence) and 'the unswerving punctuality of chance', I might be best suited to simply sit down and read your casebook on Torts from which you lifted these pages, for these wider evidences of what James called 'the high brutality of good intentions'.

However all this comes out, you have again my warm thanks.

With very best regards,
Bill

Cardozo: Benjamin Cardozo's opinion *Palsgraf v. Long Island Railroad* (1928) is considered a legal classic, and is referred to twice in *FHO* (29, 579).

casebook on Torts: William L. Prosser et al.'s *Cases and Materials on Torts*, 7th ed. (Foundation Press, 1982), a classic text originally published in 1943, and the source for many of the legal citations in *FHO*.

'the high brutality of good intentions': title of an essay on Henry James by William H. Gass (1958), and a phrase WG will continue to use occasionally.

To Clive Suter

[A student at Keele University in England who had sent WG his Master's thesis, "God Damned Holy Shit: Wasteful Reproduction in William Gaddis' J R" (1985).]

Wainscott, New York 11975
27 April 1986

Dear Clive Suter.

Thank you for your letter & the accompanying thesis. I do remember our meeting and your speaking of it what seems like a very long (& cold) time ago, & from reviews that have been sent me I gather that *Carpenter's Gothic* has been quite well received which of course is pleasing.

I've given your thesis 2 readings with obvious enjoyment: it is a thesis *with* a thesis (which unhappily is not always the case, some of them I've seen mere laborious retelling of the 'plot'). But in others such as this one I am always intrigued by what I learn, as for example the Marc Shell quote p. 3, marvelous. Your examination of Gibbs is I think awfully good &, again, rare (he is after all central to the book).

However not to pursue it point by point, the extremely well knit details & citations of your argument have absorbed me in this fascinating way: with the rise, or at least the rise in cohesion of the political right in America, my work has more frequently been characterised as an assault on capitalism, with the unspoken implication of communism as its only alternative. What it comes down to, as some woman in a recent piece in *Commentary* touched upon, is whether in each system the abuses are inherent, or whether one or the other system is amenable to its abuses being corrected & therefore essentially sound. For communism, or rather the nearest approach to it on a visit to Soviet Russia last fall, I think the abuses are inherent and those of the totalitarianism it spawns inevitable; & I had thought that I thought, & that my work was directed at the abuses—& thus the (naive) hope of their correction—in our own system as essentially sound. However through reading your thesis here and now in the light, or perhaps the darkness, of 'free enterprise' totally unleashed by our present Administration, deficit ridden, corporate takeovers in the hundred millions which serve no productive purpose whatever, the widening gap between 'private wealth & public squalor' everywhere apparent (to say nothing of our Pentagon, NASA &c monsters), I have got to wonder, & that line 'he builded better than he knew' comes to mind, at least to keep the mind working for which I thank you. There's a line somewhere in *The Recognitions* about the present constantly reshaping the past & this may be it.

with best regards,
William Gaddis

Marc Shell quote: "America was the historical birthplace of widespread paper money in the Western world, and a debate about coined and paper money dominated

American political discourse from 1825 to 1845. [...] The paper money debate was concerned with symbolization in general, and hence not only money but also with aesthetics. [...] With the advent of paper money certain analogies, such as the one that 'paper is to gold as word is to meaning,' came to exemplify and to inform logically the discourse about language. For example a call was made by critics for a return to gold not only in money but also in aesthetics and language. [...] While a coin may be both symbol (as inscription or type) and commodity (as metallic ingot), paper is only (or virtually all) symbolic. Thus Wittgenstein chooses to compare meaningless sounds with scraps of paper rather than with unminted ingots" (*Money, Language and Thought* [University of California Press, 1982], pp. 5–6, 18–19; Suter's ellipses).

some woman in [...] *Commentary*: Midge Decter in the November 1985 issue, pp. 34–36.

'he builded better than he knew': see note to 13 June 1984.

present constantly reshaping the past: see note to Sheri Martinelli letter (Summer 1953).

To Steven Moore

[*Two acquaintances of mine from New Hampshire, Clifford Mead and Richard Scaramelli, planned to visit me in New Jersey and wondered if I could arrange for the three of us to visit WG. In the postscript to my letter asking if a visit was feasible, I had asked, "Who in the world is Peter Taylor and what's he doing with your PEN/Faulkner award?"—for much to my (and many others') surprise, CG, though nominated, was passed over in favor of Taylor's latest book,* The Old Forest and Other Stories.]

Wainscott, New York 11975
25 May '86

Dear Steve Moore.

The PEN/Faulkner award & ceremonies turned out to be, in my jaundiced northern eyes, something resembling the Southern Christian Readership Conference: 1 judge Texan; 1 Virginian; & Alice Adams fighting the good fight. Peter Taylor, whose work I didn't know, all short stories apparently, a gentle elderly gent from Charlottesville &c. Made quite clear to us by m.c. Mississippian Hodding Carter that its whole thrust was to put Washington (a real southern town as I often forget till I revisit) on the culture map, shake off the yankee (NY) yoke. Uh huh.

To your real query: I am here with only occasional forays to NY & unpredictable at that. You'd all 3 be welcome to come out for lunch though it is a hell of a distance, if you call first (516-537-0743) we should be able to work something out here or possibly NY though I've no immediate plans for going into town.

yours,
W. Gaddis

Alice Adams: an acquaintance from WG's Harvard days (see letter of 9 March 1947). The other two judges were Richard Bausch and Beverly Lowry.

Hodding Carter: W. Hodding Carter III (1935–), Southern journalist and travel writer.

To Richard Scaramelli

[*When Mead, Scaramelli, and I visited Gaddis on May 30th, Dick dropped off a draft of a long article he had written on the school Gaddis attended as a boy and its director, John Kingsbury (now in the Gaddis collection at Washington University). Largely a historical account of Merricourt, the essay ventures a few conjectures on Kingsbury as a possible model for the Rev. Gwyon. During our visit, Dick asked a number of questions about this period, and WG displayed an astonishing memory of names and incidents fifty-five years in the past.*]

Wainscott, New York 11975

1 June 1986

Dear Richard Scaramelli.

That is quite a piece of homework, thank you for letting me read it. A few points:

p. 2,9 I think 7 rather than 8 years boarding there

p. 15 & passim, Mr Kingsbury was not a tall or big man though for his authority & stress on 'doing it right' a formidable figure for a small boy (you did not sit on the edge of your bed to tie your shoes, you sat on the chair; the bed was to lie down on & sleep). Looking back, I can see him as a very gentle man, no nonsense or sentimentality but not dour either, & as distant from cigars or schnapps as possible; religion was not a constant or oppressive presence let alone mythic meanderings, he saw things as they were. The 'John H.' is so far as I know coincidence. The 2 syllable/Kingsbury (p. 16) quite farfetched; & the 1883 date pure coincidence, as is (p. 17) the YMCA connection. He'd never (19) espouse false religion.

p. 18, further extreme coincidence: I hadn't known till now of his earlier marriage, such things would never have been discussed before us (p. 19)

p. 22, the 'preface' draft was dropped because it was pretentious

pp. 25,6 The Whitford material news to me, do. (p. 31) Timothy Dwight though most amusing.

I hope you all got home before midnight.

Yours,

W. Gaddis

To Michael Urban

[*A fan in the hospital for lymphoma. His mother asked WG to send signed books to him.*]

Wainscott, New York 11975
13 December 1986

Dear Michael.

I've just learned of your illness which inevitably recalled me to mine some 50 (! I find hard to believe) years ago, 2 years of what was at last resignedly diagnosed as a 'tropical fever of unknown origin' (I'd then never been in the tropics), told I'd accumulated the most voluminous case history in New York Hospital, and finally sent home without prospects when I demanded that my dog be brought in for a visit; after which things gradually mended with no more explanation than what it was all about in the first place. Lord, when I remember those hospital days waking bright as a penny sitting bolt upright learning/practicing Old English lettering doing Do Not Disturb signs for the nurses (& I still vividly recall in all of age 14's confusion lusting after Miss McElvar, I see her now coming in for the night shift with a fling of red lined blue cape) and by evening a temperature of around 103° & pains not generally earned till about age 80...

At any rate, & since you've read *The Recognitions*, it's all there (from page 41 on) written 12 or so years later as what, I wonder looking back, revenge certainly but perhaps not, as I must have meant it at the time, on the well intended medical blundering efforts, but on the gratuitous absurdity of the illness itself & equally, I must now suppose, of some glimpse of some part of the human spirit that refuses to accept it. Of course, as I note above, the actual (& equally gratuitous) solution was nothing as to the Heracles solution in the novel but it clearly did provide this material of innate indignation, indeed of human outrage at the accidental human condition & thus confirming its deterministic paradox that 'everything happens for some reason', in this case to produce 'one more damned, thick square book' of whatever merit but some sort of testimony, its reviews at the time notwithstanding.

Well I think of Mark Twain in his late dark years clinging to humour in its deepest sense as courage in its best, & doubt we can do better than that.

again with warm hopes & good wishes,
William Gaddis

To Judith Gaddis

[*In his first letter to Judith since August 1980, WG enclosed this in a copy of* CG. *After they separated, Judith moved to Key West, became involved in the arts scene there, was director of a small historic house museum, and eventually became a board member of the Key West Literary Seminar.*]

24 January 1987

Dear Judith,

well this time you should really read the book to the end if only because it doesn't *end* (note no period at the last page) which in a way is what it's all about (though I don't plan a sequel) but since I'm off on this there are a few points of ambiguity which for the 'reading public' (Ch. Lehmanhaupt) I'm glad to leave that way, having always said You can't go running after your book saying what I really meant was &c . . . but after some of the reviews I've got to realize that perhaps some points were more obscure than I'd intended although (1) I thought it clear enough that Liz, bad health, talk of high blood pressure, obviously alone in the house when she goes down, that the robbery was committed earlier, her head hits the table ('blunt instrument'), kitchen's orderly enough but when she's found next morning (Mme Socrate has been told to come very early) the floor is strewn with placemats &c (Mme Socrate had seen where she kept her household $) & finally the check cashed in Haiti, obviously (I thought) she rushed back there into the dark & had a fatal heart attack, but too many read it that Paul killed her! Poor fellow, again reviewers finding him mean bad brutal &c where I found him desperate confused desolated as much or more a victim as anyone & his dependence (not simply $ly) painfully clear upon her & the last person to do her in as the FBI (& similarly dimwitted or only careless readers) adduce; then (2) is (as many inferred) McCandless 'mad'? spent some time in a hospital though what sort is only implied, may have had a breakdown? but I didn't think 'mad' unless I am which may be the good question; finally the point I think probably everyone missed so I must take some blame, wherein at the last where the woman shows up & introduces herself as Mrs McCandless this is *not* Irene but his first wife (old enough to have a 25yr old son) and that, muddy enough I admit, she & Liz each mistake the other for Irene who is never more than the constant presence haunting the house & McCandless, & Liz who in effect moves into Irene's role in her desperate attempt to rescue her own shattered identity. So there it is. I'm finally resigned to the apparent fact that I shall never reach 'the man at the airport' but perhaps some doctoral students will be kept busy with it. [...]

And I've been fortunate finally I must say & as you probably know from Rust & others if only *I* would just cut down on the drink & quit the smokes as I've been postponing these 10 years. So I am being dragged somewhat reluctantly by circumstances to start another book though fortune keeps interrupting: where those 12 years ago with a comedy indicting 'free enterprise' abuse got me that trip to Japan, with the last book indicting just about everything else the USIA invites me to go to Australia too good to turn down, aside from all that all goes calmly though I am appalled how the time passes as one grows older. I did appreciate your message, Key West seems 1000 years ago & I've often enough thought & hoped things have gone well for you there but not written since this is quite simply not a scene that encourages correspondence, otherwise though happy to hear you sounding well & bright as I remember.

with love,
W.

USIA [...] Australia: United States Information Agency; see 12 April 87 for WG's impressions of Australia and New Zealand.

To William H. Gass

[WG accepted the following invitation; see 7 October 1987.]

30 January 87

BILL —do you know anything about this gang? they are celebrating Berlin's 750th anniversary most of this spring-summer-fall & have sent me pages & pages mit Luftpost im Drucksak &c describing it all, writers, doodle-sackpipers & everything + invitation for 8–14 November as you see, did you get one? & can you / could you and Mary go? And if you didn't can I write desperately to recommend you? I assume my name got to them because Rowolt Verlag took *Carpenter's Gothic* (but apparently 'Mr Heepe' is having difficulties). Have you a German publisher? PLEASE don't abandon us to the Krauts in our hour of need!

It would be very friendly, so that we come into dialogue, I will be happy to hear from you bitte, genug und

mit Freundschaft
WG

Had I mentioned? USIA sending me (if I pay Muriel's carfare) to Australia/ NZ whole month of March.

---

mit Luftpost im Drucksak: airmail printed matter, though the final word should be *Drucksache*.
doodlesackpipers: German variant of bagpipers.

Mr Heepe: Hans Georg Heepe (1936–2009), longtime editor at Rowolt who specialized in publishing German translations of American authors.
bitte, genug und mit Freundschaft: broken German for "please, enough and with
friendship."

To Mary McCarthy

[*American novelist and critic (1912–89), an old friend of WG. She taught one semester a
year at Bard College from 1986 until her death. "Leon" is Leon Botstein.*]

Wainscott, New York 11975
4 February 1987

Dear Mary,
finally just a note of regret that I never managed to get up to Bard during
your reign there, I talked to Leon who sounded elated with you[r] efforts and
I must say all things considered how I admire you for taking it on and carrying it off. But what busted up our fall plans was an invitation to Sofia from
the Bulgarian Writers' Union, where we heard the US denounced and vilified
by 200 'writers' from 50odd countries though we did get a stop in Paris to see
Sarah now in probably her last year there (and just harried to move to 6 rue
de l'Assomption (chez Foisnel), 75016).
More and more amazed at how fast time passes and the sense of the past
devouring the present as though frantic to consume it, we see Liz Hardwick
and hope to see you both somewhere along the line,
very best wishes
William Gaddis

Liz Hardwick: Elizabeth Hardwick (1916–2007), American critic and fiction writer.

To John and Pauline Napper

12 April 87 (can it be?)

Dear John & Pauline,
Well we are back from all things Australia whence perhaps you had a
picture postcard? & New Zealand which is quite stunning especially perhaps
after Australia, I don't for a moment mean to be unkind everyone treated us
splendidly & we didn't after all see such great attractions as the Great Barrier
Reef &c but the sheer green of NZ & the people with a little of Maori showing through rather more seductive than Australia's good white cheery USA
brawn: what it was all about was our US govt information agency sending
me out to talk for USA as I wished & did about "writing", the dissident tradi-

WG in Paris. Top: with his daughter Sarah on the Île St.-Louis, Quai de Bourbon, 1985 (photo © Mellon Tytell); bottom: at Odile Hellier's Village Voice Bookstore, with Ivan Nabokov, actress Dominique Sanda (who read from *CG*), and Christian Bourgois, 1988 (photo by Flavio Toma).

tion in American literature (my theme) &c &c to a point I never want to hear my voice in public again, ready to drop out with the Trappists or better perhaps get back to this damn typewriter where I belong. [...]

But at any rate the rather gorgeous news from [Sarah] is that all this while, 3 years? that she's been working at her degree from Parson's design school there in Paris she has also (really) been working at a novel on the sly, I hadn't a word of it though I knew she was trying at stories but here she comes to my agent (again without my interference) who is very struck thence to a publisher ready to "make an offer" as they say, imagine! All I know of it is that it's somewhat 'autobiographical' (as all first novels but mine?) so may read myself into a doddering well meaning drinking & smoking old fellow on the board-walk—perhaps I hope for too much?—at any rate something of *hers* done quite her own & what better for that vital self regard, any money (though never) aside: point is it is really damned difficult for a 'young person' (how she hates that description) to get a first novel up front & for the ruthlessness of NY publishing I know no favour to me, the connection may simply have got it read faster but that's all. [...]

Our immediate next steps are quite unclear but for the 90% likelihood of renting out the Long Isld stylish/Oblomovka place for the summer, Muriel's asthma not at all good there last year + the endless round of cocktail/dinner ++ the rental itself which cannot be discounted especially with the end of my MacArthur, I can't believe the 5 year term of it has passed! So I must get down to another damned book trying to echo Sam'l Butler's —I do not look for them, they come to me wanting to be written ... for which I've got plente-ous notes but no Page 1 Chapter I so for June-September must seek a place for that hope & having heard myself chatter in the antipodes some silent peak in Darien all yet to be resolved, which may even end up right here in Manhat-tan with a terrace & all air conditioning that people kill for hardly that bad after all though glimpses of peace over the bay at Wellington & sheep of Christchurch lead one astray where Butler after all got his first breath, as against the glimpse from our pedestal of how much time is left where I must say your both example of courage & good cheer sets me a mark. (I have just now been drinking whisky & reading again *Howards End* which may account for something?)

love & all the rest,
Willie

---

working at a novel: her novel *Swallow Hard* was published by Atheneum in January 1991.
Oblomovka: the title character's estate in Goncharov's *Oblomov*, one of WG's favorite novels.

silent peak in Darien: the final line of Keats's "On First Looking into Chapman's Homer" finds him, like Cortez, "Silent, upon a peak in Darien."

Butler: in his twenties Butler immigrated from England to New Zealand to set up a successful sheep run.

Howards End: E. M. Forster's 1910 novel.

To Donald Oresman

[*Accompanied by a draft of "Szyrk v. Village of Tatamount et al," published in October in the* New Yorker, *and eventually in* FHO *(30–40).*]

Wainscott NY 11975

6 May 1987

Dear Donald Oresman,

Barbara W. gave me your home address with word that you haven't been as well as might & certainly should be, & I thought you might be diverted by the trouble I've got myself into with the LAW.

All innocently—as anyone confronting the law cries out—drawing upon (not as a co-conspirator such as we read about these days) your generous Case Book and Prosser as well as my 250 lb. *AmJur*, I set out on this troubled sea where the artist's small boat arrogance rows against the tide of sentimental greed with the distracted results attached.

Now in the doctrine of res ipsa loquitur (misused on p. 2) it should be clear that the octogenarian Judge Crease is 1) somewhat senile, 2) enjoys writing opinions for the sheer writing of them, and that 3) in the course of the projected novel—in which this is very much of a subplot—his decision must face, indeed invite reversal on appeal. Well I've shown it to a couple of lawyers and even a county judge & clearly in its present form the judge should not only be reversed but certified. Making matters worse, as matters can only be made, I light heartedly showed (not submitted) it to someone at the *New Yorker* who, with a little 'fixing up' (literary not legal, to make it a 'story') at the end, is enthusiastic for its possible publication. Oh Lord.

Because heaped upon this our month's trip to Australia, and the accumulated trivia that has devoured time since, leaves me now trying to get back to it thoroughly muddled over the generous critical suggestions by these lawyers & judge: not a temporary injunction but restraining order; "the standard for preliminary relief must first be addressed"; the infant James B cannot be sued but must have a guardian (ad litem?); get copy of Harvard *Blue Book* for rules of case citations etc; the disorder of dismissal of charges related to the case itself and the order of procedure from the original complaint, the hearing (is this judgment the result of a hearing?) to trial, appeal & God knows what, (speaking of co-conspirators).

Do you know that John Irving for his novel *Ciderhouse Rules* involving abortion actually took a course at Yale on obstretics? A sobering thought in this context but for the moment I send this along to you for as I say some kind of diversion, disruption of equally absurd oppressions,

with warm regards,
W. Gaddis

AmJur: the set of *American Jurisprudence* Oresman had sent him.

res ipse loquitur: legal Latin (should be *ipsa*), "the thing speaks for itself."

ad litem: a person appointed by the court to act "for the lawsuit" (*ad litem*) on behalf of another.

Harvard *Blue Book*: *The Bluebook: A Uniform System of Citation*, compiled by the Harvard Law Review Association et al. WG owned the 14th edition (1987).

To Candida Donadio

Wainscott NY 11975
19 July 1987

Dear Candida.

Here is the card that of course never quite got mailed at its source, the stunning island where some farmer dug up the Venus de Milo (the Milos Aphrodite they call it); but then all the islands were stunning, Naxos, Thera, Kea, must have been 8 or ten Cyclades we called on, if ever I went 1st class all the way it was this trip, the only curse my short breath climbing ruins & the shipboard cough, got to do something about it as I've been saying for 10 years.

It was another 2 weeks away from the typewriter but worth anything even though I haven't a place for it in 'the work' (but may of course always squeeze one in); & so now, in this clean simple tree-surrounded air-conditioned-if-I-want-it studio there remains *no* excuse but laziness for my not finally really getting down to work.

Of course the Sifton/Knopf number adds *spice* doesn't it! added to Mehta's enthusiasm for the last book at Picador to say nothing of Sarah's loyal diligent efforts, if only she & I had the current high taste for vulgarity just picture the DAD & DAUGHTER photo feature in *People* magazine . . . But it does, touch wood, look like everything is falling into place after those God knows how many years of tormented uncertainty every step of which you were painfully aware & never gave up.

Maschler! Well splendid, good news, *always remembering* his handling of the *J R* cash & contract to which Sarah herself was of course privy at the time as I pounded the deck at FIRE ISLD shouting for money to pay the grocery bill as the pound sterling fell, and fell … so however good his offer if accepted we must keep him on a short leash. Marvelous. (And Deutsch? Picador?)

As I get my work in hand here this next month or so I will let you know & we can plan 'strategy'—I'm probably worth more to Elisabeth at Knopf than I would have been at Viking? &c&c&c … (& just to crown everything, Gottlieb OUT).

Love from the catbird seat,
Willie

---

a place for it […] squeeze one in: WG squeezed in a reference to the Melos Aphrodite (as it's more properly spelled) on p. 34 of *FHO*.

Sifton/Knopf number […] Mehta: in 1987 publisher Sonny Mehta lured Sifton away from Viking to join him as executive vice president of Knopf. "A self-described perfectionist," writes Thomas Meier, "Sifton alienated some of her colleagues almost from the start by sending a memo at Mehta's suggestion to then chairman [Robert] Bernstein about the inefficient ways that manuscripts passed through Knopf" (*Newhouse: All the Glitter, Power, and Glory of America's Richest Media Empire and the Secretive Man Behind It* [St. Martin's Press, 1994], p. 219). The British paperback edition of *CG* was published by Picador, which Mehta headed before he went to Knopf.

Maschler: see note to 29 May 1976.

Gottlieb: in 1987 he left Knopf to edit the *New Yorker*.

To Arthur Kerr Brown

[*A student of Elaine Safer, Dr. Brown had written to Gaddis while working on his dissertation "The Past as Prologue: A Study of the Allusive Techniques of John Barth and William Gaddis" (Univ. of Delaware, 1989).*]

Wainscott NY 11975
19 July 1987

Dear A. K. Brown.

Thanks for your letter & continuing interest in my work. I don't know how practicable your notion of getting together to discuss my work may prove to be, after some recent travel I am pretty much settled out here on the tail end of Long Isld making every effort to get down to cases on another book with the usual distractions which I'm trying to keep to a minimum & a long trip from New York (let alone North Chatham) & quite honestly cannot afford the time to get into a correspondence about past work as I trust you will understand. The 'sources' of *Carpenter's* Gothic* seem to me quite evident in the book itself as opposed to other aspects of it (such as the gap between 'the truth and what really happens') which, again, I don't want to elucidate except—as a good example—the query in your PS: the *Boston Globe* is just about as good at getting it right as it was reviewing *The Recognitions* 30 years earlier. An entire theme of *Carpenter's Gothic* embraces getting it wrong, as Paul exemplifies, & in the end Liz is the only person who does get it right & in a world where getting it wrong prevails ('contras' = 'freedom fighters') she must be eliminated. Of course reading her as a murder victim is nonsense & the most obvious instance of getting it wrong, by the police the papers & your *Globe* reviewer: your interpretation clearly gets it right as numerous evidences plainly there in the text attest.

Let me know if you've similar specific queries & I will try to respond in brief, always bearing in mind I feel strongly that eventually the interpretation is the reader's, that one cannot/should not try to run after a book saying 'What I really meant was . . .' &c though the *Globe* interpretation you refer to above was simply too egregious (&, in its way, a *part* of the book itself) to let pass.

Yours,
William Gaddis

*Note the title's apostrophe, not Carpenters as you have it.

Boston Globe : Mark Feeney found it "apocalyptic, topical, heavy-handed, a kind of jeremiad." *R* was unfavorably reviewed in the *Globe* by Edward A. Laycock on 13 March 1955, p. 72.
'contras' = 'freedom fighters': then-President Regan used "freedom fighters" to describe the U.S.-funded right-wing rebel groups attempting to overthrow the Marxist government in Nicaragua. Others at the time more accurately described the Contras as brutal thugs.

To Sarah Gaddis

[Wainscott, NY]
21 July 87

Dear Sarah.

Enfin! The first day in, how long . . . since February I think, of total peace, silence, solitude [...] & here I sit in my air conditioned studio with no obligations in sight but the blank page in the typewriter, a feeling you may now empathise with! And of course all of the recent obligations have been of the best: go to Australia; your visit; isles of Greece . . . perhaps something in my bleak Calvinist soul saying Stop these pleasures! down to work!

And again, how abruptly the future becomes the past, how the present devours it, how it all speeds up as one grows older: how Australia loomed, how your visit excited, how the Aegean and those Greek islands are now themselves an island in a sea of memory; & how, on that very sea I was already writing you in my head how quickly come and gone your visit here, & did we make the most of it sitting silent, reading in this glass living room, 'living every, every minute' as your old favourite *Our Town* had it, & I think we must have. I suppose it is all haunted for me, and so for you & for Matthew, by those fleeting visits & abrupt separations after school Tuesday and Thursday at the old house at Croton (little pies from Ritchie's & homework), the Budin camp, the trip back from Saltaire, the Sunday pm drive from Piermont to that grey Greyhound station in New Haven, in which of course I invested all of my own childhood: the train at Grand Central to Berlin Connecticut age 7 & the desolation of every town along the way as the lights went on: your mother once said in one of her fits of pique & I suppose for good reason —I will not have you living these children's lives for them! But apparently that's what we do & perhaps not too bad a thing after all if it does lead to some kind of understanding of our own childhoods & the pain & love of those around us then in their efforts to save us, or better to try to equip us to save ourselves, rehearsing all those cheerful embraces at train stations, bus stations, airports, and the desolation that followed, & the loneliness constantly racked by —Did I do the right thing? As I look back on that winter you put in alone at Pennington & think now How could I have permitted it! And so somehow it all becomes an examination of our childhoods & strangely enough the more so as one grows older—I've talked with Saul about it & in fact at this moment Sigrid is in Germany seeking clues to hers—underlying my 4th novel as it does your first: do we want to write novels & simply use this material? or is the attempt to sort all this out what drives us to write them.

Well, speaking of that here's an item. (CONFIDENTIAL FOR NOW) Louis Auchincloss wants to write a piece on my work (& me) for the *NY Times Magazine*. I know that MHG will howl & you may too! Everything I've always avoided, shied from, a few 'personal details' &c. HOWEVER. 1) He is a class act, not a celebrity junk journalist a la *Vanity unFair*, real probity, novelist & lawyer, steeped in the world of class, money, Edith Wharton's world, WASP forthright generous aristocrat & I say all this *not* for its social cachet but for his crisp approach 'nothing in it for him', not using me to build his reputation nor his to build mine & not the 'celebrity' trip. It springs from his strong feeling that *J R* is one of the great novels in its preoccupation with $/USA & his wish (demand!) that it reach a wider audience, rescue it from the academic critics & deliver it to the Middle Class which the *NYT Magazine* reaches. By the 100 thousands. 2) In the next few months you know I will be offering this next novel (sketch & outline) for a new contract somewhere

& a piece such as his could raise the stakes a good deal on the advance, deliver me from being an 'intellectual', 'writers' writer', PhD material &c, to the wider audience they seek. (Also one cannot discount the possibility of the illiterate movie people seeing its promise for their $$$ ends.) + his assurance of nothing in the piece I do not want there, which is also to say that you (or MHG) do not want there, so we have time to sort out anything from "He has a daughter who has been living and studying in Paris in recent years" to "While Mr Gaddis takes evident satisfaction in his work, his real pride is reserved for his children. His lovely daughter Sarah, residing in Paris, is completing a much talked about novel already signed with Alfred Knopf, which ..." (Exactly the stuff Louis would never write but) whatever will make sense to you, point being whatever emerges that your (& MHG's) accomplishments are your *own* which is true. Anyhow I do honestly think that the time of being the reclusive unapproachable writer is not only over but to press it on could very well appear as a coy play for attention, NOT that you'll see me (us) playing tag in *People* magazine. Certainly I was reclusive for years & for damned good reason but this seems a time simply to be forthright & here the point which is essential is that Louis is concerned with the *work* itself, not with cute. It's a matter of a few months & I'll keep you informed.

And now this (imagine our correspondence gradually becoming writerly exchanges about publishing?): NEWS: Elisabeth Sifton has just left Viking. For KNOPF. And of course I'm a writer she'd like very much to take with her. You're there. Mehta was strong for *Carpenter's Gothic*. Gottlieb's OUT. All pretty wild. I don't expect to make any move for 3 or 4 months & will discuss every step with you beforehand but good Lord at last we may be coming out on top! & again, most primarily & to be preserved for the truth it is as individuals, you for your own efforts & talents, MHG for his, me for mine, & everything I can do to shun the danger you may both see as prospering 'in my shadow', ie the kind of crap that the cheap press loves.

To other matters, will you be able to get away from Paris this summer? If not for a long stretch at least for long weekends (taking your work with you), I hope so. I can remember Paris in August as sweltering heat; but of course you have the Bois so it's not like being locked up in the rue Dauphine where I was.

Out now to lay in a few groceries for the promised appearance of Julia [Murphy] driving out with MHG today or tomorrow wishing of course that you were here now that things have settled down. But our real settling down is I guess settling down to work again, mine the problem of getting started and yours of finishing which is what I would urge upon you, finishing one complete draft even if there are a few rough spots since you can always go back

& put things in/take things out but there is a great sense of satisfaction getting that first draft done. However we all work at our own rates & I know there's no telling someone else what & how to do it, as I know you will.

much love
Papa

---

desolation of every town along the way: see headnote to 24 October 1933.

Pennington: Sarah lived in Pennington, NJ, while attending school.

Saul [...] Sigrid: Saul Steinberg (see headnote to 21 January 1990) and his partner, photographer Sigrid Spaeth.

Louis Auchincloss: American novelist, lawyer, and historian (1917–2010). "Recognizing Gaddis" appeared in the *New York Times Magazine* on 15 November 1987, and was reprinted (with new material) as "William Gaddis" in his *The Style's the Man: Reflections on Proust, Fitzgerald, Wharton, Vidal, and Others* (Scribner's, 1994), 11–25.

To Donald Oresman

[*On the same day that he wrote this update on "Szyrk v. Village of Tatamount et al," WG sent a similar, shorter letter to his friend Judge Pierre Leval, for whom see headnote to 10 August 1993.*]

Wainscott, New York 11975
6 August 1987

Dear Donald.

Since your kind letter in May I have finally got back to this item with a good deal of juggling around, and even wonder if some of it, in the interests of 'technical correctness' has made it a little the less 'vivid' (as you warn). Nonetheless there were some major points to be addressed such as 'temporary restraining order' and 'preliminary injunction' and 'summary judgment' which I think I've now got straight. By happy chance for the last of them (summary judgment) Saul Steinberg passed along to me a copy of his just obtained against Columbia Pictures promoters distributors & advertisers for copyright infringement using his well known *New Yorker*'s myopic view of America poster in promoting a movie called *Moscow on the Hudson* (Opinion by U.S.D.J. Louis L. Stanton) so lucidly written that I lifted those portions bodily.

Still I'm sure there are still enough errors for a reversal on appeal (as intended), particularly the citations (do they correspond to Virginia law? &c, a couple of lawyers suggested I get the Harvard *Blue Book* but I've refrained), but I did find a paperback (Scribner's) *Law Dictionary*. And there's still enough evidence of an aging judge who immensely enjoys the sound of his own writing, parody run-on sentences &c though whether he 'takes judicial notice' too often (& incorrectly) I'm not sure.

And why didn't plaintiff's lawyers claim *Cyclone 7* as a protected statement under the 1st Amendment? Well that will be the issue when it all gets to the Supreme Court (where this aged judge will just have been seated & a la Renquist refuses to recuse himself) later in the novel if we ever get there. (At that point Mr Szyrk *wants* the thing removed since he's sold it to Holland for a Holocaust memorial, & the Village demands to keep it since it has become a big tourist attraction.) And so now I am simply trying to get down to the real novel itself for which this is simply an appendix though constantly tempted elsewhere, such as an action for defamation and infringement by the Episcopal church v. Pepsi-Cola claiming the latter is an anagram of Episcopal &c&c&c...

I hope you are well, meanwhile this may provide diversion and of course any blue penciling would be a welcome, as you suggest & if so inclined.

warmest regards,
Bill Gaddis

Cyclone 7: a steel structure by an artist named Szyrk at the center of these legal battles in *FHO*, carried over from *J R* (671–72).
Renquist: William *Rehnquist* (1924–2005), seated on the Supreme Court in 1986. Judge Crease doesn't make it that far in the novel.
Episcopal church v. Pepsi-Cola: unfortunately, WG didn't finish this subplot for *FHO*.

To Steven Moore

[I had sent WG a draft of what would eventually be published as chapter 1 of my William Gaddis *(Twayne, 1989), asking him to vet it for any factual errors regarding his biography and requesting permission to quote from his writings and letters.]*

[Wainscott, NY 11975]
12 August 87

Dear Steven Moore.

To yours of 17 July: yes, permission to quote the passages you note (though I think footnote 20 should be ascribed simply to Thos Mirkowicz, Miss Logan simply sat in, 'observed', later wanted to publish the whole thing in the US as I'd expressly ruled out.)

Other items from a quick scanning:

bottom of p3, I'd already entered Harvard when war broke out, simply stayed there.

WG (with Muriel Murphy behind him) and Steven Moore at the publication party
for Joseph McElroy's *Women and Men*, New York City, May 1987
(photo © Miriam Berkley).

last line some 2 years for little over a year

p4 line 3, I still feel this pressure of trying… for I still have this trying
below: What lines from *Junkie*?

p5 bottom, some raw material for the raw materials (really very little)

p10 I should have said Elizabethan drama

p14 your interesting emphasis on Firbank; Henry Green yes but *not* CP-
Snow, the most wooden fiction I've ever encountered

p16 Hawthorne, better assumptions: *the Blithedale* (sp?) *Romance* and a
story I believe called the Artist of the Beautiful. And quite a good deal more
of Twain, *Christian Science* comes to mind, many short (journalistic) pieces
as on King Leopold's Congo, late story about a man unsure whether he's on
a ship dreaming of home or vice versa. Certainly *Tom Sawyer*.

p.18 why limit Shakespear to those 2 (& 'perhaps' even *Lear*!)? Most of
Shakespear certainly, favourite is still *As You Like It*.

p22 I don't recall the 'none of us grew &c' as J R's company, simply saw it
pass on a truck one day

I don't know regarding quotes from the books, you might ask Viking's
Permissions dept (remind them I own rights to first 2 & give my permission).
But I should think the 'fair use' rule must still apply provided the quotes aren't
too long, ie tending toward the body of the piece, & are for fair critical purposes.

Finally no to taking time for a short critical piece & for now don't especially want the PEN reprinted.

Also have got to tell you that when in Budapest last year an interview with an American Literature scholar named Zoltan Abady-Nagy which turned out well & has filled the hole for the nagging *Paris Review*, next spring perhaps? Not critical as your work but informed & got the thing out of the way.

Yours,

WG

---

2 years for little over a year: his time at the *New Yorker*. The magazine's personnel department had informed me that WG worked there from 26 February 1945 until 29 April 1946.

Junkie: in *R*, a character identified only as the "attractive girl with the Boston voice" recommends Benzedrine in the exact same words as the character Mary in William Burroughs's novel *Junkie* (1953). Cf. *R* 631 and 640 with the Penguin edition of *Junky* (1977), p. 14.

raw material: I had written that WG's jobs in industry in the late 1950s and 1960s provided the raw materials for *J R*.

Elizabethan drama: he had said "Jacobean" drama in his interview with Miriam Berkley, from which I was quoting.

CPSnow: I was listing British writers whom WG had *read*, not necessarily those who influenced him.

better assumptions: I had speculated on what Hawthorne WG may have read (*The Scarlet Letter* and *The Marble Faun* have been cited by other critics). The rest of this paragraph refers to my listing of other American writers WG had read.

Shakespear: as a result of his "quick scanning," WG misread this paragraph: I was not listing all the Shakespeare plays he had read, but arguing that his work belonged to the same tradition of vitriolic satire that included (among Shakespeare's works) *Troilus and Cressida, Timon of Athens*, and perhaps *King Lear*.

short critical piece: I was guest-editing a special issue of the *Review of Contemporary Fiction* entitled "Novelist as Critic" and invited WG to contribute an essay, or—if he couldn't take the time to write something new—to allow me to publish his 1986 PEN address "How Does the State Imagine?" (*RSP* 123–26).

To Sarah Gaddis

22 August 1987

Dear Sarah.

Much the same here, day after day in the trees it's like being in Michigan, as you recall, utterly *un*Hamptons, how I wish I could just pick up this nifty little studio up with me teeth and set it up at Wainscott. [...]

[H]ow do you like the musical chairs going on on the publishing scene: there's Ivan Nabokov abruptly off to some new (German owned?) publishing conglomerate & my new boss at AlbinMichel a young lady who turns out to be the daughter of Jim Salter. (*In margin*: about your age, her name is Nina, you may already have heard from her?) And you? for you and Candida to sort out. Meanwhile here's Elis. Sifton at Knopf, will I follow her there? This time I'm not kidding, with the time I've got left there's none for sentimental 'loyalties' as the old days in publishing, for them it's been Hollywoodized = it's all $$$$$, so likewise me & in a very fortunate spot when I decide to seek a contract, 'in demand' good Lord, you can remember the bad days & there were so damned many of them. Touch wood.

& Speaking of that slippery world, the latest on Spot-trapped-in-the-steel-sculpture-Cyclone 7: I rewrote it with some comments from a couple of lawyers, showed it again to Linda A. very pleased, could she show it to "Bob" [Gottlieb]? So she did. So he wants it. So I told her I hate the idea of contributing in any way to his success at getting 'the magazine' to a fresh start but then thought, well look: I had to pay that bastard $10 thousand for the rights back to *J R* so I'll begin to recoup it this way, only condition that I deal with her only and have nothing to do with him at all. So far so 'good'. (I just hate to think that he thinks he's scored but will go on spreading unkind words about him wherever possible.) The book itself goes very well now in extensive outline & getting very complicated of course. [...]

Much love always,

Papa

Ivan Nabokov: Ivan Nabokov (1932–), younger cousin of the novelist, became Editorial Director at Editions Christian Bourgois. He had previously been Editorial Director for Foreign Literature at Editions Albin Michel, and subsequently held the same position at Editions Plon, where, under his Feux Croisés imprint, he also published French translations of *J R* and *AA*.

Jim Salter [...] Nina: James Salter (1925–2015), American novelist best known for *A Sport and a Pastime*; after Albin Michel, Nina Salter (1957–) was an editor for Calmann-Levy and Éditions des Deux Terres.

Linda A: Asher, fiction editor at the *New Yorker* at the time, and a noted translator from the French. She was married to WG's old editor Aaron Asher.

To Louis Auchincloss

[*For his* New York Times Magazine *piece, WG sent him* In Recognition of William Gaddis, *Aldridge's* American Novel and the Way We Live Now *(which reprints his* J R *review), other reviews, a corporate speech, and* "Szyrk v. Village of Tatamount et al."]

Wainscott, New York 11975
23 August 1987

Dear Louis.

If you haven't tossed out the whole noble notion of rehabilitating *J R* for the 'general public', I risk discouraging you further with this self serving bundle where you may find something useful.

Item: book of essays, the first 19pp with more biographical material than I'd have wished, essays 8, 11, 12, 13 may be the most pertinent.

Item: book by critic John Aldridge, pp 46–52.

Item: batch of reviews, from the scathing reception of *The Recognitions* through the kinder welcome given the next 2 books (though see 'George Steiner' in the *New Yorker*).

Item: the only corp. speechwriting I've come up with for Eastman Kodak reproduced in this brochure (& they always paid within '5 business days').

Item: simply for your own passing entertainment, as I would hope, a crude tribute to your other profession in the form of a judicial Opinion, one of many projected for my present novel in the works; also for the fact that the part justifying summary judgment (pp 3,4) is lifted bodily (I understand these Opinions are 'public property'? though perhaps it should have a citation?) from the case of artist Saul Steinberg v. Columbia Pictures et al. for pirating his *New Yorker*'s well known myopic view of the USA in advertising a dumb movie, found for plaintiff by U.S.D.J. Louis L. Stanton & I now learn to be your cousin! (The *New Yorker* interested in taking it.)

Back to *J R* which incidentally came out 2 or 3 years before the desecration of television's *Dallas* in J.R. Ewing's vicious greed, as contrasted to (with?) the *original* J R's cheerful innocent hunger. He may incidentally reappear on the scene in a fall *NY Times Book Review* business book issue, these years later now age 23 working for the Department of the Budget explaining this Administration's policy to a Congressional Hearing committee.*

Have you still an appetite for this most generous proposal? and especially in the light of a hoped for minimum of 'human interest' (ie about '*me*') as opposed to the books themselves—though I suppose there's something to be said for my teaching a course at Bard College in the late 70s on The Theme of Failure in American Literature . . .

warm wishes to Adele from us both,
W G

* his was after all the original 'Reaganomics'.

Eastman Kodak [...] brochure: probably "Educational Technology Shapes the Future ... Are You Ready?," depicted on pp. 30–31 of *RSP*.

Dallas: popular TV series that ran from 1978 to 1991.

fall *NYTimes Book Review*: "Trickle-Up Economics: J R Goes to Washington" appeared on p. 29 of the 25 October 1987 issue; reprinted in uncut form under its original title "J R Up to Date" in *RSP* (63–71).

Adele: Auchincloss's wife.

To Sarah Gaddis

Wainscott
17 Sept. 87

Dear Sarah.

What a great treat to hear your report of Deauville, not only for the high life part of it but essentially what sounded in all you said like a further grasp at what we've called taking over your own life & the self esteem that must be a part of that: & so, so fitting that it should crown a birthday! one of the best you've had. Which brings in the negative note you've brought in a few times talking about the 'jealousies' & lacks of generous attitudes toward your well-earned good fortune you've felt among some people around you. Well, there's nothing to be done about it, just that feeling of disappointment that's hard to shake off. For the most extreme example in my own life of course I cite Martin [Dworkin]; our last contact was many months ago & I finally just decided damn it all, he has always looked at the underside of any (well-earned!) good fortune of mine, never had a good word for either *J R* or the last one (& only for the first one because of what he considers his own monumental 'contributions' to it), I don't even know that he's read them; point is there's nothing to be done or gained so why go on with it? These things do eat away at one if we let them so the best we can do is to try to have learned something, to rescue that & cross the rest out.

Now: regarding the assortment enclosed, [...] Next a piece of rabid nonsense from *Esquire* picturing the world you are entering as a starry universe (I get in there under Leo, the Hamptons & Ursae Majoris) (but alas not Comets), the whole thing designed to inflame exactly what we talk about above (envy, jealousy &c).

& finally the *Szyrk* Opinion (not in final form, a good many alterations needless to say made on the phone yesterday with Linda A who has been terribly concerned about the dog's fate so I've supplied a sort of life support system for it—little does she know that later in the book lightning will strike *Cyclone 7* & all America will greet Spot's demise 'with an outpouring of grief' ...). I hope it amuses you.

Anything else is a footnote to our talk on the phone. The Schnabel business is all pretty wild & wait till you see the thing! I'm already anticipating unkind remarks from colleagues, if it appears somewhere, re someone (me) who has always kept privacy (avoided Elaine's) suddenly going public —to say nothing of Louis A's piece if they use it . . . (Again imagine Martin seeing the Schnabel! that I had surely finally sold out!) But simply enough, with negotiating for another contract on the next book coming up, why not?

Certainly you can relax about all that for a while, you'll have plenty of time

Julian Schnabel, *Portrait of William Gaddis* (1987).
Oil, plates, bondo on wood, 60" x 48". Courtesy of the artist.

& I'm sure many changes of mind between now & your publication date. I haven't talked with Candida (ie 'interfered') but hope you have some progress ($) on the English deal. I have just got a copy of *Carpenter's Gothic* in Swedish (titled *Träslott*, whatever that means) so sent one along to Torsten. I mean who else can read it?

see you very soon, with much love
Papa

Deauville: prestigious seaside resort town in northwestern France.

Esquire: a chart in the August issue (pp. 55–56) depicting the "Literary Power Game," viewable here: https://classic.esquire.com/article/1987/8/1/the-universe-today.

Schnabel [...] wait till you see the thing: *William Gaddis* (1987), an oil portrait with broken crockery by American artist Julian Schnabel (1951–); see Hallowe'en 1991 for more on the painting, and see WG's brief tribute to Schnabel in *RSP* (137–39).

Elaine's: famous Upper East Side restaurant where literary (and other) celebrities hung out.

Träslott: "wooden castle," a house style that resembles carpenter gothic. Translated by Caj Lundgren, *Träslott* was published by Legenda (Stockholm).

Torsten: Torsten Wiesel (1924–), Swedish-born co-recipient of the Nobel Prize in physiology in 1981. He taught at Rockefeller University in the 1980s and later married Jean Stein.

To Gregory Comnes

[*A professor of literature and philosophy (1948–) at Hillsborough Community College in Tampa, Florida, who had sent WG the J R chapter of his doctoral thesis, eventually published in revised form as* The Ethics of Indeterminacy in the Novels of William Gaddis *(University Press of Florida, 1994).*]

Wainscott, New York 11975
29 September 1987

Dear Gregory Comnes.

I have just read your paper (Fragments of Redemption) again and find it quite extraordinary, certainly far more informed than all but perhaps 2 or three of the numerous dissertations &c I've seen. And whether the book deserves it or not I must finally admit that it does demand a careful reading (recalling a review by 'the late' John Gardner who read the passage on the unfinished work as invalid as evidence of "In all fairness (sic) Gaddis was apparently uneasy about bringing out *J R*.", among many other misreadings.) Unfortunately but of course, many more will have read his words than yours.

This is to say nothing of all you bring to it, some I must confess as surprise

(& delight) to me. No, though the name is vaguely familiar, I do not recall to have ever read Walter Benjamin, for the most glaring such instance; & probably the better so, I should have got myself even more entangled but how profoundly intriguing these parallels are, if only they might illuminate those who seek and demand 'influences'—I am constantly regaled with my influence on Pynchon & vice versa—unable, apparently, to accept the notion of 2 writers preoccupied with similar ideas quite independently. Just as, in the case of *Agapē Agape*, I recently came across what it might have become in the hands of Hugh Kenner's *The Counterfeiters* and felt, well damn! that settles it, mine will never be done; though something still remains that drives me to tear out & save anything I come across on mechanization & the arts to add to the 30 year hoard. All of it relating, in that never to be finished work* & in fact to the finished work *J R* itself, to the epitaph** (p 724) when the ceiling has fallen in on the painting, —look! if you could have seen what I saw there! You seem to have done so, and a good deal more at that.***

*Notwithstanding, I shall certainly look out for Benjamin's essays you mention (Art in the Age of Mechanical Reproduction, The Destructive Character) adding a bit to the pain of work undone though, looking back, better for me to have worked it into a fiction than my (& Gibbs') original intention.

**cf *The Recognitions*' epitaph in its last 2 lines.

***for a fleeting instance, the further explication of the prolonged E-flat opening *Das Rheingold* and its extension to Mozart & Freemasonry.

(Though, to pick, Isadore Duncan (your p28) was to play on *Isadora* as a confused/confusing echo in the inarticulate reader's mind, an insolent solacement in effect.

thank you again and warm regards,
William Gaddis

Walter Benjamin: German philosopher-critic (1892–1940). WG eventually read Benjamin and cites him in *AA*.

Agapē Agape: the nonfiction book WG had worked on, not the novella published posthumously.

The Counterfeiters: subtitled *An Historical Comedy* (Indiana University Press, 1968), a wide-ranging study of mechanization and the arts.

Duncan [...] *Isadora*: American dancer (1878–1927).

To Klaus Modick

[*German writer and translator (1951–). With Martin Hielscher (1957–) he translated CG as* Die Erlöser *("The Redeemers," Rowohlt, 1988) and with Marcus Ingendaay trans-*]

lated J R *(Zweitausendeins, 1996), as well as a German edition of my* Reader's Guide
(Zweitausendeins, 1998).]

Wainscott NY 11975
7 October 1987

Dear Klaus Modick.

Thank you for your letter of 29 September just received. By happy chance
I had just spent the morning with your colleague in translating *Carpenter's
Gothic*, Martin Hielscher, here visiting the US. We discussed the problems
of translation at length and I believe cleared up any remaining small points.
A title, for example, must be in your & Rowolt's hands as knowing what
sounds provocative in German, though I think *A Locked Room* sounds like
our Nancy Drew girl detective and *Patchwork* conveys little or nothing. *Das
Holzschloss* does at least sound substantial.

I appreciate the pains you have gone to to produce a faithful & careful
translation, but the vagaries of the publishing world will always elude me. As
I mentioned, the Swedish took exactly 1 year from contract to finished book,
though I cannot judge the quality of the translation of course; on the other
hand, I have just received the Spanish edition of *The Recognitions* (*Los Reconocimientos*), and read Spanish well enough (as well as being familiar with the
text of course) to see that they have done a very creditable job of it. Thus why
Rowolt cannot publish *Carpenter's Gothic* before spring and possibly not
until fall a year hence is to me one of publishing's mysteries. In fact perhaps
that is why sometimes smaller publishing firms are preferable to the elaborate
complications and schedules of large firms like Rowolt.

Incidentally, it would surprise me if Rowolt has the rights to either of my
books, as you mention. I recall many years ago perhaps around 1962, they paid
a small sum for an option on *The Recognitions*, subsequently 2 translators gave
up on it & I was told they now had a 3rd who had 'translated *Moby Dick* into
German' so were quite certain it would work out, & I never heard from them
again. Of course that option has long since expired; and I do not recall them
making any offer on *J R*. However I will ask my agent here to check on that
& Rowolt might also want to check their files.

Martin Hielscher was also kind enough to give me the copies of the magazine *Das Schreibheft* you speak of containing translations from *The Recognitions*. Of course this is pleasing and flattering & might even help to gain an
audience for the book itself, though I don't recall them having any permission
or making any payment as is the custom here.

My plans for Berlin are unclear until I have them from the people there,
an Alice Franck and Renate Selmer who are with the 750th BERLIN Program,

I believe it runs 5–14 November. I may make a stop for a reading at Bonn but plan then to go straight to Paris for a few days and then home. So I may never meet you until your visit to the US whenever that occurs.

with best regards
William Gaddis

Das Holzschloss: like the Swedish *Träslott*, literally "wooden castle."

Spanish edition of *The Recognitions*: translated by Juan Antonio Santos, published by Alfaguara (Madrid).

Das Schreibheft: the final six pages of *R* were published in number 29 of this German literary journal as "Wiedererkennen," translated by Bernd Klähn.

750th BERLIN program: see 30 January 1987.

To Sarah Gaddis

[Wainscott, NY]
21 December '87

Dear Sarah,

for the number of times I think of you during the day and days I am appalled at how long it has been since I've written, even a note. Not as though I've been consumed at the typewriter snapping out page 104, 206, even 31 … quite the opposite: days spent simply staring at this pile of books, notes, brilliant insights, & finally getting nothing down on paper even a note to you let alone whoever else. It is all simply this phase you have tasted & I blithely say —It'll pass, don't worry… until it happens to me again. That's what is curious, it's always as though it had never happened before.

My timing has come off exactly as planned: preparing the ground with the piece in the *New Yorker*, Louis A's piece in the *NYT* magazine, interview any day now in the *Paris Review* and a 30 or so page draft opening of the novel with a couple of pages 'outline' submitted to Viking to clear their option, they make an offer, we call it too low and now—this very day in fact—Candida is sending it out to other publishers who are breathing hard, Elis. Sifton & Aaron Asher in the lead but others too so that in the next few weeks there will be the contract & a substantial advance & I wake at night—that 3 o'clock in the morning business—with the What do you think you're doing! age 65 starting the whole mad thing over again? with this trash heap of notes & paper? Looking at the whole project with 'fear and loathing'… Or may it be that I need that kind of pressure, the money drifting away & the kindly editor asking How is it coming along? It's like these fellows running for president, all the energy enthusiasm Brilliant Ideas &c go into the campaign & then inevitably one of them's elected sitting there thinking Holy Jeez what have I done! what

WG, Donald Barthelme, and Walter Abish, West Berlin, November 1987.

do I do now? Or thinking: I've done it, haven't I? Got a nicely high reputation for my work, why threaten it with this mess . . . not like the old days either when I had to have that $200. Why not just, Come on old boy, relax, you've done your work, go to parties, get on the lecture circuit, go to conferences, Berlin, Moscow, get your picture in the papers, be seen in *Vanity Fair* with the luminaries . . . but it simply doesn't work that way.

No, this isn't a complaint, all just as I've repeated to you (from Arthur Miller), It comes with the territory. I wish I had those lines of Eliot's about every start is a new beginning, "a raid on the inarticulate with shabby equipment, always deteriorating . . ." And so I can only think that there is something to the whole idea of the necessity for the artist to put himself in peril, & that that is what provides the energy for the work, as opposed say to the steady drone of a James Mitchner (who gave Swarthmore a cool million) but God knows, we shouldn't read the apparent smugness of others for granted, he may have some perilous moments too.

So here we are. A new year fairly packed with perils we have arranged ourselves—and of course Matthew is in here too!—which will call on us for the best we've got; and with all the evidence I have to believe we wouldn't have it any other way. Well, you & he both know of my support in your perils every step of the way, but you may not be so aware of the strength you give to me and how fortunate I count myself for having it, having you both there and for the people you've become.

my love always,
Papa

---

that 3 o'clock in the morning business: WG gave Sarah a copy of *The Crack-Up*, where Fitzgerald writes, "In a real dark night of the soul it is always three o'clock in the morning, day after day."

'fear and loathing': a phrase adapted by Hunter S. Thompson (1937–2005) from Kierkegaard's book *Fear and Trembling* (1843), alluding to the exhortation "Work out your own salvation with fear and trembling" (Philippians 2:12).

Arthur Miller), It comes with the territory: a phrase popularized (if not originated) by Miller in *Death of a Salesman* (1949): "A salesman is [*sic*] got to dream, boy. It comes with the territory."

those lines of Eliot: from "East Coker"; see 27 December 1948 for the complete passage.

To James Cappio

[James Cappio (1953–) was a law clerk at the time to Chief Judge Charles L. Brieant (1923–2008), and later practiced law at Cahill Gordon & Reindel and elsewhere before moving to Canada, where he became a legal editor. He sent WG an opinion he had ghost-

written for Judge Brieant that cites a passage from J R *(201.20–33); see* Carl Marks & Co., Inc v USSR *665 F.Supp 323 (S.D.N.Y. 1987), at 324–25. WG enclosed with the following letter a copy of the* New Yorker *version of "Szyrk v. Village of Tatamount et al." (12 October 1987), adding by hand: "I should note that Judge Crease is about 90 years old—and have begun to suspect that his opinions are written by his law clerk who is (cf. Wagner in Goethe's* Faust*) about as diligent & ill-informed as I am."*]

235 East 73 Street
New York, New York 10021
10 January 1988

Dear Jim Cappio.

What a marvelous birthday gift! Enshrined in an Opinion (& clearly a significant & important one at that) by Brieant CJ—why, it's infinitely more gratifying than, say, a PEN/Faulkner Award (where I was a runner-up), something about having a place in the World as opposed to self-congratulatory literarydom.

You will see from the attached (I gather you hadn't come across it) that my remarks are not at all fatuous: at this late date I have got myself hopelessly enthralled by the law, having read Cardozo's classic Palsgraf v. Long Island R. Co. a year or 2 ago & been seduced by a world wherein "reality may not exist at all except in the words in which it presents itself" (Ziff L., *Literary Democracy* 294, Dallas 1982) & now hopelessly out of my depth in gifts of Prosser & the 82 vol. *American Jurisprudence* 2d for a novel in the form of a network of lawsuits of every variety, & of which this *Szyrk* Opinion is the first. (I should note that it will be reversed on appeal & am now trying to dig up the grounds, which I'm sure are plentiful.)

And so of course I would enjoy meeting & thanking you & falling deeper into this morass. We have just come in from the country & I'm trying to get myself & my 'work' into some kind of order but if you'll call when it suits you we can work something out. And yes I do know John Holdridge, have not seen him for some time but he's a good pal of my son from whom I have rousing reports, he is quite a fellow & really out there on the barricades. Finally I can even claim to have encountered Judge Motley, years ago as a member of a US Court jury pool where the lawyers for both sides promptly rejected me but I was greatly impressed by her.

If it is seemly to do so, & assuming Judge Brieant is still about & you see him, do tell him of my great pleasure, many many thanks for your efforts & for your letter.

Yours,
W. Gaddis

Literary Democracy: a book by Larzer Ziff, quoted on p. 30 of *FHO*. Regarding Melville's *Confidence-Man*, Ziff writes: "His theme drives toward pure wordplay; reality
may not exist at all except in the words in which it presents itself."

John Holdridge: a lawyer known for his active opposition to capital punishment.

Judge Motley: Constance Baker Motley (1921–2005), African American activist, lawyer, judge, and politician. She hired Cappio as a law clerk.

To Sarah Gaddis

23 Jan. 88
Dear Sarah.

Here is my annual letter. Or so it is beginning to seem, a year between them:
I realize how long it is since you moved, & how few time(s) I've addressed you
at rue tickeytun, to count my letters on the finger of one hand. Of course I
could say "I've been waiting for these infernal pen refills to find their way
from Germany to Parsippany NJ" to here & only hope they fit & work. Tif-
fany must have a store in Paris? If these don't work I would march right in
there & make a scene (like the Board member who quit over them).

Or I could say, "I've been waiting for these *Paris Review* people to send
their new issue with the interview" which is, in part, true. It does just seem
damned chatty doesn't it. I mean I've by now read a number of critical pieces
and dissertations on my work which I find far more filled with insight, wit,
clear thinking and interesting connections than this folderol which almost
seems to trivialize the work; but it scarcely matters. The purpose after all was
simply to do one fairly long interview in a 'serious' place & get it out of the
way so that when people come with this same threat I can simply direct them
to this one without appearing to be some reclusive nut, to say this one pretty
much covers all I've got to say about my work though of course that is not
true either, that's the problem with interviews, those 2nd thoughts (as, p. 59,
What moved you to write *J R*? why didn't I say a large part of energy came
from revenge on that horrid town that Massapequa became, the vandalism
that was really traumatic &c.) But that's the advantage of a fiction, that one
can go back and insert, clarify, rewrite, until it's a whole.

Which is what I'm rather stumblingly doing now: folders with ribbons &
ribbons of paper laying out the step by step of Oscar's car accident insurance,
his copyright lawsuit, Lily's divorce, her malpractice suit, a dozen suits springing from the ill fated outdoor sculpture *Cyclone 7*, & many many more. I am
rather aghast at what I've let myself in for in areas where I am marvelously
ignorant. Most of my contemporaries seem to be fiddling around publishing
reminiscences about what an interesting fellow I was at fifteen, how I Became
a Writer &c. Yawn. All this trepidation obviously over having pretty much

got (though I haven't yet signed) what I wanted in this contract with S&S, everyone saying great, wonderful, me saying my God what have I done!

So I've been trying to face the health area seriously, had a thorough physical examination where obviously the effects of the smoking show (though no scary spot on the lung &c). For this past week I've been trying to prove to all concerned, MHG Muriel you me &c that we aren't dealing with an alcoholic, have had only 1 or 2 drinks daily (+ a glass of wine once or 2ce when guests at dinner), I certainly would enjoy a 3rd or 4th as of yore but do not feel driven to it or the need to go to some 'drying out' place. No, the real problem & battle is the tobacco, one more try this week going to see a hypnotist & if that doesn't work I will take more extreme measures. Though MHG would like to see the more extreme measures right now he at least sees me making serious efforts along these lines for I think the first time, which I think gives him better spirits, planning to have him & some of his rowdy friends (Jeff, Jack &c) in on the 28th.* No words of course for all that your and his love and concern have done and are doing in all this so I'm working on the deeds.

with much love
Papa

*no, now he says one of their 50¢ Indian restaurants

---

rue tickeytun: she lived at 38 rue Tiquetonne.

vandalism: WG's studio next to his mother's Massapequa house was vandalized on 8 November 1960 by some teenagers, an event dramatized in *J R* (137–43).

contract with S&S: Simon & Schuster acquired the novel in 1987 for $275,000 ($670K in today's terms).

Jeff, Jack: Jeff and John Holdridge (mentioned in the previous letter).

To Mary McCarthy

6 February 1988

Dear Mary.

Many thanks for your note and enclosure. As I get older I must say I recall more frequently my mother's Panglossian view that 'everything happens for the best' (she also counseled me to always remember that there is more stupidity than there is malice in the world) —here demonstrated once again. I too found our 'translator' rather painfully self important, & was less surprised than annoyed when he quit on *Carpenter's Gothic* to work in films where he saw more money thereby delaying publication with the search for a new translator. However during that delay Ivan Nabokov fled Albin Michel for, is it Presses de la Cité (more money) where he's taking the book on condition

he also signs up *J R*. I'd liked the girl Nina Salter at A-M- for her straightfor-
wardness (& a stunning lunch at the Closerie des Lilas) but could not deprive
J R the opportunity to speak french.

Meanwhile I am pressing my luck here signing up for another (& I trust
mercifully last) novel, after many gyrations, with Simon & Schuster, now all
that's left to do is to sit down & write it. [...]

best wishes from us both to you and Jim,
Willie

'translator': unidentified; the task was taken over by novelist Marc Cholodenko
  (1950–), who also did *J R* (Paris: Plon, 1993).
Ivan Nabokov [...] Nina Salter: see 22 August 1987.
Jim: diplomat James R. West, McCarthy's second husband.

To Donald Oresman

Wainscott, New York 11975
16 June 1988

Dear Donald,

I haven't thanked you or even acknowledged your earlier mailing, very
aware time was passing but now quite embarrassed to see that it was a good
month ago. Your brief succinct treatise on law & equity clears that up for me
for the moment & appreciated accordingly as is all the Salinger material; &
in fact it is your further good offer regarding complaint & answer in a case
that accounts for my procrastination, thus:

In the central case in the novel, the main character has written an unproduced Civil War play and is suing a movie company; the issues are infringement
and 'fair use'. Since when I work I always need to know where I'm going, I
decided to work out the Appeals Court decision (reversing the District Court)
first, which won't occur until about chapter VI, & then work toward it. This
may not have been too wise: I am now flailing about among Sheldon v. Metro-
Goldwyn Pictures (Learned Hand); Harold Lloyd Corp. v. Universal Pictures
Co; Murray v. National Broadcasting Co.; & my correspondent (a young law
clerk in the office of Constance Baker Motley) has even supplied Bright Tunes
Music Corp. v. Harrisongs Music, Ltd. The Hand material is marvelous &
my case largely based on (lifted from) that. Then to go back to Chapter II &
work toward it, involving the letters & private papers (Salinger) & the briefs
&c where rather than content I will only need form ("As and For a First Cause
of Action" kind of thing) which should not go on at too great lengths if I can
only restrain myself, and for which I guess almost any such brief, complaint
& answer &c will serve as a model. From the foregoing it's apparent how I

double even triple the amount of work for myself but at this point despair of starting out fresh.

Your last mailing, the Serra v. G.S.A. appeal, is a delight with such straight-face lines as the work now "coated with what the artist refers to as 'a golden amber patina' and what the sculpture's critics refer to as 'rust'." And the nice twist on the First Amendment privilege as now belonging to the Government, all most useful plunder when I get back to Szyrk.

We go to Italy in August presumably to work on this at that Rockefeller Foundation compound at Bellagio, meanwhile plodding onward and when I have any fragment that looks half finished I'll send it along for your amusement.

with best regards,
Bill Gaddis

Salinger material: J. D. Salinger had recently sued British author Ian Hamilton for unauthorized use of his letters in a forthcoming biography.

Sheldon v. Metro-Goldwyn [...] Murray v. National Broadcasting Co.: all cited on pp. 406–8 and 412–13 of *FHO*, where WG also quotes from Judge Hand's *Nichols v. Universal Pictures Corporation*.

Bright Tunes Music Corp. v. Harrisongs Music: ex-Beatle George Harrison was sued for unconsciously adapting the melody of "He's So Fine" for his song "My Sweet Lord." WG didn't use this material.

Serra v. G.S.A.: sculptor Richard Serra unsuccessfully sued the General Services Administration to prevent removal of his *Tilted Arc* (1981) from its site in Lower Manhattan.

To Don DeLillo

[*American novelist (1936–) who in 1982 praised Gaddis in a* New York Times *profile "for extending the possibilities of the novel by taking huge risks and making great demands on readers." DeLillo would later attend WG's memorial service and contribute a brief tribute to the portfolio about WG that* Conjunctions *published in 2003.*]

Wainscott, New York 11975
19 July 1988

Dear Don DeLillo.

Why in the world have I waited till the day your *Libra* gets its nihil obstat from Christopher Lemondrop to send you a note. It showed up in galleys in New York 2 or 3 months ago when things were ghastly (health) about the time I saw you, I looked into it then & should certainly have written without waiting to read it through because my response was immediate, it is a terrific job. I don't know all your work & also hesitate to say to any writer whatever comparing one of his works to another but in this case must tell you I find it far far beyond *White Noise*. Obviously if we take our work seriously we do not try to clone one novel to its predecessor so comparisons are indeed odious, & equally obviously the constantly shattered & reknit & fragmented again style of this new book appeals to me rather more than the linear narrative, when it's always 9 o'clock in the morning at 9 am & 3pm at 3 in the afternoon if you see what I mean; but the hard cover arrived here a couple of weeks ago & I've just read it & confirmed all my earlier impression, its marriage of style & content—that essential I used to bray about to 'students' in those grim days—is marvelously illustrated here I think & especially as it comes together at the end as we know it must, speaking of the 'nonfiction' novel if we must but why must we, except that concept does embrace the American writer's historic obsession getting the facts down clear (from "tells me more about whales than I really want to know" to Dreiser tapemeasuring Clyde's cell at Sing Sing, or Jack London's "Give me the fact, man, the irrefragable fact!") & again one marvels at what you've marshaled in this impressive piece of work. We'll be out of the country for August but may hope to see you in town in the fall, meanwhile high marks.

best regards,
WG

Christopher Lemondrop: Christopher Lehmann-Haupt's approving review of De-Lillo's ninth novel appeared in the 18 July 1988 issue of the *New York Times*.

"tells me more about whales [...]": obviously a response to *Moby-Dick* (1851), but source unknown. WG notes Melville's poor critical reception in *FHO* (39) and *AA* (55).

Dreiser tapemeasuring: near the completion of *An American Tragedy* (1925), Dreiser toured Sing Sing prison where Chester Gillette, a factory worker accused of murdering a young woman, and the model for his novel's Clyde Griffiths, was interred.

Jack London's [...] fact!: from *The Iron Heel* (1908). WG quotes the same line in *J R* (571).

To Donald Oresman

[*Accompanied by Judge Bone's opinion, discussed in WG's previous letter to Oresman, and eventually published on pp. 399–416 of* FHO.]

Wainscott, New York 11975
4 August 1988

Dear Donald.

While I enclose this item for your passing entertainment, I believe it is a good deal less amusing than the earlier *Szyrk* Opinion. Satire as in that case assumes a certain distance, whereas here this Opinion is more imitation than parody. That is because not simply does it play an important part in the novel, but because the Civil War 'play' referred to does actually exist (and fragments of it will appear in the book) and as I lifted material from Judge Learned Hand both in quoting and bodily lifting from his Opinions, I found myself filling with righteous indignation as evidence of this piracy mounted and felt at times like I had seen the infringing movie. I am still paranoid enough about it to refrain showing this about too widely for fear that someone will steal the whole thing literally (as a war picture) lock, stock and barrel: as a lawyer in the novel tells its protagonist, —You can't copyright the Civil War, Oscar... [*FHO* 17] At any rate this for the moment is simply a draft and I am back entangled with the novel's text where Oscar is just getting together his Complaint.

I haven't yet approached the book's next legal confrontation, whether it will involve product liability (in Oscar's being run over by his own car), or the reversal of his father Judge Crease's opinion in *Szyrk*, or begin to face the Episcopal Church v. Pepsico(la) for all kinds of infringement (mainly I suppose the Lanham Act) exploiting the (subliminal) possibilities of the trade name's anagram (Pepsicola/Episcopal) getting into quite deep waters, whether as Judge Pierre Laval suggests, the court's consideration of the complaint constitutes in itself a forbidden 'establishment' of a religion, whether a religion can be guilty of laches &c; let alone digging up chores of the corporate origins of Pepsico (I wrote them once for a corporate history but got only some slick Annual Report material in return); let alone writing the whole thing and having Pepsico and the Episcopals sue *me*...

At any rate we are off for the Rockefeller's 54 acre Study Center on Lake Como (Bellagio) to ponder these problems more deeply and hope to return in September with something to report.

with warmest regards,
Bill Gaddis

Lanham Act: 1946 law prohibiting trademark infringement, false advertising, etc.
laches: unreasonable delay in seeking legal claims or damages.

To Gregory Comnes

[*Greg, his wife Judith Chambers (1943–), Joseph Tabbi (see next letter), and I met with Gaddis for a few hours on the afternoon of 6 October 1988 at his Manhattan apartment. The Comneses brought him a T-shirt with the last line of* J R *printed on the front ("Hey? You listening?"). At this time Greg was revising his dissertation and afterward asked some questions about influences, which elicited this postcard, without salutation.*]

5 Nov. 88

To your queries:

I'd never come upon Walter Benjamin till this same query from 2 or 3 directions this past year or so, & at that point looked his work up.

Rilke no comment but I doubt of any greater concern than other liftings.

I have no notion of what GMHopkins 'ideas' are (the danger of 'tracing down' sources, ask Steven M.).

I enjoyed meeting you all & your wife's charming letter, & for the shirt

Yours

W. Gaddis

To Joseph Tabbi

[*Tabbi (1960–), a doctoral student at the University of Toronto, was revising a chapter on J R from his dissertation for publication and wrote asking about WG's background reading in mechanization and communication (aside from Wiener's* Human Use of Human Beings*). He also asked if he could send him the published essay.*]

235 East 73rd str.
New York NY 10021
13 March 1989

Dear Joseph Tabbi.

To your queries of 28 February these unsatisfactory responses:

Regarding Walter Benjamin, I have read nothing but his mechanization & the arts essay which was called to my attention only within the past 2 or 3 years & thus aeons after researches & readings on the subject for the player piano project (& *J R*); but found the parallels most striking.

Unfortunately I cannot go down the shelves of my library since it is almost entirely—or for those years quite entirely—locked away in a house I have rented out. Doubtless many of them would recall themselves to me on sight; they were very far ranging & having largely to do with organization (Hull House, crime, John D Rockefeller &c); Hollerith (sp?), early punched card innovations (from Jacquard(sp?)'s loom & Thos J Watson (pere) selling pianos off a truck; Plato's warnings & exclusion of the artist; Babbage (sp?); v. Neumann(sp?)(which I found largely beyond my comprehension); & I cannot recall his wellknown name doing time/motion studies in the very early 1900s for industrial efficiency: all these flood back but there was far far more *however* all this was done *before* (though spilling a little over into) the composition of *J R* for the never to be completed *Agapē Agape* whose premises—measurement & quantification as indexing thence dictating order & performance (cf. McNamara's Vietnam body counts)—have long since caught up with us. Alas it will never be realized but in massive notes & marked margins in the hands of some beleaguered doctoral candidate, since I am now immersed in an equally mad enterprise.

I cannot say how I became interested in player pianos, it all started about 1947 in hopes of a (rejected) piece for the *New Yorker*'s Onward & Upward with the Arts & gathered winds from there well into the 60s. RIP

I am of course always interested in seeing intelligent commentaries on *J R*.

Yours

William Gaddis

Hull House: WG's library contained Jane Addams's *Twenty Years in Hull House* (Signet, 1961).

Hollerith: Herman Hollerith (1860–1929) is credited with developing the modern tabulating machine in the late nineteenth century.

Jacquard [...] Babbage: Joseph Marie Jacquard (1752–1834) invented a loom in which the hooks lifting the warp threads were controlled by cards perforated to a desired pattern, a technique adapted by later by Charles Babbage (1792–1871) for an early calculating machine.

Thos J Watson: (1874–1956), founder of IBM.

v. Neumann: John von Neumann (1903–57), Hungarian-born American mathematician, noted for his work on the theory, design, and construction of computers.

wellknown name: E. L. Thorndike (see *J R* 581).

McNamara's Vietnam body counts: Robert McNamara (1916–2009), Secretary of Defense under Kennedy and Johnson. See WG's caustic remarks on him in *RSP* 50–52.

To Rodger Cunningham

[*A professor (1948–) of English at Sue Bennett College in Kentucky. On the basis of his dissertation "Cabala to Entropy: Existentialist Attitudes and the Gnostic Vision in William Gaddis's* The Recognitions *and Julio Cortazar's* Rayuela" *(Indiana University, 1980), I had invited him to contribute to* In Recognition of William Gaddis, *but Kuehl found his submission somewhat inaccessible and (his main objection) too awkwardly written to include in our book. It was eventually published, in somewhat revised form, as "When You See Yourself: Gnostic Motifs and Their Transformation in* The Recognitions," *Soundings (71.4 [Winter 1988]: 619–37), which he sent to WG.*]

Wainscott, New York 11975

10 May 1989

Dear Rodger Cunningham.

Just a note to thank you for sending along your Gnostic observations in When You See Yourself. I do think it unfortunate that they didn't see fit to include it in the *In Recognition* &c volume, it is indeed light shed from another direction & doesn't seem that 'inaccessible' (a word that is anathema here) &, as sometimes happens in these cases, I learn things I was unaware of.* The concluding analysis of the end of the book breaking off 'where perfection is still possible' is interesting, in the light of this recollection: I worked then (as now) with fairly detailed outline notes & had literally at hand notes for what would have been perhaps another 20 or 30 pages (not the discarded final chapter) when, sitting back one night to review my progress, read that last sentence ('...though seldom played.') & was stunned, elated, dismayed, by the realization of the fact that this was the end of the book, for all of its strivings &c it ended, that is to say it ended itself, right there. Anything further would have been the (to me inexcusable) author stepping in & elucidating & thus milking, painting the lily (gilding the gold), killing with kindness, destroying the whole thing & *its* intent & integrity (that pompous & essentially dishonest wretch "John Gard(i?)ner"'s whine regarding nihilism notwithstanding, cf. his ridiculous reading of *J R* (*NY Rev. of Books*), the plagiarist for 'moral fiction' indeed). *The Hymn of the Pearl bird/letter parallel is especially remarkable. I very much liked & have enshrined your closing quote (Aunque sepa los caminos...),

Yours,

W. Gaddis

The Hymn of the Pearl: an early Gnostic fable incorporated into the apocryphal Acts of Thomas.

closing quote: the epigraph page in the bound galleys of *FHO* read "Aunque sepa los caminos / yo nunca llegaré a Cordoba" (Although I may know the roads / I will never arrive at Cordoba—quoted by Cunningham from R. D. Laing's *Facts of Life*, originally from Federico García Lorca's poem "Canción del jinete"), but the published book has a remark by Henry David Thoreau instead (first used in *R*).

To Steven Moore

[*My* William Gaddis *was published by Twayne in May 1989, at which time I sent WG a copy. I also told him I had left New Jersey for Illinois to work for Dalkey Archive Press/* Review of Contemporary Fiction.]

Wainscott, New York 11975

14 June 1989

Dear Steven Moore.

    Many thanks for sending me your book. On a brief examination it looks like it should put an end to such industry for a good while & the exhaustive range of references is quite impressive (though I confess I've made a number of starts at the classic seminal Melville's *Confidence Man* & not progressed & must give it another try).

A bright moment addition to your charting of trivia last week when I was given a Governor's Arts Award, aegis of NYS Council &c with a fancy turn-out at the Metropolitan Mus. & fancy company (Miles Davis, Baryshnikov (sp?)) & I must say I was quite impressed by Mr Cuomo, quick, humour, energy, informed (but will it sell books?).

Did I congratulate you on your new publishing arrangement & (I think) sensible flight from East Coast vendettas (though I doubt I could survive the trip), & wish you good luck with it.

all best regards
W Gaddis

Miles Davis, Baryshnikov: superb trumpeter and dancer, respectively.
Mr. Cuomo: Mario Cuomo (1932–2015), governor of New York from 1983 to 1994.

To Sarah Gaddis

14 June 1989

Dear Sarah.

Another 'souvenir'! But the evening itself was quite impressive, the 'presentations' in an auditorium at the Met. Museum by the Governor whose high praise for my work won me over to him completely & I would vote for him tomorrow... seriously though he is a very impressive fellow, sharp, quick, listens, humour &c, & then a very large reception afterwards in a vast Met indoor court (just off the 'armour' collection), lots of handshaking &c & I think Matthew had a 'good time', said he thought (as did others) I had made a very good (the best) acceptance brief speech (in which I thanked them for the award, then said I had been leery of awards ever since *J R* won the Natl Book Award which I thought might sell books though MHG told me most people thought the NBA stood for Natl Basketball Assn & then 'my publisher' told me the book was already pegged as elitist (ie difficult) & since the NBA was regarded as an elitist award it might frighten off any who still might have bought it). Lots of warm laughter. If there is one thing I have learned in 'public speaking' it is that audiences simply ache to laugh, give them any excuse to & they will. Anyhow now I have this heavy knee high steel sculpture which will go nice with my Schnabel portrait [...].

It has been pouring rain here day after day which has not helped my spirits sitting down to the typewriter, looking over what I've written so far &

thinking about recasting the whole thing; piles of legal papers notes books & dismay that I have got in over my head again with maybe still time to get in and cut material before it gets into a floundering draft rather than after. I believe assume trust & hope that yours is in much better shape as it must be having got as far as you have & I hope able now as I've said to cut & restore some of the sharpness & dry wry observations of what you actually went through in 'those days'...

MHG is deeply involved in his film project (which I have not read), I only worry what is at stake as it is for you & was for me with *The Recognitions* and I guess all of us trying to do anything well of inevitably so much riding on it, with the fear (from my own experience obviously) of the day when the world shrugs or simply turns its back—but those are the risks we take. [...]

much love always,
Papa

To Paul Ingendaay

[*German critic and translator (1961–), brother of WG's German translator Marcus Ingendaay (1958–). Paul had sent WG his essay on his work, "Zauberer ohne Publikum"* (Magician without an Audience), Das Schreibheft 32 (November 1988), among others.]

Wainscott, N.Y. 11975
[postmarked 25 August 1989]

Dear Paul Ingendaay,

a short note to thank you first for writing, and then for sending me, your pieces on my work. Of course I cannot read them, aber... my German being shreds of rote from 40 years ago the opening lines of your Zauberer ohne Publikum (Magician without a public? like the *Mann ohne Eigenschaften*? (whence we have Mr Eigen in *J R*)) reverberate with some Grimm moment in *The Recognitions* wo die Wünschen noch gehollffen hat, lebte ein König, dessen tochter warum alle schön... well, there go my credentials but it sounds better than it looks.

I agree with you, of the 3 I prefer *J R* but largely probably because of how fond I became of the boy himself; but the most difficult I should think for translation though it is right now presumably going into French, and with less evidence Italian & Spanish as well, Spanish have done a very servicable job with *The Recognitions*. It seems odd to me that the Germans (or is it only Rowolt?) have such problems with me, they (Rowolt) gave the first book 2 or 3 tries about 20 years ago & gave up as too difficult; now I've understood decided to wait & see how this *Erlöser* fared in the marketplace before doing any others (which is good J R cautionary business practice). [...]

with best regards,
William Gaddis

Mann ohne Eigenschaften: *The Man without Qualities*, Robert Musil's huge, unfinished novel (1930–43).

wo die Wünschen [...] schön: from the Grimm Brothers' "Frog King," as quoted in *R* (273). See 17 December 1950.

To David Markson

[*A postcard, without salutation or return address.*]

5 Oct. 89

Only you can fully appreciate my son Matthew haunting the sites of young film writing aspirants, only to meet—to be invited to dinner by, in fact—yes, Harry Joe Brown...plus ça change, which I'm afraid will also go for your Guggenheim try. Meanwhile since Si Krim 2 classmates of mine have gone 'on tour' as we (the living) say. Sobering,

Gaddis

Harry Joe Brown: see letter to Markson of ca. February 1966.

Si Krim: WG's old friend Seymour Krim (1922–89), a highly regarded editor and essayist in the 1960s, committed suicide on August 30.

To John and Pauline Napper

Wainscott, New York 11975
21 December 89

Dear John and Pauline.

[...] How many times we've thought of you but the weeks the months even the years go by justlikethat each taking a toll, you remember my old and eccentric (though not really by English standards) friend Barney Emmart in September and 2 more classmates since while strokes and cancers and divorces abound elsewhere and one hesitates to ask are you well? and are you both well?

Approaching seventy (!!!) is nothing like I'd envisaged God knows, still spry but short of breath and with both whisky and cigarettes flatly ruled out

I cannot say I'm enjoying it all that much wondering why in God's name I ever signed up to write another novel but I did and even worse about a world of which I discover I know nothing, the law; but I've taken their money and am now waist deep. [...]

love and warm wishes
Willie

To James Cappio

[*Cappio had sent WG an analysis of his draft of the Judge Bone opinion. This letter was accompanied by a four-and-a-half legal-page outline of the legal procedure for one aspect of* FHO.]

Wainscott
5 January '90

Dear Jim:

Do not panic!

Let me explain, first. In the early summer I got stuck in the novel in the novel sense not the legal, it was just beginning to sound wooden, and I broke it off to write a subsequent sequence which I greatly enjoyed, Oscar being deposed by the defendants' counsel Mister Mudpye, a token minority number in a large wasp blueribbon firm, enjoyed it so much that it runs 50 pages. More than 'based on', 'drawn from' &c&c, it is much of it line for line lifted from* Saul Steinberg's deposition in his suit v. Columbia Pictures. *and another legal horror (assuming Saul's acquiescence) how Mister Mudpye's "real life" original (with Pryor Cashman Sherman & Flynn) will feel at being so parodied or are depositions fair game[?]

Meanwhile I read and reread your meticulous informed & delightful dissection of the Crease appeal decision, its misuse of Murry v. NBC &c, and

a) grasped or at least for the first time got a sense of the bramble patch I have marched so blithely into, and

b) realized I must throw out the grand design I had hatched in my early enthusiasm (roughly, to compress *AmJur* (or at least Prosser) into a 'novel'), whereupon

c) I went into a blue funk, from which my struggles to emerge have now got me as far as the brown study down the hall, whence this.

I thoroughly appreciate your repeated assurance (in *Crease* supra) that you mean only to clarify 'real world' law not direct my course, but that I might wish to know the former & where I'd strayed intentionally or otherwise (artistic license? sheer sloppiness? plain ignorance?), the point my main mentor has stressed from the start (Donald Oresman at Paramount, Simon-Schuster &c: "Did getting *Arrowsmith* medically correct make it a better novel?") But I have got this damned affliction as witness *J R* for (what Bill Gass despises as) 'verisimilitude' or its semblance wherein events in the 'real' world of business (read, the law) while not plausible are essentially possible, ie an 11yr.old 'could' buy up by mail the controlling majority of a defaulted bond issue at 7¢ on the dollar, &c.

Thus re the attached assuming for the moment that you are not ready to call the whole thing quits here is my hopeful notion: It is as you will see at a glance my attempt at a simple 'procedural' outline for Oscar's infringement case. I certainly do not ask or want you to deliver a 10 page written commentary but would this be feasible? to call you when 'convenient' and run through the steps for any major gaffes? as, (in 6), would law firm A be obligated (by law? ethics?) to tell firm B it has discovered fraudulence in the credibility of a member of B's staff? (though God knows I'm a long way from that scene)... And so forth.

I will call to try to explain further and will understand if your secretary responds 'Mister Cappio is not taking any calls...'

warm regards & "happy new year"
Gaddis

"real life" original: attorney Stephen F. Huff, mentioned later (p. 570).
Arrowsmith: satiric 1925 novel by Sinclair Lewis about the medical profession.

To Donald Oresman

Wainscott NY 11975
21 January 1990

Dear Donald,

many thanks for Judge Leval (in fact I went to that lecture) and Ron Hubbard and the excuse to break this long silence.

Somewhere about the early summer I was abruptly overwhelmed by the enormity of the project I had set myself, its threat to come apart at the evident seams, and the legal complexities for which I was unprepared [...]. In this case it was a reading of my appeals court (Judge Bone's opinion which you saw) decision for infringement for my protagonist Oscar by a meticulous young law clerk (for Judge Motley) since recruited by Cahill Gordon &c (who has admired my work to the extent of once inserting a citation from *J R* into Judge Breiant(sp?)'s opinion washing out Russian Imperials). His admonition has been similar to yours, ie: I will try to give you the relevant 'real world' points of law but please do not let this impede your fiction.

Nonetheless it all sent me 'back to the drawing board' as they aptly phrase it and I think very much to the novel's eventual good; and I am heartened by the memory that this has happened before with both my earlier long novels—the teeming research, the putting it aside with 'what have I got myself into!'—and the thing finally emerging in its own shape.

At any rate, toward the end of the year I sent along the draft bundle to the point it had reached to my S&S editor Allen Peacock as seemed only fair at this point, and had lunch with him just last week and found him quite pleased with it despite some obvious repetitions and disjointed elements (after all it is a draft) and I have always shrunk from showing unfinished work; but bearing all that in mind if you have any interest in looking at it at this stage of course you are welcome though I have hated to waste your time with unresolved ends or requests I am not ready to make immediate use of.

These eventually include Church of the Holy Trinity v. United States; Zorach v. Clauson; McGowan v. Maryland; Disney v. Air Pirates. But obviously the most intriguing current eruption must be Buchwald v. Paramount* aspect (*NYTimes* 15 Jan '90) B's lawyer took it on contingency but the judge didn't require punitive damages (or 'reasonable attorneys' fees'?) and the legal costs already exceed B's winnings, which is just where I have foreseen my protagonist Oscar heading.

On the side here I am probably heading myself for an expensive education with filmdom: one currently quiescent item with an option on *Carpenter's Gothic* with Keith Barish which he wants to turn over to a Larry Gagosian if I will modify our agreement in which they now indemnify me to read instead that I indemnify them and everyone else in sight (so I've said if they want to go on with this nonsense they must pay my lawyer's consultations: silence); and the other embracing efforts by a young screen writer to option *J R* for a possible deal with the gang at Guber Peters which seems ridden with pitfalls. Rather than arming one's self to sue, what seems to me paramount (excuse!) these days is to arm one's self against being sued. I have certainly got some tigers by the tails.

Well, thank you for reading this far. I had hoped to have something more conclusive before reaching you again, and now with Muriel in town I am staying on here in the grey sky country empty house for a bit with no preoccupations but those skirted above.

very warmest regards and wishes for the new year
Bill Gaddis

*which seems to me very much to resemble Murray v. NBC, black star and all.

Ron Hubbard: founder of Scientology (1911–86); many lawsuits pursued him during his lifetime and his cult after his death.

Cahill Gordon &c: Cahill Gordon & Reindel, a prominent Wall Street law firm established in 1919.

Allen Peacock: he acquired the novel in 1987 but left Simon & Schuster in November 1990. The following March, Peacock (1954–) went to work for Henry Holt, where he would later acquire *AA*.

Buchwald v. Paramount: journalist Art Buchwald successfully sued Paramount Pictures for breach of contract over the 1988 movie *Coming to America*.

Keith Barish: American film producer (*Endless Love, Sophie's Choice, Ironweed,* et al.).

Larry Gagosian: high-profile American art dealer.

Guber Peters: American film production company (*The Color Purple, The Witches of Eastwick, Caddyshack II*, et al.).

To Saul Steinberg

[*Romanian-born cartoonist and illustrator (1914–99), best known for his work for the* New Yorker. *He was an old friend of Muriel Murphy, who introduced him to WG in 1982. As WG noted earlier (6 August 1987), Steinberg's famous* View of the World from 9th Avenue *cover for the* New Yorker *(1976) inspired the poster for the movie* Moscow on the Hudson *(1984), which led to a lawsuit for copyright infringement against Columbia Pictures. (The lawyers for Columbia claimed protection under parody, but the court found in favor of Steinberg.) The case is cited in* FHO *(31) and, as WG had informed Cappio, a deposition from the case was the model for the one between Oscar, Basie, and Pai (pp. 185–234), referred to below as "the Deposition."*]

Wainscott, NY
21 January 1990

Dear Saul.

Rather than wait any longer on the formerly reliable chance of our all getting together for dinner with the vagaries of town or country, the weather &c where the promptings of conversation may serve to clarify one's thoughts, I am trying to clarify some of mine by getting them down on paper here in some kind of order.

I have long been intrigued, and more recently troubled by, the collisions in human affairs caused by misunderstanding and 'getting it wrong' (this is in fact largely what *Carpenter's Gothic* and especially the character Paul are all about); and I say 'troubled by' because in this past year it seems to have come home to roost on all sides: with Muriel, my son, and I'm sure elsewhere I don't yet know about. Thus 'the Deposition'.

Earlier in the summer my work on this law novel was not prospering, as I began to be aware of the complex mess I'd got myself into and the overwhelming source material I had assembled, including of course yours with Columbia where the Huff-Rembar deposition I thought offered a marvelous vehicle for parody of the vagaries of the legal process itself rather than the real people involved excepting insofar as it was heightened by your as always elegantly precise care for words and meanings harassed by the language at its most obfuscating in the mouths of otherwise intelligent lawyers, all this to the point where I felt in some odd way duty bound to pursue the parody as close as I could consistent with my protagonist's (Oscar's) dilemma.

Aside from the curious parallel of Columbia's brief attempt to (mis)use parody as a defense, there emerged (in this 'getting it wrong' mode) the essential irony—irony being still to my old fashioned eye at the heart of fiction, certainly comic fiction—which this letter is at such obvious pains to deal with, where in the light of our many past conversations and my impression from them of pretty complete license with the legal pages, motions, interrogations, memoranda, depositions &c that all this was a prank which we, you and I, were playing on not any person but on the process; and it was in that spirit that I devoted most of July and August, and that I pressed the results on you a couple of months ago.

Thus I was concerned when I got the thing back from you with accompanying cordial items but without comment, and remain so, more so in fact since I have gathered that my concern was justified. All this I failed to recognize at the time since by the early fall some sort of gap seemed already to have opened which Muriel and I remarked, she of course more sensitively and more informed by your long association than I, but we worried for it and simply hoped, that from wherever the chill descended—whether your own private affairs where we hesitated to intrude, or evidences of our own abrasions spreading discomfort around us—it would all fade in a natural recovery of our old bonhomie. I suspect the latter (our own abrasions), for which I must assume the main responsibility I suppose, and am acutely aware as you must be of your immense importance in Muriel's life at its every level.

For myself, if I may be allowed to put it this way, our friendship over this past decade has been one of the most surprising gifts Muriel has brought to me, making this apparent rupture doubly difficult since, again, I trust you know my awareness of my strong sense of indebtedness to you in at best an uneven exchange and at, again, so many levels, from such worldly arenas as the Academy to sheer relish in conversation embracing even some painful glimpses of self revelation, and moments of enlightenment, of which this may be one.

with all possible warm regards,
Gaddis

To Marc Chénetier

[*French literary critic (1946–) who taught and wrote about WG's work throughout his long, distinguished career. The following undated note is handwritten at the top of a photocopy of WG's "Trickle-Up Economics: J R Goes to Washington" and was accompanied by a copy of the uncut version (RSP 62–71), which was translated by Chénetier's student Brigitte Félix as "J R se met à la page" and published in* Europe *733 (May 1990): 112–19.*]

[April 1990]

Dear Marc Chenetier—

I am sorry to be so late responding to your letter of 14/03 but some recent confusion moving about and the question whether I might dig up something to send you for your edition of *Europe*— afraid this would not suit even if there were still time (though you're welcome to use it) but thought that it might amuse you in any event,

best regards
William Gaddis

To Joseph Tabbi

[*Tabbi sent WG his essay "The Compositional Self in William Gaddis'* JR," Modern Fiction Studies *35.4 (Winter 1989–90): 655–71.*]

Wainscott, New York 11975
1 May 1990

Dear Joseph Tabbi.

Thank you for sending me your Compositional Self piece from *Modern Fiction Studies*. It certainly reflects a wide and careful reading & I find the analyses & conclusions very much to the point & obviously pleasing to me.

My one moment of annoyance came with your very mild reprimand on p659 "It was, I think, erroneous and perhaps unfair of John Gardner to conclude in the *New York Review of Books*, simply from one character's conceit of the unfinished work as a kind of invalid, that Gaddis himself 'was apparently uneasy about bringing out *J R*.'" The whole point of that image was of course precisely the opposite, like most of Gardner's points in that appallingly perverse misreading of the book right through to the end where he concludes how easy it is to portray the artist as ground down by commerce when, again, the point is precisely the opposite in Gibbs, Eigen & Bast constantly putting obstacles in their own paths to avoid facing the completion & consequences of the creative act head on, as crystalized in Bast's resolution at the very end to do so. The whole 'review' was a transparent stunt he has pulled elsewhere (see his on was it Walker Percy's? *Lancelot*), the flattering & utterly phony appreciative buildup packed with strawmen to be demolished in the conclusion ('it fails as art'), a regular Procrustian bed tended by a man I have always been convinced simply eaten out by envy & I have never quite understood how he was allowed to run around loose for so long patronizing his betters, the epitome of course being his ridiculous number on 'moral fiction' (what was *J R* if not exactly that?). Now I grant it would be awfully difficult to be so vain a fellow publishing a novel the year the Pulitzer Prize—about his level if he'd ever got a prize (see Bill Gass on the Pulitzer in the *NY Times BR* a few years ago)—the year that is that they fail to give one in fiction because they find no worthy candidate, even worse I should imagine than seeing it go to some other pedestrian contender since there is very much the heart of the cancer: his writing was simply pedestrian, which he tried to make up for / divert attention from by providing bizarre (to his lights) characters like his 'magician' in *October Light* & some book about a giant boy locked up in a closet. Interestingly enough he was a great admirer of *The Recognitions* early on which finally soured, & perhaps it was the theme of forgery that spoke to him, later to blossom in borrowings & plagiaries, a little Sir Arthur Eddington here, some murky business about the *Canterbury Tales* there, so to find the poor bastard 'perhaps' erroneous & unfair is gentle handling indeed.

Addendum: poor George Steiner too (speaking of paranoia), in his own embarrassing attempt at fiction, some nonsense about carting Adolf Hitler out of the woods in Argentina was it? Brought to mind the Arab into Spanish proverb into English: Sit in the doorway of your house & watch the bodies of your enemies carried by... a long sitting but amply rewarded. (He apparently never noticed the inconsistency in calling a book unreadable & then reviewing it presumably having read it—though there was evidence otherwise.)

I doubt you expected such an outburst in return for your kind gesture in sending me your piece singling out one fleetingly brief passage from the thoughtful & estimable whole but quite obviously it's been rankling for a long time. Otherwise I thank you for calling my attention to Melville's *Pierre* which I read ages ago if then & will look it up now.

with regards,
William Gaddis

Your Faulkner epigraph is marvelous.

Walker Percy's? *Lancelot:* Gardner reviewed this novel in the 20 February 1977 issue of the *New York Times Book Review*; like his review of *J R*, it is reprinted in Gardner's *On Writers and Writing* (1994).

Bill Gass on the Pulitzer: "Pulitzer: The People's Prize," reprinted in Gass's *Finding a Form* (Knopf, 1996), 3–13 (which mentions WG on pp. 8 and 12). No Pulitzer Prize in fiction was given in 1971, the year Gardner published *Grendel*.

'magician': the magician is actually in Gardner's *Sunlight Dialogues*, not *October Light* (1976). The giant boy is in *Freddy's Book* (1980).

Sir Arthur Eddington: English astronomer, cited by WG in *FHO*.

Steiner [...] fiction: *The Portage to San Cristobal of A. H.* (1981).

Faulkner epigraph: "It is my ambition to be, as a private individual, abolished and voided from history, leaving it markless, no refuse save for the printed books."

To Susan Barile

[A young woman who, as the letter notes, abandoned law school to become a writer. To support herself she worked at various New York City bookstores, including Gotham Book Mart; see headnote to letter of 13 November 1991.]

> Wainscott, New York 11975
> 2 May 1990

Dear Susan Barile.

Thank you for your letter & for your generous appraisal of my work; but there are so many pitfalls in a writer's life that having inadvertently encouraged you to pursue it inevitably makes me somewhat uneasy & I can only wish you luck.

I suppose this strikes me especially right now because just as you abandon law school I have become entangled with another novel involving lawsuits of every variety—the one at the center embracing copyright infringement—through having been seduced by reading opinions which I find real gems in the use of the language proceeding on to the fine points of the law which seems to be nothing but fine points & find it a little late to be starting my legal education.

Good luck to us both,

> Yours
> William Gaddis

To Saul Steinberg

> Wainscott
> 2 July 1990

Dear Saul.

Well, I have greatly missed seeing you, both for the pleasure & illuminations of the old comraderie fallen under the shadow of 'unfinished business' in these troubled times. It was a bleak winter out here adrift on a sea of doubts & the work not going well—barely going at all in fact—so much so that even with the entire spring passed taking the Academy with it only now the pall is lifting & that not by grace but force of will if it can be sustained. Clearly a part of all this has been that fragment of work on which I spent last summer and which, to my total & unhappy surprise, took painful shape as another in the series 'the high brutality of good intentions' from which I still earnestly hope we can be rescued, much less any 'harm' intended or so far as I can see even faintly implied as I am sure a reading of the entire 300-odd page MS to date would bear out if you are inclined to consider such a chore. At the least I should very much like for us to sit down together when it suits you, if it suits you, & hope to hear from you about such a possibility.

yours most sincerely,

Gaddis

To Howard Goldberg

[*Editor of the* New York Times's *Op-Ed page. This cover letter accompanied WG's essay "This Above All," on the Silverado Savings & Loan scandal of 1990, which was rejected; published posthumously in RSP (110–13).*]

Wainscott, New York 11975

30 July 1990

Dear Howard Goldberg.

I think Mike Levitas warned you that this would appear on your desk.

You will see that something in me seems hellbent on getting US ex rel. Gerald Mayo in there but this time I think the flow from his in forma pauperis to the homeless to Reagan's get-rich credo (to Keynes' everybody getting rich/ for foul is useful to S&L to &c &c) follows closely and earnestly hope you agree. So closely in fact right through to the end that it would be very painful to cut further* (as I have already done from the earlier notes and drafts even given up Ed Meese in the process) in trying not to take full advantage of Mike Levitas' generous provisos regarding length getting up in the 12-1500 area (QED) though when the figure rose higher he did qualify with 'since you trust Howard Goldberg's editing' as I do but obviously desperately hope that (what I read as) the tight coherency of the piece will stay your hand . . .

Holding my breath, I am

with best regards,

Yours

W. Gaddis

*I would yield the opening sentence if so pressed.

Mike Levitas: Mitchell Levitas (1929–2019), another editor of the Op-Ed page and former editor of the *Times Book Review*.

US ex rel. Gerald Mayo: i.e., the court case *UNITED STATES ex. rel. Gerald Mayo v. SATAN AND HIS STAFF* (1971). Mayo is the devil-blaming plaintiff mentioned on p. 430 of *FHO*.

in forma pauperis: legal Latin: "in the manner of a pauper"; i.e., at no cost.

Keynes: economist John Keynes (1883–1946), as quoted in E. F. Schumacher's *Small Is Beautiful*: speculating in the 1930s that someday everyone would be rich, Lord Keynes cautioned, "The time for all this is not yet. For at least another hundred years we must pretend to ourselves and to every one that fair is foul and foul is fair; for foul is useful and fair is not" (Harper & Row, 1973, p. 24).

Ed Meese: Attorney General under Ronald Reagan.

opening sentence: "We will find justice in the next world; in this world we have the law"—paraphrased as the opening sentence of *FHO*.

To Sarah Gaddis

[*In response to reading the bound galley for her forthcoming novel, published the following January, in which WG is portrayed as Lad Thompkins, and his Harvard friend Douglas Wood (see 14 March 1957) as Douglas Kipps. Sarah was still living in France at this time.*]

23 August 1990

dear Sarah,

Well! I have just finished a slow reading of *Swallow Hard*. It's no longer a book by a girl about a girl growing up but a real book written by a young woman about a girl, yes, but people and places and feelings and things I never knew you knew—I don't mean 'facts of life' or family secrets but life's secrets & secret places some of them quite touching and some of them quite painful & done with a sense & use of language that so exquisitely suits & conveys them with never a bit of self indulgence, so clean, certain of itself & underivative of others' styles so full & entirely itself in its haunting sense of desolation utterly uncluttered by sentimentality especially in those very last lines which are so spare & simply stunning.

I remember reading those last lines in your MS & commenting on their effectiveness but is this the same book I read? or am I the same or not the same person who read it? This latter I find very disconcerting because I'm quite aware that this past year or so in my various states of being there have been gaps, gaps of memory & attention & concentration all over the place but still, this book is so much more full than I remembered, not simply of people but of insights & fraught impressions & deeper glimpses & the staunch ('Firm and steadfast; true' as the dictionary defines it) quality that Marvin Cherney grasped in his painting & is there still.

All the Fire Isld part of course I remember but not the extent to which you evoked that village & house & the people careening around from room to room (all I see missing is the Monopoly under that paper lampshade) but the atmosphere of it is all there so marvelously yet never overdone which is as true of the rest of the book's familiar scenes & places, & how curious we will be to learn what it evokes for 'the reader' who was not there but here again, all that is evoked by sheer invention so far as I know, I mean there never was a Peninghen was there? So for me throughout there is the repeated shock of recognition buffeted by that of fabrication & all of it running smooth & seamless. And the people. Your Douglas must be the most remarkable creation in the book, for turning a 'real' person into a character elaborated in your invention of who he was and who—for those of us who knew him—he might have been, so well might have been if he had soared on the wings you've given him, an utterly believable character for 'the reader' & as equally real a poignant evocation of the fellow we knew. And the way you have juxtaposed him with her father Lad (I remember most vividly when I was in the mad & drinking & yes, I admit self pitying throes of that prolonged divorce, Douglas saying in the blunt way you have captured so well: Did you think it was going to be easy? meaning of course not the divorce but life: it pulled me up short, & still does when I recall it not infrequently because I think I did & in some demented way still do). Thus the brooding smoking cut off Lad/father you've given us: again, so understated & unsentimentalized & unindulgently but there at the end (page 311) right to the core.

Which I think, this juxtaposition of Douglas & Lad, gives your last line "... and almost drowned, and made a man a hero" such stunning effect because so suddenly & abruptly & believably it is all there; & I cannot imagine anyone reading it without feeling a blow to the pit of the stomach but at the same time an overwhelming & lingering sense of the inevitable beauty of it.

And thus all of this considered I think your original title that you've ended up with *Swallow Hard* is the right one, it's sharp & intriguing when you pick the book up and continues to reverberate when you've finished reading it & put it down; & what else is to be said about it for now. Except what a pain to have to wait till February! But that, as we know, 'comes with the territory'.

Except that you have a well earned Happy Birthday ahead! Because it will be one not of tinseled presents but one you have made yourself with all of your own courage & diligence & talent, & I know if anyone outside yourself can know the cost of all that to you, a pretentious thing to say but if not as aware perhaps at least aware of the part my own delinquencies & clumsy & so often futile attempts to keep the peace, have played. So you have every reason to be as proud of yourself as I am of you when you face the gang at Deauville & Lord knows some familiar faces, I have heard that Sidney & Pidie Lumet will be there, he is a warm fellow (despite my earlier annoyance with him for Matthew's budding career speaking of my clumsy attempts) & Pidie is absolute tops, straight as can be. I forget who else but understand you may even get Gloria Jones, enough said, you can handle that.

The world prospects are something else now that they are spilling over into our own lives, USA was already becoming a financial nightmare but now with the millions a day Iraq adventure really alarming, my concern for your situation with the steady decline of the dollar if you are going to try to continue to carry that apartment yourself & my own situation when for the first time next January there will be no check from Simon & Schuster since the final one is due when I turn in the 'finished' MS which is (as always with my works) 'not quite finished', my Italian publisher silent on the $15 thousand he has owed me since spring & the movie prospects in the usual unresolved chaos but the Lord knows, looking back, we are certainly all much better off than we have been. There have been some rocky times here but I think we are straightening them out & Matthew is in very good form working away at his projects & the great good fortune of Katarina.

with my love as always, your proud
Papa

Marvin Cherney: American painter (1925–67), a family friend.
Sidney & Piedie Lumet [...] Gloria Jones: see notes to 9 June 1984.
Iraq adventure: President Bush began sending US troops to the Middle East shortly after Iraq invaded Kuwait on 2 August 1990.
Katarina: Matthew's girlfriend at the time.

To James Cappio

22 September 1990

Dear Jim,

I wonder how many times I have not written you (though you are at the top of a long list), appalled at the time that has passed & I cannot explain but can possibly recount. First I believe was my abrupt halt after your fine long detailed dissection of the Bone opinion reversing Oscar's loss of his case on appeal, originality vs novelty &c. (I daren't even look it up now for the date.) It was that I believe that made me stop and realise the immense morass I'd got myself into, the reams of material, of hundreds of marked passages in

AmJur & Prosser & I thought, like Mr Gibbs in his (my) *Agapē Agape*, what in God's name did I think I was doing! [*J R* 586] To be clear here: I was very aware of your sensitive & generous concern that I not feel you were correcting/interfering with the work but were simply trying, as I wished you would do, to make me aware of any legal gaps in case I wished to amend them. And all along about that time other breakdowns came along, in threatened health, confidence, the 'what use is any of it' that apparently comes upon many enough writers late in their careers. Unproductive months, a bleak & grey winter spent out here alone largely, each day starting Now I shall get to it, ending Perhaps tomorrow, then.

Meanwhile to the work itself, my realisation that in my absorption with 'the law' & absurd notion of a novel almost entirely of legal memorandums briefs opinions &c my real attention & any surviving remnants of 'talent' should return to a novel's real essentials: plot springing from character, character must be consistent but plot should cause surprise (Forster), what happens next? And in that desolate months-long search which should have taken a week gradually finding the clues in your Bone letter: Oscar's (black) lawyer permits (or later says he did) the NYS law regarding originality (patents) to prevail intending to turn about & win on appeal (I haven't got all that quite straight in my head yet, just how it will work), meanwhile it's revealed that he (the black lawyer Mr Basie) is a fraud, never passed the bar, learned law in prison &c, Oscar threatens his firm, finally his father the old Judge Crease reads the lower court's decision & spots the flaws (which you spotted) steps in & directs the (successful) appeal (Bone recast) not out of love for Oscar whom he's angry with for having exploited the family in his awful play but for love of the law; meanwhile having had his own troubles back with *Cyclone 7* struck by lightning which killed the dog Spot (negligence? Act of G*d?) &c about where I'm at now, sometimes a week for a paragraph when things are going well...

More and more prompted by those lines in *Four Quartets* where the words slip slide perish will not stay in place, where it's all been done before better & elsewhere such a stunning passage I can't believe I don't have it here at hand but you certainly know it.

I heard, again how long ago! that you were no longer with Cahill but that's all, I hope this reaches you. And getting hold of myself again I will write, at latest when I have *James B. (Infant) v. Village of Tatamount*, Crease, J. in some sort of shape [*FHO* 285–93]. Perhaps starting tomorrow,...

with thanks always for your time and patience,

I hope things are going well—
W Gaddis

plot should cause surprise (Forster): "characters, to be real, ought to run smoothly, but a plot ought to cause surprise"—*Aspects of the Novel* (Harcourt, Brace, 1927), 137—a phrase cited by Judge Bone in *FHO* (411).
lines in *Four Quartets*: see endnotes to 7 September 1950.

To Judith Gaddis

[1 October 1990]

Dear Judith,

no I don't "think one ever can" get one's life in order, at least in my experience of it so far (& most of those I see around me) though they strive: here's Matthew living up near the GW [George Washington] bridge in a bloodthirsty neighborhood working at movie scripts, I keep telling him he's too nice a person to get mixed up with that bunch ("I know, Pop") and he is, compassionate's the best word & with a kind of wisdom, just very decent though (or because of) these qualities don't provide great financial returns; & Sarah still trying to get things in place has been living in Paris these 5 or 6 years after her escape-marriage collapsed (like going to live with the Shaws dinner-at-6) but speaking of Fire Isld she's written a novel titled *Swallow Hard* which about sums it up, you & Matthew are not included but the 'father' appears in old tennis shoes, smoking, writing books that don't sell too well, but touching & distant both, to be published in February & the early Saltaire days house full of drinking friends quite vivid as you'll see. And the drinking I think looking back was a great part in "what went wrong", I only realized recently what a large part it played in a good 40 years of my life, now haven't had a scotch & soda &c for 1½years though a little wine along the way, & the smoking & its effects still the on-again off-again plague. I can no more imagine that I'm approaching 70 than you as 50 & I find time goes more quickly & is harder to understand, part of it I know is approaching the end of a 4year book contract with of course the thing not at all near delivery, I suddenly got fascinated by the law for a novel in which everybody is finally suing everybody else & it took me a couple of years to realize the mess I'd got myself into, books & books & judicial opinions briefs depositions & marked passages piled high now trying to work my way out of it all so we don't have another aborted Secret History of the Player Piano but the law is a very complicated & often comic scene or at least I hope to make it so.

Well, your word of Paz—that most unacceptable event we are obliged to accept, Barney Emmart gone, Bernie Winebaum—but beyond her 'eccentricities' the moment I think of Paz is with a lift of spirits & thank heavens for such an abrupt & simple end & how touched I am at her last thought for me. Lord we all did try, how we tried! & you I believe most of all till it simply became untenable & it took me a long time to understand that & to grasp your courage. And of course I think of you not infrequently & all our good days & always with the hope you are well because you so deserve well & even the 'contentment' you sought from the start & I could not grasp, your letter was generous & so like I always remember you & I will let you know as things prosper or at least go on,

W.

—————

James Cappio

[*Enclosed was a draft of the second Crease opinion, mentioned in WG's last letter to Cappio. In a handwritten postscript he adds:* "*The* New Yorker *declined, having had enough of Spot—*"]

3 Nov. 90

Dear Jim,

many thanks for your letters & new treatise. I have read that some 40 thousand enter law school each year, about the same number leaving the profession over stress, distress, &c&c & so much I suppose for your departure from Cahill but it is a shock that you haven't landed elsewhere, or is there a (divinity?) that shapes our ends rough hew them how we may? For now I just hope that you'll stay around town a bit longer to keep an eye on me.

So to keep the lines of communication back in operation I attach the attached for your entertainment. Having drafted it I've now taken a step back to lay the ground for it in the novel's terms, just a few but tortured pages then on to the Main Action again.

Looking at the attached I red underlined a couple of phrases unsure if they are correct usage, otherwise the same madness prevails (having got into 'bailment' when a tenant here reneged & left possessions I was ready to sell or destroy but was warned we were inadvertant bailees, thus we learn).

But I will be back in touch after the above low hurdle.

best regards,
W.G.

—————

a (divinity?) that shapes our ends: *Hamlet* 5.2.10.

To Sarah Gaddis

14 March '91

Dear Sarah.

This morning I decided to approach it all differently: daily I've got up, tea & come straight to the typewriter to take up where I left off yesterday's frustration, thinking Work Must Come First, then letters &—but what this has led to over what's now weeks is neither letters nor the work; I have never that I recall been so stuck, a day or 2 on 3 or 4 lines & even those unsatisfactory. So now at 8 am I've reversed things, at least will get one letter off to you before the day collapses. [...]

Well not being practical folk sitting down to apply our talents to sex greed & violence best seller success in the American Way, we have chosen an odd path for ourselves, me complaining at this end over these frustrations entirely of my own making & you there having done an honest piece of work in the so far as I know silent aftermath. Individually you get very good grades: Helen (Mrs E.L.) Doctorow with many words of praise for your book (she having written a novel), Karen Saks, all impressed by your work & want to see you Move Onward. Louis Auchincloss the most teacherly: Well Will, I have just finished reading your daughter's book, she is most certainly a writer & now that she has exorcised you, having killed you off at the end, I hope she will go on to the wider world. And so, now given your proven talent & ability, that does seem to be the next challenge, getting away from, out of one's self to create entire fictions & characters (although these inevitably are made up of bits & pieces of one's self & one's own observations), but necessarily plot & story, where as Forster says, plot arising from character, that character must be consistent but plot should cause surprise. It has always seemed to me, though I have never really managed it, what a treat to get hold of an essentially simple situation & then watch the story write itself. For instance the one of *Gaslight*, the man marries the wealthy woman & then sets about driving her crazy, convincing her fearing & convincing herself that she is going mad & he is trying desperately to help, the only one she can trust & turn to &c. Well maybe all this is going too far but you see what I mean. A Plot. Something Matthew and I have talked about regarding his own work & medium, the movies, where it is more especially important I think, not just for suspense but that suspense must always be present (not necessarily the murder mystery sort) but simply What will happen next? To create characters the reader will, first, believe, & second, care about what happens to. Why so many movies are so ridiculously bad, the character scarcely believable but even if so you really don't give a damn what happens to him as in most of these violence prone shoot out movies, who cares?

Also this business of character & plot as of particular importance at the stage you are at now if you wish to be: having proved that you can write, publish, & get Sunday *NY Times* reviewed, to work out & outline a 'story' & write a chapter or 2 for an advance on another novel. Not a reflection on your work but simply the times we live in that whereas a few years ago there were almost immediate paperback offers when a novel came out, now (according to my editor at Simon & Sch) far far fewer. (Any day now both *J R* & *The Recognitions* OP, out of print.) Well it's the world we've chosen & not an easy row to hoe as yr grandmother would have said. [...]

I just learned that Mark Twain took 3 years off between halves of finishing *Huckleberry Finn*, some comfort.

much love
Papa

Helen [...] a novel: as Helen Henslee, Mrs. Doctorow published a novel entitled *Pretty Redwing* (1982).

Karen Saks: i.e., Keren, second wife of stage and film director Gene Saks until his death in 2015.

Gaslight: 1944 film directed by George Cukor, based on a play by Patrick Hamilton, and the source of the term "gaslighting."

To Griselda Ohannessian

[*Managing Director of New Directions (1927–2011). After Stuart Klawans's "Out of Print, but Not Forgotten" appeared in the* Voice Literary Supplement *in April 1991—expressing outrage at the "out of stock indefinitely" status of WG's first two novels—WG received several inquiries from publishers. (WG wrote Klawans a thank-you note on 7 May 1991.) This letter underscores the importance of New Directions's avant-garde titles to writers of WG's generation.*]

Wainscott, New York 11975
7 May 1991

Dear Ms Ohannessian.

Thank you for your inquiry regarding reprint possibilities for my 2 novels discussed in the *VLS* article, which has provoked a good deal of interest. I have put the whole matter in the hands of my agent Candida Donadio & eventually we will work out some resolution; meanwhile looking back to my reading in the late 'forties I recall among the best, such things as *The Wanderer*, Kafka's *Amerika* &c, under the New Directions imprint & whether or not we may work out anything in this current instance find your interest gratifying.

Yours,
William Gaddis

The Wanderer [...] *Amerika*: Alain-Fournier's *The Wanderer* (*Le Grand Meaulnes*) was published by New Directions in 1946, and Kafka's unfinished novel in 1940.

To John Napper

Wainscott, New York 11975
Hallowe'en 1991

Well! dear John,

what a treat & a pleasure & a confirmation your news brings that you're both still with us but, with the Albemarle catalogue, triumphantly so! as the pictures themselves express in just these terms; their (your) clarity & vitality but (as I read them) underneath lurking something awfully wrong.

My own plods on at the usual glacial pace (426pp to date) but with What's Dreadfully Wrong out there for all to see. I got far far deeper into 'the law' than intended, enough research for 10 books as usual & now struggling to surface once I at last realized that perhaps The Reader is not so utterly entranced by the mad elegance of a well written court Opinion as I, to say nothing of the intricacies of the (this is all) civil law itself; I mean I'd rather read Prosser on *Torts* than most novels (except of course the 19^{sie} Russians...

Imagine: I was actually in England for a couple of days in the spring. By misadventure. I hadn't seen Sarah for some long time so heard about a $199. round trip to Paris, by 'stand by' & indeed I did: getting there was easy, spent 4 fine days, then 2 days 'standing by' at deGaulle; finally got on a plane to Boston but 'we stop in London' & indeed we did, all put off the plane at Heathrow, in to a minute bed&breakfast nr Victoria, another day standing by at Heathrow, another bed&breakfast night nr Victoria & quite unable to see anyone so of course ended up spending the simple return trip fare on these shenanigans & really got back to my own bed vowing never to travel again, preferring "a fool to make me merry than experience to make me sad, and to travel for it too."

Now, regarding the enclosure, if you are prepared to be amused? appalled? My 'portrait' done on a large expanse of broken crockery by Julian Schnabel: could anything be more remote from your *Recognition* (#11)? Well. He wanted to do it, having dipped into *The Recognitions* & simply gave it to me, a large forthright generous fellow I got quite fond of but his other & much heralded (others say 'hyped') 'abstracts' are utterly beyond me as is all of what's going on in the galleries these days. To say nothing of 'poetry'.

So we've no choice but to persist & know that we will last. Your spry photo in the elegant Albemarle is most heartening. I haven't had a glass of spirits for more than 2 years though a little wine for the stomach's sake, still fight the tobacco back & forth & its toll is apparent (especially dragging a bag through the endless corridors of Heathrow). Congratulations!

and love to you both,
Willie

Albemarle catalogue: published to coincide with Napper's exhibit at the Albemarle Gallery in London, 16 October–22 November 1991.

"a fool [...] travel for it too": so says Rosalind in *As You Like It* (4.1.25–26).

a little wine for the stomach's sake: 1 Timothy 5:23 (quoted in *R* 24).

To Erika Goldman

[*An editor at Scribner's who requested a blurb for John Aldridge's* Talents and Technicians: Literary Chic and the New Assembly-Line Fiction *(1992), on American fiction of the 1980s, including WG's.*]

Wainscott, New York 11975
7 November 1991

Dear Erika Goldman.

Thank you for sending me John Aldridge's *Talents and Technicians*. I don't write (or seek) jacket blurbs but in this case think you & certainly John Aldridge would agree in the light of his long generous appraisal of my work, renewed in these pages, it could appear especially self serving & in fact prove counterproductive.

Well, that said, I read it straight through with pleasure & bleats of satisfaction, a very much needed corrective succinctly putting forth what many feel but haven't had his patience in actually examining the material & bearing down with critical intelligence, right from the earliest pages' vital distinction between critics & reviewers & the latters' encroachment upon or rather displacement of the former in our current 'literary' climate which seems to have gone unremarked for the major deleterious factor it has willy nilly become.

My own patience with the material under fire here was provoked by curiosity & exhausted quite early with a try at Raymond Carver's 'story' about the birthday cake, manipulated sentimentality &c & I looked in vain in these pages' exploration of the self fulfilling/defeating plague of Teaching Creative

Writing—my own brief & depressing foray among undergraduates to witness—for the debt Carver apparently felt to a major minimalist in terms of talent John Gardner whose numbing influence seems to persist beyond the grave.

Taken altogether, Aldridge's thesis recalls to me lines of a poet (Roy Campbell?) of generations ago as 'They use the bridle and the curb all right, but where's the bloody horse?'

Good luck with publishing the book & please give John Aldridge my best personal regards when you are in touch with him,

yours,
William Gaddis

Carver's 'story': "A Small, Good Thing" (in *Cathedral*, 1983), regarded as one of his best.

Roy Campbell: Anglo-African poet (1901–57). His poem "On Some South African Novelists" begins: "You praise the firm restraint with which they write— / I'm with you there, of course: / They use the snaffle and the curb all right, / But where's the bloody horse?"

To Susan Barile

[Barile planned to open a bookstore called "Noted with High Regard Though Seldom Read" (after the last line of R), and wanted WG to read at the store's opening, but the store never came to be. She was then working at Gotham Book Mart, whose rare-book department was curated by Andreas Brown (1933–2020), mentioned below.]

Wainscott, New York 11975
13 November 1991

Dear Ms. Barile.

I apologize for being so late about answering your inquiry & generous estimate of my work.

To the 'readings': I avoid giving them (& sitting through them) but appreciate your invitation. The one at the luncheon out here in the spring was a local library benefit & a favour to a friend, & as far as that goes I didn't read from my but Dostoevski's work, a long comic scene of a literary luncheon fete in *The Possessed*. I do recall talking with your friend there & sorry to hear about your illness deferred bookstore project but certainly the Gotham should fill the bill as it always has done & of course it's pleasing to hear of the inquiries for my books & your efforts on their behalf.

The *Village Voice* piece came as a happy surprise to me & did in fact elicit inquiries from ½dozen publishers, still fiddling with Viking/Penguin over whether they'll renew their imminently expiring license or sign off, given the chaotic state of publishing Lord knows the outcome but I hope to in a week or so.

Please too give my best regards to Andreas Brown who gave me generous advice some years ago on the equally mad area of my 'archive' on which I've still taken no action except to relentlessly add to it as this present work trundles on at my usual overburdened glacial pace.

with kind regards
William Gaddis

To William H. Gass

[*Gass spent 1991–92 at the Getty Center for the History of Art and the Humanities in Santa Monica, California, completing his novel* The Tunnel. *All misspellings are* sic.]

9 January '92

der Bill, well, by jing! I herd someplace you got a job someplace pumping gas at some Getty station way off to hell & gone and here's your newyars greting to prove it certainly makes me feel better & a dam site better way to make a living for wife & kids than that writing game I met this Mrs Getty once boy ther is some dish you would lik to sink your choppers into those white alabastard sholders white columnar thighs to brake a bulls back I'll say but there was other people in the room so the opportunity did not presnt itself still shows up in my dreams tho'

Real glad to have your address tho' if anything coms up I see its at Santa Monica I guess where that boy asked for a Jewsharp for Honnika but something went wrong he ended up with a harmonica that's the way it goes old top there are probably a clutch of those stars of stage & screen around too stopping at your station I bet you get a chance to pump them up haha

Well I am still out here in the woods nobody to sport with but some dam Canada geese fly over all grey and chill Muriel is mainly in the city warmth because I am still trying to get thru' this damn book a real fools errand I have grown to lothe it but have taken mony from S&S so cant quit as we say in for a penny in for a pound & I don't mean Ezra, managed to get thru' 1991 without erning one red ¢ so the social security folks come right thru' on the dot that is one good thing about this weird country where they pay a executive $1 million salary for running a car company that loses $1 billion the same year its one day sunny the next day rain life's too dam funny for me to explain. So maybe the day will come when you can speak to your boss & see if I can get a billet there too some day sounds a dam site better than camping out here near locals like Peter Matthiessen nearby in Sagaponack that is the Indian word for where the nuts fall and sure enogh here we are. Even my daughter Sarah just quit the 8 years high life over at Paris France she is stiffing the culture shock & expects to show up out at California too any day with all the young folk like yourselves are you still with that same wife Mary I hope you count your blessings speking of this sullen craft somebody called it would be something if we both finished these god dam books this same year 1992 I hope to Christ mine is still called The Last Act & this time I mean it let me tell you, Jesus Jack the child is black what a party that would be, I havent had a real drink I mean spirits lo these 3 years now just a few oz of wine in the evening like that little bastard John Tower if you remember him they said if he's a ladys man thers a chance for all of us gone are the days when I have been to Ludlow fair & left my necktie God knows where tho' it all shows up in my FBI files Ive been getting from Freedom of Information Act most of it blacked out but the rest to make a temperance mother weep, tho' Muriel still does, sees even the drop of wine as poison they say you cant win them all but why not.

Well thanks for letting me get this off my chest if you got this far & let me know if theres anything I can do for you here I am in the mood to shoot someone so dont be too persnickety as we say hello to Mary I can hear her laugh now & it is something to give a man courage even if it is at him & really cheer a fellow up give her my best to you too——

Gaddis

Getty station: Getty Oil used to have gas stations in the northeast until the mid 1980s.

Mrs Getty: Teddy Getty Gaston (1913–2017).

Jewsharp [...] harmonica: from a limerick: "There was an old Jew from Salonika / Who for Christmas wanted a harmonica. / His wife, to annoy him, / Said 'Christmas's for goyim, / But I'll give you a Jew's harp for Hanukkah.'"

its one day sunny [...] to explain: from Don Marquis's *the lives and times of archy and mehitabel* (1940).

this sullen craft: from Dylan Thomas's poem "In My Craft or Sullen Art."

The Last Act: the working title of *FHO*. Other titles he contemplated are "Damages," "Articles of War," "The Last Clear Chance," and "True Wars Are Never Won."

Jesus Jack the child is black: an old Dublin catch-phrase, used in the Penelope chapter of Joyce's *Ulysses* (18.163).

John Tower: an ugly Republican senator (1925–1991), known for his womanizing and heavy drinking.

Ludlow fair: from Housman's poem "Terence, This Is Stupid Stuff": "Oh I have been to Ludlow fair / and left my necktie God knows where" (ll. 29–30).

To Ann Patty

[*Publisher (1953–) and Editorial Director of Poseidon Press, an imprint of Simon & Schuster that she founded in 1982. After Allen Peacock left S&S, FHO was passed along to her. Poseidon went under in 1993; FHO, published on 17 January 1994, was one of its last titles.*]

Wainscott, New York 11975

13 September '92

Dear Ann Patty,

thank you for your letter (lately reached me at this address) & its kind wish for a 'lovely summer' which in fact turned out quite otherwise, the only lasting & pertinent item to emerge from the chaos being that the book has not prospered as much as I'd hoped & intended but I now have some 200 pages beyond what you have in your folder & its plotless plot right now reaching a boiling point: would you care to see it?

And thank you for the Erickson book whose story interests me (what a time Quayle would have with the situation!) which I've put aside for the moment though for the record I've never written a 'blurb' (& don't solicit them) so that won't affect its sales not that it would.

Oh I would pray for the fall '93 publication date you mention for me though God knows the gaps between even the completed text & that grand moment (especially borne in upon me by Penguin's next-summer note for *The Recognitions* & *J R* in their Classic Series with the corrected film already in hand from the earlier ed.).

Well back to work

with best regards

W Gaddis

Erickson book: Steve Erickson's *Arc D'X* (1993), a surreal dystopian novel.

Quayle: American politician (1947–), vice president under the first Bush and the subject of a squib by WG that had just appeared in the August issue of *Esquire* (*RSP* 114).

To Gregory Comnes

[*For the visit WG refers to, see headnote to 5 November 1988. Comnes had finished revising his dissertation and sent a copy to WG. The Comnes kept in touch with WG during his final years, and in April 1993 spent two days with Sarah and him in Key West, "during which he spun tales ranging from his time spent with Robert Graves to musing how perfect Macaulay Culkin would have been in a movie version of* J R" (*email 23 August 2022*).]

Wainscott, New York 11975
15 October 1992

dear Greg Comnes,

indeed I remember your visit (& at risk of sounding rude more for that breathtaking beauty in your company than, say, Walter Benjamin) but had not counted on the extraordinary issue from it that you have sent me, in the shape of Agape Agape & Indeterminacy, & am struck & gratified by the argument grasped & glossed in your accompanying letter regarding "how, if at all, being moral had any legitimacy in the postmodern world" & "the willingness of people to act without the sanction of absolutes" all of which, I believe, continue to occupy (read "obsess") me to an even further (read "despairing") degree in my 500+ page work in hand which opens with the fine old saw "You get justice in the next world, in this world you have the law" trying desperately now to surface from the deluge of my usual vastly overresearched material to wind the thing up for "another damned, thick, square book."

Thus in no particular order: I hadn't meant to "fuss" over your allusions to Walter Benjamin: it has been remarked elsewhere his obvious influence on my work & thought though—as I must have told you to my embarrassment—I hadn't known of him, & certainly would have been pilloried for plagiary had I ever completed my own *Agape Agape: the Secret History of the Player Piano* which became (cf. Gibbs) a casualty of overresearch; but then of course in my ignorance Benjamin had already clearly, concisely, brilliant & briefly covered the ground.

Gregory and Judith Comnes

And thus in this mixture of frustration & revelation we constantly find ourselves preempted by those "selves who could do more" and did, as Frank on the greatest of them: "Not to believe in God and immortality, for the later Dostoevski, is to be condemned to live in an ultimately senseless universe; and the characters in his great novels who reach this level of self awareness inevitably destroy themselves because, refusing to endure the torment of living without hope, they have become monsters in their misery." (& to see this rambunctious agony played out in our own time stagger through the marvelous new Stannard biography of Evelyn Waugh vol. 2)

And thus as I've grown older (how one cowardly shrinks from saying simply & forthrightly "grown old" as in When Dostoevski was my age he'd been dead for a decade) my youthful romantic preoccupations with love redemption not to say 'God' have quite given way to simply struggling with, documenting & surviving the senseless universe op.cit. in pursuing Gibbs' dilemma both in work and 'real life' over how we who cry out for order seem to lead the most disorderly existences (as, in a recent note from Bill Gass, "We must get together and celebrate something, even if it's only our weary selves and our out-of-whack lives.").

And so on to another old saw, the Hollywood star: We've talked enough about me now let's talk about you, what did you think of my last movie?

Waugh's late years are my bedside reading otherwise I daren't turn what is left of my mind & time on earth to any more serious reading than the daily paper until this literally Last Act is done. The reach of your letter is quite enough; but I believe, with it & spotting through* your MS & rather staggering bibliography, I am even more overwhelmed by the foreboding that the future is already here, & thus while I frequently enough see my work cited in a postmodern context I cower in the notion of a traditional novelist to such a degree that, sitting back & looking at this work in hand, I am often enough depressed at the notion that it will be dismissed as behind the times much as this letter on a 20year old portable in the face of word processors computer screens &c in the hands of 10year olds leave me outdistanced by an eon. I have to say then that seeing what you have done makes the blood race, makes up in some part for me the reassurance of "what is worth doing" & I hope you must not take it amiss that I do not for now pursue it all further here but simply send this along with thanks & appreciation & my very best regards to you

and the stunning blonde, of course
W. Gaddis

*I did give a passing glimpse at it to 2 fellows you might recognize Frederick Karl & Walter Abish passing through who were more at home with the allusions & citations & pronounced it 'eminently readable'...what will be its disposition? a univ. press? (or even a Dalkey Archive

---

Walter Benjamin: WG would work in references to Benjamin in *AA*.

Frank: from Joseph Frank's *Dostoevsky: The Years of Ordeal, 1850–1859* (Princeton UP, 1983), 159.

Stannard: Martin Stannard, *Evelyn Waugh: The Later Years 1939–1966* (New York: Norton, 1992).

a univ. press: as noted earlier, it was eventually published by the University Press of Florida in early 1994.

To Steven Moore

[*In September 1992 I sent WG two copies of Dalkey Archive's edition of Jack Green's* Fire the Bastards!, *disregarding Green's earlier refusal to grant permission to reprint his work. (It was in the Public Domain, hence Green's permission wasn't legally necessary.) As this letter makes clear, WG was still upset that I had sold his letters the previous year.*]

Wainscott

15 October 1992

dear Steven Moore,

    sorry to be so late thanking you for sending the finished copies of the Jack Green opus (might even have added an appendix page of the review parodies of *The Recognitions* in *J R*) held back probably by the conflict in my head & history between vain pleasure at seeing Green's work preserved & circulated on the one hand & on the other my strong feelings over a writer's wishes for & implicit rights to his work & privacy however legally encroached upon over which I've tangled with (Judge) Pierre Leval from the Salinger case onward, goes I suppose with an oversensi[ti]vity over seeing one's private letters sold where I suppose a case can be made for 'making a market' for the eventual 'archive' as patrimony.

    Penguin Classic eds. of the above apparently not due till next summer.

    I have received an extraordinary & detailed exegesis from Greg Comnes with which you're probably familiar but am too consumed with the work in hand to give it the thorough attention it demands & I am sure deserves.

Yours,

WG.

Pierre Leval: see headnote to 10 August 1993.

Penguin Classics eds.: new editions of *R* and *J R* appeared in the summer of 1993, the former with an introduction by William H. Gass, the latter one by Frederick R. Karl.

———

To Ivan Nabokov

[*See note to 22 August 1987. He had published the French translation of* CG *that year and was preparing for* J R *in 1993 (both translated by novelist Marc Cholodenko, who would later translate* FHO *as well.) The following is a fax, a medium WG had just begun using.*]

27 October 1992

Dear Ivan,

what a great pleasure hearing your voice this morning bursting with good news and enthusiasm! These are the citations I mentioned if they may be of any use to you and *J R* even though they embrace both books. I do not solicit (or give out) 'blurbs' but once they appear independently it seems valid to use them.

These are citations that were written proposing my membership in The American Academy and Institute of Arts and Letters (Bellow, 1984) and then for the inner American Academy of Arts and Letters itself (McCarthy, 1989); Bellow has given his permission and McCarthy God rest her soul would I know.

Aesop's vixen, pleased with her numerous litter, asked the lioness how many offspring she had. The lioness said, "One. But a lion." Gaddis has published two novels, each of them a lion. These are bold, powerful books ambitious in conception and elegant—leonine—in execution.

—Saul Bellow

William Gaddis is pure prodigy. He has a fantastic ear for American speech with the strictest attention and exactitude such an ear demands but, strangely crossed with that, the wildest of imaginations. He is horrid and funny. His three novels—*The Recognitions, J R,* and *Carpenter's Gothic*—are massive in ambition and dazzling in execution. They are fierce with integrity.

—Mary McCarthy

Whatever their use 'commercially' you may only imagine how deeply pleased I was when I first saw them (& remain so!). And with what an appetite I look forward to seeing your 'press kit' and the cover posthaste even a xerox—and of course the book itself (a prepublication copy?) and yourself early next year.

very best regards,
William Gaddis

To Saul Bellow

Wainscott, New York 11975
31 October 1992

Dear Saul,

a note of real thanks to you for your generosity in the use of your Academy citation by the Penguin people for the reissue of *The Recognitions* and *J R* in their 'Classic Series'.

Since I have always avoided writing and soliciting 'blurbs' I felt the notion of this request shadowed by an infringement both on friendship and good manners, since presumably these citations bear the confidentiality of the higher order of clubs; but as Saul Steinberg—another man for the scrupulously chosen word and image—observed in his good offices here, it would be a pity to see the marvelously conceived endorsement moulder away in the Academy's vaults and so I am elated now as I was when first saw it.

In licensing the rights to this 'Classic Series' it was quite clear that their list is mainly posthumous, meaning I assume they may dispense with the annoyance of paying royalties or deal bluntly with 'the estate of' unfettered by the unreasonable price the author himself might place on his wistful vision of inkstained immortality where we find even Sidney Sheldon leading the pack demanding publication on acid-free paper. But having now been relegated as a 'classic' in this age of Madonna (& Sidney Sheldon) your imprimatur so cleanly marks the line between literature and the deluge of sheer books and it's that which I find inordinately gratifying in this battle to simply last them out.

Bearing down myself though on both 3 score & 10 and the shattered ending of what increasingly looks like 'another damned, thick, square book' it's difficult to hold at bay the despair of finding it an episodic sitcom as the word and indeed the world now has it and the wish for the day to say goodbye to all that.

Notwithstanding, as all these considerations begin to strike closer to the bone they inform me of the quite serious cast of my best wishes to you for good health and yet longer work and life,

William Gaddis

Sidney Sheldon: American TV producer and best-selling novelist (1917–2007). In 1989, Sheldon and nearly a hundred other writers and publishers signed a pledge to use "acid-free paper for all first printings of quality hard-cover trade books."

goodbye to all that: perhaps only coincidentally the title of Robert Graves's early memoir (1929).

To Jack Green

[*After I sent Green copies of the Dalkey edition of* Fire the Bastards!, *he wrote me an insulting letter threatening legal action—which I ignored, knowing nothing would come of it—and mailed a copy of his letter to WG.*]

Wainscott, New York 11975
20 November 1992

Well Jack Green,

long live intransigence! What are we dealing with: in a splendid (as always) phrase from Bill Gass 'the high brutality of good intentions'? Hovering as I have always done between the limelight & obscurity this butterfly of the divided self (a basic theme of 'another damned, thick, square book'* I am finishing now) pinned to the wall by Steven Moore's attentions, 2 books past on my work & future threat of publication of my letters even & 'biography'? which is dull stuff I would proclaim having just finished v. II of Stannard's marvelous *Evelyn Waugh*.

You see by the enclosed that indeed I did receive copies of his publication as what he must have felt my curt note witnesses (I have not heard from him since) every letter of mine (Dear Miss Tillingast Thank you so much for your perfumed and generous estimate of my work, might I ask you to send me a snapshot of yourself naked) being worth $1 or so to the patrimonial archive, Lord! to have the thunderous integrity of Samuel Butler say (his fine novel published posthumously) or even Sir Richard Burton's wife burning his papers (for all the wrong reasons) or what about Nietzsche's crazy sister's recreation, Hauptmann's (& even Heidrich(sp?)'s) widows + Mary Hemingway's uxorial rehabilitative efforts, on to Mme Pasteur ('Oh Looie! all Paris is talking…')

God knows how I got off on all this, not a glass of spirits in 3 years but a little wine for the stomach's sake trying desperately to close out the * above now at 500++ 8½x14 pages much, in fact, dealing with copyright (a man's illfated play stolen for The Movie) law but law law everywhere as usual over researched having been given the 84 vol. *AmJur* (next step down from *Corpus Juris*) hoping against hope (whatever that fine cliche may mean) to be done with it by year's end & perhaps my own but otherwise expect to be in NY later in the winter & would be a tonic to see you again with fair warning.

best regards
W. Gaddis

Butler […] posthumous novel: written in the 1880s, *The Way of All Flesh* was not published until 1903, a year after his death.

Sir Richard Burton's wife: Isabel Burton burned many of his papers and manuscripts "to protect his reputation."

Nietzsche's crazy sister's recreation: Elisabeth Förster-Nietzsche published his writings in mangled form after his death in 1900. See *AA* 77–78.

Hauptmann: after the death of German dramatist Gerhart Hauptmann (1862–1946), his widow kept his archives secret.

Heidrich: in 1951, the widow of Nazi official Reinhard Heydrich turned down an offer by a Welsh writer to split the royalties 50-50 on a book about her husband.

Mary Hemingway: authorized the posthumous publication of novels that her husband Ernest (1899–1961) may not have wished to be published.

Mme Pasteur: holding rights to the French chemist's name, his widow allowed another scientist to call his laboratory Institut Pasteur du Brabant.

To Muriel Oxenberg Murphy

[One of several letters and faxes WG sent to Mrs. Murphy over the next few years as their relationship deteriorated. Two of hers to him are reprinted in her Excerpts, *pp. 202–4.]*

[undated fax, 1992/1993?]

OR—accepting your good point that Ibsen has given us the 2nd act curtain only with Nora stamping out the door resolute? or in despair?—of course her (fictional 'ideal') husband Helmer is left in utter despair & confusion finally understanding "what has really happened" as GBShaw tells us "and sits down alone to wonder whether that more honourable relation can ever come to pass between them." But she has, after all, "learnt to coax her husband into giving her what she asks by appealing to his affection for her: that is, by playing all sorts of pretty tricks until he is wheedled into an amourous humor" (and my! Claire Bloom certainly could in Joyce's phrase make his mickey stand for him) . . . suppose, in his confused crushed angered self pity Helmer wonders whether she has taken a leaf from an egregious best seller of the 60s called *Games People Play* and is in effect daring him to come after her, invite her back, enlist family friends & seek 'professional help' shrinks & priests all to yield to the burden of the crippling proposition that it's hardly over unless *he* wants it to be? Still mightily confused 'after all he's done for her' trips he's taken her on, gifts he's tried to give her, friends and unspeakable practices & delights they've shared and all she has given him, does wretched Helmer left sitting there simply pour a glass of schnapps (it being Scandanavia)? or stand up and walk out the door himself up the country road breathing deeply on this beautiful fall day, same old squirrels, same old bunny rabbits scampering from his path, trying to clear his head thinking & hoping that with the help of the Great Script Doctor in the sky that this may be a 4 act play after all?

Ibsen [...] GBShaw: WG quotes from the conclusion of Shaw's analysis of Ibsen's 1879 play *A Doll's House* in *The Quintessence of Ibsenism* (Brentano's 1928), 92.

Claire Bloom: the English actress (1931–) played Nora both on stage and in the 1973 film version of *A Doll's House*.

Joyce's phrase make his mickey stand: a few pages from the end of Molly Bloom's monologue in *Ulysses*.

Games People Play: a 1964 book by Dr. Eric Berne on the psychology of human relationships.

To Saul Steinberg

[*Typed on the back of a rough draft of a paragraph on page 570 of* FHO *that cites lines from Longfellow's* Hiawatha.]

Wainscott, NY
4 January 1993

Dear Saul,

it is not a paper shortage here that prompts this (overleaf) as my letter paper but it occurred to me you might be amused by these desperate notes for the morass I'm engulfed in out here trying perhaps unsuccessfully & surely unnecessarily to join up fragments of Longfellow's *Hiawatha* with the tenants of a home aquarium in this last ditch effort to roll up this whole ball of wax (speaking of mixed metaphors) which keeps me from coming into town this week for not merely the pleasure but the happy need of your company at one of our simple dinners together which have meant a great deal to me as perhaps never more than now with the opportunity to thank you for your overpowering gift & so much else.

Muriel returns on Saturday from her London trip with her companion & I have the rather desperate but not entirely impossible hope of finishing the near final draft of this project which has oppressed our house like a contagious illness for so long ridden of course with the deep fear of its being too late to save the situation or any human part of it if I could ever have done so which you were subjected to in its latest & most painful manifestation at the Century: all I may have learned from it is that my daughter's torments here on these occasions have blinded me to her own very perilous condition anywhere & that that must be my first assignment, especially given what have increasingly seemed to become my futile and too often intemperate efforts to resolve or at

least to deal effectively with the domestic situation which now embraces this
3rd party 'analyst' to in my view a quite bizarre degree. Of course I may have
got the whole thing backwards if indeed the topsy-turvy world we see on the
evening news is the real one.*

Well enough for now of this burden on your ~~generosity~~ friendship which
you have shown us both in so many ways over what have become so many
years, I look forward to seeing you in a short time and in a better climate for
my wishes to you for a 'happy new year',

with every high regard,
Gaddis

PS I have reread & still think Updike might have framed exactly the points
he claims undraped by the 'melancholy' he himself inhabits.

*And so I go back where I came from, to reading Eliot,
> To explore the womb, or tomb, or dreams; all these are usual
> Pastimes and drugs, and features of the press:
> And always will be, some of them especially
> When there is distress of nations and perplexity
> Whether on the shores of Asia, or in the Edgware Road

(1943)

---

the Century: the Century Club in Manhattan.
Updike: reference unknown. See headnote to the fax dated 5 August 1996.
Eliot [...] in the Edgware Road: from part 5 of "Dry Salvages."

To Donald Oresman

Wainscott, New York 11975
18 Jan. '93

Dear Donald,

first to thank you for 'this year's sheaf' of literary pointers from which I
happily gather you are well & fully operational; next to report that I turned
in the last of the full (629pp) MS of this sometime law novel last week to the
attention of Ann Patty at Poseidon whither I was diverted when the young
Alan Peacock left the S&S fold. What she will make of it I do not know.

I recall, as I have continually throughout the process, your prompting that
what was at stake here was a *novel* & not an agonizedly accurate legal treatise
(Was *Arrowsmith* any the better for Lewis's having checked every blister &
catheter with the doctors? you asked) & so it has come about with *The Last
Act* (a rather weak title I think & expect to change).

And so, as is hardly unusual, during the daily desperate course of it over the past 2 or 3 years, it changed of its own accord in that direction away from the series of legal briefs & opinions I had originally & haplessly envisioned, although the characters are from first to last entangled in legal thickets from the sublime to the ridiculous & the 'story' just as I planned it right through the last despairing outcry. (Was there a retort ascribed to Joyce when asked regarding *Ulysses*, What's it about? 'It's not about something, it *is* something'?)

At any rate I am getting my breath for the patchwork yet to be done amidst bright spots on the publishing horizon: both *The Recognitions* & *J R* appearing in the Penguin XXth Century Classic series around May, & a trip before that to Paris for the publication of *J R* in the French language which I can scarcely imagine.

And so perilous as it may be I am finally able to try in some way to thank you for your concern & repeated patient & willing efforts at encouragement right from your first mailing of Palsgraf v LIRR through the now dogeared casebook on torts—still left now with the drained feeling of not having got in the prolonged brief on Episcopal Church of America v Pepsico (aka 'Pepsicola') though the case is there fleetingly, as with others, recalling Tolstoy's dismayed outcry waking the day *War & Peace* went to press with My God! I left out the yacht race!

with very best regards and hopes of seeing you soon
Bill

To Ann Patty

[*Selections from the first two acts of WG's old play* Once at Antietam *appear in* FHO; *he enclosed the third and final act.*]

235 East 73rd str.
New York 10021
24 February "93

dear Ann Patty,
here (literally) is the last act. You will see, it is quite heavyhanded, inflated &c rising to heights almost, in fact, as bad as O'Neill. But it is perhaps what Oscar as we now know him from the book might have written (even to Oedipus' blinding at the end). (There are references to items cut from the passages quoted in the book such as his daughter, the watch & tobacco case which may confuse.) However I am terribly pleased at your comment that you love reading the play whenever you come to it in the book & relieved that you don't find it obtrusive since it should function, like the Opinions, as documentation;

& like them, set in a different type, skimable or skipable for the LemonHaupts in the audience. I had omitted it both for the length & with some esoteric notion of 'the melancholia of things completed' as well as for its highblown pretensions but am curious what your impression will be.

From a quick review of your comments they all seem to me very well taken, helpful useful &c—with perhaps an exception or two when I come to them— very much to the point. Especially the Basie/Mudpye repetition of the O'Neill references which had in fact just struck me after finishing the thing looking back & thinking how did I let this happen? So I'd already faced the chore of somehow rectifying it. (I agree on somehow tying up the O'Neill estate suit at the end.)

I see your point regarding the length of the Deposition, had also already thought of trimming for instance Mudpye's police/criminal symbiosis allegory; but every time I've been through the whole thing I've found it about the fastest reading in the book perhaps for its profound absurdity as legal procedures go (most depositions of this nature running 1 or 2 or more hundred pages); & again, in a different typeface, lightning skimable but to the heart of the pivotal issue for the 'serious reader' & the horde of disillusioned lawyers out there.

What do you think of this title for the book: *Once at Antietam* ?

I am here drudging away & at your call on shortest notice, as yet unclear how long my patchwork will take & want your rough schedule whenever you have it.

Needless to say your concluding 'brilliant, amazing, important novel' is most heartening.

Yours,
W. Gaddis

'the melancholia of things completed': a line from Nietzsche's *Beyond Good and Evil* that WG first used in *R* (69, 599) and again in *J R* (486).

To Muriel Oxenberg Murphy

Sunday evening
[February/March 1993?]

Dear Muriel,

Maybe a way of putting it is that I think you have 'star quality' and I am trying to understand what I mean by that, but I think I have always thought that, the first time we met and when we met again and every day since but having got it into those two words I see what a marvelously complex idea it is and a difficult one—that I had simply accepted it when we came together counting my blessings every day and night and it is true you never leave my thoughts happy or proud troubled or fearful whatever they are or all of these at once and so as I say so difficult to try to face and figure out and satisfy except at last how terribly and sadly apparently true how I have not succeeded and, apparently again, till this last year or so taken for granted that I had—you must imagine it was quite painful to hear you write off the times we've had together here there and places in the world I've taken you as a mere decade alcoholic haze with "I've had better times" but what a dreadful thing it would be to lose it now. Well it's surely enough raining out there and I am trying to get my work done and to figure out 'star quality'* here for starters, perhaps you can?

With much love, at least I hope you know that,
W.

not to be confused with 'star complex', 'star struck' &c—

To Muriel Oxenberg Murphy

[A fax: the first half refers to two essays published in the February 1993 issue of Dædalus—*which WG received as a member of the American Academy of Arts and Sciences—and the second half evokes the sights he and Mrs. Murphy saw during their travels the previous decade.]*

3 March 93

The almost forgotten blessing of sleeping in a real bed again....

how subtly one's horizons shrink, lower, close in, constrict & finally suffocate—& how the metaphor of the real open landscape can suddenly release it, turn it wide & free to the lost illusion of all kinds of possibilities with the sun rising in an open sky spreading the day out before you freed from Miko Dwyer's speculations on social scientific hypotheses & the brilliant insights of M Csikszentmihalyi's observation that "Human beings appear to value two distinct sets of conditions. The first is pleasure, and it consists of genetically determined stimulation that the organism seeks out...The second condition that people seek out is enjoyment. Enjoyment differs from pleasure in that it is not a homeostatic process..."

good God, can one imagine a greater damper for sheer JOY?

I thought I heard Buddy Bolton shout

Open up these windows, let some of this foul air out...

I loved the one I discovered all this with here over the pond,

or on the Acropolis
or the Nevsky prospect
and the Kremlin gate
and the hotel courtyard in the rue Jacob
overlooking Lake Como
or Butler's pass to New Zealand's South Island & Erewhon beyond
and the Tiber
and the Danube
and the Rhine, the Thames, the Seine
and the morning and the evening
cannot be dismissed as an alcoholic haze,
believe me.

Miko Dwyer's speculations: the name sociologist Thomas J. Cottle gives to a ten-year-old girl who speculates that adults must *give* children joy, which she hasn't known since her grandmother died; see his "Witness of Joy," *Dædalus* 122.1 (Winter 1993): 135–36.

M Csikszentmihalyi's observation: on p. 40 of the same issue of *Dædalus*. Mihaly Csikszentmihalyi (1934–2021) was a Hungarian-American psychology professor best known for his book *Flow: The Psychology of Optimal Experience* (Harper & Row, 1990), where he offers similar observations.

I thought I'd heard [...] foul air out: a couplet from Jelly Roll Morton's rendition of "Buddy Bolton's Blues," composed by African-American jazz cornetist Charles Bolden (*sic*, 1877–1931).

Butler's pass to [...] Erewhon: Butler's *Erewhon* is set in New Zealand.

To Donald Oresman

Wainscott, NY
20 April 1993

Dear Donald,

'No good deed goes unpunished' as they say, hence in gratitude for your last researches here in the spirit of Sarah Bernhardt's positively last farewell appearance.

Does LEXIS® NEXIS® go so far back as 1834 to provide the context for Baron Parke's classic phrase 'going on a frolic of his own' as cited by Prosser in Joel v. Morrison, 1834, 6 C. & P. 501, 172 Eng.Rep 1338[?]

I'm glad you find *A Frolic of His Own* 'by far the best' [of proposed titles] & am quite settled on it. The above information is hardly vital since the phrase is explained loosely far into the text dialogue [398] & might even be used as an epigraph if easily available the fuller context might provide even further entertainment, if not we shall certainly survive (carrying the notion further as one is inclined to do waking at 3 am, 'going on a frolic of his own' is in a world governed by laws really what the artist is eventually all about.

> best wishes again,
> Bill Gaddis

Sarah Bernhardt: French actress (1844–1923).

LEXIS® NEXIS®: online search services for legal documents and newspaper articles, respectively, now called LexisNexis.

Joel v. Morrison: a case cited by Prosser in his *Torts*: "In 1834 Baron Parke uttered the classic phrase, that a master is not liable for the torts of his servant who is not at all on his master's business, but is 'going on a frolic of his own.'"

To James Cappio

21 May 1993

Dear Jim Cappio.

Many thanks for your note (& enclosures). I too have been feeling pangs of conscience over the hiatus.

The book is done. Its title is

A Frolic of His Own

which came to me in reading Master & Servant lore, the Master ('God'?) liable for his Servant (Jesus)'s tort while on the master's business (Know ye not that I am on my Father's business?) but not if the servant is off 'on a frolic of his own' (Joel v. Morrison, 1834, 6 C & P. 501, 172 Eng.Rep. 1338 by Baron Parke).

The 640pp MS went in to Simon&Schuster/Poseidon in Feb after months of 5am days, copyread & marked for printer, returned to me for queries (Apr), returned to Poseidon via Federal Express, who lost it. A week of agony. They found it minus p. 638, 3 days recasting that, & it is now presumably in the hands of the printers; Poseidon (ed. Ann Patty) appear very pleased, most cooperative with me regarding various type faces (text, opinions &c), art title page &c & there should be galleys in a couple of weeks about the time I go in for prostatectomy to then review & revise at my convalescent leisure assuming of course that in the course of things I have not gone off on a frolic* of my own.

I would hope to get you a set of galleys but this mayn't be feasible & have to wait for the bound ones but will keep you advised (*nisi),

> very best regards,
> Gaddis

Know ye not [...] Father's business?: Luke 2:49.

nisi: Latin, "unless," used in legal proceedings.

To Robert Coover

[*Fabulist fictionist (1932–) and a professor at Brown University since 1980. Stephen Wright (1949–) is another innovative novelist; his superb first novel,* Meditations in Green, *appeared in 1983.*]

Wainscott, New York 11975

19 June 1993

Dear Bob.

I am glad to recommend Stephen Wright for any opening there may be on your teaching staff at Brown in the area of writing on the strength of my memory of having been impressed a few years ago reading through his novel *Meditations in Green.* I haven't seen his subsequent works but the very fact of his having published a second and finished a third rather lengthy novel makes clear that he is committed to the work in all its wonder and drudgery and should, after evident talent, I think be the first qualification for spreading our plague among the young who want not to 'be writers' but to write.

with regards,

W. Gaddis

To William H. Gass

[*Gass invited WG to participate in a symposium on "The Writer and Religion" that would be held at the International Writers Center at Washington University in October 1994. WG delivered a lecture entitled "Old Foes with New Faces," which was published the following year in the* Yale Review, *again in* The Writer and Religion, *ed. Gass and Lorin Cuoco (Southern Illinois University Press, 2000), and reprinted (minus its final page) in RSP 88–108.*]

Wainscott

25 Jne "93

Dear Bill,

your invitation is irresistable—caveats about the 'literary reading' aspect of course though I assume we'll have tangled with that in Hollywood (which does sound like 'a gas' if you pardon the expression I look forward to it) in fact, I was dizzied enough at first reading that I took it for this ('93) October as a launching pad for publication of a novel touching on this same topic* to appear in January following but of course by the appointed date all AMER-ICA will have read it & a bounty (cf Rushdie) on my head from the vested interests as noted below.

And so I will hope to appear at your doorstep much like Prince K. in D's *Uncle's Dream* arriving at Mordasov 'so decrepit, so worn out, that as one looked at him the thought instinctively occurred to one that in another minute he might drop to pieces' having, last week, a 10year lithium battery pacemaker installed beneath the clavicle as a cautionary step before next week's shaving of the prostate with other repairs to follow ('the Prince had made a brilliant debut, he had led a gay life, flirted, had made several tours abroad, sang songs, made puns, and had at no period been distinguished by the brilliance of his intellectual gifts. Of course he had squandered all his fortune, and found himself in his old age without a farthing.')

*to the contrary notwithstanding I felt it wise to put you on notice of the sort of goods you are bargaining for & so enclose a sample here—it is as you see galley time at Oblomovka-by-the-Sea where it would be a great treat if you were passing through but failing that

the warmest wishes to you both,
Willie

Hollywood: WG and Gass had been invited there for a program the following January; see 6 February 1994.

Rushdie: Islamic extremists pronounced a death sentence on British writer Salman Rushdie (1947–) after the publication of *The Satanic Verses* in 1988.

D's *Uncle's Dream*: an 1859 novella by Dostoevsky. (Prince K. is a senile aristocrat.) The quotations are from the beginning of chapter 2, in Constance Garnett's translation (pp. 229–30 in *The Short Novels of Dostoevsky* [Dial Press, 1945], which Gaddis purchased in his twenties).

To Peter Friedman

[*A New York City attorney and a fan of WG's fiction; having heard he was working on a novel about lawyers, Friedman wrote to offer any legal assistance he might need.*]

Wainscott, New York 11975
30 July 1993

Dear Peter Friedman.

Thank you for your generous offer and most impressive (both in extent & legal bent) resume in connection with the morass of legal fiction I'd got myself into; however we may both probably count our blessings that it comes along too late or it might have taken another 5 years & thousand pages from both our lives.

As of today, under the title *A Frolic of His Own* (Joel v. Morrison, 1834, 6 C.&P. 501, 172 Eng.Rep. 1338) the entire 600+ pages of turmoil is in the hands of Poseidon / Simon & Schuster in the form of corrected galleys waiting to be cut & bound, packaged & remaindered over the months to come (publication date probably January '94) & thank the Lord to have it out of my hands.

Quite contrary to the received opinion of legal language as purposely obfuscatory I had come to admire its tortuous (no pun intended) struggles for precision & contingency ("holding these rights in perpetuity throughout the world and elsewhere"), was handed Palsgraf v. Long Island Railroad &, once hooked, on to Prosser & thence a gift of every human foible in *AmJur*'s all 84 vols. till finally a couple of years ago I sobered up to the fact that I was writing a novel of civilization & its discontents not a compendium of western law & finally surfaced a few months ago to my great relief & that of those around me albeit with decisions never to be reached & opinions never to be written. Which may be just as well.

At any rate I hope you will find the final product entertaining & perhaps even, as Conrad had it, with that little bit of truth we'd forgot to ask for.

Yours,

W. Gaddis

---

civilization and its discontents: title of a late work by Sigmund Freud (1930).

Conrad: from his preface to *The Nigger of the 'Narcissus'* (1897): "My task which I am trying to achieve is, by the power of the written word, to make you hear, to make you feel—it is, before all, to make you see. That—and no more, and it is everything. If I succeed, you shall find there according to your deserts: encouragement, consolation, fear, charm—all you demand; and, perhaps, also that glimpse of truth for which you have forgotten to ask." WG quotes this passage in both *J R* (449) and *FHO* (363).

To David Ulansey

[*A professor of philosophy and religion, author of* The Origins of the Mithraic Mysteries: Cosmology and Salvation in the Ancient World *(Oxford University Press, 1991). The letter is damaged; the brackets enclose tentative reconstructions.*]

Wainscott, New York 11975
30 July 1993

Dear David Ulansey,

most thoughtful of you to send me the copy of your *Mithraic Mysteries* which I'm now happily able to peruse at leisure rather than with the frantic research bent I'd have approached it those decades ago—1949 or so [having just] read Robert Graves' *White Goddess* &c, [living] in Spain & embarked on what became *The Recognitions*, went up to call on Graves in [Deya] (Mallorca) hoping for help in finding some [alterna]tive religion which a despairing rock bound [Protestant] preacher might turn to, a futile mission in that regard (Graves was still immersed in god & goddess & we somehow got off into the Salem witch trials) but the great treat of time spent with the man himself who became in a way, through his youthful enthusiasm, the physical model for Reverend Gwyon. At any rate I finally stumbled on what I thought the perfect vehicle in Mithraism & what seemed mercifully small amount of information on it but sufficient to my purposes probably all for the best since had your work been available I'd probably have become submerged & perhaps never surfaced. Thank you again,

Yours,
W. Gaddis

To Pierre N. Leval

[*A jurist (1936–) who had just been appointed to the United States Court of Appeals for the Second Circuit (New York, Connecticut, and Vermont), known in literary history for his role in J. D. Salinger's case against Ian Hamilton's use of quotations from the author's letters in his forthcoming biography; Judge Leval found it within the bounds of fair use, but his decision was reversed on appeal, a finding WG supported. The "Beatrice" of the first sentence was his mother.*]

Wainscott, New York 11975
10 August 1993

Dear Pierre,

discussing the unreliability of the *NY Times* with Beatrice here over dinner last night but this morning's edition does confirm the fine news she'd already given us of your elevation to the US Court of Appeals ("considered just a question of time" says the paper, indeed!) but we are not so blasé and find it most exciting and send our warmest congratulations.

It is even more impressive in the light of my own district court judge who dies on the eve of his confirmation for a seat on the appeals court at age 97 ('an interim appointment') in the book which is at last finished and going into print under the title *A Frolic of His Own* (Joel v. Morrison, 1834, 6 C.&P. 501, 172 Eng.Rpt. 1338); and it would have been appropriate to thank you for your generous interest and support on some sort of acknowledgment page but then I thought better of it since it must inevitably contain some legal howlers that would hardly reflect well on your good offices.

I will hope for the chance to see you out here before the summer is over, meanwhile Muriel sends her love and best wishes to you both and again, congratulations.

Bill

———

To Sarah Gaddis

14 August '93

Dear Sarah,

I have your letter & I know you are discouraged, have known it of course for this long time & know it all well because as you know I've been there myself—right from our start really from just the time you were born, living till then with and for this Great Book I was writing, had written, saw it drop like a shot & started a new life 'raising a family'; 2 years writing a long play & saw it as hopeless; 7 years writing another Great Book & saw it drop like a shot . . . & another marriage with it . . . easy enough now to say, the 2 books as 'classics', that it was all worth it but I certainly didn't know that at the time—& with Eliot writing 50 years ago 'Trying to learn to use words, and every attempt Is a wholly new start, and a different kind of failure . . . and now, under conditions That seem unpropitious' and that was 50 years ago, the times are certainly far less promising now for publishing good work or making good movies with MHG in facing the same vast tide of trash overwhelming all & everyplace, publisher or film studio, interested only in the 'bottom line' including my own Simon & Schuster I just thank heaven I got the book finished & got the advance when I could, all spent now but I could hardly ask for a deal like that again & may even sell a few copies.

All of which isn't really what all this is all about anyway, it's more about stopping & regrouping rather than 'giving up' as you say, giving up hopes & illusions perhaps but not the thing itself to 'always do it and be drawn to it' as you say again but, again as I've done more than once, to know when the time comes to give it a rest & turn one's efforts & energies elsewhere when one's own work done under conditions of desperation cannot be as good as it should be & eventually will be. I must say the whole area of foundation work does seem more suitable to you than anything I've ever heard & I should think your resume sounds made for it. The Lannan people I've talked with (notably Patrick himself) sound extraordinarily cool civilized thoughtful & steady calm in this chaotic corner (the arts) of this chaotic world & these chaotic times we live in & that any help they can give you sincere & real & to your credit seeing things in you that perhaps you've somewhat lost track of & I'm glad you're pursuing it & giving it a chance out there [Los Angeles] before you give up on the place itself, a little more time for it before you think of another major move. I must quickly make a minor one (to the post office) & will send you word of the nutty adventures at this end when I have it probably next week or so, wait & pray,

> much love always
> Papa

Eliot [...] unpropitious: from part 5 of "East Coker."
Lannan [...] Patrick: son of J. Patrick Lannan, who established the Lannan Foundation in 1960. In 1986 his son expanded the foundation's literary philanthropy.

To Judith Gaddis

[*Enclosed in a copy of* Flaubert–Sand: The Correspondence *(Knopf, 1993).*]

> [late August 1993]

Dear Judith,

I'd been reading this back in last rather grim winter & since your letter in the spring mentioning your imminent trip to France and Mme Sand's environs had meant to send it long before now, suddenly seeing that September when you plan to go is only days away. It is certainly one of the more touching friendships spawned by literature & its discontents & clearly I felt more than a little kinship with Flaubert though here of course the 17 year age difference is reversed & it's she who has the children & he the mother...

I look at the book I've just finished & wonder if it has any relation to life as we've lived & known it (though I'm sure the reviewers will straighten me out on that when it finally appears around the end of the year)... certainly it embraces little of the generous warmth of this letter of yours; & in a way the only real mirrors I have are Sarah & Matthew who are neither of them having an especially smooth or easy or happy time of it. It's all rather like the epigraph I'd chosen (but have since replaced) for this new novel: aunque sepa los caminos, yo nunca llegaré a Córdoba—in spite of knowing all the roads, I will never get to Cordoba.

I probably exaggerated the hospital episodes [heart trouble] from my own apprehensions & communicated elsewhere what Modern Medicine regards as quite routine & proved to be no more than thoroughly unpleasant discomfort, plumbing repairs in a word, but I have deeply felt your wonderfully generous love & concern & so we go forward counting our blessings as it were, I hope your France trip is a marvelous one,

> W

To Clare Alexander

[*Publishing Director at the London office of Penguin Viking. The Bosch artwork WG suggests below was indeed used for the cover of the UK edition, which appeared in June 1994. The artwork for the US edition, a family in-joke, was a "painting" from Sarah Gaddis's childhood.*]

Wainscott, New York 11975
17 September 1993

Dear Ms Alexander.

I was happy to have your letter with word that you will be publishing *A Frolic of His Own* in Britain next spring, and your courtesy in consulting me about the cover. Regarding the fax you speak of receiving of the US book jacket you may have seen an early & somewhat jumbled version (not to speak of the poor quality of faxed art in general) & I have asked Simon & Schuster to send you a fairly finished proof which I am quite pleased with.

Elsewhere I'm sure you've seen the really splendid covers on the new Penguin XXth Century Classic eds. of *J R* & *The Recognitions*, products of a frenzy of faxed exchanges between me & Michael Millman at Penguin New York, in fact looking over our rejections I come across the enclosed detail from H. Bosch's gigantic *Garden of Delights* which* I have found rather haunting & may intrigue you for the moment; & as anything turns up elsewhere I shall surely let you know.

The good Lord only knows where I shall be next spring when you publish, I should certainly like going down to Kew in Lilac time better than anything but there are so many contingencies I daren't think of them now. Meanwhile I look forward to continuing with this exchange.

with best regards,
W. Gaddis

*a point being to bring out the ironic rather than frivolous use of the fine word 'frolic' in cover art & lettering so it doesn't promise just another damn silly book like those engulfing the market here.

H. Bosch's gigantic *Garden of Delights*: *The Garden of Earthly Delights*, a triptych (87 x 153 inches) Bosch painted sometime between 1490 and 1510, which WG would have seen at the Prado in Madrid.

going down to Kew in Lilac time: the fifth stanza of Alfred Noyes's poem "The Barrel-Organ" begins "Go down to Kew in lilac-time, in lilac-time, in lilac time" (quoted in *ODQ*).

To Robert Creeley

[*American poet and critic (1926–2005), then teaching at SUNY Buffalo. The final paragraph refers to WG's designation by Governor Mario Cuomo as the official New York State Author for 1993–95, which entailed a trip to SUNY Albany for a ceremony.*]

Wainscott, New York 11975

20 September 1993

Dear Bob,

many thanks for your note & for taking interest in this agreeable plight we share: coming up with more \$\$ for the detritus than we ever did from the published work (Oh! to have the intransigent integrity of Justice OW Holmes ordering all his papers burnt & letting his Opinions stand for themselves nobody's business how he got there . . . of course he left most of his estate to the US Treasury though with taxes what they are we are doing practically the same thing.)

I've had various 'feelers' regarding my 'archives' even a visit from one of those Santa Barbara dealers a few years ago but have wanted to finish this last 586pp novel *A Frolic of His Own* now in bound proofs for Jan 94 publication & get all that dead matter back before considering the next move, & had had in fact a feeler from this Minkoff (mentioning yours) a couple of months ago saying he thought it's worth a good deal of money whatever that means, I responded with some estimate of the bulk of it (goes back complete to the MS &c of *The Recognitions*) but never heard again from him so heaven knows whom he's got now 'much interested' in buying, he knows where I am.

You won't happen to be in Albany around 10 November (I think is the date) will you? to see me canonized New York State Author (+ check) from the Governor? I'd be delighted if so,

best regards

Willie

Justice OW Holmes: Oliver Wendell Holmes (1841–1935), mentioned often with approval in *FHO* (23, 46, 109, 286, 429, 443, 472, and on 574 the quip about leaving his estate to the US Treasury).

Minkoff: George Robert Minkoff, a New York rare-book dealer and writer (not to be confused with the Robert Minkoff who wrote his dissertation on *R*.) WG never did sell his archives during his lifetime.

WG at the New York State Writers Institute, 10 November 1993,
upon being named State Author for 1993–95 (photo by Luanne Ferris).

To the Editors, *Iowa Review*

Wainscott NY 11975

28 September 1993

Dear Editors.

Thank you for the distinction you so generously heap upon me in your recent letter regarding your forthcoming issue on 'experimental fiction'. I fear however that in this deluge of critical approaches and categories—high modern, post-modern, deconstruction, post-structural, where I frequently see my work discussed at length—'experimental' is the one which I find specifically unsuited, due to my sense of the decline in the use and meaning of 'experimental' and 'experiment' from the blunt dictionary definition as 'A test made to demonstrate a known truth' to which I should happily subscribe, to the rather loose embrace of writing pursued willy-nilly in some fond hope of stumbling on those strokes of brilliance which that perfect poet Keats mistrusted even in himself observed with "It is true that in the height of enthusiasm I have been cheated into some fine passages; but that is not the thing."

From the start almost a half century ago I have believed (& Keats to witness) that I knew exactly what I am doing: as 'known truth' for example, that style must match content, hence the fragmentation in *The Recognitions*; language and disorder, and authorial absence going back to Flaubert, in *J R*; exercising the cliche in *Carpenter's Gothic*; language and order in *A Frolic of His Own*.

Thus it would be quite unseemly (not to say inflammatory) for me to name as 'carrying the torch of the experimental movement' writers who might well feel that they too know exactly what they are doing as I trust you will understand, as I trust you will further understand that I have no wish or intention of disparaging your enterprise, or of belittling your generous appraisal of my work. I have no short stories recent or otherwise, I do not wear T shirts, but can at least respond to your notion regarding 'the work of new and established visual artists who use text in their works' with the enclosed from Julian Schnabel's *Recognitions* Series (there are a half dozen or so of them nicely reproduced in his catalogues &c) which you may find pertinent.

With best regards,

W. Gaddis

Keats [...] not the thing": assessing himself in a letter to B. R. Haydon (8 March 1819), Keats wrote: "I am three and twenty with little knowledge and middling intellect. It is true that in the height of enthusiasm I have been cheated into some fine passages;

but that is not the thing" (so reads *ODQ*, WG's source; other editors read the last three words as "nothing"). Also quoted in *J R* (486).

Julian Schnabel's *Recognitions* Series: a 1987 suite of paintings featuring words or phrases from *R*, published in catalogue form as *Reconocimientos Pinturas del Carmen/The Recognitions Paintings del Carmen* (Kunsthalle Basel, 1989).

To Muriel Oxenberg Murphy

[*A fax handwritten in all caps and spaced thus:*]

> [Wainscott, NY]
> [2 November 1993]

THIS IS THE FIRST DAY THAT I HAVE FELT <u>WELL</u>
A CAR PASSES WITH A 6-POINT BUCK TIED
    ACROSS THE HOOD
THE SEDGE IS WITHERED AND GONE ACROSS
    THE POND—ONLY BARE RUINED CHOIRS
    OF BRANCHES
I VOTED
I HOPE YOU DID NOT VOTE
    FOR JUDGE PHYLLIS GANGEL
AND THAT YOU ARE WELL
AND AT PEACE
AND AN END TO THE DAY WITH A BRISK
    CORRECTIVE TO ALL THE PRAISE FOR THE
    BOOK FROM ELSEWHERE
ON A "RATHER TINNY NOTE" FROM OUR
FRIENDS AT
THE KRICKET REVIEW

WHAT A MISFORTUNE NOT TO SHARE
SO BEAUTIFUL A DAY OF COLOURS
SILENCE SERENITY HERE WITH YOU
AND YOUR CONSTANT CONCERN FOR
MY HEALTH BUT I AM AS MUCH
CONCERNED OVER YOURS WORN DOWN
EXHAUSTED NOT GOOD FOR THE
EQUALLY IMPORTANT MENTAL &

SPIRITUAL WELL BEING
I HOPE YOU CAN LET UP
SOON
SOON
     LOVE
        W

---

bare ruined choirs: from Shakespeare's Sonnet 73; see 30 Nov. 1979.

Judge Phyllis Gangel: a lawyer who in 1989 became an acting justice of the New York Supreme Court of New York County in 1989, and in 1993 was elected a justice.

"rather tinny note" [...] Kricket Review: *Kirkus*'s largely negative review of *FHO* (1 November 1993) concludes "all that finally seems left is a rather tinny note of pissed-off energy and formal subordination." As WG notes in his letters of February 1994, the novel was otherwise well received.

To Donn O'Meara and William Carnahan

[*A fax sent to each of these old friends. It begins with the opening lines of Tennyson's "Tithonus" (1859), a figure from Greek mythology who asked for and received immortality from his lover Eos, goddess of dawn, but forgot to ask to remain forever young. Now withered and decrepit "Here at the quiet limit of the world" (l. 7), he is transformed by Eos into a grasshopper.*]

19 November "93

And here The woods decay, the woods decay and fall, / The vapours weep their burthen to the ground, / Man comes and tills the field and lies beneath, / And after many a summer dies the swan . . . literally, literally; & did I ever mention that a ½ century ago I changed my middle name on Harvard's transcripts from 'Thomas' to 'Tithonus' there conjuring the day when through Eos' intervention I'd secure immortality forgetting, in our lust, to stipulate eternal youth, until the day comes round (Here at the quiet limit of the world) when, pitying, the Dawn to the rescue has him transformed into the grasshopper with its relentless immortal tdzzzk, tdzzzk, tdzzzk . . .

now designated New York State's official State Author ($10 thousand, to help pay the taxes on) the Lannan award ($50 thousand), another damned thick square book

meanwhile the electrical and plumbing ravages attended to: a pacemaker, prostate resection, inguinal hernia I tell you it's all metaphor.

In fact, I may well have looked you up last July had not the prostate venture kept me wandering the corridors of New York Hospital, a bag of bloody urine tied to my leg, from joining Eos (Muriel Oxenberg) tripping to a working (filming) visit to the archaeological dig at Ashkelon stopping off at the Wailing Wall to have a good cry; & despite Eliot's dictum that old men ought to be explorers I find the notion of travel increasingly unattractive echoing, I believe, your own reservations

OR EVEN —not a glass of spirits lo these 4 years (but a glass of wine for the stomach's sake) still fighting the tobacco monster breathless at the thought of staggering up those heights at Bellagio ever again,

Aunque sepa los caminos,
yo nunca llégare a Córdoba

as the original epigraph for this imminent (january) last book which I replaced at the last minute with Thoreau (to Emerson):

What you seek in vain for, half your life, one day you come full upon, all the family at dinner. You seek it like a dream, and as soon as you find it you become its prey.

tdzzzk tdzzzk tdzzzk ...
with corresponding best wishes,
WG

Lannan award: he received its Lifetime Achievement Award earlier in 1993 and flew to Los Angeles to receive it.
Ashkelon: ancient coastal city in Israel, about 50 miles west of Jerusalem's Wailing Wall.
Eliot's [...] explorers: from part 5 of "East Coker."
Aunque [...] Thoreau: see note to 10 May 1989.

To Charles Monaghan

[*Monaghan informed WG that his publisher for the British edition of* R, *Timothy O'Keeffe, died on 11 January 1994. Monaghan had also had just read* A Frolic of His Own, *published in January.*]

[22 January 1994]

Sorry to hear about Tim O'Keeffe but we are beginning to get more such news daily, last time I saw him was at London pub some years ago & did the drink help him along? I've had no spirits (wine only) these 4 years & can't say I like it but thanks for your note & glad you liked the book

—Gaddis

To William H. Gass

[*On 18 January 1984 the Lannan Foundation sponsored an event in Los Angeles at which Gass spoke on WG, who then spoke briefly. See 13 April 1994 for more.*]

6 Feb. '94

dear Bill, dear Mary,

dear God that was a week that was & I am eternally grateful that you were both there both for our brief times together over Power Breakfast at that ridiculous hotel & the Tuesday evening Occasion when my health mental & physical seemed to ebb like the Bay of Fundy getting out alive with my honorarium still pricked by such regrets as what must have appeared consummate rudeness to your Lord John pal pressing books on me to sign in the backstage dark with someone's faulty fountain pen after his cordial invitations &c probably just as well the gas stove expired at the restaurant where Patrick Lannan had booked dinner for 40 & I understand he is turning his philanthropic attentions from paintings to such social concerns as the homeless (or the 'underserved' in foundationspeak).

I am delighted at the prospect of Knopf seizing *The Tunnel* especially just having read they are trimming their list & augmenting their publicity staff, quite opposite to S&S who are finally unbending for ½page ad in the *NYT Book Review* only with a really stunning array of reviews to draw from, *NY Review of Books Washington Post* 4 pages in the *New Republic* nothing seize the day about S&S I suppose they think with such free notices why advertise & so sic transit my 15minute fame: Think not the struggle naught availeth as the 6figure reprint sale fades & aunque sepa los caminos, yo nunca llegare a the man at the airport (though there may be a 5.5 aftershock in the *London Review of Books* you say, adding to my happily shouldered indebtedness to you).

Back to LA I did stay on till Sunday & opportunity to spend some time with Sarah which made it all worthwhile in her wholly fresh job/car/people life thank the good Lord, life here at daggers drawn goes on a good deal calmed, looking forward immensely to seeing you in May.

meanwhile with great affection,

Gaddis

that was a week that was: *That Was the Week That Was* was a short-lived but influential television program in both the UK and the US in the early 1960s.

Lord John pal: Herb Yellin; see 12 March 1979.

Knopf seizing *The Tunnel*: originally contracted to Ticknor and Fields, they changed their mind and after a brief period in limbo—during which I asked Gass if Dalkey Archive could publish it—the novel was acquired by Knopf, who let it go out of print a few years later, at which time Dalkey Archive reissued it in paper.

New Republic: Sven Birkerts's "Down by Law" appeared in the 7 February issue.

Think not the struggle naught availeth: the opening line of Arthur Hugh Clough's once-popular poem of encouragement, "Say Not the Struggle Naught Availeth" (1855; *ODQ*).

6figure reprint sale: Scribners acquired it for less, and reset the book (down from 586 to 509 pages) to reduce printing costs.

5.5 aftershock: early in the morning of the 17th, a magnitude 6.7 earthquake struck the area.

London Review of Books: Michael Wood reviewed *FHO* in its 12 May 1994 issue.

To John W. Aldridge

New York, NY 10021
9 February 94

dear Jack Aldridge,

a great pleasure to hear from you on this more or less occasion mainly of course with your good opinion of the new book & 'as up there with (my) very best', some of the reviewers even grudgingly conceding its being more 'accessible'; & since I've made a show of neither writing nor soliciting 'endorsements' your advance copy like them all went out with my short rein on the publisher to not even suggest such a thing to those on the list I gave them incl. yours, if Auchincloss & Heller simply couldn't restrain themselves we all come off with a clean & happy slate.

I assumed (as I presumed you would) that
or should it be

I presumed (as I assumed you would) that you hardly courted the warm embrace of the *NY Times* not, as you note, for scolding them over assigning novels to novelists & poets to poets but for putting their star daily reviewer on display as the quintessential symptom of the far greater plague to which you call attention—& in which the publishers (like their movie studio counterparts) are hardly blameless for its spread—wherein the field of criticism has been usurped by reviewers (see *A Frolic of His Own* foot of page 217) with the bland acquiescence of a lazy 'readership' for a fitting extrapolation of entropy where at last everything = everything else. Of course right now I'm hardly in a position to complain personally since Michiko Kamikaze (as she's known locally) did, as some other reviewers, treat the book 'respectfully' if somewhat grudgingly & sublimely humourless in her earnest approach &, heaven knows, I've been beyond fortunate in the *NY Review of Books, Washington Post, Boston Globe, Phila Inquirer* even 4 not entirely rave but thoughtful pages in the *New Republic* & so, I think Gertrude Lawrence said, what we lose on the swings we can make up on the roundabouts.

In light of the above it's very good news that you're taking on Cormac McCarthy who is a rare one & well worth more serious attentions (some day I'll tell you the pig joke he told me), meanwhile we're in town for now if you're both passing through before this insane winter weather gives in to the hounds of spring.

with all best regards
Gaddis

Auchincloss & Heller: brief statements by both novelists appear on the front and rear dust-jacket flaps, respectively.

page 217: the lawyer Madhar Pai corrects Basie: "I did not say book critics I said reviewers, there's a world of difference although the reviewers are delighted to be referred to as critics unless they're on the run, then they take refuge in calling themselves journalists."

Michiko Kamikaze: Kakutani (1955–) wrote about new fiction for the daily *New York Times,* where she reviewed *FHO* on 4 January 1994.

Gertrude Lawrence: WG forgot that he had already used this line with Aldridge in his letter of 28 January 1976.

Cormac McCarthy: Aldridge's essay "Cormac McCarthy's Bizarre Genius" appeared in the August 1994 issue of the *Atlantic Monthly.*

the hounds of spring: a once-famous image from Swinburne's verse drama *Atalanta in Calydon* (1865). WG had used the phrase as early as 1953.

To Clare Alexander

New York, New York 10021
13 February 1994

Dear Clare.

While US applause may echo rather hollow in the British press I nonetheless enclose a dozen or so reviews & interviews which may be of use in promoting your publication of *A Frolic of His Own* in June.

The reviews vary from respectful to quite marvelous, Jonathan Raban in the *NY Review of Books* is really stunning & such provincial capitals as Boston & Philadelphia happily intelligent & high spirited. The interviews, to which I submitted with some trepidation, turn out quite merciful & that in the *Washington Post* is surely all one could wish for. There is also a ½page ad finally scheduled for the *NYTimes Book Review* representing the whole extent of Simon & Schuster's such efforts to date which seems rather feeble response with the enclosed material to draw on & especially short sighted in a country the size of this one where the *Washington Post* & *Los Angeles Times* have been so generous, & the smaller literary press quite overlooked.

Snow banked outside the windows makes the possibility of your bringing me to London in June daily more attractive & I look forward to hearing from you about further developments.

kind regards,
W. Gaddis

Jonathan Raban in the *NY Review of Books* : "At Home in Babel" in the 17 February issue, pp. 3–4, 6.

Washington Post: "America's Greatest Novelist?" by John Schwartz, which appeared on the front page of the Style section of the *Post* on 3 February 1994.

Los Angeles Times: reviewed by Richard Eder in the 9 January 1994 issue.

To Paul Ingendaay

[*The author/translator's critical study was published by Wissenschaftlicher Verlag in 1993.*]

New York, New York 10021
13 February 1994

Dear Paul Ingendaay,

your *Romane von W* G** is indeed a handsome piece of work & thank you for sending it to me. We seem to have been exchanging letters for rather a while & I've almost the feeling that you may have spent as much time & energy disentangling my work as I've put in creating the tangles, those of this last book at any rate which has got off to a far better start critically & in sales than its predecessors in large part I think for having been labeled more 'accessible' & even, reviewers finally admit, highly comic.

Your pointing out the arboreal carnage interwoven in *J R* of course rears again in the new book with its concluding screaming parody of *The Cherry Orchard* occasioned, in fact, by precisely such a horror at the far (but scarcely far enough) end of our driveway at the heretofore tranquil place on Long Island day after day saws trucks bulldozers for the last 2 years I worked on the book there, no underestimating the destructive power of money in the wrong hands (where it usually is) & the powerlessness of 'art' in collision, hardly news but always news to me.

I'm needless to say more than curious looking forward to see what emerges from Rowohlt's efforts with those legal opinions rendered into German! & I'm further sure that your efforts on my work's behalf must have encouraged Naumann's taking on this new assignment, for which I remain most grateful to you.

> with my best regards again,
> —Gaddis

The Cherry Orchard : Anton Chekhov's final play (1904).

Rowohlt's […] Naumann's: Michael Naumann of the German publishers Rowohlt acquired rights to *FHO*, publishing it in Nikolaus Stingl's translation in fall 1996 as *Letzte Instanz* (The Last Act, WG's working title).

To Michael Millman

[The editor at Penguin who oversaw the 1993 Penguin Classics reissues of R *and* J R. *Penguin would add* CG *to their classics line in March 1999.]*

> Wainscott
> 2 March 94

dear Michael Millman—

Candida has forwarded to me your letter regarding the new book & the shortfall on the 2 old ones—"puzzled" at how few copies of those have been ordered by bookstores recently—but why "puzzled"? When ½ the country thinks they're still out of print and—as you observe yourself—need *ads* to *remind them* of the new epiphanies. Along these lines I enclose my letter to "my editor" at S&S (not yet acknowledged)—

What seems such a damned shame in both cases is the marvelously successful effort that went into making the books themselves—yours with the 2 'classics', covers (which should have so splendidly framed even a small ad) &c, & the designers compositors copyreaders &c at S&S producing such a marvelous 'product' & after that everyone collapsing (you may have seen the off register "colour" ½page in the *Times BR*—I ask you!).

> best regards,
> W. Gaddis

To Gregory Comnes

[Comes had written to ask (1) if WG would autograph his copy of FHO, *and (2) if WG had received his* Ethics of Indeterminacy. *This note is undated and lacks a salutation.]*

Wainscott, New York 11975
[March 1994]

NEW (for me) WORD: APORIA (from a Gertrude Himmelfarb rvw)
     "difference, discontinuity, disparity, contradiction, discord, ambiguity, irony, paradox, perversity, opacity, obscurity, anarchy, chaos"
                    LONG LIVE!
1) Surely, send the book for signing
2) I have your (signed) book & thank you
3) I have your note with it & don't know what you mean with "all & sundry are busy complimenting me on the caustic comment made about my book" This is Jonathan Raban?
Ah!

                    Gaddis

Himmelfarb rvw: the word and definition are from Kakutani's review of historian Gertrude Himmelfarb's book *On Looking into the Abyss* in the *New York Times*, 1 March 1994, C19.

Raban: in the opening paragraph of his review of *FHO* in the *New York Review*, Raban refers to "the professional Gaddisites, a solemn crew themselves given to sentences like 'Read from this perspective, *The Recognitions* demonstrates the essential alterity of the world, the meta-ethical virtue of agapistic ethics'" (from p. 49 of Comnes's book).

To John H. Snow

[*A Harvard classmate (1924–2008) who later became a clergyman and author. He wrote to express his admiration for* FHO.]

Wainscott, New York 11975
13 March 1994

dear Reverend John,

     how is it that we who have so desperately sought to rescue/impose order seem in the summing up to have led the most disorderly of lives? Your letters (now & a couple of years ago) breathe a kind of self contentment—longlasting wife, real estate, retirement work—which I gave up on long ago & which may point to our essentially opposite orientations: yours grounded on absolutes (as you've demanded from the start) vs. my attempt to "provide an honest vision of an essentially indeterminate landscape[,] a postmodern world without absolutes" &c (v. Comnes, *The Ethics of Indeterminacy in the Novels of W*G*, Univ. Florida Press 1994 [p. 15]) for which I learn a new word "aporia" from a review of a theoretical opponent named Himmelfarb (sic) meaning "discontinuity, disparity, contradiction, discord, ambiguity, chaos" (she's against it). Of course you have borne a tragedy which may only have confirmed your stance (like the patriotic parents who lost sons in Vietnam) either of which I am sure would have destroyed me confirming *my* stance. Think not the struggle naught availeth &c ... Or is another word for it 'romantic' re your account of Mowery of whom I lost track long ago, or Bill Davison, d[itt]o. Dear old Barney Emmart, diabetic & other illnesses but I think finally a spirit severely damaged following a very bad mugging in Spain, a man of such wit & tenderness & a great loss dead as he was while still alive. Jacob Bean too who of course started off in the Divinity School &, in a manner of speaking, returned to it toward the end in an alcoholic haze of devout P.E. devotions as blindness overtook him, a gentleman in the most generous sense of the word. Thus regarding 'our 50th' D.V. but I doubt that I am, since I feel so strongly that it is not the college I went to but from their relentless mailings (inc. *H* Magazine*) has become a vast selfpromoting multinational corporation with [*lacuna in manuscript*] & no place whatsoever for me.

Like yourself I have had the body's plumbing & electrical functions refurbished & am now casting about through the vast store of detritus those 4 books have left behind to see whether there lurks somewhere another 'wanting to be written' (as Samuel Butler had it), nearer I fear to Flaubert than I ever knew.

[unsigned]

---

you have borne a tragedy: the death of Snow's son.
Think not the struggle: see 6 February 1994.
Mowery: Eldred Mowery, a mutual friend, had died recently.
Bill Davison: the man WG drove to Mexico with in 1947.
P.E.: elsewhere WG uses this abbreviation for Protestant Ethic.

To Polly Roosevelt

[*The wife of a CIA officer (the grandson of Theodore Roosevelt), Ms. Roosevelt was born Mary Lowe Gaddis; she apparently saw WG's interview in the* Washington Post *and wrote to see if they were related.*]

Wainscott, New York 11975
14 March 1994

Dear Ms. Roosevelt.

Thank you for writing: I too am just into my 70s & so understand the haste involved & only wish I could be of more help regarding your inquiry.

In fact I can really be none at all. Had you asked about my mother's side (Williams, Hough, Meredith &c) I could have gone on chapter & verse, largely Quaker stock moving from the Carolinas to Indiana in one of those schisms before the Civil War & gradually drifting back to the East Coast, my mother age about 18 to a brief college career at Sweetbriar & thence to New York where she met this dashing fellow & married at 22 & he wasn't much older in the high spirits of the 20s, little fliers on Wall Street (where he overworked) which seemed to go on theatre tickets & finally a breakdown & they separated when I was about 3 brought up by my mother's family & I didn't see him again until I was in my 20s when we got reacquainted or I should say acquainted but I never did pursue his lineage with him, thought it was largely Scotch Irish (as much also on my mother's side with England & Wales) but met his ancient mother who was German Catholic which I later understood hadn't set too well with the Williams side, recalling an equally ancient thee-&-thou great aunt of mine whose visits east from Fountain City Indiana in the 30s we would try to spark with trips up to the Roosevelt shrine at Oyster Bay (we lived on the South Shore) & there, I'm afraid, I must leave you.

There were other Gaddis uncles of his involved in NY state politics especially in the Dewey years & all of their fortunes might have changed mightily had he won that presidential election [in 1948] when who knows, all sorts of revelations might have surfaced & we might even have met. Meanwhile my best wishes for your & your sister's good health (since that's what it all seems to be coming down to at last),

with warm regards
William Gaddis

To Arthur A. Hilgart

[*A businessman, radio host, and patron of the arts (1936–2010) who occasionally corresponded with WG. After an unidentified reference to "Alcott," WG clarifies some points in* FHO.]

Wainscott, New York 11975
14 March 1994

dear Hilgart,

the healing power of Pepsi is splendid but the Alcott frolic is quite beyond anything—years of reviews of my work have shown me how rare is the careful reader, ergo:

No, Trish didn't marry both men, it's simply another turn on 'getting it wrong' which preoccupies me (see *Carpenter's Gothic*): Lily has simply blurted out that Trish said she'd got married & Christina takes for granted it's Madhar Pai (she'd married Bunker). No, Basie had nothing to do with Judge Crease getting hold of the opinion, he's simply got it through channels & of course on the lookout for it. And no, Harry wasn't in the accident caused by Lily (p.523); his death (515) is meant to be left in the realm of predictable, with Lily (491), unexplained fact lost & overwhelmed in the clutter of trivia (his Turnbull & Asser shirts) surrounding it.

Speaking of 'careful reading' here's an item that was on my mind from the book's start: the careful threading of the 'hairy Ainu' Harry & Christina in bed through her embarrassment with Basie's cheerful ignorance to the blow that finally strikes her down (582) with the young lawyer's — . . . no. No that's not the Harry I knew. Perhaps some doctoral candidate will find it.

Kind regards,
W. Gaddis

'hairy Ainu': a reference to Japan's Ainu tribe: see *FHO* 119–20.

WG with Poseidon publisher Ann Patty, at the National Book Awards,
16 November 1994 (Miriam Berkley).

6. *AGAPĒ AGAPE*
1994–1998

To Sarah Gaddis

[*At this time, Sarah was working in the press office of the Los Angeles County Museum of Art, which was mounting an exhibition of William S. Burroughs's "shotgun paintings."*]

Wainscott
30 March 94

dear Sarah,

I know what you mean about meaning to sit down & write a long letter but the weekends end up with errands & & & except that I've got no real excuses, think I'll call & the time difference interferes then make the weekend try but the line's busy which frustrates but really pleases me because it means that you are busy & leading a real life after the time you've put in on one so poorly furnished; but I forget, we (esp east coast here) forget about earthquakes till another 5.6 is all over the evening news diverted, today, by people staring vacantly at homes & the sad small lives laid to waste in Georgia tornados—I mean here I am still dining out on my earthquake anecdote until you remind me that for you & those around you it is a constant presence, your remark about a subliminal lack of concentration in people & things they forgot to do or did wrong & knowing your earlier distress over them admire you going right on, but at this cost, it is like some overwhelming fiction (the terms I think in) esp the Hollywood set image inserting epoxy in the walls like I felt that one night of it in the "Ritz Carlton".

But thank you for the packet you sent reviews & all, I hadn't known of St Moore's for the *Nation* & have certainly done well but trying to get S&S to spend another 50¢ on an ad is hopeless, they say they'll make a big splash when they bring it out as the lead book in their new fancy Scribner's (which they took over) trade paperback series end of the year... another year! Lord how they go by. The woman on book jackets is quite intriguing I only wish she'd seen ours but Sarah the ART world I confess is simply beyond me aware that

I am a minority of 1 & how oddly a leading postmodernist in fiction but Bill Burroughs with his 'lost images' in the catalogue . . . & to think I've got a copy of his first paperback *Junkie* inscribed (in soft pencil) 'To Bill Gaddis who knew me before I knew myself'. . . at any rate I am so pleased (& proud) that you are out in front with what's going on in the world & handling it so well stress & all, stress of course being a vital part of it or what is the art itself all about? And not to add to it though I know it must be something you & the women you work with must discuss frequently but I do (like most parents I'm sure) worry about you & all the wildness loose in the world, things like carjackings (do you lock your car doors when you get in? take a careful look at shopping mall parking lots?) the list is endless & could drive one crazy & there's finally no hiding place.

I mainly wander about literally & figuratively (in the head) vaguely considering what to do, I mean work on, next, going through old notes & papers, does anyone need *A Secret History of the Player Piano*? & getting something together to speak about in Albany the 14th & the college at Stonybrook later, part of the price of my NYState Authorhood & the money already gone to pay taxes on the Lannan prize . . . Your brother incidentally is right now presumably in New Orleans, sketch for a film project on his pal Jack's legal tussles & I'm simply glad of his getting out of town finally for a few days' change.

much love always
Papa

St Moore's for the *Nation*: "Reading the Riot Act," postdated 25 April 1994, pp. 569–71.

To James M. Morris

[*Author and editor-at-large for the* Wilson Quarterly. *At the urging of feminist Betty Friedan (a Hamptons friend of WG and Mrs. Murphy), he invited WG to give a lecture at the Woodrow Wilson Center in Washington, DC. WG gave a casual talk there on 7 December 1994.*]

Wainscott, New York 11975
10 April 1994

Dear Mr Morris.

Thank you for your letter & your invitation to talk. I am sorry to be so long responding but take refuge in the welcome provision that it may be later this year or even early next.

Most welcome however is the proposal that it be for a talk rather than a 'reading'. On occasions when I've been asked to do the latter I've answered if at all with an offer to speak on why I do not give readings &—shades of Dylan Thomas 'traveling 200 miles just to recite, in my fruity voice, poems that would not be appreciated & could, anyway, be read in books'—don't see why anyone else does except for the toxin of this 'in performance' culture. My only concern would be that since what I put on the page is more structured & disciplined than the informal somewhat rambling nature of a talk, transcribing such a talk for publication as you mention puts me off a bit but I'm sure could be resolved.

Further, from the material you enclosed, the aims & atmosphere of the Wilson Center sound most congenial to my ways of thinking & I hope we can work something out along the lines you suggest; & finally, thanks for your warm estimate of my books especially this last.

Yours,

W. Gaddis

Dylan Thomas: the quotation is from Philip Larkin's essay "Subsidizing Poetry," as WG indicated in a 1990 interview.

To Michael Silverblatt

[*Creator and host of* Bookworm, *a literary radio program broadcast since 1989 by KCRW in Los Angeles, and underwritten by the Lannan Foundation. He hosted the January event at which Gass and WG spoke. At this time, Lannan's Jeannie Kim expressed concerns about the program's direction; the Kurt mentioned below was her assistant.*]

Wainscott NY 11975
13 April 1994

Dear Michael,

word has reached me of some of the pressures you are under involving Lannan's literary program & I hope they will dissipate before things come to some sort of bureaucratic grief.

I thought (& was later told) that our presentation in January came off quite successfully, & I certainly felt I had you & Bill Gass to thank for making it more than just another of these ubiquitous 'readings'. Gass is for me our foremost writer, a magician with the language, & it was he who'd told me before I came out there of your deep commitment to literature as your thoughtful probing confirmed, opposed to the interviewer asking whether one uses a word processor & on which side of the paper do you write?

What it all finally comes down to I suppose is what sort of writer & what sort of audience such a program wishes to attract, the difference between entertainment & exploration of ideas, of what writing & the serious writer are all about or an audience that can say I saw Irving Wallace in person on television last night, all adding up to how seriously such a literary program's sponsor's name is taken by its peers & any serious writer quickly spots the difference. We're not up there reciting recipes for tapioca pudding to make some insecure bureaucrat look good after all.

A propos, when you see Kurt will you thank him for sending me the Heaney version of *Philoctetes* we'd discussed out there, now here again is a really good man with real ties to literature who is far too valuable to be relegated as someone's nameless bureaucratic 'assistant' in what armed service slang appropriately refers to as Mickey Mouse. In situations like this one I think there's a lot to be said for running a loose ship.

Good luck and best regards,
W. Gaddis

Irving Wallace: best-selling American novelist (1916–90).
Heaney version of Philoctetes: *The Cure at Troy* (1990) is the Irish poet and translator Seamus Heaney's adaptation of Sophocles' *Philoctetes*.

To Isabel and John Butterfield

[*Old British friends whom WG saw while in England for the publication there of* FHO.]

Wainscott, New York 11975
30 June 1994

dear Isabel & John,

how can civility—the mere civility of a note of gratitude to old & dear friends—have fallen to such low estate as it nears a month since I have left you?

In some part it may be explained (if not excused) in the enclosed FAX I just faxed to my publishers, having flown (literally) from that week of order & indulgence, of correct & thoughtful & generous behaviour on all sides, to be plunged immediately back into the Psychopathology of Everyday Life maintained all too familiarly here, leaving the accoutrements of civilised life where we left them behind 200+ years ago. Dinner in the House of Lords! I mutter to gaping friends over undergrilled fish & marble-hard potato salad; addressing a select (albeit rather small) audience in London University's Senate Room; devouring a haunch of beef in the shade of Evelyn Waugh at the Hyde Park Motel, recounted over hash at a kitchen table; a Publication Dinner (roast wood pigeon) at Lauceston Place, retailed to my publisher here who has never come up with so much as a burger at Burger King... All of it crowned by your warm embrace, it was a stunning time.

And I have got to say (in an immediate & similarly inexcusably delayed note to her) how deeply struck & touched I was by Mathilde's warmth & care & sheer courage had never reached me so strongly, what we call 'character' I suppose in its lonely strength, 'blood will tell' as archie told mehitabel, breaks your heart.

The road ahead (ahead?) here is off like the course of, who was it? mounting his horse & 'riding off in all directions', tempting the novelist to descend to yet untold depths ('The writer will always sell you out' says Joan Didion) though I hasten to add you both must come off quite unscathed in the event, if event there is to be frankly at the moment I've scarcely the appetite for it though the possibility nay perhaps the necessity of grovelling for another advance suggests itself so me & mine are not to be seen in the Edgeware Road singing 'Back and side go bare, go bare, but belly God give thee good ale...'

with love and thanks again
as these things become more precious,
Willie

Psychopathology of Everyday Life: title of one of Freud's best-known books (1901).

as archie told mehitabel: the free-verse-typing cockroach (properly, archy) and his alley cat friend from Don Marquis's popular newspaper columns of the 1910s and 1920s.

'riding off in all directions': Stephen Leacock; see 30 June 1969.

'The writer [...] says Joan Didion: correctly, "writers are always selling somebody out," the concluding sentence of her preface to Slouching Towards Bethlehem (1968).

'Back and side [...] good ale': from a song in William Stevenson's Elizabethan comedy Gammer Gurton's Needle: "Back and side go bare, go bare / [...] / But belly God send thee good ale enough" (ODQ).

To Stanley Elkin

[Elkin's 1985 novel The Magic Kingdom features a character named Charles Mudd-Gaddis, an eight-year-old geriatric who "dreams of his first birthday. He dreams the cake and dreams the candles, dreams the balloons and dreams the streamers; he dreams the toys, he dreams the clapping. And dreams he's three, the little boy, who would have been a man by now—twenty, twenty-one. Then dreams the girl, six, to him a woman. And now he's five and pushing forty. Ah, to be thirty-four again! he dreams. And dreams he's seven and confusion comes, that white aphasia of the heart and head. And dreams in awful clarity it's now, and can't recall how old he really is."]

9 November '94

dear Stanley,

I had been vaguely troubled by Mudd-Gaddis since first stumbling upon him & seeing you again in such fine fettle thought to get back & give him a closer look. And was stunned. How do you do it? How (p. 80) did you *know*!

Staggers. Though perhaps 10 years ago it mightn't have fit so well, but prescient my God it's I, it's me today that brief touching elegant agonizing profile believe me real age 72 is daily more infringed by that blond pageboy off to boarding school age 5 & the confusion *does* come, "that white aphasia of the heart and head" sheer poetry, break those 10 lines up into 20 & what a poem it is (looking about today at what passes for 'poetry') in its 'awful clarity' for a stupefying epitaph however you may have meant it (in decon-struction's disavowing the author's intent) I have taken it to heart.

good weather & warmest wishes to you both

Gaddis

Mudd-Gaddis: Mudd was taken from the news anchor Roger Mudd, whom Elkin knew when younger. Elkin later told WG, "I often use the names of friends [...] be-cause of the sound their names make on the page'" (Dougherty, *Shouting Down the Silence*, 36).

To Judith Gaddis

[*Typed on the back of a Harvard newsletter regarding WG's 50th class reunion. FHO won the National Book Award for fiction on 16 November 1994.*]

Wainscott
15 Jan. '95

Dear Judith,

response of sorts to your long delightful multitypeface (this is still the toy Olivetti I gave Sarah off to George School) letter & handsome letterhead (see other side) of, dare I say it? last September... but frankly it seems much lon-ger ago than that, upheavals on every front: outrage at the publisher's failure to advertise, then the Book Award (sound painfully familiar? but not entirely broke this time); health coming & going, travel slowed by those decades of tobacco but no whisky now for some 5 years (a little wine with dinner); the last couple of months a kind of running horror of being asked to give 'read-ings' & getting up to give a presentation on why I don't give readings & don't think anyone else should, why did we invent the printed page? the whole vain nonsense of 'writers in performance', everything is performance; & 'book signings'... none of it to do with the work itself, please! [...]

And now when it would seem that one could finally sit down & gape at the Golden Years the success of this last book makes a profitable opportunity for a next one which I suppose must be taken advantage of though I've no idea what it would be 'about' but as J R said at some point —Even when you win you have to keep playing [p. 647]. [...]

and so good to hear you sounding well & in such good spirits
W.

—————

To Sarah Gaddis

[*Typed on the back of a photocopy of an article on WG in the French newspaper* Le Monde.]

Wainscott
7 Feb. 95

Dear Sarah,

well! Which would we prefer, *Le Monde* or the 'Pulitzer Prize' —I'll settle for the French, after what Oscar had to say about the Pulitzer on page 369 and these people picked up and attributed to *me*! Well, so long Pulitzer (I think they hand them out in April) (in case anyone got as far as p. 369 which I'd doubt, Oscar is right). Lord knows what this Book Critics Award thing is, I think no $$ just the 'prestige' (who needs it)...

At least, after hearing you on the phone last night, I can reread your letter & feel that *at least* you can take a good deal of satisfaction in your work & how well you have done it & that there are some serious people around who are aware of it & appreciate it but believe me recalling those 5 Pfizer years, & now seeing your 'boss' (from outside thank God) so perfectly cloned in this cheery dense utterly self-centered 'cute' bird-brain at S&S I feel for you, how consistently these ridiculous people get themselves into positions of power is one of the great sad commentaries on our times but all this is cold comfort I know + the fact that they can turn quite vicious if 'crossed'... the only revenge probably a short novel about such a scene but of course that's been done too (though there's always room for one more if well done: *take notes*! (right down to the lipstick smear on her teeth as I did with Miss Flesch in *J R* who was 'inspired' by this ghastly woman at Pfizer)...)

Meanwhile I'm simply fiddling around trying to dredge up some idea for a project both to keep my mind in 1 piece & to embark on a regular income from S&S or Knopf &c, & very sadly meanwhile here again Candida in

difficulty in hospital with a leg/foot operation, some rare circulatory problem
that will leave her impaired & a long and painful haul & I am trying to
convince her to sell her agency & retire &c, count our blessings as they say
but at what cost!

much love again,
Papa

Pulitzer on page 369: "—The Pu, good God talk about being famous for five minutes
the Pulitzer Prize is a gimcrack out of journalism school you wrap the fish in tomorrow, talk about the great unwashed it's got nothing to do with literature or great
drama it's the hallmark of mediocrity and you'll never live it down [...]." WG's low
opinion of the Pulitzers is also expressed in his letter of 1 May 1990 and in *AA*
(60–62).
Book Critics Award: the National Book Critics Circle gives out awards every spring.
FHO was a finalist for the 1994 fiction award but lost to Carol Shield's *Stone Diaries*.
Miss Flesch in *J R*: a "curriculum specialist" at J R's school, later hired as "project director" (and Thomas Eigen's boss) at Typhon International (=Pfizer). Miss Flesch's
lipstick-smeared teeth are noted at her first appearance in the novel (p. 22).

To Muriel Oxenberg Murphy

*[A fax without salutation entitled "In the Style of Thomas Bernhard." WG describes the
end of their relationship in the manner of the Austrian writer's 1970 novel* The Lime
Works, *in which the narrator tells the disjointed story of an eccentric writer named Konrad who has just killed his wife, drawing on hearsay by characters like Konrad's acquaintance Fro. The opening paragraph is from pages 128–29 of Sophie Wilkins's translation
(Knopf, 1973); WG photocopied the same passage and sent it to Greg Comnes in 1996 with
a note saying "You may see where I have found my Cicero for all future engagements."
WG's final novel* AA *is very much "in the style of Thomas Bernhard."]*

Feb. 17 '95

"Words ruin one's thoughts, paper makes them ridiculous, and even while
one is still glad to get something ruined and something ridiculous down on
paper, one's memory manages to lose hold of even this ruined and ridiculous
something. Paper can turn an enormity into a triviality, an absurdity. If you
look at it this way, then whatever appears in the world, by way of the spiritual
world so to speak, is always a ruined thing, a ridiculous thing, which means
that everything in this world is ridiculous and ruined. Words were made to
demean thought, he would even go so far as to state that words exist in order
to abolish thought... In any case, words were bringing everything down,

Konrad said. Depression derives from words, nothing else . . . It was comforting, one of those rare times when one feels that everything is possible again, Konrad is supposed to have said to Fro. Suddenly everything . . .
—Thomas Bernhard, *The Lime Works*

. . . is sad, Konrad said to Fro, that was not my word, Konrad said, it was not my word but it was the perfect word, it was the word that took in everything, the whole past present even perhaps the future while looking for the words to forestall that future because none of this was new, it had been going on for months, even years, even all the years since the dreadful third party came into the picture to help, I want you to help me with her the dreadful third party said gradually shifting the burden over months and finally years having to explain, having to account, being called to account Konrad told Fro, but every explanation or rather every attempt at explanation only demanded further explanation which was disregarded, every appeal was disregarded, shrugged off by the dreadful third party, the last thing I ever want to do is hurt her I told Fro, hurting her is absolutely the last thing I want to do so that finally it seems (I am told) all I do whatever I do or say hurts her until I hardly know what I am saying (or doing) which is the last thing I want to do (or say) because the next to the last thing I want to do is to enrage her but as the years go by and turn into months and finally the months turn into weeks everything I do or say seems to eventually enrage her I tell Fro, I'm going to run down and get the newspaper I'll be back in a minute in my coat, standing there in my coat she is suddenly enraged because I thought there would be an interview with me in the newspaper (of course there wasn't I tell Fro), none of my small triumphs seem to please her when I had thought they would please her when what I thought would please her is usually met with silence or even derision or even what seems like contempt because it means that I have put other obligations first, that is what hurts her and angers her, wouldn't any woman feel that way I ask Fro? Is there anything surprising about *that*? That I put other obligations or what I think are obligations before my obligations to her, work obligations social obligations (contracts) the house obligations to her house here but she is not the house she is not talking about the house the house has nothing to do with her so that every attempt at explanation demands further explanation, with Q & A with a siege a veritable siege of Q & A living under siege at every encounter overflowing with conditions ultimatums assignments all totally unpredictable because the only thing that is predictable is its unpredictability overflowing with evidence of commission and omission which are always my sins of commission and omission I tell Fro, thoughtlessness carelessness memory lapses for insignificant moments or what I thought were insignificant moments become momentous events harbouring secrets which would only complicate things and which always complicate things on trial being on trial when One is not aware of being on trial because one is always on trial and any gesture of autonomy even the simplest gesture or the most complicated one becomes an evasion of control, or being controlled leading to assignments ultimatums conditions, there must be no conditions Eric is supposed to have said, I tell Fro, he (Eric) is a doctor and not only a doctor but a serious person making the statement "there must be no conditions" looking for relief, looking for blessed relief in the morning paper which may explain everything I tell Fro, here is a headline in the morning paper MEN AND WOMEN USE BRAIN DIFFERENTLY, STUDY DISCOVERS ("Using a powerful new method for glimpsing the brain in action") which may explain everything...

---

third party: the psychoanalyst WG mentions in his letter of 4 January 1993, apparently named Eric.

headline in the morning paper: an article by Gina Kolata in the 16 February 1995 issue of the *New York Times*.

To Candida Donadio

[*Sometime after April 1995, WG moved to a small house in East Hampton, where he lived for the rest of his life.*]

> [#1 Boat Yard Road
> East Hampton, NY 11937]
> 10 August (full moon, watch
> out!) 1995

Dear Candida,

so these are the Golden Years! Most reading seems to be obituaries, Elkin, Friedrich, Bazelon, most social events wakes, most news pain & abandonment still the sun comes up in the morning & goes down at night. I am quietly holed up in my 4 room house out here by an East Hampton boatyard (Muriel reels between Wainscott & NY) each day finding a new way to exercise my bad judgment: the latest was saying Yes to a request from the Natl Endowment for the Arts to serve on a 'panel' for fiction grants which means reading 275 x 30pp (= 8250 pages) of 98% hopeless MSS + writing a brief commentary for each, why why why did I do it!

Mainly though preoccupied with 'getting my affairs in order', while I try to figure out where my 'career' goes from here, meanwhile trying to corner

WG's final home on Boat Yard Road.

what assets I have so the kids can make sense of things when the time comes. The past 4months entangled with selling the house in Piermont with every possible hitch, not least will be paying something like 41% IRS/NYS taxes on the sale; my other tangible asset being the boxes & boxes of my socalled 'archive' which we've talked of my selling for years now the time seems to have come. MSS, notes, galleys, correspondence &c and then this occurred to me: to complete it, what of our correspondence over the years, decades, from my letters to you over outrage with the Jovanovichs & Gottliebs of this world on & on & on (I've most I think of yours to me), are these packed away in some sort of dead file and could I ask for them back? They would fill out the endless ups & downs of this writer's life & provide such a terrific record of the battle-field, could you let me know?

I think of you & yours often enough & painfully, have reports from your office that things are going along 'as well as can be expected' as they say, my own discomforts pale beside yours of course, the sciatica gone I think & in its wake a 'colonoscopy' & now they would like to do a stomach-oscopy, & wondering what/how your plans are taking shape & by now how real any of it really is, do write or call & let me know.

                                        love
                                        Willie

obituaries: Stanley Elkin died in May 1995, Otto Friedrich a month earlier, and composer Irwin Bazelon on 2 August 1995.

Natl Endowment for the Arts: see WG's essay on the experience in *RSP* 115–19.

To Jeff Bursey

[*The Canadian novelist and literary critic (1963–) had sent a letter to the editor of the* New York Times Book Review *protesting Columbia professor and novelist* Robert Towers' *review of* FHO *(9 January 1994, 1, 22), which was not printed. A year and a half later—by which time Towers had died—Bursey sent a copy of his letter to WG.*]

16 Sept '95

dear Jeff Bursey,

thanks for your letter to the *Times* book review; it certainly won't change things but they do need to be *reminded* . . .

The problem with academic reviewers like Towers (especially those in the modest/failed novelist category who 'teach') seems consistently to be (as Christina remarks [*FHO* 11]) being taken seriously, hosannas for Melville (or on whomever they wrote their dissertation) but ponderous damns with faint praise for unruly contemporaries: Tom Clancy, anyone?

best regards,

W. Gaddis

Tom Clancy: best-selling novelist (1947–2013) of techno-military thrillers.

To Judith Gaddis

[*In October WG sold the Piermont house and sent Judith a check for her portion.*]

East Hampton, NY 11937
29 Nov. '95

dear Judith,

well! as my grandmother used to say, "one fire = 3 moves" & that is certainly the case with Piermont (the moves I mean) & what has disappeared over these 40 years, Massapequa, Saltaire, Piermont . . . usually only myself to blame especially in the last case, people who've had a fire say that for years afterward they keep abruptly missing things: start with the attic in Piermont where I went with Matthew & a sturdy young man with a van (if you remember our van ride getting lost from my mother's 19th str.), some things came down I'd forgotten (Chinese dolls) but where, *where* an original Lionel train set (probably worth some $900 now), I can *see* it where I'd put it, but no; painfully, that wonderful balloon picture I sought specifically, instead only the big phlox painting from grandmother house in Woodstock; of the 2 stove plant lithographs of Napper that hung in the guest room, only one; &c &c —could one of my awful string of tenants have climbed through the ceiling for them? Madness. [...] Records? God knows. An original roll of sheets from 1st printing of *The Recognitions*? ditto; a filing cabinet (next to last tenants)? same. Afghan throws & quilts by my grandmother's hands? Well maybe, maybe those or some of those are with Sarah's things in storage in Princeton since *her* divorce 100yrs ago. And the Roliecord camera I carefully hid somewhere in the house & never saw again. The mulberry tree was finally cut down, greatly overgrown & dropping its berries ankle deep.

So here I sit among relics: the small lazy susan from scrabble days at the Saltaire dinner table, chipped survivors of Quimper from the hooligan children's raids in Massapequa 40 years ago...it all wrenching, wrenching, wrenching as you say, in every case it seems traceable to my own delinquency in the name of a writer's obsession with finishing a book, & another book, at the agony & expense of everyone around him. I'm glad at any rate that that mortgage check helped to close out these dim latter Piermont days & leave us both with a good many many sunlit memories there together all, really, as tangible in their way as furniture & of far greater value, sunt lacrimae rerum (there are tears for things) notwithstanding. [...]

Of absent friends, I just gradually lost touch with the Nappers (he'd be well in his 80s by now & probably is), Martin [Dworkin] I finally simply gave up on, he had alienated everyone he knew in terrible bitterness & I finally realized he is really quite mad. And then there are the obituaries, Otto Friedrich, Stanley Elkin, Terry Southern, & back to (mad) Barney Emmart & whose last words were these?: Si ça c'est la morte, ce n'est pas drole...(errors forgiven, not my language though I've been invited to Paris next May by some Pompidoux people if I'm still in 1 piece), who knows?

Meanwhile (Life is what happens to us while we are busy making other plans) I am trying to embark on another project (book), a new agent after a generation with Candida whose health has badly sagged all quite a painful scene, but that is not a note I cared to end on, better your being "excited about finally being a grown-up" (though I'm not sure I can wholly recommend it, was it Hemingway who said 'growing up is a very difficult thing and but few survive it')? Always the encouraging word,

love
W.

sunt lacrimae rerum: a phrase from Virgil's *Aeneid* (*ODQ*).

Si ça c'est la morte, ce n'est pas drole: "If this is death, it isn't funny."

Pompidoux people: the Centre Georges Pompidou, a cultural complex.

Life is what happens [...] other plans: attributed to Allen Saunders in the January 1957 issue of *Reader's Digest*.

a new agent: Andrew Wylie (1947–).

Hemingway [...] few survive it': another one of Jack Gibbs' epigraphs (*J R* 486) but untraced.

To Larry M. Wertheim

[*A lawyer (Kennedy & Graven) and adjunct professor of law at William Mitchell College of Law in Saint Paul, Minnesota. He sent WG a copy of his essay "Law as Frolic: Law and Literature in* A Frolic of His Own," *William Mitchell Law Review 21.2 (1995): 421–56, to which the page numbers below refer.*]

East Hampton, NY 11937
12 March 1996

Dear Larry Wertheim,

(predictably) failing best cellardom, the time effort hopes &c that go into a piece of work like this last frolic of mine may however rarely provoke rewards a good deal more substantial than *Today Show* celebrity & this law review article of yours certainly ranks. It is a delight to me in its seizures on detail & nuance, width of its grasp & peripheral reading both in my earlier work & elsewhere & I suppose paramount to the novelist (or should be) believing & feeling for the characters.

That said, running through it item by item as they leap forth, in fact (423) despite reviews headlined Scathing Indictment of Law & Lawyers in the current mode, it's been more warmly & happily embraced by lawyers which of course I'd intended & hoped for.

Your mention (425) that 'the plot can largely be retold as a series of lawsuits' recalls an initial notion I had of making it simply that, no narrative dialogue &c but the story emerging from an entanglement of complaints depositions brief[s] &c which thank heavens I abandoned, already stigmatized as 'difficult' as I am.

Curiously (427, 438, 443) the Eugene O'Neill entry was kind of a post hoc affair. I'd long since worked out the substitute/self murder equation, & even such details as the stiff father/major a judge, the cheek scar/head wound &c &c; then late along the way reread the O'Neill play which I (like Oscar) found contrived awkward stilted & altogether pretty bad BUT was honestly really startled at the correspondencies ('substantial similarities') with *my* tale: unconscious plagiary (but still culpable?) that Hand mentions? Because I had written papers in college & diagramed O'Neill/Greek drama/Freud. And then at the last minute it occurred to me that obviously the O'N. estate would sue Oscar & even, once the deed was done, wondered if (in 'real life') they would sue me. And so (443) while Oscar's homage apologia embraces Plato I don't think I meant it to O'Neill.

Regarding (428) the Episcopal/Pepsico suit: I'd originally intended it to be a prominent, if ancillary, feature of the book & had-&-have collected the vast amount of ammunition for this reductio-ad-absurdum version of rendering unto Caesar &c but was finally so overwhelmed by this additional prospect (as also realizing I could push the reader just so far) that I finally escaped it as the 'lost' brief at the end but God knows if I'm around for long enough it may yet surface as so rich with implications for our ridiculous times.

(Incidentally: for the sort of small prank I sometimes cannot resist & to keep my interest from flagging, I doubt any reader noted but picture his treat if he did, the confusion of the young lawyer & the lost brief (446) over the 2 Harrys ("That's not the Harry I knew" *Frolic* paper ed. 506) harks back to the rather salacious exchange between Christina & Basie (id. 107 & 206) regarding the hairy Ainu, which finally sends Christina over the edge.) And speaking of Mr Basie I meant him as a man with a good deal of dimensions, cunning & compassion, saves Oscar from himself as it were, & 'living' parallel to the finally hunted down John Israel in the play.

Oscar's lawsuit was well in (my) hand researched, outlined, determined outcome &c some time before Buchwald (434) & (as you note) distinct from it as breach of contract rather than plagiary though I did at the end pick up from Buchwald the 'creative accounting' details for Oscar's 'pyrrhic victory' (444). (Incidentally I believe Paramount even had the gall to claim that the 'idea' for that really lousy movie was EMurphy's.)

In light of the above & all of your marvelous insights, summation & care I hate to point out that it is Tatamount (id.29) not Tantamount (426) & not Frickert (428) but Fickert (id.373) I believe I stole from an old routine of Jonathan Winters. Ah, but a man's reach should exceed his grasp, or what's a heaven for?

My thanks to you again, with warm regards
William Gaddis

O'Neill play: *Mourning Becomes Electra* (1931), based loosely on the Oresteia of Aeschylus. Oscar calls it "a clumsy warmed over schoolboy parody of Euripides with a few vulgar Freudian touches thrown in for good measure" (*FHO* 96).

Buchwald [...] EMurphy's: as noted earlier (21 January 1990), Eddie Murphy's *Coming to America* was the subject of a lawsuit brought by journalist Art Buchwald.

Jonathan Winters: one of the stand-up comedian's many personas was a grouchy old woman named Maude Frickert [*sic*], a recurring character on *The Jonathan Winters Show* (CBS, 1967–69).

Ah [...] for?: the most memorable line from Robert Browning's poem "Andrea del Sarto" (1855).

To Thomas Überhoff

[A fax to the editor at Rowohlt Verlag who was overseeing Nikolaus Stingl's German translation of FHO *(Letzte Instanz, 1996). In a rare explication of his own prose, WG attempts to untangle a long sentence on page 304 as Oscar nods off while watching a television nature program on*

a lackluster member of the Cistaceae or rockrose family, Helianthemum dumosum, more familiarly known in its long suffering neighborhood as bushy frostweed for its talent at surviving the trampling by various hoofed eventoed closecropping stock of the suborder Ruminantia, to silently spread and widen its habitat at its neighbors' expense like some herbal version of Gresham's law in Darwinian dress demonstrating no more, as his head nodded and his breath fell and the crush of newsprint dropped to the floor, the tug at his lips in the troubled wince of a smile might have signaled no more than, or better perhaps the very heart of some drowned ceremony of innocence now the worst were filled with passionate intensity where —we share something then don't we, no small thing either —That's good to know, demonstrating simply the survival of the fittest embracing here in bushy frostweed no more than those fittest to survive not necessarily, not by any means, by any manner of speaking, the best [...].

Überhoff also asked what kind of "rockets" were used in the Civil War.]

East Hampton, NY 11937
12 May 1996

Dear Mr Überhoff.

Thank you for your inquiry: no question that that is about as dense a sentence as I have ever written, for which I apologize to Mr Stingl (but not to the reader!). I shall try to 'shed some light' which may simply confuse things further.

Overall, the 'density' is calculated to reflect the *silent spread* of *bushy frostweed*, here representing disorder & vulgarity (Ortega y Gasset's 'mass man' proclaiming his rights to be vulgar) *widening its habitat at its neighbors' expense*, i.e., Oscar's elitism & search for order, as bad money driving out good in

Gresham's Law: thus the wincing defeat of Oscar's (play=ceremony of) innocence as portrayed in Yeats' poem The Second Coming wherein "The ceremony of innocence is drowned; / The best lack all conviction, while the worst / Are full of passionate intensity", Yeats being the bond that brings Oscar & Basie closer (*no small thing either* as noted elsewhere (p.88) in the book). And so the metaphor of bushy frostweed for *the worst full of passionate intensity* (see Oscar's diatribe on pp. 96–7) demonstrating here that *survival of the fittest*, rather than *the best* ('plays of ideas'), means *no more than those fittest to survive* & quite possibly, as we see all around us, the worst.

Well! have I simply compounded our difficulties? It may be the most expeditious course just to translate the whole passage word-for-word and leave it all for some brilliant graduate student to decode in his doctoral PhD dissertation.

The 'rockets' you ask about were probably to illuminate targets (or incendiaries?) from "the rockets' red glare" in our Star Spangled Banner written during the War of 1812 (vs. Britain).

And finally, I am quite stunned by your "little brochure for the booksellers", it is extremely handsomely done, I'd never seen that picture in the overcoat before & needless to say my vanity runneth over, could I presume to ask you to send me ½dozen more copies? (The design of the book's jacket is also marvelous but of course vanity prevails), you may imagine how I look forward to publication!

With warm regards,
William Gaddis

Ortega y Gasset's mass man: see his *Revolt of the Masses* (1930).
Gresham's Law: cited in several of WG's writings and interviews.

To Alice Mayhew

[*An editor at Simon & Schuster who had sent a bound galley of James Knowlson's* Damned to Fame: The Life of Samuel Beckett *to solicit a blurb. The last paragraph reveals that WG had decided to resurrect his player piano project from the 1940s; his new agent Andrew Wylie sold the proposal to the ever-generous Allen Peacock, then at Henry Holt, for a $150,000 advance. It was to be a nonfiction work entitled* Agapē Agape: The Secret History of the Player Piano, *and tentatively scheduled for publication in the fall of 1998.*]

East Hampton, NY 11937
21 June 1996

Dear Alice,

many thanks for sending me the *Beckett* book; however having tried these

40 years to get the word around that I've never & don't do or solicit blurbs, here again to save you further trouble. As opposed to (already published) quotes from responsible critics & reviews I just don't believe these blurbs help much, too often obvious as doing pals a good turn or returning a favour or hitching a ride on someone else's bandwagon.

So we appear directly opposed: S&S favouring blurbs & (in my own recent experience) disdaining advertising, whereas I'd disdain the former & embrace the latter, not that an ad goes out & sells books but I do think that, appropriately placed, it announces one to those who have missed initial reviews; reminds those where good reviews have slipped their minds in the weekly avalanche of new books; but perhaps most important—as I indicated to that enigmatic cipher assigned as my S&S "editor" following *A Frolic*'s widespread splendid reviews to which he deigned a reply some 5 weeks later—it tells potential readers *and* booksellers that the publisher is pleased even proud to be publishing this book and that he stands behind it.

Our Germans seem to agree as you see from the attached prepared for its imminent publication there mailed to critics &, can I have heard them right? to 8000 booksellers!

Thanks again for the *Beckett*, I look forward to it but will take time to give it the attention it obviously deserves since I'm almost totally occupied right now on a project exactly 50 years in the gestation only now moving its slow thighs &, as I hope, its hour come round at last.

with best regards
W. Gaddis

---

moving its slow thighs [...] at last: the "rough beast" of Yeats's "The Second Coming," mentioned in WG's fax to Überhoff.

To John Updike

[American writer (1932–2009) who attended Harvard in the early 1950s and, like WG, contributed to the Harvard Lampoon. *WG attached a letter by Ormonde de Kay in response to a harsh review of the Everyman omnibus edition of Updike's Rabbit novels by Harvard professor Robert Kiely that appeared in "The Browser" column of the July/August 1996 issue of* Harvard Magazine. *A number of letters to the editor condemning Kiely's piece were printed in the next issue, but not de Kay's.]*

East Hampton, NY 119375
August 1996

Dear John,

should 'they' (*Harvard Magazine*) fail to print this I thought you might be cheered by the outcry attached from a classmate & *Lampoon* activist as appalled as was I at "Browser"'s jeremiad not for what was said there—we must be inured to those by now—but where, those of your own house as Matthew has it somewhere. It is arrogantly not a general circulation magazine but one addressed to an exclusive audience: those alums who buy Harvard chairs & Veritas cocktail sets, have prospered sufficient to sail the Aegean in comfort & swell the class gift buoyed up by puff pieces on colleagues' wizard works in astrophysics, butterfly pinning &c, all of it underscored by those canons of decency which 3 centuries of Harvard have essentially been all about, & every one of which this episode violates. But this today is not the Harvard College we took in; rather some $6billion multinational conglomerate flailing about in a corresponding ethical vacuum (for I'd indict the editor(s) as or even beyond Bowser himself), though I'd never faintly imagined the extent of the motley invasion that Ormonde documents here.

Auguri!

and best regards,
W. Gaddis

---

your own house as Matthew has it: Matt. 10:36: "And a man's foes shall be those of his own household."
Auguri!: Italian, "best wishes."

To Miriam Berkley

[*A professional photographer who had interviewed WG for* Publishers Weekly *in 1985 and shot several photos of WG over the years. The one he praises below was reproduced on the jacket of Peter Wolfe's* A Vision of His Own: The Mind and Art of William Gaddis *(Fairleigh Dickinson UP, 1997).*]

East Hampton, NY 11937
9 November '96

dear Miriam Berkley.

Where to start? The apology or the 3 cheers... well, on the happier note I must say that if this were obituary time from all the pranks the camera has played upon me I should hands down the picture—more of a portrait really—of which you so kindly (& rare among photographers) sent me the large

William Gaddis, 1996   Miriam Berkley

print, I believe it the bottom far left on contact sheet #4: it is in all my crude
vanity the most straight no-nonsense item in the archive & I do thank you
(paging the *NYTimes*).

The apology is of course self evident in the time I have taken to thank you
& return the contacts. For no reason I can imagine I spent the 2nd ½ of August at Southampton Hospital with a 'compartmental syndrome', a torn calf
muscle which swelled the whole left calf marvelously with bad blood & tissue,
enter the 'sports medicine' surgeon to cut open 2 long gashes & remove the
detritus leaving 2 splendid scars & a foot still ½ numb to this day. I'd pictured
going to Frankfurt (Rowohlt had said they would 'send someone over to get
me'!) but with the leg & other items unmentionable I pretty much lost my
appetite for it & fell into a blue funk only now emerging from it. I felt very
badly about it since both Rowohlt & Zweitausendeins had made such handsome books & been so generous I can only hope they felt rewarded by the raft
of stunning reviews as obviously I was. *The Recognitions* is due out (by 2001)
before too long & *A Frolic* &c in France (Plon) this spring. [...]

many many thanks again,
W Gaddis

To Gregory Comnes

[Enclosed with a packet of German reviews of translations of J R *and* FHO. *The salutation's exclamation point mimics that in German letters.]*

East Hampton, NY 11937
3 December 1996

dear Gregory Comnes!

from a last year's letter of yours I gather you read German? or is it only
Eigen (threatening suit v. J R Corp.)—much enough like 'my' German in the
hands (mouth) of Gibbs on the train, since I can read practically none of the
enclosed though it generally looks friendly, & I thought might amuse you &/
or give you fodder...

At any rate I have found it astounding, an entire REBIRTH...& in
German(y), far cry from Michiko Kamikaze & Co. I did not feel quite up to
going to the Frankfurt book fair (Rowohlt even said they would send someone over to get me!) but a bad leg ('compartmental syndrome') interfered,
nonetheless the books seem to have prospered mightily & *The Recognitions*
due for the spring.

Indian giver as always, I send you this bundle with the request that you
return it eventually, something to while away these long winter evenings.

Soon enough (Christmas eve) I expect to go to Miami for a week or so then Key West for January & Feb, I cannot handle another winter's snow & dark here again & will be in touch once I have something resembling an address there, meanwhile

Auguri!
—Gaddis

Eigen [...] v. J R Corp.: in July 1994 Comnes sent WG a mock e-mail document in which Thomas Eigen, represented by J. R. Vansant, threatens to take action against WG for misrepresenting his work in *FHO*.

To Liesel and Molly Friedrich

[*The daughters of WG's old friends Otto and Priscilla Friedrich, whose memorial service on 24 May 1995 he had missed. Liesel read aloud a eulogy that WG had sent for the occasion, available online at* ottofriedrich.com/wp-content/uploads/2014/03/William-Gaddis-Tribute.pdf.]

East Hampton, NY 11937
13 December 1996

dear Liesl & Molly,

when I called the house that Monday afternoon aware, first, of the commotion of voices people phone ringings kitchen doings more people, where's the bathroom? can you move your car? is there any gin? preparing for Tuesday morning's event &, second, aware that I wouldn't get there or even, finally, that either of you would pick up the phone answered nonetheless by a young lady, Julia was it? Molly's daughter? most courteous but *so* young, which crept in upon me as I fell into an old man's plaint over how the loss of old close & faithful friends somehow diminished one's own sense of being to which she responded not with some dismal platitude for this self-serving notion but rather a positive cheerful alternative which I must say reduced me still further—ah youth!

Nonetheless it is true. Vanity? fear? the chill memento mori in old Spain's 'vida sin amigo, muerte sin testigo'? But however it is immensely true for me at any rate in the loss of Otto & Priscilla, almost half a century, imagine! of every kind of up & down on all hands, extraordinary courage on their parts & a kind of idiotic 'it can't happen here' on mine from Paris to Massapequa leaving me feeling somewhat like the Easter Bunny Who Overslept, Priscilla running a rather distracting household, I in the cellar saying No water today, I have to sink a new well & install new pump, & Otto walking that rainswept mile to the LIRR to the *NY Daily News* but still, my abiding memories are of wide lawns in the sun & 2 small unclothed beauties gamboling by, how deeply fond my mother was of you both & of Priscilla especially. I've always regretted that Otto never got round to writing the short & venomous book he contemplated on what happened to that sweet old town. I last saw him at a party of Ted Morgan's on a sunny New York rooftop, one whole side of him still as a board but that incorrigibly warm even twinkling smile of, well, generosity?

Generosity, yes, yes that was probably what I felt most from them both putting their own travails aside for it, as that last & indelible time I saw Priscilla &, of course, both of you that sunny afternoon I got out to Locust Valley thank heavens, limping around with my own absurdities & —Willie? can we get you something? some cheese? some ham? in that charming room, sun crisp slipcovers books books books & Priscilla as always filled with brisk good cheer & all of you concerned for me & not the loss that still hung in the air, & how glad I am that I had that last long chat with Priscilla (aside from a few subsequent phone calls when, expecting to find her in extremis, instead hear her plan for an October trip where was it, Turkey? & again, she is off for Block Island; & again, this parting bit of advice: Just remember, Willie, you don't have to do what the doctors tell you …

Character? Courage (which I suppose is a part of character)? So one can easily see how, for example, Margaret [Williams] loved and admired her (with a rather wild kind of courage herself) & the efforts she made to get out there from New Hampshire to see her, makes us all want to go back (or feel we should) & read Emerson on Friendship.

So at any rate there you both are at this immense juncture & the responsibilities ahead that go with it but good heavens look at this terrific bunch of genes you've inherited to meet them. The last line in a marvelous BBC adaptation of Galsworthy's *Forsyte Saga*, after dealing with every kind of betrayal, financial disaster, passions runs amock &c, the family lawyer who had overseen all this, Soames, asks "What was it all for?" but I think we know: since Nature's mission is prolongation of the race, the tribe, the family &c it is this next generation that all these travails are 'for', from my & Otto & Priscilla's generation you both, and Niki & Amelia too, & even that brief light of Tony, and Sarah, and Matthew, 'for' the next generation you all bring along. We do & will always owe you all so much for what you have given us.

Auguri! and love,
Willie

'vida sin amigo, muerte sin testigo': "life without a friend, death without a witness" (*R* 112).

the Easter Bunny Who Overslept: title of a children's book cowritten by the Friedrichs (1957), often reprinted and reillustrated.

Ted Morgan: French-American historian and biographer (1932–), whom WG had
known for years. He admired Morgan's biography of Somerset Maugham (1979) and
in 1983 recommended him for a Guggenheim, without success.

Locust Valley: the Friedrichs' residence on Long Island.

Emerson on Friendship: an 1841 essay.

BBC adaptation of Galsworthy *Forsyte Saga*: a 26-part serial broadcast in 1967 adapted
from John Galsworthy's trilogy of novels (1906–21).

To Don DeLillo

East Hampton, NY 11937
21 September 1997

dear Don,

the 'physics' of baseball is an astounding piece of work & as though served
up for my nefarious purpose, many thanks for going to the trouble of getting
it to me; as for the generously signed copy of your new grand entry I think
you know the measure of my appreciation,

very best regards,
Gaddis

---

the 'physics' of baseball: *The Physics of Baseball* is a 1990 book by Robert K. Adair, a
Yale professor of physics, and is cited in *AA* (47); "your grand new entry" is DeLillo's
eleventh novel, *Underworld* (1997).

To Christopher Knight

[*A critic (1952–) who contributed to* In Recognition of William Gaddis, *Knight sent WG
a copy of his book* Hints & Guesses: William Gaddis's Fiction of Longing *(Univ. of
Wisconsin Press, 1997). The following typed letter begins with a handwritten note at top:*]

My letter carefully written to you almost a month ago, and then as carefully
packed with other papers for the journey home at any rate here it finally is

Key West, Fla.
25 April [1998]

Dear Christopher Knight.

I am sorry being so long about thanking you for sending your *Hints &
Guesses* & for the work itself. I won't go into the somewhat bizarre circumstances that have contributed to the long delay but rather the great pleasure

Top: Saul Steinberg, Judith Gaddis, and WG, Key West, 1997.
Bottom: Matthew Gaddis, WG, and Sarah Gaddis, Key West, 1998.

& rewards I had on first examining it, & have even now not yet read it thoroughly through.

However what is immediately evident is your readiness (nay, appetite!) for pursuing situations beyond their appearances (as background of American Gothic (pp. 165fol.) even if contradictory; or better perhaps the citations of cases, pursuing outside references; or picking up on small but vital details consistently missed by 'reviewers' (as Cruickshank/Lester (obvious) leap from CIA to industrial espionage); also my attempt at the Holmes/Crease///Hand marvelous collision. Those for random starters.

Incidentally I thought it might amuse you (177fol.) *Jane Eyre* sequence, my attempt to find a writing style to conjure up a reading/visual style in such total contrast to the actual bed scene: this attempt to impose her fiction upon the reality almost coming to grief through editor's failure to get permission for the already written sequence using *Lost Horizon* only to be denied (didn't like the sex-context) at the very last minute by Hilton's estate so I broke my neck rushing through every public-domain distinctive prose passage & think it worked (though not so well as the original).

Such the pitfalls. I regret, once again, being so brief & perfunctory with this response to what I find around the top of works I've seen on mine, with on the one & happy hand reaching back to what you have made from our first encounter & I an agonized paranoid/shy (guest), to the opposite which I might have anticipated with some academic collisions under my belt now the inevitable sharp words that must emerge between those selling apples & those selling oranges.

I am incidentally heavily involved just now in a book on the player piano (the one Gibbs didn't write in *J R*) tangled for the moment in contract difficulties (my work incidentally doing immensely well in Germany (where they *read*) and even should we all survive all (meaning *all*) the notes for the Pepsi-Cola-Episcopal case, God help us all & thank you again,

> Warm regards
> William Gaddis

---

our first encounter: WG had visited John Kuehl's class at NYU when Knight was a
  graduate student there.

To Gregory Comnes

> East Hampton, NY 11937
> 17 July 1998

Greg,

The Plutarch on Herodotus Father of Lies is a sheer delight, how else would

I have got hold of it & I do thank you (as well as followups) fits in so beautifully with my (also Plato's in banishing Homer?) assault on/embrace of the
'fictions' adorning the naked animal; also & obviously I do enjoy a bit of
malice & Plutarch is a marvel at it here...

More to follow eventually but I wanted to get this off at least, warm best
to you both,

WG

Plutarch on Herodotus: in his essay "On the Malice of Herodotus," 1st-century-A.D.
  Greek biographer Plutarch dismissed much of the history written by 5th-century
  B.C. Herodotus, called by some the Father of History.
Plato's in banishing Homer: in Plato's *Republic,* Socrates says Homer would not be
  studied in his ideal state. See *AA* 76.

To Steven Moore

*[I had sent WG a copy of my essay "Sheri Martinelli—A Remembrance" (Anais vol. 16,
pp. 92–103), which was based on information supplied by his old Greenwich Village friends
Vincent Livelli, Chandler Brossard, and Sheri herself (whom I knew for the last dozen
years of her life before her death in 1996; she supplied the "mama's boy" remark). He typed
but did not send this letter: "not mailed (or he'd probably sell it)" he wrote at the bottom.
It was found after his death in a copy of the magazine Gargoyle I sent him later that summer, which contains a much expanded version of my Martinelli memoir (#41, pp. 28–54).]*

18 July 1998

Steven Moore

Thanks for sending your version of Sheri. I hadn't known of the range of
her later acquaintance & admirers, as Ginsberg whom I'd known over the
years till he dropped but never heard they'd met, let alone all the other stars
you mention I hope more accurately portrayed here than myself "quite smit-
ten with her" (p99) certainly but that she "didn't reciprocate (my) interest,
regarding (me) as something of a mama's boy" hardly bares dignifying especially
as backed by the similarly invidious "literally" since "my father left (my mother)
when I was 3." He did not leave her. They separated. Or is this plain carelessness as elsewhere (trusting you see the difference), hardly anyone's business
but in these times of internet easily entered as 'information' once it's been
introduced as 'fact' much enough like (p100) the mention of 'revenge fantasy'
as the equally loaded alternative of Sheri's 'indifference' to me (compare
Plutarch's 'On the Malice of Herodotus').

"You had to be there" as they say & as your Village scene illustrates the danger of having not: the under current of the drug ambience, Stanley Gould, Anton Rosenberg (dead a few weeks ago), Eddie Shu the heavy drug connexion, hardly the 'rival' you imply. No, no, you had to be there, hardly 'indifference' but life & book were Sheri being celebrated, that winter of '47 I was perhaps unwisely contemplating some sort of permanent arrangement at her decision, instead a telegram among my papers signaling her nonappearance with 'sister Judith is in town' & I left that night for Panama, to Spain as you note the year following. No, those were youthful grand and often wild times. You had to be there.

Ginsberg [...] dropped: the poet had died the previous year.

'revenge fantasy': at the end of *R*, WG kills off Esme, the character based on Martinelli.

Anton Rosenberg: Village hipster, painter, and jazz musician (1926–98), called "Julien Alexander" in the same Kerouac novel WG appears in (*The Subterraneans*).

Eddie Shu: jazz musician (1918–86) and Martinelli's drug dealer; he appears in *R* as Chaby Sinisterra (called Gism in early drafts).

To Gregory and Judith Comnes

[*After WG decided to convert* AA *from a nonfiction study to a novella, he received a commission from Deutschland Radio to write a play for broadcasting, so he sent them the penultimate draft of* AA *as a one-act monologue entitled* Torschlusspanik, *which means the fear of doors closing, of opportunities lost. It was translated by Marcus Ingendaay and broadcast under Klaus Buhlert's direction on 3 March 1999, three and a half months after WG died. The book version of* AA *contains the Pulitzer diatribe mentioned below (60–62), which is the cover letter that accompanied a copy of the play. In his archives there is an "Outline for the remainder of 'Torschlusspanik', Book One of Agape Agape," that envisions the "continuation" he mentions.*]

East Hampton, NY 11937
1 Sept. 98

dear friends,

I could & might as well have sent this off a while ago but had hoped to get in a diatribe on Pulitzer (done but not the right pace) but more important this is as you will see a sort of compleat in itself, ie with a beginning middle & end, & since it now cast as the opening of the (book) the carryover from this to the continuation both character(s?)wise & features, the youth & mentor the history as lie (gossip) the &c&c&c is proving difficult so run through this if you wish for the time being,

WG

EPILOGUE

WG FINISHED *AA* just as he was hospitalized in Southampton for a variety of ills. He died on the morning of December 16th, two weeks before what would have been his 76th birthday. A memorial tribute was held on 6 May 1999 at the American Academy of Arts and Letters in New York City, at which Sarah Gaddis, Louis Auchincloss, William H. Gass, Joy Williams, Julian Schnabel, and D. A. Pennebaker spoke; the proceedings were published in *Conjunctions* 33 (Fall 1999): 149-60. Washington University purchased WG's archives in March 2002, and in October of that year Viking/Penguin published *Agapē Agape* and WG's collected essays, *The Rush for Second Place*. Since then, new editions of his novels have been reprinted, translations of his books continue to appear, and a few of the stories WG wrote in the 1940s have been published, along with a full-length biography and a steady stream of criticism and commentary.

The Gaddis summer house on Fire Island.

AFTERWORD

IT IS A long journey to read a volume of letters, and so it has been for me with this one, a selection of my father's correspondence that reveals his life in high times and low, sometimes in painful magnification.

Long before I knew his work, I knew my father's writing through his letters—a use of language that involved control and precision and striking passages of beauty, whether observing the natural world or describing loss or how it is to grow up. And now that I have read the whole collection, I see that this beauty is present even when—perhaps especially when—he is angry, or feels abandoned or betrayed, and is wounded.

Included in the collection are thirty or so letters out of some three hundred that he wrote to me. He frequently addressed envelopes in his unique calligraphic hand, and these were startling to receive when I was growing up, almost medieval looking, a work of art; the result of time he spent convalescing from an illness in adolescence. His letters were handwritten or else he used a manual typewriter. I never received an e-mail from him, and don't imagine he ever wrote one.

He wrote to me as early as 1964, while traveling; but his regular letters began after my parents divorced and my mother remarried and we moved to Massachusetts. Although they were to be a stabilizing force in my life, they were not easy for me to read and absorb early on. Rich in emotion and description, with an emphasis on values and the importance of being out in the world, the letters were serious in nature, difficult for a twelve-year-old girl growing up in another household. Their very existence underscored the fact of our living apart, and often I felt his anger at this, his frustration and helplessness, as much I did his devotion and concern and wisdom. He himself grew up without a father present in his life, and in one letter, he described his wistfulness taking the train back and forth to a small Connecticut boarding school when he was a young child. From this I knew how deeply it affected him to put my brother and me on a train after a weekend visit with him. He could have simply told me how he felt, but that would have been handing a child the burden of a parent's loneliness. So instead he wrote about his boyhood experience of loneliness.

I knew his loneliness perhaps because I knew him through his letters; when he was low, he wrote about it. He drove convertibles after my mother left him: a navy blue Pontiac with a white top, a burgundy Chevy with a white top, a bronze Ford XL with a black top. Years later, he told me that owning those cars was a way for him to feel a bit of flash and dash to keep himself together and to make us think he was together, even as he was plagued with money worries, running out of advances while working on *J R*, taking jobs writing corporate speeches to pay tuitions, mortgages, child support.

During these years, he picked us up every other Friday at the train or bus station in New Haven or Stamford, Connecticut, and drove us back to Croton, later Piermont. After a weekend of cribbage and *Perry Mason*, perhaps a movie, and going over homework, he drove us back to the train on Sunday. Then he followed up on our visit with a letter—or else wrote a furious letter like the one he wrote to Jovanovich, his publisher, in April, 1970, which is staccato in intensity even with its run-on sentences.

J R took my father twenty years to write—my childhood and adolescence. I particularly remember the summers, when he loaded cartons of the manuscript into the car, and we drove to Bay Shore and boarded the ferry to Saltaire, Fire Island. He managed to hold onto that house for over fifteen years, rebuilding it when it was condemned following a severe storm in the Sixties that brought it down off its pilings.

In person, my father was quiet, deliberate, with a dry sense of humor. He was thoughtful, gentle. He listened. He encouraged me to write. He planned ahead and was rarely impulsive. Yet he could be impatient and short-tempered. He was a driven man, intense in what he demanded and what he gave. He eschewed sentimentality, yet he quoted from Thornton Wilder's *Our Town*, telling me to live "every, every minute." In terms of the world, he wanted to belong, yet stubbornly remained an outsider. Even in good times, he had that cautionary sense of "waiting for the other shoe to drop," using that expression.

In addition to letters, I received birthday collages, Valentines, cartoons of political figures made from photos clipped from the *New York Times*. As I grew up and made my own life, his letters, handwritten or typed single-spaced, sometimes on the backs of discarded manuscript pages, reflected back to me things I said in my own. They were now part of an exchange, became a correspondence we both counted on and enjoyed, except for periods of upheaval in his life, when for me they were cause for worry.

Having kept track of my trove of letters for years, letting go wasn't easy. Before packing them off to the archive at Washington University, I organized and catalogued them. Some I matched with envelopes, but some didn't have dates, or postmarks on envelopes were illegible, which meant that a few thick packets of empty envelopes went along as well. Envelopes are curious things, with their stamps and postmarks. They are documents; artifacts. In this case a record of my father having lived in New York State his entire adult life, and for me, a long list of addresses in New York, Massachusetts, Pennsylvania, New Jersey, California, France, and North Carolina.

It is deeply moving to see my letters in the context of this book. But I was most affected by the first section, my father writing to my grandmother. I had read some of these letters, but didn't realize the scope of them, how they charted my father's travels as a youth abroad. And having met Margaret Williams, I was riveted when reading about my father's hopes to marry her. I hadn't known it was so serious between them. I found myself worried for this callow adventurer who was so sure of himself as a writer, but who (it was clear from the letters before he knew it himself) was going to lose the girl.

His voice early on sounds familiar to me, as do his concerns. In his twenties, in a letter from 1/15/48, he is already using the word "Lord" ("Lord how I miss New York") as if he were an old man looking back. Writing from the Canal Zone at twenty-six years of age, he is conscious of time passing and defensive when my grandmother says his plans sound "glorious." He is "disconcerted" by this word, and says he is "(1) earning and saving (2) thinking reading and writing—which is not time wasted dreaming." Anxiety and self-denial—these traits were with him throughout his life.

Other letters were a revelation. I hadn't known of Pop's correspondence with Katherine Anne Porter; and though I knew growing up that the British painter John Napper and his wife Pauline were close friends of ours (we went to John's exhibitions in New York, and I visited them on my 1978 honeymoon), I didn't realize what a very long and intimate dialogue they maintained over the decades through letters.

When life got complicated, he wrote letters to get under control situations that were out of control; and regarding publishers and scholars, to set the record straight. I found his letters to scholars interesting, considering he was known for being unwilling to discuss his work.

During the last three years of my father's life, my brother Matthew and I alternated caring for him, at Boat Yard Road in Easthampton and in Key West, where Pop and his second wife Judith had rented a house once, and where we were reunited with Judith again. Key West was a magical, sunny world where he worked on his final novel, where doctors and friends were in close proximity and old friends came to visit. We were set to go down there for a third winter in the fall of 1998, when he began to decline definitively.

I was based in Asheville, North Carolina, during those years, flying north or south every month or two to be with my father. In December, my fiancé, John Twilley, and I rented a house in Sag Harbor to be near him. We arrived on December 15th. He was in the hospital, Matthew there with him, and his old pal, John Sherry. His condition had worsened, and that evening, we were permitted to take him home to Boat Yard Road. He died early the next morning, December 16th, 1998.

As one grows older, photographs become important, for themselves and for the memories they bring. The best photographs of the early years were taken by Martin Dworkin; I can remember him at Fire Island, following us on the boardwalks in his sandals and socks, several cameras around his neck. Chelsea Pennebaker's photo of the three life-long friends was taken at her father's birthday party; it is difficult to see my father looking so frail, but wonderful to remember how those friendships sustained him. As for the photo Mellon Tytell took of my father and me in Paris, it was a cold day and we walked around the Île St. Louis, and she caught exactly what it was like to have him visit me there.

—SARAH GADDIS
June 5, 2012

INDEX

Parke, Henry, 22, 54–55, 359

Parke, James, 1st Baron Wensleydale, 601–2

Parke, Marilyn, 7, 22, 54–55, 131–32, 134, 358

Parker, Bruce and Tommy, 156, 197, 199

Parker, Helen, 139, 155–56, 166, 197–99, 234–35, 238–39

Partisan Review, 238, 254, 401, 403, 469

Pasmezoglu, Ariadne (Paz), 344–46, 350–51, 394, 404, 579

Pasteur, Louis and Marie, 594–95

Patty, Ann, 588, 597–98, 602, 624

Peacock, Allen, 568, 582, 588, 597, 643

Peale, Norman Vincent, 431

"Peanut Vendor, The," 370–71

PEN/Faulkner Award, 525, 553

PEN International, 518–19, 520

Pennebaker, Donn A., 80, 268–59, 520, 655, 660

People, 492–94, 495, 534, 538

Percy, Walker, 572

Petrillo family, 19

Pfizer International, xi, 269, 271, 278, 293, 314, 633

Philadelphia Inquirer, 618

Philip II, 127, 145

Phillips, Carol, 458

Piaget, Jean, 298–99

Picador, 534–35,

Picasso, Pablo, 479–80

Pirandello, Luigi, 102, 106, 151

Pius XII, 194, 196

Plato, 275, 289, 373, 374, 560, 641, 653

Playhouse 90, 145

Plimpton, Freddy Espy, 519, 521

Plimpton, George, 389, 463, 519

Plon, Éditions, 543, 647

Plutarch, 652–53

Poe, Edgar Allan, 249, 343

Poets & Writers, Inc., 437–38

Pope, Alexander, 238

Porgy and Bess (Gershwin), 31

Porter, Arabel J., 314, 315

Porter, Katherine Anne, xiii, 51, 90–91, 92, 100–105, 107, 114, 116–19

Poseidon Press. *See* Simon & Schuster

Postman Always Rings Twice, 119

Potter, Carole, 25

Poulaille, Henri, 461

Pound, Ezra, 135, 586

Prado, Museo del, 135, 174, 210, 609

Prairie Schooner, 273, 290, 293, 303, 451

Praz, Mario, 451–52

Preminger, Otto, 350–51

Prescott, H.F.M., 168

Prescott, Peter S., 508–9

Prosser, William L., 523, 533, 566, 578, 583, 598, 601, 605

Publishers Weekly, 353–54, 378, 382; WG interview in, 505–6

Puccini, Giacomo, 234

Pulitzer Prize, 572–573, 633–34, 654

Puzo, Mario, 389

Pynchon, Thomas, 297, 322, 334, 337, 368, 440–41, 445, 468, 470, 513; WG's alleged influence on, 462, 548

Pyrrho, 70–71

Quayle, Dan, 588

Quesenbery, William Doyle, Jr., 360

Quintet, 420–21

Raban, Jonathan, 616, 618, 621

Ramuz, C.F., 103, 106

Randolph, John, 124

Rapture, The (Anderson), 482

Ray, William, 494

Reagan, Ronald, 438–39, 498; Administration of, 477, 480–81, 485–86, 489–90, 524, 536; "Reaganomics," 544, 574

Recognitions (Roman novel), 184, 242, 244

Reeve, Benjamin, 374–75

Rehnquist, William, 540

OTHER NEW YORK REVIEW CLASSICS

For a complete list of titles, visit www.nyrb.com.